ECLIPSE MODELING PROJECT

eclipse

the eclipse series

SERIES EDITORS Erich Gamma ▪ Lee Nackman ▪ John Wiegand

Eclipse is a universal tool platform, an open extensible integrated development environment (IDE) for anything and nothing in particular. Eclipse represents one of the most exciting initiatives hatched from the world of application development in a long time, and it has the considerable support of the leading companies and organizations in the technology sector. Eclipse is gaining widespread acceptance in both the commercial and academic arenas.

The Eclipse Series from Addison-Wesley is the definitive series of books dedicated to the Eclipse platform. Books in the series promise to bring you the key technical information you need to analyze Eclipse, high-quality insight into this powerful technology, and the practical advice you need to build tools to support this evolutionary Open Source platform. Leading experts Erich Gamma, Lee Nackman, and John Wiegand are the series editors.

Titles in the Eclipse Series

Richard C. Gronback, *Eclipse Modeling Project: A Domain-Specific Language (DSL) Toolkit*
978-0-321-53407-1

Diana Peh, Nola Hague, and Jane Tatchell, *BIRT: A Field Guide to Reporting, Second Edition*
978-0-321-58027-6

Dave Steinberg, Frank Budinsky, Marcelo Paternostro, and Ed Merks, *EMF: Eclipse Modeling Framework*
978-0-321-33188-5

Jason Weathersby, Tom Bondur, Iana Chatalbasheva, and Don French, *Integrating and Extending BIRT, Second Edition*
978-0-321-58030-6

Naci Dai, Lawrence Mandel, and Arthur Ryman, *Eclipse Web Tools Platform: Developing Java™ Web Applications*
978-0-321-39685-3

David Carlson, *Eclipse Distilled,*
978-0-321-28815-8

Eric Clayberg and Dan Rubel, *Eclipse Plug-ins, Third Edition,*
978-0-321-42672-7

Jeff McAffer and Jean-Michel Lemieux, *Eclipse Rich Client Platform: Designing, Coding, and Packaging Java™ Applications*
978-0-321-33461-9

Erich Gamma and Kent Beck, *Contributing to Eclipse: Principles, Patterns, and Plug-Ins*
978-0-321-20575-9

For more information on books in this series visit www.informit.com/series/eclipse

ECLIPSE MODELING PROJECT

A Domain-Specific Language Toolkit

Richard C. Gronback

✦Addison-Wesley

Upper Saddle River, NJ • Boston • Indianapolis • San Francisco
New York • Toronto • Montreal • London • Munich • Paris • Madrid
Cape Town • Sydney • Tokyo • Singapore • Mexico City

Library of Congress Cataloging-in-Publication Data:

Gronback, Richard C.
  Eclipse modeling project : a domain-specific language (DSL) toolkit / Richard C. Gronback.
    p. cm.

  ISBN 0-321-53407-7 (pbk. : alk. paper) 1. Computer software—Development. 2. Eclipse (Electronic resource) 3. Programming languages (Electronic computers) I. Title.
  QA76.76.D47G785 2009
  005.1—dc22
                    2008050813

ISBN-13: 978-0-321-53407-1
ISBN-10: 0-321-53407-7
Text printed in the United States on recycled paper at Courier in Stoughton, Massachusetts.
First printing March 2009

Associate Publisher
Mark Taub

Acquisitions Editor
Greg Doench

Managing Editor
Kristy Hart

Project Editor
Jovana San Nicolas-Shirley

Copy Editor
Krista Hansing Editorial Services, Inc.

Indexer
Erika Millen

Technical Reviewer
Simon Archer

David Orme
Daniel Holt

Publishing Coordinator
Michelle Housley

Cover Designer
Sandra Schroeder

Compositor
Nonie Ratcliff

Dedicated to my father, Philip Richard Gronback, Sr.
November 2, 1948–December 8, 1997

Contents

Foreword

Just like a pearl, the Eclipse Modeling Project has grown organically as layers around a central core. From the humble beginnings of the Eclipse Modeling Framework (EMF) (initially part of the Eclipse Tools Project) along with the Graphical Modeling Framework (GMF) and the Generative Modeling Tools (GMT) (both initially part of the Eclipse Technology Project), the Modeling Project coalesced to become one of Eclipse's most exciting and diverse projects. The depth and breadth of its technology is vast and even its rate of growth continues to increase. The Eclipse Modeling Project has truly become a Swiss Army knife for state-of-the-art model-driven software development.

The sheer volume of useful modeling technologies that the Eclipse Modeling Project includes makes mastering a significant portion of it a daunting task. Even determining which specific available technologies are useful for solving any particular problem is a challenge exacerbated by the fact that, as a rule, the documentation tends to lag far behind the development work. As such, this book fills a fundamentally important need in the modeling community: a coherent vision of how all this powerful technology can be best exploited to build domain specific languages (DSLs). In other words, the focus of this book is on pragmatic applications illustrated by way of concrete examples rather than on abstract modeling concepts and theories. This pragmatic focus reflects that of the Modeling Project overall—that is, a focus on building powerful frameworks that real programmers use every day. I'm sure this influential book—with its interesting examples and its excellent reference material—will become a key part of every toolsmith's technical arsenal.

EMF provides a sound basis for abstract syntax development and even includes a crude but effective XML-based concrete syntax. But, that is only the start of the journey, and the second edition of the *Eclipse Modeling Framework* book covers this basic material well. This book effectively picks up where EMF leaves off with an in-depth exploration of alternative forms of concrete syntax, particularly graphical syntax, model-to-model transformation (such as Query

View Transformation Operational Mapping Language), and model-to-text transformation (such as Xpand). It rounds out the DSL picture with a holistic view of everything it takes to build a complete model-based product line.

It has been my great pleasure and honor to work closely with Richard C. Gronback as the Modeling Project coleader for the past few years. He has a keen mind and a sharp wit. This book reflects it well. I've learned a great deal from him, and I'm sure readers of this book will as well.

—Ed Merks, Ph.D.
President, Macro Modeling

Preface

About This Book

This book covers a relatively new collection of technologies that focus on developing domain-specific languages (DSLs) using the Eclipse Modeling Project, offering a first look at a range of Eclipse projects that have not yet been covered in detail within this context. Although the core of these technologies has been available for several years in the Eclipse Modeling Framework (EMF), diagram definition and model transformation are emerging technologies at Eclipse. These are complemented by upcoming textual syntax development frameworks, which likely will be covered in detail in subsequent editions of this book.

This book delivers a pragmatic introduction to developing a product line using a collection of DSLs. A model-based, largely generative approach is designed to accommodate future adjustments to the source models, templates, and model transformation definitions, to provide customized solutions within the context of the product line. To illustrate this approach, this book presents a set of sample projects used to define a requirements product line.

Audience

This book targets developers and architects who want to learn about developing DSLs using Eclipse Modeling Project technologies. It assumes a basic understanding of the Java programming language, Eclipse plug-in development, and familiarity with EMF. This book's target audience are those interested in learning about the Eclipse Graphical Modeling Framework (GMF), Model-to-Model Transformation (M2M) Query/View/Transformation Operational Mapping Language (QVT OML), and Model-to-Text Transformation (M2T) Xpand project components.

The book is divided into introductory, hands on, and reference sections. Readers who want an overview of the Eclipse Modeling Project and development of DSLs in the context of an Eclipse-based product line should read Part I, "Introduction." Readers who want to follow along in a tutorial fashion to learn how to use the projects listed earlier should read Part II, "Developing Domain-Specific Languages." Readers also can reference the sample project solutions in this section to get an overview of the techniques. Part III, "Reference," serves as a resource for readers who want a deeper understanding of Graphical Editing Framework (GEF), GMF, Xpand, and QVT OML while they are completing Part II or developing their own DSL-based projects.

Readers who want to experience the benefits of a commercial version of the technologies presented here can download the Borland Together product. There they will find enhanced domain modeling, refactoring, diagram development, transformation authoring and debugging, workflow, and generation capabilities in a well-integrated DSL Toolkit.

Sample Code

The Modeling Amalgamation Project (Amalgam) at Eclipse holds the sample code from this book and is available as sample projects in the DSL Toolkit download. This package also includes all the prerequisites required for developing the sample applications.

Visit the Amalgam project Web site for more information on obtaining the DSL Toolkit: www.eclipse.org/modeling/amalgam.

Feedback

The examples in this book are maintained within the Modeling Amalgamation Project at Eclipse. Feedback on their content—and, therefore, this book's content—is welcome on the project newsgroup, http://news.eclipse.modeling. amalgam. Alternatively, feel free to contact the author directly at richard. gronback@gmail.com.

Acknowledgments

This book would not have been possible without the help of many great people, especially because its contents are based almost exclusively on the work of others. I have worked over the years with a number of terrific people, but this book all started with a team of exceptional developers that comprised the initial Borland contingent of the GMF project: Artem Tikhomirov, Alexander "Vano" Shatalin, Boris Blajer, Dmitry Stadnik, Max Feldman, Michael "Upstairs" Golubev, and Radek Dvorak. Our small team led the way into the world of Eclipse contribution from Borland, thanks to the support of our management at the time, Raaj Shinde and Boz Elloy.

Our colleagues from IBM were also instrumental in the success of GMF and have been a pleasure to work with over the years. Thanks to Fred Plante, Anthony Hunter, Christian Damus, Linda Damus, Mohammed Mostafa, Cherie Revells, and the rest of the GMF runtime team.

I have greatly enjoyed working with Ed Merks, who helped form the top-level Eclipse Modeling and served as co-leader of its PMC. Thanks also to Kenn Hussey, Paul Elder, Jean Bezivin, Sven Efftinge, and Frederic Jouault, all on the PMC representing the breadth of projects within Modeling, for making our project the success it has become.

Today the modeling team at Borland has expanded its Eclipse contribution to other technologies covered in this book. Thanks to Artem for pushing us toward Xpand, and to the openArchitectureWare team who initially developed it, particularly Bernd Kolb who was most helpful during the writing of the Xpand chapter. Thanks to Radek for taking on the task of open sourcing and improving our QVT Operational Mapping Language implementation, along with the talented Sergey Boyko and Alexander Igdalov. Thanks to Michael for taking on the task of developing UML diagrams using GMF for contribution to the MDT project, along with the excellent help of Sergey Gribovsky and Tatiana Fesenko. It has been a privilege working with Konstantin Savvin and the rest of our team in Prague and St. Petersburg over the past few years.

This book also served as an exercise to develop requirements for our commercial DSL Toolkit—thanks to our current management team, Steve McMenamin and Pete Morowski, for providing excellent support and encouragement. Thanks also to Tom Gullion and Ian Buchanan for being fantastic stewards and product managers for the Together product line.

Thanks again to those who reviewed portions or all of this book and provided valuable feedback, particularly Karl Frank and Angel Roman. I especially want to thank Artem Tikhomirov and Alex Shatalin for their support and feedback while writing this book. At Addison-Wesley, thanks to Greg Doench for his support and encouragement during the publishing process, and to Jovana San Nicolas-Shirley and Krista Hansing for making it readable. And thanks to Ian Skerret, who introduced me to Greg during EclipseCon 2007 and got the ball rolling.

On the home front, extra special thanks go to my wife, Pam, and son, Brandon, who afforded me the time and peace to work evenings and weekends, even through the winter holiday season of 2007. And finally, I must thank my parents for providing a strong foundation and the best possible example to live by.

About the Author

Richard Gronback is the chief scientist for modeling products at Borland Software Corporation, where he manages both open source and commercial product development. Richard represents Borland on the Eclipse Board of Directors and Planning and Architecture Councils, co-leads the Modeling project Project Management Committee (PMC), and leads the GMF and Amalgam projects. Richard holds a Bachelor of Software Engineering degree in computer science and engineering from the University of Connecticut. He was a reactor operator in the U.S. Navy before entering his current career in software.

PART I

Introduction

This part of the book focuses on the big picture of the Eclipse Modeling Project and the development of domain-specific languages (DSLs) using a subset of its technologies. This overview serves as the basis for understanding how the projects and components work together before we get our hands dirty in Part II.

CHAPTER 1

Introduction

This book provides an overview of the capabilities of the Eclipse Modeling Project that you can leverage when working with domain-specific languages (DSLs). First it gives an introduction to the Eclipse Modeling Project, followed by a discussion of DSLs and their application in the context of the Modeling project. Although this book does not cover all projects within Modeling, it includes projects and components that cover the range of Model-Driven Software Development (MDSD) technologies that you need to start developing your own DSL and custom tool set. Throughout the book, you will develop a set of sample applications to cover Modeling project functionality for each topic. Finally, the book provides a reference section to cover more of the in-depth technical detail of the technologies and projects that comprise the DSL Toolkit.

1.1 About Modeling

Although we sometimes think of modeling as nothing more than a tool for drawing documentation pictures or for use within the Unified Modeling Language (UML) (in the case of big "M" modeling), or as purely an academic pursuit, we can apply modeling to virtually any domain and can use model-driven approaches to increase productivity and quality, particularly when using them in a domain-specific manner. This book does not focus on the general topic of models, modeling, metamodels, meta-metamodels, super-models, model-driven software development, and so on; instead, it focuses on these topics as they relate to using the Eclipse Modeling Project as a DSL Toolkit. In other words, this book focuses on the practical application of MDSD with what is available today in the Modeling project. You can find other sources of information on the topics of modeling, DSLs, and MDSD; I suggest several later in Part III, "References."

As David Frankel pointed out in *Model Driven Architecture: Applying MDA to Enterprise Computing* [45], a critical aspect of the success of MDSD is using a common metamodel. In our case, Eclipse Modeling Framework's (EMFs) Ecore is this metamodel (or meta-metamodel, depending on your perspective). Beginning with Ecore (and leveraging the facilities of EMF for defining, editing, querying, and validating models), I describe how a Toolsmith can begin to develop a DSL. Using several of the other Modeling projects, you will add diagramming, transformation, and generation capabilities to a DSL, resulting in a full-featured toolset that a Practitioner can use. Throughout the book, I use the roles Toolsmith and Practitioner to distinguish between those who develop DSL tools using the Modeling project and those who use these tools in practice.

Terminology

Before going further, it's important to understand some key terminology used in this book. The structure of a DSL is captured in its *metamodel,* commonly referred to as its *abstract syntax.* A metamodel is just a model that provides the basis for constructing another model. Although both are models, one is expressed in terms of the other; in other words, one model is an *instance of* or *conforms to* the other. In this book, a DSL's abstract syntax is defined using EMF's Ecore model, which is, therefore, its metamodel and the model used to define all DSLs in this book. A model created in terms of our DSL's abstract syntax is commonly referred to as an *instance* model; the DSL is then the metamodel, which makes Ecore the meta-metamodel. The Ecore model is expressed in terms of itself, but this book doesn't give this a name or assign an absolute numbering scheme to the levels, as the Object Management Group (OMG) does. For our purposes, you can simply think of Ecore as the *metamodel* that a Toolsmith uses to define a DSL's *abstract syntax,* leaving the Practitioner to create *instance* models of the DSL.

The term *abstract* syntax refers to a metamodel, so it often has a corresponding *concrete* syntax in the form of text or diagram notation. These are referred to as *textual concrete syntax* and *graphical concrete syntax,* respectively. A textual syntax enables users to work with instance models just as they would other text-based programming languages. A graphical syntax enables users to work with instance models using a diagram surface; the most popular is the UML. Abstract syntaxes are defined using Ecore models, which themselves are persisted in XMI format— this could technically be considered a concrete syntax, although it's sometimes called a *serialization syntax.*

After defining the DSL's abstract syntax in terms of Ecore, we can leverage a variety of the Modeling project's capabilities that are designed to work with Ecore models. Nearly everything involved in developing a DSL Toolkit revolves around EMF's capabilities, including diagram definitions, transformation definitions, code-generation templates, model serialization and persistence, and more. In addition, many of these capabilities are developed using EMF models. For example, Graphical Modeling Framework (GMF) uses a collection of EMF models (DSLs themselves) in generating domain-specific modeling surfaces. QVT's abstract and concrete syntax are defined with EMF models, and so on. Before going deeper into the individual projects you'll leverage within the context of this book, let's take a step back and look at domain-specific languages and the Eclipse Modeling Project as a whole.

1.2 Domain-Specific Languages

A DSL is a language designed to be useful for a specific set of tasks. Much has been written on the general topic of DSLs, with the domain-specific aspect being the most controversial and reminiscent of discussions regarding "meta-ness." Just as *metamodel* is a relative term to describe a model that is used as the basis for another model, the term *domain-specific* is used in a relative sense. Domain specificity is determined by the designer of the language—in our case, the Toolsmith.

For example, you might consider the UML to be a general-purpose language that consists of several domain-specific languages for state machines, structural definition, use cases, and so on. Others might consider all of UML to be a domain-specific language covering the domain of software development. However you look at it, UML is a modeling language that, in the sphere of MDSD, is used to generate source code in the form of a general-purpose programming language. General-to-general mappings typically don't work well, so additional specificity is typically applied at one end or both ends. A common approach is to make the modeling language more specific and target a stable framework, as in the case of using a UML Profile for developing Java EE applications. An alternative is to start small, creating your own domain-specific language that includes just what you need.

COMMENT

Any plan to standardize a general-purpose model or set of models will likely continue to fail because humans inherently need to express their own creativity (Not Invented Here [NIH] syndrome). Furthermore, the level of investment required to learn a large and complex language, become familiar with the associated tools, and then incorporate them into a development process makes the approach too costly for many. Therefore, when modeling is advantageous but using standards-based modeling languages is not, the alternative is to use tooling that facilitates the creation of DSLs.

1.2.1 Why Develop a DSL?

Definitions and perspectives aside, why would you choose to develop your own DSL? Most people prefer to begin with something small and grow it as required, which is likely how the UML itself got started. The key difference today is that UML and its associated tooling is now large and complex, whereas tools for rapidly developing custom domain-specific products are more readily available. That said, in the process of creating, maturing, and extending your DSL or family of DSLs, you might end up with something akin to UML. The difference is that you're using your organization's family of models, transformation definitions, and generation facilities, which are tailored to your exact needs.

Don't interpret this the wrong way: My intention is not to disparage UML. The point is that whether your DSL is defined using the UML or a smaller language such as Ecore, you can create a set of tooling around your DSL in a largely generative manner. Historically, this was not the case: Modelers were forced to buy expensive, inflexible, closed modeling tools that inevitably required customization. Today Toolsmiths can develop custom tooling using the capabilities of a strong open source foundation provided by the Modeling project. This changes the playing field for modeling tools and MDSD in general.

Finally, because a library of models and model transformations likely will be available for reuse, the capability to assemble DSL-based applications that build on MDSD techniques becomes even more attractive. For example, the GMT project [37] has already begun building such a library. Thanks to the use of available DSLs, along with a growing number of target application frameworks, the resulting abstraction gap has sufficiently shrunk to the point at which MDSD is an increasingly attractive approach to delivering software.

1.3 Model-Driven Software Development

MDSD can make use of many approaches and technologies. The Modeling project provides many such technologies for use in MDSD, whether standards based (such as when using UML2, Object Constraint Language [OCL], and Query/View/Transformation [QVT] implementations) or non-standards based (such as when using Xpand, Atlas Transformation Language [ATL], and so on). Technically, Ecore itself is a "near-standard" implementation of the Essential Meta-Object Facility (EMOF) metamodel. Discussions continue on aligning Ecore and EMOF, as well as on the need for a Complete Meta-Object Facility (CMOF) implementation within Modeling.

Not unlike the early days of domain and object modeling, the current idea of MDSD is to focus on developing and refining the model of a particular domain to provide a standard vocabulary for use in development. The key difference is that, in the context of generative programming techniques, much of the work that goes into developing a domain model (or DSL) can be used to produce working software.

Volumes have been written on this subject [41], so I don't cover it again here; this book focuses on the practical reality of what can be done in this area using the Modeling project. Still, it's worth discussing a couple relevant points: the OMG's Model-Driven Architecture initiative (discussed in Appendix B, "Model-Driven Architecture at Eclipse") and software product lines, or software factories.

1.4 Software Product Lines and Factories

Perhaps the most compelling reason to leverage the Modeling project as a DSL Toolkit is related to the development of software product lines. Using the Modeling project to develop custom DSL tooling still requires significant effort, so the most likely scenario for adoption is to produce a series of products, each with a set of defined variation points. Using the facilities of the Modeling project to produce a one-off custom DSL-based application is significantly easier today than it was just a few years ago. However, the effort required to design a DSL, author transformations and templates, and so on yields a greater return when a product line is produced. Much has been written on the subject of product line engineering, feature models [39], and the related concept of software factories [40].

The sample applications developed in this book represent a simplistic example of how a series of models is used to define various aspects of the software requirements domain. The process and tooling needed for software requirements largely depend on the methodology a team uses for development, so requirements solutions need to be quite flexible. Traditionally, this has meant providing tooling with extensibility points and open application programming interfaces (APIs), which typically were not powerful enough or stable enough to meet a wide range of customer requests.

Instead of developing large, complex APIs for client customization needs, consider the alternative approach of software factories. Give your clients, or perhaps your services organization, a core set of models, transformations, and code-generation templates to target a stable underlying application framework such as Eclipse or Java EE. Developing the domain models to suit clients—or, in the case of the sample applications here, the process methodology used—means that the application delivered is designed up front to meet their needs. Selecting variation points is complemented by customizing the underlying generation facilities to provide the required functionality. In the case of a true product line, in which the functionality is largely the same from client to client, the richness of the generator improves over time to the point that setting top-level parameters (instead of low-level framework modifications) achieves greater customization. This is where the promise of model-driven software development lies: a reduced cost of application development through domain-specific models or generative techniques.

Today there's still a long way to go before this vision can be realized. This book focuses on what is available today and, specifically, what is available to enable DSL development using the Eclipse Modeling Project, which we cover next.

1.5 The Eclipse Modeling Project

The Eclipse Modeling Project is a relatively new top-level project at Eclipse. In contrast, the core of the project, EMF, has been in existence for as long as the Eclipse platform itself. Today the Modeling project is largely a collection of projects related to modeling and MDSD technologies. This collection was formed to coordinate and focus model-driven software development capabilities within Eclipse. The introduction of the Amalgamation project ushered in the beginnings of a DSL-focused development environment, although it has a long way to go before mainstream developers can use it. Documentation certainly lags behind implementation within Modeling—hence, the need for this book.

The Modeling project is organized logically into projects that provide the following capabilities: abstract syntax development, concrete syntax development, model-to-model transformation, and model-to-text transformation. A single project, the Model Development Tools (MDT) project, is dedicated to the support of industry-standard models. Another project within the Modeling project focuses on research in generative modeling technologies. These are outside the scope of this book, except where explicitly referenced.

Figure 1-1 is an image originally proposed as the logo for the Modeling project. A better logo was contributed by Gen Nishimura, but this image gives a sense of the structure of the modeling project and its functional areas. As you can see, EMF is at the center, providing abstract syntax-development capabilities. EMF Query, Validation, and Transformation complement the EMF core functionality, as do Teneo and CDO for database persistence of model instances. Surrounding the abstract syntax-development components are model-transformation technologies, both model-to-text (Java Emitter Templates [JET] and Xpand) and model-to-model (QVT and ATL). Beyond those lie concrete syntax development: GMF used for graphical representation and Textual Modeling Framework (TMF) used for textual representation of models. Finally, a series of orbiting projects and components represent models, capabilities, and research initiatives available from the Modeling project.

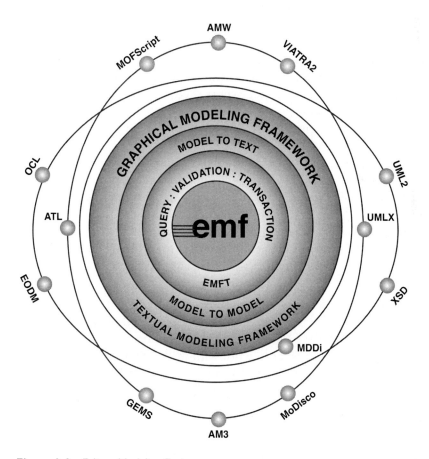

Figure 1-1 Eclipse Modeling Project

1.5.1 Abstract Syntax Development

The core of a DSL is its abstract syntax, which is used in the development of almost every artifact that follows, including graphical concrete syntax, model-to-model transformations, and model-to-text transformations. Typically, the first element of a DSL to be developed is its abstract syntax; for this we use the Eclipse Modeling Framework (EMF).

EMF Project

EMF's Ecore model serves as the metamodel for defining our DSL. We can further refine the structure and semantics of our DSL using Object Constraint Language (OCL), in addition to providing support for transactions, query, and validation.

Much has been written on the subject of little languages, domain-specific languages, language workbenches [29], and so on. Models provide a superior language-definition format to traditional approaches such as BNF because a model described in terms of Ecore is more expressive and can have a number of concrete syntaxes defined for generating textual and graphical editors. Chapter 3, "Developing a DSL Abstract Syntax," covers the use of EMF in developing a DSL abstract syntax.

Several components available from the Modeling project extend and complement the core capabilities of EMF. Within EMF are components that provide query, validation, and transaction features, in addition to an implementation of Service Data Objects (SDOs). An incubation project named EMF Technology (EMFT) exists for the sole purpose of providing extensions to the core functionality of EMF. When technologies developed within the EMFT project mature sufficiently, they can graduate into EMF itself or another project within Modeling, or they can become full-fledged projects on their own.

Model Transaction

The Model Transaction component of EMF provides transactional support for editing EMF models. Managing access to a transactional editing domain enables multiple clients to read and write models. A transaction workspace integration allows the transaction layer to work with the Eclipse undoable operations framework. Section 10.7, "Command Infrastructure," includes more information on the transaction framework in the context of its use in GMF.

Model Validation

A Model Validation framework complements the transaction framework, to provide model integrity support. Although EMF core provides basic validation support, an enhanced Validation Framework component is available to provide batch and "live" validation of domain model instances. By default, constraints can be defined in Java and OCL, although additional languages can be provided. The audit and metric features of GMF for diagrams leverage the Validation Framework; Section 4.3.5, "Audits and Metrics," discusses this.

Model Query

As in a database, the contents of a model instance commonly need to be queried. EMF models can be queried using provided Java APIs, but the Model Query component of EMF provides OCL- and SQL-like alternatives. Model Query provides only a programmatic interface, but the Model Search component of the EMFT project aims to provide integration with the Eclipse Search UI.

Model Search

The Model Search component of the EMFT project provides rich model-search capabilities and integrates into the familiar Eclipse Search dialog. Model search provides regular expression- and OCL-based search for EMF and UML2 models. Search results are provided in the familiar search results view and include result filtering support.

Model Compare

As with working with source code, working with models within a team inevitably leads to the need for comparison and merge support. The EMF Compare component of the EMFT project provides generic compare and merge support for any Ecore-based model. Compare uses the standard Eclipse comparison framework to provide a familiar environment for comparing two versions of a model.

Persistence Alternatives

EMF has a flexible resource interface that allows the default XMI serialization to be replaced with alternatives, including database persistence. One such capability comes from Teneo, an EMFT project that leverages Hibernate (or Java Data Objects [JDO]/Java Persistence Objects [JPOX]) to provide object-relational mapping and persistence for EMF models. CDO is another object-relational mapping technology that allows for database persistence; a new component, Java Content Repository (JCR) Management, allows for the persistence of EMF model instances in a Java Specification Request (JSR)-170-compliant repository.

1.5.2 Concrete Syntax Development

The abstract syntax for a DSL usually must be presented for use by humans, so one or more concrete syntaxes must be developed. By default, EMF provides XMI serialization of model instances, but you might want to provide an alternative serialization syntax as well. You also might choose to define a textual concrete syntax used for serialization.

GMF Project

The GMF project provides a *graphical* concrete syntax. Using GMF, a Toolsmith can develop the graphical notation for a DSL and map it to the abstract syntax. These models generate a feature-rich diagram editor. Chapter 4, "Developing a DSL Graphical Notation," covers the development of diagrams for DSLs using GMF.

TMF Project

Those who prefer a *textual* concrete syntax can use the TMF project. After extracting grammar from the domain model, you can leverage generators that target the Eclipse platform to produce high-quality textual editors, complete with syntax highlighting, code completion, builders, and so on. Chapter 5, "Developing a DSL Textual Syntax," covers the development of textual editors for DSLs.

1.5.3 Model Transformation

As satisfying as it is to define a DSL and generate a custom textual or graphical editing environment, we typically want to produce some output from our instance models. We include the development of model transformations in the context of a DSL Toolkit because, without them, the story is incomplete. The Modeling project provides both model-to-model and model-to-text transformation components.

Model-to-Model Transformation (M2M) Project

Using the abstract syntax definition of our DSL, we can define model transformations to produce other models or generate textual output. In the case of the former, you will develop model-to-model transformations using the QVT Operational Mapping Language (OML), although the Model-to-Model Transformation (M2M) project offers alternatives such as ATL and QVT Relations. You will develop model-to-model transformations using QVT in Chapter 6, "Developing Model-to-Model Transformations."

Model-to-Text Transformation (M2T) Project

Alternatives exist within the Modeling project for model-to-text transformation. Perhaps the most well-known is the Java Emitter Templates (JET) component, which EMF itself uses. Xpand is an increasingly popular template engine, used extensively by the GMF project. You will develop model-to-text transformations using Xpand in Chapter 7, "Developing Model-to-Text Transformations."

1.5.4 Model Development Tools (MDT)

The MDT project within Modeling does not fall into any previous categorization. The focus of this project is to provide so-called big "M" modeling capabilities—that is, those based on industry-standard models, such as those produced by the OMG.

Currently, MDT consists of several components, each of which I briefly describe next. Although this book touches on some of these components, the range of functionality that MDT provides deserves a book of its own. Until such time, you can find documentation for these components on the Modeling Web site and wiki pages.

XML Schema (XSD)

An important component within the MDT project that extends the capabilities of EMF is XSD. Many XSDs are available for application- and industry-standard models, so it is useful to import them into EMF and work with them as you would any Ecore model. Special annotations are added to the model created when importing an XSD, which allows EMF to serialize these model instances as valid XML documents that conform to their schema definition. Section 6.7.1, "Importing an XSD," uses the XSD for XHTML to produce a report using model-to-model transformation.

UML2

The UML2 component provides an EMF-based implementation of the OMG's UML2 metamodel. This component serves as the de facto "reference implementation" of the specification and was developed in collaboration with the specification itself. The UML2 component also provides support for UML Profiles. Although this component focuses on the implementation of the metamodel, it provides an enhanced version of the EMF-generated editor. UML2 diagramming functionality is left to the UML2 Tools component.

Noted that although this book focuses on Ecore as the metamodel for creating the abstract syntax of DSLs, the UML2 metamodel provides another option.

In fact, it provides multiple options because a DSL can be defined using a lightweight or heavyweight extension of the UML2 metamodel.

UML2 Tools

The UML2 Tools component of MDT provides diagramming to complement the metamodel implementation provided by the UML2 component. These diagrams are implemented using the Graphical Modeling Framework and provide an extensive set of additional examples of how to use GMF's tooling and runtime. Not all of the UML2 diagrams are yet provided; the current list includes Class, Component, Activity, Deployment, Composite Structure, State Machine, and Use Case.

Object Constraint Language (OCL)

The OCL is commonly used to query and define constraints for models. As you will see in this book, OCL can also be used in custom templates to provide runtime behavior, initialize features in models, define model audits and metrics, and serve as the basis of transformation and expression languages. The OCL component of MDT provides the basis of these capabilities and is covered throughout the book.

By itself, the OCL component of MDT provides an implementation of the OMG's OCL 2.0 specification, provides bindings for Ecore and UML2, and comes with an interactive Console view to allow for testing OCL statements on model elements.

Business Process Modeling Notation (BPMN2)

The OMG plans to unite the Business Process Modeling Notation (BPMN) and Business Process Definition Metamodel (BPDM) into a single BPMN2 specification. This forthcoming component of MDT plans to provide an implementation of the underlying metamodel, again similar to the UML2 component. Diagramming for BPMN is currently provided in the SOA Tools project and plans to update this support to leverage this metamodel implementation.

Information Management Metamodel (IMM)

This component aims to provide metamodel and profile implementations for the upcoming IMM specification from the OMG, again similar to the UML component. The implementation will be based on EMF's Ecore metamodel, with integration and exchange capabilities. The Eclipse DataTools project (DTP) likely will provide diagramming of data models in the future.

1.5.5 Generative Modeling Technologies

Essentially a top-level project itself, GMT is a project within the Modeling project that holds a wide range of research-focused components that deal with modeling and model-driven software-development technologies. The GMT project serves as an incubator for the Modeling project, where components are free to exit GMT and become Modeling projects on their own or can be added to another Modeling project.

For example, the Xpand template engine described in this book originated with the openArchitectureWare component within GMT but has graduated to the M2T project. ATL is a model-to-model transformation technology that has graduated to the M2M project. Similarly, TCS and Xtext are two GMT components that form the basis of the new TMF project. This book does not cover the individual components within GMT; visit the GMT project home page at www.eclipse.org/gmt to learn more.

1.5.6 Amalgamation

The Modeling Amalgamation Project (Amalgam, for short) was recently added to Modeling to provide a set of modeling-specific packages to ease download and installation. These packages enable the user to avoid a series of updates because Modeling components are fine-grained and maintained on many separate download pages and update sites. Amalgam is also chartered to provide some common user interface (UI) elements and integrations that would not otherwise be appropriately maintained in another project. The examples from this book are available from Amalgam because they span a range of project capabilities. In fact, the DSL Toolkit download from Amalgam is specifically configured to be used in the context of this book's examples, which you can extract into the Toolsmith's workspace as samples.

1.5.7 Project Interaction

As an Eclipse open source project, the Modeling project operates under the process and guidelines outlined by the Eclipse Foundation. Modeling projects have contributors from a wide range of organizations, including commercial enterprises, academic organizations, and individuals. You can interact with projects at Eclipse in many ways, but you should keep some important things in mind. First, newsgroups are typically your best source of information, and you should search them before posting a new question. Using a good newsgroup reader that has no limits on the amount of history that it maintains locally is superior to searching via the Web interface, although that works as well. Second are the project wiki pages, which recently have become far more popular than the Eclipse Web site for content because they are easier to maintain and facilitate immediate contribution. Most projects have developer and release engineering mailing lists, but don't use these unless you're a developer on the project. If you post a question to a mailing list, you'll likely be directed to the newsgroup.

Contributions are welcome, of course, and they're best attached to a Bugzilla in the form of a patch. Guidelines govern contributing patches on the wiki. It's best to confer with a developer on the project before contributing code, and remember that you must follow intellectual property guidelines for all contributions. If you're contributing a patch or feature, be sure to include unit tests to cover the code, when applicable. Finally, remember that contributions come in various shapes and sizes. Documentation is just as welcome as code because there's always a shortage of documentation.

The best starting point for learning more about Eclipse and how to get involved is to visit the Web site, the wiki, newsgroups, mailing lists, and the new-comers FAQ page, in particular: www.eclipse.org/home/newcomers.php.

1.6 Summary

As you can see, the Modeling project has a wide array of modeling technologies. Diversity is an important part of the Eclipse ecosystem, and the Modeling project is the poster child of diversity, considering the range of commercial, academic, and individual contributors to the project. Furthermore, the Modeling project continues to improve relations with specification organizations, such as the OMG. This book focuses specifically on using a subset of Modeling project technologies within the context of creating a DSL Toolkit, but it's possible to do much more with what's provided in Modeling.

On the larger topic of domain-specific languages and model-driven software development, the rest of this book focuses on providing a view and extended tutorial of what capabilities exist today. Although the Modeling project has come a long way from its beginnings with the Eclipse Modeling Framework, it has a long way to go before the functionality provided by its many components used together as a DSL Toolkit will rival the richness of the JDT for Java development. Arguably, no project at Eclipse will ever achieve this lofty goal, but we hope to provide considerable improvement in Modeling in the next few years. The areas for improving the JDT are narrowing, and the possibilities and functionality of modeling are just beginning. So let's get started.

CHAPTER 2

Modeling Project as a
DSL Toolkit

To discuss using the Modeling project as a DSL Toolkit, this chapter first covers some of the basics of domain-specific languages, model-driven software development, and the installation of the requisite modeling project components. In the abstract, a DSL Toolkit needs to enable a Toolsmith to define the domain model itself, a diagram, a textual notation, model-to-model transformations, and model-to-text transformations. The Modeling project provides these through the Eclipse Modeling Framework (EMF), Graphical Modeling Framework (GMF), Model-to-Model Transformation (M2M), and Model-to-Text Transformation (M2T), respectively. Used together, they relate as shown in Figure 2-1, with the domain model (abstract syntax) being the basis of all artifacts. Figure 2-1 displays a simple notation for these abstract elements that I use throughout the book.

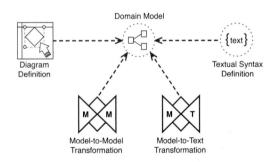

Figure 2-1   DSL Toolkit artifacts—abstract

Figure 2-2 provides a more concrete example (but still speaks in terms of the *abstract* elements) and shows the artifacts used by our Toolsmith in developing the mindmap application. Note that artifacts the Toolsmith develops might or might not be deployed to the Practitioner. For example, Figure 2-2 shows model-to-text templates used to generate model code and others invoked by the Practitioner on model instances. A Practitioner might want to alter the output from an M2M or M2T, so the latter are typically deployed to allow for customization. Technically, all DSL artifacts can be deployed for extension and regeneration.

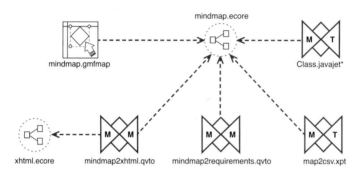

Figure 2-2   Abstract DSL artifacts—Toolsmith

When I discuss the Practitioner's use of these artifacts, I alter the notation slightly to indicate instances of each. Specifically, I fill in areas of each notation element to distinguish an *instance* from its *abstraction,* which is "hollow" in comparison. In the case of Figure 2-3, the Practitioner works with an instance of the mindmap model through its diagram and can export the model using model transformations. The first is an M2T template that results in a Comma-Separated Values (CSV) file. The second produces an HTML report using an Extensible HTML (XHTML) model. An M2M transformation results in a Requirements model that can be transformed to HTML using an M2T transformation.

To get an overall picture of what I described previously in the process of developing a DSL Toolkit, Figure 2-4 represents a general flow. Of course, some elements are purely optional, and the process is intended to be iterative. Again, a DSL Toolkit in the context of this book includes the tooling required for developing of all aspects of a domain-specific language, including model transformations and code generation. The important point to keep in mind is that models, transformations, and templates are iteratively developed with the goal of providing as much generation as practical. We probably won't see fully generated applications in the near future, although many aspects of the tooling that you'll produce in the context of this book are just that. As the tooling and techniques improve, complete product lines likely will be mostly generated over time.

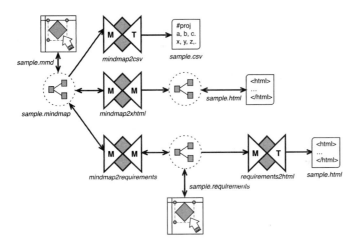

Figure 2-3 Instance DSL artifacts—Practitioner

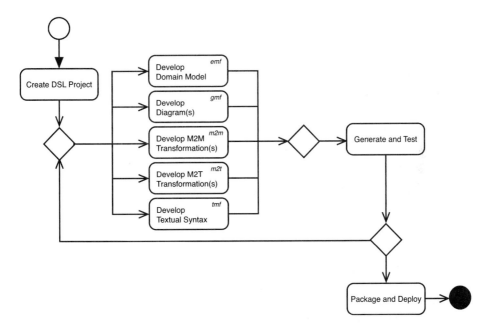

Figure 2-4 DSL Toolkit development workflow

As always, the use of the toolkit begins with creating a new project to hold the DSL artifacts. The Amalgam DSL Toolkit download provides a DSL project type, although it's possible to begin with a regular Eclipse plug-in project and add the appropriate natures and builders. The structure provided by the DSL project is not mandatory, but it nicely organizes artifacts into model, diagram, template, and workflow folders.

Development of the domain model (the DSL abstract syntax) follows and is stored in its EMF `.ecore` and `.genmodel` files. With the domain model available, the Toolsmith can then create the collection of models used to define a diagram using GMF, develop transformation definitions using Query/View/Transformation (QVT) or ATL, develop code (text) generation templates using Xpand or Java Emitter Templates (JET), and create the artifacts required for generation of a text editor.

After they are created, the corresponding generator models are used to produce plug-ins for deployment. Generally, it is not recommended that the DSL project itself be the target of code generation because doing so would complicate cleanup and regeneration. The deployment artifacts should also provide actions to invoke templates and transformations. Standard Eclipse packaging of plug-ins as features or product definitions can be used to deploy the DSL tooling to a practitioner's workbench.

2.1 Installation

Before you can get started using the Modeling project as a DSL Toolkit, you must install it and configure the sample projects. This book is based on the Ganymede release of Eclipse (version 3.4), although some references are made to features found in the Galileo release, due out in June 2009. The easiest way to get started is to download the DSL Toolkit from the Amalgamation project at www.eclipse.org/modeling/amalgam/. Alternatively, you can begin with the Modeling package download from the Eclipse Packaging Project (EPP), available at www.eclipse.org/epp/ganymede.php. EPP provides a number of preconfigured Eclipse downloads targeted at Java, Java EE, C/C++, Plug-in Development, Reporting, and Modeling. The modeling package is defined and maintained by the Amalgamation and is configured with all of the Eclipse simultaneous release projects from Modeling, although it doesn't include everything you need to complete the samples in this book. Therefore, I recommend using the tailor-made Amalgam DSL Toolkit download. This book identifies additional dependencies for installation as required.

2.2 The Sample Projects

You can install the sample projects from the Welcome screen of the DSL Toolkit package or by using the standard example wizard in the New dialog. If the Amalgam DSL Toolkit is not used, you can get the sample projects from CVS at http://dev.eclipse.org in the /cvsroot/modeling repository under org.eclipse. amalgam. I recommended that you create the projects in the book from scratch and develop them along with the content, leaving the extraction of the completed samples for reference or a quick start. Furthermore, the namespace for the projects from Amalgam differs from what is described in the book. The book uses an org.eclipse.dsl.* namespace because it is shorter than the org. eclipse.amalgam.examples.dsl.* namespace in the provided solutions, which is a more appropriate namespace to be checked into Eclipse CVS. This also allows both sets of projects to be located in a single workspace, facilitating reference to the solution artifacts.

The sample projects in this book are provided in the context of a fictitious Eclipse Requirements Project (ERP). It is a top-level project, with several projects built using the Eclipse Modeling Project as a DSL Toolkit. In other words, it's a model-based requirements project, consisting of several related models used throughout the process of requirements elicitation, management, scenario, and business domain modeling. So in the process of describing how to use the capabilities of one top-level project at Eclipse, I'll be developing another. Keep in mind that these are fictitious projects and that certain decisions on their implementation were made to illustrate the capabilities of the Modeling project and focus less on developing a usable set of requirements tools, as can be found in the Eclipse Open Requirements Management Framework (ORMF) and Open System Engineering Environment (OSEE) projects.

The ERP contains the following four projects, each described here in minor detail in terms of what capabilities from the DSL Toolkit are illustrated during their development: the Requirements Elicitation Project (REP), Requirements Management Project (RMP), Requirement Scenario Project (RSP), and Business Domain Modeling (BDM) project.

The REP includes a simple mindmap [36] application, used for requirements elicitation. A mindmap is based on a simple domain model (DSL) and graphical notation, yet it can be incredibly powerful when used for brainstorming and organizing topics during the initial phases of a project (any project, not just software). A mindmap is also used as the basis of the GMF tutorial online, as an updated version of that tutorial. Our sample demonstrates the development of the mindmap domain model and associated diagram. It also illustrates the transformation from the mindmap model to a text document, an HTML report, and the requirements model of the next project, as seen in Figure 2-5.

The RMP includes an Eclipse rich client application for working with a requirements DSL, as seen in Figure 2-6. We also develop a diagram to show traceability, as well as an M2T for reporting requirements information. Requirements can be linked to additional detail in scenario diagrams, the next project in our fictitious ERP.

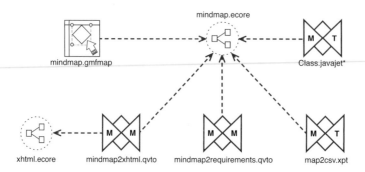

Figure 2-5   Mindmap DSL artifacts

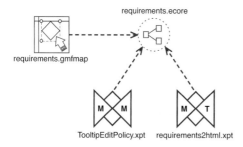

Figure 2-6   Requirements DSL artifacts

The RSP provides scenario-modeling capabilities using the standard Business Process Modeling Notation (BPMN), as seen in Figure 2-7. Scenario diagrams can be used to elicit requirements, in addition to providing dynamic modeling to enhance our last project. We transform scenario diagrams into Test and Performance Tools Platform (TPTP) manual test cases using QVT.

The BDM project provides a high-level business domain–modeling capability to refine our requirements in the context of business domains, as seen in Figure 2-8. This DSL is inspired by the *Java Modeling in Color with UML* book by Coad, et. al. [46]. It has a diagram similar to that of a UML class diagram, yet it provides a higher-level abstraction and set of constraints for object modeling within the context of a domain-neutral component, as described in the book. Throughout this book, the terms *BDM* and *color modeling diagram* are synonymous. We also develop a set of transformation definitions to produce Java Persistence API (JPA) code from these models.

To wrap up the sample and provide detail for our deployment section, the RMP project components are deployed as an Eclipse product definition.

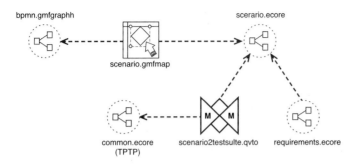

Figure 2-7 Scenario DSL artifacts

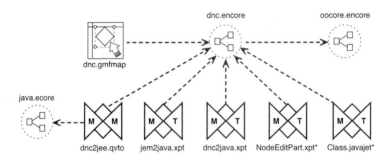

Figure 2-8 Color modeling DSL artifacts

Extending this set of sample projects involves many possibilities, such as producing BPEL from BPMN-based scenario diagrams, transforming business domain and scenario diagrams to and from their UML counterparts, transforming scenarios to Eclipse cheat sheets, extending the mindmap to display task information with a diagram better suited for temporal display (such as a Gantt chart), synchronizing tasks in mindmaps with Bugzilla entries using an M2M, and so on. All of these come to mind as feasible options using familiar techniques and a common metamodel by leveraging the Modeling project for DSL and model-driven software-development techniques. Of course, these extensions are left as exercises for the reader.

Figures 2-9 through 2-11 illustrate sample application artifacts and how they relate, using the notation introduced earlier. From the Practitioner's perspective, mindmap, scenario, and business models are created and viewed with corresponding diagrams. The requirements model can be produced from a mindmap model and edited with a diagram and corresponding editor. The mindmap and requirements models can produce reports using M2M and M2T transformations.

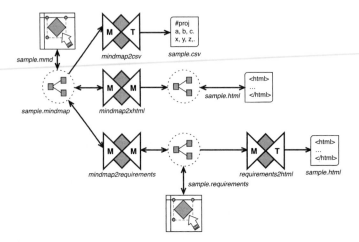

Figure 2-9   Mindmap and requirements DSL instances

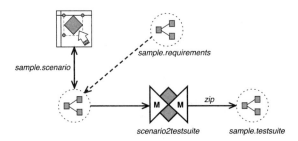

Figure 2-10   Scenario DSL instance

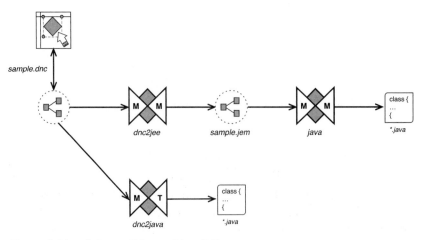

Figure 2-11   Color modeling and Java DSL instances

A scenario model is transformed into a TPTP Manual Test model, for use in its editor. Scenario models can also be embedded within requirements models.

The business model is transformed first to a Java EMF Model (JEM) and then to text as Java class files. Alternatively, the business model is transformed directly to Java classes using Xpand templates.

Figure 2-12 shows a Practitioner's workspace with each of the artifacts represented. The four open diagrams in the editor are the mindmap in the upper left, the scenario in the upper right, the requirements in the lower left, and the color modeling diagram in the lower right. The outline view shows the content of the requirements editor, which is also visible using the Selection page in the editor itself.

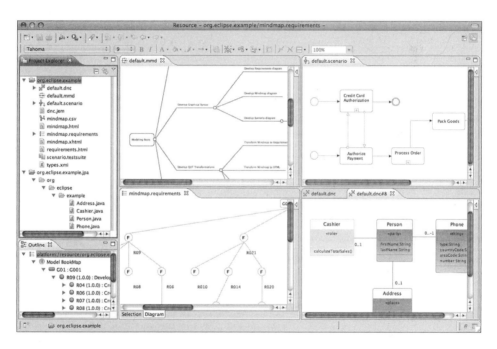

Figure 2-12   Practitioner's view of sample projects

The workspace has two projects, with the second being the target of the Java code generation from the color model instance. The main project contains all the Practitioner models and generated artifacts, other than Java. The mindmap CSV output, requirements HTML report, mindmap XHTML report, intermediate JEM, and TPTP test suite are all found in the `org.eclipse.example` project. Also seen is a `types.xmi` file used by the color business domain model.

2.3 Summary

In this chapter, we introduced a fictitious set of DSL-based projects that are used in the context of a product line for examples to follow. As you will see, maximizing the use of models and model-based technologies for a product line can lead to increased productivity and enable customization options not found in traditional methods of product development.

PART II

Developing Domain-Specific Languages

This part of the book takes the reader through a series of tutorial-like steps of developing a product line using domain-specific languages. From abstract syntax developed using Eclipse Modeling Framework (EMF), to graphical concrete syntax developed using Graphical Modeling Framework (GMF), to model-to-model transformation using Query/View/Transformation (QVT), to model-to-text transformation using Xpand, each technology is illustrated using a series of sample projects. At the end, we present a chapter that focuses on deploying the samples.

CHAPTER 3

Developing a DSL Abstract Syntax

In this chapter, we walk through the development of a domain-specific language (DSL) using the Eclipse Modeling Framework (EMF) and supporting components. Specifically, we develop the DSL's abstract syntax using the Ecore metamodel. But first we cover some basics on what to consider when creating a DSL and the different implementation strategies you might want to employ when using EMF. Next, we provide an overview of EMF, leaving detailed information to the book [38] dedicated to this purpose. We cover some additional components of EMF and Model Development Tools (MDT) that enable you to further refine DSLs, and we develop a series of domain models for use in the sample projects.

DISCLAIMER

The domain models developed as samples are constructed to illustrate certain features of the associated tooling and, as such, should not necessarily be considered "best practices" in some cases.

3.1 DSL Considerations

Many considerations are involved in creating a DSL. Does a model already exist that is close enough? If so, can an existing model be extended, or is it fixed? Does the model need to be based on a standard? Does the DSL lend itself to graphical display and editing? Does the DSL require a textual syntax and editor? Will a product line be built on the DSL, and perhaps others? Is the Ecore metamodel expressive enough to suit your needs for a DSL? How can you model dynamic behavior?

BEST PRACTICE

Leverage existing models, when appropriate. XML Schema Definition (XSD) and EMF are very popular technologies, and EMF can import just about any XSD, so search for existing domain models before you reinvent the wheel. Also consider publishing your domain model if you think that others might find it useful, if only as part of your application's API to aid in integration.

A key consideration is the amount of flexibility you need or will tolerate in the DSL. As you can see in the examples, sometimes a change in the domain model makes your transformation definitions much easier to write. Also, frameworks such as GMF have certain limitations—or, rather, were designed with particular use cases in mind. Your particular style of modeling might not lend itself well to graphical representation, but a few changes might allow mapping to diagram elements much easier. For example, certain mappings in Query/View/Transformation (QVT) and template expressions can be facilitated by adding derived features or methods to the domain model. Complex queries using Object Constraint Language (OCL) (and, therefore, useful ones in QVT and Xtend) can be added to the domain model with code generated for their implementation at runtime. Having a feature available in the model will greatly simplify transformations and templates that access them.

TIP

Don't be afraid of modifying your domain model to make working with templates, transformations, and diagram definitions easier. Unless you're using a model that cannot be altered, the Toolsmith will appreciate being able to make certain design decisions in the domain model to suit the tooling, instead of having to create workarounds or write custom code to use the tooling with a domain model.

This is not to say that you should let the tooling influence your DSL to an extent you are not comfortable with. The question is, how do you maintain a satisfactory level of "purity" in your DSL when considering the additional complexity associated with developing and maintaining the other Model-Driven Software Development (MDSD) artifacts? In general, the more complex the metamodel (DSL) is, the more complex the transformation definitions, templates, and diagram definitions are.

A set of conventions and best practices for the definition of DSLs, transformations, and templates likely will arise, as it has for Java and other popular programming languages. With conventions and best practices comes tooling to support refactorings, static analysis, and cleanup. At this stage of the Modeling project's evolution, operations are still quite manual and even error prone. As an open source project that forms the basis for commercial products, Eclipse eventually will see more advanced features pushed down into it, thereby improving the Toolsmith experience.

3.2 Eclipse Modeling Framework

From the project description, EMF is "a modeling framework and code generation facility for building tools and other applications based on a structured data model." This pretty much sums it up, but there's a lot to know about EMF. I highly recommend that you first read, or at least have available, the book on EMF [38] to better understand its use in the context of this book. Alternatively, reading through the online documentation and tutorials on EMF should make its use in this book easy to follow. In other words, the examples in this book only scratch the surface of what is possible using EMF.

You can create models using EMF in many ways. You can use the provided editor (a tree with properties view) or import a set of annotated Java classes. An Ecore diagram is available from the EMFT project. If you have the XSD component installed, you can import an XSD file. If you have the Unified Modeling Language (UML) version 2 (UML2) component installed, you can import a UML2 model. If you have Graphical Modeling Framework (GMF) installed, you can use its example Ecore diagram editor. If you download and install Emfatic [42], you can work in a textual syntax and synchronize with your Ecore model. In the future, you will be able to design your own concrete textual syntax for Ecore, or any model, using the Textual Modeling Framework (TMF) project.

Regardless of the method you choose for importing or working with your domain model, you will find an `.ecore` file in your workspace—that is, unless you take a purely programmatic approach. If you open this file in a text editor, you will see that it is an XML Metadata Interchange (XMI) serialization of your Ecore-based model. By default, EMF enables you to edit models in a basic (generated) tree editor with a Properties view. You can easily generate a similar editor for your own model.

Before getting into more detail, let's take a look at the Ecore metamodel.

3.2.1 Ecore Metamodel

The EMF book describes the Ecore metamodel in detail, but here you find a simplified diagram for reference (Figure 3-1), along with some discussion of the more relevant aspects used as we develop our DSL abstract syntax. It's a fairly simple model, which is part of its strength. In most cases, you can compensate for the lack of features in Ecore by using some of the more advanced modeling techniques, which are discussed in the EMF book. A longstanding topic of debate among EMF users is the lack of an EAssociation class, but we don't get into that here.

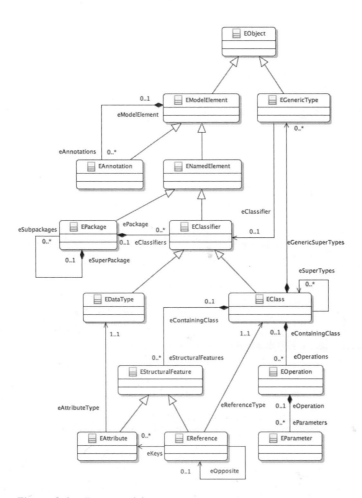

Figure 3-1   Ecore model

Annotations

Sometimes it's important to add information to a model element for documentation purposes, or to provide parameters to be considered during transformation or generation. EAnnotations provide these for all model elements in EMF. An EAnnotation has a **Source** field, which serves as a key, and a list of **References**. An EAnnotation may have zero or more **Details Entry** children, which have **Key** and **Value** properties. This simple capability of annotating models is quite flexible and turns out to be useful for many purposes, including XSD support.

Another particularly useful application of annotations is to declare OCL constraints, method bodies, and derived feature implementation, as discussed in Section 3.2.4, "Applying OCL."

3.2.2 Runtime Features

The EMF runtime includes facilities for working with instances of your models. No strict dependencies exist on the Eclipse platform for the runtime and generated model and edit code, so these bundles can be used outside of the Eclipse workbench. As bundles, they can be deployed in any Equinox OSGi container, even within a server environment.

The generated code for your model has a dependency on the underlying EMF runtime components. A significant benefit is gained from the generated Application Programming Interface (API) and model implementation working with the provided runtime features. An efficient observer pattern implementation is provided to alert listeners to model change events. A generated reflective API provides an efficient means of working with models dynamically. In fact, EMF can be used in a purely dynamic fashion, requiring neither an .ecore model nor code generation. Finally, it's possible to have static registration of a dynamic package, but that's an advanced use case left to the EMF documentation.

When working with model instances, changes can be recorded in a change model that provides a reverse delta and allows for transaction support. A validation framework provides for invariant and constraint support with batch processing. The Model Transaction and Validation Framework components provide enhanced transaction and validation support, respectively.

For persistence of models, the EMF runtime provides a default XML serialization. The persistence layer is flexible, allowing for XMI, Universally Unique Identifiers (UUIDs), and even a zip option. A resource set consists of one or more resources, making it possible to persist objects in multiple files, including cross-containment references. Proxy resolution and demand loading improve performance when working with large models across resources. Additionally, use of EMF Technology (EMFT) components Teneo and CDO allow for the persistence of models to a relational database.

The generated editor for EMF models includes a multipage editor and properties view. Drag-and-drop support is provided, as is copy/paste support. A number of menu actions are available in the generated editor, including validation
invocation and dynamic instance model creation. Each generated editor comes
with a default creation wizard. Figure 3-2 shows an example of the editor,
including a context menu showing options to create new elements, cut, copy,
paste, delete, validate, and so on.

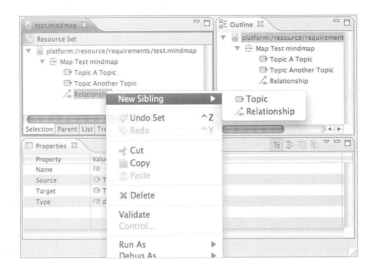

Figure 3-2   EMF-generated editor

3.2.3 Code Generation

From an *.ecore (Ecore) model, you need to produce a generator model and
supply additional information required for code generation. An EMF generator
model has a *.genmodel file extension and is essentially a decorator model for
a corresponding *.ecore model. This generator model is fed to Java Emitter
Templates (JETs) that are used to write Java and other files. JET is the Java Server
Pages (JSP)-like technology used by default when generating text from Ecore
models. This book does not cover it in detail, but a tutorial is available online
[51] if you want to know more.

You can customize the existing generation output using custom templates.
Furthermore, you can extract constraint, pre-/post-condition, and body implementations from OCL annotations for use in generation and invocation at runtime. This is not a native EMF capability, but you can add it using the MDT OCL
component. You will use this technique in the context of the sample projects.

When regenerating code, the JMerge component is used to prevent overwriting user modifications. Generated Java code is annotated with `@generated` javadoc style tags to identify it and distinguish it from user code. Removing the tag or adding NOT after the tag ensures that JMerge will not overwrite the modified code. Typically, using `@generated NOT` is preferred because it allows the Toolsmith to identify code that was generated and modified, as opposed to newly added code. Note that not all code benefits from merging. Specifically, `plugin.xml` and `MANIFEST.MF` files need to be deleted before an update can occur.

3.2.4 Applying OCL

Many opportunities arise for using OCL in EMF models. Class constraints, method bodies, and derived feature implementations can all be provided using MDT OCL and EMF dynamic templates. The approach of using OCL and custom templates in this book comes from an Eclipse Corner article [44] and has been modified only slightly to conform to a similar approach taken to leverage OCL added to models in QVT, as discussed in Section 6.5.6, "Leveraging OCL in EMF Models." The templates are generic and can easily be added to any project that needs to provide OCL-based implementations in its generated model code. It is also worth noting that GMF uses OCL extensively in its models, employing an EMF Validator to maintain the integrity of its models.

To add an OCL expression to a model element, we begin by adding a normal EAnnotation. For the `Source` property, enter `http://www.eclipse.org/2007/OCL`. This URI allows our custom templates and QVT engine to recognize this annotation as OCL, where it can expect to find `Details Entry` children of type `constraint`, `derive`, or `body`. Note that the original article [44] used `http://www.eclipse.org/ocl/examples/OCL` as the URI.

Depending on the context, add the appropriate `Key` (EMF `constraint` key, `derive`, or `body`) to a child `Details Entry` of the EAnnotation and specify the OCL in the `Value` property. For invariant constraints, the OCL annotations complement the normal EMF constraint annotations by providing implementation for the validation framework to enforce constraints.

TIP

To test your OCL, it's helpful to use the Interactive OCL Console with a dynamic instance of your model, as discussed in Section 1.5.4, "Object Constraint Language." Be sure to select the proper model element for the expression, as well as the proper metalevel in the console.

To invoke the provided OCL at runtime, you must use custom JET templates for your domain model. The generated code retrieves the OCL statement from the model element and invokes it, evaluating the result. An alternative to this is to generate a Java implementation of the OCL during generation and avoid invoking the OCL interpreter at runtime.

The referenced article covers the details of the custom templates, so they are not covered here. Also, the templates are included in the book's sample projects and are touched upon during the development of the sample projects. For now, we take a look at just the derived feature implementation, both before and after using the OCL with a custom template approach. First, consider the default generated code for a derived reference—in this case, the rootTopics reference from the MapImpl class in our mindmap example.

```
/**
 * <!-- begin-user-doc -->
 * <!-- end-user-doc -->
 * @generated
 */
public EList<Topic> getRootTopics() {
    // TODO: implement this method to return the 'Root Topics'
    // reference list
    // Ensure that you remove @generated or mark it @generated NOT
    // The list is expected to implement
    // org.eclipse.emf.ecore.util.InternalEList and
    // org.eclipse.emf.ecore.EStructuralFeature.Setting
    // so it's likely that an appropriate subclass of
    // org.eclipse.emf.ecore.util.EcoreEList should be used.
        throw new UnsupportedOperationException();
}
```

Let's add the following OCL statement to the derived feature using the previous convention. Here we see the annotation within the mindmap.ecore model in its native XMI serialization. Note that this OCL statement could be simplified by using the parent eOpposite relationship on our Topic's subtopics reference, which was added to facilitate the diagram definition of Section 4.3.5, "Subtopic Figure."

```
<eStructuralFeatures xsi:type="ecore:EReference"
  name="rootTopics" upperBound="-1" eType="#//Topic" volatile="true"
  transient="true" derived="true">
  <eAnnotations source="http://www.eclipse.org/2007/OCL">
    <details key="derive"
      value="let topics : Set(mindmap::Topic) = self.elements->
               select(oclIsKindOf(mindmap::Topic))->
               collect(oclAsType(mindmap::Topic))->asSet() in
```

```
                 topics->symmetricDifference(topics.subtopics->
                 asSet())"/>
    </eAnnotations>
</eStructuralFeatures>
```

Before regeneration, we need to make some changes in the genmodel. To allow the OCL plug-in to be added to our generated manifest dependencies, we need to add `OCL_ECORE=org.eclipse.ocl.ecore` to the `Model Plug-in Variables` property of the genmodel root. Also, we need to set the `Dynamic Templates` property to `true` and enter the templates path (such as `/org.eclipse.dsl.mindmap/templates/domain`) to the `Template Directory` property. After we generate, we can see the following implementation in our `MapImpl` class.

```java
private static OCLExpression<EClassifier> rootTopicsDeriveOCL;

private static final String OCL_ANNOTATION_SOURCE =
  "http://www.eclipse.org/2007/OCL";

/**
 * <!-- begin-user-doc -->
 * <!-- end-user-doc -->
 * @generated
 */
public EList<Topic> getRootTopics() {
  EStructuralFeature eFeature =
    MindmapPackage.Literals.MAP__ROOT_TOPICS;

  if (rootTopicsDeriveOCL == null) {
    Helper helper = OCL_ENV.createOCLHelper();
    helper.setAttributeContext(MindmapPackage.Literals.MAP, eFeature);

    EAnnotation ocl = eFeature.getEAnnotation(OCL_ANNOTATION_SOURCE);
    String derive = (String) ocl.getDetails().get("derive");

    try {
      rootTopicsDeriveOCL = helper.createQuery(derive);
    } catch (ParserException e) {
      throw new UnsupportedOperationException(e.getLocalizedMessage());
    }
  }

  Query<EClassifier, ?, ?> query =
    OCL_ENV.createQuery(rootTopicsDeriveOCL);

  @SuppressWarnings("unchecked")
  Collection<Topic> result = (Collection<Topic>) query.evaluate(this);

  return new EcoreEList.UnmodifiableEList<Topic>(this, eFeature,
    result.size(), result.toArray());
}
```

The generated code checks to see if the `OCLExpression` for this derivation has been created already; if not, it initializes it by retrieving the statement from the `EAnnotation` and its detail with key `derive`. Then the expression is evaluated and the list of `Topic` elements is returned.

As mentioned in the article, some improvements could be made to this approach, but it illustrates the usefulness of adding OCL statements to your EMF models. It's not hard to imagine how a significant portion of an application could be generated from a model adorned with OCL for invariant constraints, method bodies, and derived features. In GMF, we can see how OCL is used to augment the diagram-mapping model to provide for constraints, feature initialization, audit definition, and model metric definition.

BEST PRACTICE

Adding constraints and validation is essential in model-driven software development. Although you can place validation code within QVT, Xpand templates, and so on, it's most useful to ensure that your model instance is well formed when created, or before moving to a model transformation.

3.2.5 Dynamic Instances

A powerful feature of EMF, and one that is useful to a Toolsmith developing a new DSL, is the capability to create dynamic instances of a model. The reflective framework of EMF is leveraged to allow instantiation of a model element without generating code beforehand. This can be done from within the default Ecore editor by selecting an element and choosing the `Create Dynamic Instance` context menu item. The instance is stored in an XMI file within the development workspace, so the generation or launch of plug-ins is not required to test a model or, more importantly, to test Xpand templates and QVT transformations under development. This is one important distinction when comparing JET to Xpand. Dynamic instances are used in the context of our sample projects.

BEST PRACTICE

Use dynamic instance models for development as much as possible. Xpand templates, QVT transformations, and the OCL console can all work with dynamic instance models and avoid making Toolsmiths generate code and

---

invoke a runtime instance to test their work. GMF diagrams still require code generation to develop effectively, although generated diagrams are capable of working with dynamic instances.

Figure 3-3 is an example of a dynamic instance model for our mindmap domain model, along with the Properties view. It's similar in functionality to the generated EMF editor, although it requires the metamodel to be loaded and reflected upon, as you can see from the loaded `mindmap.ecore` resource file.

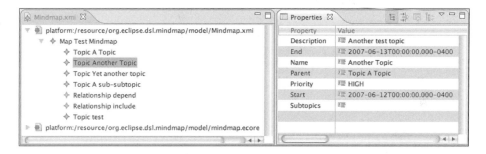

Figure 3-3 Mindmap dynamic instance model

TIP

You can view any Ecore model using the **Sample Reflective Ecore Model Editor**, so there's little need to generate the EMF .editor plug-in. This applies to XMI dynamic instances, such as GMF-based diagrams files where both the domain and notation models are persisted in a single file. Simply right-click the file and select **Open With** → **Other** → **Internal Editors** → **Sample Reflective Ecore Model Editor**.

3.3 Developing the Mindmap Domain Model

We develop a simple mindmap DSL and use it throughout the book to provide an example of how to use components of the Modeling project as a DSL Toolkit. This model forms the base of our fictitious Requirements Elicitation Project (REP).

This is the beginning of those sections in the book that you can follow in a tutorial fashion. Solution projects are available to save time, although you should be able to begin from scratch and produce these solutions on your own. It's up to you to follow along or simply review the solutions as we proceed.

Figure 3-4 is a diagram of the basic mindmap DSL we create in this section. Not much explanation should be required here because you can easily see that a `Map` class serves as the container for `Topics` and `Relationships`, which both extend from `MapElement`. The following sections provide details on setting up a DSL project and creating this model, along with the other DSL artifacts associated with the project.

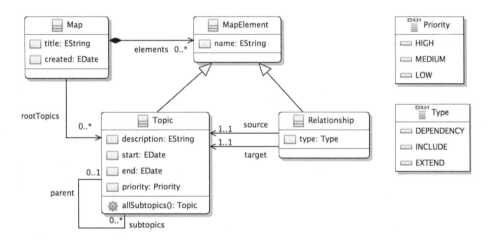

Figure 3-4   Mindmap domain model

3.3.1 Project Setup

Before getting started defining our mindmap domain model, we need a new project. Although EMF and GMF provide their own project wizards, we use the DSL Project Wizard provided by the Amalgam project to hold our DSL artifacts. You can create an equivalent project by starting with a plug-in project and adding the required dependencies, natures, and builders. The DSL project is also a plug-in project, as we'll eventually want to deploy the project to facilitate revisioning and extension. Furthermore, Xpand and workflow files currently need to be located in source paths to be developed, so we need a Java project anyway. In the future, this should not be required.

For our mindmap project, switch to the DSL perspective and use **File → New → DSL Project** to create a new project named `org.eclipse.dsl.mindmap`. The wizard creates a set of folders: `/model`, `/diagrams`, `/templates`, `/transformations`, and `/workflows`. Not all of these folders are required for each DSL project, but we use them for our mindmap. The wizard also adds natures and builders for QVT and Xpand/Model Workflow Engine (MWE).

3.3.2 Creating the Mindmap Domain Model

As mentioned earlier, creating an Ecore model involves many starting points. If we had an existing XML Schema for our domain, we could import it and EMF would take care of serializing documents conforming to the schema. If we used the UML2 project and associated the UML2 Tools class diagram to model our domain, we could import it to create an EMF model. We begin using "classic" EMF to create our mindmap DSL from scratch.

Typically, we'd begin with **File → New → Other → Eclipse Modeling Framework → Ecore Model** (Ctrl+3 → Ecore Model). However, the DSL Toolkit from Amalgam provides some wizard redefinitions to facilitate DSL development and defines capability definitions to hide the original UI contributions from various Modeling projects. To create our model, we select the `/model` folder and use the **File → New → Domain Model** (Ctrl+3 → Domain Model) wizard, which is really just the GMF Ecore diagram wizard. Name the model and diagram files `mindmap.ecore` and `mindmap.ecore_diagram`, respectively. Optionally, you can use the Ecore Tools component, available from the EMFT project. It provides some capabilities beyond those that the GMF example editor provides.

Before we begin to model the domain, we need to set some defaults in our mindmap Ecore model. First, right-click on the blank diagram surface and select **Show Properties View**. This shows the properties for the root package in our new Ecore model. Each Ecore model has a single root package, under which we can create a number of additional subpackages. In our case, we set the properties accordingly: `name` and `Ns Prefix` should be set to `mindmap`; `Ns URI` should be set to `http://www.eclipse.org/2008/mindmap`.

Using Figure 3-4, model the mindmap domain using the palette and Properties view. It's a straightforward model to implement, with only a couple noteworthy items: First, the `MapElement` class is abstract; second, the `rootTopics` relationship is derived, transient, and volatile. We implement this derived reference using OCL in Section 3.3.5, "Adding OCL."

The diagram surface has many features to explore, as discussed in Section 10.1, "Overview." You should note a few things, however, when using the Ecore diagram to create the mindmap domain model:

Aggregation links create a reference with the `Containment` property set to `true`, in contrast with Association links, which are noncontainment references.

Setting the upper bound property of a link to –1 creates a **many** relationship and causes the link to be displayed with the familiar 0..* notation.

References with `eOpposites` are shown in Figure 3-4 as a single connection, whereas the Ecore diagram shows two separate links.

3.3.3 *Creating the Mindmap Generator Model*

With our `mindmap.ecore` model complete, we can validate it and create a generator model. To validate it, open the model in the **Sample Ecore Model Editor** and right-click on the root package. Select **Validate** and confirm that no errors exist. If there are errors, correct them and continue. We look into adding validation for our mindmap model later, which leverages a similar validation framework provided for all Ecore models.

To create `mindmap.genmodel`, right-click the `mindmap.ecore` file in Explorer view and select **New → Other → Domain-Specific Language → Domain Generator Model** (Ctrl+3 → Domain Gen). Note that the original EMF wizard is found in **New → Other → Eclipse Modeling Framework → EMF Model** (Ctrl+3 → EMF Model). We started by selecting our `mindmap.ecore model`, so the wizard defaults to the same folder and provides the name we want. It also recognizes that we are importing an Ecore model, but we have to load it ourselves, curiously. We have only one root package, so we can finish the wizard and take a look at the generator model properties.

EMF generator models include several properties to consider. For our mindmap, we need to change only a couple from their default settings. In the root, change the `Compliance Level` from 1.4 to 5.0 (if it's not already set to 5.0) and change the `Model Directory` to be `/org.eclipse.mindmap/src`. (Note that this changes the edit, editor, and tests properties as well.) We need to manually change the `Model Plug-in ID` property to `org.eclipse.mindmap`, however. In the properties for the Mindmap root package, we need to set the `Base Package` property to `org.eclipse` to match our new plug-in namespace.

This gets us started, so we can move on to code generation. Later, we return to our mindmap model and add constraints, validation, and other enhancements.

3.3.4 Generate and Run

The last thing to do is generate our mindmap plug-ins and code. Technically, we don't need to generate code at this time because we plan to leverage dynamic instances as long as we can in the development of our DSLs. However, for those new to EMF, it's worthwhile to continue with generation at this point to see how things work. This is accomplished by right-clicking the root of the `mindmap.genmodel` in the editor tree and selecting **Generate All**. This generates our model code, edit code, editor code, and test skeletons, each in their own plug-in projects. We don't need the generated editor code because a diagram provides our primary means of working with mindmap instance models. For now, we can continue by running the generated editor to verify our model and configuration.

To run our plug-ins and test the functionality of our editor, we need to be in the Plug-in Development Environment perspective to gain access to the appropriate Run option. Select **Run** → **Open Run Dialog** (Ctrl+3 → Run C) and create a new Eclipse Application run configuration named `requirements` in a directory named `runtime-requirements`. Figure 3-5 is an image of this dialog. Figure 3-6 shows the **Arguments** page with some arguments for launching on Mac OS X. We use this launch configuration throughout our development of the sample projects, hence the general `requirements` name.

TIP

If you get tired of adding arguments to your launch configurations each time you create one, navigate in the Preferences dialog to **Plug-In Development** → **Target Platform** → **Launching Arguments** and enter them in the field provided. These values will be copied into any new launch configuration you create.

Run this configuration to launch a new instance of Eclipse with the new plug-ins installed. We could trim the plug-in list to launch only those plug-ins we need for our application. This makes launching faster and keeps us aware of our underlying plug-in dependencies. In Chapter 8, "DSL Packaging and Deployment," we fine-tune our launch settings before creating our product configuration.

In the runtime workbench, create a new project and follow **New** → **Example EMF Model Creation Wizards** → **Mindmap Model,** giving it whatever name you want and selecting Map as the Model Object. The default EMF-generated editor appears upon finish, ready for you to create new Topic and Relationship instances within the map.

You again need to open the Properties view to set model element properties and establish subtopics and relationship links. Notice that validation is available for our model instances and enforces the basic structural features defined in our model. For example, we declared 1 for the upper and lower bounds on source and target references of our Relationship class. Creating a new Relationship instance in our model and invoking the **Validate** menu option brings up a dialog that points out that these required features were not set. As we enhance our model further, EMF and the Validation Framework will provide additional validation, as used by GMF for diagram validation.

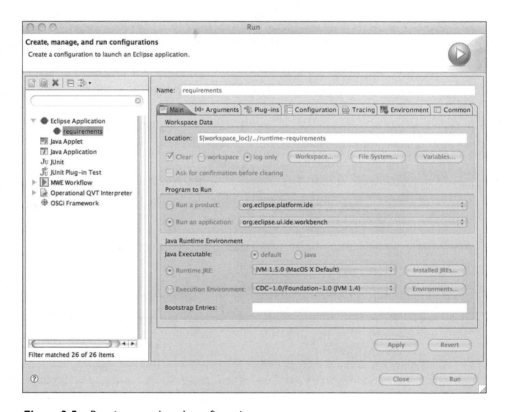

Figure 3-5　Requirements launch configuration

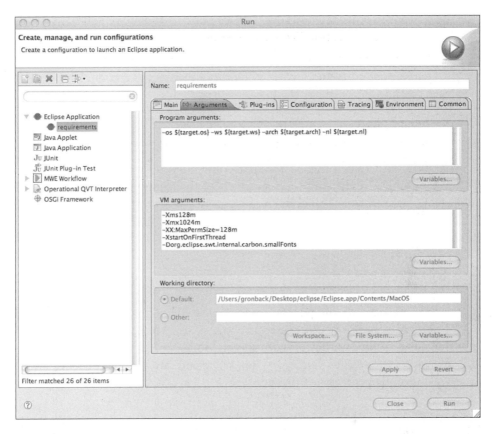

Figure 3-6   Requirements launch configuration arguments

3.3.5 Adding OCL

As you should recall, we added a derived, transient, volatile `rootTopics` reference in our `Map` class. Section 3.2.4, "Applying OCL," described the basics of adding OCL and using dynamic templates to generate implementations for invariant constraints, method bodies, and derived features. The example in that section covered the `rootTopics` implementation using OCL and used a set of dynamic templates that we use in this context as well. At this time, rename the default templates folder to be a templates-domain source folder in the mindmap project, and copy the templates provided in the solution into this folder. We'll have additional templates later for deployment, so we can separate them into different root folders. Each DSL project that uses OCL to refine its domain model will reuse this set of templates. Then return to Section 3.2.4 and configure the `mindmap.ecore` model to use OCL to implement the `rootTopics` feature.

We can leverage OCL in our model in additional places to provide an implementation and avoid having to modify our generated code. Let's begin by adding a method that returns the full set of subtopics for a given `Topic`.

Finding All Subtopics

Currently, our model has a `subtopics` reference on each `Topic`, along with a method, `allSubtopics()`, that is intended to return a list of all of a `Topic`'s subtopics—that is, its subtopics, all of their subtopics, and so on. All methods declared in an Ecore model require an implementation to be provided, so we turn to OCL, where the implementation of this method is trivial, thanks to the non-standard `closure` iterator in MDT OCL:

```
self->closure(subtopics)
```

We need to add an `EAnnotation` to the method in our model with `Source` equal to `http://www.eclipse.org/2007/OCL`. A child `Details Entry` is added to the annotation with the previous expression as its `Value` property and with a `Key` value of `body`. When we regenerate our model code, we can see that our implementation is provided:

```java
/**
 * The parsed OCL expression for the body of the
 * '{@link #allSubtopics <em>All Subtopics</em>}' operation.
 * <!-- begin-user-doc -->
 * <!-- end-user-doc -->
 * @see #allSubtopics
 * @generated
 */
private static OCLExpression<EClassifier> allSubtopicsBodyOCL;

private static final String OCL_ANNOTATION_SOURCE =
  "http://www.eclipse.org/2007/OCL";

/**
 * <!-- begin-user-doc -->
 * <!-- end-user-doc -->
 * @generated
 */
public EList<Topic> allSubtopics() {
  if (allSubtopicsBodyOCL == null) {
    EOperation eOperation =
      MindmapPackage.Literals.TOPIC.getEOperations().get(0);
    OCL.Helper helper = OCL_ENV.createOCLHelper();
```

```
helper.setOperationContext(MindmapPackage.Literals.TOPIC,
  eOperation);
EAnnotation ocl = eOperation.getEAnnotation(OCL_ANNOTATION_SOURCE);
String body = ocl.getDetails().get("body");

try {
  allSubtopicsBodyOCL = helper.createQuery(body);
} catch (ParserException e) {
  throw new UnsupportedOperationException(e.getLocalizedMessage());
}
}

Query<EClassifier, ?, ?> query =
  OCL_ENV.createQuery(allSubtopicsBodyOCL);

@SuppressWarnings("unchecked")
Collection<Topic> result = (Collection<Topic>) query.evaluate(this);

return new BasicEList.UnmodifiableEList<Topic>(result.size(),
  result.toArray());
}
```

Again, here we see the boilerplate OCL code that configures an OCLExpression if it's the first invocation, and then it invokes the expression obtained from the annotation. We leave the mindmap model at this point and move on to develop the second domain model in our product line.

3.4 Developing the Requirements Domain Model

In a similar fashion to our mindmap model, we create a new org.eclipse. dsl.requirements DSL project here to hold our requirements model. This forms the base of our fictitious Requirements Management Project (RMP). We create the new requirements.ecore model using the Domain Model Wizard and GMF Ecore diagram, and we complete it to match the diagram and description of Figure 3-7.

Basically, a model contains a collection of RequirementGroups, which contain a number of children groups and Requirements. Requirements have child references and contain Version and optional Comment elements. A number of enumerations for Priority, State, Type, and Resolution are also in the model. A Requirement can also have a number of dependent requirements, which become the basis for our dependency diagram. Note that the author attributes are simple strings. We could create a Team model and reference these elements to assign to our requirements and comments. We also could have a separate Discussion model to use here and in our mindmap, as a topic might have an associated discussion thread. Many possibilities exist, but for the purposes of our sample application, we keep it simple.

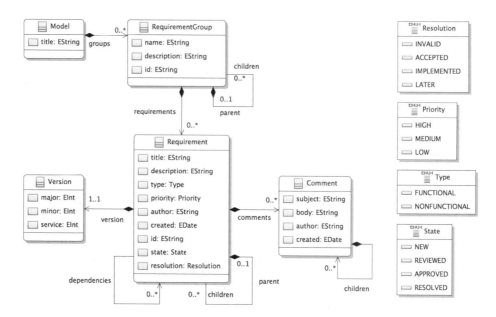

Figure 3-7 Requirements domain model

3.4.1 Requirements Generator Model

We create a `requirements.genmodel` in the usual manner, using the new **Domain Generator Model (Ctrl+3 → Domain Gen)** wizard and selecting our `requirements.ecore` model as the input. We'll make some adjustments to this genmodel and to the generated Edit code because we intend to use the generated EMF editor as part of our solution.

For the display string of a requirement in the editor selection tree, we want to have it be id `(major.minor.service):title`, where `major`, `minor`, and `service` are from the contained `Version` element. We'll be using the Properties view to edit the details of the requirement, so we'll have plenty of horizontal space to use in the editor, allowing even longer requirement titles to fit. Another option is to navigate using the Project Explorer view, but this is narrow and does not allow for much information display. Furthermore, we'll have a second tab in the editor to display a requirements dependency diagram, which will also require a bit of editor space. To accomplish the task, we'll select the requirement element in the genmodel and change its `Edit Label Feature` to be our `id:EString` attribute. Unfortunately, we cannot set two attributes to display for the label, as we can for GMF diagrams. This means we have to modify the generated code.

Before generation, we need to check the other properties and make changes accordingly. As with the mindmap and other models, we want to generate our model, edit, and editor code to their own projects, so we can change the **Model Plug-in ID** and **Model Directory** properties to be `org.eclipse.require-ments.model`. We generate the three plug-ins and open the `org.eclipse.requirements.provider.RequirementItemProvider` class from our Edit plug-in. Modify the `getText()` method as seen next. Note that if we wanted to preserve the generated method to allow the label feature of the generator model to have an effect, we could use the `getTextGen()` method approach, as described in the EMF documentation.

```
/**
 * This returns the label text for the adapted class.
 * Modified to show id (major.minor.service) : title
 *
 * @generated NOT
 */
@Override
public String getText(Object object) {
  StringBuilder sb = new StringBuilder();
  sb.append(((Requirement)object).getId());
  sb.append(" (");
  Version version = ((Requirement)object).getVersion();
    if (version != null) {
      sb.append(((Requirement)object).getVersion().getMajor());
      sb.append(".");
      sb.append(((Requirement)object).getVersion().getMinor());
      sb.append(".");
      sb.append(((Requirement)object).getVersion().getService());
    } else {
      sb.append("0.0.0");
    }
    sb.append(") : ");
    sb.append(((Requirement)object).getTitle());
    String label = sb.toString();
    return label == null || label.length() == 0 ?
      getString("_UI_Requirement_type") : label;
}
```

We've eliminated the redundant `Requirement` prefix from our label because we're using a custom icon to distinguish `Requirements` from `Requirement Groups`, `Comments`, and so on. For our `RequirementGroup` element, we can similarly modify the `getText()` method to display only the `name` attribute; we can modify the `Comment` element to display `created`, `author`, and `subject`.

3.5 Developing the Scenario Domain Model

Because we're basing the notation for our Scenario diagram on the Business Process Modeling Notation (BPMN) standard, we could simply use its description of the underlying domain model and semantics to develop our DSL. A better approach would have been to find an XSD for BPMN and simply import it into EMF. Unfortunately, no such schema is published with the specification—even worse, a new specification from the OMG, the Business Process Definition Metamodel (BPDM), is slated to provide a domain model for BPMN2. Also unfortunate is that this specification has no serialized format that we can use and is overly complicated for our Scenario DSL. This leaves us to create our own scenario model.

In a new `org.eclipse.dsl.scenario` project, we can create our `scenario.ecore` model as the base of our fictitious Requirements Scenario Project (RSP) project. Figure 3-8 is the model to create using our Ecore diagram.

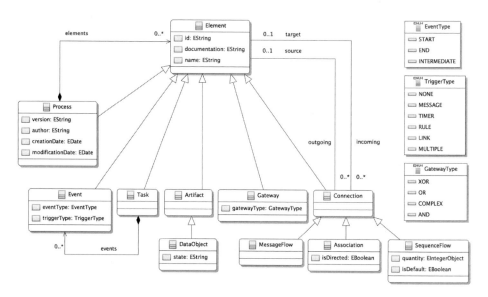

Figure 3-8   Scenario domain model

Elements of a scenario model are maintained in the `Process` class, which itself extends `Element`. A `Connection` maintains target and source references for `Elements` that are connected in `Sequence` or `Message` flows. An `Association` also connects elements. `Elements` come in a variety of types, including `Tasks`, `Events`, `DataObjects`, and `Gateways`. These elements all map in a straightforward manner to notation elements because the model is inherently graphical in nature. The model is actually similar to the description provided in the BPMN specification, although it is a subset.

3.6 Developing the Business Domain Model

Plenty of options exist for developing the domain model that will form the base of our fictitious Business Domain Modeling (BDM) project. We want something less complicated than the Unified Modeling Language (UML) model for structural class modeling, but something expressive enough to generate code either directly or through an intermediate model. Also, the model should constrain the user to the supported methodology and domain of business models. For the purposes of this book, the four archetypes described for business domain modeling in *Java Modeling in Color with UML* [46] seem like a good option. Figure 3-9 is a partial image of the Domain-Neutral Component (DNC) model, created with the editor we develop in Section 4.6, "Developing the Color Modeling Diagram." Of course, a black-and-white rendering of a color modeling diagram in the printed form of this book is not very compelling.

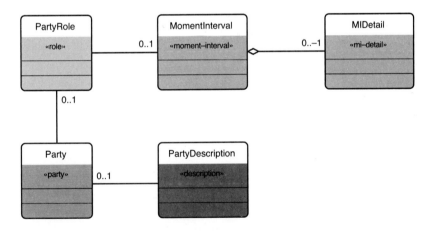

Figure 3-9   Color archetypes

Basically, a set of archetypes is used to model moment-interval, role, party, place, thing, and description elements and their relationships. The relationships and several described patterns of interaction are provided in the book, which we want to facilitate in our modeling environment. First, however, we need an underlying model (a DSL).

This DSL is strongly rooted in a general object-oriented DSL, so we begin with just that. Figure 3-10 is an `oocore.ecore` model that we extend to add our archetypes and other DNC elements. Why begin with a general object-oriented DSL? Well, we might decide to use this model as the basis for another DSL in the future. Why not simply extend Ecore itself, you might ask? Well, it contains elements that we really don't need or want, leaving us with all those *E*-prefixed elements and their properties. Besides, it's straightforward to develop our own object-oriented DSL. We can use the Java EMF Model (JEM) as a transformation target, giving us a chance to see what a model that extends Ecore is like.

Adventurous types can create a new `org.eclipse.dsl.oocore` DSL project and create the `oocore.ecore` model, as we have done previously. Complete the model using Figure 3-10 as a reference. Otherwise, simply copy the `oocore.ecore` domain model from the solutions into your project. Finally, create a new `org.eclipse.dsl.dnc` DSL project to hold our `dnc.ecore model` that will extend our core model.

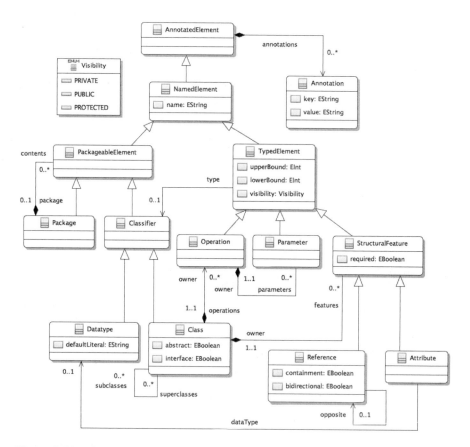

Figure 3-10   Object-oriented core domain model

With our base model complete, we can create our dnc.ecore model. To reference our oocore.ecore model in our newly created dnc.ecore model, we need to use the EMF **Load Resource** context menu in the default EMF editor. Fortunately, the dialog that appears now contains options to **Browse Registered Packages, Browse File System**, and **Browse Workspace**. At one time, you needed to enter platform:/ URIs into the field to load a registered package. In our case, the oocore.ecore model is easily found in our workspace.

In creating our DNC model (Figure 3-11), several options exist, as always. You've seen that using an enumeration to define the type is one solution, as was used in the Mindmap domain model's Relationship class and Type enum. This approach has some drawbacks, including the loss of polymorphic behavior in our templates and transformation scripts. To illustrate the differences, let's go ahead and create an Archetype abstract class that extends our oocore::Class class. Each of our archetypes will extend the Archetype class. We also add an Association class that extends oocore::Reference and add a property to signify aggregation. Although it is not a true Association class in the UML sense, it aids us in developing our diagram and hiding some complexities of the underlying model to the Practitioner. As we develop the diagram and other DSL artifacts, we'll revisit this model and refine it as necessary, potentially pulling up some functionality into the domain model to aid in our color modeling and model transformations.

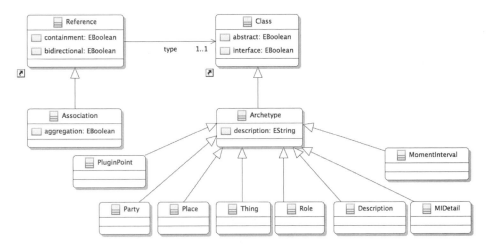

Figure 3-11   Domain-neutral component domain model

3.7 Summary

This chapter explored the capabilities of EMF as the means of describing our DSL abstract syntax. Although we leave the details of EMF to its own book, we covered enough to get started developing our sample projects. The benefits of leveraging a common underlying metamodel and generation capabilities should become clear as we continue to develop the DSL projects.

At this point, we have starter domain models for our fictitious ERP, plus a reference to a fifth oocore DSL. We now move on to describing how to create graphical concrete syntax for those we want to provide diagrams for, understanding that we will most likely revisit and enhance the EMF models we created in this chapter.

CHAPTER 4

Developing a DSL Graphical Notation

In many cases, a domain-specific language (DSL) can be represented using graphical nota-
tion. Of course, not every DSL has such an application, nor is it the case that all aspects
of a single DSL can be sensibly represented in a graphical manner; a combination of
graphical and textual could be the best solution. This chapter explores the capabilities of
the Graphical Modeling Framework (GMF) project, first covering some basics of design-
ing a graphical notation.

4.1 Design Considerations

You must consider many things when selecting a graphical concrete syntax (notation) for a DSL, including scalability, information density, and semantic inter-
pretation of your notation. You can find many examples, both good and bad,
from existing notations to use as a guide, although some of the best notations
might not yet have been realized, given the restriction that we typically work in
just two dimensions. This section gives you some idea of how to best represent
your DSL using a graphical notation.

RECOMMENDATION

Leverage known notations where possible. With the popularity of several
modeling notations, certain shapes and figures already have meaning to
many people. Also, try not to provide a diagram element when it serves no
purpose in recognition or semantic meaning for the model. Textual elements (external labels) might be the best way to provide the required
information—and you don't always have to surround them by a border or
even include an associated graphic.

4.1.1 Notation Design

Most people are familiar with the work of Edward Tufte (/www.edwardtufte. com/) on the visual display of information. Although Tufte originally focused on the display of data, many of the concepts he presented can apply to the development of a graphical notation for your DSL.

If you've read Tufte's books or attended his lectures, you know that he recommends that everyone use 30-inch monitors or better. Being confined to an undersized, low-resolution monitor will kill your dreams of effectively modeling any domain using a diagramming surface. The human brain is capable of processing a large amount of high-density information, more so than we are likely to display using the current 2D limitations of our underlying Graphical Editing Framework (GEF) infrastructure. A proposed addition to GEF promises to provide support for 3D, which should introduce an opportunity to improve, yet complicate, the current situation.

One of Tufte's key messages is to not include gratuitous or redundant notational elements in your display of information. For example, consider the Unified Modeling Language (UML) use case diagram. Actors are associated with use cases, yet each actor is represented by a stick figure along with a role name label. Typically, the stick figure is larger than the label. Why not just have the text label indicating the role name and a link representing its association? Why do we need the stick figure at all? Or, if we must have a graphic, why not a simple label icon? Because the stick figure is typically the same for all actors, no additional information is conveyed, and because the only other main figure is the use case oval connected by a line, it would not be hard to distinguish role names from their associated use cases. The point is, we should strive to eliminate "noise" when designing a graphical notation. Just because we have nifty tools such as GMF to produce graphical notations doesn't mean we should abandon these basic principles. Arguably, GMF's default settings should produce "clean" diagrams instead of illustrate all its bells and whistles. Another example to consider when designing your notation is the Ecore diagram and several diagrams like it that use icons to adorn each attribute and method. In the absence of a distinguishing characteristic that indicates visibility, cardinality, or navigability, simply including an icon for these elements is gratuitous. Icons do provide a degree of visual appeal ("eye candy") for the diagram, but there should always be an option to hide such elements.

The book *The UML Profile for Framework Architectures,* by Marcus Fontoura, et al., offers a published example of how to improve the density of information of a UML class diagram. In the book, an alternative display of inheritance information is added to a class to indicate either a flattened or a hierarchical representation. Instead of simply adding a static icon for an attribute or method, a box is colored and positioned near each feature to denote visibility, refinement, abstraction, and so on. It's a powerful visual effect that would be straightforward to implement using GMF.

Inlining graphics and text is another recommendation from Tufte, inspired at least in part by Galileo's records of observed astronomical phenomena. Galileo included small, text-sized images of his observations within the sentences. Tufte's sparklines are another example of inlining graphical information within text. In designing graphical notations, consider including text and graphics in ways that leverage this method of enriching the display of information. For example, consider how metric data could be added in the form of a sparkline to a UML class element.

Color is another powerful aspect to consider when designing a graphical notation. Today color printers are common, which supports more use of color in notation, without the redundant use of text or other means of indicating the same meaning. This book illustrates the use of color in the sample business domain diagram, as inspired by the book *Java Modeling in Color with UML,* by Peter Coad, et al. The book quotes Tufte and others in a discussion on the proper use of color, stressing the importance on its thoughtful application and advising against using too many colors. In general, two to four colors is best. A gradient range of a single color on some diagrams can be effective because it is sometimes difficult to decide on colors to distinguish elements when there is no natural analog to consider. For example, in the book *Object-Oriented Metrics in Practice,* by Michele Lanza and Radu Marinescu, metric values of classes are displayed using degrees of darkness, making certain elements come to immediate focus. Other measures determine the relative size and shape, resulting in a powerful visual effect.

In summary, you must consider many aspects when designing a graphical notation. Many good examples—and many poor examples—exist. Most people can tell the difference, although you definitely should take into account advice from Tufte and other recognized experts, along with feedback from your Practitioners, of course.

4.1.2 *Filters and Layers*

A diagram that displays all the information about a model isn't likely very readable. We've all seen large, complex models with hundreds or thousands of nodes and links that end up looking like a Rorschach inkblot test. The overview, zoom, and printing of large wallpaper diagrams can do only so much to help you understand such models. We need ways to filter out information that is unnecessary or not of interest. UML diagramming tools have some familiar filters, where various levels of detail are shown in Class diagrams, for example. Analysis-level detail typically includes only element names, while an implementation view includes visibility, multiplicity, and type information.

The Mylyn project at Eclipse provides a capability to filter out "noise" in an Eclipse workspace based on what the developer is actively working on. Tasks are associated with workspace elements that remain visible, while other elements are dimmed or hidden altogether. Some discussion regards the application of Mylyn technology to diagrams, although nothing has yet been developed. Contributions to this area would be welcome because extending this metaphor to modeling in general has great potential.

GEF provides layering in diagrams, although not much has been done to exploit this mechanism to "lift" or "lay down" information on a diagram, as was done historically with transparencies using overhead projectors and today with presentation animation effects. We need a more well-defined way of defining diagrams of multiple layers, which could come in handy when considering the decoration of models as they move from more abstract to more concrete during model-driven software-development scenarios. This and other ideas to improve the filtering and rationing of information presented on a diagram are points to seriously consider when defining your notation, along with an effective layout algorithm.

4.1.3 Layout

Arguably, the most important factor in providing usable diagrams is layout. Layout algorithms are numerous and can be tuned to suit a specific notation, although sometimes custom layouts must be developed. Keep in mind that fixed or semifixed layouts might be the best option for certain types of diagrams. Our mindmap diagram uses an automatic layout because the last thing the Practitioner wants to do while rapidly brainstorming is stop to adjust the position of a topic using the mouse. At the same time, class diagram layouts are fairly mature but still cannot suit the needs of each modeler, so this requires the capability to adjust the position of diagram elements. Not many modelers would be satisfied with a fixed-layout class diagram.

Links cause the difficulty in layout, in most cases. Links that cross are often considered bad form, yet jumps in links that cross are not a great solution, either. Consider using ellipses (...) to show that a link exists but is not shown until selected or after a filter is removed. Another possibility is to make visible certain types of links during mouseover events, allowing a diagram to easily be viewed in detail but only when desired.

4.1.4 Synchronization

Layout can go a long way toward making diagrams more readable and can even convey semantic information. Keep in mind that diagrams represent a view of the underlying model. In the case of large, complex models, it's often best to have multiple diagrams, or views, of the model. You can use filters to accomplish these views, as mentioned earlier, or the views can be distinct diagram instances that the Practitioner creates. The question of synchronicity comes up frequently at this point because sometimes we want the diagram to update automatically based on changes to the underlying model, sometimes we want changes to be made only manually, and sometimes we want a hybrid approach in which elements on the diagram should update but no new elements should be added. We explore synchronization options in GMF in Section 11.4.2, "Synchronized."

4.1.5 Shortcuts

Toward the goal of creating specific views of our model, we often need to create shortcuts, or aliases, of model elements on diagrams that are essentially imported from another diagram or model. Support for shortcuts on diagrams is common, as is the capability to have more than one notation element represent the same underlying domain model element. We explore these options as we develop our sample diagrams. Shortcuts are supported in diagrams generated with GMF and are covered in Section 11.4.2, "Contains Shortcuts To and Shortcuts Provided For."

4.2 Graphical Modeling Framework

Before GMF, many had undertaken the task of binding the model aspect of the GEF's Model-View Controller (MVC) architecture to an EMF model. An IBM Redbook was written [43], a sample was provided by the GEF project, and numerous commercial and academic institutions implemented solutions, some of which included a generative component. GMF came about as the result of this need for an easier way to develop graphical editors using GEF and an underlying EMF model.

Today GMF consists of two main components: a runtime and a tooling framework. The runtime handles the task of bridging EMF and GEF while providing a number of services and Application Programming Interfaces (API) to allow for the development of rich graphical editors. The tooling component provides a model-driven approach to defining graphical elements, diagram tooling, and mappings to a domain model for use in generating diagrams that leverage the runtime.

4.2.1 GMF Runtime Component

GMF has two runtime options. The first is commonly referred to as just the runtime; the second is referred to as the "lite" runtime. The former provides extensive capabilities for extension, and the latter focuses on providing a small installation footprint and is largely generative. These two runtimes represent two distinct philosophies of how to provide a diagramming runtime. Even more fundamentally, perhaps, they illustrate two approaches to Model-Driven Software Development (MDSD) in general.

The full runtime was originally developed as an extensible framework for creating diagrammatic editors on Eclipse Modeling Framework (EMF) and GEF. This runtime was originally designed and developed to provide rich extensibility options for clients. It includes a rich set of APIs, extension-points, a service layer, and many enhancements to the underlying EMF and GEF runtimes. The full runtime can be used with or without the tooling and generation features of GMF. The default target of the tooling and generation component is the full runtime.

Details on the GMF runtime, its APIs, and extension-points are described in Chapter 10, "Graphical Modeling Framework Runtime." Although it's not necessary to understand the inner workings of the GMF runtime during the initial phase of development using the tooling and generation component, you will eventually need to provide functionality that goes beyond what is generated.

The GMF Lite Runtime

Whereas the full runtime provides a rich published API, numerous extension-points, a service provider layer, and more, the lite runtime is just the opposite. The motivation for the lite runtime was to provide as much of a generated implementation for diagramming as possible, with a minimal runtime code base. The current implementation of the lite runtime consists of a single runtime plug-in, with a single extension-point for supporting diagram shortcuts.

To provide compatibility with GMF diagrams created for the full runtime, the lite runtime uses the same notation model. In theory, a diagram produced with an editor generated using the lite runtime option will open in an editor generated to the full runtime. Some missing features in the lite runtime prevent full interoperability, but it does work, to an extent.

To target the lite runtime when using the tooling, you must first deselect the **Utilize Enhanced Features of the GMF Runtime** and **Use IMapMode** options when creating the generator model. When generating diagram code from the generator model, use the **Generate Pure-GEF Diagram Code** option.

The lite runtime requires a single `org.eclipse.gmf.runtime.lite` plug-in for deployment, along with its dependencies, which include the Eclipse platform core, EMF, GEF, EMF Transaction, and tabbed properties view. Although it is not as feature rich as the full runtime, it offers a core set of runtime capabilities, including diagram properties, preferences, shortcuts, and validation. For tooling, the lite runtime has its own set of Xpand templates for generation, found in the `org.eclipse.gmf.codegen.lite` plug-in, available in the GMF Experimental SDK feature.

4.2.2 GMF Tooling Component

As you will see, GMF was itself developed as a DSL Toolkit. From the beginning, it was decided that the tooling for GMF would be as model driven and bootstrapped as possible. In short, a diagram is defined using a collection of models (DSLs) that drive code generators targeting either the full runtime or the lite runtime. One of the remaining tasks to complete the story is to use Query/View/Transformation (QVT) in the transformation from its mapping model to generation model, to considerably improve the extensibility of GMF's tooling.

Figure 4-1 illustrates the main components and models used on the tooling side of GMF. To begin, a GMF project is created and references a domain model. A graphical definition model designs the figures (nodes, links, compartments, and so on) that will be used to represent domain model elements on the diagram surface. A corresponding tooling definition model supports palette tool definition and other tooling for use in diagramming. The mapping model binds elements from the graphical and tooling definitions to the domain model. A transformation from the mapping model to the generator model is followed by the generation of a diagram plug-in.

Note that it is possible to design and run GMF diagrams without a domain model, which can be useful for those who want to experiment with notation design and not be burdened with mapping it to a domain. Each of these models is described in some detail in the following sections, and Chapter 11, "Graphical Modeling Framework Tooling," includes a complete reference for each model. Following the basic overview of each model, we turn to learning more about them in the context of developing our sample application diagrams.

Graphical Definition Model

The graphical definition model consists of two parts and defines the graphical elements found on a diagramming surface. The first part is a Figure Gallery, which defines figures (shapes, labels, lines, and so on) that the Canvas elements later reference to define nodes, connections, compartments, and diagram labels. An important point is that figure galleries can be reused. Many diagrams require similar-looking elements, such as a rounded rectangle with center label, or connections that are a solid line with open arrowhead decoration on the target end.

Defining a number of figures and sharing galleries within your organization or larger community means less time spent reinventing the wheel. For UML2, a set of figures are defined and available for reuse from the UML2 Tools component of the Model Development Tools (MDT) project.

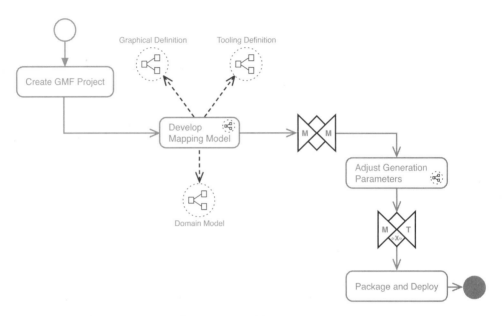

Figure 4-1   Graphical Modeling Framework workflow

The mapping model references figures defined in the gmfgraph model. When the mapping model is transformed to the generator model, figure code is generated and included within the gmfgen model itself. When code is generated, edit parts will contain figures as inner classes. This is the default behavior when working with GMF, although it is not necessarily the recommended approach.

Another lesser-known feature of the graphical definition model is the capability to export figures to a standalone figure plug-in. This can also satisfy reuse because these plug-ins can be shared by several diagrams and among a community as a binary form of the figure gallery. To create a figure plug-in from a gmfgraph model, either use the **Generate Figures Plug-In** context menu action, or start by creating a new plug-in project and select the **Figure Definitions Converter** template in the plug-in project wizard. Section 4.5.5, "Generating the Figures Plug-In," covers the use of a standalone figure plug-in.

A complication that arises when using a standalone figures plug-in is that it creates a "mirror" of the gmfgraph model. This adds one more model to the picture that needs to be synchronized, so it's recommended that you first define all your figures and generate the plug-in that contains the associated `mirror.gmfgraph` model. The mapping model uses the mirrored model instead of the original graphical definition model. With this approach, the mapping model passes class name references to the generator model, not actual classes. The generated code simply references the figure classes in their own plug-in and is not written out as inner classes within generated edit parts. This process imposes the additional step of regenerating the figures and mirrored model upon a change to the graphical definition. A future version of GMF will hopefully do away with the serialized class method and make generating a standalone figures plug-in work more seamlessly in the workflow.

To ease the design of figures, a WYSIWYG (what you see is what you get) style of editor is included in the experimental Software Development Kit (SDK). It is not complete, but it illustrates the bootstrapping of GMF and a method for customization using a decorator model described in detail in Section 4.2.3, "Dynamic Templates." Use of the graphical model editor is also helpful for understanding layouts and how they work when composing complex figures.

Tooling Definition Model

Diagrams typically include a palette and other periphery to create and work with diagram content. The purpose of the tooling definition model is to specify these elements. The tooling model currently includes elements for the palette, the toolbar, and various menus to be defined for a diagram. Unfortunately, in the current release of GMF, the generator uses only the palette element. If additional capabilities are required until this functionality is completed, advanced properties view UI elements can be designed using an extension to the generator model and custom templates, as discussed in Section 4.6.6, "Color Preferences." Note that it is also possible to exclude the palette altogether from a diagram definition, thereby creating a read-only diagram. Of course, the pop-up bars and connection handles features should be disabled as well in this case.

Mapping Model

Perhaps the most important of all models in GMF is the mapping model. Here, elements from the diagram definition (nodes and links) are mapped to the domain model and assigned tooling elements. The mapping model represents the actual diagram definition and is used to create a generator model. Typically a one-to-one mapping exists among a mapping model, its generator model, and a particular diagram.

The mapping model uses Object Constraint Language (OCL) in many ways, including initializing features for created elements, defining link and node constraints, and defining model audits and metrics. Audits identify problems in the structure or style of a diagram and its underlying domain model instance, and metrics provide measures of diagram and domain model elements.

Generator Model

As mentioned in the overview, the generator model adds information used to generate code from the mapping model and is somewhat analogous to the EMF genmodel. Both can be reproduced and reloaded from their source models, although the EMF genmodel is a true decorator model. The GMF generator model is more of a many-to-one model transformation than a decorator model.

As a mapping model is transformed into a generator model, it loses knowledge of the graphical definition and gains knowledge of the runtime notation model. This minimizes the number of dependencies linked from the generator model and separates concern among the models. Currently, the transformation is performed using Java code, but it is planned to be reimplemented using QVT to give Toolsmiths easier customization, as mentioned earlier.

A trace facility exists in the experimental SDK to aid in generating visual IDs when new nodes are added and the generator model is updated. A reconciler preserves other user-modified elements in the generator model upon retransformation from the mapping model. Many of the commonly modified properties are preserved, although not all of them are, so be aware of this when making changes to the generator model.

As with EMF, you can use custom code-generation templates in GMF. The main difference here is that EMF uses Java Emitter Template (JET) as its template engine, and GMF uses Xpand. Chapter 14, "Xpand Template Language," covers Xpand, which also is used throughout Chapter 7, "Developing Model-to-Text Transformations." You can find information on how to use dynamic templates in GMF in Section 4.2.3, "Dynamic Templates," and in our sample diagram in Sections 4.3–4.6.

When using the full runtime as a generation target, a number of extension-points are contributed to in the generated diagram code. You will likely want to explore the generated plug-in manifest and source code.

TIP

Sometimes you must open and modify GMF definition models in a text editor. When doing so, add new elements that are part of a list of items to the end of the list, because GMF models use relative position references. For example, if you're copying a figure from one .gmfgraph model to another, add it after the last descriptors element in the file.

4.2.3 Customization Options

You can extend the GMF generator in several ways, all of which are analogous to how you can use and provide for extensibility in your DSL tooling. The next sections discuss code modification, extension-points, dynamic templates, and decorator models, and illustrate them in the sample applications.

Code Modification

As GMF utilizes JMerge to protect Toolsmith modifications of generated code from being overwritten, the same practice of placing NOT after @generated tags in code can be used as with EMF. Additionally, GMF provides merge capabilities for plugin.xml and MANIFEST.MF files, which is a nice feature that EMF should consider adopting.

Extension-Point

When targeting the full runtime for generation, provided extension-points can be used to extend diagrams generated using the tooling component of GMF. This approach has the benefit of being completely separate from the generated diagram and code. For example, a parser provider for our color modeling diagram's attribute elements is provided in this manner, as discussed in Section 4.6.7, "Custom Parsers." The service-provider aspect of the runtime allows for the addition or overriding of behavior in diagrams, such as the addition of EditPolicies to an EditPart, as illustrated in Section 10.9.3, "Custom EditPolicy."

Dynamic Templates

Also as in EMF, you can leverage dynamic templates to provide customized output from GMF code generators. You can extend or override both the templates used to generate figure code and the templates used to generate diagram code using so-called dynamic templates.

GMF uses Xpand extensively. To override a template for diagram generation, you must put it in the same directory structure (namespace) that GMF uses. The easiest way to see the templates and their structure is to import the org.eclipse.gmf.codegen plug-in into your workspace using the **Import As → Source Project** option from the Plug-Ins view. Note also that GMF templates contain «DEFINE» entries for extraMethods and additions with corresponding «EXPAND»s to allow for extensibility. When using the «AROUND» construct for aspect-oriented features of Xpand, GMF requires placing these templates under an /aspects folder below the root in order to be found. GMF recently added a new "composite template" approach that makes it possible to augment an existing template if found in the same namespace, effectively merging its content with the original. Sections 4.6.5, "Gradient Figures," and 4.6.6, "Color Preferences," describe the use of custom templates with GMF in detail.

Decorator Model

A more advanced—and possibly most conceptually "pure"—method for customizing or extending the output of GMF code generators is to use a decorator model. Basically, the GMF generator model is wrapped in a root XML Metadata Interchange (XMI) element to allow additional decorator model instances to coexist and to enable elements of the generator model to reference them. Xpand templates used to generate diagram code are augmented with custom templates that are invoked when these references are encountered.

The GMF graphical definition model has a bootstrapped diagram editor to allow for WYSIWYG-style figure development. It was implemented using custom templates and also includes a decorator model for use in defining its form-based properties view. This serves as an example of how to use decorator models in the context of GMF, but also for any other occasion in the context of using a DSL Toolkit where extensions are required to an existing model used for generation. Section 4.6.6, "Color Preferences," covers the steps in using decorating models in GMF.

Model Extension

With the addition of the child extenders feature in EMF 2.4, it's possible to have your contributed model elements of customizations to the GMF models available in the default editor. GMF 2.1 has been regenerated with these generator model settings, thereby allowing your extensions to contribute to GMF editors. The UML2 Tools project has extensions defined for GMF models and makes use of this new capability.

4.2.4 Dashboard

GMF comes with a dashboard view that streamlines the workflow of dealing with its collection of models. The dashboard is available from **Window → Show View → Other → General → GMF Dashboard** (Ctrl+3 → gmfd), or you can open it when creating a new GMF project. Figure 4-2 shows the dashboard used in the context of the mindmap diagram sample project.

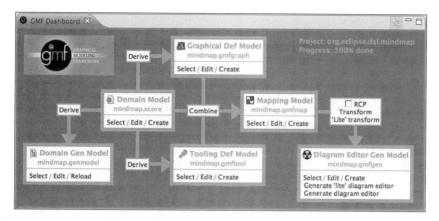

Figure 4-2 GMF Dashboard view

Each model can be selected, created, or edited within the dashboard, including EMF *.ecore and *.genmodel models. Invoking GMF and EMF wizards is accomplished using the hyperlink actions throughout, making the dashboard helpful not only in understanding the workflow, but also in streamlining the invocation of transformation and generation actions during diagram development.

4.2.5 Sample Application Diagrams

The best way to learn how to use GMF is by example, as with most new technology. The following sections explore most aspects of GMF-based diagram definition in the context of our sample projects, by design. Comments throughout should illustrate the techniques for developing diagrams, enumerate their relative pros and cons, and provide the basis for becoming well versed in GMF tooling.

Because diagramming is central to mindmaps, I pay special attention to this diagram, particularly layout and other usability elements. The requirements dependency diagram is similar to the mindmap, but the underlying model structures are different, so we explore how this impacts our mapping model. The scenario diagram enables us to explore the concept of diagram partitioning. Finally, our business domain modeling diagram explores compartments, customization, and more advanced labeling techniques.

4.3 Developing the Mindmap Diagram

Our diagram for the mindmap DSL defined earlier is rather straightforward: It is a simple "box and line" style of diagram, but one that serves us well in introducing GMF. We start out with a simple default diagram definition to first understand the basics, and then we iterate through several enhancements, including layout and advanced figures.

4.3.1 Mindmap Graphical Definition

Building on Section 3.3, "Developing the Mindmap Domain Model," you should have a mindmap DSL project and the generated EMF plug-ins from the mindmap domain model in your workspace. We put our GMF models in the diagrams folder, so begin by right-clicking that folder and selecting **New → Other → Models → Graphical Definition Model** and naming it `mindmap.gmfgraph`. If you're not using the DSL Toolkit, you'll find the standard GMF wizard in **New → Other → Graphical Modeling Framework → Simple Graphical Definition Model**. Use **Find in Workspace** to quickly locate our mindmap.ecore model and select **Map** as the **Diagram Element**. The next page of the wizard presents elements discovered within the domain model and a guess at what would be appropriate for each: node, link, label, or nothing. Make the dialog look like Figure 4-3 so that we'll create a node for the **Topic** element with a label for its name attribute and link for subtopics, and a link for the **Relationship** element with labels for its name and type. Finally, click **Finish**.

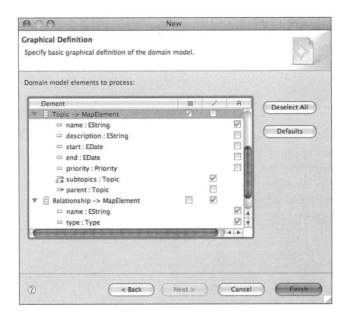

Figure 4-3   Graphical Definition Wizard

The model derived from the wizard has a canvas named mindmap, a node for our **Topic** element, two connections, and three labels. Each corresponds to an element in the figure gallery. For now, we don't modify what the wizard has produced because we first want to get through the entire process. Later, we'll come back and refine the graphical definition.

4.3.2 Mindmap Tooling Definition

Similar to the process of examining the domain model to produce a starter graphical definition, a wizard enables you to create a tooling definition model, as seen in Figure 4-4. Begin again by right-clicking the diagrams folder and navigating to **New → Other → Models → Tooling Definition Model;** name it `mindmap.gmftool`, locate the `mindmap.ecore` model, and select **Map** as the **Diagram Element.** The wizard should correctly determine the required tooling: a node tool for the **Topic** element, and link tools for both the **Relationship** element and the subtopics relationship within **Topic.** Deselect the link suggested for the parent reference.

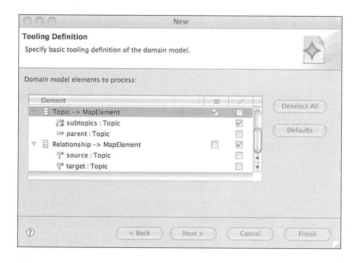

Figure 4-4 Tooling Definition Wizard

With the tooling model open in its editor, you can see that the wizard created a single tool group and creation tools for each of these. We might want to create separate groups for links and nodes, but for now we'll leave the model as is.

4.3.3 Mindmap Mapping Model

Once again, we use a GMF wizard to get us started. Right-click on the diagrams folder and select **New** → **Other** → **Domain-Specific Language** → **Diagram Definition** to begin creating a GMF mapping model. Note that you can begin a diagram definition directly from this wizard because it enables you to create a new palette model and select an existing graphical definition model. Provide the name `mindmap.gmfmap` and select `Map` as the class to represent the canvas. Accept the default `mindmap.gmftool` model and select our `mindmap.gmfgraph` model on the next page. On the Mapping page, modify the wizard defaults and move `Relationship` to the Links list, leaving just `Topic` in the Node list. Remove all but `subtopics` and `Relationship` from the Links list, as shown in Figure 4-5.

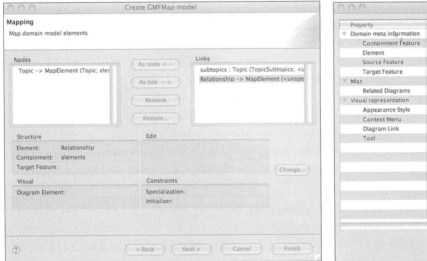
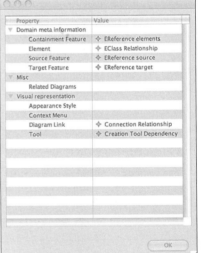

Figure 4-5   Mapping Model Wizard

Notice that for each selection of Node and Link, you can change the wizard's mapping. A limitation on Nodes exists: The dialog that displays with **Change** shows only the mapping for the top-level node, not the node mapping or labels. Try this now with the `Relationship` link, setting the `Source Feature` to the

source reference and the `Target Feature` to the `target` feature. Also ensure that the proper Tool and Diagram Link are selected. Upon **Finish**, browse the mapping model in the editor. Check each property to verify that all are correct, and use the **Validate** action from the context menu.

Regarding our two types of links, notice that they illustrate the two most common methods of providing link mappings for a diagram. The subtopics reference maps to a link that shows the relationship between `Topic` elements. In this case, we need to indicate only the `Target Feature` in our link mapping, leaving the other properties blank. The relationship link shows how to map a link to a domain model class—in this case, our `Relationship` class. To complete the mapping definition, we need to specify the `Element` and its `Containment Feature`, `Source Feature`, and `Target Feature` for the link.

Let's go through the mapping model in some detail, because it often causes confusion. Beginning with the `Canvas Mapping` element, you can see that the `Map` domain `Element` will be represented by the mindmap `Diagram Canvas` from our `mindmap.gmfgraph` model. Similarly, the diagram canvas will have a `Palette`, represented by our `mindmap.gmftool` model's `mindmapPalette` element. Note that the `Menu` and `Toolbar Contributions` properties are blank because GMF has not yet implemented them, as seen in Table 4-1.

Table 4-1 Mindmap Canvas Mapping

Element	Property	Value
Mapping		
Canvas	Domain Model	Mindmap
	Element	Map
	Palette	Palette mindmapPalette
	Diagram Canvas	Canvas mindmap

For our `Topic` node, we see in the properties of the `Top Node Reference` that new instances of `Topic` elements are to be maintained in the `elements` containment reference of our `Map` class, as shown in Table 4-2. The `Children Feature` property is left blank because we retrieve and store our `Topic` elements directly from the `elements` containment feature.

Table 4-2   Mindmap Topic Mapping

Element	Property	Value
Mapping		
Top Node Reference	Containment Feature	Map.elements : MapElement
Node Mapping	Element	Topic -> MapElement
	Diagram Node	Node Topic (TopicFigure)
	Tool	Creation Tool Topic
Feature Label Mapping	Diagram Label	Diagram Label TopicName
	Features	MapElement.name : EString

Below the `Top Node Reference` mapping is the `Node Mapping` for the `Topic` class itself. The `Topic` class, which is a subclass of `MapElement`, is used for the node's `Element`. The `Topic` node from our `mindmap.gmfgraph` is used for the `Diagram Node`, which we see references the `TopicFigure` from the `Figure Gallery`. Finally, the `Node` requires a `Tool`, so we select the `Topic Creation Tool` from our palette defined in our `mindmap.gmftool` model. Note that the `Appearance Style` and `Context Menu` properties are left blank because GMF has not yet implemented them.

The `Topic` displays its name using a label, which is defined in the child `Feature Label Mapping` element. The `Diagram Label` property is selected to the `TopicName` label in our graphical definition and displays the value of the `Topic`'s `name:EString` attribute. Both the `Edit` and `View Method` properties are set to the default `MESSAGE_FORMAT` value, meaning that the Java `MessageFormat` class provides the underlying implementation for parsing, editing, and displaying our label. In the case of our `Topic` label, a single attribute is displayed, with no other characters required.

With the node mapping complete, let's look at the subtopics link mapping. In our domain model, `Topics` are related to other "sub" `Topics` using the `subtopics` reference. Simple references such as this are straightforward to map in GMF because we only need to set our `Target Feature` property to this reference in our domain model, as seen in Table 4-3. Our next link mapping discusses the remaining `Domain meta information` properties. The `Diagram Link` and `Tool` properties are set as you would expect, to the `TopicSubtopics Connection` from our graphical definition, and to the `TopicSubtopics Creation Tool` in our tooling definition, respectively.

Table 4-3 Mindmap Subtopic Link Mapping

Element	Property	Value
Mapping		
Link Mapping	Target Feature	Topic.subtopics : Topic
	Diagram Link	Connection TopicSubtopics
	Tool	Creation Tool TopicSubtopics

The `Relationship Link Mapping` is more involved than our `TopicSubtopics Link Mapping` because we are mapping a domain class to the link, not just a reference within a class, as seen in Table 4-4. In this case, the `Relationship` class in our domain model is the domain `Element`, with the element's `Containment Feature` of our `Map` being where we will store new `Relationship` instances created with each link. Using a class to represent a relationship in our domain model essentially gives us what an `EAssociation` in Ecore itself would provide. The `Source` and `Target Feature` properties map in a straightforward manner to our `source : Topic` and `target : Topic` references, respectively. As with the `TopicSubtopic` link mapping, we map our `Diagram Link` and `Tool` properties to their corresponding graphical and tooling model elements. Again, `Appearance Style` and `Context Menu` go unused; Section 4.5, "Developing the Scenario Diagram," discusses the `Related Diagrams` property.

Table 4-4 Mindmap Relationship Link Mapping

Element	Property	Value
Mapping		
Link Mapping	Containment Feature	Map.elements : MapElement
	Element	Relationship -> MapElement
	Source Feature	Relationship.source : Topic
	Target Feature	Relationship.target : Topic
	Diagram Link	Connection Relationship
	Tool	Creation Tool Relationship
Feature Label Mapping	Diagram Label	Diagram Label RelationshipName
	Features	MapElement.name : EString

(continues)

Table 4-4   Mindmap Relationship Link Mapping (continued)

Element	Property	Value
Feature Label Mapping	Diagram Label	Diagram Label RelationshipType
	Features	Relationship.type : Type
	Read Only	true
	View Pattern	«{0}»

The graphical wizard created child label figures for our relationship link, but the mapping wizard does not provide label link mappings. We need to add these manually before proceeding. Create a new child `Feature Label Mapping` to the `Relationship Link Mapping` and fill in accordingly, for the Relationship name attribute.

Add another `Feature Label Mapping` to the link, but this time set it to `Read Only` and alter the `View Pattern` to add <<guillemets>> to the type name. With the basics of our initial diagram mapping understood, we're ready to move on to generation.

4.3.4 Mindmap Generator Model

The last model to create in developing our mindmap diagram is the GMF generator model. As mentioned, this model is analogous to the EMF genmodel and contains additional parameters used for generating our diagram plug-in. Technically, the GMF generator model is a bit more complex and is really the result of a many-to-one model transformation. To produce our `mindmap.gmfgen` model from our `mindmap.gmfmap` model, right-click the mapping model and select **Create Generator Model** to open the wizard. The default name and location are fine, as is the selection of the mapping model. The `mindmap.genmodel` should also be selected by default but could indicate a warning about the relative date of the genmodel to its ecore model. If required, reload the genmodel at this time; GMF utilizes references found there for its own code generation. On the last page of the wizard, leave the defaults as is and click **Finish** to complete.

Open the new `mindmap.gmfgen` model in the editor so we can adjust a couple of its properties prior to generation. In the `Gen Editor Generator` properties, set the `Diagram File Extension` to `mmd` in place of the default `mindmap_diagram`, as seen in Figure 4-6. Also, we select `true` for the `Same File For Diagram and Model` property. The default behavior persists them into separate files, which we consider for other diagrams.

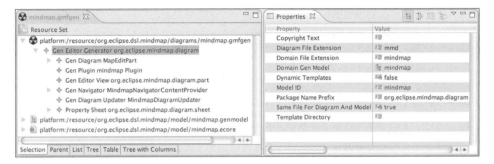

Figure 4-6 Mindmap GMF generator model

At this time, we leave the remaining defaults for the generator model and generate code by right-clicking the `mindmap.gmfgen` model and selecting **Generate Diagram Code**. A new `org.eclipse.mindmap.diagram` plug-in appears, and because we already have a launch configuration from our domain model, all we need to do is run.

A wizard is generated for our mindmap diagram, which we use to create and populate a simple map. Figure 4-7 is an example of what you can see and do at this point.

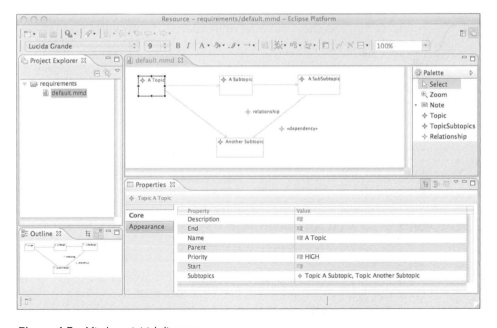

Figure 4-7 Mindmap initial diagram

Now that we've proven that we can quickly create a basic diagram to allow for graphical editing of our DSL, let's go back and explore in detail more of the options available using GMF.

BEST PRACTICE

At this point, it's a good idea to consider how to best work with a collection of GMF models. EMF has no real refactoring support, per se, so it's important to understand that changes to a model with references to another won't be propagated as you might expect. However, EMF does allow you to work on several models within a single resource set, in which case it does a much nicer job of keeping models in synch. To accomplish this in GMF, it's best to work within the mapping model editor. This way, changes to tooling, gmfgraph, the domain, and the mapping model should not result in broken models because they are all in the same editor and resource set.

4.3.5 Improving the Mindmap Diagram

So far, we've used the default settings that GMF provides and have established that everything is working. Now let's go back and refine our models to get closer to what we want from our mindmap diagram. The label icons are superfluous, as are the full rectangles for our subtopics, so let's begin by improving our notation elements and regenerating the diagram. Before completing this section, you might want to review the GMF tooling models described in Chapter 11.

Updating the Graphical Definition

Using our mapping model editor instance and expanding our `mindmap.gmfgraph` node, create a new `Figure Descriptor` named `TopicFigure` in the `Figure Gallery`. To this descriptor, add a child `Rounded Rectangle` named `TopicFigure`. Adjust both the `Corner Height` and `Width` properties to 15. Add a `Stack Layout` to the `Rounded Rectangle` to center our label in the rectangle. Add a child label named `TopicNameFigure`, and to keep the label from getting too close to our left and right edges, add an `Insets` child to the rectangle and set the `Left` and `Right` properties to 5. We want to have the default line color set to blue, but we won't use the `Foreground Color` elements because we want the default color to be reflected in the diagram preferences.

We set default values in our diagram preferences in Section 4.3.5, "Diagram Preferences."

We can delete the original rectangle figure descriptor assigned to the `Node Topic` and select our new rounded rectangle descriptor. As with the original `TopicFigure`, we need to add a `Child Access` to the `Figure Descriptor` and set its `Figure` to our `TopicNameFigure`. In the `TopicName Diagram Label`, set the label's `Accessor` property to the `getFigureTopicNameFigure Child Access` created earlier for the `Topic`'s name label. The label currently has its `Element Icon` property set to `true`. This is the default, but because the icon adds no information at this point, it's just noise; set this property to `false`, and do the same for the `RelationshipType` and `RelationshipName` labels. To provide a reasonable default size for our `Topic` nodes, we add a `Default Size Facet` element to its `Node` element, with a child `Dimension` element. We give it a default size of `Dx = 80, Dy = 40`. That's it for our `Topic` node.

We also want to change the look of our relationship links. We want to use a dashed line and open arrow decoration on the target for our relationships, and just a solid line with no decoration for our subtopic. Later, we'll add a circle decoration to the target of our subtopic link, but that requires writing some custom code. For now, change the name of our `Polyline Decoration` to `RelationshipTargetDecoration` and select this decoration as the `Target Decoration` for our `RelationshipFigure`. Change the `Line Kind` of our `RelationshipFigure` to `LINE_DASH` and remove the target decoration from our Subtopics connection figure.

Table 4-5 shows the current state of the graphical definition; only properties that changed from their default values are shown.

Table 4-5 Mindmap Relationship Link Mappings

Element	Property	Value
Canvas	Name	mindmap
Figure Gallery	Name	Default
Polyline Decoration	Name	RelationshipTargetDecoration
Figure Descriptor	Name	TopicSubtopicsFigure
Polyline Connection	Name	TopicSubtopicsFigure
	Target Decoration	*unset*
Figure Descriptor	Name	RelationshipFigure

(continues)

Table 4-5   Mindmap Relationship Link Mappings (continued)

Element	Property	Value
Polyline Connection	Name	RelationshipFigure
	Line Kind	LINE_DASH
	Target Decoration	Polyline Decoration RelationshipTargetDecoration
Label	Name	RelationshipNameFigure
Label	Name	RelationshipTypeFigure
Child Access	Figure	Label RelationshipNameFigure
Child Access	Figure	Label RelationshipTypeFigure
Figure Descriptor	Name	TopicFigure
Rounded Rectangle	Name	TopicFigure
	Corner Height	15
	Corner Width	15
Stack Layout		
Insets	Left, Right	5, 5
Child Access	Figure	Label TopicNameFigure
Node	Name	Topic
	Figure	Figure Descriptor TopicFigure
Default Size Facet		
Dimension	Dx, Dy	80, 40
Connection	Name	TopicSubtopics
	Figure	Figure Descriptor TopicSubtopicsFigure
Connection	Name	Relationship
	Figure	Figure Descriptor RelationshipFigure
Diagram Label	Name	TopicName
	Figure	Figure Descriptor TopicFigure
	Element Icon	false
	Accessor	Child Access getFigureTopicNameFigure

Element	Property	Value
Diagram Label	Name	RelationshipName
	Figure	Figure Descriptor RelationshipFigure
	Element Icon	false
	Accessor	Child Access getFigureRelationshipNameFigure
Diagram Label	Name	RelationshipType
	Figure	Figure Descriptor RelationshipFigure
	Element Icon	false
	Accessor	Child Access getFigureRelationshipTypeFigure

Updating the Tooling Definition

Expand the `mindmap.gmftool` node in the mapping model. We want to have two groups of tools in our palette. The first will have the Topic node creation tool; the second will have our links, including a stack of tools for our different types of relationship links (dependency, include, extend). This is a simple matter to accomplish in our model using copy and paste, with some renaming. The only special property you need to set is the `Stack` property to `true` for our `Relationships Tool Group`. Note that if you want to have each group in a drawer, you must set the `Stack` property to `true`. Figure 4-8 shows what your tool model should look like at this point. Note that if a particular tool should be the default one available, you must use the `Active` property to select it. In our case, the dependency tool is first on the list and is a reasonable default.

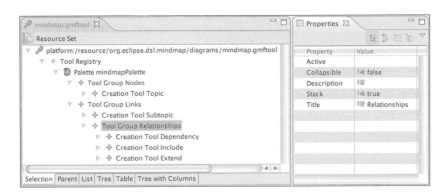

Figure 4-8 Mindmap GMF tooling model

Updating the Mapping Definition

The main change we need to make to our mapping definition is to our Relationship link. Our DSL includes a `Type` enumeration with three literals: `DEPENDENCY`, `INCLUDE`, and `EXTEND`. We now have three separate tools for these relationship types, so we need to create a mapping for each. Begin by modifying the existing relationship link mapping to be our dependency link, and then copy/paste the element and adjust for the include and extend mappings. Table 4-6 shows what the dependency mapping looks like after our changes.

Table 4-6   Updated Mindmap Relationship Link Mapping

Element	Property	Value
Link Mapping	Containment Feature	Map.elements : MapElement
	Element	Relationship → MapElement
	Source Feature	Relationship.source : Topic
	Target Feature	Relationship.target : Topic
	Diagram Link	Connection Relationship
	Tool	Creation Tool Dependency
Constraint	Body	self.type = Type::DEPENDENCY
Feature Seq Initializer	Element Class	Relationship → MapElement
Feature Value Spec	Feature	Relationship.type : Type
Value Expression	Body	Type::DEPENDENCY
	Language	ocl
Feature Label Mapping	Diagram Label	Diagram Label RelationshipName
	Features	MapElement.name : EString
Feature Label Mapping	Diagram Label	Diagram Label RelationshipType
	Features	Relationship.type : Type
	View Pattern	«{0}»

As you can see, the link mapping now has some additional child elements. First, we add a `Constraint` to indicate using OCL that `self.type = Type::DEPENDENCY`. This enables us to identify each of our `Relationship` mappings so that the generator can create code to distinguish nodes based on their type attribute. Also, we add a `Feature Seq Initializer` child element along with `Feature Value Spec` and `Value Expression` that sets the value of the type attributes upon link creation.

At this point, we only need to copy/paste the dependency link mapping and alter the properties accordingly for `INCLUDE` and `EXTEND` links. When complete, validation and update of the generator model from the mapping model, followed by code regeneration, will enable us to run and test our updated diagram. This will become a familiar sequence, which begs for the creation of a single action to streamline the process. The Dashboard view comes in handy for this purpose.

Topic Figure Layout

Before we run the diagram, we need to make some tweaks to the generated code if we want our `Topic` name labels to be centered in their rounded rectangle and wrap. The code we use is from the `GeoShapeFigure` class in the runtime. In the `TopicEditPart` class, adjust the constructor for the inner `TopicFigure` class as follows:

```
/**
 * Modified to adjust stack layout
 *
 * @generated NOT
 */
public TopicFigure() {
  this.setLayoutManager(new StackLayout() {
    public void layout(IFigure figure) {
      Rectangle r = figure.getClientArea();
      List children = figure.getChildren();
      IFigure child;
      Dimension d;
      for (int i = 0; i < children.size(); i++) {
        child = (IFigure) children.get(i);
        d = child.getPreferredSize(r.width, r.height);
        d.width = Math.min(d.width, r.width);
        d.height = Math.min(d.height, r.height);
        Rectangle childRect = new Rectangle(r.x + (r.width - d.width) /
          2, r.y + (r.height - d.height) / 2, d.width, d.height);
        child.setBounds(childRect);
      }
    }
  });
  this.setCornerDimensions(new Dimension(getMapMode().DPtoLP(15),
  getMapMode().DPtoLP(15)));
  this.setBorder(new MarginBorder(getMapMode().DPtoLP(0),
    getMapMode().DPtoLP(5), getMapMode().DPtoLP(0),
    getMapMode().DPtoLP(5)));
  createContents();
}
```

To allow our `WrapLabel` to wrap, we need to slightly modify the `createContents()` method as follows:

```
/**
 * Modified to enable text wrapping
 *
 * @generated NOT
 */
private void createContents() {
  fFigureTopicNameFigure = new WrappingLabel();
  fFigureTopicNameFigure.setText("");
  fFigureTopicNameFigure.setTextWrap(true);
  fFigureTopicNameFigure.setAlignment(PositionConstants.LEFT);
  this.add(fFigureTopicNameFigure);
}
```

Figure 4-9 shows our diagram. Note the relationship stack of tools in the palette and note that the `mindmap.ecore` literal values for our relationship `Type` enum have been changed to lowercase. Alternatively, we could have changed the case within our label code, or even shortened the literal values to be just d, e, or i.

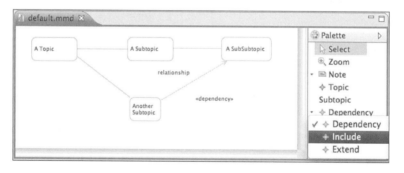

Figure 4-9   Mindmap relationship links

Adding Custom Layout

A major requirement for a mindmap diagram is good layout, preferably automatic. A fixed layout is fine for our needs, although more advanced layout strategies that are pseudo-fixed are possible. Mindmaps should be arranged in a tree, typically with both left-to-right and right-to-left flows to the sides of the central `Topic`. The default layout for GMF-generated diagrams is top-to-bottom. The layout we need is similar, if you consider that mainly the orientation of the layout needs to be changed from vertical to horizontal. This is exactly what the GMF runtime's `LeftRightProvider` class provides, so we use it as a starting point.

We could add the following modifications to our generated diagram plug-in, but as mentioned earlier, this would make regeneration and maintenance more difficult. Instead, here we create a new `org.eclipse.mindmap.diagram.custom` plug-in project using PDE and put our modifications in this separate plug-in.

Let's back up a minute and discuss the big picture of diagram layout and our needs for the mindmap. You've seen that the main toolbar for all GMF diagrams has a layout button, with a corresponding context menu on the diagram canvas. The runtime provides these by default for all diagrams, so it's a matter of adding our own provider for the layout service to invoke. We begin with the `layoutProviders` extension-point and contribute the following to our `plugin.xml` manifest. Section 10.4.10, "Layout Service," discusses the layout service.

```
<extension point="org.eclipse.gmf.runtime.diagram.ui.layoutProviders">
  <layoutProvider class="org.eclipse.mindmap.diagram.layout.
    MindmapDefaultLayoutProvider">
    <Priority name="Low"/>
  </layoutProvider>
</extension>
```

We've set the priority of our provider to `Low`, which is one level above `Lowest`. Now we need to implement the `MindmapDefaultLayoutProvider`, as shown here:

```
public class MindmapDefaultLayoutProvider extends LeftRightProvider {

  public static String DEFAULT_LAYOUT = "Default";

  public boolean provides(IOperation operation) {
  // enable this provider only on mindmap diagrams
  if (operation instanceof ILayoutNodeOperation) {
    Iterator<?> nodes = ((ILayoutNodeOperation)
      operation).getLayoutNodes().listIterator();
    if (nodes.hasNext()) {
      View node = ((ILayoutNode) nodes.next()).getNode();
      Diagram container = node.getDiagram();
      if (container == null ||
        !(container.getType().equalsIgnoreCase("mindmap")))
      return false;
    }
```

```
    } else {
      return false;
    }
    IAdaptable layoutHint = ((ILayoutNodeOperation)
      operation).getLayoutHint();
    String layoutType = (String) layoutHint.getAdapter(String.class);

    return LayoutType.DEFAULT.equals(layoutType);
  }
}
```

As you can see, our default provider simply extends the runtime-provided `LeftRightProvider` and only needs to override the `provides()` method to enable our provider for mindmap diagrams. We'll further modify this provider later to get the layout we want, but for now, this is all we need to get started. Besides the need to provide both left-to-right and right-to-left layout of topics about a centered root, we want to ignore dependency links when performing a layout. More specifically, we want to lay out topics in a tree structure while arranging relationship links to avoid topics; relationship links will be optionally hidden and should not be considered during main layout.

When deployed, this provider replaces the default layout provider that the menu item and toolbar invoke. Section 4.3.5, "Subtopic Figure," explores what is required to programmatically invoke layout on a diagram as we create subtopics using a keyboard shortcut.

Subtopic Figure

For our notation, we want root `Topic` elements to be displayed with a rounded rectangle, and subtopic elements to be displayed with a single underline. Our domain model has no notion of distinct `Topic` and subtopic elements, so this means we end up with two figures for the `Topic` element that will change depending on the structure of the elements. Furthermore, we might decide that *n*-level subtopic elements should have yet another notation, so we focus on a solution that is general. Currently, the models of GMF cannot handle this type of definition, whereby a different figure represents a domain element based on its state. This is a planned enhancement for GMF, but in the meantime, we begin by adding a new subtopic figure.

The subtopic figure is a rectangle with only the bottom border drawn, thereby appearing as an underline for our subtopic name. The makeup of this figure is somewhat complicated. Table 4-7 details our subtopic figure and node properties. Note the use of `CustomBorder`, which uses a provided runtime figure.

Table 4-7 Mindmap Subtopic Figure

Element	Property	Value
Figure Gallery	Name	Default
Figure Descriptor	Name	SubtopicFigure
Rectangle	Name	SutopicFigure
	Fill	false
	Outline	false
Border Layout		
Insets	Left	10
Rectangle	Name	SubtopicNameRectangleFigure
	Fill	false
	Outline	false
Border Layout Data	Alignment	CENTER
	Vertical	true
Stack Layout		
Custom Border	Qualified Class Name	org.eclipse.gmf.runtime.draw2d.ui. figures.OneLineBorder
Custom Attribute	Name	position
	Value	org.eclipse.draw2d. PositionConstants.BOTTOM
Label	Name	SubtopicNameFigure
Insets	Bottom, Left	5, 5
Child Access	Figure	Label SubtopicNameFigure
Node	Name	Subtopic
	Figure	Figure Descriptor SubtopicFigure
Default Size Facet		
Dimension	Dx, Dy	50, 10
Diagram Label	Name	SubtopicName
	Figure	Figure Descriptor SubtopicFigure
	Accessor	Child Access getFigureSubtopicFigure
	Element Icon	false

Our tooling model does not require changes because we don't want to allow for the explicit creation of subtopic nodes; we want to have them visualized when subtopic links are made. Our mapping model needs a new top-level node mapping, as shown here along with our original `Topic` mapping. With two node mappings for a single domain model element, we need to define a constraint for each so that the generated code can distinguish between them, as seen in Table 4-8. This is especially important when diagrams are created from existing models, to remove ambiguity and to allow for the proper notation to be assigned. In the case of our mindmap, `Topic` elements with no `parent` are considered "root" `Topic`s and use the rounded rectangle figure. Those that have a parent, which is the `eOpposite` of the `subtopics` reference, will be rendered with our new underline figure.

Table 4-8   Updated Mindmap Node Mappings

Element	Property	Value
Mapping		
Top Node Reference	Containment Feature	Map.elements : MapElement
Node Mapping	Element	Topic → MapElement
	Diagram Node	Node Topic (TopicFigure)
	Tool	Creation Tool Topic
Constraint	Body	self.parent = null
	Language	ocl
Feature Label Mapping	Diagram Label	Diagram Label TopicName
	Features	MapElement.name : EString
Top Node Reference	Containment Feature	Map.elements : MapElement
Node Mapping	Element	Topic → MapElement
	Diagram Node	Node SubTopic (SubTopicFigure)
Constraint	Body	self.parent <> null
	Language	ocl
Feature Label Mapping	Diagram Label	Diagram Label SubtopicName
	Features	MapElement.name : EString

Regenerating our diagram and testing reveals some problems. Although it's possible to create subtopic links, the target figure is not immediately updated. If we use the provided refresh action by pressing F5, we see that the figure updates and its location is preserved. If we create a relationship link, the diagram *is* refreshed automatically because of the canonical update of the `Map` itself. We want the image to automatically update when a subtopic link is created or removed, and for layout to be invoked when using the palette or an action. As with most things in GMF, we can solve our problem in many ways.

If we look at our `MapCanonicalEditPolicy` class, we see the `refreshSemantic()` method, which is invoked by our refresh action. The generated code overrides this method and the `isOrphaned()` method from `CanonicalConnectionEditPolicy` to incorporate knowledge of our mapping constraints into the logic. If you look into the code, you'll see that view elements that have no corresponding semantic element are deleted, while semantic elements with no view have one created. As soon as a subtopic connection is made between two `Topics`, our constraints prompt the deletion of our target `Topic` view because its visual ID no longer matches its semantic constraint. We could override the methods in this `EditPolicy` and its superclass to transfer the location of the original view to the updated view. This is feasible but would require the copy and paste of a lot of code because many of these methods are marked as `final` in the runtime.

Another option is to implement our own connection tool used in the palette that could invoke a delete-and-create-view-command to update our `Topic` figure after link creation. This would not solve our problem of switching the view back when the subtopic link is removed, although it would be a clean way of creating an updated figure in the same location. This approach is covered in the UML2 Tools project, which provides actions to toggle alternative notations of some UML elements, such as Interface. Specifically, take a look at the `ChangeNotationAction` class, in the `org.eclipse.uml2.diagram.common` plug-in. There, the original view element's location is passed to the create-view-request, to avoid the positioning problem.

We know that the view needs to change when an element is added or removed from a `Topic`'s subtopics reference list, so we can watch for events on this feature and invoke a refresh on our `MapCanonicalEditPolicy`. Furthermore, we can add code to the `EditPolicy` to invoke a diagram layout when subtopics are added, or when `Topics` are added or removed from the diagram.

In each of our `Topic` `EditParts`, we override the `handleEvent Notification()` method and invoke the `refresh()` method on our `MapCanonicalEditPolicy` class, to let the generated code update the view on our `Topic` elements.

```
@Override
protected void handleNotificationEvent(Notification notification) {
  int type = notification.getEventType();
  Object feature = notification.getFeature();
  if (MindmapPackage.eINSTANCE.getTopic_Subtopics().equals(feature) &&
    (type == Notification.ADD || type == Notification.REMOVE)) {
    CanonicalEditPolicy canonicalEditPolicy = (CanonicalEditPolicy)
      getParent().getEditPolicy(EditPolicyRoles.CANONICAL_ROLE);
    canonicalEditPolicy.refresh();
    if (getParent().getEditPolicy(
EditPolicyRoles.CANONICAL_ROLE) instanceof MapCanonicalEditPolicy) {

((MapCanonicalEditPolicy)canonicalEditPolicy).layout();
    }
  }
  super.handleNotificationEvent(notification);
}
```

In our `MapCanonicalEditPolicy` class, we override `handleNotifi-
cationEvent()` and look for additions or removals from our Map's elements
feature and invoke a new `layout()` method. Finally, we modify the
`refreshSemantic()` method to invoke layout if it's detected that a new view
was created in the process.

```
@Override
protected void handleNotificationEvent(Notification event) {
  int type = event.getEventType();
  Object feature = event.getFeature();
  if (MindmapPackage.eINSTANCE.getMap_Elements().equals(feature) &&
    (type == Notification.ADD || type == Notification.REMOVE)) {
    layout();
  }
  super.handleNotificationEvent(event);
}

/**
 * @generated NOT
 */
protected void refreshSemantic() {
  List createdViews = new LinkedList();
  createdViews.addAll(refreshSemanticChildren());
  List createdConnectionViews = new LinkedList();
createdConnectionViews.addAll(refreshSemanticConnections());
  createdConnectionViews.addAll(refreshConnections());

  if (createdViews.size() > 1) {
    // perform a layout of the container
    DeferredLayoutCommand layoutCmd = new
      DeferredLayoutCommand(host()
      .getEditingDomain(), createdViews, host());
    executeCommand(new ICommandProxy(layoutCmd));
  }
```

```java
    createdViews.addAll(createdConnectionViews);
    makeViewsImmutable(createdViews);
    if (createdViews.size() > 0) {
      layout();
    }
  }

  public void layout() {
    TransactionalEditingDomain ted =
      TransactionUtil.getEditingDomain(getDiagram());
    final View diagram = getDiagram();
    final AbstractEMFOperation operation = new AbstractEMFOperation(ted,
      "Mindmap layout", null) {
      protected IStatus doExecute(IProgressMonitor monitor,
        IAdaptable info) throws ExecutionException {
        LayoutService.getInstance().layout(diagram, LayoutType.DEFAULT);
        return Status.OK_STATUS;
      }
    };
    PlatformUI.getWorkbench().getDisplay().asyncExec( new Runnable() {
      public void run() {
        try {
          operation.execute(new NullProgressMonitor(), null);
        } catch (ExecutionException e) {
          // TODO Auto-generated catch block
          e.printStackTrace();
        }
      }
    });
  }
```

This gets us a lot closer to our desired behavior of having a fixed layout. Certain actions, such as resizing topics manually, represent another opportunity to update layout. For now, we move on to a new topic.

Custom Connection Figure

Although you can define many figures using the GMF graphical definition model, some figures require custom code. Additionally, you might want to reuse existing figures in GMF diagram definitions, as you saw with `CustomBorder`. To illustrate this capability, here we use a custom figure for the target decoration of our subtopic link. This is the source code for a simple circle figure that we'll add to a new `org.eclipse.mindmap.diagram.figures` package in our diagram plug-in:

```java
public class CircleDecoration extends Ellipse implements
RotatableDecoration {
  private int myRadius = 5;
  private Point myCenter = new Point();
  public void setRadius(int radius) {
```

```
    erase();
    myRadius = Math.abs(radius);
    bounds = null;
    repaint();
  }

  public void setLineWidth(int width) {
    super.setLineWidth(width);
  }

  public Rectangle getBounds() {
    if (bounds == null) {
      int diameter = myRadius * 2;
      bounds = new Rectangle(myCenter.x - myRadius,
        myCenter.y - myRadius, diameter, diameter);
      bounds.expand(lineWidth / 2, lineWidth / 2);
    }
    return bounds;
  }

  public void setLocation(Point p) {
    if (myCenter.equals(p)) {
      return;
    }
    myCenter.setLocation(p);
    bounds = null;
  }

  public void setReferencePoint(Point p) {
    // ignore, does not make sense to rotate circle
  }
}
```

To use this figure, we'll create a new Custom Decoration in our figure gallery named CircleDecoration with a Qualified Class Name of org. eclipse.mindmap.diagram.figures.CircleDecoration. In the Source Decoration property of our TopicSubtopicsFigure, we'll select this decorator and then regenerate our mindmap.gmfgen model from our mindmap. gmfmap file.

Adding a Subtopic Action

Adding new subtopics to our mindmap is not very convenient right now. The mouse and palette are required to first create a Topic and then a connection, seriously impeding our "brainstorming" ability. We want to use the keyboard as much as possible to add and insert new Topic elements. Adding keyboard short-cuts and menu items to elements involves straightforward Eclipse platform code that we can add to our customization plug-in. Note that here we don't use the contributionItemProviders extension-point that the runtime provides because of some outstanding issues with keyboard binding at the time of this writing.

First, we add the object contribution to our `org.eclipse.mindmap.diagram.custom` plug-in manifest, as shown. Only our `Topic EditPart` classes need the contribution because it makes sense to add a new subtopic only from the context of an existing `Topic`. The only nodes on our diagram are either `Topics` or `Subtopics`, so we use their superclass `ShapeNodeEditPart` for the `objectClass`. We're defining an **Insert** menu item, with a child Subtopic action. We could have created a single menu item (Insert → Subtopic), but this gives us a placeholder for other possible additions, such as Insert → Parent Topic.

```
<extension point="org.eclipse.ui.popupMenus">
  <objectContribution adaptable="false"
    id="org.eclipse.mindmap.diagram.ui.objectContribution.TopicEditPart"
    objectClass="org.eclipse.gmf.runtime.diagram.ui.editparts.
      ShapeNodeEditPart">
    <menu
      id="MindmapInsert"
      label="&amp;Insert"
      path="additions">
      <separator name="group1"/>
    </menu>

    <action
    class="org.eclipse.mindmap.diagram.part.MindmapCreateSubtopicAction"
      definitionId="org.eclipse.mindmap.insertSubtopic"
      enablesFor="1"
      id="org.eclipse.mindmap.popup.MindmapCreateSubtopicActionID"
      label="&amp;Subtopic"
      menubarPath="MindmapInsert/group1">
    </action>
  </objectContribution>
</extension>
```

The declared action class is `MindmapCreateSubtopicAction`, which we have defined next. It enables only a single `Topic` selection because it doesn't make sense to invoke the action for multiple selected `Topic` elements. Before diving into the action code, we complete our definition by contributing to the `commands` and `bindings` extension-points.

```
<extension point="org.eclipse.ui.bindings">
  <key
  commandId="org.eclipse.mindmap.insertSubtopic"
  contextId="org.eclipse.mindmap.diagram.ui.diagramContext"
  schemeId="org.eclipse.ui.defaultAcceleratorConfiguration"
  sequence="M1+I"/>
</extension>
```

```
<extension point="org.eclipse.ui.commands">
  <command
  id="org.eclipse.mindmap.insertSubtopic"
  name="Insert Subtopic"
  description="Inserts a new subtopic"
  categoryId="org.eclipse.ui.category.edit"/>
</extension>
```

We're using the **Ctrl+I** (**Cmd+I** on the Mac) key combination to insert new subtopics, and we're using the provided edit category for the command. Also note that we are using the `contextId` that is declared in our generated diagram plug-in for use with the F5 diagram refresh action. This is the implementation of our create subtopic action:

```
public class MindmapCreateSubtopicAction implements
IObjectActionDelegate {
  public final static String ID =
    "org.eclipse.mindmap.popup.MindmapCreateSubtopicActionID";
  private ShapeNodeEditPart selectedElement;
  public void run(IAction action) {
    if (selectedElement == null) {
      return;
    }
    CompoundCommand cc = new CompoundCommand("Create Subtopic and
      Link");

    // create the new topic for the other end
    CreateViewRequest topicRequest =
      CreateViewRequestFactory.getCreateShapeRequest(
      MindmapElementTypes.Topic_2001,
      selectedElement.getDiagramPreferencesHint());
    MapEditPart mapEditPart = (MapEditPart)
      selectedElement.getParent();
    Command createTopicCmd = mapEditPart.getCommand(topicRequest);
    cc.add(createTopicCmd);

    // create the subtopics link command
    IAdaptable topicViewAdapter = (IAdaptable) ((List)
      topicRequest.getNewObject()).get(0);
    CreateConnectionViewAndElementRequest ccver = new
    CreateConnectionViewAndElementRequest(
      MindmapElementTypes.TopicSubtopics_4001,((IHintedType)
      MindmapElementTypes.TopicSubtopics_4001).getSemanticHint(),
      selectedElement.getDiagramPreferencesHint());
    ICommand createSubTopicsCmd = new
      DeferredCreateConnectionViewAndElementCommand(ccver, new
        EObjectAdapter((EObject) selectedElement.getModel()),
        topicViewAdapter, selectedElement.getViewer());

    cc.add(new ICommandProxy(createSubTopicsCmd));
    selectedElement.getDiagramEditDomain().getDiagramCommandStack()
      .execute(cc);
```

```
// here, update view to subtopic
final EditPartViewer viewer = selectedElement.getViewer();
final EditPart ep = (EditPart) mapEditPart.getChildren()
  .get(mapEditPart.getChildren().size()-1);

if (ep != null) {
  viewer.setSelection(new StructuredSelection(ep));
  viewer.reveal(ep);
  Display.getCurrent().syncExec(new Runnable() {
    public void run() {
      Request der = new Request(RequestConstants.REQ_DIRECT_EDIT);
      ep.performRequest(der);
    }
  });
}
}

public void selectionChanged(IAction action, ISelection selection) {
  selectedElement = null;
  if (selection instanceof IStructuredSelection) {
    IStructuredSelection structuredSelection = (IStructuredSelection)
      selection;
    if (structuredSelection.getFirstElement() instanceof
      TopicEditPart || structuredSelection.getFirstElement()
      instanceof Topic2EditPart) {
      selectedElement = (ShapeNodeEditPart)
        structuredSelection.getFirstElement();
    }
  }
}
}
```

Starting at the bottom with the `selectionChanged()` method, we set our `selectedElement` field to be that of the currently selected `Topic`. The `run()` method of our action class does all the work to create the compound command for creating our new subtopic and associated link, invoking the diagram layout, and finally activating the in-place editor. The code is fairly straightforward, aside from the details of what goes on within the `DeferredCreateConnection ViewAndElementCommand` when executed. For this, it's recommended that you set a breakpoint and follow its execution, if interested, as is the case with much of the GMF runtime code.

One troubling point of our implementation are the references to `MindmapElementTypes TopicSubtopics_4001` and `Topic_2001`. These are generated visual IDs that are produced by the tooling of GMF and are subject to change, unfortunately. A better solution here is to create custom templates that would enable us to generate this action and, therefore, eliminate the possibility that our custom action code will break after some future change to the generated diagram code. Section 4.4.5, "ToolTips," covers the use of custom templates for diagram generation.

Adding Fixed Anchor Locations

By default, connections made between `Topics` and their subtopics anchor on the target using one of several anchor points. Although this works well for many diagrams, we don't want this in the mindmap. The situation is helped to an extent by our automatic layout, which nicely anchors links to the right and left of the topics, but that's not quite where we want them in the case of subtopics. Figure 4-10 is a simple example to illustrate the problem before the layout is added. As you can see, the target decorators are positioned where the default chopbox anchor point is calculated, using the center of the figure as a reference point. This applies to the outgoing source end as well.

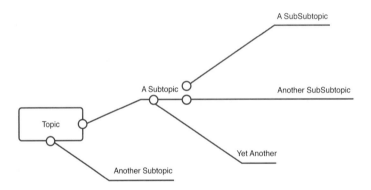

Figure 4-10   Mindmap chopbox anchors

Preferably, lines should connect at a fixed point for all Topic elements to the left of the text at the target end. The source end should have the line connect at a point to the right of the text. Following are `SourceFixedConnection Anchor` and `TargetFixedConnectionAnchor` classes that you can add to the generated `TopicEditPart` and `Topic2EditPart` classes. A root `Topic` never needs a target anchor: After a subtopic connection is made, the figure changes. We're going to ignore relationship links from our layout and don't want them to be anchored the same as subtopic links, so we're applying our anchors only to subtopic connections. The code we use is basically stripped-down versions of the `FixedConnectionAnchor` provided with the GEF Logic Diagram example. First, consider the additions to `TopicEditPart`:

```
private ConnectionAnchor sourceAnchor;

@Override
public ConnectionAnchor getSourceConnectionAnchor(ConnectionEditPart
        connEditPart) {
    if (sourceAnchor == null) {
```

```
      sourceAnchor = new SourceFixedConnectionAnchor(getNodeFigure());
    }
    return sourceAnchor;
  }

public class SourceFixedConnectionAnchor
    extends AbstractConnectionAnchor {

    public SourceFixedConnectionAnchor(IFigure owner) {
      super(owner);
    }

    public Point getLocation(Point reference) {
      Point right = getOwner().getBounds().getRight();
      Point p = new PrecisionPoint(right.x + 1, right.y - 1);
      getOwner().translateToAbsolute(p);
      return p;
    }
  }
}
```

The overridden getLocation() method provides the main functionality. To install on our EditPart, we override getSourceConnectionAnchor(), and in our Topic2EditPart, we override getSourceConnectionAnchor() as well.

```
private ConnectionAnchor targetAnchor;
private ConnectionAnchor sourceAnchor;

@Override
public ConnectionAnchor getTargetConnectionAnchor(
ConnectionEditPart connEditPart) {
  if (targetAnchor == null) {
    targetAnchor = new TargetFixedConnectionAnchor(getNodeFigure());
  }
  return targetAnchor;
}

@Override
public ConnectionAnchor getSourceConnectionAnchor(
ConnectionEditPart connEditPart) {
  if (sourceAnchor == null) {
    sourceAnchor = new
    SourceFixedConnectionAnchor(getNodeFigure());
  }
  return sourceAnchor;
}

public class SourceFixedConnectionAnchor extends
    AbstractConnectionAnchor {

    public SourceFixedConnectionAnchor(IFigure owner) {
      super(owner);
    }
```

```
  public Point getLocation(Point reference) {
    Point right =
      getOwner().getBounds().getBottomRight();
    Point p = new PrecisionPoint(right.x + 1, right.y - 1);
    getOwner().translateToAbsolute(p);
    return p;
  }
}

public class TargetFixedConnectionAnchor extends
  AbstractConnectionAnchor {

  public TargetFixedConnectionAnchor(IFigure owner) {
    super(owner);
  }

  public Point getLocation(Point reference) {
    Point left = getOwner().getBounds().getBottomLeft();
    Point p = new PrecisionPoint(left.x + 10, left.y - 1);
    getOwner().translateToAbsolute(p);
    return p;
  }
}
```

Figure 4-11 shows an updated image of our mindmap that, again, uses our default layout. Clearly, this is an improvement, but we still have some tweaking to do. Note that although the left-to-right anchor and layout have been implemented, we need to modify the implementation if we are to support right-to-left layout as well.

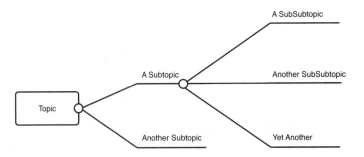

Figure 4-11   Mindmap fixed anchors

Diagram Preferences

Our generated diagram code includes preference settings that are accessible from the Eclipse preference dialog in a Mindmap Diagram category. Diagram general, appearance, connection, ruler, grid, and printing preferences are all available from a set of contributed preference pages. In our generated `org.eclipse. mindmap.diagram.preferences` package is code that supports further extension and enables us to set defaults. For example, if we want all the mindmap diagram lines to be blue by default, we can adjust our `DiagramAppearance PreferencePage` class as follows:

```java
public class DiagramAppearancePreferencePage

    extends AppearancePreferencePage {

    private static RGB LINE_COLOR = new RGB(90, 140, 255);

    /**
     * @generated
     */
    public DiagramAppearancePreferencePage() {
      setPreferenceStore(MindmapDiagramEditorPlugin.getInstance().
        getPreferenceStore());
    }

    public static void initDefaults(IPreferenceStore store) {
      AppearancePreferencePage.initDefaults(store);
      PreferenceConverter.setDefault(store,
      IPreferenceConstants.PREF_LINE_COLOR, LINE_COLOR);
    }
}
```

We can set more preferences and add new preferences. Section 4.6.6, "Color Preferences," looks at how to modify code-generation templates to add custom preferences for the color modeling diagram.

Audits and Metrics

GMF provides the capability to define OCL-based audits and metrics for the domain and diagram models. Using the mapping definition model, we can define diagram audits and metrics for both domain and notation model elements. What's generated leverages the EMF Validation Framework. To begin, we open our mindmap.gmfmap model in the editor, right-click on the `Mapping` element, and add a new `Audit Container` child. To the container, add the two audit rules in Table 4-9.

Table 4-9   Mindmap Audit Definition

Element	Property	Value
Mapping		
Audit Container	Description	A set of mindmap model audits.
	Id	mindmap.audits
	Name	Mindmap Audits
Audit Rule	Description	Topics should not have subtopic relationships that form a cycle.
	Id	cycle
	Message	A cycle was detected in the subtopics of this Topic.
	Name	Subtopic Cycle
	Severity	WARNING
	Use In Live Mode	false
Constraint	Body	not self->closure(subtopics)->includes(self)
	Language	ocl
Domain Element Target	Element	Topic -> MapElement
Audit Rule	Description	All Topic elements require a valid name.
	Id	name
	Message	Topic has no name.
	Name	Topic Name
	Severity	ERROR
	Use In Live Mode	true
Constraint	Body	not self.name.oclIsUndefined() and self.name <> ''
	Language	ocl
Domain Element Target	Element	Topic -> MapElement

We've defined two audits using OCL. The first detects cycles in `Topic` subtopic relationships using MDT OCL's `closure()` iterator. If the topic is within the set of all subtopics, a cycle is formed. The `Severity` of this audit is set to `WARNING` and it is not used in `Live Mode`, meaning that the Practitioner must manually invoke the **Diagram** → **Validate** menu item to run the audit. The second audit detects invalid Topic names, which, in this case, are limited to empty name strings and those that are not initialized. A more elaborate audit could be created to ensure that valid `Topic` names are entered. The severity is set to `error` and the audit is defined as a "live" audit. This means that it will be invoked automatically when changes are made to the specified domain element. As you'll see in the generator model, an additional option is available to provide immediate UI feedback: A dialog will pop up to alert the Practitioner that the change made violates a constraint.

Moving to metric definitions, right-click the `Mapping` node again and add a child `Metric Container` element. Populate the container with the elements and property settings in Table 4-10.

Table 4-10   Mindmap Metric Definition

Element	Property	Value
Mapping		
Metric Container		
Metric Rule	Description	The number of direct subtopics for the selected Topic
	High Limit	5.0
	Key	NOS
	Low Limit	0.0
	Name	Number of Subtopics
Value Expression	Body	self.subtopics->size()
	Language	ocl
Domain Element Target	Element	Topic -> MapElement

Metrics are defined with upper and lower limits and are based on the result of the OCL statement. In this case, we're counting the number of direct subtopics of a `Topic`. We could define another that counts the total number of subtopics using the `closure()` iterator we used earlier.

At this point, we can re-create our `mindmap.gmfgen` model from the mapping model and observe new `Gen Audit Root` and `Gen Metric Container` elements. More interesting are the options related to validation in the `Gen Diagram` element. Under the `Diagram` category are the `Validation Enabled` and `Validation Decorators` properties that we set to `true` here. Also notice the `Live Validation UI Feedback` property mentioned earlier. Here we set this to `true` as well, just to see the result. In the `Providers` category are a number of additional options related to validation and metric priorities and providers. The `Metric Provider Priority` property needs to be set to a value higher than `Lowest`, so we set it to `Medium` and regenerate our diagram.

In the runtime, you'll find `Validate` and `Metrics` items in the `Diagram` menu. To test our audits and metrics, create a set of `Topic` elements with subtopics connecting them in a circle. At this point, our layout should be indication enough that cycles are a bad idea, as Figure 4-12 illustrates. Ideally, we'd add a link constraint to prevent cycles altogether. Nevertheless, run the **Validate** action and observe in the Problems view the warning of a cycle. Also notice the warning decorations added to each Topic; each violates the audit.

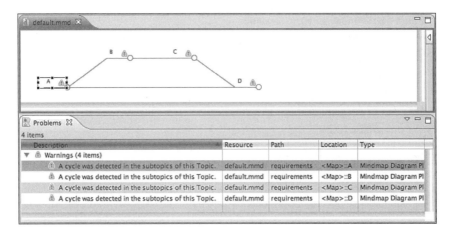

Figure 4-12   Mindmap audit violations

Rename one of the Topics to a blank value and observe the live validation dialog, shown in Figure 4-13.

Invoke our diagram metrics and observe the Mindmap Diagram Metrics view, listing each `Topic` and providing the metric value in the **NOS** column, as seen in Figure 4-14. Those with values above the upper limit are displayed in red, and those below the lower limit are displayed in blue.

In our preferences, we now have a `Model Validation` category with options for live validation, in case the Practitioner chooses not to have a dialog pop up on each violation, as seen in Figure 4-15. Each constraint is also listed, with information on what it checks and the option to disable each, as seen in Figure 4-16.

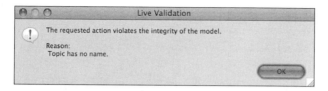

Figure 4-13 Mindmap live validation

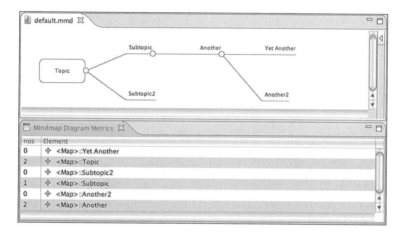

Figure 4-14 Mindmap metrics

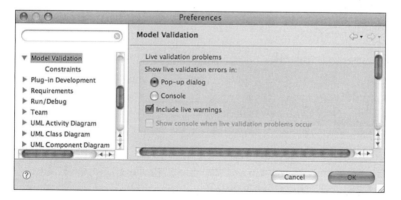

Figure 4-15 Mindmap validation preferences

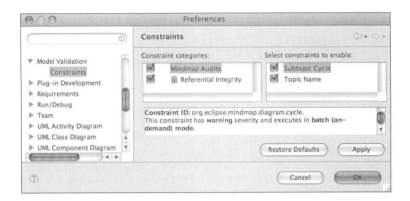

Figure 4-16   Mindmap validation constraint preferences

Note that audits and metrics defined using GMF are GMF-specific only when they're written against the notation model. Otherwise, the generated code can be refactored for use in the domain model without a diagram. You will find the Validation Framework quite useful, particularly considering the extensibility provided with its declarative nature. You can add other audits and metrics by augmenting the generated `plugin.xml` file, or even from another plug-in. This is how our earlier audits and metrics are declared, not including the decorator and marker declarations:

```
<extension point="org.eclipse.emf.validation.constraintProviders">
  <?gmfgen generated="true"?>
  <category id="mindmap.audits" mandatory="false"
    name="Mindmap Audits">
    <![CDATA[A set of mindmap model audits.]]>
  </category>
  <constraintProvider cache="true">
    <package namespaceUri="http://www.eclipse.org/2008/mindmap"/>
    <constraints categories="mindmap.audits">
      <constraint id="cycle"
        lang="OCL"
        name="Subtopic Cycle"
        mode="Batch"
        severity="WARNING" statusCode="200">
        <![CDATA[not self->closure(subtopics)->includes(self)]]>
        <description><![CDATA[Topics should not have subtopic
relationships that form a cycle.  ]]>
        </description>
        <message><![CDATA[A cycle was detected in the subtopics of
this Topic.]]>
        </message>
        <target class="mindmap.Topic"/>
      </constraint>
```

```xml
          <constraint id="name"
            lang="OCL"
            name="Topic Name"
            mode="Live"
            severity="ERROR" statusCode="200">
            <![CDATA[self.name <> '']]>
            <description><![CDATA[All Topic elements require a valid
name.]]>
            </description>
            <message><![CDATA[Topic has no name.]]></message>
            <target class="mindmap.Topic"/>
          </constraint>
        </constraints>
      </constraintProvider>
    </extension>

    <extension point="org.eclipse.emf.validation.constraintBindings">
      <?gmfgen generated="true"?>
      <clientContext default="false"
        id="org.eclipse.mindmap.diagram.DefaultCtx">
        <selector class="org.eclipse.mindmap.diagram.providers.
          MindmapValidationProvider$DefaultCtx1"/>
      </clientContext>
      <binding context="org.eclipse.mindmap.diagram.DefaultCtx">
        <constraint ref="org.eclipse.mindmap.diagram.cycle"/>
        <constraint ref="org.eclipse.mindmap.diagram.name"/>
      </binding>
    </extension>

    <extension id="MetricContributionItemProvider" name="Metrics"
      point="org.eclipse.gmf.runtime.common.ui.services.action.
      contributionItemProviders">
      <?gmfgen generated="true"?>
      <contributionItemProvider checkPluginLoaded="true"
       class="org.eclipse.mindmap.diagram.providers.MindmapMetricProvider">
        <Priority name="Medium"/>
         <partContribution
           id="org.eclipse.mindmap.diagram.part.MindmapDiagramEditorID">
           <partMenuGroup menubarPath="/diagramMenu/" id="validationGroup"/>
           <partAction id="metricsAction"
             menubarPath="/diagramMenu/validationGroup"/>
                 </partContribution>
           </contributionItemProvider>
    </extension>
```

You can find the generated code corresponding to these contributions in the classes `MindmapMetricProvider` and `MindmapValidationProvider`; both are in the `org.eclipse.mindmap.diagram.providers` package. They are not described in detail here, so take a look at the provided sample code and the documentation on the EMF Validation Framework for more information.

4.4 Developing a Requirements Diagram

We want a simple diagram that displays requirements so that we can visualize their relationships and dependencies. We first develop the diagram to be stand-alone, and then we integrate it as a tab in the generated EMF editor to illustrate the approach. Eventually, we want the requirements editor to be primarily form based.

4.4.1 Diagram Definition

Beginning with the Graphical Definition Model Wizard, we create a new `requirements.gmfgraph` model in our `/diagrams` folder of the `org.eclipse.dsl.requirements` project. In the wizard, be sure to select the `Model` class as the diagram element. Table 4-11 shows the completed model, indicating values that changed from their default.

Table 4-11   Requirements Figure Definition

Element	Property	Value
Canvas	Name	RequirementCanvas
Figure Gallery	Name	RequirementGallery
Polyline Decoration	Name	OpenArrow
Figure Descriptor	Name	Circle
Rectangle	Name	CircleOuterRectangle
	Fill	False
	Outline	False
Stack Layout		
Ellipse	Name	Circle
Label	Name	CenterLetter
Basic Font	Face Name	Arial
	Height	10
	Style	BOLD
Margin Border		
Insets	Left, Top	6, 5
Child Access	Figure	Rectangle CircleOuterRectangle

Element	Property	Value
Child Access	Figure	Ellipse Circle
Child Access	Figure	Label CenterLetter
Figure Descriptor	Name	SolidLine
Polyline Connection	Name	SolidLine
Figure Descriptor	Name	BasicLabel
Label	Name	BasicLabel
Child Access	Figure	Label BasicLabel
Figure Descriptor	Name	DashedLineWithOpenArrow
Polyline Connection	Name	DashedLineWithOpenArrow
	Line Kind	LINE_DASH
	Target Decoration	Polyline Decoration OpenArrow
Foreground Color	Value	Blue
Figure Descriptor	Name	RoundedRectangleCenterLabel
Rounded Rectangle	Name	RoundedRectangleCenterLabel
	Corner Height	8
	Corner Width	8
Stack Layout		
Maximum Size	Dx, Dy	50, 20
Minimum Size	Dx, Dy	50, 20
Preferred Size	Dx, Dy	50, 20
Insets	Bottom	5
	Left	5
	Right	5
	Top	5
Label	Name	CenterLabel
Child Access	Figure	CenterLabel
Node	Name	Requirement
	Figure	Figure Descriptor Circle
	Resize Constraint	NONE

(continues)

Table 4-11   Requirements Figure Definition (continued)

Element	Property	Value
Default Size Facet		
Dimension	Dx, Dy	20, 20
Node	Name	RequirementGroup
	Figure	Figure Descriptor RoundedRectangleCenterLabel
	Resize Constraint	NONE
Default Size Facet		
Dimension	Dx, Dy	50, 20
Connection	Name	RequirementChild
	Figure	Figure Descriptor SolidLine
Connection	Name	GroupRequirement
	Figure	Figure Descriptor SolidLine
Connection	Name	Dependency
	Figure	Figure Descriptor DashedLineWithOpenArrow
Connection	Name	GroupChild
	Figure	Figure Descriptor SolidLine
Diagram Label	Name	RequirementTitle
	Figure	Figure Descriptor BasicLabel
Diagram Label	Name	RequirementGroupName
	Figure	Figure Descriptor RoundedRectangleCenterLabel
Diagram Label	Name	RequirementType
	Figure	Figure Descriptor Circle

Note that the `Resource Constraint` property is set to `NONE` on both the `Requirement` and `RequirementGroup` nodes. This makes the node nonresizable. Another option to make an element nonresizable is to add `org.eclipse.gef.editpolicies.NonResizableEditPolicy` to the `Primary Drag Policy Qualified Class Name` property of the corresponding `Gen Top Level Node` property in the gmfgen model. Alternatively, you can use the `NonResizableEditPolicyEx` class from the GMF runtime.

A complication here is the label on the `RequirementGroup`, which, although nested within a nonresizable figure, causes the figure to grow by default as the text exceeds the width of the figure. To address this, the children `Maximum Size`, `Minimum Size`, and `Preferred Size` elements are added to the `Rounded Rectangle` to prevent resizing.

Notice that we have "hard-coded" the dependency link blue. Optionally, we can create a preference for this type of connection to allow the user to modify it, as you saw in the mindmap diagram Section 4.3.5, "Diagram Preferences."

4.4.2 Tooling Definition

The tooling definition is straightforward, as always. We need two groups again: one for Nodes and the other for Links. Because of our numerous connection types, we need several Link tools, depending on their source and target types. Figure 4-17 shows the palette model. Here, we are more interested in simply displaying dependency relationships and are not so interested in allowing for the creation of elements on the diagram, so we could exclude a palette definition altogether.

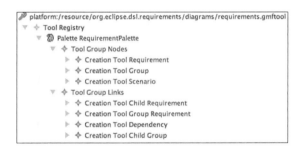

Figure 4-17   Requirements tooling definition

4.4.3 Mapping Definition

The structure of the requirements model differs from that of the mindmap model, in that children of `RequirementGroups` and `Requirements` are maintained in containment references of the elements, not in containment references of the root element. Thus, you can see how the mapping differs in this example. Figure 4-18 is our domain model to use as a reference through this discussion.

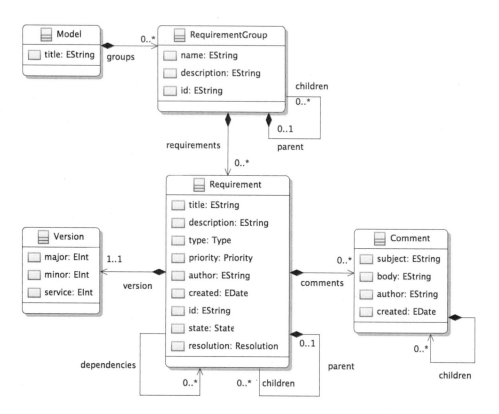

Figure 4-18   Requirements domain model

The `Canvas Mapping` is straightforward, as Table 4-12 shows.

Table 4-12   Requirements Canvas Mapping

Element	Property	Value
Mapping		
Canvas Mapping	Domain Element	requirements
	Element	Model
	Palette	Palette RequirementPalette
	Diagram Canvas	Canvas RequirementCanvas

For `RequirementGroups`, we have two mappings. The first represents groups that are contained in our canvas `Model` domain element; the second represents subgroups that are maintained as children of other groups.

The first mapping uses the `groups` reference of the Model class as the `Containment Feature`. The child `Node Mapping` is straightforward and listed in Table 4-13.

Table 4-13 RequirementGroup Node Mapping

Element	Property	Value
Mapping		
Top Node Reference	Containment Feature	Model.groups : RequirementGroup
Node Mapping	Element	RequirementGroup
	Diagram Node	Node RequirementGroup (RoundedRectangleCenterLabel)
	Tool	Creation Tool Group
Constraint	Body	parent.oclIsUndefined()
Feature Label Mapping	Diagram Label	Diagram Label RequirementGroupName
	Features	RequirementGroup.id : EString

Notice from the table that we have a `Constraint` added to this node mapping, indicating that the parent reference must be null for this mapping to hold. We use the OCL expression `parent.oclIsUndefined()` to accomplish this. The second `RequirementGroup` mapping specifies that the parent must be a `RequirementGroup` using `parent.oclIsTypeOf(requirements:: RequirementGroup)`. If we had an `eOpposite` relationship with our `Model` class as we do between `RequirementGroup` and its children, we could have used `parent.oclIsTypeOf(requirements::Model)` in the first mapping.

For the first mapping, we specify a `Tool`, and in the second we rely on a `Link` to create a subgroup when drawn between two root groups. The `Feature Label Mapping` uses the `id` attribute, although with a fixed size of our `RequirementGroup` node, we expect the label to be truncated in the display. We'll add ToolTips later, to allow diagram browsing to reveal the full name string.

Jumping to the second `RequirementGroup` mapping, we see in Table 4-14 that no `Containment Feature` is specified for the node.

Table 4-14   Second RequirementGroup Node Mapping

Element	Property	Value
Mapping		
Top Node Reference	Containment Feature	*Intentionally not set*
Node Mapping	Element	RequirementGroup
	Diagram Node	Node RequirementGroup (RoundedRectangleCenterLabel)
	Tool	*Intentionally not set*
Constraint	Body	parent.oclIsTypeOf(requirements:: RequirementGroup)
Feature Label Mapping	Diagram Label	Diagram Label RequirementGroupName
	Features	RequirementGroup.id : EString

Note that no `Tool` is specified for this mapping. We've specified a node that uses the same figure as the previous `RequirementGroup` mapping but that will be created after a link is drawn between two groups. Note that this is not an example of the "phantom" node concept discussed in Section 11.3.3, "References, Containment, and Phantom Nodes." In this case, all nodes added to the diagram canvas are legitimate because they're being held in the `Model`'s `groups` containment reference. We're just switching the containment feature from this to the `children` containment reference of `RequirementGroup` after a link is drawn between two groups.

Although we could achieve this change in containment for a node in other ways, this approach maximizes our use of generated code. We've defined constraints for each so that the generated code can uniquely specify each view mapping for the underlying semantic element. The `Feature Label Mapping` is the same as for the first `RequirementGroup` node mapping.

The `Link Mapping` for `RequirementGroup` specifies the `children` containment reference for subgroups, when drawn. The rest of the mapping is straightforward, as Table 4-15 shows.

Table 4-15 RequirementGroup Link Mapping

Element	Property	Value
Mapping		
Link Mapping	Target Feature	RequirementGroup.children : RequirementGroup
	Diagram Link	Connection GroupChild
	Tool	Creation Tool Child Group

Our `Requirement` node mapping *does* illustrate the "phantom" node concept. In this case, `Requirement` elements added to the diagram surface are not immediately placed in a valid containment reference; the `Canvas` is mapped to the `Model` class, which does not hold `Requirements` directly. A `Requirement` can be contained only in a `RequirementGroup` or as a child of another `Requirement`. So we specify the `Top Node Reference` with no `Containment Feature`, but we create two links that specify each of the two valid containments, as seen in Table 4-16.

Table 4-16 Requirement Node Mapping

Element	Property	Value
Mapping		
Top Node Reference	Containment Feature	*Intentionally not set*
Node Mapping	Element	Requirement
	Diagram Node	Node Requirement (Circle)
	Tool	Creation Tool Requirement
Feature Seq Initializer	Element Class	Requirement
Reference New Element Spec	Feature	Requirement.version : Version
Feature Seq Initializer	Element Class	Version
Feature Value Spec	Feature	Version.major : EInt
Value Expression	Body	1
	Language	ocl
Feature Label Mapping	Diagram Label	Diagram Label RequirementTitle
	Features	Requirement.id : EString

(continues)

Table 4-16   Requirement Node Mapping (continued)

Element	Property	Value
Feature Label Mapping	Diagram Label	Diagram Label RequirementType
	Features	Requirement.type : Type
	Read Only	true
	View Pattern	{0}

As you can see, `Node Mapping` uses the `Feature Seq Initializer` element to create a new `Version` instance upon creation of a `Requirement` and set its `major` attribute to 1. This is a nice capability of GMF that would be beneficial in EMF as well. Table 4-16 gives the details of the `Requirements Node Mapping`.

The Requirements node has two `Feature Label Mappings`. The first is for an external label used to display the `Requirement`'s id attribute. The second is a `Read Only` label used to display the `type` of the `Requirement` in the center of its circle graphic, as Figure 4-19 shows. This works because we changed the `Literal` property of each `Type` enumeration to be a single letter: F in the case of FUNCTIONAL, N in the case of NONFUNCTIONAL. This is a simple solution, although it's trivial to modify the generated code to return the first character or simply supply a character based on the selected enum.

Now we turn to our two `Requirement` link mappings. First is the mapping for `Requirements` that are maintained in the `requirements` feature of our `RequirementGroup` class, as shown by the `Target Feature` property setting. It uses the same `Diagram Link` we'll use in the next mapping, but it has its own `Tool`, as seen in Table 4-17.

Table 4-17   Requirement Link Mappings

Element	Property	Value
Mapping		
Link Mapping	Target Feature	requirements : Requirement
	Diagram Link	Connection GroupRequirement
	Tool	Creation Tool Group Requirement
Link Mapping	Target Feature	children : Requirement
	Diagram Link	Connection RequirementChild
	Tool	Creation Tool Child Requirement

The second mapping uses the `children` containment reference as the `Target Feature` and has its own `Tool`. Our final mapping is for `Dependency` links. As you will recall from our graphical definition, these are blue dashed lines with open arrow head target decorations. We can use them to indicate dependency references between `Requirements`, as shown in Table 4-18.

Table 4-18 Requirements Dependency Link Mapping

Element	Property	Value
Mapping		
Link Mapping	Target Feature	dependencies : Requirement
	Diagram Link	Connection Dependency
	Tool	Creation Tool Dependency

4.4.4 Generation

As before, we can right-click on our mapping model and select **Create Generator Model** to bring up the transformation dialog. The default `requirements.gmfgen` in the `/diagrams` folder is fine, so we proceed to the **Select Mapping Model** page, where our `requirements.gmfmap` model is already loaded. On the next page, we find that our `requirements.genmodel` is already selected and loaded as well. On the final page, we keep the defaults **Use IMapMode** and **Utilize Enhanced Features of GMF Runtime**, and then click **Finish**.

We now leave the default generation properties for the moment and generate our diagram plug-in using the **Generate Diagram Code** option from the file's context menu. Launching the runtime workspace lets us create a new requirements diagram using the generated wizard found in the **Examples** category of the **New** (**Ctrl+N**) dialog. Figure 4-19 is a sample diagram.

You'll notice right away that creating two `RequirementGroup` objects on the diagram, followed by linking these groups using the `Child Group` tool, requires pressing F5 to invoke a refresh to see the link. We need to modify the generated code to invoke a canonical update to avoid this, as we did in our mindmap with the override of `handleNotificationEvent()`.

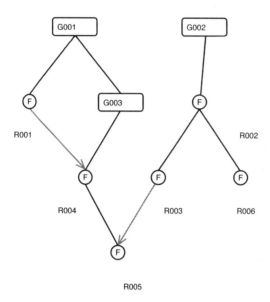

Figure 4-19   Requirements dependency diagram

4.4.5 ToolTips

Because we have decided not to clutter our dependency view by displaying only the ID of each `Requirement` and `RequirementGroup`, we need to populate a ToolTip with the `Requirement`'s title. This provides a convenient way to browse the diagram with the mouse but not have to select each element and look in the Properties view to see its information. For now, we just display the `title` attribute value in a `Label` by modifying the `createMainFigure()` method of the `RequirementEditPart` class, as follows:

```
/**
 * Creates figure for this edit part.
 *
 * Body of this method does not depend on settings in generation model,
 * so you may safely remove <i>generated</i> tag and modify it.
 *
 * @generated NOT
 */
protected NodeFigure createMainFigure() {
  NodeFigure figure = createNodePlate();
  figure.setLayoutManager(new StackLayout());
  IFigure shape = createNodeShape();
  figure.add(shape);
  contentPane = setupContentPane(shape);
```

```
    String text = ((Requirement) resolveSemanticElement()).getTitle();
    Label tooltip = new Label(text);
    tooltip.setBorder(new MarginBorder(getMapMode().DptoLP(0),
      getMapMode().DptoLP(5), getMapMode().DptoLP(5),
      getMapMode().DptoLP(5)));
    figure.setToolTip(tooltip);
    return figure;
}
```

This works but suffers from the fact that if the `title` attribute is modified, the ToolTip does not reflect the change. We could override `handleNotificationEvent()` in our `EditPart` and update the ToolTip when changes are made, but a better solution is to leverage a custom `EditPolicy`. Furthermore, this is something we'll potentially need for our `RequirementsGroup` because it is also a fixed-size shape that requires selection and the Properties view currently to get the full text. Instead of continuing to modify the generated code, this seems like a good opportunity to add a decorator model to our `requirements.gmfgen` model to specify ToolTips and their displayed attributes for selected elements. We begin by creating a simple `tooltip.ecore` model in the `/diagrams` folder of our requirements project, with just a root `Model` element that contains a collection of ToolTip elements, which, in turn, contains a number of `DisplayElements`. The important aspect of the model is the reference from the ToolTip to the GMF generation model's `CustomBehaviour` class, as shown in Figure 4-20 using a diagram shortcut.

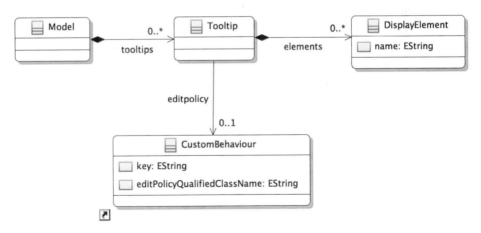

Figure 4-20   ToolTip model

We plan to implement a custom `EditPolicy` for our ToolTip, which is the standard GEF approach for adding behavior to an `EditPart`. It might seem like overkill when you see the actual implementation, but this gives us an opportunity to illustrate this extension approach.

The GMF generator model enables us to define `Custom Behaviour` elements as children of `Gen Top Level Node` elements. We need to add a reference from our `Tooltip` class to this element in the GMF generator model. Using the **Load Resource** menu followed by the convenient **Browse Registered Packages** button brings up the dialog shown in Figure 4-21. It takes a few seconds to populate, but when it does, we select our GMF GenModel from the list. Be sure to select **Runtime Version** and not **Development Time Version**, and then accept the corresponding warning that models referenced in this manner will not appear as a root in the editor. Selecting **Runtime Version** means that references to this loaded model will use the registered package Namespace URI instead of a `platform:/` URI, as is the case when selecting **Development Time Version**.

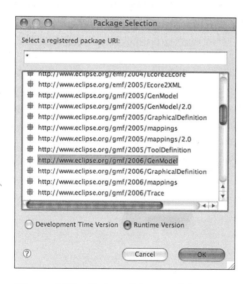

Figure 4-21 Package Selection dialog

We now create an `editpolicy` reference from our `Tooltip` class to the `CustomBehaviour` class in the loaded GMF GenModel. To reference the text we need to display in our ToolTip, we add a reference to the Ecore `EAttribute` element. Similar to our earlier procedure, we first use the **Load Resource** menu item to add the `http://www.eclipse.org/emf/2002/Ecore` model to our

resource set using the **Runtime Version,** and we create a new reference to our
`ToolTip` class named `textAttribute` of type `EAttribute`.

In our `requirements.gmfgen` model, navigate to the `Gen Top Level Node RequirementEditPart` element and add a new child `Custom Behaviour` element. It's a simple element, with just `Key` and `Edit Policy Qualified Class Name` properties, which we set to `"TooltipPolicy"` (the quotation marks are required) and `org.eclipse.requirements.diagram.edit. policies.RequirementsTooltipEditPolicy`, respectively. The parameter used to install an `EditPolicy` is a String, which typically comes from constants defined in either the GMF runtime's `EditPolicyRoles` interface or GEF's `EditPolicy` interface. Look at the policy roles defined here before you create your own. If you reuse a defined constant, you don't need to wrap it in quotes.

Next, we need to create a Dynamic Instance of our ToolTip model for use in generating our custom `EditPolicy`. This is much more convenient than the alternative, which is to create a `tooltip.gen` model and generate model code, followed by deploying that model into the environment. From the Ecore editor, we right-click our `Tooltip` element and select **Create Dynamic Instance** and select our `/diagrams` folder for the new `Tooltip.xmi` model. In the **Sample Reflective Ecore Model Editor,** use Load Resource to load our `requirements. genmodel` from the workspace. Now we can select the `Custom Behaviour` element that we added previously for our `Editpolicy` property. This is where the option of using the `Runtime Version` in our loading of the GMF GenModel earlier becomes important, for if we left the reference as `platform:/plugin...`, we would not have seen our `Custom Behaviour` element in the list.

Finally, set the `textAttribute` property of our `Tooltip` instance to the `title:EString` attribute of our Requirements class, which was loaded into the resource set when we loaded the `requirements.gmfgen` model.

TIP

When selecting the `title:EString` attribute for our `textAttribute` reference, we had to select it from a large list of possibilities in the Properties view, several of which had the required `name:Type` but with no indication that it was from our Requirements class. First, to narrow the list, type `title` into the field to filter the possibilities. Second, verify that the proper element was selected by opening the model in a text editor.

After we add the `Custom Behaviour` element to the generation model, the generated code references the `ToolTip` class. The GMF generator knows nothing of our custom template, and there's no way currently to add new template definitions to the execution environment. We need to create our own workflow and run a second-generation step to produce the referenced ToolTip `EditPolicy` class. Section 14.1.16, "Workflow Engine," covers workflows, but for now, just use **File → New → Other → Model Transformation → Workflow Definition** to create a `tooltip.mwe` file in the `/workflows` folder. Next you can see the workflow used to invoke our template following the normal GMF diagram generation; it includes a number of model references. As such, it's necessary to add the following plug-ins as dependencies of our project in the `MANIFEST.MF` file: `org.eclipse.gmf.codegen`, `org.eclipse.gmf.runtime.notation`, and `org.eclipse.gmf.validate`. Curiously, you also need to add `org.eclipse.core.runtime`, `org.eclipse.jdt.core`, and `org.eclipse.jface.text`.

```xml
<?xml version="1.0"?>
<workflow>
  <property
    name="model"
    value="platform:/resource/org.eclipse.dsl.requirements/
      diagrams/Tooltip.xmi" />
  <property name="out"
    value="../org.eclipse.requirements.diagram/src" />

  <!-- set up EMF for standalone execution -->
  <bean class="org.eclipse.emf.mwe.utils.StandaloneSetup">
    <platformUri value="../" />
    <RegisterGeneratedEPackage
      value="org.eclipse.gmf.codegen.gmfgen.GMFGenPackage"/>
    <RegisterGeneratedEPackage
      value="org.eclipse.gmf.runtime.notation.NotationPackage"/>
  </bean>

  <component class="org.eclipse.emf.mwe.utils.Reader">
    <uri value="${model}" />
      <modelSlot value="model" />
  </component>

  <!-- generate code -->
  <component class="org.eclipse.xpand2.Generator">
    <metaModel id="mm"
      class="org.eclipse.xtend.typesystem.emf.EmfRegistryMetaModel"/>
      <expand value="TooltipEditPolicy::Main FOR model" />
      <outlet path="${out}">
        <postprocessor
          class="org.eclipse.xpand2.output.JavaBeautifier" />
```

```
    </outlet>
  </component>

</workflow>
```

We need a template named `TooltipEditPolicy.xpt` that we can place in a `/templates-diagram` folder of our `org.eclipse.dsl.requirements` project. This folder needs to be added as a source path in the project; as does the `/diagrams` folder, we've placed our `tooltip.ecore` model and corresponding dynamic instance there. Following is the content of the Xpand template file, which could use some improvement. Chapters 7 and 14 cover Xpand, so we don't get into the details here.

```
«IMPORT tooltip»
«IMPORT gmfgen»
«IMPORT ecore»

«EXTENSION Utils»

«DEFINE Main FOR Model»
«FOREACH tooltips AS tooltip»
«EXPAND EditPolicy FOR tooltip»
«ENDFOREACH»
«ENDDEFINE»

«DEFINE EditPolicy FOR tooltip::Tooltip»
«FILE editpolicy.editPolicyQualifiedClassName.replaceAll("\\.", "/") +
    ".java"-»
package «packageName(editpolicy.editPolicyQualifiedClassName)»;

import org.eclipse.draw2d.ColorConstants;
import org.eclipse.draw2d.MarginBorder;
import org.eclipse.draw2d.RoundedRectangle;
import org.eclipse.draw2d.Shape;
import org.eclipse.draw2d.StackLayout;
import org.eclipse.draw2d.geometry.Rectangle;
import org.eclipse.draw2d.text.FlowPage;
import org.eclipse.draw2d.text.ParagraphTextLayout;
import org.eclipse.draw2d.text.TextFlow;
import org.eclipse.gef.Request;
import org.eclipse.gef.editpolicies.GraphicalEditPolicy;
import org.eclipse.gef.requests.LocationRequest;
import org.eclipse.requirements.Requirement;
import org.eclipse.requirements.diagram.edit.parts.RequirementEditPart;

public class «className(editpolicy.editPolicyQualifiedClassName)»
extends GraphicalEditPolicy {
```

```java
    Shape tooltip;
    RequirementEditPart rep;

    @Override
    public void showTargetFeedback(Request request) {
        if (tooltip == null && request instanceof LocationRequest) {
            rep = (RequirementEditPart) getHost();
            Requirement req = (Requirement)
              rep.resolveSemanticElement();

            tooltip = new RoundedRectangle();
  tooltip.setBackgroundColor(ColorConstants.titleGradient);
            tooltip.setLayoutManager(new StackLayout());
            tooltip.setBounds(new
Rectangle(getHostFigure().getBounds().getBottomRight().x,

getHostFigure().getBounds().getBottomRight().y, 200, 100));
            tooltip.setBorder(new MarginBorder(3));

            FlowPage flowPage = new FlowPage();
            TextFlow textFlow = new TextFlow();
            textFlow.setLayoutManager(new
ParagraphTextLayout(textFlow,
ParagraphTextLayout.WORD_WRAP_TRUNCATE));
            flowPage.add(textFlow);
            tooltip.add(flowPage);
            textFlow.setText(buildText(req));
            addFeedback(tooltip);
        }
    }

    private String buildText(Requirement req) {
        String title = req.getTitle() == null ? "" :
req.getTitle();
        String author = req.getAuthor() == null ? "" :
req.getAuthor();
        String text = "Title: " + title + "\n\n" + "Author: " + author;
        return text;
    }

    @Override
    public void eraseTargetFeedback(Request request) {
        if (tooltip != null) {
            removeFeedback(tooltip);
            tooltip = null;
            rep = null;
        }
    }

}
«ENDFILE»
«ENDDEFINE»
```

The template makes use of an Xtend utility named `Utils.ext`, whose contents are shown here for those who are interested. Again, later chapters cover the details of Xpand, Xtend, and Workflow.

```
String packageName(String fqn) :
    fqn.subString(0, (fqn.length - className(fqn).length)-1)
;

String className(String fqn) :
    fqn.split('\\.').last()
;
```

For completeness, this is the content of the `Tooltip.xmi` file used to complement our GMF generation with a custom `EditPolicy` that presents `Requirement` `title` and `author` attributes in a ToolTip on mouseover events:

```
<?xml version="1.0" encoding="ASCII"?>
<tooltip:Model xmi:version="2.0" xmlns:xmi="http://www.omg.org/XMI"
  xmlns:xsi="http://www.w3.org/2001/XMLSchema-instance"
  xmlns:tooltip="http://www.eclipse.org/2008/tooltip"
  xsi:schemaLocation="http://www.eclipse.org/2008/tooltip
  tooltip.ecore">
  <tooltips>
   <editpolicy
href="requirements.gmfgen#//@diagram/@topLevelNodes.1/@behaviour.0"/>
    <elements name="Title">
      <textAttribute
        href="../model/requirements.ecore#//Requirement/title"/>
    </elements>
    <elements name="Author">
      <textAttribute
        href="../model/requirements.ecore#//Requirement/author"/>
    </elements>
  </tooltips>
</tooltip:Model>
```

We can execute the workflow by right-clicking the `tooltip.mwe` file and selecting **Run As → MWE Workflow**. After execution, our new `TooltipEdit Policy` is generated into our requirements diagram project. Don't forget to regenerate the diagram code from the `requirements.gmfgen` model as well; the code required to install our custom editpolicy on the `Requirement` `EditPart` needs to be generated. If we launch the diagram, we can test the result, as Figure 4-22 shows.

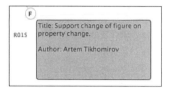

Figure 4-22   Requirement ToolTip

4.4.6 Integrating EMF and GMF Editors

For our requirements diagram, we want it to be a page within a multipage editor rather than a standalone diagram. The reason is that it's more of a dependency visualization diagram than a requirements editing environment, although it does have editing capabilities. An Eclipse Corner article [47] provides much of the detail on how to accomplish integrating EMF and GMF editors this way, so we imitate that approach here.

Sharing File Extension

To begin, we need to open our `requirements.gmfgen` model and make some changes, as shown in Figure 4-23. The `Diagram File Extension` property should match the `Domain File Extension`—in this case, `requirements`. Also, we need to change the `Same File For Domain And Model` property to `true`.

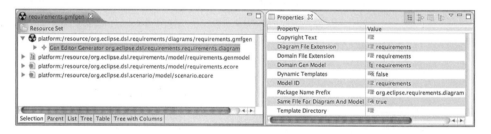

Figure 4-23   Requirements GMF generator model

At this point, regenerate the diagram code and launch the runtime workbench. Create a new Requirements Diagram using the GMF-generated wizard and populate it with some data. Right-click the `.requirements` file you created and select **Open With → Requirements Model Editor**, which is the EMF-generated editor. You'll find that the model has two roots: one for the domain model and the other for the diagram notation model. Note that if you try to create a new Requirements model using the GMF-generated wizard at this point, you'll get an error stating "Resource contains no diagram." Also, if you have an existing .requirements model in your workspace and attempt to initialize a diagram for it using the context menu, it will work fine. If you subsequently reopen this .requirements model in the EMF-generated wizard, you'll notice that the diagram notation model has been added as a second model root.

Furthermore, if you open the two editors simultaneously, you will notice the following behavior. Changes made in the EMF editor do not appear in the diagram until the EMF editor has been saved. As soon as you save the EMF editor, you'll notice a dirty marker appear on the diagram editor. Newly added elements are found in the upper left and require diagram layout. Likewise, the EMF editor does not see changes made to the diagram until the diagram is saved. Switching to the EMF editor results in a refresh that collapses the tree, though no dirty marker appears on this editor. The two editors are at least aware of changes made to the files they have open, but it's not quite good enough. Let's return to our development workspace and continue.

Sharing an Editing Domain

Although both editors use an EditingDomain, they use their own; the EMF editor uses an AdapterFactoryEditingDomain, and the GMF editor uses a TransactionalEditingDomain. We need them to share a single TransactionEditingDomain, so we must modify the generated EMF editor code. To use this class, we need to add the org.eclipse.emf.transaction plug-in to our list of Require-Bundle dependencies in the MANIFEST.MF file. Now open the org.eclipse.requirements.presentation.RequirementsEditor class found in the generated org.eclipse.requirements.model.editor plug-in. Mark the initializeEditingDomain() method as @generated NOT, and replace the code that creates a new BasicCommand Stack with the creation of a new TransactionalEditingDomain; then use its getCommandStack() method to add the listener. At the bottom of the method, cast the TransactionalEditingDomain to the expected AdapterFactory EditingDomain, making the method appear as follows:

```
/**
 * This sets up the editing domain for the model editor.
 * Modified to share TransactionalEditingDomain with diagram.
 *
 * @generated NOT
 */
protected void initializeEditingDomain() {
  // Create an adapter factory that yields item providers.
```

```
adapterFactory = new ComposedAdapterFactory(
  ComposedAdapterFactory.Descriptor.Registry.INSTANCE);

adapterFactory.addAdapterFactory(new
  ResourceItemProviderAdapterFactory());
adapterFactory.addAdapterFactory(new
  RequirementsItemProviderAdapterFactory());
adapterFactory.addAdapterFactory(new
  ReflectiveItemProviderAdapterFactory());

TransactionalEditingDomain domain =
  TransactionalEditingDomain.Factory.INSTANCE.createEditingDomain();
domain.setID("org.eclipse.requirements.EditingDomain");

// Add a listener to set the most recent command's affected objects
// to be the selection of the viewer with focus.
domain.getCommandStack().addCommandStackListener(new
  CommandStackListener() {
    public void commandStackChanged(final EventObject event) {
      getContainer().getDisplay().asyncExec(new Runnable() {
        public void run() {
          firePropertyChange(IEditorPart.PROP_DIRTY);
          // Try to select the affected objects.
          Command mostRecentCommand = ((CommandStack)
            event.getSource()).getMostRecentCommand();
          if (mostRecentCommand != null) {
          setSelectionToViewer(mostRecentCommand.getAffectedObjects());
          }
          if (propertySheetPage != null
            && !propertySheetPage.getControl().isDisposed()) {
              propertySheetPage.refresh();
          }
        }
      });
    }
  });

// Create the editing domain with a special command stack.
editingDomain = (AdapterFactoryEditingDomain) domain;
}
```

Open your requirements.gmfgen model and locate the Editing
Domain   ID property in the Editor category of the Gen   Diagram
ModelEditPart element part. Set the value of this property to the same ID we
previously set for the TransactionalEditingDomain, as seen in Figure 4-24.

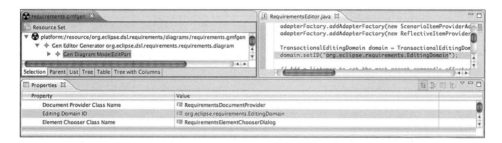

Figure 4-24 Requirements editing domain

With our editors sharing a common editing domain, now we turn to each of our pages in the multipage editor because they need a reference to this shared domain. Fortunately, GMF comes with a FileEditorInputProxy class that we can use to initialize each of the pages. First, we need to add a dependency from our EMF editor plug-in to our `org.eclipse.requirements.diagram` plug-in and re-export all the `org.eclipse.gmf.runtime.*` plug-ins from the diagram editor manifest. After this, navigate to the `init()` method of the RequirementsEditor class. Mark the method with `@generated` NOT and modify accordingly (changes in bold):

```
/**
 * This is called during startup.
 * Modified to pass FileEditorInputProxy as input for
 * TransactionalEditingDomain support.
 *
 * @generated NOT
 */
@Override
public void init(IEditorSite site, IEditorInput editorInput) {
    IEditorInput input = editorInput;
    if (input instanceof IFileEditorInput) {
        input = new FileEditorInputProxy((IFileEditorInput) input,
            (TransactionalEditingDomain) editingDomain);
    }
    setSite(site);
    setInputWithNotify(input);
    setPartName(input.getName());
    site.setSelectionProvider(this);
    site.getPage().addPartListener(partListener);
    ResourcesPlugin.getWorkspace().addResourceChangeListener(
        resourceChangeListener, IResourceChangeEvent.POST_CHANGE);
}
```

With our diagram becoming just another page in a multipage editor, we need
to modify its generated code a bit to take into account the passed
`FileEditorInputProxy`. Open the `org.eclipse.requirements.`
`diagram.part.RequirementsDocumentProvider` class and replace all uses
of `org.eclipse.ui.part.FileEditorInput` with `org.eclipse.ui.`
`IFileEditorInput`, with the exception of the method `handleElement`
`Moved()`. Don't forget to mark each section with `@generated NOT`.

Next, we need to modify the `createEmptyDocument()` method so that it
uses the passed `EditingDomain` instead of creating its own. Actually, we have
the original method delegate to a new method that takes an input parameter and
modify the `createDocument()` method to pass its parameter as follows
(changes in bold):

```
/**
 * @generated NOT
 */
protected IDocument createDocument(Object element) throws CoreException
{
  // ...
  IDocument document = createEmptyDocument(element);
  setDocumentContent(document, (IeditorInput) element);
  setupDocument(element, document);
  return document;
}

/**
 * Modified to use passed EditingDomain
 *
 * @generated NOT
 */
protected IDocument createEmptyDocument() {
  return createEmptyDocument(null);
}

/**
 * Use passed EditingDomain from input
 */
protected IDocument createEmptyDocument(Object input) {
  DiagramDocument document = new DiagramDocument();
  if (input instanceof FileEditorInputProxy) {
    FileEditorInputProxy proxy = (FileEditorInputProxy) input;
    document.setEditingDomain(proxy.getEditingDomain());
  } else {
    document.setEditingDomain(createEditingDomain());
  }
  return document;
}
```

Refactoring the Editor

Back to our EMF-generated `RequirementsEditor`, we see that each page is created as an anonymous subclass of `ViewerPane`. This causes problems when trying to integrate our diagram into a page, so we can create an *abstract* `RequirementsEditorPart` class to use as a superclass for converting each page into its own `EditorPart`. Create the new class in the `org.eclipse.requirements.presentation` package that extends `EditorPart` and implements `IMenuListener` and `IEditingDomainProvider` as follows:

```java
public abstract class RequirementsEditorPart extends EditorPart

implements IMenuListener, IEditingDomainProvider {

  protected RequirementsEditor parentEditor;

  public RequirementsEditorPart(RequirementsEditor parent) {
    super();
    this.parentEditor = parent;
  }

  protected static String getString(String key) {
    return RequirementsEditorPlugin.INSTANCE.getString(key);
  }

  public EditingDomain getEditingDomain() {
    return parentEditor.getEditingDomain();
  }

  protected BasicCommandStack getCommandStack() {
    return ((BasicCommandStack) getEditingDomain().getCommandStack());
  }

  protected AdapterFactory getAdapterFactory() {
    return ((AdapterFactoryEditingDomain) ((FileEditorInputProxy)
      getEditorInput()).getEditingDomain()).getAdapterFactory();
    }

  protected void createContextMenuFor(StructuredViewer viewer) {
    MenuManager contextMenu = new MenuManager("#PopUp");
    contextMenu.add(new Separator("additions"));
    contextMenu.setRemoveAllWhenShown(true);
    contextMenu.addMenuListener(this);
    Menu menu = contextMenu.createContextMenu(viewer.getControl());
    viewer.getControl().setMenu(menu);
    getSite().registerContextMenu(contextMenu, new
      UnwrappingSelectionProvider(viewer));

    int dndOperations = DND.DROP_COPY | DND.DROP_MOVE | DND.DROP_LINK;
    Transfer[] transfers = new Transfer[] {
      LocalTransfer.getInstance() };
    viewer.addDragSupport(dndOperations, transfers, new
      ViewerDragAdapter(viewer));
```

```
    viewer.addDropSupport(dndOperations, transfers, new
      EditingDomainViewerDropAdapter(getEditingDomain(), viewer));
}

public void doSave(IProgressMonitor monitor) {
  // nothing to do here - this is handled by the parent editor
}

public void doSaveAs() {
  // nothing to do here - this is handled by the parent editor
}

public void init(IEditorSite site, IEditorInput input) throws
    PartInitException {
    setSite(site);
    setInput(input);
}

public boolean isDirty() {
  return getCommandStack().isSaveNeeded();
}

public boolean isSaveAsAllowed() {
  return true;
}

public void menuAboutToShow(IMenuManager manager) {
  // pass the request to show the context menu to the parent editor
  ((IMenuListener) parentEditor.getEditorSite()
  .getActionBarContributor()).menuAboutToShow(manager);
}

public abstract void setInput(Object input);
}
```

We actually don't want to use all of the EMF-generated pages in our multi-page editor. We'll use just a selection tree and a diagram, so we can remove the rest. We create a new SelectionTreeEditorPart that extends our RequirementsEditorPart and migrate code from its original anonymous sub-class of ViewerPane from the RequirementsEditor class, as shown here:

```
public class SelectionTreeEditorPart extends RequirementsEditorPart {

  protected TreeViewer viewer;

  public SelectionTreeEditorPart(RequirementsEditor parent) {
    super(parent);
  }

  public void setInput(Object input) {
    viewer.setInput(input);
  }
```

```
public void createPartControl(Composite parent) {
  viewer = new TreeViewer(parent, SWT.MULTI);
  viewer.setContentProvider(new
    AdapterFactoryContentProvider(getAdapterFactory()));
  viewer.setLabelProvider(new
    AdapterFactoryLabelProvider(getAdapterFactory()));
  viewer.setSelection(new
    StructuredSelection(getEditingDomain().getResourceSet()
      .getResources().get(0)), true);
  getEditorSite().setSelectionProvider(viewer);
  new AdapterFactoryTreeEditor(viewer.getTree(),
    getAdapterFactory());
  createContextMenuFor(viewer);
    }

public void setFocus() {
  viewer.getTree().setFocus();
  }
}
```

We can refactor the `RequirementsEditor.createPages()` method now to use our `SelectionTreeEditorPart` class. As mentioned, we eliminate all but one of the standard EMF-generated pages, including the parent tree view, which means that we can eliminate the inner `ReverseAdapter FactoryContentProvider` class altogether. Following is our `createPages()` method, which initializes the `selectionTreeEditorPart` class attribute that we'll add to the class. We'll return to this method to add our diagram page later.

```
/**
 * This is the method used by the framework to install your controls.
 * Modified to include diagram page and use standalone
 * EditorPart classes for each page.
 *
 * @generated NOT
 */
@Override
public void createPages() {
  // Creates the model from the editor input
  createModel();

  // Only creates the other pages if there is something to be edited
  if (!getEditingDomain().getResourceSet().getResources().isEmpty()
    && !(getEditingDomain().getResourceSet().getResources().get(0))
    .getContents().isEmpty()) {
    try {
      int pageIndex;

      // Create selection tree viewer page
      selectionTreeEditorPart = new SelectionTreeEditorPart(this);
      pageIndex = addPage(selectionTreeEditorPart, getEditorInput());
      setPageText(pageIndex, getString("_UI_SelectionPage_label"));
```

```
      selectionTreeEditorPart.setInput(getEditingDomain()
        .getResourceSet());
    } catch (PartInitException e) {
      RequirementsEditorPlugin.INSTANCE.log(e);
    }

      // Removed all remaining pages original generated here

   getSite().getShell().getDisplay().asyncExec(new Runnable() {
      public void run() {
        setActivePage(0);
      }
    });
  }
  //. . .
}
```

Selection Handling

Before we clean up our `RequirementsEditor` class, we need to fix the selection handling we disrupted by splitting up the editor. `MultiPageEditorPart`
already provides a mechanism to handle selection changes, so we can refactor the
code to use it. We add a `MultiPageSelectionProvider` selection
`Provider` attribute to the class and initialize it in the constructor. We then set
this instance as the sitewide provider in the `init()` method, thereby eliminating
the need for the editor to implement `ISelectionProvider`. Changes are
in bold.

```
MultiPageSelectionProvider selectionProvider;

private int diagramPageIndex;

/**
 * This creates a model editor.
 * Modified to initialize selection provider.
 *
 * @generated NOT
 */
public RequirementsEditor() {
  super();
  initializeEditingDomain();
  selectionProvider = new MultiPageSelectionProvider(this);
  selectionProvider.addSelectionChangedListener(new
    ISelectionChangedListener()
    {
    public void selectionChanged(SelectionChangedEvent event) {
      setStatusLineManager(event.getSelection());
      IEditorPart activeEditor = getSite().getPage().getActiveEditor();
      if (selectionProvider.getMultiPageEditor().equals(activeEditor)
```

```
          && getActivePage() == diagramPageIndex) {
          diagramEditor.updateSelectionActions();
      }
    }
  });
}

public void init(IEditorSite site, IEditorInput editorInput) {
  // . . .
  site.setSelectionProvider(selectionProvider);
  // . . .
}
```

The `selectionChanged()` method calls upon a new `updateSelection` `Actions()` method that we add to our `RequirementsDiagramEditor`, which appears here:

```
public void updateSelectionActions() {
  updateActions(getSelectionActions());
}
```

In the `handleActivate()` method, we need to leverage the `selection` `Provider` as well (changes in bold):

```
/**
 * Handles activation of the editor or its associated views.
 * Modified to use selection provider.
 *
 * @generated NOT
 */
protected void handleActivate() {
  // Recompute the read only state.
  if (editingDomain.getResourceToReadOnlyMap() != null) {
    editingDomain.getResourceToReadOnlyMap().clear();

    // Refresh any actions that may become enabled or disabled.
    selectionProvider.setSelection(selectionProvider.getSelection());
  }

  // . . .
}
```

Our `setCurrentViewer()` method becomes much simpler because it no longer needs to deal with selection handling.

```
/**
 * This makes sure that one content viewer, either the current page or
 * the outline view, if it has focus, is the current one.
```

```
 * Modified to remove selection handling.
 *
 * @generated NOT
 */
public void setCurrentViewer(Viewer viewer) {
  if (currentViewer != viewer) {
    currentViewer = viewer;
  }
}
```

Finally, we need to refactor our handleContentOutlineSelection()
method.

```
/**
 * This deals with how we want selection in the outline to affect
 * the other views.
 * Modified to update selection handling.
 *
 * @generated NOT
 */
public void handleContentOutlineSelection(Iselection selection) {
      if (!selection.isEmpty() && selection instanceof
    IStructuredSelection) {
    List selectedElements = ((IStructuredSelection)
      selection).toList();
    if (getActiveEditor() == selectionTreeEditorPart) {
      // For the selection viewer, select the same selection
      selectionProvider.setSelection(new
        StructuredSelection(selectedElements));
    } else {
      // For others, set the input directly.
        ((RequirementsEditorPart)getActiveEditor())
      .setInput(selectedElements.get(0));
    }
  }
}
```

Our editor no longer is responsible for being an ISelectionProvider, so
we can eliminate this interface from the implements list and all associated code.
Attributes selectionChangedListener, selectionChangedListeners,
and editorSelection can be removed, along with their associated
methods addSelectionChangedListener(), removeSelectionChanged
Listeners(), getSelection(), and setSelection(). We no longer need
the currentViewerPane or the viewers, so we can remove these (except
currentViewer) as well. We also can remove the setFocus() and isDirty()
methods.

Finally, we can add the diagram to a page in our editor. Back in create
Pages(), enter the following code and corresponding RequirementsDiagram
Editor diagramEditor class attribute:

```
private RequirementsDiagramEditor diagramEditor;

public void createPages() {
    // . . .
      try {
        int pageIndex;
        // . . .
        // Create diagram viewer page
        diagramEditor = new RequirementsDiagramEditor();
        pageIndex = addPage(diagramEditor, getEditorInput());
        setPageText(pageIndex, "Diagram");
      } catch (PartInitException e) {
        RequirementsEditorPlugin.INSTANCE.log(e);
      }
    // . . .
}
```

We need to revisit our handleContentOutlineSelection() method to
take into account the diagram page because we want to map the selection to the
proper EditPart on the diagram (changes in bold):

```
public void handleContentOutlineSelection(ISelection selection) {
    if (!selection.isEmpty() && selection instanceof
      IStructuredSelection) {
      List selectedElements = ((IStructuredSelection)
        selection).toList();
      if (getActiveEditor() == selectionTreeEditorPart) {
        // . . .
      } else if (getActiveEditor() == diagramEditor) {
        // For diagrams, map to the appropriate EditPart
        ArrayList<Object> selectionList = new ArrayList<Object>();
        for (Object selectedElement : selectedElements) {
          if (selectedElement instanceof EObject) {
            String elementID = EMFCoreUtil.getProxyID((EObject)
              selectedElement);
            selectionList.addAll(
              diagramEditor.getDiagramGraphicalViewer()
              .findEditPartsForElement(elementID,
              IGraphicalEditPart.class));
          }
          selectionProvider.setSelection(new
            StructuredSelection(selectionList));
        }
      } else {
        // . . .
      }
    }
}
```

If we launch the runtime workbench and open one of our existing `.requirements` models, we will see that our editor now has two pages: one the familiar Selection page, the other our new Diagram page. Although it's working, we need to fix a few more items, including the Properties view, which currently does not respond to diagram selections. Also, you'll notice that the diagram toolbar is missing and that the Outline view has no diagram overview.

Properties View

The explanation for the Properties view not working is obvious. GMF editors use the tabbed properties by default, but EMF uses the "classic" view. We can update the `RequirementsEditor` to implement `ITabbedPropertySheet PageContributor`, add method `getContributorId()`, and update `getPropertySheetPage()`. Note that we need to change the type of `propertySheetPage` to `PropertiesBrowserPage`.

```
/**
 * This is the property sheet page.
 * Modified to support tabbed properties.
 *
 * @generated NOT
 */
protected PropertiesBrowserPage propertySheetPage;


/**
 * This accesses a cached version of the property sheet.
 * Modified to support tabbed properties view.
 *
 * @generated NOT
 */
public IPropertySheetPage getPropertySheetPage() {
  if (propertySheetPage == null) {
    propertySheetPage = new PropertiesBrowserPage(this) {
      public void setActionBars(IActionBars actionBars) {
        super.setActionBars(actionBars);
        getActionBarContributor().shareGlobalActions(this, actionBars);
      }
    };
  }
    return propertySheetPage;
}

public String getContributorId() {
    return diagramEditor.getContributorId();
}
```

This fixes our diagram page but breaks our tree selection page. The reason is that the contribution to the `*.tabbed.propertySections` extension-point made in the diagram editor plug-in does not include the raw EMF model types in our model. We need to add them, as shown here:

```
<extension
point="org.eclipse.ui.views.properties.tabbed.propertySections">
  <?gmfgen generated="false"?>
  <propertySections contributorId="org.eclipse.requirements.diagram">
      <!-- ... -->
   <propertySection
      id="property.section.domain"
      tab="property.tab.domain"
      class="org.eclipse.requirements.diagram.sheet.
        RequirementsPropertySection">
        <input type="org.eclipse.gmf.runtime.notation.View"/>
        <input type="org.eclipse.gef.EditPart"/>
        <!-- ... -->
        <input type="org.eclipse.requirements.Model"/>
        <input type="org.eclipse.requirements.Requirement"/>
        <input type="org.eclipse.requirements.RequirementGroup"/>
        <input type="org.eclipse.requirements.Comment"/>
        <input type="org.eclipse.requirements.Version"/>
      </propertySection>
   </propertySections>
</extension>
```

TIP

GMF's code generation provides merge capabilities for `plugin.xml` and `MANIFEST.MF` files in addition to `*.java` files, so be sure to mark modified sections accordingly to prevent overwrite. We changed the generated attribute of the gmfgen processing instruction to `false`, with the other alternative being to remove it altogether. This is analogous to adding `@generated NOT` to Java code that is modified.

While we're here, let's remove the `org.eclipse.ui.editors` contribution from our diagram plug-in manifest because we no longer need it.

Menus and Toolbar

To address the issues with menus and toolbars, we can add two classes provided in the article to our `org.eclipse.requirements.presentation` package: `RequirementsMultiPageActionBarContributor` and `SubAction BarsExt`. These are slightly refactored from the originals and are not covered here. Basically, the first class is a composite `ActionBarContributor` that handles switching between pages where each has its own contributor. The second class is a utility class used by the first. To use these classes, we need to modify two methods—first, the `getActionBarContributor()` in `RequirementsEditor`:

```
/**
 * Modified to support MultiPageActionBarContributor
 *
 * @generated NOT
 */
public EditingDomainActionBarContributor getActionBarContributor() {
  return (RequirementsActionBarContributor)
    ((RequirementsMultiPageActionBarContributor) getEditorSite()
    .getActionBarContributor()).getTreeSubActionBars().getContributor();
}
```

In `RequirementsEditorPart`, we need to modify `menuAboutToShow()` as well:

```
public void menuAboutToShow(IMenuManager manager) {
  // pass the request to show the context menu on to the parent editor
  ((RequirementsActionBarContributor)
    ((RequirementsMultiPageActionBarContributor) parentEditor

.getEditorSite().getActionBarContributor()).getTreeSubActionBars()
    .getContributor()).menuAboutToShow(manager);
}
```

The new contributor needs to be registered in our editor contribution, replacing the original:

```
<extension point="org.eclipse.ui.editors">
    <editor
      id="org.eclipse.requirements.presentation.RequirementsEditorID"
      name="%_UI_RequirementsEditor_label"
      icon="icons/full/obj16/RequirementsModelFile.gif"
      extensions="requirements"
      class =
"org.eclipse.requirements.presentation.RequirementsEditor"
      contributorClass="org.eclipse.requirements.presentation.
    RequirementsMultiPageActionBarContributor">
    </editor>
</extension>
```

Our edit menu actions are still in need of repair. Again, we need to "upgrade" the EMF-generated editor by having `RequirementsEditor` implement `IDiagramWorkbenchPart`, with each of its methods delegating to our `diagramEditor`:

```
public Diagram getDiagram() {
  return diagramEditor.getDiagram();
}

public IDiagramEditDomain getDiagramEditDomain() {
  return diagramEditor.getDiagramEditDomain();
}

public DiagramEditPart getDiagramEditPart() {
  return diagramEditor.getDiagramEditPart();
}

public IDiagramGraphicalViewer getDiagramGraphicalViewer() {
  return diagramEditor.getDiagramGraphicalViewer();
}
```

Our diagram plug-in manifest contains contributions to `globalAction-HandlerProviders`, each using the ID of the diagram editor. We need to either modify the IDs to be that of our EMF editor (now multipage), or copy this contribution to the other editor manifest, change the IDs, and make the priorities higher than the diagram editor. We opt for the second approach here, pasting the entire `globalActionHandlerProviders` section into the `org.ecilpse.requiremements.model.editor` `plugin.xml` file, replacing the three `Priorities` with `Low` and changing each of the `ViewIds` to `org.eclipse.requirements.presentation.RequirementsEditorID`.

Creation Wizard

Recall the "Resource contains no diagram" error we received when attempting to create a new Requirements model using the EMF-generated wizard. The EMF-generated wizard knows nothing about creating the diagram, which is an instance of the GMF notation model. We need to modify the `performFinish()` method to create and initialize a diagram when the domain model is created (changes in bold).

```
/**
 * Do the work after everything is specified.
 * Modified to include diagram.
 *
 * @generated NOT
 */
@Override
public boolean performFinish() {
```

```java
try {
  // Remember the file.
  final IFile modelFile = getModelFile();

  // Do the work within an operation.
  WorkspaceModifyOperation operation = new WorkspaceModifyOperation()
  {
    @Override
    protected void execute(IprogressMonitor progressMonitor) {
      try {
        // Create a resource set.
        ResourceSet resourceSet = new ResourceSetImpl();

        // Get the URI of the model file.
        URI fileURI = URI.createPlatformResourceURI(
          modelFile.getFullPath().toString(), true);

        // Create a resource for this file.
        Resource resource = resourceSet.createResource(fileURI);

        // Add the initial model object to the contents.
        EObject rootObject = createInitialModel();
        if (rootObject != null) {
          resource.getContents().add(rootObject);
        }

        // Create the diagram.
        Diagram diagram = ViewService.createDiagram(rootObject,
          ModelEditPart.MODEL_ID,

RequirementsDiagramEditorPlugin.DIAGRAM_PREFERENCES_HINT);
        if (diagram != null) {
          resource.getContents().add(diagram);
          diagram.setName(fileURI.lastSegment());
          diagram.setElement(rootObject);
        }

        // Save the contents of the resource to the file system.
        Map<Object, Object> options = new HashMap<Object, Object>();
        options.put(XMLResource.OPTION_ENCODING,
          initialObjectCreationPage.getEncoding());
        resource.save(options);
      } catch (Exception exception) {
        RequirementsEditorPlugin.INSTANCE.log(exception);
      } finally {
        progressMonitor.done();
      }
    }
  };
  // . . .
}
```

We'll use this Wizard exclusively to create requirements models, so we can remove the newWizards contribution in our diagram plug-in manifest.

Navigator and Outline

The **Project Explorer** view in the **Resource** perspective enables us to drill down into our .requirements file and navigate its contents. However, if we attempt to do this, we'll get ClassCastExceptions in the error log because we have a diagram contents contribution to the navigatorContent extension-point that doesn't know how to handle domain model elements. To fix this issue, we simply set the activeByDefault property of this contribution to false, as shown in Figure 4-25. More is involved in making the navigator truly useful, but this at least avoids the exceptions.

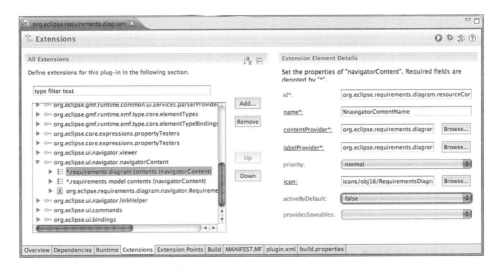

Figure 4-25   Requirements navigator extension

Our selection trees in the editor and the **Outline** view both show diagram content. Later we'll want to fix the **Outline** view so that it again gives us the "bird's-eye" view of the diagram when the diagram page is selected, but for now we just filter diagram content from our tree viewers. The process is the same for both, so we only show the changes made to SelectionTreeEditorPart. createPartControl() here. The same change needs to be made to RequirementsEditor.getContentOutlinePage(). As shown here, it's simply a matter of adding a ViewerFilter that excludes instances of Diagram from the view (changes in bold).

```
@Override
public void createPartControl(Composite parent) {
  viewer = new TreeViewer(parent, SWT.MULTI);
```

```
//  . . .
ViewerFilter[] outlineFilters = new ViewerFilter[1];
outlineFilters[0] = new ViewerFilter() {
  @Override
  public boolean select(Viewer viewer, Object parentElement, Object
    element) {
    return !(element instanceof Diagram);
  }
};
viewer.setFilters(outlineFilters);
//  . . .
}
```

At this point, we can run our editor and test its functionality. We still have some bugs to work out, but it's largely functional at this point.

Properties Revisited

The default generated properties from both EMF and GMF are simple tables, with the exception of diagram element properties that use form-based property sheets. The default is fine for certain property types, but it's painful to deal with long text strings such as a requirement's description property. Even the EMF generator model's `Property Multiline` option is painful because you need to first open a dialog from the Properties view. In this section, we generate a custom property sheet tab that we can use to provide a large text area for the description property.

To begin, open the `requirements.gmfgen` model and navigate to the `Property Sheet` element. Create a new `Custom Property Tab` element and populate it according to Table 4-19. Note that we're interested in only the `Requirement` class, so we enter its domain model class and corresponding diagram `EditPart` class.

Table 4-19   Requirements Custom Property Tab

Element	Property	Value
Gen Editor Generator		
Property Sheet		
Custom Property Tab	Human Readable Label	Description
	Identifier	description
	Implementation Class	RequirementDescriptionPropertySection

Element	Property	Value
Typed selection filter	Generated Types	abstractNavigatorItem
	Types in selection	org.eclipse.requirements.Requirement, org.eclipse.requirements.diagram.edit.parts. RequirementEditPart

When we regenerate our diagram, we find the following additions to the plugin.xml file and the default generated property section class. Note that if you marked the propertySections element as generated="false" during the steps to combine editors, you don't see the new property section. To regenerate in this case, set the value to true after backing up the changes and merge manually afterward.

```
<extension
point="org.eclipse.ui.views.properties.tabbed.propertyContributor">
        . . .
        <propertyCategory category="visual"/>
        <propertyCategory category="extra"/>
    </propertyContributor>
</extension>

<extension point="org.eclipse.ui.views.properties.tabbed.propertyTabs">
    . . .
    <propertyTab
        category="domain"
        id="property.tab.domain"
        label="%tab.domain"/>
    <propertyTab
        category="extra"
        id="property.tab.description"
        label="%tab.description"/>
    </propertyTabs>
</extension>

<extension
point="org.eclipse.ui.views.properties.tabbed.propertySections">
    <?gmfgen generated="false"?>
        . . .
        <propertySection
            id="property.section.description"
            tab="property.tab.description"
            class="org.eclipse.requirements.diagram.sheet.
              RequirementDescriptionPropertySection">
            <input type="org.eclipse.requirements.Requirement"/>
            <input type="org.eclipse.requirements.diagram.edit.parts.
              RequirementEditPart"/>
            <input type="org.eclipse.requirements.diagram.navigator.
              RequirementsAbstractNavigatorItem"/>
```

```
      </propertySection>
    </propertySections>
</extension>
```

The generated class extends the runtime's `AdvancedPropertySection` class. This provides the same table style of property view we're trying to replace, so we can delete the class content and have it extend the provided `AbstractBasicTextPropertySection` class, as shown here. This class provides a simple text field with code that sets up a forms-based property sheet, just as we wanted. Some changes we've made include the use of a text area and not a single line text field. Also, we have overridden the `unwrap()` method to identify our `Requirements` class or edit part properly, ensuring that the sheet will work when selections are made in both the diagram and tree view.

```java
/**
 * @generated NOT
 */
public class RequirementDescriptionPropertySection extends
AbstractBasicTextPropertySection {

  @Override
  protected String getPropertyChangeCommandName() {
    return "RequirementDescriptionChangeCommand";
  }

  @Override
  protected String getPropertyNameLabel() {
    return "";
  }

  @Override
  protected String getPropertyValueString() {
          String description = ((Requirement)
getEObject()).getDescription();
          return description == null ? "" : description;
      }

  @Override
  protected void setPropertyValue(EObject object, Object value) {
    ((Requirement) getEObject()).setDescription((String) value);
  }

  protected Text createTextWidget(Composite parent) {
    Text text = getWidgetFactory().createText(parent,
      StringStatics.BLANK,
      SWT.MULTI | SWT.H_SCROLL | SWT.V_SCROLL | SWT.WRAP);
    FormData data = new FormData();
```

```
    data.left = new FormAttachment(0, 0);
    data.right = new FormAttachment(100, 0);
    data.top = new FormAttachment(0, 0);
    data.bottom = new FormAttachment(100, 0);
    data.height = 100;
    data.width = 100;

    text.setLayoutData(data);
    if (isReadOnly()) {
      text.setEditable(false);
    }
      return text;
  }

  @Override
  protected EObject unwrap(Object object) {
    if (object instanceof Requirement) {
      return (EObject) object;
    }
    if (object instanceof EditPart) {
      Object model = ((EditPart) object).getModel();
      return model instanceof
        View ? ((View) model).getElement() : null;
    }
    if (object instanceof View) {
      return ((View) object).getElement();
    }
    if (object instanceof IAdaptable) {
      View view = (View) ((IAdaptable) object).getAdapter(View.class);
    if (view != null) {
      return view.getElement();
    }
  }
  return null;
  }
}
```

Figure 4-26 shows the result. Although we still have some work to do, this gets us started converting our table view to forms view properties. If you're interested in developing a model to define the property sheets and using custom templates to generate these form-based sheets, take a look at the GMF graphical definition model editor. This editor provides WYSIWYG editing of figures when developing diagrams, but it is still in the "experimental" SDK. It also supports the definition and generation of forms-based property sheets and editors through the use of a collection of models found in the org.eclipse.gmf.formtk plug-in.

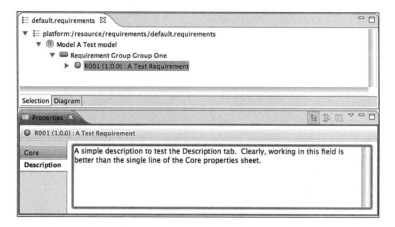

Figure 4-26   Requirement description Properties tab

One thing about the **Properties** view that we notice in our generated GMF diagrams is that the **Properties** view cannot handle the selection of multiple diagram elements. For example, try selecting multiple topics in our Mindmap diagram or selecting multiple requirements in our Requirement diagram. The **Core** tab of the **Properties** view goes blank. To resolve this, open the `RequirementsPropertySection` class in our requirements diagram. It's located in the `org.eclipse.requirements.diagram.sheet` package. To enable multiselection, we need to have the `getPropertySource()` method return an instance of `EMFCompositePropertySource` instead of the generated `PropertySource` default. This is the method showing the change:

```
/**
 * Modified to allow for multiselection
 * @generated NOT
 */
public IPropertySource getPropertySource(Object object) {
  if (object instanceof IPropertySource) {
    return (IPropertySource) object;
  }
  AdapterFactory af = getAdapterFactory(object);
  if (af != null) {
    IItemPropertySource ips = (IItemPropertySource) af.adapt(object,
      IItemPropertySource.class);
    if (ips != null) {
      return new EMFCompositePropertySource(object, ips,
        "Requirements");
    }
  }
  if (object instanceof IAdaptable) {
    return (IPropertySource) ((IAdaptable)
```

```
        object).getAdapter(IPropertySource.class);
    }
    return null;
}
```

This displays the properties of selected items for edit in the **Properties** view, but only if they are of the same type. However, we want only properties that make sense to change on multiple elements at a time to be editable. It doesn't make sense to change all the requirement IDs to the same value, for example. We leave this refinement as a future enhancement and move on to our next diagram.

4.5 Developing the Scenario Diagram

As mentioned already, we want to leverage the BPMN notational elements for our Scenario diagram. Unfortunately, no BPMN2 diagramming component exists within MDT, and the BPMN project within the SOA Tools project uses an older version of GMF and does not generate its figures to a standalone plug-in. Fortunately, this gives us an opportunity to show how this is done as we develop this diagram.

4.5.1 Graphical Definition

The BPMN specification defines many notational elements. We start with those to be used in our scenario diagram, but the idea is to create a figures plug-in that can be reused as a reusable library for any BPMN-based diagram. To begin, we create a new `org.eclipse.dsl.bpmn` project and, within it, a new `bpmn.gmfgraph` model in the `/diagrams` folder. In this case, we're interested in only the graphical definition, which we can use to generate a standalone plug-in and `mirrored.gmfgraph` model that we'll be referencing in our scenario diagram definition.

TIP

Some workflow issues arise when dealing with standalone figure bundles, so it's typically easier to first develop the default way using figures generated and included in the generator model. When the diagram is mostly completed, generate the figure bundle and load the `mirrored.gmfgraph` model into your mapping model to change references.

Each of the elements defined in our graphical definition is covered in a later subsection. Although we could define them all and then do the tooling and mapping, it's typically better to work iteratively. So although in each section it appears as though it was all done in a waterfall manner, the figures, their tooling, and their mappings actually were all done one or two at a time with many gmfmap→ gmfgen→ code iterations in between.

Also, notice the use of Figure Ref elements in the graphical definition. BPMN has several elements that contain common internal notation, so this reuse capability prevents copying/pasting/updating figures. For example, the envelope image in Figure 4-27 can appear within three different Event types.

Figure 4-27   Figures with inner elements

TIP

Notice that myUseLocalCoordinates is set to false by default when using Figure Ref, so you might want to change it to true if your figure contains another figure. This was the case with our envelope inner element; otherwise, it did not appear within the parent circle.

Task and Subprocess

We begin by creating a Task figure, which will be similar to our mindmap Topic figure, including the modifications we'll do to fix the stack layout and text wrapping covered in Section 4.3.5, "Topic Figure Layout." Figure 4-28 shows these elements, along with their figure and node settings, beginning with a Task. Table 4-28 shows the detail of the Task figure definition.

Figure 4-28   Scenario task figures

Table 4-20 BPMN Task Figure Definition

Element	Property	Value
Figure Gallery	Name	BPMN Figures
Figure Descriptor	Name	NamedRoundedRectangle
RoundedRectangle	Name	NamedRoundedRectangle
Stack Layout		
Minimum Size	Dx, Dy	80, 40
Preferred Size	Dx, Dy	80,40
Insets	Bottom, Left, Right, Top	5, 5, 5, 5
Label	Name	Name
Child Access	Figure	Label Name
Node	Name	Task
	Figure	Figure Descriptor NamedRoundedRectangle

We don't want `Task` items to be sized below a defined minimum, which is also the preferred size. As such, we don't need to set a `Default Size Facet` on the node element. As mentioned, `Tasks` can have border items, as shown in Figure 4-28. The `Affixed Parent Size` property used to enable this capability is set on the border item itself, as described in Section 4.5.1, "Events."

A `Subprocess` is similar to a `Task` element, with the addition of a small box with a plus sign located at the bottom center. Additional decorators are defined in the specification to indicate looping, parallelism, and so on, but these are not covered here. Table 4-21 defines the `Subprocess` figure and node.

Table 4-21 BPMN Subprocess Figure Definition

Element	Property	Value
Figure Gallery	Name	BPMN Figures
Figure Descriptor	Name	CollapsedNameRoundedRectangle
Rounded Rectangle	Name	CollapsedNameRoundedRectangle
Border Layout		
Minimum Size	Dx, Dy	80, 40
Preferred Size	Dx, Dy	80, 40

(continues)

Table 4-21   BPMN Subprocess Figure Definition (continued)

Element	Property	Value
Insets	Bottom, Left, Right, Top	0, 5, 5, 5
Rectangle	Name	NameArea
	Fill	False
	Outline	False
Border Layout Data	Alignment	CENTER
	Vertical	True
Stack Layout		
Label	Name	ProcessName
Rectangle	Name	CollapseArea
	Fill	False
	Outline	False
Border Layout Data	Alignment	END
	Vertical	True
Grid Layout		
Insets	Bottom, Left, Right, Top	0, 0, 0, 5
Figure Ref	Figure	Rectangle ExpandBox
Child Access	Figure	Label ProcessName
Rectangle	Name	ExpandBox
	Fill	False
Grid Layout Data	Grab Excess Horizontal Space	True
Stack Layout		
Maximum Size	Dx, Dy	10, 10
Minimum Size	Dx, Dy	10, 10
Preferred Size	Dx, Dy	10, 10
Insets	Bottom, Left, Right, Top	0, 1, 0, –1

Element	Property	Value
Label	Name	Plus
	Text	+
Node	Name	CollapsedSubprocess
	Figure	Figure Descriptor CollapsedNamedRoundedRectangle

We need to point out a few things in this graphical definition. First, a `Figure Ref` element points to the `ExpandBox` figure at the root of the `Figure Gallery`. The reason for this reference is that we will likely create additional subprocess figure elements to include decorations for additional types, thereby allowing reuse of this figure. Note that the plus symbol (+) itself for the box is an ordinary `Label` element, not a polyline. Using text elements such as this is not always a good idea because diagram scaling might not work as desired. Its use here is illustrative.

Also note the use of layout elements to achieve a text area on top with the `ExpandBox` figure centered at the bottom of the Subprocess node. A combination of Grid, Border, and Stack layouts is used.

TIP

When working with complex figures, it's helpful to add a line border or fill to see how layout and placement work. See Section 9.1.3, "Painting," for information on how GEF figures are composed.

Gateways

The `Gateway` item is a simple diamond but is decorated by an internal figure depending on the type: exclusive, inclusive, or parallel. The exclusive gateway has no decoration, and the specification has variants we don't implement here. The inclusive gateway has a heavy-lined inner circle figure, and the parallel gateway has a "plus" sign at its center, as seen in Figure 4-29. Table 4-22 defines each figure, as well as an image of the exclusive, inclusive, and parallel gateway figures (from left to right).

Figure 4-29   BPMN gateway figure definitions

Table 4-22   BPMN Gateway Figure Definitions

Element	Property	Value
Figure Gallery	Name	BPMN Figures
Figure Descriptor	Name	BasicDiamond
Rectangle	Name	BasicDiamond
	Fill	False
	Outline	False
Stack Layout		
Polygon	Name	Diamond
Template Point	X, Y	15, 0
Template Point	X, Y	0, 15
Template Point	X, Y	15, 30
Template Point	X, Y	30, 15
Figure Descriptor	Name	DiamondPlus
Rectangle	Name	DiamondPlus
	Fill	False
	Outline	False
Stack Layout		
Polygon	Name	Diamond
Template Point	Same points as above *	
Polyline	Name	Vertical
Template Point	X, Y	15, 8
Template Point	X, Y	15, 22
Polyline	Name	Horizontal
Template Point	X, Y	8, 15
Template Point	X, Y	22, 15

Element	Property	Value
Figure Descriptor	Name	DiamondCircle
Rectangle	Name	DiamondCircle
	Fill	False
	Outline	False
Stack Layout		
Polygon	Name	Diamond
Template Point	Same points as above *	
Rectangle	Name	HeavyOutlineCircle
	Fill	False
	Outline	False
Stack Layout		
Insets	Bottom, Left, Right, Top	7, 7, 7, 7
Ellipse	Name	Circle
	Line Width	3
Node	Name	ExclusiveGateway
	Figure	BasicDiamond
	Resize Constraint	NONE
Default Size Facet		
Dimension	Dx, Dy	30, 30
Node	Name	InclusiveGateway
	Figure	DiamondCircle
	Resize Constraint	NONE
Default Size Facet	Same as above	
Node	Name	ParallelGateway
	Figure	DiamondPlus
	Resize Constraint	NONE
Default Size Facet	Same as above	

* It should be possible to use a `Figure Ref` element here to point to a single `Diamond` figure definition, as we use elsewhere. At the time of this writing, the generated code is incomplete.

Note that the figures are fixed in size, although it would be possible to define each as scalable figures. Also note that each will be fully generated, with no template or code modification.

TIP

Use the `Default Size` facet of a node element to give it the desired size upon creation. In the figure definition, you can also set maximum, minimum, and preferred sizes.

Events

As with `Gateways`, many flavors of `Event` notation elements exist, as shown in Figure 4-30. The basic shape is a circle, with the outline determining its type. A normal outline (single line) represents a Start Event, and a thick border outline represents an End Event. A double outline represents an Intermediate Event. Within the circle, numerous "triggers" are defined in the spec, although only the definition of a message trigger (envelope) is provided here. Following are examples of Start, Intermediate, and End Event elements and their corresponding Message trigger alternatives. Table 4-23 gives figure and node definitions.

Figure 4-30   BPMN events

Table 4-23   BPMN Event Figure Definitions

Element	Property	Value
Figure Gallery	Name	BPMN Figures
Figure Descriptor	Name	BasicCircle
Rectangle	Name	BasicCircle
	Fill	False
	Outline	False
Stack Layout		

Element	Property	Value
Ellipse	Name	Circle
Figure Descriptor	Name	DoubleCircle
Rectangle	Name	DoubleCircle
	Fill	False
	Outline	False
Stack Layout		
Ellipse *	Name	Circle
Figure Descriptor	Name	HeavyOutlineCircle
Rectangle	Name	HeavyOutlineCircle
	Fill	False
	Outline	False
Stack Layout		
Ellipse	Name	Circle
	Line Width	3
Figure Descriptor	Name	BasicCircleWithEnvelope
Rectangle	Name	BasicCircleWithEnvelope
	Fill	False
	Outline	False
Stack Layout		
Ellipse	Name	Circle
FigureRef	Figure	Polyline Envelope
Figure Descriptor	Name	DoubleCircleWithEnvelope
	Same as DoubleCircle above with Fig Ref to Envelope	
Figure Descriptor	Name	HeavyOutlineCircleWithEnvelope
	Same as HeavyOutlineCircle above with Fig Ref to Envelope	
Polyline	Name	Envelope
Template Point	X, Y	5, 6
Template Point	X, Y	14, 6
Template Point	X, Y	14, 13
Template Point	X, Y	5, 13

(continues)

Table 4-23   BPMN Event Figure Definitions (continued)

Element	Property	Value
Template Point	X, Y	5, 6
Template Point	X, Y	9, 10
Template Point	X, Y	10, 10
Template Point	X, Y	14, 6
Node	Name	StartEvent
	Figure	Figure Descriptor BasicCircle
	Resize Constraint	NONE
Default Size Facet		
Dimension	Dx, Dy	20, 20
Node	Name	EndEvent
	Figure	Figure Descriptor HeavyOutlineCircle
	Otherwise, same as StartEvent node	
Node	Name	IntermediateEvent
	Figure	Figure Descriptor DoubleCircle
	Otherwise, same as StartEvent node	
Node	Name	MessageStartEvent
	Figure	Figure Descriptor BasicCircleWithEnvelope
	Otherwise, same as StartEvent node	
Node	Name	MessageIntermediateEvent
	Figure	Figure Descriptor DoubleCircleWithEnvelope
	Otherwise, same as StartEvent node	
Node	Name	MessageEndEvent
	Figure	Figure Descriptor HeavyOutlineCircleWithEnvelope
	Otherwise, same as StartEvent node	

Element	Property	Value
Node	Name	BorderedIntermediateEvent
	Figure	Figure Descriptor DoubleCircle
	Affixed Parent Side	NSEW
	Otherwise, same as StartEvent node	
Node	Name	BorderedMessageIntermediateEvent
	Figure	Figure Descriptor DoubleCircleWithEnvelope
	Affixed Parent Side	NSEW
	Otherwise, same as StartEvent node	

*Note that the `DoubleCircle` definition is identical to the `BasicCircle`. We modify the generated code in Section 4.5.4, "Intermediate Event Outline," to draw the second outline.

These figures are fairly straightforward, with the most complex part being the definition of the `Envelope`. Note that in addition to reuse of the `Envelope` using `Figure Ref` elements, figure reuse takes place in `Node` definitions (for example, as I used in the `DoubleCircle` node for both the standalone and border item `Intermediate Event`).

Connections

BPMN has several connection types, including Association, Message Flow, and Sequence flow, which are covered here. These are straightforward definitions, with the exception of the source decoration on the Message Flow—we need to code it by hand and reference it as a `Custom Figure`. Figure 4-31 shows images of each connection we define in Table 4-24: Normal Sequence Flow, Default Normal Sequence Flow, Association, Directed Association, and Message Flow (from top to bottom).

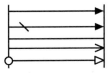

Figure 4-31 BPMN connection types

Table 4-24   BPMN Connection Figure Definitions

Element	Property	Value
Figure Gallery	Name	BPMN Figures
	Implementation Bundle	org.eclipse.bpmn.figures *
Figure Descriptor	Name	SolidLineClosedArrow
Polyline Connection	Name	SolidLineClosedArrow
	Target Decoration	Polygon Decoration ClosedArrow
Polygon Decoration	Name	ClosedArrow
Background Color	Value	black
Template Point	X, Y	0, 0
Template Point	X, Y	−1, 1
Template Point	X, Y	−1, −1
Template Point	X, Y	0, 0
Figure Descriptor	Name	DashedLineOpenArrow
Polyline Connection	Name	DashedLineOpenArrow
	Target Decoration	Polyline Decoration OpenArrow
	Line Kind	LINE_DASH
Polyline Decoration	Name	OpenArrow
Template Point	X, Y	−1, 1
Template Point	X, Y	0, 0
Template Point	X, Y	−1, −1
Figure Descriptor	Name	DashedLine
Polyline Connection	Name	DashedLine
	Line Kind	LINE_DASH
Figure Descriptor	Name	DashedLineCircleAndHollowPoint
Polyline Conection	Name	DashedLineCircleAndHollowPoint
	Target Decoration	Polygon Decoration ClosedArrow
	Source Decoration	Custom Decoration CircleDecoration
	Line Kind	LINE_DASH
Polygon Decoration	Name	ClosedArrow

Element	Property	Value
Background Color	Value	white
Template Point	X, Y	0, 0
Template Point	X, Y	−1, 1
Template Point	X, Y	−1, −1
Template Point	X, Y	0, 0
Custom Decoration	Name	CircleDecoration
	Qualified Class Name	org.eclipse.bpmn.figures. CircleDecoration
Custom Attribute	Name	radius
	Value	3
Figure Descriptor	Name	SolidLineSlashAndClosedArrow
Polyline Connection	Name	SolidLineSlashAndClosedArrow
	Source Decoration	Polyline Decoration Slash
	Target Decoration	Polygon Decoration ClosedArrow
Polyline Decoration	Slash	
Template Point	X, Y	−2, −1
Template Point	X, Y	−1, 1
Figure Descriptor	Name	SimpleLabel
Label	Name	SimpleLabel
Connection	Name	Association
	Figure	Figure Descriptor DashedLine
Connection	Name	DirectedAssociation
	Figure	Figure Descriptor DashedLineOpenArrow
Connection	Name	NormalFlow
	Figure	Figure Descriptor SolidLineClosedArrow
Connection	Name	Message
	Figure	Figure Descriptor DashedLineCircleAndHollowPoint

(continues)

Table 4-24 BPMN Connection Figure Definitions (continued)

Element	Property	Value
Connection	Name	DefaultNormalFlow
	Figure	Figure Descriptor SolidLineSlashAndClosedArrow
Diagram Label	Name	Name
	Figure	Figure Descriptor SimpleLabel

* We specify the `Implementation Bundle` property here as we reference a `Custom Figure` for our `Message Flow` source decorator. This allows the generated code to include the proper plug-in dependency while we develop the diagram. When the standalone figures plug-in is generated, this value automatically is entered into the generated `mirrored.gmfgraph` model, and we separate our custom code into its own project source path.

Note the `Diagram Label` and associated `Label` figure. This label is generic for all external labeling needs, such as that used by the `Normal Flow` connections in the mapping model. This represents another form of reuse because this single external label is used for connections and our `Data Object` node, as shown in the next section.

Data Object

A Data Object in BPMN refers to an artifact that can be associated with a flow object using an Association link or can be passed with a sequence flow. The notation is a simple document and uses the traditional dog-ear corner. Figure 4-32 shows an example of the Data Object being used in both directed and nondirected associations; Table 4-25 gives its figure and node definition.

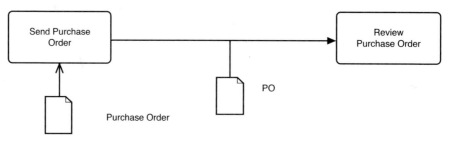

Figure 4-32 BPMN data object

Table 4-25 BPMN Data Object Figure Definition

Element	Property	Value
Figure Gallery	Name	BPMN Figures
Figure Descriptor	Name	Document
Rectangle	Name	Document
	Fill	False
	Outline	False
Stack Layout		
Polygon	Name	DogEarPage
Template Point	X, Y	16, 0
Template Point	X, Y	20, 4
Template Point	X, Y	20, 25
Template Point	X, Y	0, 25
Template Point	X, Y	0, 0
Template Point	X, Y	16, 0
Template Point	X, Y	16, 4
Template Point	X, Y	20, 4
Child Access	Figure	Label SimpleLabel
Node	Name	DataObject
	Figure	Figure Descriptor Document
	Resize Constraint	NONE
Default Size Facet		
Dimension	Dx, Dy	20, 25

Aside from the list of `Template Points`, this figure definition is nothing special. Note the use of `Default Size Facet` again, as well as NONE for the `Resize Constraint`. The default size of a node is 40×40, which would leave our document within a larger rectangle when selected. Not only does this look odd, but it also prevents connections from reaching their true target.

4.5.2 Tooling Definition

We have several types of certain tools, so here we exploit the use of stacks in our scenario diagram palette definition. We also show in our mapping model that we can reuse a tool to create more than one type of node, even without a stack of tools or a pop-up menu. In this case, the Events that are placed either on the diagram or on the border of a Task use the same tool; the target of the mouse determines the proper context for the tool, to determine the correct node to create.

BEST PRACTICE

When designing a palette, try not to get too carried away with drawers and stacks. If all your tools can easily fit into the vertical space expected to be available given the default height of the diagram, there's really no need for drawer functionality. Similarly, stacking tools can be more of a burden to the user than a benefit, so be sure to test your palette on a Practitioner to get feedback on its usability.

Figure 4-33 shows our `scenario.gmftool` model and its generated palette. A palette with one of its stacked tools expanded is also shown. Creating the model is straightforward; the only noteworthy step is to set the `Stack` property to `true` for nested `Tool Group` elements. Note that the palette shows nondefault icons, which are added in Chapter 8, "DSL Packaging and Deployment."

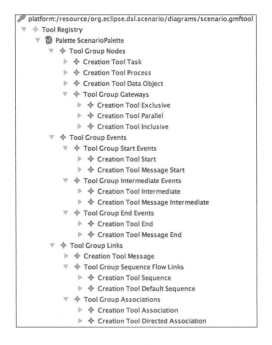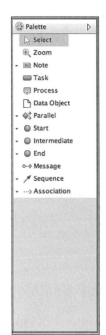

Figure 4-33   Scenario palette definition

TIP

Be sure to not give `Tool` entries the same name, even when they are in different groups or stacks. If you do, the generated code will produce message strings with the same name. The solution is to alter the generator model or give unique names to `Tool` entries in the model and change the properties file later.

4.5.3 Mapping Definition

The mapping definition for the scenario diagram is fairly straightforward because the main `elements` containment reference of the `Process` class will be used to store all elements other than border events, which are stored in the events containment reference of the `Task` class. Each of these sections follows that of the graphical definition section and discusses the mapping of each major diagram element, leaving the particulars to be explored in the supplied sample code. Table 4-26 shows the mappings with details for the `Canvas Mapping`.

Table 4-26   Scenario Canvas Mapping

Element	Property	Value
Mapping		
Canvas Mapping	Domain Model	scenario
	Element	Process -> Element
	Palette	Palette ScenarioPalette
	Diagram Canvas	Canvas BPMN

Task and Subprocess

`Task` mapping is the most complicated because of the border items of a `Task`, although it is straightforward, given the mappings we've accomplished so far in the book. Table 4-27 shows the mapping structure.

Table 4-27   Scenario Task Mapping

Element	Property	Value
Mapping		
Top Node Reference	Containment Feature	Process.elements : Element
Node Mapping	Element	Task -> Element
	Diagram Node	Node Task (NamedRoundedRectangle)
	Tool	Creation Tool Task
Feature Label Mapping	Diagram Label	Diagram Label TaskName
	Features	Element.name : EString
Child Reference	Containment Feature	Task.events : Event
Node Mapping	Element	Event -> Element
	Diagram Node	Node BorderedIntermediateEvent (DoubleCircle)
	Tool	Creation Tool Intermediate
Constraint	Body	eventType = EventType:: INTERMEDIATE and triggerType = TriggerType::NONE
Feature Seq Initializer	Element Class	Event -> Element
Feature Value Spec	Body	EventType::INTERMEDIATE
	Feature	Event.eventType : EventType
Feature Value Spec	Body	TriggerType::NONE
	Feature	Event.triggerType : TriggerType
Child Reference	Containment Feature	Task.events : Event
Node Mapping	Element	Event -> Element
	Diagram Node	Node BorderedMessageIntermediateEvent (DoubleCircleWithEnvelope)
	Tool	Creation Tool Message Intermediate

Element	Property	Value
Constraint	Body	eventType = EventType:: INTERMEDIATE and triggerType = TriggerType::MESSAGE
Feature Seq Initializer	Element Class	Event -> Element
Feature Value Spec	Body	EventType::INTERMEDIATE
	Feature	Event.eventType : EventType
Feature Value Spec	Body	TriggerType::MESSAGE
	Feature	Event.triggerType : TriggerType

Two `Child Reference` elements represent the two `Event` border items: `BorderedIntermediateEvent` and `BorderedMessageIntermediate Event`. These elements are stored in the `Task`'s `events : Event Containment Feature`. For their `Node Mapping`, they use their corresponding `Node` definition but the same `Creation Tool` we use for these events when placed on the diagram surface (Intermediate and Message Intermediate).

To distinguish border `Events`, as they represent instances of the same `Event` class from our domain model, we use `Constraint` and `Feature Seq Initializer` elements. As shown in the mapping, both the `eventType` and `triggerType` attributes are specified in the constraint and feature initialization.

The `CollapsedSubprocess` node is mapped in much the same manner, yet it has no `Child Reference` elements. Section 4.5.6, "Subprocess Partition," covers how to use the `Related Diagrams` property of the `Node Mapping`, enabling us to double-click on a `Process` element and open it in a new diagram.

Gateways

All `Gateway` elements map in a similar manner because they all represent a `Gateway` domain element initialized to different `GatewayType` enumeration literals. Table 4-28 gives the mapping, where, again, the `Top Level Node Containment Feature` is set to our `Process elements:Element` reference.

Table 4-28   Scenario Gateway Mappings

Element	Property	Value
Mapping		
Top Node Reference	Containment Feature	Process.elements : Element
Node Mapping	Element	Gateway -> Element
	Diagram Node	Node ExclusiveGateway (BasicDiamond)
	Tool	Creation Tool Exclusive
Constraint	Body	gatewayType = GatewayType::XOR
Feature Seq Initializer	Element Class	Gateway -> Element
Feature Value Spec	Body	GatewayType::XOR
	Feature	Gateway.gatewayType : GatewayType

Events

Again, we can map each of our `Event` nodes to their corresponding `Event` domain element and add a `Constraint` and `Feature Seq Initializer` to set the `eventType` and `triggerType` attributes accordingly. All of the six `Event` mappings are done in the same manner, as seen in Table 4-29.

Table 4-29   Scenario Event Mapping

Element	Property	Value
Mapping		
Top Node Reference	Containment Feature	Process.elements : Element
Node Mapping	Element	Event -> Element
	Diagram Node	Node StartEvent (BasicCircle)
	Tool	Creation Tool Start
Constraint	Body	eventType = EventType::START and triggerType = TriggerType::NONE
Feature Seq Initializer	Element Class	Event -> Element
Feature Value Spec	Body	EventType::NONE
	Feature	Event.eventType : EventType
Feature Value Spec	Body	TriggerType::NONE
	Feature	Event.triggerType::TriggerType

Connections

We must define five `Link Mapping` elements, with all but the Message Flow mapping following the pattern given. For Message Flow, only one type exists, so there is no need to add the child `Constraint` and `Feature Seq Initializer` elements as with the rest. Each link maps to the `Connection` class in the domain element, with our usual `Containment Feature` of the `Process elements:Element` reference. A `Source Feature` and `Target Feature` are specified, mapping to the `source:Element` and `target:Element` references, respectively. The appropriate `isDirected` constraint and initializer are set for the `Association` mappings, while the `isDefault` property is checked or initialized for the `Sequence Flow` mappings. Each `Link Mapping` has an external `Feature Label Mapping` for the name attribute, as seen in Table 4-30.

Table 4-30   Scenario Link Mappings

Element	Property	Value
Mapping		
Link Mapping	Containment Feature	Process.elements : Element
	Element	Association -> Connection
	Source Feature	Connection.source : Element
	Target Feature	Connection.target : Element
	Diagram Link	Connection DirectedAssociation
	Tool	Creation Tool Directed Association
Constraint	Body	isDirected = true
Feature Seq Initializer	Element Class	Association -> Connection
Feature Value Spec	Body	true
	Feature	Association.isDirected : EBoolean

Data Object

The Data Object mapping is the most basic, with just a `Node Mapping` for the `DataObject` domain element to its corresponding `DataObject` node and `Creation Tool`, along with a `Feature Label Mapping` for its `name: EString` attribute.

4.5.4 Generation

As usual, we invoke the transformation from mapping to generator model using the context menu **Create Generator Model** on our `scenario.gmfmap` model. In the generator model, we change the `Diagram File Extension` property to `scenario`, and we set the `Same File For Diagram And Model` property to `true`, as seen in Figure 4-34.

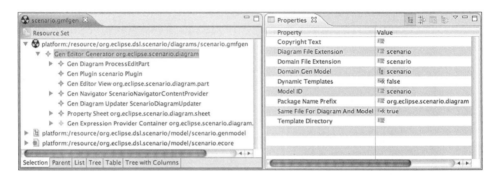

Figure 4-34   Scenario GMF generator model

We next generate our scenario diagram plug-in and move on to making some of the necessary code changes—or you can run the diagram now to see how it looks.

Border Item Adjustment

Our border item `Event` nodes are offset by default so that the edge of the node meets the edge of the parent. For our `Event` nodes, we want them to straddle the border, so we must modify the `addFixedChild()` method of the parent `TaskEditPart` class to set the offset to half the diameter of the `Event` circle figure. The modified method follows, showing the general `EventXEditPart` modification, where `X` is replaced by the number of each side-affixed event. A better solution would be to use `childEditPart.getSize().width/2` to calculate the offset. Changes appear in bold.

```
/**
 * Modified to add border offset for overlapping event nodes
 *
 * @generated NOT
 */
protected boolean addFixedChild(EditPart childEditPart) {
  if (childEditPart instanceof TaskNameEditPart) {
```

```
    ((TaskNameEditPart) childEditPart).setLabel(getPrimaryShape()
      .getFigureRoundedRectangleNameLabel());
    return true;
  }
  if (childEditPart instanceof EventXEditPart) {
    BorderItemLocator locator = new BorderItemLocator(getMainFigure(),
      PositionConstants.NONE);
    locator.setBorderItemOffset(new Dimension(getMapMode().DPtoLP(10),
      getMapMode().DPtoLP(10)));
    getBorderedFigure().getBorderItemContainer().add(
      ((Event2EditPart) childEditPart).getFigure(), locator);
    return true;
  }
  return false;
}
```

Figure 4-35 shows the result of the change, showing the before and after versions.

Figure 4-35 Task border item

Intermediate Event Outline

Our graphical definition model has no "double line" option, so we need to write some custom code to create a double outline for our intermediate event. We can do this in several ways, including nesting figures. It seems easiest to simply override the `outlineShape()` method in our generated `Ellipse` figure. Following is the modification made to accomplish this, though it won't work if we have a line width other than 1. Fortunately, we know that we won't, because otherwise we'd take the time to put the additional logic in the templates and provide a decorator model for our graphical definition model. The following code is found in the generated `Event2EditPart` class. After generating the figures plug-in in Section 4.5.5, "Generating the Figures Plug-In," you can find the code to modify in `org.eclipse.bpmn.figures.DoubleCircle` and associated `DoubleCircleWithEnvelope`.

```
/**
 * Modified to draw double outline, assuming lineWidth == 1
 *
 * @generated NOT
 */
```

```
private void createContents() {
  Ellipse circle0 = new Ellipse(){
    @Override
    protected void outlineShape(Graphics graphics) {
      super.outlineShape(graphics);
      Rectangle inner = Rectangle.SINGLETON;
      inner.width = getBounds().width - 5;
      inner.height = getBounds().height - 5;
      inner.x = getBounds().x + 2;
      inner.y = getBounds().y + 2;
      graphics.drawOval(inner);
    }
  };
  this.add(circle0);
}
```

Figure 4-36 shows an example of our Scenario diagram to this point.

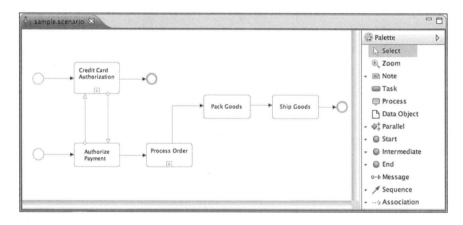

Figure 4-36   Scenario diagram

4.5.5 Generating the Figures Plug-In

We must generate a standalone figures plug-in for use in our diagram. As mentioned earlier, this is the preferred way to develop GMF diagrams, but it comes at the expense of a slightly complicated workflow. Begin by right-clicking on the bpmn.gmfgraph model and select **Generate Figures Plug-In**. Specify the name org.eclipse.bpmn.figures for the plug-in name and select the **Use IMapMode** and **Utilize Enhanced Features of GMF Runtime** options before clicking **Finish,** as seen in Figure 4-37.

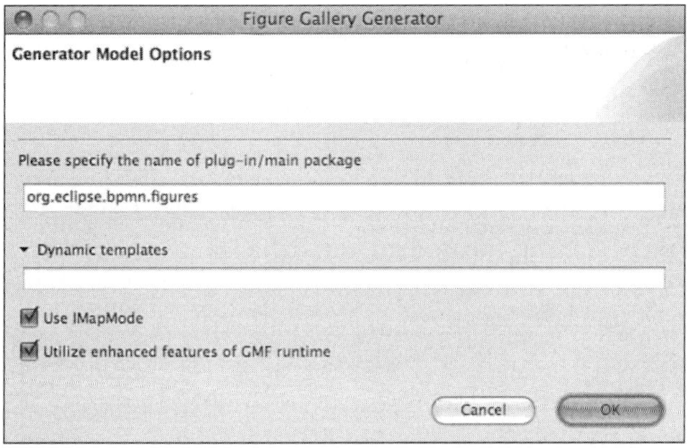

Figure 4-37   Figure Gallery Generator dialog

Upon finishing, you will observe a new plug-in project with generated figures code and a `mirrored.gmfgraph` model. If you compare this model to our original, you'll note that it contains identical canvas elements (nodes, connections, diagram labels), but the figures are all declared as custom with references to their generated classes.

From now on, when working with figures, you need to regenerate the plug-in and `mirrored.gmfgraph` model. The complication here is that the model is not in the same resource set as your gmfmap model, and changes are not reflected in referenced elements. This means it's a good practice to design your figures up front; if you do make a change, be sure to return to your mapping model after regeneration and update any references that might have been impacted. The mapping model references only canvas elements, not elements within the `Figure Gallery`, so it is cause for concern only when changing nodes, compartments, links, and diagram labels.

TIP

Recall from our earlier discussion that working with generated figure plug-ins introduces the complication of synchronizing with an external `mirrored.gmfgraph` model. Currently there's no way of using GMF to change elements in a gmfgraph model, regenerate the `mirrored.gmfgraph` and figures, and have the changes propagated to the mapping model within the same resource set. Currently, the best approach when working with `mirrored.gmfgraph` models is to remove references from the gmfmap model first, and then update the source gmfgraph and regenerate the mirror. New elements will appear at the end of the containment lists and, therefore, not break anything.

At this point, we're ready to change our `scenario.gmfmap` model to use the `mirrored.gmfgraph` now located in our `org.eclipse.bpmn.figures` project. Unfortunately, GMF does not provide a **Migrate to Standalone Figures** utility GMF, so we're left to make the changes manually in a text editor. In our case, it's a straightforward search and replace of all `bpmn.gmfgraph` occurrences with `platform:/resource/org.eclipse.bpmn.figures/models/mirrored.gmfgraph`; we can use **Validate** to ensure that we didn't make a mistake. Note that we use the `platform:/resource/...` URI type and not the usual relative path. If we were referencing a deployed plug-in in our environment or target, we'd use `platform:/plugin/...` instead, which should make updating this mapping model easy if we deploy these figures.

We have to do a couple more things before we regenerate our diagram. Recall that we previously had figures generated during the gmfmap → gmfgen transformation, so our figures are currently located in our `EditParts` as inner classes. First, we want to relocate our custom `CircleDecoration` class into our new figures plug-in, but in a new `src-custom` source folder. This makes our regeneration easier because we don't have to worry about deleting this custom class. Also, this class will be available to other diagrams that want to use the decoration for other links. In fact, we can go back to our Mindmap diagram and reference this decoration. After we copy the class into the `/src-custom/org/eclipse/bpmn/figures` folder, our generated figures code will compile without error.

The second thing we do is move the `bpmn.gmfgraph` model to our generated figures plug-in. This keeps the original source model near its mirror and makes the source figures available to those who are creating diagrams and want to extend them instead of using only the mirror's custom figure elements. We can later modify the graphical definition and regenerate the figures code into this same project.

BEST PRACTICE

When using generated figure plug-ins and `mirrored.gmfgraph` models, it's a good idea to include the original graphical definition in the generated plug-in for later regeneration and to make it available for source-level reuse of the figures. Note that subsequent regeneration of the figures plug-in

> onto itself creates a new `mirrored.gmfgraph` model in the root of the plug-in, so be sure to move it to its original location in the `/models` folder in place of the previous version.

Now that we've separated figures from our model, we can re-create our generator model and regenerate the scenario diagram. Notice that the updated `scenario.gmfgen` model no longer contains serialized figures, but references our `org.eclipse.bpmn.figures` plug-in, which has been added to our diagram's dependency list. At this point, we need to reimplement the changes we made to our intermediate event figures (`DoubleCircle` and `DoubleCircleWithEnvelope`) in Section 4.5.4, "Intermediate Event Outline." And we need to modify our `NamedRoundedRectangle` and `CollapsedNamedRoundedRectangle` figures to adjust the stack layout and enable text wrapping of our labels, as described in Section 4.3.5, "Topic Figure Layout." If you choose to delete the diagram plug-in entirely, you also need to make the changes to the `TopicEditPart` for overlapping events in Section 4.5.1, "Graphical Definition."

4.5.6 Diagram Partitioning

This section covers the two main use cases for *diagram partitioning,* which the `Related Diagrams` property of a `Node Mapping` supports. First, we simply allow subprocess elements on our scenario diagram to open a new diagram editor page where the subprocess will be modeled. Second, we add the capability for a `Requirement` element on our requirements dependency diagram to reference and open a scenario diagram.

Subprocess Partition

It's as simple as setting the `Related Diagrams` property in our scenario. gmfmap model for the `Subprocess Node Mapping` to its `Canvas Mapping` for the subprocess partition to work. In the `scenario.genmodel`, this results in an `Open Diagram Behaviour` element being added to our `Gen Top Level Node` for the subprocess node, as shown in Figure 4-38.

These default generated values give us the desired behavior of double-clicking on a subprocess node to open an new diagram instance in the editor. After doing so, open the diagram file in a text editor and notice that, for each partition, a diagram element exists within the file.

Figure 4-38   Scenario open diagram edit policy

Looking at our generated policy class, you can see that it uses the `HintedDiagramLinkStyle` from the notation model. If you look at the generated `Process2ViewFactory`, you can see how this style is added to our `Subprocess` view element.

```
/**
 * @generated
 */
protected List createStyles(View view) {
  List styles = new ArrayList();
  styles.add(NotationFactory.eINSTANCE.createShapeStyle());
  {
    HintedDiagramLinkStyle diagramFacet = NotationFactory.eINSTANCE
      .createHintedDiagramLinkStyle();
    styles.add(diagramFacet);
  }
  return styles;
}
```

When we define the next partition, it will be to another diagram type, where the code will include a call to `setHint()` so that the open diagram action knows the type of diagram to open.

Requirement to Scenario Partition

It's slightly more complicated to have a related diagram be of a type other than the one specifying the partition, but not a lot more. We want to have a scenario diagram associated with a requirement and opened from the requirement dependency diagram. To do this, we need to associate a `Process` element in our scenario model from our `Requirement` element. This is necessary for two reasons: The node that has the `Related Diagrams` property set must be of the same type as that representing the canvas of the target diagram, and, as such, there must be a reference into which created domain elements of that type can be added when elements are added to the diagram.

NOTE

This example is a bit contrived but illustrates the approach. Typically, this technique is used if there are multiple views (diagrams) for a single domain model, such as the UML. Perhaps a better example would be to associate state characteristics with our business domain model elements and create a diagram partition for each class to represent its state behavior.

Opening our `requirements.ecore` model, we use **Load Resource** to load our `scenario.ecore` model into the resource set. To the `Requirement` class, right-click and add a new `EReference` named `scenario` of type `Process`. Set the `Containment` property to `true`. Reload the `requirements.genmodel` and add a reference to the `scenario.genmodel` before clicking **Finish**. Right-click on the `requirements` package root in the genmodel and regenerate the model, edit, and editor code. If you're interested, launch and test the requirements editor, adding a new `Process` to a `Requirement` instance. If you do, you'll notice that no properties exist for the new `Process` element, which should remind you to add the `org.eclipse.scenario.Process` input type to the diagram plug-ins `propertySections` contribution. Otherwise, we move on to modify our requirements diagram definition to allow new scenario diagram partitions.

Beginning with the `requirements.gmfgraph` model, we now create a new `BasicDiamond` figure in our gallery. This is much the same as our `BasicDiamond` figure in the `bpmn.gmfgraph` model, although it's smaller because we intend to add it as a side-affixed node to our `Requirements` circle. Table 4-31 lists the additions.

Table 4-31 Diamond Figure Definition

Element	Property	Value
Canvas		
Figure Gallery		
Figure Descriptor	Name	BasicDiamond
Rectangle	Name	BasicDiamond
	Fill	False
	Outline	False

(continues)

Table 4-31 Diamond Figure Definition (continued)

Element	Property	Value
Stack Layout		
Polygon	Name	Diamond
Template Point	X, Y	5, 0
Template Point	X, Y	0, 5
Template Point	X, Y	5, 10
Template Point	X, Y	10, 5
Node	Name	Scenario
	Affixed Parent Side	NSEW
	Resize Constraint	NONE
Default Size Facet		
Dimension	Dx, Dy	10, 10

In our `requirements.gmftool` model, we add a new creation tool in the `Nodes` group for the `Scenario` element by copying another tool and pasting into the group.

In the mapping model, to select our scenario diagram canvas for the `Related Diagrams` reference, we need to use **Load Resource** again and load `scenario.gmfmap` into the resource set. Next, we create a new `Child Reference` to our `Requirement Node Mapping` and set its `Containment Feature` property to our new `scenario:Process` reference. The child `Node Mapping` settings are found in Figure 4-39. Unfortunately, when selecting the `Related Diagrams` property, a dialog appears with two `Canvas Mapping` entries. The scenario canvas should be the second one on the list, but we can do our usual verification by opening the model in a text editor.

We're ready to re-create our `requirements.gmfgen` model using the normal sequence, but don't generate the diagram code just yet. Open the generator model and navigate to the `Gen Child Side Affixed Node ProcessEditPart` element, where you can see the generated `Open Diagram Behaviour` element. The `Diagram Kind` property of the generated `Open Diagram Behaviour` element defaults to `FIXME put GenEditorGenerator.modelID value here`. Similarly, the `Editor ID` property defaults to `FIXME put GenEditorView.id value here`. We replace these with `scenario` and `org.eclipse.scenario.diagram.part.ScenarioDiagramEditorID`, respectively, as shown in Figure 4-40. Fortunately, these properties are preserved when updating

the .gmfgen model. Note that if we planned to have multiple open diagram policies, we'd rename the default OpenDiagramEditPolicy to something such as
OpenScenarioDiagramEditPolicy, to distinguish between them.

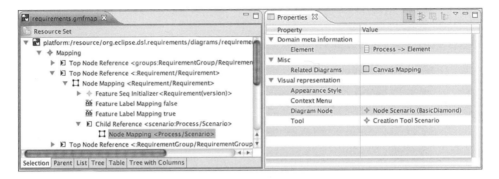

Figure 4-39   Scenario-related diagram mapping

TIP

When working with diagram Styles, be sure to create new elements
when testing their behavior. Existing View elements were initialized and
persisted before new Style code was added to the ViewFactory.

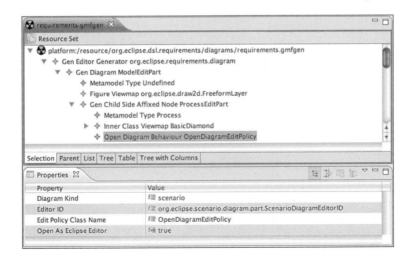

Figure 4-40   Scenario open diagram edit policy

The string 'scenario' matches the semanticHints attribute of the Scenario diagram's provider declaration, as shown next. When the ViewService is consulted to create the new diagram for the Process element reference, it uses this hint to create the diagram, as discussed in Section 10.4.1, "View Service."

```
<extension point="org.eclipse.gmf.runtime.diagram.core.viewProviders">
  <?gmfgen generated="true"?>
  <viewProvider
  class="org.eclipse.scenario.diagram.providers.ScenarioViewProvider">
    <Priority name="Lowest"/>
    <context viewClass="org.eclipse.gmf.runtime.notation.Diagram"
      semanticHints="scenario"/>
    <context viewClass="org.eclipse.gmf.runtime.notation.Node"
      semanticHints=""/>
    <context viewClass="org.eclipse.gmf.runtime.notation.Edge"
      semanticHints=""/>
  </viewProvider>
</extension>
```

TIP

When testing behavior that initiates on double-click, such as an open diagram edit policy, be sure that the root figure is selected. If you're not sure, use the mouse to drag around the element to select it and then double-click.

In the RequirementsEditor class, we need to add an adapter factory for our Scenario integration. The following line added to initializeEditingDomain() does the trick:

```
adapterFactory.addAdapterFactory(new
        ScenarioItemProviderAdapterFactory());
```

We now can regenerate our diagram code and launch. Add a new Scenario element to a Requirement in a sample diagram and double-click it. A new diagram should open in an adjacent editor tab, as shown in Figure 4-41.

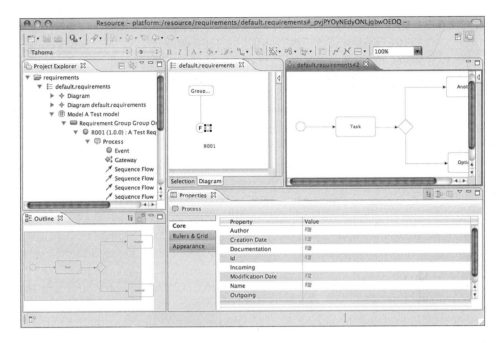

Figure 4-41 Requirements diagram partition

At the moment, we're persisting a process model instance within our requirements model instance, contained within the associated `Requirement` instance. We could set the `requirements.genmodel` to use `Containment Proxies`, which would let us specify a new resource (file) for persisting new `Process` instances. This would also let us store these models independently and even initialize a new standalone scenario diagram for each process. This doesn't work out of the box, but you can implement it using custom code.

4.5.7 Database Persistence

As mentioned in the overview of Modeling project components, we can persist models to other than a local file. Two components within the EMFT project allow for database persistence of EMF models: Teneo and Connected Data Objects (CDO). In this section, we use Teneo to persist our scenario diagram and domain model instance to a Derby database using Hibernate. The process for persisting both EMF models and GMF diagrams is presented in tutorials linked from the Teneo Web site, with the latter inspiring the content here.

After installing Teneo, we need to create plug-ins in our workspace that wrap the Hibernate and Derby libraries. This is as simple as adding empty plug-in projects and dropping the `*.jar` files from each into a `/lib` folder and setting up the manifest to include the archives and expose their packages. It's also necessary to add an `Eclipse-BuddyPolicy:  dependent` property in the Hibernate bundle manifest. In the scenario model plug-in, we can add dependencies to these plug-ins and to the `org.eclipse.emf.teneo.hibernate` plug-in, reexporting each.

With the dependencies established, we need to create an empty scenario database. The DataTools project makes this simple and is described in the tutorial. It's a matter of configuring the Derby-embedded driver and declaring a path to where the database will reside. When the simple ping works, the database is ready for Teneo to use.

As in other diagram extensions, we create a separate `org.eclipse.scenario.diagram.db` plug-in to hold our additional classes required to enable database persistence. In the `/src` directory, we add a `teneo.properties` file that will contain the connection string information and Teneo options we need. These will ultimately be presented in the user interface, but for now we can simply use a properties file, as shown here. Adjust the `driver_class`, `url`, and `dialect` properties as necessary to match your environment.

```
teneo.mapping.inheritance = JOINED
hibernate.connection.driver_class=org.apache.derby.jdbc.EmbeddedDriver
hibernate.connection.url=jdbc:derby:/derby/databases/scenario
hibernate.connection.username=
hibernate.connection.password=
hibernate.dialect=org.hibernate.dialect.DerbyDialect
```

Because of the GMF notation model's use of multiple inheritance, Teneo needs an additional `annotations.xml` file in the `/src` folder to map these elements to a relational store. This shows the contents of the file:

```
<?xml version="1.0" encoding="utf-8"?>
<persistence-mapping xmlns="http://www.eclipse.org/emft/teneo"
  xmlns:xsi="http://www.w3.org/2001/XMLSchema-instance">

  <epackage
   namespace-uri="http://www.eclipse.org/gmf/runtime/1.0.1/notation">

    <eclass name="ShapeStyle">
      <entity extends="LineStyle"/>
    </eclass>

    <eclass name="DiagramStyle">
```

```
    <entity extends="PageStyle"/>
  </eclass>

  <eclass name="ConnectorStyle">
    <entity extends="RoutingStyle"/>
  </eclass>
</epackage>

</persistence-mapping>
```

A curious feature in the notation model implementation requires another change for Teneo to function properly. See bug 159226 in Eclipse Bugzilla and the GMFEListPropertyHandler class in the sample project for more information. Hopefully by the time you read this, the bug will be resolved and the custom handler will no longer be required.

To initialize Teneo, we create a StoreController class. The class is provided in the sample project and comes largely from the original tutorial. You can easily generate this class and the remaining code required to use Teneo in combination with GMF using a decorator to the generator model and custom templates.

In the StoreController, a URI is defined using the datastore name and query using the hbxml scheme, which initializes a HibernateXMLResource class. In this case, our scenario data store is queried to load the Process element of the domain model and Diagram element of the notation model into the resource root.

```
public static final URI DATABASE_URI = URI.createURI(

"hbxml://?dsname=scenario&query1=from Process&query2=from Diagram");
```

An instance HbSessionDataStore class is created and initialized as shown next in the contents of our initializeDataStore() method. The EPackages used include the domain model, the GMF notation model, the Ecore model, and the Ecore XML type model. The teneo.properties with connection information and annotations.xml are also loaded and used in the initialization. This method and the corresponding closeDataStore() method should be called from our plug-in Activator's start() and stop() methods, respectively.

```
final HbSessionDataStore localDataStore = new HbSessionDataStore();
localDataStore.setName("scenario");
HbHelper.INSTANCE.register(localDataStore);

final EPackage[] ePackages = new EPackage[] {
ScenarioPackage.eINSTANCE, NotationPackage.eINSTANCE,
```

```
    EcorePackage.eINSTANCE, XMLTypePackage.eINSTANCE };
    localDataStore.setEPackages(ePackages);

    try {
      final Properties props = new Properties();
      props.load(this.getClass().getResourceAsStream("/teneo.properties"));
      props.setProperty(PersistenceOptions.PERSISTENCE_XML,
      "/annotations.xml");
      localDataStore.setProperties(props);
    } catch (IOException e) {
      throw new IllegalStateException(e);
    }

    localDataStore.getExtensionManager()
      .registerExtension(EListPropertyHandler.class.getName(),
      GMFEListPropertyHandler.class.getName());

    localDataStore.initialize();
```

At this point, we need to write an action that will initialize our models and open our diagram editor. You can add the code found in the sample class OpenScenarioDBEditor to a wizard that enables the user to input the connection string information currently held in the teneo.properties file but for now is used in a simple action from the main menu. This code and corresponding contribution to the actionSets extension-point found in the sample project comes from the original tutorial.

Finally, some slight changes to the diagram editor are required because it expects to be working with file-based model resources. By overriding the following methods, the editor can accommodate the database resource that Teneo provides:

```
@Override
public void setInput(IEditorInput input) {
    try {
                    doSetInput(input, true);
        } catch (CoreException x) {
                    Shell shell = getSite().getShell();
                    ErrorDialog.openError(shell, x.getMessage(),
    x.getMessage(), x.getStatus());
        }
    // set the resource in the resourcetoreadonly map
    final ResourceSet rs = getEditingDomain().getResourceSet();
    for (Resource res : rs.getResources()) {
      ((AdapterFactoryEditingDomain) getEditingDomain())
      .getResourceToReadOnlyMap().put(res, Boolean.FALSE);
    }
}

@Override
```

```
// implement a simple with no save-as dialogs
public void doSave(IProgressMonitor progressMonitor) {
  updateState(getEditorInput());
  validateState(getEditorInput());
  performSave(false, progressMonitor);
}
```

At this point, with our database created earlier, we can launch the runtime instance and open a new diagram using the **Database → Open Scenario Diagram** menu. As with the file-based version, you can modify, close, and reopen the diagram. In fact, the two versions continue to function properly, although the database version presents some complications when working with transformations. With some custom code, you can overcome this by loading and exporting models from the database to a local file, or by modifying the invocation method for QVT, as the default launch configuration expects files.

Additional functionality is added to the scenario diagram in Section 10.9, "Extending Diagrams."

4.6 Developing the Color Modeling Diagram

Our final sample application diagram is similar to a UML Class diagram, which gives us an opportunity to explore GMF compartment support for attributes and operations. We want this business domain modeling diagram to be simple, so we leave out some features of the UML and even object-oriented programming, such as navigability and strong aggregation. To begin, we need to consider how to represent the different archetypes using color. Starting with the figure gallery, we could create a distinct figure for each archetype and indicate the proper coloration. Unfortunately, this "hard-codes" the color and results in a fair amount of duplication, even if we use the `Figure Ref` element. We'd prefer a single archetype figure with a corresponding node in the graphical definition. Furthermore, we'd prefer to give users the opportunity to select the default shade of each archetype color using diagram preferences.

Concerning the mapping model, we know from our previous diagrams that adding constraints to node mappings determines their uniqueness and allows the canonical update of the diagram to function properly. If our domain model used a simple enumeration type to distinguish archetypes, we could initialize the value of the archetype's type enum value using a `Feature Seq Initializer`. The problem is that the generated code will generate a figure class for each archetype, and by using the type enum in the constraint, a change of the value in the Properties will cause the view to be "orphaned" when the update takes place. A new view will be created for the element and placed by default in the upper-left corner of the diagram. This is clearly not what we want.

Another factor to consider with the enumeration approach is to map a single archetype node and hand-code changes in color based on enumeration value changes. This would greatly reduce the amount of generated code, but it leaves us wondering how often users would want to change an archetype type. If they did, the constraints and other factors we attribute to the archetype would have to change, potentially causing a ripple effect on connections and more. With the enumeration approach, to prevent users from changing the type, we could make the type attribute read-only in our EMF genmodel. In our case the domain model has a specific subclass for each archetype, making mapping straightforward and eliminating the need to provide feature initialization for each mapping. Furthermore, the generated code is much easier to deal with when using distinct subtypes for each archetype. As you'll see, they generate `EditPart` names such as `MomentIntervalEditPart` instead of a series of `ArchetypeEditPart`, `Archetype2EditPart`, and so on, as is the case when using enumeration literals to distinguish type. We saw this in our Mindmap diagram when the `Relationship` class used an enumeration to distinguish among dependency, include, and extend types.

4.6.1 Diagram Definition

Unlike the previous diagram-definition models that referenced the domain model when creating a graphical definition, we can simply create a blank `dnc.gmfgraph` model in our `/diagrams` folder of the `org.eclipse.dsl.dnc` project by skipping the pages in the **Graphical Definition Wizard** that select a model.

As mentioned earlier, we can define a single archetype figure and node to be used for each of the mappings. Our archetype figures will use compartments for attributes and operations. Coloration and gradients will be accomplished using custom templates. Let's start with our archetype definition, shown in Table 4-32.

Table 4-32   Archetype Figure Definition

Element	Property	Value
Figure Gallery	Name	DNC Figures
Figure Descriptor	Name	ArchetypeFigure
Rounded Rectangle	Name	ArchetypeFigure
Insets	Bottom	5

Element	Property	Value
Rounded Rectangle	Name	InnerRectangle
	Fill	False
	Outline	False
Flow Layout	Force Single Line	True
	Major Alignment	CENTER
	Major Spacing	0
	Match Minor Size	True
	Minor Alignment	CENTER
	Minor Spacing	0
	Vertical	True
Rectangle	Name	NameArea
	Fill	False
	Outline	False
Grid Layout	Equal Width	True
	Num Columns	1
Label	Name	Name
Grid Layout Data	Grab Excess Horizontal Space	True
	Grab Excess Vertical Space	True
Basic Font	Height	11
Rectangle	Name	StereotypeArea
	Fill	False
	Outline	False
Grid Layout	Equal Width	True
	Num Columns	1
Minimum Size	Dx, Dy	80, 0
Label	Name	Stereotype
Grid Layout Data	Grab Excess Horizontal Space	True
	Grab Excess Vertical Space	True
Basic Font	Height	11

(continues)

Table 4-32   Archetype Figure Definition (continued)

Element	Property	Value
Child Access	Figure	Label Name
Child Access	Figure	Label Stereotype
Figure Descriptor	Name	BasicRectangle
Rectangle	Name	BasicRectangle
Figure Descriptor	Name	ListItemLabel
Label	Name	ListItemLabel
Insets	Left, Top	5, 2
Node	Name	Archetype
	Figure	Figure Descriptor ArchetypeFigure
Compartment	Name	Attributes
	Figure	Figure Descriptor BasicRectangle
Compartment	Name	Operations
	Figure	Figure Descriptor BasicRectangle
Diagram Label	Name	Stereotype
	Figure	Figure Descriptor ArchetypeFigure
	Element Icon	False
	Accessor	Child Access getFigureStereotype
Diagram Label	Name	Name
	Figure	Figure Descriptor ArchetypeFigure
	Element Icon	False
	Accessor	Child Access getFigureName
Diagram Label	Name	ListItem
	Figure	Figure Descriptor ListItemLabel
	Element Icon	False

Our archetype figure is similar to a standard class figure. It has a name compartment and stereotype, although the placement of the stereotype is below the name in the case of our color modeling diagram. This is both to be different, and the result of a snag with applying gradients (discussed in Section 4.6.5, "Gradient Figures"). Note that we have defined `ListItemLabel` with an `Inset` element that keeps our attribute and operation compartment list items from aligning too close to the edge of the outer rectangle. We've done similarly in the outer rectangle, adding an Inset to keep the lowermost operation from being too close to the bottom of the rounded rectangle. Also note that our `ListItem Diagram Label` element has no `Accessor` selected, leaving its `External` attribute as `true`. Unlike other labels within nodes, selecting the `BasicRectangle` as the `Diagram Label` figure and adding a child accessor to the `ListItemLabel Figure Descriptor` causes the generated compartment to not function properly.

TIP

Compartments require the proper layout in the parent figure in order to look correct. The parent figure should use a Flow Layout with vertical orientation and force a single line option if the compartments are to be as typically seen in UML Class nodes.

Also note our use of `GridLayout` and `GridDataLayout` elements throughout. These let us accomplish the layout of our archetype name and its stereotype label so that they remain centered in our rectangle. Our compartments for attributes and labels use basic rectangle figures. Note that we don't bother setting their fill and outline properties to `false` because compartment figures defined will generate an extension of the runtime's `ResizableCompartmentFigure` that takes care of rendering compartments properly. The `EditPart` generated will extend `ListCompartmentEditPart`, and the attribute and operation labels within these compartments will implement `CompartmentEditPart`, using `WrappingLabel` for the figure. Taking advantage of the runtime's compartment support saves us some work because it provides proper layout, collapse, expand, and filtering functionality.

We also define a package figure and node, which is similar to the `Archetype` figure, aside from the fact that it uses a regular outer `Rectangle` and not a `RoundedRectangle`. Also, we'll later map only one compartment to our package figure, to list subpackages. Because we have so much potential duplication in defining this figure, we turn to the `Figure Ref` element to avoid redundancy, as shown in Table 4-33.

Table 4-33   Package Figure Definition

Element	Property	Value
Figure Gallery	Name	DNC Figures
Figure Descriptor	Name	PackageFigure
Rectangle	Name	PackageFigure
Insets	Bottom	5
Figure Ref	Figure	Rounded Rectangle InnerRectangle
Child Access	Figure	Label Name
Child Access	Figure	Label Stereotype
Node	Name	Package
	Figure	Figure Descriptor PackageFigure
Compartment	Name	Packages
	Figure	Figure Descriptor BasicRectangle
Diagram Label	Name	PackageName
	Figure	Figure Descriptor PackageFigure
	Accessor	Child Access getFigureName
	Element Icon	False

Clearly, using the graphical definition model's `Figure Ref` element saves us a bit of work and encourages reuse. Moving on to our links, Table 4-34 gives the definitions of our `Association` and `Aggregation` connections. We use the `Generalization` link from the provided `classDiagram.gmfgraph` model, provided by GMF. We don't need to reference it here—only in our mapping definition to follow.

Table 4-34   Generalization Link Definition

Element	Property	Value
Figure Gallery	Name	DNC Figures
Figure Descriptor	Name	SolidLineHollowDiamond
Polyline Connection	Name	SolidLineHollowDiamond
	Source Decoration	Polygon Decoration DiamondFigure
Polygon Decoration	Name	DiamondFigure

Element	Property	Value
Background Color	Value	White
Template Point	X, Y	−1, −1
Template Point	X, Y	−2, 0
Template Point	X, Y	−1, 1
Template Point	X, Y	0, 0
Figure Descriptor	Name	BasicLink
Polyline Connection	Name	BasicLink
Figure Descriptor	Name	BasicLabel
Label	Name	BasicLabel
Connection	Name	Aggregation
	Figure	Figure Descriptor SolidLineHollowDiamond
Connection	Name	Association
	Figure	Figure Descriptor BasicLink
Diagram Label	Name	LinkTarget
	Figure	Figure Descriptor BasicLabel
Diagram Label	Name	LinkTarget
	Figure	Figure Descriptor BasicLabel
	Element Icon	False
Alignment Facet	Alignment	BEGINNING
Label Offset Facet	X, Y	0, −10

These connection definitions are straightforward, although you might have noticed that we don't use link name labels in the diagram. We might add them later, but for now we want to keep our diagram as simple and uncluttered as possible.

The final elements that require definition at this point are the `Annotation` note and link. This time, we use a dashed line connection figure provided in the GMF `classDiagram.gmfgraph` model. To reference this or any other `.gmfgraph` model, right-click on the editor surface and select **Load Resource** from the menu. Enter the URI to the model in the dialog, as shown in Figure 4-42.

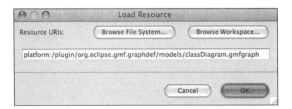

Figure 4-42   Load Resource dialog

Table 4-35 gives the definitions of the annotation note figure and associated link. When selecting the `Figure` for the `AnnotationLink Connection`, you'll find the `DashedLineConnection` now available, along with all other `Figure Descriptors` from our loaded `classDiagram.gmfgraph` model.

Table 4-35   Annotation Figure Definition

Element	Property	Value
Figure Gallery	Name	DNC Figures
Figure Descriptor	Name	AnnotationFigure
Rectangle	Name	AnnotationFigure
	Line Kind	LINE_DASH
Flow Layout	Force Single Line	True
	Major Alignment	CENTER
	Major Spacing	0
	Match Minor Size	True
	Minor Alignment	CENTER
	Minor Spacing	0
	Vertical	True
Insets	Left, Right	5, 5
Figure Ref	Figure	Rectangle StereotypeArea
Figure Ref	Figure	Rectangle NameArea
Child Access	Figure	Label Stereotype
Child Access	Figure	Label Name
Node	Name	Annotation
	Figure	Figure Descriptor AnnotationFigure

Element	Property	Value
Connection	Name	AnnotationLink
	Figure	Figure Descriptor DashedLineConnection
Diagram Label	Name	AnnotationLabel
	Figure	Figure Descriptor AnnotationFigure
	Accessor	Child Access getFigureName
	Element Icon	False

Notice again the use of the `Figure Ref` element. This time, we reuse the stereotype area and name area from our `Archetype` figure, but we list in reverse order because we want our `Annotation` to have a stereotype-like label at the top of the rectangle, with an area for the key and value below. As you can see, we chose a dashed line for the link to the annotation as well as for the rectangle outline. This lightens the appearance of the note, enabling us to focus on the annotation key and value, not to mention the color archetypes, which are the main focus points of the diagram overall.

This completes our initial graphical definition for the color modeling diagram. Next, we look at the palette definition.

4.6.2 Tooling Definition

Begin by creating a new `dnc.gmftool` model in the `/diagrams` folder using the provided wizard. You can use the **Tooling Definition Model Wizard**, as before, which enables you to derive tooling from the domain model. Or as in the graphical definition wizard, simply skipping the domain model selection pages results in an empty new model.

For the palette of our color modeling diagram, we group archetypes together and then stack the moment interval and moment interval detail within the group. We also stack our three "green" archetypes: party, place, and thing. You'll find plug-in points and the package tool in this first tool group because they are main diagram nodes. Attributes and operations are listed next in their own group, followed by a group containing our association, aggregation, and generalization links. The most infrequently used tools are contained in the last group, where we put the annotation node and link. Figure 4-43 shows the palette definition next to an image of the palette itself.

Figure 4-43   Color modeling palette definition

4.6.3 Mapping Definition

Create a new dnc.gmfmap model in the /diagrams folder using the **Diagram Definition** (Ctrl+3 → Diagram Def) Wizard. Select the dnc.ecore model as the **Domain Model** and for now select the Archetype class for the canvas mapping. We can't select the oocore::Package element at this time because the wizard does not load the oocore.ecore model when selecting our dnc.ecore model. In the subsequent pages, select the dnc.gmftool and dnc.gmfgraph models as our tooling and graphical definition models, respectively. On the **Mapping** page, we can see another symptom of the wizard not resolving the oocore.ecore model. The list of discovered **Nodes** and **Links** is not what we expect, unfortunately. For now, just move the Association node to the Link side and remove the contents of the **Links** list. We need to correct our Canvas mapping and finish the remaining nodes manually.

With the dnc.gmfmap model open in the editor, adjust the Canvas Mapping to be as shown in Table 4-36.

Table 4-36 DNC Canvas Mapping

Element	Property	Value
Mapping		
Canvas Mapping	Domain Model	dnc
	Element	Package → PackageableElement
	Palette	Palette DNC Palette
	Diagram Canvas	Canvas dnc

We'll return to our `Association` link mapping later. At this point, we enter a new `Top Node Reference` element to define the mapping for our moment interval archetype. Complete the mapping for this node according to Table 4-37. We'll use this as the basis for all archetype mappings and use the `Referenced Child` property to avoid unnecessary duplication. This enables us to point to another node mapping that is already defined, rather than create another fully defined node mapping.

Table 4-37 Moment-Interval Archetype Mapping

Element	Property	Value
Mapping		
Top Node Reference	Containment Feature	Package.contents : PackageableElement
Node Mapping	Element	MomentInterval → Archetype
	Diagram Node	Node Archetype (Archetype Figure)
	Tool	Creation Tool Moment-Interval
Feature Label Mapping	Diagram Label	Diagram Label ArchetypeName
	Features	NamedElement.name : String
Feature Label Mapping	Diagram label	Diagram Label Stereotype
	Features	Archetype.description : String
	Read Only	True
	View Pattern	«moment-interval» *
Child Reference	Compartment	Compartment Mapping <Attributes>
	Containment Feature	Class.features : Feature

(continues)

Table 4-37   Moment-Interval Archetype Mapping (continued)

Element	Property	Value
Node Mapping	Element	Attribute → StructuralFeature
	Diagram Node	Diagram Label ListItem
	Tool	Creation Tool Attribute
Feature Label Mapping	Diagram Label	Diagram Label ListItem
	Features	NamedElement.name : String
Child Reference	Compartment	Compartment Mapping <Operations>
	Containment Feature	Class.operations : Operation
Node Mapping	Element	Operation → StructuralFeature
	Diagram Node	Diagram Label ListItem
	Tool	Creation Tool Operation
Feature Label Mapping	Diagram Label	Diagram Label ListItem
	Features	NamedElement.name : String
	View Pattern	{0}()
Compartment Mapping	Children	Child Reference <features:Attribute/ListItem>
	Compartment	Compartment Attributes (BasicRectangle)
Compartment Mapping	Children	Child Reference <features:Operation/ListItem>
	Compartment	Compartment Operations (BasicRectangle)

* The use of the `Feature Label Mapping` element for our stereotype labels in all archetypes, package, and annotation mappings is a workaround for the fact that it's not possible to leave the feature blank, or provide a default string value, if we want to use a regular `Label Mapping` or `Design Label Mapping` element. With the `Read Only` property set to `true` and the `View Pattern` set to the stereotype string we want displayed, it really doesn't matter what feature is mapped, actually. This approach prevents us from having to create multiple label definitions in our graphical definition model and would likely cause us to create multiple archetype figure definitions.

Subsequent archetypes are mapped in a similar manner, each using the `Referenced Child` property, as mentioned earlier. Table 4-38 shows the mapping for the `Role` archetype; we don't show the remainder, to save space. Only the mapped domain `Element` property of the `Node Mapping`, `Creation Tool`, and stereotype label `View Pattern` should differ for each archetype. In the case of the `PluginPoint` archetype, feature initializers for both the `interface` and `abstract` properties are set to `true`.

Table 4-38   Role Archetype Mapping

Element	Property	Value
Mapping		
Top Node Reference	Containment Feature	Package.contents : PackageableElement
Node Mapping	Element	MomentInterval → Archetype
	Diagram Node	Node Archetype (Archetype Figure)
	Tool	Creation Tool Role
Feature Label Mapping	Diagram Label	Diagram Label ArchetypeName
	Features	NamedElement.name : String
Feature Label Mapping	Diagram label	Diagram Label Stereotype
	Features	Archetype.description : String
	Read Only	True
	View Pattern	«role»
Child Reference	Compartment	Compartment Mapping <Attributes>
	Containment Feature	Class.features : Feature
	Referenced Child	Node Mapping <Attribute/ListItem>
Child Reference	Compartment	Compartment Mapping <Operations>
	Containment Feature	Class.operations : Operation
	Referenced Child	Node Mapping <Operation/ListItem>
Compartment Mapping	Children	Child Reference <features:Attribute/ListItem>
	Compartment	Compartment Attributes (BasicRectangle)
Compartment Mapping	Children	Child Reference <features:Operation/ListItem>
	Compartment	Compartment Operations (BasicRectangle)

The `Package` mapping is also quite similar, with the exception that it has only one compartment mapping and that it makes use of the diagram partitioning feature by specifying a `Related Diagrams` property, as you learned in Section 4.5.6, "Diagram Partitioning." Including this mapping feature means that package elements on the diagram can be double-clicked to open a new diagram canvas to display the contents of the package. See Table 4-39.

Table 4-39   Package Mapping

Element	Property	Value
Mapping		
Top Node Reference	Containment Feature	Package.contents : PackageableElement
Node Mapping	Element	Package → PackageableElement
	Related Diagrams	Canvas Mapping
	Diagram Node	Node Package (Package Figure)
	Tool	Creation Tool Package
Feature Label Mapping	Diagram Label	Diagram Label PackageName
	Features	NamedElement.name : String
Feature Label Mapping	Diagram label	Diagram Label Stereotype
	Features	NamedElement.name : String
	Read Only	true
	View Pattern	«package»
Child Reference	Compartment	Compartment Mapping <Attributes>
	Containment Feature	Package.contents : PackageableElement
Node Mapping	Element	Package → PackageableElement
	Diagram Node	Diagram Label ListItem
	Tool	Creation Tool Package
Feature Label Mapping	Diagram Label	Diagram Label ListItem
	Features	NamedElement.name : String
Compartment Mapping	Children	Child Reference <contents:Package/ListItem>
	Compartment	Compartment Packages (BasicRectangle)

Annotations are mapped next. Note that we'll again use the "phantom node" concept here because the annotation link determines the archetype that will contain the annotation. Although it's possible to attach annotations to every model element, we provide for only archetype annotations at this time. Some complications arise when attaching links to compartment items. Table 4-40 shows the Annotation node and link mappings.

Table 4-40 Annotation Mapping

Element	Property	Value
Mapping		
Top Node Reference	Containment Feature	*Intentionally left blank*
Node Mapping	Element	Annotation
	Diagram Node	Node Annotation (AnnotationFigure)
	Tool	Creation Tool Annotation
Feature Label Mapping	Diagram Label	Diagram Label AnnotationLabel
	Editor Pattern	{0} = {1}
	Edit Pattern	{0} = {1}
	Features	Annotation.key : String, Annotation.value : String
	View Pattern	{0} = {1}
Feature Label Mapping	Diagram Label	Diagram Label Stereotype
	Features	Annotation.key : String
	Read Only	true
	View Pattern	«annotation»
Link Mapping	Target Feature	AnnotatedElement.annotations : Annotation
	Diagram Link	Connection AnnotationLink
	Tool	Creation Tool Annotation Link

Now we return to the Association link that the wizard created. Complete the mapping as shown in Table 4-41, taking note of the initialization of our element, including a Java initializer that we'll need to provide code for later.

Table 4-41   DNC Association Mapping

Element	Property	Value
Mapping		
Link Mapping	Containment Feature	features : Feature
	Element	Association → Reference
	Target Feature	TypedElement.type : Classifier
	Diagram Link	Connection Association
	Tool	Creation Tool Association
Constraint	Body	self.aggregation = false
	Language	ocl
Feature Seq Initializer	Element Class	Association → Reference
Feature Value Spec	Feature	Association.aggregation : EBoolean
Value Expression	Body	false
	Language	ocl
Feature Value Spec	Feature	Reference.opposite : Reference
Value Expression	Body	*
	Language	java
Feature Value Spec	Feature	Reference.bidirectional : Boolean
Value Expression	Body	true
	Language	ocl
Feature Value Spec	Feature	NamedElement.name : String
Value Expression	Body	self.opposite.owner.name.toLower()
	Language	ocl
Feature Label Mapping	Diagram Label	Diagram Label LinkTarget
	Editor Pattern	{0}..{1}
	Edit Pattern	{0}..{1}
	Features	TypedElement.lowerBound : Integer, TypedElement.upperBound : Integer
	View Pattern	{0}..{1}

* The body of the generated method for a Java initializer can be provided in the model. Later, we'll need to set the `GenJavaExpressionProvider` element's `injectExpressionBody` property to `true` in our generator model for the following code to appear in our output. Note the use of fully qualified class names, which the generator cleans up.

```
org.eclipse.oocore.Reference opposite =

org.eclipse.oocore.OocorePackage.eINSTANCE.getOocoreFactory()

.createReference();
        opposite.setOpposite(self);
        opposite.setBidirectional(true);
        opposite.setType(self.getOwner());
        opposite.setName(self.getOwner().getName().toLowerCase());
        ((org.eclipse.oocore.Class)
self.getType()).getFeatures().add(opposite);
        return opposite;
```

For our `Association` element, we set a constraint based on the `aggregation` property to distinguish these links from our `Aggregation` links. We also initialize the **aggregation** property to `false`, set the `bidirectional` property to `true`, and create the `opposite` end `Reference` using the injected Java code above; after that, we set the name of the reference to the name of the opposite. An important side effect of using an `Association` to create an opposite `Reference` in this case is that we won't get a duplicate link drawn, as would be the case if we specified a `Reference` type for the link. The reason is that no link mapping is defined for a plain `Reference`.

As you can tell, the links in the color modeling diagram remove a lot of the underlying complexity present in the domain model. Features are initialized to values that limit the range of modeling capabilities, keeping it simple for the Practitioner. We can expose more functionality in the future, but for now we will create bidirectional links and allow for only the specificity of target cardinality. Our `Association` class is not as powerful as what the UML provides, but that's not the point of this diagram.

TIP

Feature initialization occurs in the order of listing, so if an initialization of a feature depends on another feature being initialized first, be sure to list them in the proper order.

Our `Aggregation` link is similar to a regular association, except for the initialization of the aggregation property to `true` and the hollow diamond decorator at the source end. Another difference is with respect to link constraints, which here prevents aggregation relationships from being created to archetypes of differing type. The exception is the most common aggregation relationship in color models—that is, between a Moment Interval and a Moment Interval Detail. Table 4-42 shows the mapping.

Table 4-42   Aggregation Link Mapping

Element	Property	Value
Mapping		
Link Mapping	Containment Feature	Class.features : StructuralFeature
	Element	Association → Reference
	Target Feature	TypedElement.type : Classifier
	Diagram Link	Connection Aggregation
	Tool	Creation Tool Aggregation
Constraint	Body	self.aggregation = true
	Language	ocl
Feature Seq Initializer	Element Class	Association → Reference
Feature Value Spec	Feature	Association.aggregation : EBoolean
Value Expression	Body	true
	Language	ocl
Feature Value Spec	Feature	TypedElement.upperBound : EInt
Value Expression	Body	−1
	Language	ocl
Feature Value Spec	Feature	Reference.opposite : Reference
	Body	*Same as body above*
	Language	java
Feature Value Spec	Feature	Reference.bidirectional : Boolean
	Body	true
	Language	ocl

Element	Property	Value
Feature Value Spec	Feature	NamedElement.name : String
	Body	self.opposite.owner.name.toLower()
	Language	ocl
Feature Label Mapping	Diagram Label	Diagram Label LinkTarget
	Editor Pattern	{0}..{1}
	Edit Pattern	{0}..{1}
	Features	TypedElement.lowerBound : EInt, TypedElement.upperBound : EInt
	View Pattern	{0}..{1}
Link Constraints		
Target End Constraint	Body	*
	Language	ocl

   * Here's the sad truth about creating a constraint to prevent aggregation links from targeting types other than the source—or, in the case of moment intervals, other than moment intervals or moment interval details. OCL gives us no simple solution, such as `oppositeEnd.oclIsTypeOf(self)`. The reason is that the argument to `oclIsTypeOf()` must be a type literal, leaving us with this rather large expression:

```
(oppositeEnd.oclIsTypeOf(dnc::MomentInterval) and
self.oclIsTypeOf(dnc::MomentInterval))
or
(oppositeEnd.oclIsTypeOf(dnc::MomentInterval) and
  self.oclIsTypeOf(dnc::MIDetail))
or
(oppositeEnd.oclIsTypeOf(dnc::Role) and self.oclIsTypeOf(dnc::Role))
or

(oppositeEnd.oclIsTypeOf(dnc::Party) and self.oclIsTypeOf(dnc::Party))
or

(oppositeEnd.oclIsTypeOf(dnc::Place) and self.oclIsTypeOf(dnc::Place))
or

(oppositeEnd.oclIsTypeOf(dnc::Thing) and self.oclIsTypeOf(dnc::Thing))
or

(oppositeEnd.oclIsTypeOf(dnc::Description) and
self.oclIsTypeOf(dnc::Description))
```

Regarding `Target End Constraint` and `Source End Constraint` elements, it's important to realize that these constraints are evaluated based on mouse position during the act of creating the link. For example, the `source end constraint` is evaluated when starting the link, so the context is that element. The `oppositeEnd` variable isn't known yet, so don't reference `oppositeEnd` in a source end constraint. Likewise, the `target end constraint` is evaluated when the mouse hovers over a target element when drawing the link. At this point, the `oppositeEnd` environment variable has a value.

Our final mapping is for the generalization link, shown in Table 4.43. Recall that we'll be using the provided `Connection` from the `classDiagram.gmfgraph` model. Normally, we'd have to load this model using the **Load Resource** action, as done before in the graphical definition model. But because that model includes a reference to the `classDiagram.gmfgraph` model and is open in our mapping model resource set, the connection is already available to our mapping model.

Table 4-43   Generalization Mapping

Element	Property	Value
Mapping		
Link Mapping	Containment Feature	Class.superclasses : Class
	Diagram Link	Connection SolidConnectionWDstClosedArrow
	Tool	Creation Tool Generalization
Link Constraints		
Source End Constraint	Body	self.superclasses->isEmpty()
	Language	ocl
Target End Constraint	Body	*
	Language	ocl

* As was the case with the `Aggregation` constraint, this is the verbose OCL constraint for generalizations:

```
oppositeEnd <> self and not superclasses->includes(oppositeEnd) and
((oppositeEnd.oclIsTypeOf(dnc::Role) and self.oclIsTypeOf(dnc::Role))
or
(oppositeEnd.oclIsTypeOf(dnc::Party) and self.oclIsTypeOf(dnc::Party))
or
(oppositeEnd.oclIsTypeOf(dnc::Place) and self.oclIsTypeOf(dnc::Place))
```

```
or
(oppositeEnd.oclIsTypeOf(dnc::Thing) and self.oclIsTypeOf(dnc::Thing))
or
(oppositeEnd.oclIsTypeOf(dnc::Description) and
self.oclIsTypeOf(dnc::Description)))
```

The `Link Constraints` provide some important functionality to our link and to the Practitioner's usability of our diagram. The first constraint allows only a generalization link to be drawn from an archetype that does not yet have a superclass. In this manner, we restrict the underlying metamodel to just one superclass. Also, we prohibit cyclic inheritance by applying a target end constraint that checks to see if the oppositeEnd of the link contains the source in its superclasses list. With that, we disallow generalization to one's self. Finally, we prevent generalization relationships between archetypes of different types. In this approach to domain modeling, generalization is rarely used, and it doesn't make sense to inherit from one type of archetype to another.

4.6.4 Generation

At this point, we're ready to transform our mapping model into the generator model. Do this as before using the provided right-click menu action and corresponding wizard. If you find that the wizard cannot locate the `dnc.genmodel` file, use the **Find in Workspace** feature to locate the model and continue. Open the produced `dnc.gmfgen` model in the editor and change the `Same File for Diagram and Model` property to `true`, and change the `Diagram File Extension` property to `dnc`. Because our diagram allows for the creation of partitions to represent packages, it might be convenient to add shortcuts from archetypes in one package to another. Add the string `dnc` to the `Contains Shortcuts To` property in the `Diagram` category of the `Gen Diagram` element to provide shortcut support. Now we can run the diagram using our same launch configuration as before. Using the generated wizard, create a new DNC diagram and test its functionality. There's no color yet, but all the elements should function. Notice that you cannot specify a data type for attributes at this time with the in-place editor. We address how this is done later when we add a custom parser for attributes in Section 4.6.7, "Custom Parsers."

4.6.5 Gradient Figures

Our archetypes don't currently have any color, which is their most significant attribute. Instead of simply filling in each archetype with a background color, we use a gradient effect. GEF enables you to add a gradient to a figure but does not directly support it. Don't let that graphical definition model Gradient Facet element fool you—it is not yet implemented. Worse, this property is not available to the figure code-generation templates even if we did try to use it. So we're left to find our own way to implement gradients in our archetypes, to give them a fresh appearance.

The `fillShape()` method of our archetype figure gives us the place to add a gradient. Simply overriding this method and adding a call to `fillGradient()` does the trick, except that gradients in GEF do not respect the corners of a `RoundedRectangle` figure. This effectively reduces our rounded rectangles to regular rectangles, though with gradient. Instead of spending time figuring how to implement gradients for rounded rectangles, we can be creative and adjust the starting point of the gradient to between the archetype name and the stereotype label. (Recall the hint earlier regarding the placement of these labels?) Not only does this give us a striking visual appearance, but it also has the effect of nearly eliminating the problems GEF in respect to the corners: The top no longer has gradient applied, and it's faded enough by the bottom to make it hardly noticeable that it extends beyond the curve. Figure 4-44 is an example of the gradient, although the archetype does not yet define our foreground color. This illustrates the reason for the stereotype labels, however. Black-and-white print of our color diagrams makes it difficult to distinguish the archetypes otherwise. Additionally, the stereotypes let us distinguish between archetypes of the same color, such as Party, Place, and Thing, which are all green.

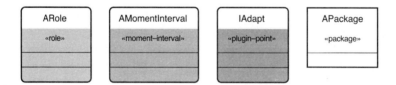

Figure 4-44   Color archetypes

This is the code modification required to create the effect:

```
protected void fillShape(Graphics graphics) {
  graphics.fillGradient(bounds.x, bounds.y + 24,
    bounds.width, bounds.height, true);
}
```

COMMENT

As we mentioned earlier, the lowering cost of high-resolution monitors has made diagramming much more palatable than even a few years ago. Similarly, the lowering cost of high-resolution color printers will hopefully encourage more use of color and eliminate redundant visual hints, such as the earlier stereotype labels. Just recall the advice on the use of color: Using too many colors is often worse than using none at all.

Now we need to generate this additional code for our archetype figures. We can leverage GMF's capability to customize the templates for figure code generation. In case you've missed it each time, the dialog presented when transforming mapping to generator model has a "Provisional" section that gives us the field to enter the path to our custom templates, as seen in Figure 4-45.

TIP

When using the "provisional" custom figures template feature, be aware that the field will not remember individual .gmfmap file settings. When you enter a path to custom templates in this field, it is applied to all mapping→generator model transformations.

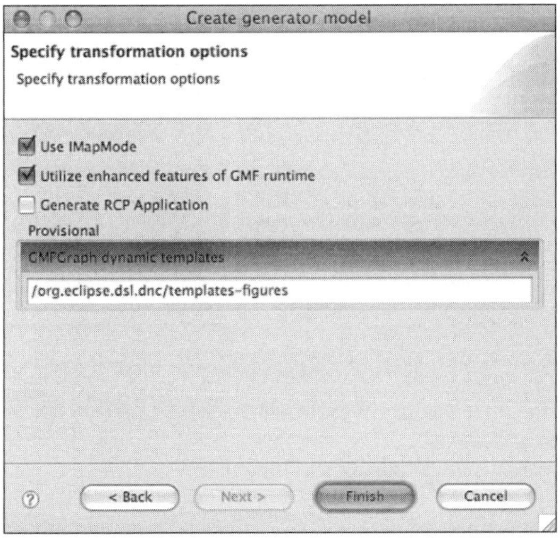

Figure 4-45   Create Generator Model dialog

The easiest way to get started modifying or augmenting GMF templates is to bring the appropriate *.codegen plug-in into the workspace. For figures, we're interested in the org.eclipse.gmf.graphdef.codegen plug-in, so switching to the Plug-Ins view of our Plug-In Development perspective, we locate it and right-click, choosing **Import As → Source Project**. Browsing the contents of this plug-in, we discover the /templates/top/Figure.xpt Xpand template. This template provides an expansion of the Extras::extraMethods «DEFINE» that looks like just what we need to add our overridden fillShape() method. The Extras.xpt template contains this «DEFINE» block that we can use to create an «AROUND» that will add our method.

```
«DEFINE extraMethods FOR gmfgraph::Figure-»
«ENDDEFINE»
```

We create a /templates-figures/aspects/Extras.xpt template in our org.eclipse.dsl.dnc project. As discussed in Section 4.2.3, "Customization Options," GMF uses the convention of prefixing the directory structure for aspects with a folder named aspects, followed by the original path to the template, as defined in the *.codegen project. In this case, we want to provide an aspect for the Extras.xpt template, which is located directly in the /templates folder. We'll use the path /org.eclipse.dsl.dnc/templates-figures/ in the wizard dialog, as shown in Figure 4-45. When the generator finds the aspects folder, it will know to add this as an aspect template path.

Following is our template, which, as you can see, uses the polymorphic feature of Xpand to add our gradient code only for RoundedRectangle figures. We need to provide the obligatory «DEFINE» for the Figure supertype as well. Also note that we're adding a useGradient Boolean to control whether to display gradients, which we can later hook up to a diagram preferences option.

```
«IMPORT "http://www.eclipse.org/gmf/2006/GraphicalDefinition"»
«IMPORT "http://www.eclipse.org/emf/2002/Ecore"»

«AROUND extraMethods FOR gmfgraph::Figure-»
«EXPAND gradient-»
«targetDef.proceed()»
«ENDAROUND»

«DEFINE gradient FOR gmfgraph::Figure»«ENDDEFINE»

«DEFINE gradient FOR gmfgraph::RoundedRectangle-»
  /**
   * @generated
   */
  private boolean useGradient = true;
```

```
    /**
     * @generated
     */
    public void setUseGradient(boolean useGradient) {
      this.useGradient = useGradient;
    }

    /**
     * @generated
     */
    public boolean getUseGradient() {
      return useGradient;
    }

    /**
     * @generated
     */
  protected void fillShape(org.eclipse.draw2d.Graphics graphics) {
      if (useGradient) {
        graphics.fillGradient(bounds.x, bounds.y + 24,
bounds.width, bounds.height, true);
      }
  }
«ENDDEFINE»
```

We can again transform our mapping model to the generator model, adding our path to the figure template in the provisional **GMFGraph Dynamic Templates** field, and regenerate our diagram code. Recall that figures are serialized within the generator model by default, although we used the standalone figures method in the Scenario diagram that eliminates the need to regenerate all the diagram code to see the change. Figure 4-44 shows the result, with the remaining task of assigning the proper color for each archetype, based on its type. We want to avoid hard-coding this into our figures, which we mentioned when creating the graphical definition model. Instead, let's see what is involved in adding color preferences for each archetype that the Practitioner can change, if desired.

4.6.6 Color Preferences

Basing the color of an archetype on its type is straightforward enough, and you can most easily accomplish this by overriding the setForegroundColor() method in each Archetype EditPart class. Recall that the gradient effect goes from our foreground to background color. For example, this simple implementation in our MomentIntervalEditPart class causes it to produce the desired gradient effect:

```
@Override
protected void setForegroundColor(Color) {
  super.setForegroundColor(new Color(null, 250, 145, 145));
}
```

We need to do a bit more for the color to be obtained from the diagram preferences, and for diagram elements to respond to changes in the default values. Plus, we again want to modify our code-generation templates so that these changes will not be overridden if we forget to add the appropriate @generated NOT tag, or if we need to delete and regenerate our diagram plug-in entirely.

BEST PRACTICE

Even though it might require a little more effort to implement, adding custom templates to implement a feature for your diagram is likely worthwhile if you find yourself regenerating clean diagram plug-ins due to refactorings, and given the reality of code merge technology limitations.

This time, we need to import the org.eclipse.gmf.codegen plug-in into our workspace as a source project, just as we did for the org.eclipse.gmf.graphdef.codegen plug-in earlier. You will find a lot of templates and extension files in this project, so consider it a resource for understanding how to use Xpand, not to mention how to modify GMF generation. Another good source of examples for working with GMF, custom templates, and extensions is the UML2 Tools project. Looking at our generated diagram code, we see that the DiagramAppearancePreferencePage class is the best location for our archetype color preferences. Currently, this page provides default font, line color, and fill color preferences, among others. We can add another group for archetype color preferences below the existing group.

As before, we first code our changes manually and then "templify" the changes in our custom templates. Looking at the AppearancePreferencePage superclass of this preference page, we see that adding our own group and color defaults should be straightforward. Using copy and paste, we insert the following code into our diagram's preference page, which started as a simple subclass designed for extension. Note that we override the addFields() method to allow for the addition of the archetype color group. To save space, some repetitive code is commented out.

```
public class DiagramAppearancePreferencePage

  extends AppearancePreferencePage{

  private String PINK_COLOR_LABEL =
    Messages.AppearancePreferencePage_pinkArchetypeColor_label;
  private String YELLOW_COLOR_LABEL =
    Messages.AppearancePreferencePage_yellowArchetypeColor_label;
  private String GREEN_COLOR_LABEL =
    Messages.AppearancePreferencePage_greenArchetypeColor_label;
  private String BLUE_COLOR_LABEL =
    Messages.AppearancePreferencePage_blueArchetypeColor_label;
  private String GRAY_COLOR_LABEL =
    Messages.AppearancePreferencePage_grayArchetypeColor_label;
  private String ARCHETYPE_GROUPBOX_LABEL =
    Messages.AppearancePreferencePage_archetypeColorGroup_label;
  public static final String PREF_MI_ARCHETYPE_COLOR =
    "Appearance.mi_ArchetypeColor";
  public static final String PREF_ROLE_ARCHETYPE_COLOR
    "Appearance.role_ArchetypeColor";
  public static final String PREF_PPT_ARCHETYPE_COLOR =
    "Appearance.ppt_ArchetypeColor";
  public static final String PREF_DESC_ARCHETYPE_COLOR =
    "Appearance.desc_ArchetypeColor";
  public static final String PREF_PIP_ARCHETYPE_COLOR =
    "Appearance.pip_ArchetypeColor";
  private ColorFieldEditor pinkArchetypeColorEditor = null;
  private ColorFieldEditor yellowArchetypeColorEditor = null;
  private ColorFieldEditor greenArchetypeColorEditor = null;
  private ColorFieldEditor blueArchetypeColorEditor = null;
  private ColorFieldEditor grayArchetypeColorEditor = null;

  public DiagramAppearancePreferencePage() {
    setPreferenceStore(DncDiagramEditorPlugin.getInstance()
    .getPreferenceStore());
  }

  @Override
  protected void addFields (Composite parent) {
    Composite main = createPageLayout(parent);
    createFontAndColorGroup(main);
    createArchetypeColorGroup(main);
  }

  public static void initArchetypeDefaults(IPreferenceStore store) {
    PreferenceConverter.setDefault(store, PREF_MI_ARCHETYPE_COLOR,
      new Color(null, 250, 145, 145).getRGB());
    PreferenceConverter.setDefault(store, PREF_ROLE_ARCHETYPE_COLOR,
      new Color(null, 238, 245, 165).getRGB());
    PreferenceConverter.setDefault(store, PREF_PPT_ARCHETYPE_COLOR,
      new Color(null, 124, 179, 77).getRGB());
    PreferenceConverter.setDefault(store, PREF_DESC_ARCHETYPE_COLOR,
      new Color(null, 86, 145, 215).getRGB());
```

```
PreferenceConverter.setDefault(store, PREF_PIP_ARCHETYPE_COLOR,
    new Color(null, 124, 124, 124).getRGB());
// Override the normal default line color
PreferenceConverter.setDefault(store,
    IPreferenceConstants.PREF_LINE_COLOR,
    new Color(null, 124, 124, 124).getRGB());
}

protected Composite createArchetypeColorGroup(Composite parent) {
    Group group = new Group(parent, SWT.NONE);
    group.setLayoutData(new GridData(GridData.FILL_HORIZONTAL));
    group.setLayout(new GridLayout(3, false));
    Composite composite = new Composite(group, SWT.NONE);
    GridLayout gridLayout = new GridLayout(3, false);
    composite.setLayout(gridLayout);
    GridData gridData = new GridData(GridData.FILL_HORIZONTAL);
    gridData.grabExcessHorizontalSpace = true;
    gridData.horizontalSpan = 3;
    composite.setLayoutData(gridData);
    group.setText(ARCHETYPE_GROUPBOX_LABEL);

    addArchetypeColorFields(composite);

    GridLayout layout = new GridLayout();
    layout.numColumns = 3;
    layout.marginWidth = 0;
    layout.marginHeight = 0;
    layout.horizontalSpacing = 8;
    composite.setLayout(layout);

    return group;
}

protected void addArchetypeColorFields(Composite composite) {
    pinkArchetypeColorEditor = new ColorFieldEditor(
        PREF_MI_ARCHETYPE_COLOR, PINK_COLOR_LABEL, composite);
    addField(pinkArchetypeColorEditor);

    pinkArchetypeColorEditor.getColorSelector().getButton().
        getAccessible().addAccessibleListener(new AccessibleAdapter() {
            public void getName(AccessibleEvent e) {
                String labelText = pinkArchetypeColorEditor.getLabelText();
                labelText = Action.removeMnemonics(labelText);
                e.result = labelText;
            }
        });

    // ... Repeat initialization of each ColorFieldEditor

}
}
```

To provide for localization, we add the strings just referenced to our Messages class and to the diagram plug-in's `messages.properties` file. Note that the default values for each archetype color are provided previously, in RGB. To initialize the preferences, we look to the generated `DiagramPreference Initializer` class. We need to have the initializer call our `initArchetype Defaults()` method, provided earlier, as shown in the modified implementation here:

```
public void initializeDefaultPreferences() {
  IPreferenceStore store = getPreferenceStore();
  DiagramPrintingPreferencePage.initDefaults(store);
  DiagramGeneralPreferencePage.initDefaults(store);
  DiagramAppearancePreferencePage.initDefaults(store);
DiagramAppearancePreferencePage.initArchetypeDefaults(store);
  DiagramConnectionsPreferencePage.initDefaults(store);
  DiagramRulersAndGridPreferencePage.initDefaults(store);
}
```

These are the additions made to the `org.eclipse.dnc.diagram.part.Messages` class:

```
/**
 * @generated
 */
public class Messages extends NLS {

  /**
   * @generated
   */
  static {
    NLS.initializeMessages("messages", Messages.class); //$NON-NLS-1$
  }

  /**
   * @generated
   */
  private Messages() {
  }

  public static String
    AppearancePreferencePage_archetypeColorGroup_label;
  public static String
    AppearancePreferencePage_pinkArchetypeColor_label;
  public static String
    AppearancePreferencePage_yellowArchetypeColor_label;
  public static String
    AppearancePreferencePage_greenArchetypeColor_label;
  public static String
    AppearancePreferencePage_blueArchetypeColor_label;
  public static String
    AppearancePreferencePage_grayArchetypeColor_label;
  //. . .
}
```

And these are the additions we made to the `messages.properties` file:

```
AppearancePreferencePage_archetypeColorGroup_label=Archetype colors
AppearancePreferencePage_pinkArchetypeColor_label=
  Pinks (moment-interval, mi-detail):
AppearancePreferencePage_yellowArchetypeColor_label=Yellows (role):
AppearancePreferencePage_greenArchetypeColor_label=
  Greens (party, place, thing):
AppearancePreferencePage_blueArchetypeColor_label=Blues (description):
AppearancePreferencePage_grayArchetypeColor_label=Plug-in point:
```

At this point, we can launch our diagram and see the properties in action, although they have no effect on the diagram because they're not incorporated into our `EditPart` code yet. Again, using black-and-white images does little to illustrate the use of color modeling, as seen in Figure 4-46.

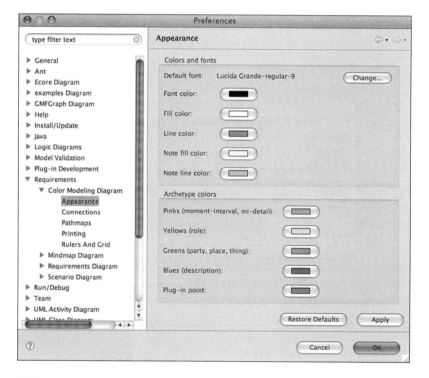

Figure 4-46   Archetype color preferences

Turning finally to our `EditPart` code, we use `MomentIntervalEditPart` as our testbed. Adding the following code makes our preferences-based color

options functional. To begin, we add an inner class, `PreferenceProperty`
`ChangeListener`, that will detect a change in the appropriate property and
invoke the `updateArchetypeColor()` method. To initialize and register this
listener, we override the `addNotationalListeners()` method.

```
private PreferencePropertyChangeListener preferenceListener;

protected class PreferencePropertyChangeListener
  implements IPropertyChangeListener {
  public void propertyChange(PropertyChangeEvent event) {
    if (event.getProperty().equals(
      DiagramAppearancePreferencePage.PREF_MI_ARCHETYPE_COLOR)) {
      updateArchetypeColor();
    }
  }
}

@Override
protected void addNotationalListeners() {
  super.addNotationalListeners();
  initPreferenceStoreListener();
}

protected void updateArchetypeColor() {
  getFigure().setForegroundColor(getPreferenceColor());
  getFigure().repaint();
}

private Color getPreferenceColor() {
  IPreferenceStore preferenceStore = (IPreferenceStore)
    getDiagramPreferencesHint().getPreferenceStore();
  org.eclipse.swt.graphics.RGB archetypeColorPreference =
    PreferenceConverter.getColor(preferenceStore,
    DiagramAppearancePreferencePage.PREF_MI_ARCHETYPE_COLOR);
  return new Color(null, archetypeColorPreference);
}

private void initPreferenceStoreListener() {
  preferenceListener = new PreferencePropertyChangeListener();
  IPreferenceStore preferenceStore = (IPreferenceStore)
    getDiagramPreferencesHint().getPreferenceStore();
  preferenceStore.addPropertyChangeListener(preferenceListener);
}

@Override
protected void setForegroundColor(Color color) {
  super.setForegroundColor(getPreferenceColor());
}
```

The overridden `setForegroundColor()` method and the preference listener both obtain the appropriate color from the preference store, as shown in

getPreferenceColor(). All that's left to do is test the functionality and then move on to templatizing the code changes. One improvement might be to restrict the color ranges for each archetype so that they still maintain their pink, yellow, green, or blue essence.

We begin our GMF diagram template spelunking in the /templates directory of the imported org.eclipse.gmf.codegen plug-in. We notice right away that there are three editparts directories: one under /templates/diagram, one under /templates/impl/diagram, and one under /templates/xpt/diagram. The last one is a legacy structure and should be ignored in favor of the /templates/impl pattern to distinguish published API vs. non-API templates. Looking into each and finding a NodeEditPart.xpt template in the first two, we open each to see the differences. In the /templates/diagram/editparts/NodeEditPart.xpt template, we see that it delegates to the /templates/impl/diagram/editparts/NodeEditPart.xpt template for generation of the class content. What interests us most, however, is the «EXPAND additions-» expansion near the end of the class. All we need to do is add the code listed earlier to our archetype EditPart classes, so this looks like a promising place to start. In fact, this expansion was designed for Toolsmiths to use for customizing the generated code, and you'll find many of them in the GMF templates. The corresponding «DEFINE» block appears at the bottom of the template and is listed here:

```
«DEFINE additions FOR gmfgen::GenNode-»
«ENDDEFINE»
```

TIP

If you need additional extensibility in GMF templates, open a bug to request the change be made.

We need to create a NodeEditPart.xpt template file in our org.eclipse.dsl.dnc project in a /templates/aspects/diagram/editparts folder. Again, we conform to the GMF convention of aspect template placement so that the generator will invoke our template. We place an «AROUND» block at the top of the template, as follows:

```
«IMPORT "http://www.eclipse.org/gmf/2006/GenModel"»
«EXTENSION Utils»

«AROUND additions FOR gmfgen::GenNode-»
«EXPAND fieldPreferencePropertyChangeListener FOR this-»
«EXPAND PreferencePropertyChangeListener FOR this-»
«EXPAND addNotationalListeners FOR this-»
«EXPAND updateArchetypeColor FOR this-»
«EXPAND getPreferenceColor FOR this-»
«EXPAND initPreferenceStoreListener FOR this-»
«EXPAND setForegroundColorMethod FOR this-»
«ENDAROUND»
```

As you can see, we're breaking up the implementation into a series of «DEFINE» blocks, each corresponding to a method. This is another best practice for using Xpand, and one you'll see throughout the GMF templates. Note, however, that the context for this custom template remains gmfgen::GenNode. This means that all EditPart classes that are generated for nodes will have these customizations added, not only archetypes. Our diagram has two other types of nodes, package nodes, and annotations. This doesn't present a problem in our case because we default all nodes not recognized as archetypes during execution as the plug-in point archetype. The «EXTENSION» at the top of our template points to our Util.ext file that contains the logic used, as shown here:

```
String toPreferenceConstant(ecore::EClass type) :
  switch (type.name) {
    case "MomentInterval" : "PREF_MI_ARCHETYPE_COLOR"
    case "MIDetail" : "PREF_MI_ARCHETYPE_COLOR"
    case "Role" : "PREF_ROLE_ARCHETYPE_COLOR"
    case "Party" : "PREF_PPT_ARCHETYPE_COLOR"
    case "Place" : "PREF_PPT_ARCHETYPE_COLOR"
    case "Thing" : "PREF_PPT_ARCHETYPE_COLOR"
    case "Description" : "PREF_DESC_ARCHETYPE_COLOR"
    default : "PREF_PIP_ARCHETYPE_COLOR"
  }
;
```

You'll see where this function is invoked shortly, but it's clear from this how each archetype is mapped to its corresponding preference constant. The first template definition invoked appears next and simply adds a field for our inner PreferencePropertyChangeListener class. Note the use of the xpt::Common::generatedMemberComment and xpt::Common::generatedMemberComent expansions throughout the template, which insert the familiar @generated tags above class, field, and method declarations.

TIP

When working with custom templates, be sure to use fully qualified template references, particularly when overriding an existing template that might have been written using local reference paths. If you don't, you will receive errors during execution because the template will not be resolved.

```
«DEFINE fieldPreferencePropertyChangeListener FOR gmfgen::GenNode-»
  «EXPAND xpt::Common::generatedMemberComment»-»
  private PreferencePropertyChangeListener preferenceListener;
«ENDDEFINE»
```

Next, we define the listener class itself, which, as you can see, needs to access the fully qualified class name for our generated appearance preference page. This listener class is the first to use our `toPreferenceConstant()` function for the passed archetype.

```
«DEFINE PreferencePropertyChangeListener FOR gmfgen::GenNode-»
«EXPAND xpt::Common::generatedClassComment-»
  protected class PreferencePropertyChangeListener
implements org.eclipse.jface.util.IPropertyChangeListener {
    public void
propertyChange(org.eclipse.jface.util.PropertyChangeEvent event) {
      if (event.getProperty().equals(
«EXPAND
xpt::diagram::preferences::AppearancePreferencePage::qualifiedClassName
FOR diagram».«modelFacet.metaClass.ecoreClass.toPreferenceConstant()»))
{
        updateArchetypeColor();
      }
    }
  }
«ENDDEFINE»
```

Note the navigation to the archetype's Ecore class using `modelFacet.metaClass.ecoreClass` in the statement. The structure of the GMF generator model is important to have handy when writing templates, and you can easily open it from the imported project, or simply open the QVTO Metamodel Explorer for navigator view access to the model. As you saw in the utility function, the name of the class maps to its preference constant, which is inserted in the generated code so that the EditPart can detect changes to its color preference. We could use a variation of this logic to avoid generating this color preference code for non-archetype nodes.

The rest of the template definition appears here. It's a straightforward templating of our handcrafted code, with the only other noteworthy aspect being the use of `toPreferenceConstant()` again in the `getPreferenceColor` definition block.

```
«DEFINE addNotationalListeners FOR gmfgen::GenNode-»
  «EXPAND xpt::Common::generatedMemberComment-»
  @Override
  protected void addNotationalListeners() {
    super.addNotationalListeners();
    initPreferenceStoreListener();
  }
«ENDDEFINE»

«DEFINE initPreferenceStoreListener FOR gmfgen::GenNode-»
  «EXPAND xpt::Common::generatedMemberComment-»
  private void initPreferenceStoreListener() {
    preferenceListener = new
PreferencePropertyChangeListener();
    org.eclipse.jface.preference.IPreferenceStore
preferenceStore = (org.eclipse.jface.preference.IPreferenceStore)
getDiagramPreferencesHint().getPreferenceStore();
        preferenceStore.addPropertyChangeListener(preferenceListener);
  }
«ENDDEFINE»

«DEFINE updateArchetypeColor FOR gmfgen::GenNode-»
  «EXPAND xpt::Common::generatedMemberComment-»
  protected void updateArchetypeColor() {
    getFigure().setForegroundColor(getPreferenceColor());
    getFigure().repaint();
  }
«ENDDEFINE»

«DEFINE getPreferenceColor FOR gmfgen::GenNode-»
  «EXPAND xpt::Common::generatedMemberComment-»
  private org.eclipse.swt.graphics.Color getPreferenceColor() {
    org.eclipse.jface.preference.IPreferenceStore
preferenceStore = (org.eclipse.jface.preference.IPreferenceStore)
getDiagramPreferencesHint().getPreferenceStore();
    org.eclipse.swt.graphics.RGB archetypeColorPreference =
org.eclipse.jface.preference.PreferenceConverter.getColor(
preferenceStore,
«EXPAND
xpt::diagram::preferences::AppearancePreferencePage::qualifiedClassName
FOR diagram».«modelFacet.metaClass.ecoreClass.toPreferenceConstant()»);
    return new org.eclipse.swt.graphics.Color(null,
archetypeColorPreference);
  }
«ENDDEFINE»

«DEFINE setForegroundColorMethod FOR gmfgen::GenNode-»
  «EXPAND xpt::Common::generatedMemberComment-»
```

```
@Override
protected void setForegroundColor(org.eclipse.swt.graphics.Color
color) {
   super.setForegroundColor(getPreferenceColor());
}
«ENDDEFINE»
```

Moving on to the preference page templates, we find the original `AppearancePreferencePage.xpt` template in `/templates/xpt/diagram/preferences`. We need to override this template, along with `PreferenceInitializer.xpt`, because they were apparently not created with extensibility in mind, as was the case with the `NodeEditPart.xpt` template. This means that we simply copy these two templates into our own `/templates-diagram/xpt/diagram/preferences` folder and modify them to suit our needs. Most of the changes required for the preference page code is straightforward copy and paste from our earlier handcrafted code, so we don't repeat it here. However, we do need to explore how GMF deals with globalization because we need to add referenced elements to our generated Messages class and `messages.properties` file. Looking at the template files, we find an `Externalizer.xpt` template in the `/templates/xpt` folder in the generator plug-in. The Externalizer template provides a centralized means by which to generate the Messages class and properties file. The template is organized in two main definition blocks, as shown here. Basically, GMF convention is to declare an `i18nAccessors` and `i18nValues` definition in templates that require localization and invoke them from the `Fields` and `Values` definitions, respectively.

```
«DEFINE Fields FOR gmfgen::GenEditorGenerator»
«EXPAND xpt::editor::CreateShortcutAction::i18nAccessors FOR diagram-»
«EXPAND xpt::editor::CreationWizard::i18nAccessors FOR diagram-»
«EXPAND xpt::editor::CreationWizardPage::i18nAccessors FOR diagram-»
   . . .
«ENDDEFINE»

«DEFINE Values FOR gmfgen::GenEditorGenerator»
«EXPAND xpt::editor::CreateShortcutAction::i18nValues FOR diagram-»
«EXPAND xpt::editor::CreationWizard::i18nValues FOR diagram-»
«EXPAND xpt::editor::CreationWizardPage::i18nValues FOR diagram-»
   . . .
«ENDDEFINE»
```

We follow suit with our properties preference page by defining similar blocks for invocation by our overridden `Externalizer.xpt` template. First, we take a look at the externalizer, which is placed in our `/templates-diagram/aspects/xpt` directory.

```
«IMPORT "http://www.eclipse.org/gmf/2006/GenModel"»
«IMPORT "http://www.eclipse.org/emf/2002/Ecore"»

«EXTENSION xpt::ExternalizerUtils»

«AROUND Fields FOR gmfgen::GenEditorGenerator»
«EXPAND
xpt::diagram::preferences::AppearancePreferencePage::i18nAccessors FOR
diagram-»
«targetDef.proceed()-»
«ENDAROUND»

«AROUND Values FOR gmfgen::GenEditorGenerator»
«EXPAND xpt::diagram::preferences::AppearancePreferencePage::i18nValues
FOR diagram-»
«targetDef.proceed()-»
«ENDAROUND»
```

Here, we create «AROUND» aspects for both the `Fields` and `Values` definitions, expand our custom template definitions, and then continue execution of the original template using `targetDef.proceed()`. This is a common approach to extensibility using Xpand. Back in our `AppearancePreference Page.xpt` template, we find the definitions.

```
«DEFINE i18nValues FOR gmfgen::GenDiagram-»
«EXPAND xpt::Externalizer::messageEntry(
"AppearancePreferencePage_archetypeColorGroup_label",
"Archetype colors")-»

«EXPAND xpt::Externalizer::messageEntry(
"AppearancePreferencePage_pinkArchetypeColor_label",
"Pinks (moment-interval, mi-detail):")-»

«EXPAND xpt::Externalizer::messageEntry(
"AppearancePreferencePage_yellowArchetypeColor_label",
"Yellows (role):")-»

«EXPAND xpt::Externalizer::messageEntry(
"AppearancePreferencePage_greenArchetypeColor_label",
"Greens (party, place, thing):")-»

«EXPAND xpt::Externalizer::messageEntry(
"AppearancePreferencePage_blueArchetypeColor_label",
"Blues (description):")-»

«EXPAND xpt::Externalizer::messageEntry(
"AppearancePreferencePage_grayArchetypeColor_label",
"Plug-in point:")-»
«ENDDEFINE»
```

```
«DEFINE i18nAccessors FOR gmfgen::GenDiagram-»
«EXPAND xpt::Externalizer::accessorField(
"AppearancePreferencePage_archetypeColorGroup_label")-»

«EXPAND xpt::Externalizer::accessorField(
"AppearancePreferencePage_pinkArchetypeColor_label")-»

«EXPAND xpt::Externalizer::accessorField(
"AppearancePreferencePage_yellowArchetypeColor_label")-»

«EXPAND xpt::Externalizer::accessorField(
"AppearancePreferencePage_greenArchetypeColor_label")-»

«EXPAND xpt::Externalizer::accessorField(
"AppearancePreferencePage_blueArchetypeColor_label")-»

«EXPAND xpt::Externalizer::accessorField(
"AppearancePreferencePage_grayArchetypeColor_label")-»
«ENDDEFINE»
```

When the Messages class and `messages.properties` files are being generated, each template that requires messages is invoked and the strings are added to these files. You need to go to the `i18nValues` blocks for declaring the default localized string values when using GMF Xpand templates. Two callback expansions are made from the template to `messageEntry` and `accessorField` in the `Externalizer.xpt` template, as shown here. The first creates a public static String entry in the generated `Messages` class file; the second creates a `key=value` entry in the `messages.properties` file.

```
«DEFINE accessorField(String key) FOR Object»
  «EXPAND xpt::Common::generatedMemberComment»
    public static String «escapeIllegalKeySymbols(key)»;
«ENDDEFINE»

«DEFINE messageEntry(String key, String message) FOR Object-»
«escapeIllegalKeySymbols(key)»=«escapeIllegalMessageSymbols(message)»
«ENDDEFINE»
```

Having provided a means by which to produce messages, we now need to access them in our generated code; this means examining another aspect of GMF's `Externalizer.xpt` template. When a message is accessed in the code generated, it needs to resolve the Messages class, which means calling back again to the `Externalizer.xpt` template so that the fully qualified path can be provided. Following is the `accessorCall` definition, used for just this purpose.

```
«DEFINE accessorCall(String key) FOR gmfgen::GenEditorGenerator-»
«getAccessorQualifier()».«getAccessorName()».
«escapeIllegalKeySymbols(key)»
«ENDDEFINE»
```

We use this in our preference page template, as shown here:

```
«EXPAND xpt::Common::generatedClassComment»
public class «EXPAND className» extends
org.eclipse.gmf.runtime.diagram.ui.preferences.AppearancePreferencePage
{

«EXPAND xpt::Common::generatedMemberComment»
private String PINK_COLOR_LABEL =
«EXPAND xpt::Externalizer::accessorCall(
"AppearancePreferencePage_pinkArchetypeColor_label") FOR editorGen»;
«EXPAND xpt::Common::generatedMemberComment»
private String YELLOW_COLOR_LABEL =
«EXPAND xpt::Externalizer::accessorCall(
"AppearancePreferencePage_yellowArchetypeColor_label") FOR editorGen»;
«EXPAND xpt::Common::generatedMemberComment»
private String GREEN_COLOR_LABEL =
«EXPAND xpt::Externalizer::accessorCall(
"AppearancePreferencePage_greenArchetypeColor_label") FOR editorGen»;
«EXPAND xpt::Common::generatedMemberComment»
private String BLUE_COLOR_LABEL =
«EXPAND xpt::Externalizer::accessorCall(
"AppearancePreferencePage_blueArchetypeColor_label") FOR editorGen»;
«EXPAND xpt::Common::generatedMemberComment»
private String GRAY_COLOR_LABEL =
«EXPAND xpt::Externalizer::accessorCall(
"AppearancePreferencePage_grayArchetypeColor_label") FOR editorGen»;
«EXPAND xpt::Common::generatedMemberComment»
private String ARCHETYPE_GROUPBOX_LABEL =
«EXPAND xpt::Externalizer::accessorCall(
"AppearancePreferencePage_archetypeColorGroup_label") FOR editorGen»;
«EXPAND xpt::Common::generatedMemberComment»
public static final String PREF_MI_ARCHETYPE_COLOR =
"Appearance.mi_ArchetypeColor";
. . .
}
```

Our final template required to provide full generation of our preferences-based archetype color feature is the `PreferenceInitializer.xpt` template. As mentioned earlier, the only change required to this template is to add an invocation of the `initArchetypeDefaults()` method, as shown next. This template contains a good deal of code that we do not require, but for now we'll leave it as is and make our single modification.

```
. . .
«EXPAND
xpt::diagram::preferences::GeneralPreferencePage::qualifiedClassName»
.initDefaults(store);

«EXPAND xpt::diagram::preferences::AppearancePreferencePage::
qualifiedClassName».initDefaults(store);

«EXPAND xpt::diagram::preferences::AppearancePreferencePage::
qualifiedClassName».initArchetypeDefaults(store);

«EXPAND xpt::diagram::preferences::ConnectionsPreferencePage::
qualifiedClassName».initDefaults(store);

«EXPAND xpt::diagram::preferences::RulersAndGridPreferencePage::
qualifiedClassName».initDefaults(store);
. . .
```

We need only to set the `Dynamic Templates` property of our `Gen Editor Generator` root element in our `dnc.gmfgen` model to `true`, and enter a `Template Directory` path of `/org.eclipse.dsl.dnc/ templates-diagram`. Regenerating our code should produce code that runs and, for the first time, renders each archetype according to its default color. Experiment with the preferences to ensure that they work and to find a set of RGB values that you find most appealing. Perhaps the best outcome of this template exercise, other than a better understanding of how GMF's code generation works, is knowing that you can delete and fully generate this feature in your diagram plug-in.

4.6.7 Custom Parsers

A popular feature of class modeling tools is the capability to specify the type after the name when entering attributes, or even complete method signatures, using the in-place editor. For our DNC diagram, we begin with the attribute field. Currently, we enter the name of the attribute using the diagram, but then we need to drop down to the properties view to select the type, which doesn't display on the diagram. We can take two basic approaches to solving the problem. One is to contribute to the `parserProviders` extension-point in the diagram or custom plug-in and implement our own `IParserProvider`. Another approach is to use the `Feature Label` mapping in the `dnc.gmfmap` model to generate code that we could modify to complete the implementation. Because we require custom parsers for our `Attribute` and `Operation` labels, we use both approaches, to illustrate the differences.

Attribute Parser Provider

For attributes, we want to enter name:Type in the label on the diagram and have it parsed properly to set the name and dataType fields of the underlying Attribute domain element. Of course, we want the label to display name:Type even when changes are made to the underlying model through the properties view, for example. To begin, we create a new (empty) org.eclipse.dnc.diagram.custom plug-in to our workspace and contribute to the parserProviders extension-point, as follows:

```
<extension
point="org.eclipse.gmf.runtime.common.ui.services.parserProviders">
<ParserProvider
     class="org.eclipse.dnc.diagram.providers.AttributeParserProvider">
           <Priority name="Low"/>
       </ParserProvider>
</extension>
```

We need to provide the AttributeParserProvider class, which extends the runtime's AbstractProvider and implements the IParserProvider interface. This is the class, which still could use some optimization but works well enough for now:

```
public class AttributeParserProvider extends AbstractProvider
implements IParserProvider {

  private IParser myParser;

  public IParser getParser(IAdaptable hint) {
    if (myParser == null) {
      myParser = new ISemanticParser() {

        public IContentAssistProcessor getCompletionProcessor(IAdaptable
          element) {
          return null;
        }

        public String getEditString(IAdaptable element, int flags) {
          Attribute attribute = getAttribute(element);
          return attribute.getName() != null ? attribute.getName()
            + ":" + (attribute.getDataType() != null ?
            attribute.getDataType().getName() : "") : "";
        }

        public ICommand getParseCommand(IAdaptable element,
          final String newString,   int flags) {
          int index = newString.indexOf(":");
          final String name;
          final String typeName;
```

```java
    if (index == 0) {
      name = "";
      typeName = newString.substring(index + 1);
    } else if (index > 0) {
      name = newString.substring(0, index).trim();
      typeName = newString.substring(index + 1).trim();
    } else if (index == -1 && newString.length() > 0) {
      name = newString;
      typeName = "";
    } else {
      name = "";
      typeName = "";
    }

    final Attribute attribute = getAttribute(element);
    final Datatype dataType = findType(typeName, attribute);

    TransactionalEditingDomain editingDomain = TransactionUtil
      .getEditingDomain(attribute);
    return new AbstractTransactionalCommand(editingDomain, "",
      Collections.singletonList(
      WorkspaceSynchronizer.getFile(attribute.eResource()))) {

      @Override
      protected CommandResult doExecuteWithResult(IProgressMonitor
        monitor, IAdaptable info) throws ExecutionException {
        if (newString.length() == 0) {
          return CommandResult.newErrorCommandResult(
            "Invalid input");
        }
        attribute.setName(name);
        attribute.setDataType(dataType);
        return CommandResult.newOKCommandResult();
      }
    };
  }

  private Datatype findType(final String typeName,
    final Attribute attribute) {
    Datatype type = null;
    if (typeName.length() > 0) {
      EList<Resource> resources =
        attribute.eResource().getResourceSet().getResources();
      for (Resource resource : resources) {
        for (EObject object : resource.getContents()) {
          if (object instanceof org.eclipse.oocore.Package) {
            type = findInPackage((org.eclipse.oocore.Package)
              object, typeName);
            if (type != null) return type;
          }
        }
      }
    }
    return type;
  }
```

```
private Datatype findInPackage(org.eclipse.oocore.Package pkg,
  String typeName) {
  for (PackageableElement element : pkg.getContents()) {
    if (element instanceof Datatype &&
      typeName.equals(element.getName())) {
      return (Datatype) element;
    }
    if (element instanceof org.eclipse.oocore.Package) {
      return findInPackage((org.eclipse.oocore.Package)
        element, typeName);
    }
  }
  return null;
}

public String getPrintString(IAdaptable element, int flags) {
  String printString = getEditString(element, flags);
  return printString.length() == 0 ? "<<...>>" : printString;
}

public boolean isAffectingEvent(Object event, int flags) {
  if (event instanceof Notification) {
    Notification emfNotification = (Notification) event;
    return !emfNotification.isTouch()
      && (emfNotification.getFeature() ==
      OocorePackage.eINSTANCE.getNamedElement_Name() ||
      emfNotification.getFeature() ==
      OocorePackage.eINSTANCE.getAttribute_DataType());
  }
  return false;
}

public IParserEditStatus isValidEditString(IAdaptable element,
  String editString) {
  return ParserEditStatus.EDITABLE_STATUS;
}

private Attribute getAttribute(IAdaptable adaptable) {
  return (Attribute) adaptable.getAdapter(EObject.class);
}

public boolean areSemanticElementsAffected(EObject listener,
  Object notification) {
  if (notification instanceof Notification) {
    Notification emfNotification = (Notification) notification;
    return !emfNotification.isTouch()
      && (emfNotification.getFeature() ==
      OocorePackage.eINSTANCE.getAttribute() ||
      emfNotification.getFeature() ==
      OocorePackage.eINSTANCE.getDatatype());
  }
  return false;
}
```

```
  public List<EObject> getSemanticElementsBeingParsed(EObject
    element) {
    List<EObject> result = new ArrayList<EObject>();
    if (element instanceof Attribute) {
      result.add(element);
    }
    return result;
  }
};}
return myParser;
}

public boolean provides(IOperation operation) {
  if (operation instanceof GetParserOperation) {
    IAdaptable hint = ((GetParserOperation) operation).getHint();
    String visualID = (String) hint.getAdapter(String.class);
    return AttributeEditPart.VISUAL_ID ==
      DncVisualIDRegistry.getVisualID(visualID)
      && hint.getAdapter(EObject.class) instanceof Attribute;
  }
  return false;
}
}
```

Starting at the bottom, we find that the `IProvider.provides()` method returns `true` if the `GetParserOperation` passed contains a hint that resolves to the `AttributeEditPart`'s visual ID and an instance of our `Attribute` class. With this parser provider registered as a service provider, its `getParser()` method is invoked to supply an implementation of `ISemanticParser`. The implementation of the parser is crude, but it functions adequately for our sample. Notice that it loads all models in the resource set that are looking for Datatypes to validate against. The idea with types is that a `types.oocore`, or similar, is provided and loaded automatically, or users are given the option to load their own types. The most important aspect of the parser is the `getParseCommand()` method. As with all model modifications that take place within the context of a GMF application, a transactional command is used within the editing domain to effect the change.

Operation Parser Provider

Our `Operation` parser provider needs to be slightly more complex than our `Attribute` parser provider, given the relative complexity of an `Operation` signature. We need to take into account the name of the operation, the return type, and each parameter name and type. As usual, we surround our parameters with parentheses and delimit them with commas. Types are followed by a colon for both parameters and return type—for example, `calculatePriceFor Quantity(item:Item, qty:Integer):BigDecimal`.

For our `Attribute` example, it was reasonable to implement the parser provider by hand, given that we had to deal with only two values. For more complex parsing, such as that required for our `Operation` parser provider, we really should define a grammar and use a parser generator to do the heavy lifting. In fact, looking again to the UML2 Tools project for examples, we find that JavaCC was used to produce parsers for UML operation fields, among others. This book does not provide the details of the implementation, but they are provided within the sample projects, including documentation throughout.

4.7 Summary

In this chapter, we explored in some detail the process of working with GMF to define a series of domain-specific diagrams. As the possible functionality of a diagramming surface may be quite extensive, we covered only some of the most popular use cases in this chapter, leaving detail about the tooling and runtime components to Chapter 11 as reference for adding your own functionality.

At this time, we move on to discuss a bit about the development of textual concrete syntaxes for our domain-specific languages.

CHAPTER 5

Developing a DSL Textual Syntax

You've seen how it's possible to create a graphical concrete syntax using Graphical Modeling Framework (GMF), but a graphical notation might not always be appropriate or sufficient for a domain-specific language (DSL). In software development, textual syntaxes are the most popular and well-supported means by which to work with programming languages, both general purpose and domain specific. Tools to generate parsers, abstract syntax trees, and semantic analysis are quite mature and plentiful. Frameworks designed to support editing, refactoring, versioning, comparison, and merging of textual languages are also common, with Eclipse representing perhaps the most popular on the planet today.

As discussed already, expressing an abstract syntax using metamodels is superior in many ways to using traditional methods of grammar definition. Fortunately, it's possible to combine abstract syntax definition, grammar specification, and the generation of textual editors that leverage a common underlying framework. Given the importance of textual syntaxes, their support in a DSL Toolkit is essential. An attractive goal is to provide support for simultaneous editing of textual and graphical elements for any language.

In the context of the Modeling project, two components within the Textual Modeling Framework (TMF) project support the development of textual syntaxes for DSLs. Furthermore, as the concept of "language workbenches" becomes increasingly popular, support continues to grow for the generation of high-quality textual editors for a provided language grammar. Within Eclipse, the IDE Meta-Tooling Platform (IMP) project aims to provide such support. In the future, the components of TMF are expected to use IMP as a complementary component for developing textual editors for languages based on an underlying Ecore-based abstract syntax.

At the time of this writing, the TMF project is just underway, and the IMP project is updating its support to allow for the generation of editors for the Eclipse 3.3 platform. Unfortunately, much work remains to be done before a comprehensive chapter on developing a DSL textual syntax can be written that will not be outdated as soon as it is published. Therefore, this chapter introduces each of the two TMF components at a high level, leaving details to the sample projects and a subsequent version of this book. In the meantime, you can visit the TMF home page and wiki to get the latest information on the development progress of these important components.

5.1 Xtext

Xtext is a component of TMF that supports the development of a DSL grammar using an Extended Backus-Naur Form (EBNF)-like language, which can use this to generate an Ecore-based metamodel, Eclipse-based text editor, and corresponding ANTLR-based parser. Unfortunately, the default nature of Xtext is to begin with a grammar and produce an Ecore model, rather than begin with an Ecore model and derive the grammar. Nevertheless, it allows for transformation to and from an Ecore-based model, thereby providing for interoperability with EMF-based technologies such as QVT Operational Mapping Language (QVTO) and Xpand. Additionally, Xtext allows a grammar specification to reference an existing metamodel by using an import mechanism, which gets us closer to the ideal case.

The Checks language is used in the context of the generated metamodel to validate the language semantics. The editor can provide validation to give the user feedback in the form of error and warning messages, complete with the expected Eclipse decorators and markers. Alternatively, validation can be provided during workflow of the model instances in the context of model-to-model or model-to-text transformation. Furthermore, Xtext registers an EMF ResourceFactory for the generated DSL file extension, allowing it to read in (but not write) an instance of the model from the textual syntax.

Although Xtext is capable of generating a functional Eclipse textual editor, complete with syntax highlighting, code assist, outline view, and so on, it does not yet use the IMP project. Hopefully, Xtext and its TMF counterpart, Textual Concrete Syntax (TCS), will provide interoperability with IMP in the future, thereby supporting the proper separation of concerns and reducing duplicated effort in the area of textual editor generation.

At the time of this writing, Xtext is available only from the GMT downloads and includes dependencies to underlying technologies that are incompatible with the versions used to develop the samples in this book. Therefore, this book does not include Xtext examples; you can visit the Xtext component Web site for examples and additional information.

5.2 TCS

The TCS component of TMF provides an alternative to Xtext in defining a textual concrete syntax for a DSL. TCS is itself a DSL that facilitates specifying a textual syntax by linking syntactic information to a metamodel. In doing so, it allows an Ecore-based model to be used with a TCS model to generate a grammar. Sufficient richness of definition allows TCS to generate both model-to-text and text-to-model capabilities.

TCS can produce an annotated grammar using an ATL transformation to be used by the ANTLR parser generator. This provides the *injector* component for text-to-model translation. An *extractor* is derived from the language metamodel and TCS model and is used to provide model-to-text translation. The extractor is based on an interpreter that may be used for any language, although it is possible to generate an extractor per DSL.

As with Xtext, TCS does not yet use the IMP project for production of its text editor. Instead, TCS uses the Textual Generic Editor (TGE), which builds upon TCS to provide the editor, outline view, and text-to-model traceability. TCS does provide a "zoo" of languages that have been defined and are available from the project Web site.

At the time of this writing, no downloads are available for TCS, although code is present in the CVS repository. Therefore, this book does not provide detailed examples or sample projects at this time. When TCS and Xtext mature and provide integration with IMP, the book's sample applications likely will include a textual syntax using one of these components.

5.3 Summary

The ability to define and generate support for textual concrete syntaxes is essential for the future of DSL tooling. With Xtext and TCS providing the beginnings of this last major element in our Eclipse DSL Toolkit, look to the TMF project website and future editions of this book for detailed information on their usage.

Next, we'll explore model transformation, beginning with model-to-model transformation using QVT Operational Mapping Language.

CHAPTER 6

Developing Model-to-Model Transformations

A model is often used as the source or target of a Model-to-Model Transformation (M2M). Within the Modeling project, the M2M project has two components to provide transformation capabilities: Atlas Transformation Language (ATL) and Query/View/Transformation (QVT). This book does not cover ATL, but it is similar to QVT. QVT is actually a collection of three transformation languages, but this book covers only the Operational Mapping Language (OML). The other languages of QVT are its Relations language and the Core language; the Relations language has just released its first build at Eclipse.

6.1 Transformation Techniques

Much has been written on model transformation and translation. Translation strives to provide semantic equivalence between two models and is beyond the scope of this book. Instead, I focus on using OML to define transformations between domain-specific languages (DSLs) and I consider several approaches to transformation and generation. As with everything, there are implementation choices to make, each with its pros and cons. In the case of transformation, we must consider where it makes the best sense to implement mappings between models. For example, consider the mapping between the notation model Business Process Modeling Notation (BPMN) and Business Process Execution Language (BPEL). The BPMN specification defines a mapping, but the Toolsmith must determine where it's best to implement it. Imagine the mapping model discussed earlier in the context of the Graphical Modeling Framework (GMF) as one possibility. In this case, a graphical definition would represent the elements of BPMN, and the domain model would be derived from the BPEL XML Schema.

Of course, the expressiveness of the GMF mapping model is insufficient to capture the complete mapping, leaving the Toolsmith to implement the rest in Java. The result would be a diagram capable of directly editing a BPEL model.

Another approach would be to create a domain model of BPMN in Eclipse Modeling Framework (EMF), for example, and map the notation directly to this model. In the case of BPMN2, this would be the BPDM metamodel. Instances of the BPMN model would be used in an M2M transformation to produce a BPEL model instance, with the transformation definition embodying the mapping from BPMN to BPEL provided in the specification. By creating an instance of the BPEL model that was derived from the XML Schema, EMF would serialize it as a valid BPEL document. Otherwise, as is the case for generating Java, an M2M transformation would result in an instance of a Java model that would have dedicated Model-to-Text Transformation (M2T) templates used to generate the compilation units as files.

Still another option would be to use this BPMN instance as input to model-to-text templates. In this case, the logic required to map from BPMN to BPEL would exist within the template language—in the case of Xpand, mostly using its Xtend language.

Many techniques must be considered when dealing with model transformation, both model-to-model and model-to-text. Chaining models through a sequence of transformations is a likely scenario, as is the case in which multiple input and/or output models are involved. Intermediate models might be required to overcome certain complexities or adapt one model for use in another predefined transformation. In fact, OML provides the capability to define a metamodel that can be used on-the-fly within the context of a transformation.

As mentioned, each of these approaches has its pros and cons. The Toolsmith must determine the appropriate technique based on stated requirements, flexibility, personal preference, maintainability, and other considerations.

6.2 Model Refactoring

Model transformation can be used for model refactoring, specifically through the use of in-place transformations. Using a transformation defined on a model that targets the same instance as the input model, it is possible to create complex refactorings.

The following is a simple example of model refactoring using QVT OML. A requirements model is passed in and out, as indicated by `inout` on both the transformation declaration and the mappings. In this case, requirement groups and their contained requirements have some of their attributes reset. Each ID attribute is reset to a sequential number, and each requirement type is set to non-functional.

```
modeltype requirements 'strict'

  uses 'http://www.eclipse.org/2008/requirements';

transformation reset(inout model : requirements);

property groupCounter : Integer = 0;
property reqCounter : Integer = 0;

main() {
  model.rootObjects()[Model].groups.map resetValues();
}

mapping inout requirements::RequirementGroup::resetValues() {
  init {
    self.id := 'G' + this.groupCounter.toString();
    this.groupCounter := this.groupCounter + 1;
    self.requirements.map resetValues();
    self.children.map resetValues();
  }
}

mapping inout requirements::Requirement::resetValues() {
  init {
    self.type := Type::NONFUNCTIONAL;
    self.id := 'R' + this.reqCounter.toString();
    this.reqCounter := this.reqCounter + 1;
    self.children.map resetValues();
  }
}
```

COMMENT

Another means by which to apply a pattern-based transformation capability to EMF models is by leveraging the Tiger project (http://tfs.cs.tu-berlin. de/tigerprj/). Although this is not an Eclipse Modeling project, it is a useful technology that uses graph transformation to map source and target model patterns to models.

6.3 Model Migration

A consideration when developing a DSL is how to provide a means for clients to migrate to future versions. Model transformation can provide the mechanism, particularly if the Toolsmith uses the recommended URI naming scheme that includes version information (typically a year). This allows the platform to recognize model versions and enables transformations to be invoked, thereby updating client models automatically or upon explicit invocation. Of course, this implies that both versions of the metamodel are deployed using a corresponding version change so that each can be loaded into the environment. Alternatively, just the old .ecore could be deployed with the newer one, as long as the transformation can locate both models.

For example, let's say that our Requirements model was refactored so that a new abstract `ModelElement` class were introduced as a superclass for `Requirement` and `RequirementGroup`. With that, our `Model` class changed its main containment reference from `groups : RequirementGroup` to `elements : ModelElement`. Furthermore, we combined our `RequirementGroup` `children : RequirementGroup` and `requirements : Requirement` containments into a single `children : ModelElement` relationship. Figures 6-1 and 6-2 are the two models for reference, beginning with the before version.

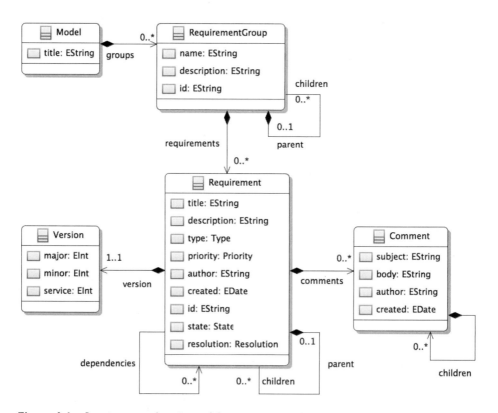

Figure 6-1   Requirements domain model

Figure 6-2 shows the version after the changes mentioned.

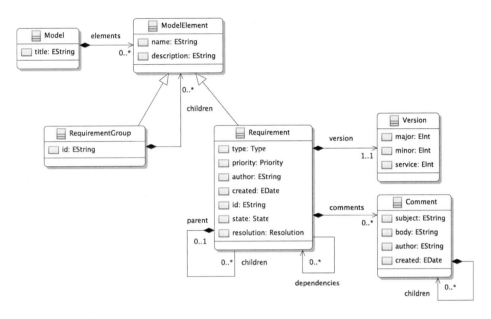

Figure 6-2   Modified requirements domain model

To provide for the migration of user models from the original version to the later version, we could deploy a transformation such as the following QVT.

```
modeltype old 'strict' uses 'http://www.eclipse.org/2008/requirements';
modeltype new 'strict' uses
➥'http://www.eclipse.org/2008a/requirements';

transformation migrate(in oldModel : old, out newModel : new);

main() {
  oldModel.rootObjects()[Model]->map toNew();
}

mapping old::Model::toNew() : new::Model {
  title := self.title;
  elements += self.groups.map toGroup();
}

mapping old::RequirementGroup::toGroup() : new::RequirementGroup {
  name := self.name;
  id := self.id;
  description := self.description;
  children += self.children.map toGroup();
```

```
    children += self.requirements.map toRequirement();
}

mapping old::Requirement::toRequirement() : new::Requirement {
    id := self.id;
    name := self.title;
    description := self.description;
    type := self.type.toType();
    children += self.children.map toRequirement();
    priority := self.priority.toPriority();
    author := self.author;
    created := self.created;
    comments += self.comments.map toComment();
    version := self.version.map toVersion();
    dependencies += self.dependencies.late resolve(new::Requirement);
    scenario := self.scenario;
    state := self.state.toState();
    resolution := self.resolution.toResolution();
}

mapping old::Comment::toComment() : new::Comment {
    subject := self.subject;
    body := self.body;
    author := self.author;
    created := self.created;
    children += self.children.map toComment();
}

mapping old::Version::toVersion() : new::Version {
    major := self.major;
    minor := self.minor;
    service := self.service;
}

query old::State::toState() : new::State {
    var state : new::State := null;
    switch {
        (self = old::State::NEW) ? state := new::State::NEW;
        (self = old::State::REVIEWED) ?
         state := new::State::REVIEWED;
        (self = old::State::APPROVED) ?
         state := new::State::APPROVED;
        (self = old::State::RESOLVED) ?
         state := new::State::RESOLVED;
        else ? assert fatal (false)
         with log('State unsupported', self);
    };
    return state;
}

-- The remaining queries toType(), toPriority(), and toResolution()
➥not shown
```

The transformation uses the URIs of the models to distinguish between them. The details of the transformation definition will become more clear after you learn more about QVT in the next section and in Chapter 13, "Query/View/ Transformation Operational Mapping Language." Afterward, you might want to return to this example.

6.4 Model Merge

QVT Operational Mapping Language is capable of dealing with multiple input and output models. One application of this is for merging models, as in the following example. Another example is in combining aspects of GMF's mapping, tooling, and domain models during transformation to its generator model. This transformation has been written and is awaiting incorporation into GMF as an alternative and more flexible means of creating the gmfgen model.

This example does not show the main body of the transformation, but the signature and main mapping indicate the intent. Here, the contents of an Eclipse product definition model are merged with the minimal content of an Eclipse Packaging Project configuration model to output a complete configuration model for use in producing a package. As shown in the transformation signature, two input models are defined along with one output model. Alternatively, the input configuration model could be filled out using the product definition model content.

```
modeltype config uses "http://www.eclipse.org/epp/config";
modeltype product uses "http://www.eclipse.org/pde/product";

transformation product2epp(in prod : product, in base : config,
  out config : config);

configuration property rcpVersion : String;

main(in inProd : product::Product,
     in baseConfig : config::DocumentRoot,
     out outConfig : config::ConfigurationType) {

  assert fatal (inProd.useFeatures)
    with log('Must use feature-based product definition');

  outConfig := inProd.map toEPPConfig();
  outConfig.updateSites := baseConfig._configuration.updateSites
    ->first().map toUpdateSites();
  outConfig.rootFileFolder := baseConfig._configuration.rootFileFolder
    ->first().map toRootFileFolder();
  outConfig.extensionSite := baseConfig._configuration.extensionSite
    ->first().map toExtensionSite();
}
```

6.5 M2M QVT Operational Mapping Language

OML is an Object Constraint Language (OCL)-based procedural language that provides a low-level method for defining model-to-model transformations. OCL provides the "Query" in QVT, and "low-level" refers to the difference between OML and its high-level counterpart, the QVT Relations language. Much as with a Java class file, an OML definition (`*.qvto` file) has a list of imported models, a main operation, a series of mappings and queries that resemble class methods, and so on. Aside from the need to be familiar with the OCL and some extensions added to produce side effects, OML should be fairly easy for most developers to get started using. Those already familiar with OCL should find it much easier to use. This section discusses the basic structure of an OML file and the language.

I've provided an implementation of the OML as a component of the M2M project. Here we look at the features of this project before going through a worked example.

6.5.1 QVT Project

QVT OML provides its own project wizard that installs the appropriate nature and builder. The DSL Toolkit project wizard from Amalgam also installs the QVT OML nature and builder. The **QVT Operational Project** wizard can be invoked from the Eclipse **New** dialog (Ctrl+N) in the **Model to Model Transformation** category. You can specify a source container for transformation location within the project structure, with the default being `/transforms`. Specifying a source container enables you to place transformation definitions in any project folder without having to specify the folder in the namespace of the definition itself, similar to a Java source folder concept.

The project wizard supports the creation of a library or transformation file during project creation. Otherwise, you can use a **QVT Operational Library** and **QVT Operational Transformation** wizard to add these elements to an existing QVT project. Figure 6-3 shows the QVT project wizard dialog.

To resolve workspace domain models, a QVT project includes **Metamodel Mappings** in its properties, as seen in Figure 6-4. Entries made here allow the engine to map an NS URI to a physical `.ecore` model in the workspace. Note that it's also possible to use an eclipse `platform:/plugin/...` or `platform:/resource/...` URI directly in a **modeltype** declaration.

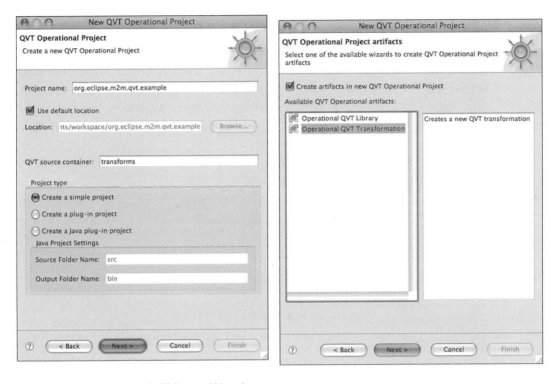

Figure 6-3   Operational QVT Project Wizard

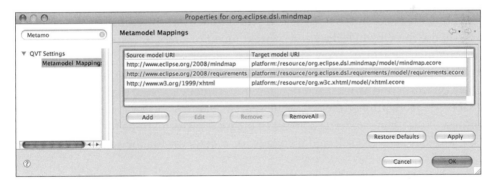

Figure 6-4   Metamodel mapping properties

6.5.2 QVT OML Editor

Eclipse M2M QVT Operational (QVTO) provides an editor for working with QVT OML (*.qvto) files, with many of the features you'd expect from an Eclipse-based editor (although there is room for improvement). Code completion, syntax highlighting, templates, navigation into metamodel browser, error markers, and more are provided. Figure 6-5 is an example of code completion available in the editor.

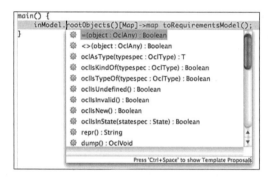

Figure 6-5   Operational QVT code completion

6.5.3 Metamodel Explorer

Metamodel Explorer view shows a list of registered Ecore models in the platform and the workspace. It provides a navigation link from the editor to this navigator. You use the **Open Declaration** context menu or press **F3** with the cursor over a metamodel element to open **Metamodel Explorer** (if it is not already open) and expand the view to the selected element. Figure 6-6 is an image of the view and shows platform and workspace registered metamodels. Note that the view has a number of navigation, filtering, and search features. Still, you can imagine a number of nice features here: actions to create transformations for selected models, mappings between selected elements, or a diagram for the selected model(s).

6.5.4 Launch Configuration

To run transformations, an Eclipse launch configuration type is added for Operational QVT. Launch configurations have three tabs for setting launch parameters: **Transformation**, **Configuration**, and **Common**. The **Transformation** tab includes the main properties, as shown in Figure 6-7. This tab specifies the launch configuration name, transformation module and trace file option, and input and output transformation parameters.

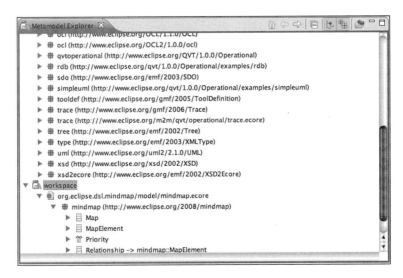

Figure 6-6 Metamodel Explorer

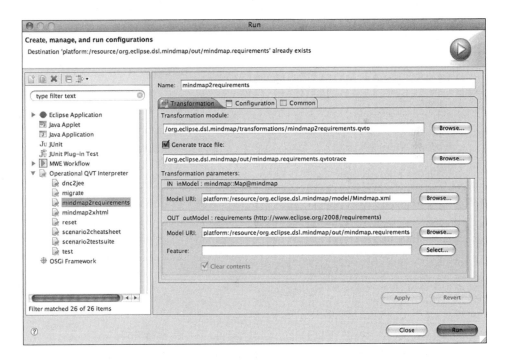

Figure 6-7 Operational QVT launch configuration

Finally, the **Common** tab shown in Figure 6-8 includes options for saving the launch configuration to a file, displaying as a **Run** favorite menu item, console encoding, and redirecting standard input and output. Saving the output to a file can be useful when using the `log()` feature of Operational QVT because the default output is to the **Console** view.

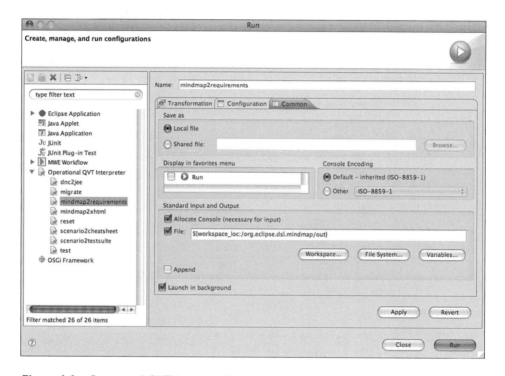

Figure 6-8   Operational QVT launch configuration—Common tab

6.5.5 Trace Model

Selecting the **Generate a Trace File** option in the launch configuration produces a `*.qvtotrace` file upon execution. Section 13.5.7, "Trace Model," discusses the trace model, which contains information on the mapping executions, including input and output instance model data.

The trace model comes with its own editor, which enables you to examine the trace in a tree view, as shown in Figure 6-9.

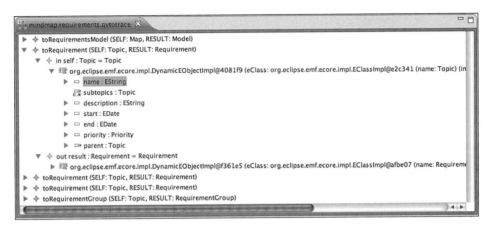

Figure 6-9   Operational QVT trace model

6.5.6 Leveraging OCL in EMF Models

As discussed in Section 3.2.4, "Applying OCL," you can add OCL to annotations in an EMF model and use them during code generation to provide implementations of constraints, method bodies, and derived features. M2M OML also can interpret OCL statements in models before generation, which greatly helps in writing QVT scripts that rely on these features. After being deployed, OCL statements are invoked on model instances and also are available to deployed transformations.

6.5.7 Ant Tasks

A set of Ant tasks is also available for invoking QVTO transformations heedlessly or in a transformation sequence with other M2M or M2T transformations, for example. The following is an example of how the `qvto.interpretedTransformation` task is configured. The order of `targeturidef` elements matches the order of models defined in the transformation signature.

```
<qvto.interpretedTransformation
    transformation="/product2epp.qvto"
    tracefile="/product2epp.qvtotrace"
    resulturiproperty="config">
    <targeturidef
        targeturi="platform:/resource/example/modeling.product"
    />
```

```
    <targeturidef
        targeturi="platform:/resource/example/modeling.config"
    />
</qvto.interpretedTransformation>
```

TIP

When launching QVT Ant tasks within Eclipse, be sure to select **Run in the Same JRE As the Workspace** on the **JRE** tab of the Ant launch configuration so that the custom tasks are found. They're located within the `antTasks.jar` file in the `org.eclipse.m2m.qvt.oml.runtime` bundle.

6.6 Transforming a Mindmap to Requirements

Returning to our mindmap example, let's use an instance of our *mindmap* model to produce a corresponding *requirements* model. Looking at the two domain models developed earlier, we can see that several elements should map nicely. When we created each DSL, we anticipated transforming from one to the other, which makes it easier but is not always the case. Using preexisting models or models that have different purposes does not typically make for such a clean mapping.

Operational QVT and Amalgam's DSL Toolkit provide projects with the appropriate nature and builder, so we don't need to manually add this nature to our DSL project. If you want to add transformations to another type of project, you can do this by opening the `.project` file in a text editor and adding the following content:

```
<buildSpec>
  <buildCommand>
    <name>org.eclipse.m2m.qvt.oml.QvtBuilder</name>
    <arguments>
      <dictionary>
        <key>src_container</key>
        <value>transforms</value>
      </dictionary>
    </arguments>
  </buildCommand>
</buildSpec>
<natures>
  <nature>org.eclipse.m2m.qvt.oml.project.TransformationNature</nature>
</natures>
```

As mentioned earlier, to have our workspace `mindmap.ecore` available to the editor, engine, and metamodel browser, we need to provide a metamodel mapping. In the project properties of `org.eclipse.dsl.mindmap`, add an entry in the **Metamodel Mappings** section using the **Browse** button to locate your `mindmap.ecore` model in the workspace. Likewise, you need to register the target `requirements.ecore` model, similar to what is shown in Section 6.5.1, "QVT Project."

Select the `/transformations` folder in our mindmap DSL project and invoke the Operational QVT Transformation wizard from **File → New → Other → Model Transformation → Operational QVT Transformation**. Note that when not using the DSL Toolkit, the wizard is found in **File → New → Other → Model to Model Transformation → Operational QVT Transformation**. Create a new `mindmap2requirements.qvto` transformation in the selected `/transformations` folder and select **Finish** to complete the wizard.

In the opened editor, you'll see the skeleton QVT, which is a simple transformation declaration statement with empty main mapping. Fill out this skeleton with the following to make it more complete:

```
modeltype mindmap 'strict' uses 'http://www.eclipse.org/2008/mindmap';
modeltype requirements 'strict' uses
'http://www.eclipse.org/2008/requirements';

transformation mindmap2requirements(in inModel:mindmap,
  out outModel:requirements);

main()
{
  inModel.rootObjects()[Map]->map toRequirementsModel();
}
```

At the top, we find the `transformation` declaration, along with `model-type` entries for our source and target models. The `modeltype` declarations include the `strict` qualifier, indicating that only models that conform with the specified URI will be accepted as inputs. The `main` entry point contains the standard form for obtaining the root model object and invoking our first mapping `toRequirementsModel()`. The use of brackets around the input model's `Map` class is shorthand notation for combined collect and select operations, which Section 13.5.3, "Imperative Iterate Expressions," covers. We expect to find a `Map` object at the root of our model, which we obtain and use as the input to the mapping that returns a requirements `Model` instance. To begin, let's just map our

Map's `title` attribute to the requirement `Model`'s `title` attribute, as shown here:

```
mapping mindmap::Map::toRequirementsModel() : requirements::Model {
    title := self.title;
}
```

The left part of the assignment represents the object being instantiated by the mapping, while the keyword `self` refers to the mappings's context object type. To run and test this simple transformation, we have at least a couple options. We can launch a runtime instance of our workbench, create a new project and instance model for our Mindmap DSL, and invoke the transformation using a launch configuration on the imported transformation. Or we can create a dynamic instance of our mindmap and model in our development workspace and test the transformation without launching. The second approach is easier, so begin by opening the `mindmap.ecore` model in the default EMF editor, right-clicking on the root element, and selecting **Create Dynamic Instance**. Save the instance file as `Mindmap.xmi` in the /model folder of our mindmap DSL project and enter some test instances. Right now, it's necessary only to set the title of the `Map` object.

We need a launch configuration to invoke our QVT transformation on the `Mindmap.xmi` instance file. Select the `mindmap2requirements.qvto` file in the navigator and, from **Run → Open Run Dialog**, create a new **Operational QVT Interpreter** configuration. Locate our `Mindmap.xmi` file as the **IN** model in **Transformation parameters**, and specify a new model adjacent to the QVT file in the /transformations folder, as shown in the dialog image in Section 6.5.4, "Launch Configuration."

From the **Run** menu, execute the transformation and observe the new requirement model and trace file in the /transformations folder. We'd need to open the created `mindmap.requirements` model in our runtime workbench to use its generated editor, so for now you can simply open it in a text editor to confirm that the contents look correct. Another option is to use the **Sample Reflective Ecore Model Editor**. You can see that our requirements model `title` is set, corresponding to the value specified in your `Mindmap.xmi` model.

Next, we must determine the desired output structure of our requirements model, given the structure of our input mindmap model. For convenience, Figures 6-10 and 6-11 show simplified diagrams of each model.

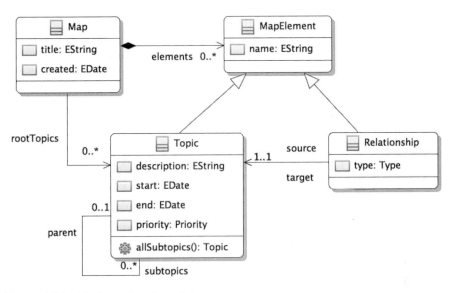

Figure 6-10 Mindmap domain model

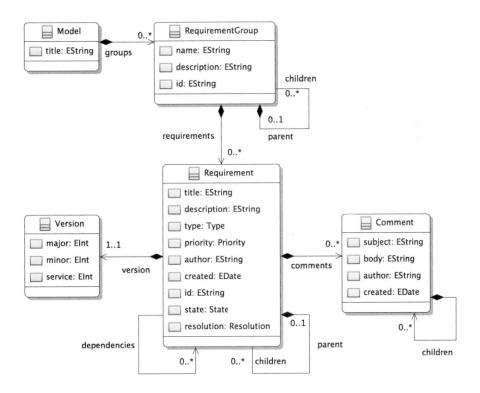

Figure 6-11 Requirements domain model

Let's say that, for each root Topic on the diagram, we want to create a RequirementGroup. For each subtopic of the root Topic, we will add a Requirement to the RequirementGroup. Finally, we'll add a dependency relationship between Requirement objects so that we have a Relationship between Topic elements that are of Type::DEPENDENCY. Recalling our requirements diagram notation, a RequirementGroup is a rounded rectangle, while child Requirement objects will be a circle connected with solid lines. Dependency links will be drawn as dashed lines with open arrow heads.

Figure 6-12 is an example diagram, to give you a better understanding of where we're headed with this transformation. Following the transformation, you can use the generated action to initialize a requirements diagram from our new model instance, to create the diagram in our runtime workspace.

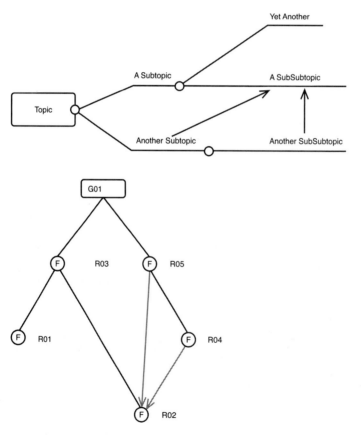

Figure 6-12   Mindmap and requirement diagrams

Although the two diagrams are similar, the structure of their domain models is quite different. The subtopics in our mindmap are contained in the canvas element (`Map::elements`) and linked using noncontainment references. In the requirements model, `Requirement` and `RequirementGroup` elements have children that are contained by their parents. Now let's take a look at the QVT that enables us to transform these models. The following is an updated `toRequirementsModel()` mapping in our `mindmap2requirements` transformation definition.

```
transformation mindmap2requirements(in inModel : mindmap,

  out outModel : requirements);

property dependencies : Set(Relationship) = null;
property reqCtr : Integer = 1;
property grpCtr : Integer = 1;

main() {
  inModel.rootObjects()[Map]->map toRequirementsModel();
}

mapping mindmap::Map::toRequirementsModel() : requirements::Model {
  init {
    this.dependencies := self.dependencies();
  }
  title := self.title;
  groups += self.rootTopics.map toRequirementGroup()->asOrderedSet();
}
```

Notice that a `dependency` property is declared at the top of the transformation and is initialized using a `dependencies()` query in the main mapping's `init{}` block. `Relationship` elements are stored within the same containment feature of our `Map` as `Topic` elements, so we can use this query to collect all those `Relationships` of type `DEPENDENCY` for use in our `toRequirement()` mapping. This is the `dependencies()` query:

```
query mindmap::Map::dependencies() : Set(mindmap::Relationship) {
  return self.elements->select(oclIsTypeOf(mindmap::Relationship))
    ->select(c | c.oclAsType(mindmap::Relationship).type =
    mindmap::Type::DEPENDENCY)
      ->collect(oclAsType(mindmap::Relationship))->asSet();
}
```

Recall that we implemented the derived `rootTopics` reference of our `Map` class using OCL in Section 3.3, "Developing the Mindmap Domain Model." We could use the OCL used to derive the root `Topics` within this QVT script, but

having it implemented in our model makes the script cleaner and eliminates the
need to repeat the code here, in code generation templates, and so on. The root
Topic elements are each mapped to RequirementGroup elements using the following toRequirementGroup() mapping. From the updated transformation
declaration shown previously, you can see two properties used as counters to
generate group and requirement indexes.

```
mapping mindmap::Topic::toRequirementGroup() :

  requirements::RequirementGroup {
  init {
    result := object requirements::RequirementGroup {
      name := self.name;
      id := 'G0' + this.grpCtr.toString();
      requirements += self.subtopics.map toRequirement();
    }
  }
  end {
    this.grpCtr := grpCtr + 1;
  }
}
```

A straightforward map of the Topic name attribute to the
RequirementGroup name attribute is followed by an invocation of the
toRequirement() mapping for each of the subtopic references. This is this final
mapping in our transformation:

```
mapping mindmap::Topic::toRequirement() : requirements::Requirement {
  title := self.name;
  children += self.subtopics.map toRequirement();
  id := 'R0' + this.reqCtr.toString();
  version := object requirements::Version {
    major := 1;
  };
  dependencies += this.dependencies->select(source = self).target.late
      resolveIn(mindmap::Topic::toRequirement,
        requirements::Requirement);
  end {
    this.reqCtr := reqCtr + 1;
  }
}
```

The Topic name attribute maps to the Requirement title, as subtopics are
recursively mapped to child Requirements. The Requirement dependencies
reference is populated with Requirement objects created from Topic elements
that are targets of mindmap DEPENDENCY relationships collected earlier. We cannot guarantee that these Topic elements have been already mapped to

Requirement objects, so we use late resolveIn to invoke this mapping at the end of the transformation. The alternative here is to map dependencies in the end{} block of our main mapping. Section 13.5.5, "Mapping Invocation," gives an in-depth discussion of resolution operators in the context of this transformation. Finally, note that Relationship references between root Topic elements are missed, which is okay because root Topics are mapped to RequirementGroup objects that have no dependency relationships.

Before testing this update to the transformation, we need to more completely populate our Mindmap.xmi dynamic instance model. Add a few Topics to the Map and include subtopic references, as well as at least one DEPENDENCY Relationship to test our mappings fully. Figure 6-13 shows a simple test model instance in our reflective Ecore editor.

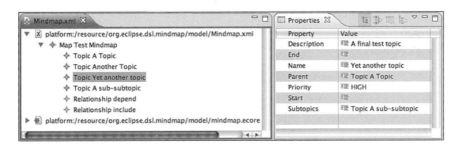

Figure 6-13   Mindmap dynamic instance model

If we deploy the transformation and run it on an actual instance of a mindmap model, the output will be a requirements model, as expected. However, combining our EMF and GMF editors for our requirements model (done in Section 4.4.6, "Integrating EMF and GMF Editors") required us to persist both the diagram and domain models within a single file. If we tried to open the resulting *.requirements file, we would get an error stating that the file contains no diagram. Fortunately, the GMF-generated diagram-initialization action takes care of the problem by initializing the diagram content and peristing the result within a *.requirements file. When deploying the diagram and transformation, we want to provide an action that takes care of this step automatically after the transformation.

6.7 Transforming a Mindmap to XHTML

To provide reporting for our mindmap, we use an xhtml.ecore model to serve as the target of a model-to-model transformation. This approach complements the one taken in Section 7.4, "Generating HTML," where we use Xpand to generate

HTML from our requirements model. In this case, we also need to import the XHTML schema into EMF to create our model. EMF then provides serialized instance models that conform to the schema, thereby producing valid HTML documents. We'll be able to work only with model-to-model transformation scripts, leaving the hassle of dealing with angle brackets for the requirements report.

6.7.1 Importing an XSD

Unfortunately, no XHTML model is present in our Metamodel Explorer view, even with the WebTools project installed. Nevertheless, a simple search for "xhtml xsd" on the Internet revealed what we need at www.w3.org/2002/08/xhtml/xhtml1-strict.xsd.

We start by creating a new `org.w3c.xhtml` **DSL Project** and copying the previous link to the Clipboard; as you will see, you don't need to download the model. Right-click the model folder and select **New → Other → Domain-Specific Language → Domain Generator Model** (Ctrl+3 → Domain Gen). Name the EMF generator model `xhtml.genmodel` and proceed to the next page in the wizard, where you select the **XML Schema** model importer. If you don't see this importer, you need to install the XSD feature from the EMF or Ganymede update site. The next page provides a **Model URIs** field where you paste the URL to the schema, followed by **Load**. On the **Package Selection** page, check the `org.w3._1999.xhtml` package in the **Root packages** table and the XMLNamespace **Referenced generator models** table, as shown in Figure 6-14.

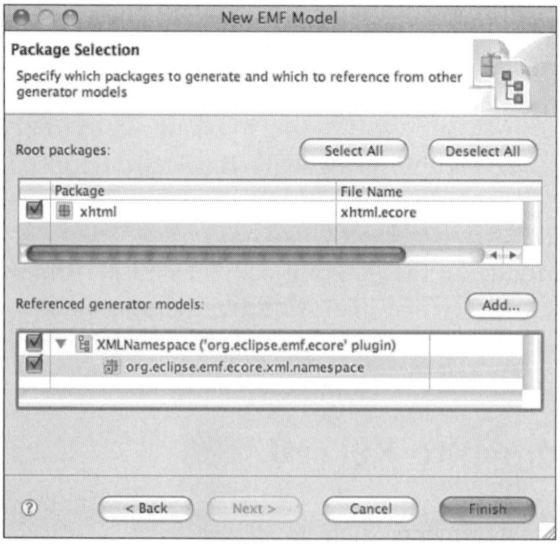

Figure 6-14   New EMF Model dialog

After **Finish,** you'll see xhtml.ecore and xhtml.genmodel in the project, with the genmodel open in the editor. Select the xhtml root package and change the Base Package property to org.w3c, replacing the org.w3._1999 derived from the schema. We use this model only as an example, so we don't spend time tweaking the remainder of the generation properties or provide much in terms of implementation enhancement beyond the defaults. If you're interested, you can take some time to browse the Ecore model that can be initialized from the schema. If you've seen HTML, the elements and attributes should look familiar.

6.7.2 Creating the mindmap2xhtml QVT

Our QVT implementation lets us work with workspace Ecore models, so there's no need to generate the XHTML model code yet. When we deploy our mindmap, however, we will need to do so. For now, we'll create a new mindmap2xhtml.qvto file in our /transformations folder of the org.eclipse.dsl.mindmap project. When you're finished with this, go to the project properties and add the local xhtml.ecore file to the **QVT Settings →
Metamodel Mappings** section so that the editor can resolve the model. Replace the default transformation content with this starter code:

```
modeltype mindmap 'strict' uses 'http://www.eclipse.org/2008/mindmap';
modeltype xhtml 'strict' uses 'http://www.w3.org/1999/xhtml';

transformation mindmap2xhtml(in inModel : mindmap,
  out outModel : xhtml);

main() {
  inModel.rootObjects()[Map]->map toXHTML();
}

mapping mindmap::Map::toXHTML() : xhtml::DocumentRoot {
  html += object xhtml::HtmlType {
    head := object xhtml::HeadType {

    };
    _body := object xhtml::BodyType {

    };
  }
}
```

So far, so good. Next we discover that there's no way to declare text between elements such as <p> or <li>, if we add their element type to the body. QVTO cannot currently deal with statements such as mixed += 'text'; because mixed is of type EFeatureMapEntry and cannot be set with a string. A workaround for this is to extend model elements that contain a string within their serialized output by XMLTypeDocumentRoot. With that, we need to delete their mixed:EFeatureMapEntry because XMLTypeDocumentRoot declares one as well. Declaring this eSuperType for the Inline and Flow classes of our xhtml.ecore model should take care of most elements we need. We'll add this supertype to more elements as needed when creating our script. Additionally, we need to change some attributes to be of type AnySimpleType (for example, colspan in ThType). A nice feature of the QVTO editor is that it recognizes model changes on-the-fly, so each update is immediately available.

Now our QVT can use the text:EString attribute of XMLTypeDocument root, as you can see in this simple test code:

```
mapping mindmap::Map::toXHTML() : xhtml::DocumentRoot {
  html += object xhtml::HtmlType {
    head := object xhtml::HeadType {

    };
    _body := object xhtml::BodyType {
      h1 += object xhtml::H1Type {
        text += 'test';
      };
    };
  }
}
```

Continuing now with our mindmap report definition, we declare a property at the top of the transformation to hold the set of Relationship elements from our mindmap. The property is initialized in the initialization section of our first mapping using shorthand [] notation for the usual collect and select operations. We use the relations property in the Topic's toContentItem() mapping to list related Topics and their relationship type.

The main mapping calls the toXHTML() mapping, which takes our Map and returns our XHTML DocumentRoot. You can see the main structure of the resulting document here, as the usual <html>, <head>, and <body> elements are constructed. The body defines a title section, content index, and list of topics, with the last two calling to their respective toIndexItem() and toContentItem() mappings. The rest of the transformation follows, with the getType() and getPriority() queries illustrating the use of the QVT switch construct. It's used frequently when dealing with enumeration types because no better alternative currently exists. Another improvement here would be to incorporate the string counter functions in QVT to produce index anchors instead of depending on Topic names, which might not be unique.

```
modeltype mindmap 'strict' uses 'http://www.eclipse.org/2008/mindmap';
modeltype xhtml 'strict' uses 'http://www.w3.org/1999/xhtml';

transformation mindmap2xhtml(in inModel : mindmap,
  out outModel : xhtml);

property relations : Set(mindmap::Relationship) = null;

main() {
  inModel.rootObjects()[Map]->map toXHTML();
}

mapping mindmap::Map::toXHTML() : xhtml::DocumentRoot {
  init {
    this.relations := self.elements[mindmap::Relationship];
  }
  html += object HtmlType {
    head := object HeadType {
      title := object TitleType {
        text += self.title + ' Report';
      };
    };
    _body := object BodyType {
      h1 += object H1Type {
        text += self.title + ' Report';
      };
      h2 += object H2Type {
        text += 'Contents';
      };
      ul += object UlType {
        li += self.rootTopics.map toIndexItem();
      };
      hr += object HrType {};
      div += self.elements[mindmap::Topic].map toContentItem();
    };
  };
}

query mindmap::Topic::getRelations() : Set(mindmap::Relationship) {
  return relations->select(r | r.source = self)->asSet();
}

mapping mindmap::Topic::toIndexItem() : xhtml::LiType {
  init {
    result := object LiType {
      a += object AType {
        href := '#' + self.name;
        text += self.name;
      };
    };
    if not self.subtopics->isEmpty() then {
      result.ul += object UlType {
        li += self.subtopics.map toIndexItem();
      };
```

```
    } endif;
  }
}

mapping mindmap::Topic::toContentItem() : xhtml::DivType {
  table += object TableType {
    tbody += object TbodyType {
      tr += object TrType {
        th += object ThType {
          align := AlignType::left;
          colspan := 4;
          a += object AType {
            name := self.name;
            text += 'Topic: ' + self.name;
          };
        };
      };
      tr += object TrType {
        td += object TdType {
          text += 'Date: ';
          text += self.start.repr();
        };
        td += object TdType {
          text += 'Priority: ';
          text += self.getPriority();
        };
        td += object TdType {
          text += 'Direct subtopics: ';
          text += self.subtopics->size().toString();
        };
        td += object TdType {
          text += 'Total subtopics: ';
          text += self.allSubtopics()->size().toString();
        };
      };
      tr += object TrType {
        td += object TdType {
          align := AlignType::left;
          colspan := 4;
          text += self.description;
        };
      };
    };
  };
  end {
    if not self.subtopics->isEmpty() then {
      result.div += object DivType {
        h4 += object H4Type {
          text += 'Suptopics';
        };
        ul += object UlType {
          li += self.subtopics.map toListItem();
        };
      };
    } endif;
```

```
      var relations : Set(mindmap::Relationship) :=
        self.getRelations();
      if not relations->isEmpty() then {
        result.div += object DivType {
          h4 += object H4Type {
            text += 'Relationships';
          };
          ul += object UlType {
            li += relations.map toListItem();
          };
        };
      } endif;
      result.br += object BrType {};
  }
}

mapping mindmap::Relationship::toListItem() : xhtml::LiType {
  text += self.getType() + ' relationship to ';
  a += object AType {
    href := '#' + self.target.name;
    text += self.target.name;
  };
}

mapping mindmap::Topic::toListItem() : xhtml::LiType {
  a += object AType {
    href := '#' + self.name;
    text += self.name;
  };
}

query mindmap::Relationship::getType() : String {
  var pri : String := null;
  switch {
      (self.type = Type::DEPENDENCY) ? pri := 'Dependency';
      (self.type = Type::INCLUDE) ? pri := 'Include';
      (self.type = Type::EXTEND) ? pri := 'Extend';
      else ? assert fatal (false)
       with log('Type unsupported', self);
  };
  return pri;
}

query mindmap::Topic::getPriority() : String {
  var pri : String := null;
  switch {
      (self.priority = Priority::HIGH) ? pri := 'High';
      (self.priority = Priority::MEDIUM) ? pri := 'Medium';
      (self.priority = Priority::LOW) ? pri := 'Low';
      else ? assert fatal (false)
       with log('Priority unsupported', self);
  };
  return pri;
}
```

Figure 6-15 is a sample output report, created from our simple dynamic instance mindmap model.

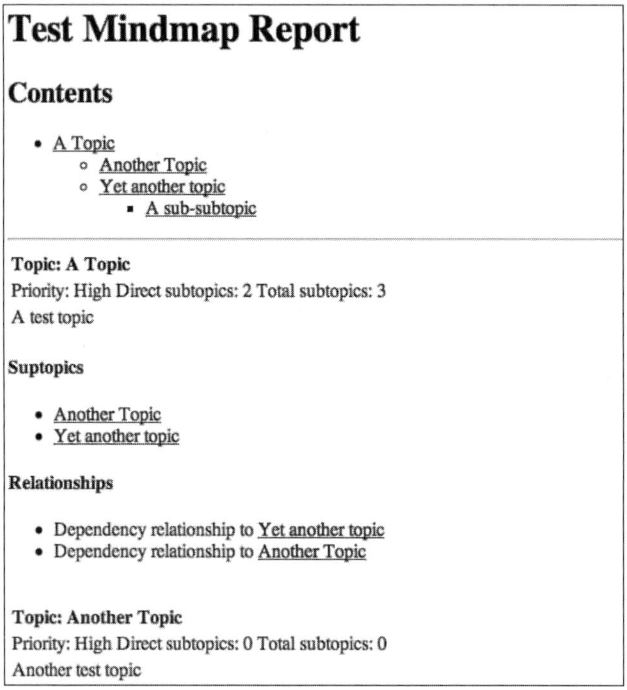

Test Mindmap Report

Contents

- A Topic
  - Another Topic
  - Yet another topic
    - A sub-subtopic

Topic: A Topic
Priority: High Direct subtopics: 2 Total subtopics: 3
A test topic

Suptopics

- Another Topic
- Yet another topic

Relationships

- Dependency relationship to Yet another topic
- Dependency relationship to Another Topic

Topic: Another Topic
Priority: High Direct subtopics: 0 Total subtopics: 0
Another test topic

Figure 6-15　Mindmap report

6.8 Transforming a Scenario to a Test Case

As it turns out, the Test and Performance Tools Project (TPTP) uses EMF extensively for its models. After some investigation, it seems we can transform our scenario diagrams into TPTP manual test cases using QVT. One complication to overcome is that TPTP uses the zip feature of EMF serialization to persist its models. So after we create a test suite model, we just need to zip the file and change the file extension to `.testsuite` to open it with the TPTP editor. Another complication is that the TPTP project has discontinued development of the Manual Test feature. To follow along in this section, you need to use the Europa edition (4.3.0) of the Testing Tools feature, not the Ganymede release. As a result, this example should be considered purely a reference and is not completed, given the uncertainty about the target.

To better understand the model used to back the TPTP Test Suite editor, we can first create one using the provided wizard and then unzip the file to examine the contents while referencing the common.ecore model. Here again, the reflective editor is useful.

TPTP's models are quite complicated, but we need to use only a small portion of the common.ecore model for our scenario of test suite transformation. Following is a look at the code for mapping straight from our scenario Task elements to TPTP manual test steps. The TPTP common model consists of several packages, hence the multiple metamodel references at the top of the definition.

To follow the transformation definition here, you likely must have the `common.ecore` model visible in the **Metamodel Explorer** or imported into your workspace. When we got a better understanding of how the model was structured, the mappings from our input scenario model were fairly straightforward to compose. The biggest complication, for which no good solution has yet been achieved, was detecting looping in our input model. QVT is not a suitable language for this type of model analysis, so I recommend using a black box approach using Java. A limited solution is shown here, along with the rest of the mappings.

```
transformation scenario2testsuite(in scenarioModel : scenario,

  out testSuiteModel : Common_Testprofile::TPFTestSuite);

modeltype scenario uses 'http://www.eclipse.org/2008/scenario';
modeltype Common_Testprofile
 uses 'http://www.eclipse.org/hyades/models/common/testprofile.xmi';
modeltype Common_Configuration
 uses 'http://www.eclipse.org/hyades/models/common/configuration.xmi';
modeltype Common_Behavior_Fragments
 uses
'http://www.eclipse.org/hyades/models/common/behavior/fragments.xmi';
modeltype Common_Behavior_Interactions
 uses 'http://www.eclipse.org/hyades/models/common/behavior/
➥interactions.xmi';

main() {
  scenarioModel.rootObjects[Process]->map toTestSuite();
}

mapping scenario::Process::toTestSuite() :
  Common_Testprofile::TPFTestSuite {
  init {
    var lifeline := object
  Common_Behavior_Interactions::BVRLifeline {
      name := '_selfLifeline';
    }
  }
```

```
    type := 'org.eclipse.hyades.test.manual.testSuite';
    persistenceId := 'HyadesFacadeResource';
    name := self.name;
    description := self.name;
    instances += object Common_Configuration::CFGInstance {
      classType := result;
      lifeline := lifeline;
    };
    behavior := object Common_Testprofile::TPFBehavior {
      name := result.name + '_behavior';
      resource := result.name + '.Test';
      interaction := object Common_Behavior_Fragments::BVRInteraction {
        lifelines += lifeline;
        interactionFragments += self.elements.selectGateways().map
          toInteractionFragment();
      }
    };
    testCases += self.elements.selectTasks().map toTestCase();
    end {
      result.testCases.setInstance(result);
    }
}

mapping scenario::Gateway::toInteractionFragment() :
Common_Behavior_Fragments::BVRCombinedFragment
  when {
    self.formsLoop(self)
  } {
  name := 'Iterate';
  interactionOperator := BVRInteractionOperator::loop;
  interactionOperands += object
    Common_Behavior_Fragments::BVRInteractionOperand {
    interactionFragments += self.collectLoopTasks().map
      toExecutionOccurrence();
    interactionConstraint := object
      Common_Behavior_Fragments::BVRInteractionConstraint {
      constraint := 'n';
    }
  }
}

mapping scenario::Task::toExecutionOccurrence() :
Common_Behavior_Interactions::BVRExecutionOccurrence {
  name := self.name + ' - invocation';
  otherBehavior := self.late
    resolveone(Common_Testprofile::TPFBehavior);
}

query scenario::Element::formsLoop(target : scenario::Gateway) :
Boolean {
  -- limit to Task elements for now
  var tasks : OrderedSet(scenario::Task) :=
    self.outgoing.target.selectTasks()->asOrderedSet();
  var loop : Boolean := tasks.completesLoop(target)
    ->includes(true);
```

```
      if not loop then {
        loop := tasks.formsLoop(target)->includes(true);
      } endif;
      return loop;
    }


    query scenario::Task::completesLoop(target : scenario::Gateway) :
    Boolean {
      self.outgoing.target.selectGateways()->includes(target);
    }


    query scenario::Gateway::collectLoopTasks() :
    OrderedSet(scenario::Task) {
      var tasks : OrderedSet(scenario::Task) :=
        self.outgoing.target.selectTasks()->asOrderedSet();
      var path : OrderedSet(scenario::Task) := null;
      var index : Integer := 1;
      while (path = null and index <= tasks->size()) {
        path := tasks->at(index).followPath(self);
        index := index + 1;
      };
      return path;
    }


    query scenario::Task::followPath(target : scenario::Gateway) :
    OrderedSet(scenario::Task) {
      var path : OrderedSet(scenario::Task) := null;
      if self.completesLoop(target) then {
        path += self->asSet();
      } else {
        var subTasks : OrderedSet(scenario::Task) :=
          self.outgoing.target.selectTasks()->asOrderedSet();
        if subTasks->isEmpty() then {
          path := null;
        } else {
          path += self->asSet();
          path += subTasks.followPath(target);
        } endif;
      } endif;
      return path;
    }


    query Common_Testprofile::TPFTestCase::setInstance(inout suite :
    Common_Testprofile::TPFTestSuite) {
      return suite.instances += object Common_Configuration::CFGInstance {
        classType := suite;
        lifeline := self.behavior.interaction.lifelines
          ->asSequence()->last();
      };
    }


    mapping scenario::Task::toTestCase() : Common_Testprofile::TPFTestCase
    {
      name := self.name;
      description := self.documentation;
```

```
    type := 'org.eclipse.hyades.test.manual.testCase';
    behavior := self.map toBehavior();
}

mapping scenario::Task::toBehavior() : Common_Testprofile::TPFBehavior {
    name := self.name + '_behavior';
    interaction := object Common_Behavior_Fragments::BVRInteraction {
      lifelines += object
Common_Behavior_Interactions::BVRLifeline {
        name := '_selfLifeline';
      }
    }
}

query scenario::Element::selectGateways() :
OrderedSet(scenario::Gateway) {
    return self->select(oclIsTypeOf(scenario::Gateway))
      ->collect(oclAsType(scenario::Gateway))->asOrderedSet();
}

-- TODO: use collectselect shorthand notation [Task]
query scenario::Element::selectTasks() : OrderedSet(scenario::Task) {
    return self->select(oclIsTypeOf(scenario::Task))
      ->collect(oclAsType(scenario::Task))->asOrderedSet();
}
```

Figure 6-16 through 6-18 are images of the input model and the resulting TPTP Manual test case, opened in its own form-based editor. The sequence has two simple loops, which you can see are transformed to test iterations. Although this short example is simplified for illustrative purposes, you can see how leveraging EMF models for multiple components leads to powerful integration possibilities using QVT and other modeling technologies introduced in this book.

TIP

When creating a dynamic instance model for models such as the scenario, it's much easier to diagram one than to use the reflective editor tree and properties view. To make it easier, launch the runtime workspace and diagram the model; then open it with a text editor and copy the elements within the root and paste them within the XMI file. Be careful not to copy over the root element.

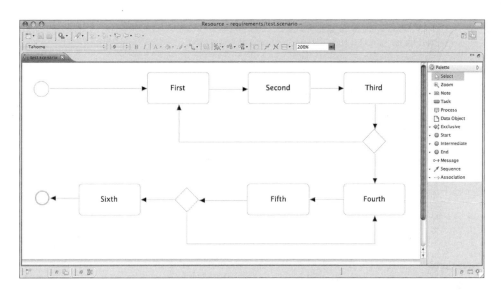

Figure 6-16   Scenario test model

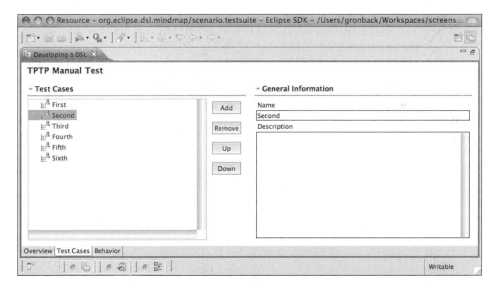

Figure 6-17   TPTP manual test

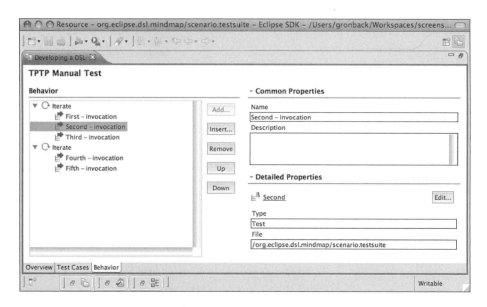

Figure 6-18   TPTP manual test behavior

To simplify the development of this transformation so that the output model is always zipped up into our `*.testsuite` file after each execution, a simple Ant build script and associated builder configuration does the trick nicely. This is the simple script to be invoked by an Ant builder configuration added to our `org.eclipse.dsl.scenario` project properties:

```
<?xml version="1.0" encoding="UTF-8"?>
<project name="org.eclipse.dsl.scenario" default="main" basedir=".">
  <target name="main">
    <zip destfile="./out/scenario.testsuite"
      filesonly="false"
      whenempty="skip" update="false">
    <fileset dir="out/">
      <include name="**/*.testprofile"/>
    </fileset>
    </zip>
  </target>
</project>
```

6.9 Transforming a Business Model to Java

When generating Java or another programming language from a model, it's typical to use model-to-text technologies, such as Xpand or JET. Ultimately, code-generation templates are required to output Java from our business domain model, so a question emerges at this point: Do we bother with an intermediate

Java model, or do we pass our DNC model straight to Xpand templates for Java generation? Or should we create a model specific for Java EE? Yet another option is to define a textual concrete syntax using TMF that provides the model-to-text transformation. These are general questions you need to consider when doing Model-Driven Software Development (MDSD), and the answer will vary depending on your requirements, technology preference, relative efficiency, or other factors. In this book, we examine two approaches. This section focuses on the transformation of a Domain-Neutral Component (DNC) model to a Java domain model. The next chapter looks at the template approach for generating Java from the DNC domain model. This enables us to examine each approach in detail and to cover the relative strengths and weaknesses of each.

First, we need a Java domain model. The WebTools project maintains a Java EMF Model (JEM), which originated in the Visual Editor project. At this point, you need to install WebTools if you're not using the DSL Toolkit from Amalgam, which includes the JEM model in its distribution. Although the model suits our needs, it also presents some challenges, such as the fact that it extends Ecore itself. We chose this model instead of implementing our own from scratch, to illustrate the challenges you might face working with an existing model, where certain restrictions and workarounds are inevitable. To make it even more "real," the version of the model used in this section included an annotation, indicating that it was indeed a work in progress.

The first step is to learn this model. The **Metamodel Explorer** provides you with a means to do this, as does the familiar process of importing the project into your workspace and generating an Ecore diagram, as shown in Figure 6-19. Keep in mind that this model extends Ecore itself, so what you see in Figure 6-19 is only the Java extension of our familiar Ecore model.

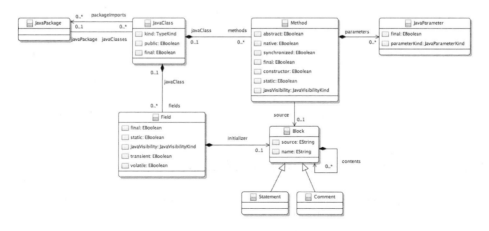

Figure 6-19 JEM model

The first step in transforming our business model to this Java model is to create a dynamic instance model from our dnc.ecore model for use in testing the QVT. The problem we immediately face is that because we have extended our oocore.ecore model but have not provided an extension of the Package class, we have no capability to create a container for our test archetypes. The referenced oocore.ecore model opens in the resource set, so we can right-click the Package class and create a new dynamic instance model; however, when we do this, we can't create archetypes. The problem is that we have no references to the dnc.ecore model in the produced model.xmi file, shown here:

```
<?xml version="1.0" encoding="ASCII"?>
<oocore:Package xmi:version="2.0" xmlns:xmi="http://www.omg.org/XMI"
  xmlns:xsi="http://www.w3.org/2001/XMLSchema-instance"
  xmlns:oocore="http://www.eclipse.org/2008/oocore"
  xsi:schemaLocation="http://www.eclipse.org/2008/oocore
  ../../org.eclipse.dsl.oocore/model/oocore.ecore">
</oocore:Package>
```

To work around this problem, we simply need to add xmlns and schemaLocation for our dnc.ecore model in this file:

```
<?xml version="1.0" encoding="ASCII"?>
<oocore:Package xmi:version="2.0" xmlns:xmi="http://www.omg.org/XMI"
  xmlns:xsi="http://www.w3.org/2001/XMLSchema-instance"
  xmlns:dnc="http://www.eclipse.org/2008/dnc"
  xmlns:oocore="http://www.eclipse.org/2008/oocore"
  xsi:schemaLocation="http://www.eclipse.org/2008/dnc dnc.ecore
  http://www.eclipse.org/2008/oocore
  ../../org.eclipse.dsl.oocore/model/oocore.ecore">
</oocore:Package>
```

Now we can open the model in our reflective editor and add archetypes, attributes, operations, associations, and references for use in testing. Figure 6-20 shows what the content of our test model.xmi looks like, although it doesn't indicate that these archetypes were created in the package org.eclipse.example.

With a dynamic instance model to use as input, we can move on to creating a transformation script to execute and see what the output looks like. The JEM model comes with no editor of its own, so we can use either the text editor or our friend the Sample Reflective Ecore Editor to view the output. Using the **Operational QVT Transformation** wizard, create a dnc2jee.qvto file in the org.eclipse.dsl.dnc/transformations directory. Alter the default transformation definition to match the following:

```
transformation dnc2jee(in modelIn : dnc, out modelOut : java);

import library Strings;

modeltype dnc uses "http://www.eclipse.org/2008/dnc";
modeltype oocore uses "http://www.eclipse.org/2008/oocore";
modeltype ecore uses "http://www.eclipse.org/emf/2002/Ecore";
modeltype java uses "java.xmi";

main() {
  modelIn.rootObjects()[Package]->map toPackage();
}
```

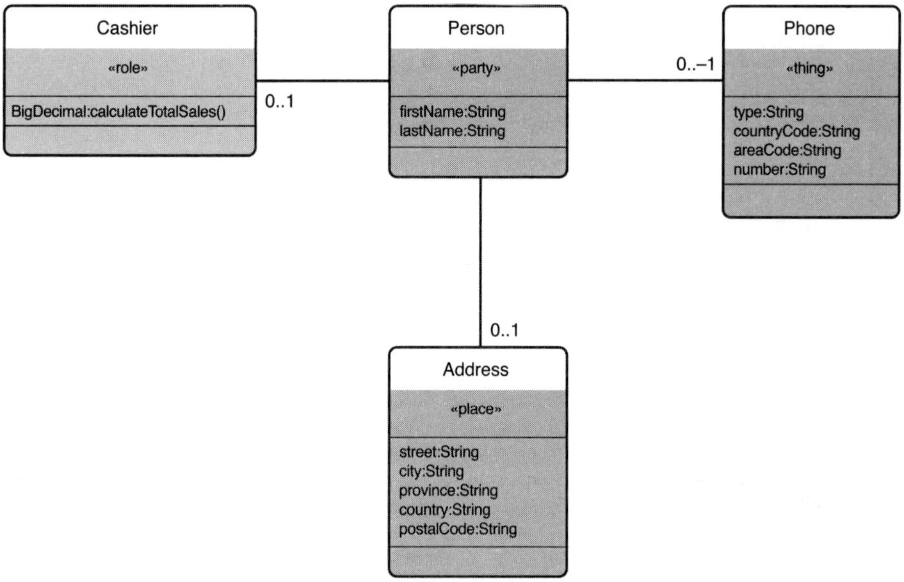

Figure 6-20   Test color model

The **Strings** library is imported because we will need it shortly. Each of our four domain models is declared in `modeltype` statements at the top of the file, just above the main mapping that invokes a `toPackage()` mapping. The package names are mapped to each other, followed by a series of mappings that convert specific archetypes to Entity or Stateful beans. Finally, subpackages are processed recursively. The rest of the transformation definition includes comments that should adequately describe how it works.

```
/**
 * Recursively map each color model package to Java package,
 * mapping each Archetype to its respective EJB type.
 */
mapping oocore::Package::toPackage() : java::JavaPackage {
  name := self.name;
  eClassifiers += self.contents[MomentInterval].map toEntity();
  eClassifiers += self.contents[MIDetail].map toEntity();
  eClassifiers += self.contents[Role].map toStateful();
  eClassifiers += self.contents[Party].map toEntity();
  eClassifiers += self.contents[Place].map toEntity();
  eClassifiers += self.contents[Thing].map toEntity();
  eClassifiers += self.contents[Description].map toEntity();
  eSubpackages += self.contents[Package].map toPackage();
}

/**
 * A mapping from an Archetype to a Java class that
 * is interited by each of the EJB mapping classes.
 */
mapping dnc::Archetype::toClass() : java::JavaClass {
  name := self.name;
  fields += self.features[Attribute].map toField(result);
  methods += self.features[Operation].map toMethod();
}

/**
 * A mapping to add obligatory Serializable implements clause
 * to each EJB class.
 */
mapping dnc::Archetype::toSerializableClass() : java::JavaClass {
  implementsInterfaces += 'java.io.Serializable'.map toClass();
}

/**
 * Map an Archetype to a @Stateful session bean, inheriting basic
 * class and Serializable features.
 */
mapping dnc::Archetype::toStateful() : java::JavaClass
  inherits dnc::Archetype::toClass
  merges dnc::Archetype::toSerializableClass {

  eAnnotations += toAnnotation('description', self.description, null);
  eAnnotations += toAnnotation('annotation', '@Stateful', null);
  classImport += 'javax.ejb.Stateful'.map toClass();
}

/**
 * Map an Archetype to an @Entity bean, inheriting basic
 * class and Serializable features.
 */
mapping dnc::Archetype::toEntity() : java::JavaClass
  inherits dnc::Archetype::toClass
  merges dnc::Archetype::toSerializableClass {
```

```
eStructuralFeatures += self.features[Association].map
  toReference(result);
eStructuralFeatures += self.features[Reference].map
  toReference(result);

eAnnotations += toAnnotation('description', self.description, null);
eAnnotations += toAnnotation('annotation', '@Entity', null);
eAnnotations += toAnnotation('annotation', '@Table(name="' +
  self.name.toUpperCase() + '")', null);

-- Add id field with getter, no setter
fields += object java::Field {
  name := self.name.toLowerCase() + 'Id';
  eType := 'int'.map toClass();
  javaVisibility := java::JavaVisibilityKind::PRIVATE;
  eAnnotations += toAnnotation('annotation', '@Id', null);
  eAnnotations += toAnnotation('annotation', '@Column(name="'
    + self.name.toUpperCase() + '_ID")', null);
  eAnnotations += toAnnotation('annotation',
    '@GeneratedValue(strategy=GenerationType.AUTO)', null);
};
methods += object java::Method {
  name := 'get' + self.name.firstToUpper() + 'Id';
  eType := 'int'.map toClass();
  javaVisibility := java::JavaVisibilityKind::PUBLIC;
  source := object java::Statement {
    source := 'return ' + self.name.toLowerCase() + 'Id;';
  };
};
end {
  result.classImport += 'javax.persistence.Entity'.map toClass();
  result.classImport += 'javax.persistence.Table'.map toClass();
  result.classImport += 'javax.persistence.Column'.map toClass();
  result.classImport += 'javax.persistence.Id'.map toClass();
  result.classImport += 'javax.persistence.GeneratedValue'.map
toClass();
  result.classImport +=
    'javax.persistence.GenerationType'.map toClass();
}
}

/**
 * Creates reference from association with annotations
 */
mapping dnc::Association::toReference(inout class : java::JavaClass) :
  ecore::EReference
  when {
    not self.opposite.oclIsUndefined() and
    self.opposite.owner.isEntity()
  } {
  name := self.name;
  eType := self.type.oclAsType(dnc::Archetype).late
    resolveone(java::JavaClass);
  lowerBound := self.lowerBound;
  upperBound := self.upperBound;
```

```
  end {
    if (not self.opposite.oclIsUndefined() and
      self.opposite.owner.isEntity()) then {
      if (self.upperBound = 1  and
  (self.opposite.upperBound = 1 or self.opposite.upperBound = 0))
      then {
          result.eAnnotations +=
  toAnnotation('annotation', '@OneToOne(targetEntity=' +
  self.opposite.owner.fullyQualifiedName() + '.class)', null);
          class.classImport +=
  'javax.persistence.OneToOne'.map toClass();
        } endif;

      if (self.upperBound = -1  and
  (self.opposite.upperBound = 1 or self.opposite.upperBound = 0)) then {
          result.eAnnotations +=
  toAnnotation('annotation', '@OneToMany(mappedBy="' +
  self.owner.name.toLowerCase() + 'Id")', null);
          result.eAnnotations +=
  toAnnotation('collection', 'type', 'java.util.Collection');
          class.classImport +=
  'javax.persistence.OneToMany'.map toClass();
        } endif;

      var columnName : String := null;
      if self.name.toLowerCase() <> self.name then {
        columnName := self.name.toColumnName();
        result.eAnnotations += toAnnotation('annotation',
  '@Column(name="' + columnName  + '")', null)
      } endif;
    } endif;
    class.methods += self.map toGetter();
    class.methods += self.map toSetter();
  }
}

/**
 * Creates reference/getter/setter from opposite reference
 * with annotations
 */
mapping oocore::Reference::toReference(inout class : java::JavaClass) :
  ecore::EReference
  when {
    not self.opposite.oclIsUndefined() and
  self.opposite.owner.isEntity() and self.opposite.upperBound = -1
  } {
  name := self.name;
  eType := self.type.oclAsType(dnc::Archetype).late
  resolveone(java::JavaClass);
  lowerBound := self.lowerBound;
  upperBound := self.upperBound;
  end {
    if self.opposite.upperBound = -1 then {
      result.eAnnotations +=
```

```
    toAnnotation('annotation', '@ManyToOne', null);
        result.eAnnotations +=
    toAnnotation('annotation', '@JoinColumn(name="' +
    self.opposite.owner.name.toUpperCase()  + '_ID")', null);
        class.classImport +=
    'javax.persistence.ManyToOne'.map toClass();
        class.classImport += 'javax.persistence.JoinColumn'.map
➥toClass();
    } endif;

    var columnName : String := null;
    if self.name.toLowerCase() <> self.name then {
        columnName := self.name.toColumnName();
        result.eAnnotations +=
    toAnnotation('annotation', '@Column(name="' + columnName  + '")',
➥null)
    } endif;
    class.methods += self.map toGetter();
    class.methods += self.map toSetter();
    }
}

/**
 * Creates getter method for Reference
 */
mapping oocore::Reference::toGetter() : java::Method {
  init {
    result := object java::Method {
      name := 'get' + self.name.firstToUpper();
      eType := self.type.late resolveone(java::JavaClass);
      javaVisibility := java::JavaVisibilityKind::PUBLIC;
      source := object java::Statement {
        source := 'return ' + self.name + ';';
      };
    };
    if (self.lowerBound = 0 or self.lowerBound = 1) and
  self.upperBound = -1 then {
      result.eAnnotations +=
    toAnnotation('collection', 'type', 'java.util.Collection');
    } endif;
  }
}

/**
 * Creates setter method for Reference
 */
mapping oocore::Reference::toSetter() : java::Method {
  init {
    var parameter := object java::JavaParameter {
      eType := self.type.late resolveone(java::JavaClass);
      name := self.name;
    };
    if self.lowerBound = 0 and self.upperBound = -1 then {
      parameter.eAnnotations +=
```

```
    toAnnotation('collection', 'type', 'java.util.Collection');
      } endif;
    }
    name := 'set' + self.name.firstToUpper();
    eType := 'void'.map toClass();
    javaVisibility := java::JavaVisibilityKind::PUBLIC;
    source := object java::Statement {
      source := 'this.' + self.name + ' = ' + self.name + ';';
    };
    parameters += parameter;
  }

/**
 * Creates field/getter/setter for attribute, with @Column
 * annotation if required
 */
mapping oocore::Attribute::toField(inout class : java::JavaClass) :
  java::Field {
  name := self.name;
  eType := self.dataType.map toClass();
  javaVisibility := self.visibility.toVisibility();
  end {
    var columnName : String := null;
    if self.name.toLowerCase() <> self.name then {
      columnName := self.name.toColumnName();
      result.eAnnotations += toAnnotation('annotation',
'@Column(name = "' + columnName  + '")', null)
    } endif;
    class.methods += self.map toGetter();
    class.methods += self.map toSetter();
  }
}

/**
 * Creates getter method for field
 */
mapping oocore::Attribute::toGetter() : java::Method {
  name := 'get' + self.name.firstToUpper();
  eType := self.dataType.map toClass();
  javaVisibility := java::JavaVisibilityKind::PUBLIC;
  source := object java::Statement {
    source := 'return ' + self.name + ';';
  };
}

/**
 * Creates setter method for field
 */
mapping oocore::Attribute::toSetter() : java::Method {
  name := 'set' + self.name.firstToUpper();
  eType := 'void'.map toClass();
  javaVisibility := java::JavaVisibilityKind::PUBLIC;
  parameters += object java::JavaParameter {
    eType := self.dataType.map toClass();
    name := self.name;
```

```
    };
    source := object java::Statement {
      source := 'this.' + self.name + ' = ' + self.name + ';';
    };
  }

  /**
   * Creates method from operation
   * TODO: handle parameters
   */
  mapping oocore::Operation::toMethod() : java::Method {
    name := self.name;
    eType := self.type.map toClass();
    javaVisibility := self.visibility.toVisibility();
    source := object java::Block {
      contents += object java::Comment {
        source := 'TODO: Implement this method';
      };
      contents += self.type.map toReturnStatement();
    };
  }

  /**
   * Creates default return statement for method
   */
  mapping oocore::Classifier::toReturnStatement() : java::Statement {
    init {
      var statement : String := null;
      switch {
        (self.oclIsUndefined()) ? statement := '';
        (self.oclIsKindOf(oocore::Class)) ? statement := 'return null;';
        (self.oclIsTypeOf(oocore::Datatype)) ? statement := 'return ' +
➡self.oclAsType(oocore::Datatype).defaultLiteral + ';';
        else ? assert fatal (false) with log('No return type found',
➡self);
      };
    }
    source := statement;
  }

  /**
   * Creates class and packaging with 'library' annotation
   */
  mapping String::toClass() : java::JavaClass {
    init {
      var segment : String := null;
      var pkg : java::JavaPackage := null;
      var parentPkg : java::JavaPackage := null;
      var pos : Integer := 1;
      while (self.indexOf('.', pos) <> -1) {
        segment := self.substring(pos, self.indexOf('.', pos));
        pos := self.indexOf('.', pos) + 2;
        pkg := segment.map toPackage();
        if parentPkg = null then {
          parentPkg := pkg;
```

```
        } else {
          parentPkg.eSubpackages += pkg;
          parentPkg := pkg;
        } endif;
      };
    }
    name := self.substring(self.lastIndexOf('.')+2, self.size());
    eAnnotations += toAnnotation('library', null, null);
    end {
      parentPkg.eClassifiers += result;
    }
}

/**
 * Creates library class from Java type
 */
mapping oocore::Classifier::toClass() : java::JavaClass {
  name := self.name;
  -- Datatypes are marked as 'library'
  eAnnotations += toAnnotation('library', null, null);
  end {
    var pack : java::JavaPackage := self._package.map toPackage(null);
    pack.eClassifiers += result;
  }
}

/**
 * Creates JavaPackage from String
 */
mapping String::toPackage() : java::JavaPackage {
  name := self;
}

/**
 * Creates JavaPackage and adds passed child
 */
mapping oocore::Package::toPackage(child : java::JavaPackage) :
  java::JavaPackage {
  init {
    result := self.name.map toPackage();
    result.eSubpackages += child;

    if self._package <> null then
      self._package.map toPackage(result) endif;
  }
}

/**
 * Creates ECore annotation for use by template
 */
query toAnnotation(type:String, key:String, value:String) :
  ecore::EAnnotation {
  return object ecore::EAnnotation {
    source := type;
    details += object ecore::EStringToStringMapEntry {
      key := key;
```

```
            value := value;
        }
    }
}

/**
 * Maps visibility to Java types
 */
query oocore::Visibility::toVisibility() : java::JavaVisibilityKind {
    if self = oocore::Visibility::PRIVATE then {
        return java::JavaVisibilityKind::PRIVATE} else
        if self = oocore::Visibility::PUBLIC then {
            return java::JavaVisibilityKind::PUBLIC} else
            if self = oocore::Visibility::PROTECTED then {
                return java::JavaVisibilityKind::PROTECTED}
            endif
        endif
    endif;
    return java::JavaVisibilityKind::PACKAGE
}

/**
 * Replaces camel case with underscore, e.g. firstName -> FIRST_NAME
 */
query String::toColumnName() : String {
    var name : String := '';
    var digit : String := '';
    var pos : Integer := 1;
    while (pos <= self.size()) {
        digit := self.substring(pos, pos);
        if digit.toLowerCase() <> digit then {
            name := name + '_' + digit;
        } else {
            name := name + digit;
        } endif;
        pos := pos + 1;
    };
    return name.toUpperCase();
}

query oocore::Class::isEntity() : Boolean {
    return self.oclIsTypeOf(dnc::MomentInterval) or
    self.oclIsTypeOf(dnc::MIDetail) or
    self.oclIsTypeOf(dnc::Party) or
    self.oclIsTypeOf(dnc::Place) or
    self.oclIsTypeOf(dnc::Thing) or
    self.oclIsTypeOf(dnc::Description);
}

/**
 * Returns dot '.' delimited package.Class string
 */
query oocore::Class::fullyQualifiedName() : String {
    var fqn : String := self.name;
    var pkg : oocore::Package := self._package;
    while (not pkg.oclIsUndefined()) {
```

```
      fqn := pkg.name + '.' + fqn;
      pkg := pkg._package;
   };
   return fqn;
}
```

Figure 6-21 is a sample output model for our test input model. What's striking is the size of the model, which seems quite disproportionate, compared to the concrete syntax of what we'll produce using our Xpand templates. Nevertheless, it took little time to produce from our business model and will provide straightforward transformation to Java compilation units, as shown in Section 7.3.1, "Using Java Model and Dedicated Template."

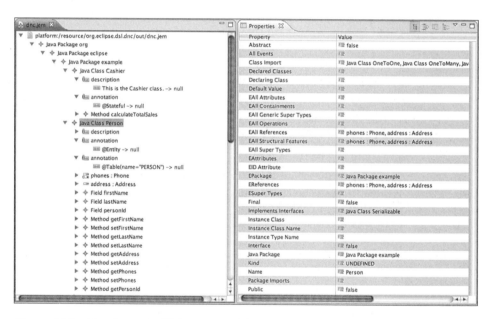

Figure 6-21   Transformation JEM output model

6.10 Summary

In this chapter, we took a look at the functionality provided by the QVT OML implementation provided by the Eclipse M2M project. We saw some of the more popular use cases for M2M, leaving M2Ts using the Xpand component of the Eclipse M2T project for the next chapter.

CHAPTER 7

Developing Model-to-Text Transformations

Working with domain-specific languages (DSLs) in the form of their abstract syntax, concrete syntax, and Model-to-Model Transformations (M2M) is great, but what we typically want to derive is a working software application, a database schema, or even some documentation from our models. This is where Model-to-Text Transformations (M2T) come into play. We typically generate code in the form of some general-purpose programming language such as Java, or even output HTML from our model instances.

As touched upon in Chapter 6, "Developing Model-to-Model Transformations," considerations must be made when selecting a transformation technology, both M2M and M2T. Either or both can fulfill your needs, with some form of workflow required in the case of the latter.

Numerous code-generation technologies are available, both within and outside Eclipse. Within the Modeling project are several facilities for code generation from models. The home for most of these components is the M2T project.

7.1 M2T Project

Two main components within the M2T project exist for code generation from models: Java Emitter Templates (JET) and Xpand. JET is the traditional template engine that was used with Eclipse Modeling Framework (EMF) and is closely aligned with Java Server Pages (JSP). It was extracted from EMF and improved into what's now referred to as JET2. We don't cover JET in this book because of space considerations. Instead, we focus on the capabilities of Xpand as a template engine to complement our DSL Toolkit.

It's worth pointing out that a third option will soon be available from M2T. The Model to Text Language (MTL) component will provide an implementation of the OMG's MOF Model to Text Language standard. Furthermore, Core and Shared components are planned for M2T, with the goal of providing shared components and a framework for the invocation of M2T transformations, regardless of the language. None of these components were available at the time of this writing, but future editions of this book might cover them.

7.1.1 Xpand, Xtend, and Workflow Components

Originally from the Generative Modeling Technologies (GMT) project, the Xpand template engine moved to M2T and is used extensively within the GMF project. In fact, GMF includes a refactored version of the Xpand engine and editor for use in GMF until the enhancements added have been incorporated into Xpand, following its move to the M2T project. More recently, the GMF project refactored its version of Xpand to remove the use of Xtend and its proprietary expression language, and replace it with Object Constraint Language (OCL) and Query/View/Transformation (QVT) Operational Mapping Language. The examples in this book likely will be refactored to use this version of Xpand in the future.

Xpand itself has basic syntax but uses an underlying expression language and Xtend to provide powerful M2T (and even M2M) capabilities. Xpand also can be used within the context of EMF Technology (EMFT) Workflow component. This component allows for an Ant-like XML representation of model transformation invocations that can be chained into a workflow. Because workflow is the easiest way to invoke Xpand templates for use in code generation, I cover it in basic detail as well. When using the GMF version of Xpand, Ant tasks can be used to invoke templates; when combined with Ant tasks provided by M2M QVTO, these make another viable workflow option.

Wizards available for creating new Xpand and Xtend files are located in the Model Transformation category when using the Amalgam DSL Toolkit download. Otherwise, they are located in the Xpand and Xtend categories of the **New** dialog, respectively. Also present is a wizard for creating Check files, which are not discussed in the context of this book. Additionally, an action is contributed to the project right-click menu to add or remove the Xpand/Xtend nature. When using this action, the following buildCommand and nature is added to your `.project` file. Note that DSL Toolkit projects come preconfigured with this nature and builder.

```
<buildCommand>
  <name>org.eclipse.xtend.shared.ui.xtendBuilder</name>
  <arguments/>
</buildCommand>

<nature>org.eclipse.xtend.shared.ui.xtendXPandNature</nature>
```

Projects with this nature are identifiable by the small O added to the upper-right corner of the project icon. Also present in the project properties is an Xtend/Xpand category, as seen in Figure 7-1. By default, Xtend/Xpand is configured for use with EMF Metamodels, although support exists for UML2 and other model types as well.

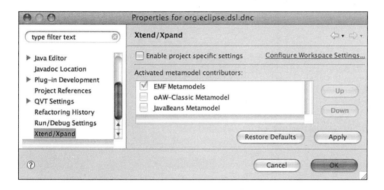

Figure 7-1   Xtend/Xpand project properties

The editor provided with Xpand provides color syntax highlighting, code completion, and a set of templates for its main elements, as shown in Figure 7-2 and Figure 7-3.

Templates are most commonly invoked with Model Workflow (*.mwe) files. The workflow component is found in the EMFT project and comes with its own wizard and editor. The wizard to create a new workflow file is found in **New →
Model Transformation → Workflow Definition** when using the DSL Toolkit. Otherwise, it can be found in **New → Modeling Workflow Engine → Workflow File**. The editor is not as full featured as the Xpand/Xtend editors, but improvements are planned.

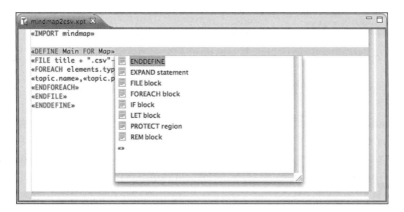

Figure 7-2   Xpand code templates

Figure 7-3   Xpand code completion

To invoke workflows on templates, you need to add the required dependencies to your project. In the future, this will hopefully not be required, nor will the use of Java source paths to locate template files and models. For now, however, the following dependencies are added to the `MANIFEST.MF` file when creating a DSL project. When using additional features, such as Java code beautifiers, you must add `org.eclipse.jdt.core`, `org.eclipse.runtime.core`, and `org.eclipse.jface.text`, in addition to plug-ins that might contain the models referenced in the workflow.

```
Require-Bundle: org.eclipse.emf.ecore;bundle-version="2.4.0",
 org.eclipse.xpand;bundle-version="0.7.0",
```

```
org.eclipse.xtend;bundle-version="0.7.0",
org.eclipse.xtend.typesystem.emf;bundle-version="0.7.0",
org.eclipse.emf.mwe.core;bundle-version="0.7.0",
org.eclipse.emf.mwe.utils;bundle-version="0.7.0",
org.apache.commons.cli;bundle-version="1.0.0",
org.apache.commons.lang;bundle-version="2.1.0",
org.eclipse.emf.ecore.xmi;bundle-version="2.4.0",
org.apache.commons.logging;bundle-version="1.0.4",
org.antlr.runtime;bundle-version="3.0.0"
```

A final note on using Xpand in our sample projects concerns the GMF variant in your environment. Until the enhancements made to Xpand for GMF are merged into the new M2T Xpand component, you will find another registered editor on the right-click **Open With** menu. Both editors are functional and can be used to develop Xpand templates. The most visible difference is the capability of the GMF version to work with NS URI import statements instead of relying on source paths in the project. GMF's Xpand also adds the notion of Xpand roots, preserved in .xpand-roots files in the workspace. Finally, GMF's Xpand leaves the direction of text generated by a template to a particular location to the workflow, not to FILE directives within a template.

Having completed the preliminary introduction to Xpand, Xtend, and Workflow elements found in your environment, let's move on to developing templates for our sample projects. You can find more information on these technologies in Chapter 14, "Xpand Template Language."

7.2 Generating CSV Files

To begin with the simplest example imaginable, we use Xpand here to output a simple comma-separated values (CSV) file from our mindmap model. The first step is to create a template in a /templates/deploy source folder of our org.eclipse.dsl.mindmap project named mindmap2csv.xpt and complete it with the following text:

```
«IMPORT mindmap»

«DEFINE Main FOR Map»
«FILE (title == null ? "map" : title) + ".csv"-»
«FOREACH elements.typeSelect(mindmap::Topic) AS topic-»
«topic.name», «topic.priority», «topic.start», «topic.end»
«ENDFOREACH»
«ENDFILE»
«ENDDEFINE»
```

The template begins with a simple import of our mindmap model and the definition of a template named Main that operates on a passed-in **Map** instance, located using the source path project settings. The FILE directive creates a new CSV file with the name equal to the title of our map. Note that the end <<guillemet>> has a hyphen before it. This indicates that white space should be stripped from the contents of this element. We need this to ensure that our CSV file has no leading spaces or empty lines.

The FOREACH directive iterates over our Topic elements, which are distinguished from our Relationship elements using the typeSelect(mindmap::Topic) operation. We refer to each Topic instance during iteration as topic and access its attributes for output, inserting commas in between.

To invoke this template on our Mindmap.xmi dynamic instance, we need to configure our project and add the following mindmap2csv.mwe file.

```xml
<?xml version="1.0"?>
<workflow>
  <property name="model"
 value="platform:/resource/org.eclipse.dsl.mindmap/model/Mindmap.xmi"/>
  <property name="out" value="out" />

  <!— set up EMF for standalone execution —>
  <bean class="org.eclipse.emf.mwe.utils.StandaloneSetup">
    <platformUri value="../" />
  </bean>

  <component class="org.eclipse.emf.mwe.utils.Reader">
    <uri value="${model}" />
    <modelSlot value="model" />
  </component>

  <!— generate code —>
  <component class="org.eclipse.xpand2.Generator">
    <metaModel id="mm"
        class="org.eclipse.xtend.typesystem.emf.EmfRegistryMetaModel"/>
    <expand value="mindmap2csv::Main FOR model" />
    <outlet path="${out}"/>
  </component>
</workflow>
```

The workflow contains two component elements, one for the EMF reader that knows about our Ecore model and the other for the generator itself. The StandaloneSetup bean is initialized to the root of the workspace. You can find information on the workflow engine in Section 14.1.16, "Workflow Engine."

7.3 Generating Java

As we've mentioned previously, you must consider at least two possibilities when generating Java, or any programming language, from models. The first is to use

M2M from a source model into a Java model, followed by Java generation using dedicated templates. The alternative is to pass the source model to a set of templates designed to output Java code. In the former, the logical mapping from one model to the other takes place in the mappings of QVT; in the latter, the logic resides in Xpand and Xtend code throughout the templates and extension files. Sometimes one approach is superior to the other; as with the two following examples, both are feasible when transforming our Domain-Neutral Component (DNC) models to Java Persistence API (JPA) code.

BEST PRACTICE

This might seen obvious, but it's typically easier to first write code that works and templify it than to try to work in a template environment from the beginning. This applies to all text output formats, not just Java.

7.3.1 Using Java Model and Dedicated Template

In this section, we develop the template used to generate Java code from our Java EMF Model (JEM) instance. We use a single template, which you can see in its entirety next, followed by the Xtend utilities used by the template.

The `Main` definition takes a collection of `JavaPackage` elements. As you can see in the corresponding workflow file used to invoke the template, the source model can contain multiple root elements, which explains the use of `Collection`. The package definition is invoked for each `JavaPackage`, which expands each `JavaClass` that is not marked with a "`library`" annotation. Subpackages are then processed recursively. The `jemUtil.ext` file contains the functions used throughout to construct fully qualified class, package, and path strings.

```
«IMPORT java»

«EXTENSION templates::java::jemUtil»

«DEFINE Main FOR Collection[java::JavaPackage]»
  «EXPAND package FOREACH this.typeSelect(JavaPackage)»
«ENDDEFINE»

«DEFINE package FOR java::JavaPackage-»
  «EXPAND class FOREACH javaClasses.select(c |
    c.eAnnotations.first().source != 'library')»
  «EXPAND package FOREACH eSubpackages.typeSelect(JavaPackage)»
«ENDDEFINE»
```

```
«DEFINE class FOR java::JavaClass-»
«FILE this.fullyQualifiedPath()-»
«IF javaPackage.isValid()-»
package «javaPackage.fullyQualifiedName()»;
«ENDIF»
«EXPAND import FOREACH classImport-»

/**
«EXPAND classComment FOREACH eAnnotations.select(a | a.source ==
  'description').details-»
 * @generated
 */
«EXPAND annotation FOREACH eAnnotations.select(a | a.source ==
  'annotation').details-»
public class «name» «EXPAND extends FOR this-»
«EXPAND implements FOR this-» {

«EXPAND field FOREACH fields-»

«EXPAND reference FOREACH eReferences-»

«EXPAND method FOREACH methods-»

«EXPAND additions-»
}
«ENDFILE»
«ENDDEFINE»

«DEFINE extends FOR java::JavaClass-»
«IF getSupertype() != null»extends
«EXPAND superClass FOR getSupertype()-»«ENDIF-»
«ENDDEFINE»

«DEFINE implements FOR java::JavaClass-»
«IF implementsInterfaces.size > 0»implements
«EXPAND superClass FOREACH implementsInterfaces SEPARATOR ","-»«ENDIF-»
«ENDDEFINE»

«DEFINE superClass FOR java::JavaClass-»
«fullyQualifiedName(this)-»
«ENDDEFINE»

«DEFINE classComment FOR ecore::EStringToStringMapEntry-»
«IF key == null || key.length == 0-»
 * TODO: Enter description of the class here...«ELSE-»
 * «key-»
«ENDIF»
«ENDDEFINE»

«DEFINE annotation FOR ecore::EStringToStringMapEntry-»
     «key» «value»
«ENDDEFINE»
```

```
«DEFINE field FOR java::Field-»
«EXPAND generatedComment FOR this-»
  «EXPAND annotation FOREACH eAnnotations.select(a |
    a.source == 'annotation').details-»
    «javaVisibility.toString().toLowerCase()» «wrapIfCollection(this)»
«name-»;
«ENDDEFINE»

«DEFINE reference FOR ecore::EReference-»
«EXPAND generatedComment FOR this-»
  «EXPAND annotation FOREACH eAnnotations.select(a |
    a.source == 'annotation').details-»
      private «wrapIfCollection(this)» «name-»;
«ENDDEFINE»

«DEFINE method FOR java::Method-»
«EXPAND generatedComment FOR this-»
  «EXPAND annotation FOREACH eAnnotations.select(a |
    a.source == 'annotation').details-»
      «javaVisibility.toString().toLowerCase()-»
«wrapIfCollection(this)» «name-»(
«EXPAND parameter FOREACH parameters SEPARATOR ','») {
            «EXPAND block FOR source»
      }
«ENDDEFINE»

«DEFINE parameter FOR java::JavaParameter-»
«wrapIfCollection(this)» «name-»
«ENDDEFINE»

«DEFINE block FOR java::Block-»
    «this.source-»
    «EXPAND block FOREACH contents-»
«ENDDEFINE»

«DEFINE block FOR java::Comment-»
    /*
     * «this.source»
     */
    «EXPAND block FOREACH contents-»
«ENDDEFINE»

«DEFINE generatedComment FOR Object-»
    /**
     *@generated
     */
«ENDDEFINE»

«DEFINE import FOR java::JavaClass-»
import «this.fullyQualifiedName() + ";\n"-»
«ENDDEFINE»

«DEFINE additions FOR java::JavaClass-»«ENDDEFINE»
```

BEST PRACTICE

Notice the additions definition and its expansion within the class body. This facilitates extension later using Xpand's aspect-oriented capability. Whenever you anticipate that a template might be extended in the future, it's a good idea to provide such extensibility points in your templates.

Here's the `jemUtil.ext` file that contains the helper functions used earlier:

```
import java;
import ecore;
String fullyQualifiedName(JavaPackage p) :
  p.eSuperPackage == null ? p.name :
  fullyQualifiedName(p.eSuperPackage) + '.' + p.name
;

String fullyQualifiedName(JavaClass c) :
  let p = fullyQualifiedName(c.ePackage) :  p != '' && p !=
  'java.lang' ? p + '.' + c.name : c.name
;

String fullyQualifiedName(Void v) : '';

String fullyQualifiedPath(JavaClass c) :
  fullyQualifiedName(c.javaPackage).replaceAll('\\.', '/') + "/" +
  c.name + ".java"
;

String wrapIfCollection(ETypedElement element) :
  let p = element.eAnnotations.select(a | a.source == 'collection')
  : p.size > 0 ?
  p.first().details.first().value + "<" +
  fullyQualifiedName(element.eType) + ">" :
  fullyQualifiedName(element.eType)
;

Boolean isValid(JavaPackage package) :
  package != null && package.name != null && package.name.length > 0
;
```

To invoke the template on our Java model, we need to configure a workflow. In this case, the JEM model is found in the environment and declared using the `RegisterGeneratedEPackage` element. Ecore is also required because it is extended by JEM. Now look at the workflow used for this example.

```xml
<?xml version="1.0"?>
<workflow>
  <property name="model" value="org.eclipse.dsl.dnc/out/dnc.jem" />
  <property name="out" value="../org.eclipse.example/src-gen" />

  <!-- set up EMF for standalone execution -->
  <bean class="org.eclipse.emf.mwe.utils.StandaloneSetup">
    <platformUri value="../" />
    <RegisterGeneratedEPackage
      value="org.eclipse.emf.ecore.EcorePackage"/>
    <RegisterGeneratedEPackage
      value="org.eclipse.jem.java.JavaRefPackage"/>
  </bean>

  <!-- load model and store it in slot 'model' -->
  <component class="org.eclipse.emf.mwe.utils.Reader">
    <uri value="platform:/resource/${model}" />
    <modelSlot value="model" />
    <!-- needed when working with multiple roots in xmi files -->
    <firstElementOnly value="false" />
  </component>

  <!-- generate code -->
  <component class="org.eclipse.xpand2.Generator">
    <metaModel id="mm"
        class="org.eclipse.xtend.typesystem.emf.EmfRegistryMetaModel"/>
    <expand value="templates::java::java::Main FOR model" />
    <outlet path="${out}">
      <postprocessor class="org.eclipse.xpand2.output.JavaBeautifier"/>
    </outlet>
  </component>

</workflow>
```

This is the output for our `Address` archetype, having been transformed from our original business model into an `Entity`.

```java
package org.eclipse.example;

import javax.persistence.Entity;
import javax.persistence.Table;
import javax.persistence.Column;
import javax.persistence.Id;
import javax.persistence.GeneratedValue;
import javax.persistence.GenerationType;

/**
 * TODO: Enter description of the class here...
 *
 * @generated
 */
```

```java
@Entity
@Table(name = "ADDRESS")
public class Address implements java.io.Serializable {

  /**
   * @generated
   */
  private String street;

  /**
   * @generated
   */
  private String city;

  /**
   * @generated
   */
  @Column(name = "POSTAL_CODE")
  private String postalCode;

  /**
   * @generated
   */
  private String province;

  /**
   * @generated
   */
  private String country;

  /**
   * @generated
   */
  @Id
  @Column(name = "ADDRESS_ID")
  @GeneratedValue(strategy = GenerationType.AUTO)
  private int addressId;

  /**
   * @generated
   */
  public String getCity() {
    return city;
  }

  /**
   * @generated
   */
  public void setCity(String city) {
    this.city = city;
  }

  // Remaining getters and setters here...
}
```

The `Person` class generates as follows:

```java
package org.eclipse.example;

import javax.persistence.OneToMany;
import javax.persistence.OneToOne;
import javax.persistence.Entity;
import javax.persistence.Table;
import javax.persistence.Column;
import javax.persistence.Id;
import javax.persistence.GeneratedValue;
import javax.persistence.GenerationType;

/**
 * TODO: Enter description of the class here...
 * @generated
 */
@Entity
@Table(name="PERSON")
public class Person  implements java.io.Serializable {

    /**
     *@generated
     */
    @Column(name = "LAST_NAME")
    private String lastName;
    /**
     *@generated
     */
    @Column(name = "FIRST_NAME")
    private String firstName;
    /**
     *@generated
     */
    @Id
    @Column(name="PERSON_ID")
    @GeneratedValue(strategy=GenerationType.AUTO)
    private int personId;

    /**
     *@generated
     */
    @OneToMany(mappedBy="personId")
    private java.util.Collection<org.eclipse.example.Phone> phones;

    /**
     *@generated
     */
    @OneToOne(targetEntity=org.eclipse.example.Address.class)
    private org.eclipse.example.Address address;

    /**
     *@generated
     */
```

```java
  public java.util.Collection<org.eclipse.example.Phone> getPhones() {
    return phones;
  }

  /**
   *@generated
   */
  public void setPhones(java.util.Collection<org.eclipse.example.Phone>
phones) {
    this.phones = phones;
  }

  // Remaining getters and setters here...
}
```

Finally, consider our Phone class, which shows the @ManyToOne opposite to our @OneToMany in the Person class:

```java
package org.eclipse.example;

import javax.persistence.ManyToOne;
import javax.persistence.Entity;
import javax.persistence.Table;
import javax.persistence.Column;
import javax.persistence.Id;
import javax.persistence.GeneratedValue;
import javax.persistence.GenerationType;

/**
 * TODO: Enter description of the class here...
 * @generated
 */
  @Entity
  @Table(name="PHONE")
public class Phone  implements java.io.Serializable {

  /**
   *@generated
   */
  private String number;
  /**
   *@generated
   */
  @Column(name = "COUNTRY_CODE")
  private String countryCode;
  /**
   *@generated
   */
  private String type;
  /**
   *@generated
   */
  @Column(name = "AREA_CODE")
```

```
private String areaCode;
/**
 *@generated
 */
@Id
@Column(name="PHONE_ID")
@GeneratedValue(strategy=GenerationType.AUTO)
private int phoneId;
/**
 *@generated
 */
@ManyToOne
@JoinColumn(name="PERSON_ID")
private org.eclipse.example.Person owner;

// Remaining getters and setters here...
}
```

7.3.2 Using the DNC Model with Templates

To compare the approaches to generating Java, we now develop a template that generates the same code as the approach in the previous section but passes an instance of our DNC model instead of using an instance of JEM produced by a QVT. This template handles only Entity beans, although that could easily be extended to generate Session beans as well.

```
«IMPORT dnc»

«EXTENSION templates::java::dncUtil»

«DEFINE Main FOR oocore::Package»
  «EXPAND package FOREACH contents.typeSelect(oocore::Package)»
«ENDDEFINE»

«DEFINE package FOR oocore::Package-»
  «EXPAND entity FOREACH contents.typeSelect(dnc::Archetype).select(a |
a.isEntity())»
  «EXPAND package FOREACH contents.typeSelect(oocore::Package)»
«ENDDEFINE»

«DEFINE entity FOR dnc::Archetype-»
«FILE this.fullyQualifiedPath() -»
«IF package.isValid()-»
package «package.fullyQualifiedName()»;
«ENDIF»
import javax.persistence.Entity;
import javax.persistence.Table;
import javax.persistence.Column;
import javax.persistence.Id;
```

```
import javax.persistence.GeneratedValue;
import javax.persistence.GenerationType;
«IF !features.typeSelect(dnc::Association).collect(a |
a.upperBound == -1).isEmpty-»
import javax.persistence.OneToMany;«ENDIF»
«IF !features.typeSelect(dnc::Association).collect(a |
a.upperBound == 1).isEmpty-»
import javax.persistence.OneToOne;«ENDIF»
«IF features.typeSelect(oocore::Reference).collect(a |
  a.opposite.metaType == dnc::Association && a.opposite.upperBound ==
  -1).isEmpty-»
import javax.persistence.ManyToOne;
import javax.persistence.JoinColumn;«ENDIF»

/**
 * «IF description.length > 0-»«description-»«ELSE»TODO:
  Enter description of the class here...«ENDIF»
 *
 * @generated
 */
@Entity
@Table(name="«EXPAND toColumnName FOR name-»")
public class «name» «EXPAND extends FOR this-»implements
java.io.Serializable«EXPAND implements FOR this-» {

«EXPAND idAttribute FOR this-»
«EXPAND attribute FOREACH features.typeSelect(oocore::Attribute)-»
«EXPAND reference FOREACH features.typeSelect(oocore::Reference)-»
«EXPAND idGetter FOR this-»
«FOREACH features.typeSelect(oocore::StructuralFeature) AS feature-»
«EXPAND getter FOR feature-»
«EXPAND setter FOR feature-»
«ENDFOREACH»

«EXPAND method FOREACH features.typeSelect(oocore::Operation)-»
«EXPAND additions-»
}
«ENDFILE»
«ENDDEFINE»


«DEFINE extends FOR oocore::Class-»
«IF !superclasses.isEmpty»extends «EXPAND superClass FOR
  superclasses.select(c | c.interface == false).first()-»«ENDIF-»
«ENDDEFINE»


«DEFINE implements FOR oocore::Class-»
«IF superclasses.select(c | c.interface == true).size > 0», «EXPAND
  superClass FOREACH superclasses.select(c | c.interface == true)
SEPARATOR ","-»«ENDIF-»
«ENDDEFINE»


«DEFINE superClass FOR oocore::Class-»
«fullyQualifiedName(this)-»
«ENDDEFINE»
```

```
«DEFINE idAttribute FOR oocore::Class-»
«EXPAND generatedComment FOR this-»
        @Id
@Column(name="«name.toUpperCase()-»_ID")
        @GeneratedValue(strategy=GenerationType.AUTO)
        private int «name.toLowerCase()-»Id;
«ENDDEFINE»

«DEFINE attribute FOR oocore::Attribute-»
«EXPAND generatedComment FOR this-»
«IF name.toLowerCase() != name-»    @Column(name="
  «EXPAND toColumnName FOR name-»")«ENDIF»
        «visibility.toString().toLowerCase()» «dataType.name» «name-»;
«ENDDEFINE»

«DEFINE reference FOR dnc::Association-»
«IF this.type.isEntity()-»
«EXPAND generatedComment FOR this-»
«IF this.upperBound == -1-»
@OneToMany(mappedBy="«this.owner.name.toLowerCase()»Id")
«ELSEIF this.upperBound == 1-»
@OneToOne(targetEntity=«this.opposite.owner.fullyQualifiedName()».class
)«ENDIF»
      private «wrapIfCollection(this)» «name-»;
«ENDIF»
«ENDDEFINE»

«DEFINE reference FOR oocore::Reference-»
«IF this.generateReference()-»
«EXPAND generatedComment FOR this-»
      @ManyToOne
      @JoinColumn(name="«this.owner.name.toUpperCase()»_ID")
        private «wrapIfCollection(this)» «name-»;
«ENDIF»
«ENDDEFINE»

«DEFINE idGetter FOR oocore::Class-»
«EXPAND generatedComment FOR this-»
        public int get«name.toFirstUpper()»Id() {
                return «name.toLowerCase()»Id;
        }
«ENDDEFINE»

«REM»Abstract - do nothing, but here to keep Xpand editor happy«ENDREM»
«DEFINE getter FOR oocore::StructuralFeature»
«ENDDEFINE»
«DEFINE setter FOR oocore::StructuralFeature»
«ENDDEFINE»

«DEFINE getter FOR oocore::Attribute-»
«EXPAND generatedComment FOR this-»
   public «this.dataType.name» get«name.toFirstUpper()»() {
    return «name»;
   }
«ENDDEFINE»
```

```
«DEFINE setter FOR oocore::Attribute-»
«EXPAND generatedComment FOR this-»
   public void set«name.toFirstUpper()»(«this.dataType.name» «name») {
    this.«name» = «name»;
    }
«ENDDEFINE»

«DEFINE getter FOR oocore::Reference-»
«IF this.generateReference()-»
«EXPAND generatedComment FOR this-»
   public «wrapIfCollection(this)» get«name.toFirstUpper()»() {
    return «name»;
    }
«ENDIF»
«ENDDEFINE»

«DEFINE setter FOR oocore::Reference-»
«IF this.generateReference()-»
«EXPAND generatedComment FOR this-»
   public void set«name.toFirstUpper()»(«wrapIfCollection(this)»
«name») {
    this.«name» = «name»;
   }
«ENDIF»
«ENDDEFINE»

«DEFINE method FOR oocore::Operation-»
«EXPAND generatedComment FOR this-»
     «visibility.toString().toLowerCase()-» «wrapIfCollection(this)»
«name-»(«EXPAND parameter FOREACH parameters SEPARATOR ','») {
   //TODO: implement method
   }
«ENDDEFINE»

«DEFINE parameter FOR oocore::Parameter-»
«wrapIfCollection(this)» «name-»
«ENDDEFINE»

«DEFINE generatedComment FOR Object-»
  /**
   *@generated
   */
«ENDDEFINE»

«DEFINE toColumnName FOR String-»
«FOREACH this.toCharList() AS char ITERATOR i-»
«IF i.counter0 == 0-»«char.toUpperCase()-»
«ELSE-»«char.asColumnNameChar()-»«ENDIF-»«ENDFOREACH-»
«ENDDEFINE»

«DEFINE additions FOR dnc::Archetype-»«ENDDEFINE»
```

This is the corresponding Xtend utility file `dncUtil.ext`:

```
import dnc;
import oocore;

String fullyQualifiedName(Package p) :
  p.package == null ? p.name : fullyQualifiedName(p.package) + '.'
  + p.name
;

String fullyQualifiedName(Class c) :
  let p = fullyQualifiedName(c.package) :  p != '' &&
  p != "java.lang" ? p + '.' + c.name : c.name
;

String fullyQualifiedName(Void v) : '';

String fullyQualifiedPath(Class c) :
  fullyQualifiedName(c.package).replaceAll('\\.', '/') +
  "/" + c.name + ".java"
;

String wrapIfCollection(Reference reference) :
  reference.upperBound == -1 ?
    "java.util.Collection" + "<" + fullyQualifiedName(reference.type) +
">" :
    fullyQualifiedName(reference.type)
;

Boolean isValid(Package package) :
  package != null && package.name.length > 0
;

String asColumnNameChar(String s) :
  s.toLowerCase() == s ? s.toUpperCase() : '_' + s.toUpperCase()
;

Boolean isEntity(Class c) :
  c.metaType == dnc::MomentInterval ||
  c.metaType == dnc::MIDetail ||
  c.metaType == dnc::Party ||
  c.metaType == dnc::Place ||
  c.metaType == dnc::Thing ||
  c.metaType == dnc::Description
;

// Currently, we only create backward reference for ManyToOne
relationships
Boolean generateReference(oocore::Reference ref) :

  ref.type.isEntity() && ref.opposite.metaType == dnc::Association &&
  ref.opposite.upperBound == -1
;
```

Finally, this the workflow file used to invoke the templates using a test dynamic instance model. This is the same model that was used to feed the dnc2jee.qvto transformation.

```xml
<?xml version="1.0"?>
<workflow>
  <property name="model" value="org.eclipse.dsl.dnc/model/model.xmi" />
  <property name="out" value="../org.eclipse.example/src-gen2" />

  <!-- set up EMF for standalone execution -->
  <bean class="org.eclipse.emf.mwe.utils.StandaloneSetup">
    <platformUri value="../" />
  </bean>

  <!-- load model and store it in slot 'model' -->
  <component class="org.eclipse.emf.mwe.utils.Reader">
    <uri value="platform:/resource/${model}" />
    <modelSlot value="model" />
  </component>

  <!-- generate code -->
  <component class="org.eclipse.xpand2.Generator">
    <metaModel id="mm"
      class="org.eclipse.xtend.typesystem.emf.EmfRegistryMetaModel" />
    <expand value="templates::java::dnc2java::Main FOR model" />
    <outlet path="${out}">
      <postprocessor class="org.eclipse.xpand2.output.JavaBeautifier"/>
    </outlet>
  </component>

</workflow>
```

BEST PRACTICE

Note the use of the JavaBeautifier in the generator component's outlet element. Generally, it's better to rely on code formatters for generated code than sacrifice readability of the template itself in an effort to generate nicely formatted output directly. However, it's often necessary to strike a balance because the Toolsmith must also be able to understand the code generated by the template.

Looking back at our two approaches, it's hard to say that one is better than the other. The template-only approach seems a bit simpler, but this ultimately depends on your personal preference and familiarity in working with QVTO and Xpand/Xtend. I did notice that many similar yet different constructs exist in OCL/QVTO and Xpand/Xtend. This makes the GMF Xpand engine's use of

OCL/QVTO an attractive alternative because you would need to know only one set of languages for all your transformation needs. Sharing a single set of QVT libraries for both M2M and M2T would be most welcome.

When we start generating method body content, the template approach without the intermediate Java model likely will be the preferred approach. Even better would be the capability for QVT to invoke an Xpand template using one of its "black box" extension mechanisms. Of course, an enhanced Java model would be required if the former approach were used because the JEM model lacks the proper fidelity to create complex statements. In the HTML example, if the domain model's serialization syntax is no different from how its instances are normally consumed, the choice of transformation options becomes more clear. In the case of HTML, an M2M from a DSL to an XHTML model requires no M2T to obtain the desired result. In fact, any XSD-based model imported into EMF provides the same characteristic. Many popular or standard XML Schemas have already been used to produce Ecore models, enhanced with additional capabilities exposed as derived features and methods.

TIP

Consult the QVTO Metamodel Explorer to see what models are registered in your environment. A full Eclipse installation contains many registered models, ranging from Web Service Definition Language (WSDL), to Enterprise Java Beans (EJB), to data models, to the Unified Modeling Language (UML). This explorer becomes handy when authoring transformations when you need to see the model structure and available features.

7.4 Generating HTML

For both our mindmap and requirements DSLs, we want to generate documentation. This can be done at least two ways using the Modeling project. First, simply use a model instance within templates to output whatever text you want—plain ASCII, HTML, or whatever. Another approach is to do a M2M to the model of another document, such as XHTML or another schema-backed format. The native serialization provided by EMF produces the output document, so all we need to do is provide the M2M. To assess the pros and cons of each approach, we use both here.

If you will generate HTML from templates, it makes sense to use JET—that is, if you've done JSP development in the past. However, we use Xpand here to illustrate its use. The following is a basic Xpand template that creates the output HTML report from a test requirements model. As we reference the scenario reference from our requirements, we need to link a source folder so that Xpand can resolve the reference. This is done in the project properties, as shown in Figure 7-4.

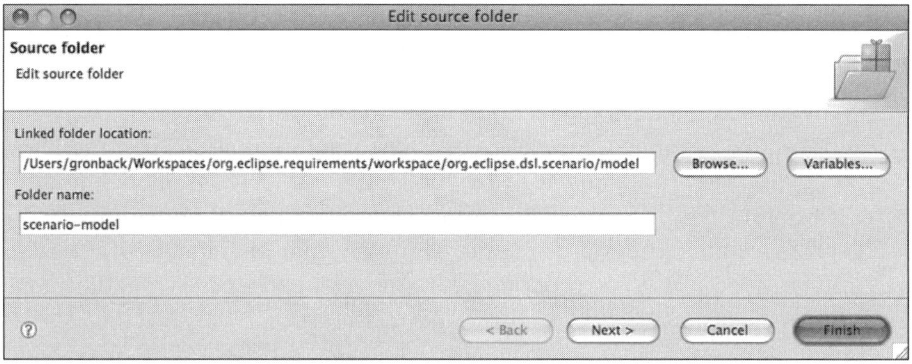

Figure 7-4   Edit Source Folder dialog

```
«IMPORT requirements»

«DEFINE Main FOR Model»
«FILE (title == null ? "requirements" : title) + ".html"»
<html>
<head><title>«title»</title></head>
<body>
<h1>«title» Report</h1>
«EXPAND index FOR this-»
<hr/>
«EXPAND groupContent FOREACH groups-»
</body>
</html>
«ENDFILE»
«ENDDEFINE»

«DEFINE index FOR Model-»
<h3>Contents</h3>
<ul>«EXPAND groupIndex FOREACH groups-»</ul>
«ENDDEFINE»

«DEFINE groupIndex FOR RequirementGroup»
<li><a href="#group«id»">«name-»</a></li>
«IF !requirements.isEmpty-»
<ul>«EXPAND requirementIndex FOREACH requirements-»</ul>
«ENDIF»
«IF !children.isEmpty-»
<ul>«EXPAND groupIndex FOREACH children-»</ul>
«ENDIF»
```

```
«ENDDEFINE»

«DEFINE requirementIndex FOR Requirement»
<li><a href="#req«id»">«title»</a></li>
«IF !children.isEmpty-»
<ul>«EXPAND requirementIndex FOREACH children-»</ul>
«ENDIF»
«ENDDEFINE»

«DEFINE groupContent FOR RequirementGroup-»
<h3><a name="group«id»">«name»</a></h3>
«IF parent != null-»<b>Parent:</b> <a
href="#group«parent.id»">«parent.name-»</a>«ENDIF»
<p>«description-»</p>
«EXPAND requirementContent FOREACH requirements-»
«EXPAND groupContent FOREACH children-»
«ENDDEFINE»

«DEFINE requirementContent FOR Requirement-»
<table width="100%">
<tr style="background: LightSteelBlue">
  <th colspan="4" align="left">
    <a name="req«id»">Requirement: «title»</a></th>
</tr>
<tr style="background: GhostWhite">
  <td><b>ID:</b> «id»</td>
  <td colspan="3">«IF parent != null-»<b>Parent:</b>
    <a href="#req«parent.id»">«parent.title-»</a>«ENDIF»</td>
</tr>
<tr style="background: GhostWhite">
  <td><b>Type:</b> «type == Type::FUNCTIONAL ? "Functional" :
➡ "NonFunctional"»
  </td>
  <td><b>Version:</b> «version.major == null ? "0" :
    version.major».«version.minor == null ? "0" :
    version.minor».«version.service == null ? "0" :
version.service»</td>
  <td colspan="2"><b>Created:</b> «created»</td>
</tr>
<tr style="background: GhostWhite">
  <td><b>Priority:</b> «priority»</td>
  <td><b>State:</b> «state»</td>
  <td><b>Resolution:</b> «resolution»</td>
  <td><b>Scenario:</b> «scenario == null ? "none" :
    scenario.name»</td>
</tr>
<tr style="background: Snow"><td colspan="4">«description-»</td></tr>
</table>
<h4>Dependencies</h4>
«IF !dependencies.isEmpty-»
<ul>«FOREACH dependencies AS dependency-»
<li><a href="#req«dependency.id»">«dependency.title»</a></li>
«ENDFOREACH»
</ul>
«ELSE»There are no dependencies for this requirement.<br/><br/>
«ENDIF»
«IF !comments.isEmpty-»
```

```
<h4>Comments</h4>
<table width="100%">
«EXPAND comment FOREACH comments-»
</table>
<br/>
«ENDIF»
«EXPAND requirementContent FOREACH children-»
«ENDDEFINE»

«DEFINE comment FOR Comment-»
<tr style="background: LightYellow"><td colspan="2">
  <b>By:</b> «author»</td><td><b>On:</b> «created»</td></tr>

<tr style="background: SeaShell"><td colspan="3">
  <b>Subject:</b> «subject»</td></tr>
<tr style="background: Snow"><td colspan="3">«body»</td></tr>
«EXPAND comment FOREACH children-»
«ENDDEFINE»
```

Figure 7.5 shows a sample generated output from the requirements report.

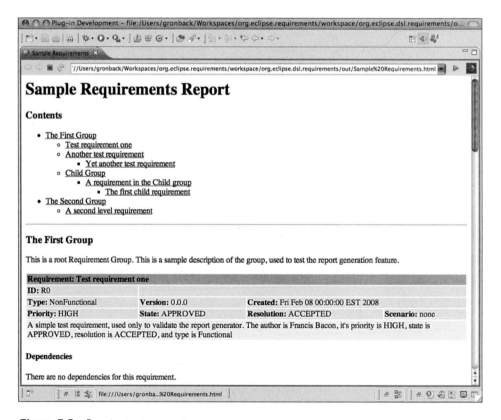

Figure 7-5   Requirements report

One thing to note when generating HTML with templates is that you have to deal with all those pesky angle brackets. The M2M approach benefited from the fact that we dealt directly with the elements and attributes, without the concern of matching brackets or even having to see them. Then again, we needed to deal with the abstract syntax that was clearly not created to be "Toolsmith friendly." Perhaps the best thing for HTML would be a textual concrete syntax and generated editor from the TMF project. In addition, it would be nice if our template editor were aware not only of our template language syntax, but also of our domain model. Perhaps someday it will be possible to generate hybrid template editors that can provide this capability.

The following is the workflow definition used to invoke our report template for this sample. Note the use of the XmlBeautifier postprocessor.

```xml
<?xml version="1.0"?>
<workflow>
  <property name="model"
            value="platform:/resource/org.eclipse.dsl.requirements/
            model/Requirements.xmi" />
  <property name="out" value="out" />

  <bean class="org.eclipse.emf.mwe.utils.StandaloneSetup">
    <platformUri value="../" />
    <RegisterEcoreFile
          value="platform:/resource/org.eclipse.dsl.scenario/
          model/scenario.ecore"/>
  </bean>

  <component class="org.eclipse.emf.mwe.utils.Reader">
    <uri value="${model}" />
    <modelSlot value="model" />
  </component>

  <component class="org.eclipse.xpand2.Generator">
    <metaModel id="mm"
        class="org.eclipse.xtend.typesystem.emf.EmfRegistryMetaModel"/>
    <expand value="requirements2html::Main FOR model" />
    <outlet path="${out}">
      <postprocessor class="org.eclipse.xpand2.output.XmlBeautifier"/>
    </outlet>
  </component>

</workflow>
```

7.5 Summary

In this chapter, we explored the Xpand component of the M2T project and its complementary workflow component from the EMFT project. Xpand provides a powerful template language and engine for code generation within the context of our DSL Toolkit and hereby completes our tour through its main elements. Next, we'll explore some of the packaging and deployment topics for our DSLs.

CHAPTER 8

DSL Packaging and Deployment

So far, we've developed a series of abstract syntax models, diagrams, and model transfor-mations. After creating a collection of domain-specific language (DSL)-related artifacts, a Toolsmith needs to test and deploy them to a Practitioner's workbench. In this chapter, we explore polishing items, packaging, and deployment options for these artifacts.

Although this book does not cover the topic, it should become obvious that much of the code you create to deploy DSLs could be generated from yet another DSL defined to model the aspects of deployment (not to mention building and packaging aspects). Feature definition, user interface plug-in, transformation invocation actions, and so on are all potential targets for a set of code-generation templates and corresponding models. When it comes to product lines, the information captured to select variation points and options for generating a set of plug-ins that represent a product are ideally captured in models and leveraged in this manner.

8.1 Deployment Preparation

Before deployment, you must tie up all loose ends. Up to this point, we've been developing our collection of requirements DSLs in a development workspace and testing in a runtime instance with all plug-ins. Let's look at a number of check-list items to make sure our DSLs are generated consistently, in preparation for feature and product definition.

8.1.1 Artwork

The most impactful thing we can do at this point is add icons and other artwork to the diagram, edit, and editor plug-ins we've generated. The default generated icons do little to convey meaning, so we can replace them with ones that do—or just remove them altogether. Remember, just because we can add icons doesn't mean we should.

I'm not a graphic artist, so let's look for another source of icons. Thousands of icons ship with Eclipse, so we can try to reuse these, although I don't recommend this for a real product. Before plug-ins were bundled in .jar files, it was simple to see all the icons that shipped with Eclipse. It's still easy to do with a simple Ant script that extracts all *.gif images from each of the **/*.jar files in the plug-ins directory. Start with a complete install of all Eclipse projects, and then prepare to scroll through thousands of icons in your file browser.

After collecting some candidate icons, we begin to replace those found in our generated plug-in projects. This is most easily accomplished by simply renaming your new icons to match the names found in the /icons/full/obj16/ directory (or similar directory). Most diagram element icons are found in their corresponding *.model.edit plug-in, and the Diagram Wizard icon is found in the *.diagram plug-in. In the case of our Requirements editor, we need to replace the image in its EMF-generated *.editor plug-in. This gets us close, but some missing ones still will require path information to be entered into our models. It's a good idea to back up the plug-in icon directories at this point, to avoid losing them upon regeneration.

Reference-based links in our diagrams are missing icons because they do not correspond to a domain model class element, as is the case with our Mindmap subtopic link. To specify the icon to use for the subtopic link, we can open the mindmap.gmftool model and navigate to our Subtopic Creation Tool. The tooling model wizard adds a large and small Default Image element to each creation tool, which normally points to the corresponding *.edit plug-in icon. We can delete these children from our Subtopic tool and create a new Small Icon Bundle Image. For the Bundle property, we can point to our org.eclipse.mindmap.model.edit plug-in and specify icons/full/obj16/Subtopic.gif for the Path property. Of course, we need to add this image to the *.edit plug-in because it was not provided. After this, we can recreate the mindmap.gmfgen model from the mindmap.gmfmap model and regenerate the Mindmap diagram. You'll find the new icon used in the palette, which just leaves updating the remainder of the tooling models for similar cases.

You won't go this far in the sample projects, but consider adding several other artwork items to your Eclipse-based product. Welcome pages, splash images, about dialog images, and more are all possibilities. Look to the branding topic in the Eclipse help system to find out more information on providing additional polish to your application.

8.1.2 Developing a User Interface Plug-In

We've tested our diagrams in the runtime workbench and our transformations in the development workbench using dynamic instance models. Now we can create an `org.eclipse.requirements.ui` plug-in that will give us a place to define a Requirements perspective, a project wizard, and the actions and object contributions we need to allow Practitioners to invoke them on their artifacts.

Wizard and Perspective

Using the **New** → **Plug-in Project** wizard, create an empty `org.eclipse.requirements.ui` plug-in in your workspace. In the **Extensions** page of the plug-in manifest editor, create a new contribution to the `org.eclipse.ui.newWizards` extension-point. Add a category to this contribution with an ID of `org.eclipse.requirements.wizards.category`. We use this ID later to unite our generated editor wizards under a common category in the **New** dialog. Now add the wizard element and name it `Requirements Project Wizard` with an ID of `org.eclipse.requirements.ui.wizards.id`. Complete the rest of the contribution to match the following—note that it specifies a Requirements perspective that we define next.

```
<extension
     point="org.eclipse.ui.newWizards">
  <category
        name="Requirements"
        id="org.eclipse.requirements.wizards.category"/>
  <wizard
        name="%_UI_ProjectWizard_label"
        icon="icons/wizard.gif"
        category="org.eclipse.requirements.wizards.category"

class="org.eclipse.requirements.ui.wizards.RequirementsProjectWizard"
        finalPerspective="org.eclipse.requirements.perspective"
        id="org.eclipse.requirements.ui.wizards.id"
        project="true">
     <description>%_UI_ProjectWizard_description</description>
  </wizard>
</extension>
```

Using the helper in the editor, or by manually entering into the `plugin.xml` tab itself, contribute the following to the `org.eclipse.ui.perspectives` and `perspectiveExtensions` extension-points.

```
<extension
     point="org.eclipse.ui.perspectives">
  <perspective
        name="%_UI_Perspective_label"
        icon="icons/wizard.gif"
        class="org.eclipse.requirements.ui.RequirementsPerspective"
        id="org.eclipse.requirements.perspective">
     <description>%_UI_Perspective_description</description>
  </perspective>
</extension>

<extension point="org.eclipse.ui.perspectiveExtensions">
  <perspectiveExtension
     targetID="org.eclipse.requirements.perspective">
     <perspectiveShortcut id="org.eclipse.ui.resourcePerspective"/>
     <newWizardShortcut id="org.eclipse.requirements.ui.wizards.id"/>
     <actionSet id="org.eclipse.jdt.ui.JavaActionSet"/>
     <actionSet id="org.eclipse.debug.ui.launchActionSet"/>
     <viewShortcut id="org.eclipse.search.ui.views.SearchView"/>
  </perspectiveExtension>
</extension>
```

We've specified a `RequirementsProjectWizard` and a `Requirements-Perspective` in our manifest that we need to implement. The implementations for each class are not covered here, but are provided in the sample projects. Consult the Eclipse help system for additional information on wizards and perspectives; their details fall outside the scope of this book. The important information required is the wizard category ID that we can use with our generator models in Section 8.1.3, "Generation Models."

Preferences

Our generated diagram preferences are each given their own root in the Preferences dialog, but we want them all to fall under a general **Requirements** category that will eventually contain more general preferences. To provide a common category each diagram can leverage, we'll define a contribution to the `org.eclipse.ui.preferencePages` extension-point as follows.

```
<extension point="org.eclipse.ui.preferencePages">
   <page
        class="org.eclipse.requirements.preferences.
           RequirementsGeneralPreferencePage"
        id="org.eclipse.requirements.preferences.category"
```

```
            name="%_UI_PreferencePage_label">
    </page>
</extension>
```

We can use the Quick Fix to have a default implementation provided for our
`RequirementsGeneralPreferencePage` class, with the important item currently being the creation of the preference category ID.

Actions

We now have a new perspective and project type for our Requirements product,
along with its four editors and corresponding creation wizard. But we don't have
a way for the Practitioner to invoke the various transformations defined by the
Toolsmith on each of the instance models that will be created. For this, we can
provide action contributions to invoke the QVT Operational Mapping Language
(QVTO) and Xpand templates on the various artifacts.

The sample projects contain actions to invoke each of our transformations,
although we can improve these a bit. At the time of this writing, QVTO scripts
are not yet available to be invoked by the Modeling Workflow Engine. The
chaining of transformations is a common use case that we could work into our
Java code, although we prefer to define it in a workflow. Furthermore, the current action to invoke a QVTO transformation simply uses the standard launch
configuration in a dialog. The most awkward part of the process is that QVTO
expects the root element of the file we invoke the action upon to be its input
model. In the case of diagrams that are persisted in the same file as the domain
model, this means simply picking the proper element within the file using the dialog. Still, it could be all done without user intervention, beyond selecting the
input model and specifying the output location.

```
<extension
      point="org.eclipse.m2m.qvt.oml.runtime.qvtTransformation">
  <transformation
        file="transformations/mindmap2requirements.qvto"
        id="org.eclipse.requirements.actions.
            TransformMindmap2Requirements.transformationId">
  </transformation>
  . . .
</extension>

<extension point="org.eclipse.ui.popupMenus">
  <objectContribution
        id="org.eclipse.requirements.actions.
            TransformMindmap2Requirements.id"
        nameFilter="*.mmd"
        objectClass="org.eclipse.core.resources.IFile">
```

```
    <action
          label="%TransformMindmap2Requirements_label"
          class="org.eclipse.requirements.actions.
                TransformMindmap2Requirements"
          menubarPath="additions"
          enablesFor="1"
          id="org.eclipse.requirements.actions.
                TransformMindmap2Requirements.actionId">
    </action>
  </objectContribution>
  . . .
  <objectContribution
        id="org.eclipse.requirements.actions.TransformMindmapToCsv.id"
        nameFilter="*.mmd"
        objectClass="org.eclipse.core.resources.IFile">
    <action
          label="%TransformMindmapToCsv_label"
          class="org.eclipse.requirements.actions.
                TransformMindmapToCsv"
          menubarPath="additions"
          enablesFor="1"
          id="org.eclipse.requirements.actions.
                TransformMindmapToCsv.actionId">
    </action>
  </objectContribution>
</extension>
```

This is the action code to invoke the mindmap2requirements transformation:

```
public class TransformMindmap2Requirements implements
➥IObjectActionDelegate {

  private IWorkbenchPart targetPart;
  private URI fileURI;

  public void setActivePart(IAction action, IWorkbenchPart targetPart)
  {
    this.targetPart = targetPart;
  }

  public void selectionChanged(IAction action, ISelection selection) {
    fileURI = null;
    action.setEnabled(false);
    if (selection instanceof IStructuredSelection == false ||
      selection.isEmpty()) {
     return;
    }
    IFile file = (IFile) ((IStructuredSelection)
      selection).getFirstElement();
    fileURI = URI.createPlatformResourceURI(
      file.getFullPath().toString(), true);
    action.setEnabled(true);
  }
```

```
public void run(IAction action) {
  try {
    EObject source = getInput();
    if (source == null) {
      String title =
          Messages.RunInterpretedTransformationAction_title;
      String message =
          Messages.RunInterpretedTransformationAction_message;
      MessageDialog.openInformation(getShell(), title,
          NLS.bind(message, fileURI.toString()));
    } else {
      URI transfUri = URI.createURI("platform:/plugin/
          org.eclipse.requirements.ui/transformations/
          mindmap2requirements.qvto"); //$NON-NLS-1$
      ArrayList<URI> paramUris = new ArrayList<URI>();
      paramUris.add(fileURI);

      IWizard wizard = (IWizard) new
          RunInterpretedTransformationWizardDelegate(
          transfUri, paramUris);
      WizardDialog wizardDialog =
          new WizardDialog(getShell(), wizard);
      wizardDialog.open();
    }
  } catch (Exception ex) {
    handleError(ex);
  }
}

private EObject getInput() {
  ResourceSetImpl rs = new ResourceSetImpl();
  return rs.getEObject(fileURI.appendFragment("/"), true);
}

private void handleError(Throwable ex) {
  MessageDialog.openError(getShell(), "Transformation failed",
      MessageFormat.format("{0}: {1}",
      ex.getClass().getSimpleName(), ex.getMessage()
      == null ? "no message" : ex.getMessage()));
}

private Shell getShell() {
  return targetPart.getSite().getShell();
}
}
```

The action used to invoke a workflow for Model-to-Text Transformation (M2T) is largely the same. The following run() method is an example of how the two differ.

```
public void run(IAction action) {
  try {
    EObject source = getInput();
    if (source == null) {
      String title = Messages.RunTransformationAction_title;
      String message = Messages.RunTransformationAction_message;

      MessageDialog.openInformation(getShell(), title,
          NLS.bind(message, file.getFullPath()));
    } else {
      final URL url = FileLocator.toFileURL(new
          URL("platform:/plugin/org.eclipse.requirements.ui/
          templates/mindmap2csv.mwe"));
      final Map<String, String> properties =
          new HashMap<String, String>();
      properties.put("model", URI.createPlatformResourceURI(
          file.getFullPath().toString(), true).toString());
      properties.put("out", Platform.getLocation().toOSString() +
          file.getParent().getFullPath());
      new WorkflowRunner().run(url.getPath(), new
          NullProgressMonitor(), properties, null);

file.getParent().refreshLocal(IResource.DEPTH_ONE, new
          org.eclipse.core.runtime.NullProgressMonitor());
    }
  } catch (Exception ex) {
    handleError(ex);
  }
}
```

8.1.3 Generation Models

Let's revisit each of our generation models, to examine the options we might have
overlooked during development and leverage our new UI plug-in.

We've seen that GMF can persist models and diagrams in either separate files
or just one. For our application, we don't need several diagrams on a single large
model instance, so we'll set the Same File for Diagram and Model property in the Gen Editor Generator element to true for all *.gmfgen models.
Also in this element is the Copyright Text property, which we populate with
the appropriate statement. Likewise, in each EMF *.genmodel file, we enter the
statement in its Copyright Text property of the root element. Note that copyright statements are output only on initial generation, forcing a delete and regeneration of our existing code. We don't necessarily need to do this for our samples
because they contain modified code that would need to be preserved and restored
after regeneration.

In the `Gen Plugin` element for each diagram, we set the `Name` property and `Provider` appropriately—in this case, a friendly name for each plug-in and `Eclipse.org` for the provider. We also set `Printing Enabled` to true because it's not enabled by default. For the `Version` property, we leave the default `1.0.0.qualifier` value because the `qualifier` suffix will be replaced by a time stamp during export and, eventually, during our headless PDE build.

By default, Graphical Modeling Framework (GMF) places its generated new diagram wizards in the Examples category. We want each of our requirements editors to fall under our new requirements category, so we can modify the diagram `.gmfgen` models to specify `org.eclipse.requirements.wizards.category` for the `Gen Diagram` element's `Creation Wizard Category ID` property, found in the `Editor` category. Eclipse Modeling Framework (EMF), on the other hand, places its generated creation wizards in its own **Example EMF Model Creation Wizards** category with the ID `org.eclipse.emf.ecore.wizard.category.ID`. Unfortunately, the EMF genmodel provides only a Boolean property either to generate a wizard or not, with no property to specify the category it should fall under. We don't expect to change it often, and because EMF does not overwrite plug-in manifest files upon regeneration, we can make the change in the generated `org.eclipse.requirements.model.editor/plugin.xml` file. Delete the nested `category` element from the `*.newWizards` contribution and change the `wizard` element's category attribute to `org.eclipse.requirements.wizards.category`.

We created a general preference category for our Requirements product that we now need to leverage in our generated diagram preferences. Unfortunately, the `Gen Standard Preference Page` element in the GMF generator model does not enable us to specify the parent `category`. We can produce a decorator model and custom templates to provide a generated approach, or we can simply add to each generated plug-in manifest the `org.eclipse.requirements.preferences.category` ID as the root page's `category`. After doing so, we see each diagram preferences under a common **Requirements** group, as shown in Figure 8-1.

Finally, not all string values can be adjusted in the generator model. This forces us to make final polish tweaks to the `message.properties` file in our generated diagram. For example, our color modeling diagram is called dnc Diagram in our new diagram wizard. Many of the default namings come from the underlying domain model—in this case, our dnc package. After using these and some other polishing items, we're ready to specify a product definition and export it for testing and use.

Figure 8-1   Requirements preferences

8.2 Defining a Product

Using the Product Definition Wizard and associated Help content, we can configure a `requirements.product` to use for deploying our product for multiple
platforms. We first configure a minimal launch configuration that includes only
those required and use it to configure the product itself. Be careful when selecting required plug-ins: The PDE's **Add Required Plug-ins** feature does not always
detect all runtime requirements.

We need to download and install the RCP delta pack into our target, to
ensure that we have the different platform launch files available. When this is
complete, we can build our product bundles from the Product Definition editor
and test on the required platforms.

Another option to building a product is to look at Amalgam's release engineering builder, which comes as another example in the DSL Toolkit. The DSL
Toolkit itself is built using this method, which begins by defining a build model
to account for the parameters required to generate build scripts from a related
product model. This model-driven build approach is in its beginning stages, so I
do not discuss this in detail at this point. The PDE's build templates could someday be Xpand templates, and the entire build process could be driven by a simple configuration model for each project or component.

8.2.1 Deploying Source

One of the reasons I chose to use a Plug-in Project type for our DSLs will now
become apparent. As you know, the Plug-ins view in Eclipse lets you import any
plug-in into your workspace. If the plug-in was packaged with source code, you

can import the plug-in into your workspace in a condition to continue develop-ment. We can apply the same concept to working with DSLs. If we properly configure our DSL projects for deployment, clients can import the source of the deployed DSL into their workspace; modify the domain model, templates, dia-gram definition, and so on; and regenerate the plug-ins to provide an update.

8.3 Summary

In this chapter, we touched upon the most basic packaging elements to consider when creating a product for your DSL. Many additional enhancements and usability issues will need to be resolved, though fall outside the scope of this book. This concludes the hands-on portion of the book.

PART III

Reference

This part of the book provides reference information on the key components used in the domain-specific language (DSL) Toolkit. Here I introduce Graphical Editing Framework (GEF) as an underlying element of Graphical Modeling Framework (GMF) and dedicate chapters to the GMF runtime and tooling components. This part also covers the Query/View Transformation (QVT) Operational Mapping Language and Xpand template language in chapters that are intended to be used throughout the development of the sample projects in Part II and later during your own DSL-based development.

CHAPTER 9

Graphical Editing Framework

The Graphical Editing Framework (GEF) is a project with the top-level Eclipse Tools Project and, as with Eclipse Modeling Framework (EMF), is one of the earliest Eclipse projects. Because no existing book is dedicated to GEF, this chapter provides an overview of the framework, based largely on the content available from the GEF documentation. This book covers GEF only to the extent required to understand Graphical Modeling Framework (GMF).

GEF consists of two plug-ins: Draw2d (`org.eclipse.draw2d`) and GEF (`org.eclipse.gef`). Draw2d, an extension of Standard Widget Toolkit (SWT), provides painting and layout functionality. GEF is built on top of Draw2d and provides an Model-View-Controller (MVC) framework for graphical editors. Although Draw2d depends on only SWT, GEF builds upon Draw2d and also supplies integration with the Eclipse platform. Note that the two collectively are commonly considered GEF and are not distinguished separately. Figure 9-1 is the Plug-in Development Environment (PDE)'s Plug-In Dependencies view, to illustrate the minimal requirements of GEF and Draw2d.

Figure 9-1   GEF dependencies

9.1 Draw2d

Figures lie at the heart of the Draw2d toolkit. Figures can consist of children figures, which are painted inside the parent's bounds and arranged by a layout manager. A `LightweightSystem` coordinates the `Canvas` with the set of figures by forwarding nonpaint events from SWT using an `EventDispatcher`. Paint events are forwarded to the `UpdateManager`, which coordinates painting and layout, as shown in Figure 9-2.

9.1.1 Figures

Because Figures figure so prominently in Draw2d, let's discuss their general responsibilities as defined in their extensive API. Following are some highlights; the rest of this section goes into more detail on their use. Figures are responsible for the following:

❍ Adding and removing child figures

❍ Adding and removing listeners (for example, coordinate, figure, focus, key, layout, ancestor, mouse, and property change listeners)

❍ Calculating whether a point falls within the figure bounds (hit testing)

❍ Locating a figure for a given location

❍ Returning the figure's border, bounds, location, ToolTip, color, font, transparency, visibility, and so on

❍ Accessing the figure's update and layout manager

❍ Painting and validating

❍ Setting and getting focus

❍ Handling events for structural changes, movement, resizing, and so on

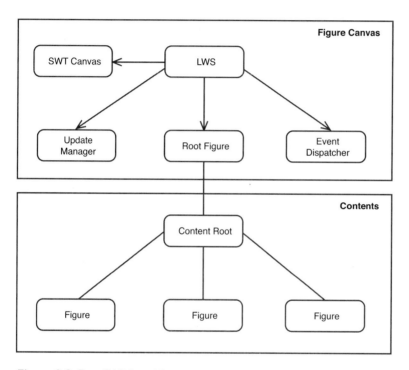

Figure 9-2 Draw2d lightweight system

Figure 9-3 illustrates a user interaction scenario to describe how these elements work together.

9.1.2 Text

In addition to figures, Draw2d has support for text. Labels (`org.eclipse.draw2d.Label`) are the primary means, while "rich text" features are also available in the `org.eclipse.draw2d.text` package. This allows for wrapping content such as a paragraph, mixing nontext with text (Tufte would love this!), supporting bidirectional support, and more.

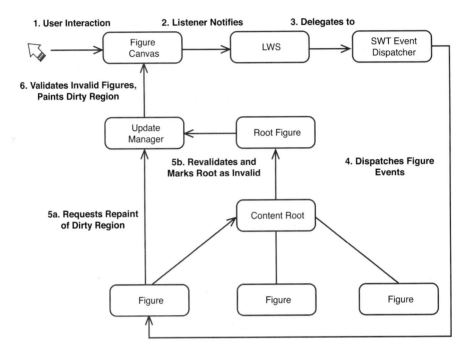

Figure 9-3 Draw2D interaction sequence

9.1.3 Painting

The following sequence illustrates the process of figure painting.

paint()—This method is declared on the interface and kicks off the painting process. First, properties are set on the graphics that children would inherit, including font and background and foreground color. Then the graphics state is pushed so that just these inherited settings can be restored when painting children. Next, the following methods are called:

paintFigure()—The figure paints itself, although figures are not required to paint at all. A simple form of painting is to fill in the bounding box with the figure's background color.

paintClientArea()—The client area is where children appear. This method should apply any changes to the graphics that affect only children, such as coordinate system modifications and translating the graphics to the client area. This method also clips the graphics to the region where children are allowed to appear.

paintChildren()—Now that the client area is set up, children are painted. After each child paints, the graphics state is restored to the incoming state so that children do not overwrite the inherited graphics settings from the parent.

paintBorder()—Finally, the figure paints decorations that should appear on top of the children. If a border has been set on the figure, it paints now.

Figures are composed in trees, structurally speaking, so they are painted by traversing the tree in depth-first order. As an example, consider the tree in Figure 9-4 and the Z-order depicted in the corresponding image to the right.

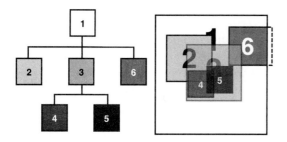

Figure 9-4   Figure composition

Children within figures cannot paint outside their parent's bounds. Clipping occurs while figures are painted and is cumulative for the entire parent hierarchy. Figure 9-5 is a simple figure hierarchy and shows the result of clipping on its rendition.

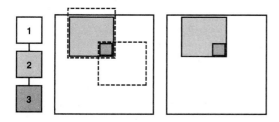

Figure 9-5   Figure clipping

9.1.4 Layout

Draw2d provides layout using two steps: first by marking figures as invalid if they need layout, and second by validating "branches" of invalid figures. Layout occurs all at once because Draw2d employs a deferred update strategy and, therefore, avoids displaying intermediate states when multiple figures become invalid.

Draw2d uses the term *validation* to perform layout. The `validate()` method can be extended to perform other functions that require integration with the update manager. When the `validate()` method is called, a figure performs its layout and then validates its children.

Layout requires information on the size of children figures, so methods are provided for querying minimum, maximum, and preferred sizes. If you know an available dimension, you can pass it as a hint to a figure when querying, which instructs the figure to consider the dimension when it returns its size requirements.

If a figure changes so that layout is required, it calls `revalidate()` to mark itself as invalid and requesting revalidation on its parent. This continues up the hierarchy and ends with an entry in the update manager's list of invalid figures. The update manager performs top-down layout by first setting the bounds of the parent and calling `validate()` on its children.

9.1.5 Connections and Routing

Draw2d provides a connection to form a line between two points. A `PolylineConnection` holds source and target `ConnectionAnchor` elements. A `ConnectionRouter` manages end and intermediate points along the line. Figure 9-6 illustrates a connection and its associated elements.

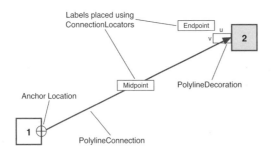

Figure 9-6   Polyline connection

The main difference between a connection and regular figures is that the `ConnectionRouter` is responsible for setting its bounds. Specialized routers can impose further constraints on a connection's bounds. Connections are typically managed by a single router instance and reside in a `ConnectionLayer`.

Anchors are used to place connection endpoints in either a fixed position or a calculated position related to some figure. For example, the `ChopboxAnchor` determines the point at which the bounds of a figure are intersected by the line traveling from some reference point to the center of the figure, as seen in Figure 9-7.

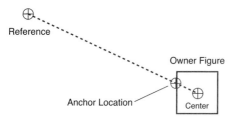

Figure 9-7   Chopbox anchor

Connections can have end decorations, such as arrowheads or labels. A `DelegatingLayout` is used to determine the placement of these decorations by delegating to a `Locator`. When adding a rotatable `PolygonDecoration` or label at the end of a polyline connection, its bounds are extended to allow these elements to be painted in addition to the line itself.

Connections affect layout because routing must occur before children can be placed. When validating a connection, a layout algorithm must remember its old bounds when determining the new, and invalidate the appropriate region in the update manager. Fortunately, the default implementation does this for you.

9.1.6 Coordinate Systems

Draw2d has two coordinate systems to consider: absolute (inherited) and relative (local). In the absolute situation (the default), figures can be compared with one another because they all use the same system. It's "inherited" in the sense that when a figure is moved, the children coordinates must be translated by the same amount. In the relative (local) situation, coordinates are relative to the bounds area of the parent, except for when the parent has insets. To use local coordinates, the parent overrides `useLocalCoordinates()` for its children. Table 9-1, from Draw2d, includes reasons you might choose to use local or absolute coordinates.

Table 9-1   Draw2d Coordinate System

Task	Absolute Coordinates	Relative Coordinates
Translate or move a figure	The figure and all its children must be translated, which can be expensive in extreme cases.	Only the figure's bounds must be updated. The children move for free.
Hit-test/determine repaint regions	No adjustments to coordinates are needed.	Some simple math is used to adjust coordinates and rectangles to and from the coordinate system's origin.
Observe the figure's "location" on the Canvas	A `FigureListener` can be used if the entire parent chain is using absolute coordinates, but this guarantee is rare.	A `FigureListener` and `CoordinateListener` must be used. You must call `translateToAbsolute` on the figure being observed to get its canvas coordinates.
Determine the bounds of a parent based on the bounds of the children	Easy—after the children have been positioned, the parent can figure out what its bounds should be.	Extremely hard—updating the parent's bounds causes the children to "move."

9.2 GEF

Whereas Draw2d provides painting and layout on an SWT canvas, GEF provides the required functionality to edit a model with figures using workbench and peripheral devices. It does this by implementing the well-known MVC architecture, as seen in Figure 9-8.

Although GEF has its own independent notion of *model*, EMF often is used to manage the underlying model. In fact, the GMF project was created precisely to combine the model aspect of GEF with GMF and build additional capabilities upon them. The *view* is largely provided by Draw2d `Figures` and SWT `TreeItems`, which leaves the *controller* as the main discussion item for this chapter.

NOTE

When discussing GMF, it gets a bit confusing when considering the terminology of GEF. In GMF, View is the main class in a diagram's notation model; it holds a reference to the domain model element it represents. Both are EMF models—together they represent the "model" discussed in the context of GEF.

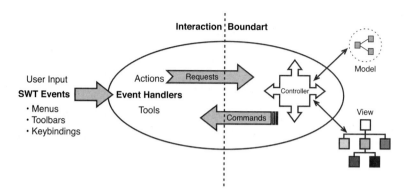

Figure 9-8   GEF MVC overview

The controller aspect of GEF is responsible for updating the view and translating UI events into requests from which commands are executed on the underlying model. Model elements that are visualized have an associated `EditPart`, which act as the controller for the element. `EditParts` contain a set of `EditPolicy` classes, which provide behavior and handle most of the actual editing of the model. An `EditPart`'s lifecycle is managed by an `EditPartViewer`, which provides the `EditPart`'s view in either graphical or tree format.

9.2.1 EditParts

Although an `EditPart` forms the controller bridge between the view and the model, it typically resembles the structure of both hierarchies. This is because the model's hierarchical structure often is represented on a diagram with nested figures. This is not always the case; sometimes elements in the model are linked by connections to sibling figure elements on the canvas. Nevertheless, we end up with three similar object structures in memory representing the model, view, and controller.

As mentioned, connections remain a special case in which the model and view do not form complementary object structures. In the case of connections, they have `EditParts` of their own and are managed by the source and target `EditParts`. A connection's figure is added to a special layer above the primary layer.

Two kinds of `EditParts` exist in GEF: graphical and tree. `Graphical EditParts` use Draw2d `Figure` objects for their view, while `TreeEditParts` use SWT `TreeItem` objects for their view. Both extend from `Abstract EditPart` and have the following main responsibilities:

❍ Create and maintain a view

❍ Create and maintain child EditParts

❍ Create and maintain connection EditParts

❍ Support editing of the model

As the controller, `EditParts` are responsible for listening to model change events and updating the view, and also for taking input from a user and updating the model. We cover both aspects in the following sections, beginning with a description of how to create the graphical view.

9.2.2 Creating the Graphical View

Let's say that you have a model created in EMF and figures using Draw2d. Now it's time to bring them together in a graphical editor. As indicated in the previous section, you need to create `EditParts` for each of the model elements you want to render in a diagram. But first you need to set up a viewer for the Draw2d `FigureCanvas`. Typically, the GEF `ScrollingGraphicalViewer` is used with a special root `EditPart`. This root `EditPart` does not correspond to a model element; it provides a context for the remaining `EditParts` and sets up the viewer. The `ScalableFreeformRootEditPart` is typically used, while GMF provides its own `DiagramRootEditPart` class to set up printing support and discrete zoom levels.

Creating EditParts

With a viewer and the root `EditPart` established, we can populate the view with content by passing in an `EditPartFactory` and our model. The `EditPartFactory` takes the base model object and creates the appropriate `EditPart` and adds it to the root, as seen in Figure 9-9. This `EditPart` is known as the contents `EditPart`; do not confuse it with the "root `EditPart`," which, as stated earlier, has no relationship with the model. The contents `EditPart` creates its `Figure`, which is added to the root `Figure`.

The contents `EditPart` creates its children `EditParts` by passing the viewer's factory, which, in turn, is used to create their children, and so on. This is done by calling `getModelChildren()` on itself, so the `EditPart` must know what model elements require `EditParts` to be created, although it is the responsibility of the `EditPartFactory` to create them. Eventually, every model object will be represented by an `EditPart` and corresponding `Figure` in the graphical viewer. In summary, you need to implement both a contents `EditPart` that will set up a diagram's backdrop figure and an `EditPartFactory` that is aware of the model and can create the contents `EditPart`.

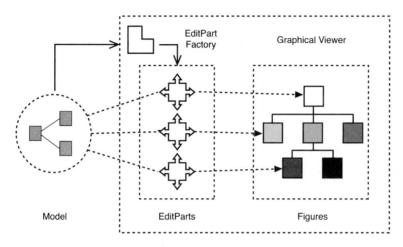

Figure 9-9   GEF EditPartFactory

Following is code from the GEF Logic Diagram example's **LogicEditor** class, showing how its `GraphicalViewer` is set up. Note that I have removed configuration code for elements not discussed (such as zoom and action configuration).

```
protected void configureGraphicalViewer() {
  super.configureGraphicalViewer();
  ScrollingGraphicalViewer viewer =
    (ScrollingGraphicalViewer)getGraphicalViewer();
  ScalableFreeformRootEditPart root = new
    ScalableFreeformRootEditPart();
  viewer.setRootEditPart(root);
  viewer.setEditPartFactory(new GraphicalPartFactory());
}
```

The contents are set in the LogicEditor's `setContents()` method:

```
getGraphicalViewer().setContents(getLogicDiagram());
```

Looking at the logic diagram's implementation of `EditPartFactory`, you can get a feel for how `EditParts` are created for corresponding model objects.

```
public class GraphicalPartFactory implements EditPartFactory {

  public EditPart createEditPart(EditPart context, Object model) {
          EditPart child = null;

    if (model instanceof LogicFlowContainer)
      child = new LogicFlowContainerEditPart();
    else if (model instanceof Wire)
```

```
      child = new WireEditPart();
   else if (model instanceof LED)
      child = new LEDEditPart();
   else if (model instanceof LogicLabel)
      child = new LogicLabelEditPart();
   else if (model instanceof Circuit)
      child = new CircuitEditPart();
   else if (model instanceof Gate)
      child = new GateEditPart();
   else if (model instanceof SimpleOutput)
      child = new OutputEditPart();
   // Note that subclasses of LogicDiagram have already
   // been matched above, like Circuit
   else if (model instanceof LogicDiagram)
      child = new LogicDiagramEditPart();
   child.setModel(model);
   return child;
   }
}
```

NOTE

As a point of clarification, the model's root is `LogicDiagram`, with a corresponding contents `EditPart` provided by `LogicDiagramEditPart`. Having *Diagram* in the model element name and diagram-related content in the class seems odd to those used to GMF, which makes a clean separation between the underlying domain (or semantic) model and the diagram (or notation) model. The GEF example uses simple serialization to persist both diagram and "domain" model information into a single file. As you'll see when looking at the GMF logic diagram example, it is implemented quite differently.

Take a look now at the `Figure` creation for the logic diagram. As mentioned, it's the `EditPart`'s responsibility to create its `Figure` and to create its child `EditParts`. Looking at our `LogicDiagramEditPart`, you can see that it provides a `FreeformLayer` as the diagram `Figure`.

```
protected IFigure createFigure() {
   Figure f = new FreeformLayer();
   f.setLayoutManager(new FreeformLayout());
   f.setBorder(new MarginBorder(5));
   return f;
}
```

As the viewer is populated, each `EditPart` has its `refreshVisuals()` method invoked to update the display of its model information. This method is also invoked when we start listening to model changes, to reflect changes in the underlying model in the diagram. Following is the `refreshVisuals()` method for our `LogicDiagramEditPart`. Note the use of the `Animation` class in the logic diagram.

```
protected void refreshVisuals() {
  Animation.markBegin();
  ConnectionLayer cLayer = (ConnectionLayer)
     getLayer(CONNECTION_LAYER);
  if ((getViewer().getControl().getStyle() & SWT.MIRRORED ) == 0)
       cLayer.setAntialias(SWT.ON);

  if (getLogicDiagram().getConnectionRouter()
     .equals(LogicDiagram.ROUTER_MANUAL)) {
    AutomaticRouter router = new FanRouter();
    router.setNextRouter(new BendpointConnectionRouter());
    cLayer.setConnectionRouter(router);
  } else if (getLogicDiagram().getConnectionRouter()
     .equals(LogicDiagram.ROUTER_MANHATTAN)) {
    cLayer.setConnectionRouter(new
      ManhattanConnectionRouter());
  } else {
    cLayer.setConnectionRouter(new
    ShortestPathConnectionRouter(getFigure()));
    Animation.run(400);
  }
}
```

The bulk of the content in the `refreshVisuals()` method of the diagram relates to connections on the diagram. This is because children of the diagram are represented by `Figures` of their own (typically called *nodes*) and have associated `EditParts` that are managed through calls to `getModelChildren()`, as mentioned earlier. `Connections` are special `EditParts` that require some additional explanation; the next section covers them.

The remaining `EditParts` in the logic diagram extend from an abstract `LogicEditPart` class that provides this general `refreshVisuals()` method implementation.

```
protected void refreshVisuals() {
  Point loc = getLogicSubpart().getLocation();
  Dimension size= getLogicSubpart().getSize();
  Rectangle r = new Rectangle(loc ,size);

  ((GraphicalEditPart) getParent()).setLayoutConstraint(this,
    getFigure(), r);
}
```

Connection EditParts

Although connection `EditParts` are largely the same as other `EditParts`, they are created and managed in a shared manner by their source and target `EditParts`. `EditParts` representing nodes on a diagram must override the `getModelSourceConnections()` and `getModelTargetConnections()` methods provided by the `AbstractGraphicalEditPart` class to return the model object representing the connection. If the corresponding `EditPart` for a connection model object has not been created by the node at the other end, GEF requests its creation from the `EditPartFactory`. The source node is responsible for creating the connection figure and adding it to the diagram.

The `Figure` created by a connection `EditPart` must implement `org.eclipse.draw2d.Connection` and typically is an instance of `org.eclipse.draw2d.PolylineConnection`. In fact, the default implementation provided by `AbstractConnectionEditPart.getFigure()` returns a new `PolylineConnection`. The connection `EditPart` maintains a reference to the source and target `EditParts` and sets its `Figure`'s anchors by casting these references to `NodeEditPart`. Following is the implementation that `AbstractConnectionEditPart` provided for `getSourceConnection Anchor()`; here, `DEFAULT_SOURCE_ANCHOR` is an `XYAnchor` at point (`10, 10`). The `getTargetConnectionAnchor()` method is implemented similarly, setting its default `XYAnchor` at (`100, 100`).

```
protected ConnectionAnchor getSourceConnectionAnchor() {
  if (getSource() != null) {
    if (getSource() instanceof NodeEditPart) {
      NodeEditPart editPart = (NodeEditPart) getSource();
      return editPart.getSourceConnectionAnchor(this);
    }        IFigure f = ((GraphicalEditPart)getSource()).getFigure();
    return new ChopboxAnchor(f);
  }
  return DEFAULT_SOURCE_ANCHOR;
}
```

To provide sensible anchor positions for your connections to use, it's important first to implement `NodeEditPart` for those nodes that support connections, and second to provide implementations for `getSourceConnectionAnchor()` and `getTargetConnectionAnchor()` to return appropriate `ConnectionAnchors`. Following is the implementation of `getSourceConnectionAnchor()` for the `LogicEditPart` in the logic diagram example. Again, `getTargetConnection Anchor()` is implemented similarly.

```
public ConnectionAnchor getSourceConnectionAnchor(ConnectionEditPart
connEditPart) {
  Wire wire = (Wire) connEditPart.getModel();
  return getNodeFigure().getConnectionAnchor(wire.getSourceTerminal());
}
```

The `refreshVisuals()` of the logic diagram's `WireEditPart` looks like the following.

```
/**
 * Refreshes the visual aspects of this, based upon the model (Wire).
 * It changes the wire color depending on the state of Wire.
 */
protected void refreshVisuals() {
  refreshBendpoints();
  if (getWire().getValue()) {
    getWireFigure().setForegroundColor(alive);
  } else {
    getWireFigure().setForegroundColor(dead);
  }
}
```

At this point, we've discussed how a model element can be displayed on a diagram using Draw2d `Figures` that are managed by extending GEF's `AbstractGraphicalEditPart` and overriding behavior appropriate for the element. Next, we look at how to edit model elements through interaction with the diagram.

9.2.3 Editing

Rendering visual elements related to an underlying model is the easy part. Providing editing support is more complicated and requires several new concepts used in GEF. Although `EditParts` remain the center of this functionality, we discuss Requests, Commands, and EditPolicies in the context of the discussion.

Requests

You can interact with the underlying model in many ways, so GEF provides an abstraction of all interaction with the `Request` class. As stated in its API documentation, a `Request` is an object used to communicate with `EditParts` that encapsulate the information `EditParts` need to perform various functions. `Requests` are used to obtain commands, show feedback, and perform generic operations.

Tools on the palette, action contributions in the UI, and programmatic interaction all create `Requests` and call upon the `EditPart` to handle the `Request`. The `EditPart` interface defines several methods that respond to `Request` objects, including those listed here.

```
EditPart getTargetEditPart(Request request);
boolean understandsRequest(Request request);
void showSourceFeedback(Request request);
void eraseSourceFeedback(Request request);
void showTargetFeedback(Request request);
void eraseTargetFeedback(Request request);
Command getCommand(Request request);
void performRequest(Request request);
```

Before safe editing of the underlying model can take place, it's important to know which `EditParts` are involved and whether they are capable of handling certain requests. Between those elements selected in the view and those under the mouse pointer (the *target*), you can capture this information using the first two API methods `getTargetEditPart()` and `understandsRequest()`.

When interacting with the diagram with a mouse—particularly when dragging a node or making connections—it's important to provide feedback to the user. The role an `EditPart` plays in these interactions is important to know when providing feedback because source and target feedback is typically distinct. This functionality is provided using the next four API methods shown earlier that are related to showing/erasing source/target feedback.

`EditParts` are responsible for returning the appropriate `Command` for a given `Request`, as provided by the `getCommand()` contract. `Commands` ultimately operate on the underlying model element within the `EditingDomain`. If a particular request cannot be performed, the `EditPart` returns a `null` or nonexecutable `Command`, which can be rendered in the UI to indicate this to the user.

Finally, the `EditPart` might just need to perform a Request. Typically, this does not result in an underlying model change; instead, it opens a dialog, collapses a compartment, or activates an in-place editor. For these cases, the `performRequest(Request)` method is called.

Commands

As mentioned, `Commands` are the primary means of effecting change in the underlying model. `Commands` encapsulate changes to the model, can be combined with other commands, and must be executed using a command stack. One of the primary complications with using GEF and EMF together has been that each framework provides its own command infrastructure. Add to that the platform's underlying command infrastructure. One of the primary benefits of using GMF is a unified command infrastructure that additionally uses the EMF Transaction API. Section 10.7, "Command Infrastructure," covers this in detail.

EditPolicies

`EditParts` delegate the handling of editing to `EditPolicy` classes, which the `createEditPolicies()` method invoked upon `EditPart` creation installs. EditPolicies handle specific editing tasks and can be reused across different `EditParts`. With the exception of `performRequest()`, each of the previous `EditPart` methods that takes a Request object is delegated to one or more of its EditPolicies.

As described in the `EditPolicy` API documentation, an `EditPolicy` is a pluggable contribution that implements a portion of an `EditPart`'s behavior. EditPolicies contribute to the overall editing behavior of an `EditPart`. Editing behavior is defined as one or more of the following: command creation, feedback management, and delegation/forwarding by collecting contributions from other `EditParts`.

In response to a given `Request`, an `EditPolicy` can create a derived `Request` and forward it to other `EditParts`. For example, during the deletion of a composite `EditPart`, that composite can consult its children for contributions to the delete command. Then if the children have any additional work to do, they return additional commands to be executed.

EditPolicies should be used to determine an `EditPart`'s editing capabilities. Although it is possible to implement an `EditPart` so that it handles all editing responsibility, using EditPolicies is more flexible and object oriented. Using policies, you can select the editing behavior for an `EditPart` without being bound to its class hierarchy, improving code reuse and simplifying code management. GMF adds the concept of an `EditPolicy` provider service, where edit policies can be contributed to an existing diagram for extensibility.

When EditPolicies are installed, they are assigned a role. Roles are simply a key, with several roles provided as constants in the `org.eclipse.gef`. `EditPolicy` interface. Some examples are CONNECTION_ROLE, CONTAINER_ ROLE, LAYOUT_ROLE, NODE_ROLE, CONNECTION_ENDPOINTS_ROLE, and COMPONENT_ROLE. Roles become important when an `EditPart` needs to substitute policies, and using them is generally good practice. Several EditPolicies are provided by default in GEF, although you can write many others to handle your particular editing functionality.

Following is the `createEditPolicies()` method found in the `Logic DiagramEditPart` class, where several provided roles are used in addition to a custom Snap Feedback role and policy.

```
protected void createEditPolicies(){
  super.createEditPolicies();

  installEditPolicy(EditPolicy.NODE_ROLE, null);
  installEditPolicy(EditPolicy.GRAPHICAL_NODE_ROLE, null);
  installEditPolicy(EditPolicy.SELECTION_FEEDBACK_ROLE, null);
  installEditPolicy(EditPolicy.COMPONENT_ROLE, new
     RootComponentEditPolicy());
  installEditPolicy(EditPolicy.LAYOUT_ROLE, new
     LogicXYLayoutEditPolicy(
     (XYLayout)getContentPane().getLayoutManager()));

  installEditPolicy("Snap Feedback", new SnapFeedbackPolicy());
}
```

9.2.4 The EditPart Life Cycle

As mentioned already, an `EditPart` begins its life when an `EditPartFactory` creates it. Specifically, it begins when the `EditPartViewer.setContents()` method is invoked; in the case of `AbstractEditPartViewer`, it calls the factory's `createEditPart()` method on the *contents* `EditPart`, which then creates all children `EditParts`. The factory sets the `EditPart`'s model by calling `setModel()` before the `EditPart` is returned.

When examining the life cycle of an `EditPart`, the `AbstractEditPart.addChild()` method provides much of the story:

```
protected void addChild(EditPart child, int index) {
  Assert.isNotNull(child);
  if (index == -1) {
    index = getChildren().size();
  if (children == null)
    children = new ArrayList(2);

  children.add(index, child);
  child.setParent(this);
  addChildVisual(child, index);
  child.addNotify();

  if (isActive())
    child.activate();
  fireChildAdded(child, index);
}
```

Adding an EditPart to a Diagram

When `EditPart` children are created, or whenever the `addChild()` method is invoked on the `AbstractEditPart` class, the `setParent()` method is called to establish the hierarchy of EditParts. This is done so that an EditPart can navigate this hierarchy, if required—for example, when it needs to obtain its viewer to access its EditPart registry.

Along with setting the parent of an EditPart during addChild(), its Figure is created by a call to addChildVisual(). Actually, the default implementation in AbstractGraphicalEditPart calls getFigure(), which calls the createFigure() method. Your EditPart must implement this abstract method.

To refresh itself for the first time following its addition to the parent EditPart, the addNotify() method is invoked. The default behavior of addNotify() performs the following:

○ Registers its model in the EditPartViewer's EditPart registry so that EditParts can find other EditParts.

○ Registers its figure in the EditPartViewer's visual part registry (used for hit testing).

○ Registers the EditPart for accessibility, if applicable.

○ Creates the EditPolicies it needs by invoking createEditPolicies(), which is abstract and requires implementation by your EditPart. In turn, the EditPart.installEditPolicy() method is invoked, passing required EditPolicies and their role.

○ Invokes addNotify() on its children and then invokes refresh(). The default implementation of refresh() invokes refreshVisuals() and refreshChildren(). As you saw earlier in the refreshVisuals() implementation in LogicEditPart, this method is intended to be overridden by your EditPart because the default implementation does nothing. The refreshChildren() method is the opposite: The default implementation should not be overridden and can be computationally expensive. Therefore, it should be invoked only when required. Following is the API documentation, to provide more detail on this method and its use.

○ The final act of addNotify() is to register the EditPart as the source or target of connections using overridden getSourceConnections() and getTargetConnections(), respectively, as applicable.

The AbstractEditPart.refreshChildren() method updates its child EditParts so that they are in sync with their model elements. This method is called from refresh() and can also be called upon notification from the model. Take care when calling this method; it can be a performance hit. When possible, call removeChild(EditPart) and addChild(EditPart, int) instead.

Activation is the final step in the process of adding a new `EditPart` to a diagram in which the `EditPart` observes changes in the model or supports editing. For this, the `EditPart.activate()` method is invoked during creation and can be invoked later following a call to `deactivate()`. The following occurs during `activate()`:

1. The `EditPart` begins to observe its model. This is done by extending this method and registering listeners on the model element.

2. The `EditPart` activates all its EditPolicies using the corresponding `activate()` method.

3. The `EditPart` activates all its children.

4. The `EditPart` notifies its listeners that it is active.

5. The `EditPart` activates all its source ConnectionEditParts.

At this point, the `EditPart` is created and activated, ready for normal use; it can be selected, provide feedback, respond to requests, return commands, and so on. The `EditPart` is deactivated upon deletion of the element or disposal of its viewer.

EditPart Disposal

To complement the `activate()` method, `EditParts` provide a `deactivate()` method. This method is also meant to be extended by your `EditPart` so that listeners registered by `activate()`can be unregistered. Otherwise, `deactivate()` undoes all that `activate()` did, by default.

Although deactivation is guaranteed to occur for viewer disposal, the following also takes place for model element deletion. Because `addChild()` was responsible for creating and initializing an `EditPart`, the `AbstractEditPart.removeChild()` method is responsible for the cleanup. This is its implementation, for reference:

```
protected void removeChild(EditPart child) {
  Assert.isNotNull(child);
  int index = getChildren().indexOf(child);
  if (index < 0)
    return;
  fireRemovingChild(child, index);
  if (isActive())
    child.deactivate();
  child.removeNotify();
  removeChildVisual(child);
  child.setParent(null);
  getChildren().remove(child);
}
```

As you can see, the process is nearly the reverse of the addChild() method. Listeners are notified that the child is being removed, the deactivate() method is called, removeNotify() is called, its model and visual are unregistered, its parent is set to null, and its children are removed. The EditPart is also removed as the source or target of any connections, although the connection itself is not removed unless both its source and target are set to null.

Note that EditParts are not recycled. Even an Undo operation causes a new EditPart object to be created, so it's important to not reference an EditPart directly with a Command, for example.

9.2.5 Tools and the Palette

Most interaction with GEF objects happens through tools selected from the palette. Tools themselves function as state machines, responding to SWT events (mouse and keyboard) to perform actions such as showing or hiding feedback, updating the cursor, obtaining commands from EditParts, executing commands, and so on. Actually, input flows from the viewer, to the EditDomain, to the active tool. Only one active tool for all viewers in the EditDomain exists—typically, the one selected in the palette.

The GEF palette is available as a standalone view (**Window → Show View → Other → General → Palette**) or within the editor itself. The palette is an optional feature, although most GEF applications use it. Figure 9-10 shows the FlyoutPaletteComposite used in the scenario diagram example.

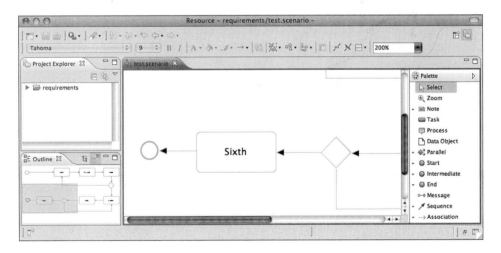

Figure 9-10   GEF palette

9.2.6 Interactions

NOTE

The content in this section is largely copied directly from the GEF programmer's guide and is provided here for convenience.

This section discusses the various types of interactions that are included in the framework and which parts of the framework are involved in supporting the interaction. An interaction can be anything that affects the model or the UI state. Many interactions are graphical, but some are not. An interaction can include the following:

- Invoking some action (usually displayed on the toolbar, menu bar, or pop-up)
- Clicking on something
- Clicking and dragging something
- Hovering over something (pausing the mouse for a certain time)
- Dropping something dragged from another source (native drag-and-drop)
- Pressing certain keys

This section discusses the participants involved in each interaction and what they do. This can include the following:

- Tools that process input
- Actions that are invoked
- The IDs and instances of requests that by tools or actions send to `EditParts`; IDs are defined on the `RequestConstants` class
- The `EditPolicy` roles designated to handle specific types of requests— these are just constants defined on the `EditPolicy` interface
- Any `EditPolicy` implementations provided in GEF for use with the interaction

Selection

Table 9-2 details the elements involved in selection interactions.

Table 9-2 Selection Interactions

Tools	Requests	Edit Policies and Roles	Actions
SelectionTool	SelectionRequest	SelectionEditPolicy	SelectAllAction
MarqueeTool	DirectEditRequest	DirectEditPolicy	
SelectEditPartTracker	REQ_SELECTION_ HOVER	SELECTION_ FEEDBACK_ROLE	
	REQ_OPEN		
*GraphicalViewer KeyHandler	REQ_DIRECT_EDIT		

The Selection Tool is the primary tool used in GEF and is often the default for an application. Although item selection might seem to be the most basic interaction, it is actually a complex topic that requires several steps to complete. Figure 9-11 is a sequence diagram that outlines the selection operation.

The Selection Tool obtains a helper called a `DragTracker` from an `EditPart` or handle below the mouse when a drag occurs. A drag is defined as a mouse button being pressed, a mouse button being released, and any events that occur in between. Events are forwarded to the delegate so that the drag can be handled differently based on where and how the drag originated. For example, clicking a handle might result in resizing a shape or moving the end of a connection. Clicking on an `EditPart` typically drags that part to a new location or parent.

Ironically, the Selection Tool doesn't select `EditPart`s. All mouse clicks are handled as drags. When the Selection Tool receives a mousedown event over a selectable `EditPart`, it asks for a drag tracker. The `EditPart` returns a tracker derived from `SelectEditPartTracker`. The tracker also receives the mousedown event, as well as any other events, until the mouse button is released. When the tracker interprets a selection gesture, it modifies the viewer's selection. Trackers even handle events such as double-click.

To continue the discussion on the selection interaction, we must first define selection. Selection is a list of `EditPart`s that an `EditPartViewer` maintains. Changes to the selection are made by invoking methods on the viewer, not by modifying the list directly. The selection is never empty. If the selection is cleared, the viewer's *contents* `EditPart` becomes the selection. The last `EditPart` in the list is considered the primary selection.

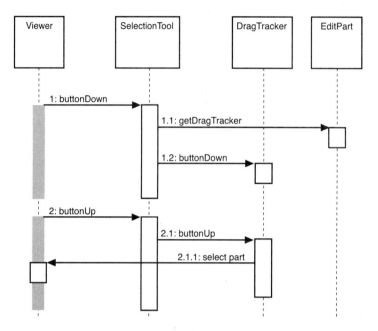

Figure 9-11   GEF mouse interaction

Closely related to selection is focus. Focus is a single `EditPart` that the `EditPartViewer` maintains. Focus is used when manipulating selection via keyboard. By moving focus, the user can navigate from one `EditPart` to another without changing the current selection. The user can add or remove the focused `EditPart` from the selection. If focus is not explicitly set, it is the same as the primary selected part.

Selection Handles

The `EditPart` is responsible for showing its selected and focused state to the user. The viewer tells `EditParts` when they are selected, when they are focused, or when they have primary selection. Typically, selection is shown by one or more EditPolicies adding selection handles. In Figure 9-12, `ResizableEditPolicy` added the handles. The black handles on the leftmost connection indicate primary selection.

Because selection handles are related to how a part can be dragged or sized—which, in turn, is related to the containing figure's layout manager—usually the parent part's `EditPolicy` installs a policy on the children for displaying the appropriate handles. For example, an `XYLayoutEditPolicy` would install a `ResizableEditPolicy` on each child of its host `EditPart`.

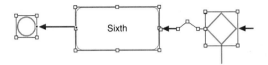

Figure 9-12   Selection handles

Connections such as `WireEditPart` in the Logic Example also change its figure's line width to help indicate selection. Both `EndpointEditPolicy` and `BendpointEditPolicy` contribute handles for connections.

Selection Targeting and Feedback

For selection to occur, the Selection Tool must first target an `EditPart` using a `SelectionRequest`. In rare cases, an `EditPart` is not selectable and targeting "falls through," hitting the `EditPart` below. During this continuous mouse targeting, the Selection Tool invokes `showFeedback()` on the current target `EditPart` by passing it a `SelectionRequest` of type `REQ_SELECTION`. Most applications should ignore this request because showing and hiding feedback as the mouse moves across a diagram can be distracting to the user. For this reason, an additional feedback request is sent with the type `REQ_SELECTION_HOVER` whenever the user pauses the mouse over an `EditPart`. Often an `EditPart` displays a pop-up shell similar to a ToolTip, displaying additional information about the part. The `SELECTION_FEEDBACK_ROLE` identifier can be used when installing policies that show such feedback.

A benefit to using these feedback requests is that the Selection Tool is smart about asking parts to erase feedback. For example, if the user starts dragging, you would not want a pop-up message to stay around. Also, selection feedback does not appear when other tools are active.

Selection Using a DragTracker

When the user actually clicks the mouse, the selection target is asked for a `DragTracker`. To allow selection, return a `SelectEditPartTracker` or its subclass `DragEditPartsTracker`, depending on whether dragging is permitted. These trackers modify selection at the appropriate time, taking into consideration the Shift and Ctrl modifier keys.

A tracker should never select the contents `EditPart` because it should never be part of a multiple selection. Therefore, it should return either a `DeselectAllTracker` or the `MarqueeDragTracker`. Remember, the selection is never empty, so the contents part is the selection when no other parts are selected.

Other Selection Requests

EditParts might be asked to perform two additional Requests related to selection. These requests are related to selection, in that they are interactions associated with clicking the primary mouse button. The first is a double-click, which is called an open request (REQ_OPEN). This interaction can be used for EditParts that you can open or expand or that can display a dialog. The other interaction is called a direct edit (REQ_DIRECT_EDIT). As an example of direct editing, imagine that a user wants to modify the text of a label. The user must first select the part and then click it again after it is selected. After a brief delay (to rule out a double-click), the request is sent.

Selection Actions

GEF provides a SelectAllAction. Given a viewer, this action selects all the contents part's children when invoked.

Selection Using the Keyboard

Keyboard selection is supported in graphical viewers by installing a GraphicalViewerKeyHandler. The key handler receives only key events that the current tool sends it. The Selection Tool forwards key events necessary for selection.

Drag trackers are not needed inside GEF's TreeViewer. The native tree handles selection already, and dragging of TreeItems is processed internally using native DND.

Basic Model Operations (Delete)

Table 9-3 details the elements involved in delete operations.

Table 9-3   Delete Operations

Tools	Requests	Edit Policies and Roles	Actions
	REQ_DELETE	COMPONENT_ROLE	DeleteAction
		CONNECTION_ROLE	
		RootComponentEditPolicy	

The only universal interaction that all GEF applications should support is delete. The workbench places a global delete action on the Edit menu, as seen in Figure 9-13. All applications should register a handler such as the included DeleteAction.

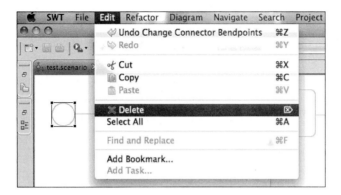

Figure 9-13   Delete menu

The `DeleteAction` sends a `GroupRequest` of type `REQ_DELETE` to the viewer's current selection. All `EditParts` should have an `EditPolicy` that either supports delete or prevents it from occurring.

Every `EditPart` is either a component or a connection. A component is a basic `EditPart` that is the child of a parent. A connection is slightly different because it is owned by its source and target.

The `COMPONENT_ROLE` key is used when installing an `EditPolicy` on a component `EditPart`. Applications can extend the provided `ComponentEdit Policy` to fill in the commands for deletion. The `RootComponentEditPolicy` should be used on the contents `EditPart`. This policy prevents the diagram itself from being deleted. Here, *root* refers to the model root and is not related to the viewer's root EditPart.

The `CONNECTION_ROLE` key is used when installing a policy on a connection `EditPart`. Applications can extend the provided `ConnectionEditPolicy` to fill in the command for deletion.

These EditPolicies should handle the tasks most closely associated with the model. In the logic example, this role is responsible for the LED's increment and decrement behavior, which adds or subtracts 1 from the LED's value.

Implementing the command that performs delete can be difficult, especially when connections are involved. The command must consider whether the object being deleted has connections or whether children of the object being deleted have connections, and delete the connections as well. But you don't want to delete the same connection twice if both source and target nodes are being deleted as part of multiple selection. The logic example's delete command addresses all these concerns.

Creation

Table 9-4 details the elements involved in creation interactions.

Table 9-4   Creation Interactions

Tools	Requests	Edit Policies and Roles	Actions
CreationTool	REQ_CREATE	CONTAINER_ROLE	CopyTemplateAction
	Create	LAYOUT_ROLE	PasteTemplateAction
		TREE_CONTAINER_ROLE	
		ContainerEditPolicy	
		LayoutEditPolicy	

A `CreateRequest` asks an `EditPart` to create a new child. The ID `REQ_CREATE` identifies the request. Creation can occur through three different methods: clicking, dragging, or pasting. The request provides the location, object, and object type being created. A `CreationFactory` provides the object and its type. The request hides the factory and provides access to the created object directly, caching it in case multiple EditPolicies need access to the created object. In some cases, the request contains a size attribute.

Producing CreateRequests

The creation tool provides a "loaded cursor" mode that attempts to create an object at the mouse location when clicking. If the mouse is clicked and dragged, the tool tracks the size of the rectangle defined by the user. The creation tool can be placed on the palette using a `CreationToolEntry`. When the mouse is released, the tool either repeats the process or switches back to the default tool.

Creation can also be performed using native drag-and-drop. The drag source can be anything, but it is typically the `PaletteViewer`. A palette entry that takes a template is added to the palette. The `TemplateTransfer` is used to transfer the template, which is just an `Object`, from the drag source to the drop target. A `TemplateTransferDragSourceListener` must be added to the `PaletteViewer`. Similarly, the viewer must have a `TemplateTransferDrop TargetListener`. Because a template is model specific, the application must extend the drop target listener to convert the template into a `CreationFactory` for the request.

A special palette entry called the `CombinedTemplateCreationEntry` supports both the creation tool and drag-and-drop styles of creation.

Consuming CreateRequests

The target `EditPart` is responsible for showing feedback and returning the command for creation. GEF provides two types of policies for handling creation. One type of policy is specific to the view in which creation occurs, either graphical or tree based. This edit policy corresponds to either the `LAYOUT_ROLE` or the `TREE_CONTAINER_ROLE`.

The other type of edit policy is specific to only the model, in case applications want to separate the portion that is shared between graphical and non-graphical creation. In most cases, any kind of shared logic is in the command implementations, making this type of policy unnecessary.

A `LayoutEditPolicy` handles the process of creation based on the container's layout manager. For example, if `XYLayout` is being used, the resulting `Command` needs to associate an (x, y, w, h) constraint with the created child. Layouts that don't use constraints require that the index of the drop location be determined. GEF provides abstract policies for the basic layout types.

The `TreeContainerEditPolicy` supports creation in a tree-based viewer. The policy is responsible for determining the index of creation and showing feedback.

The `PasteTemplateAction` can create objects without requiring the mouse. This is important for accessibility. The `CopyTemplateAction` is added to the palette. When the user invokes this action, an internal mechanism copies the transfer so that it can be pasted in a viewer. When the paste occurs, the `PasteTemplateAction` retrieves the template object, constructs a `CreateRequest`, and sends it to the selected `EditPart`. The mouse location is not available in this interaction. Paste is enabled only when the selection is exactly one `EditPart`.

When a creation command is redone, it must restore the original child that was created the first time it was executed. If it creates a new object, subsequent commands will fail upon redo when they try to modify the originally created child.

Creation Sequence

Using sequence diagrams, let's look at the sequence of events that occurs when the creation tool moves over the diagram surface using the mouse in GEF.

As you can see in Figure 9-14, as the mouse moves over the diagram, obtaining a command includes passing a request to the `EditPart`, which queries its EditPolicies. The request obtains a new object from its factory, implying that a new model object is created and loaded into the creation tool as it is moved over the diagram surface. Now we look at what happens when the mouse is clicked on the diagram surface using another sequence diagram, as shown in Figure 9-15. What's not shown in the figure is the CreationTool retrieving the EditDomain and CommandStack. The CommandStack invokes the CreateCommand execute() method, which is where the sequence picks up here.

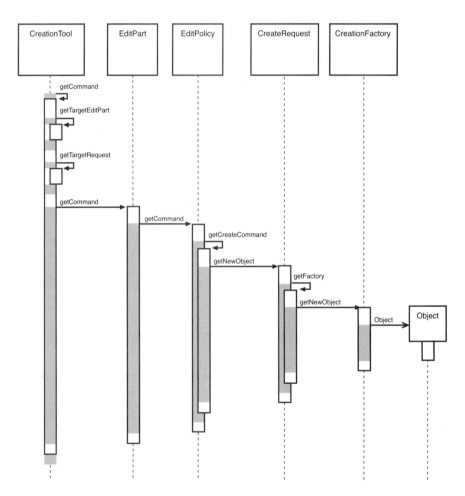

Figure 9-14   GEF creation sequence

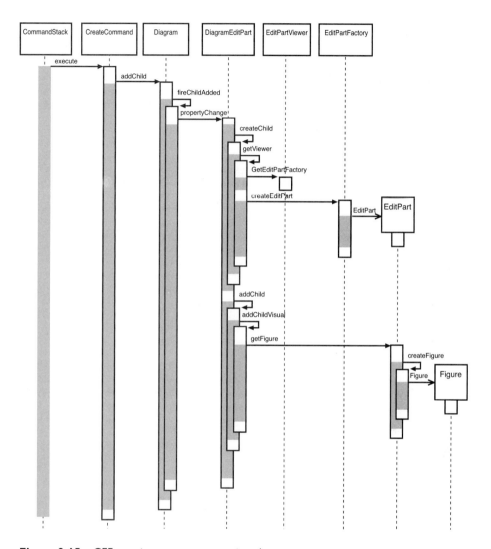

Figure 9-15   GEF creation sequence—continued

The cached object created in the mouse move operation is added to the container in the creation command execution, which triggers through events the creation of the corresponding `EditPart` and figure containment hierarchies.

Moving and Resizing

Table 9-5 details the elements involved in moving and resizing interactions.

Table 9-5 Moving and Resizing Interactions

Tools	Requests	Edit Policies and Roles	Actions
DragEditPartsTracker	ChangeBoundsRequest	LayoutEditPolicy	AlignmentAction
ResizeTracker	AlignmentRequest	ResizableEditPolicy	MatchSizeAction
	REQ_MOVE	ContainerEditPolicy	
	REQ_ADD		
	REQ_ORPHAN		
	REQ_CLONE		
	REQ_ALIGN		
	REQ_RESIZE		

The `DragEditPartsTracker` extends basic selection behavior so that the selected parts can be dragged within their graphical viewer. Dragging the selected parts results in three potential interactions: move, reparent, and clone. All three use the `ChangeBoundsRequest`, which extends `GroupRequest` to include a size delta, move delta, and mouse location.

While dragging the selection, if the tracker targets the part's original parent, the request is typed as `REQ_MOVE`. If the target changes, the interaction becomes a reparent. For a reparent, a request of type `REQ_ORPHAN` is sent to the old parent, and the new target is sent a request of type `REQ_ADD`. Pressing the Ctrl key (Alt on the Mac) always results in a `REQ_CLONE`, which is sent only to the target part.

All these requests are related, in that they require the target to process a rectangle and a mouse location. The `LayoutEditPolicy` is responsible for handling each of these request types. For layouts that use constraints, each part's original bounds are taken and modified by the size and move deltas to determine a new bounds, for which a corresponding constraint is found. For index-based layouts, the mouse location is used to establish the new index.

A `ContainerEditPolicy` can optionally contribute additional commands (not related to the layout) during ADD, ORPHAN, and CLONE requests.

Resizing

Resizing falls under the same category as changing bounds. Note that when resizing either the top or left sides, the location of the part also changes. Resizing makes sense only for layouts with constraints, such as `XYLayout`. The `ResizableEditPolicy` adds up to eight resize handles to its host. Clicking the Selection Tool on one of these resize handles prompts a `ResizeTracker` to perform a resize on the selected parts that understand a "resize." Shift and Ctrl key modifiers can constrain the resize operation.

The types of handles available on an `EditPart` depend on the layout manager in which its figure is placed. For example, parts inside a table might have handles for adjusting insets, padding, column span, or other attributes. Some layouts don't need handles, but four corner handles should be added just to indicate selection. Dragging these handles works the same as dragging the part itself.

Because of the relationship between handles and layouts, the parent's `LayoutEditPolicy` should install the `PRIMARY_DRAG_ROLE` `EditPolicy` because it defines abstract methods for this purpose. If a container changes layout managers during editing, typically the layout policy gets swapped with one for the new layout manager. The new policy then replaces the stale `PRIMARY_DRAG_ROLE` policies on each child.

The `MatchSizeAction` matches the size of the selected parts to the primary selected part's size. This action is implemented in a way similar to manually resizing the individual parts, and it uses the same request and type.

The `AlignmentAction` uses an `AlignmentRequest`, which extends `ChangeBoundsRequest`. When using a `ChangeBoundsRequest`, the part's current placement in the control (in absolute coordinates) is passed to the request, which then returns a modified version. Using this pattern, alignment can adjust each part's rectangle by different amounts. In most cases, alignment can be treated no differently from a move. This action aligns all selected parts with one of the edges of the primary selected part.

Connection Creation

Table 9-6 details the elements involved in connection creation interactions.

Table 9-6 Connection Creation Interactions

Tools	Requests	Edit Policies and Roles	Actions
ConnectionCreation Tool	CreateConnectionRequest	GraphicalNodeEditPolicy	
ConnectionDrag CreationTool	REQ_CONNECTION_ START REQ_CONNECTION_ END	NODE_ROLE	

The `ConnectionCreationTool` creates a new connection between nodes. This interaction requires the user to activate the tool (typically using the palette) and then click on two `EditParts` that support connections. Note that GMF's default behavior is a click-drag-release to create a connection. You can abort the creation by pressing the Esc key. The `ConnectionDragCreationTool` is similar, but the interaction is a single mouse drag. This tool can be returned as the drag tracker from a handle or even an `EditPart`, in some cases.

The process is separated into two parts. The first part is defining the source of the connection. The source is a node, but it also can include a specific "port" on that node. The tool uses a `CreateConnectionRequest` identified by `REQ_CONNECTION_START` to determine the target `EditPart` and ask it for a command. However, this is only the first half of creating the connection, so the command is not complete yet. The tool does not attempt to execute this command or even ask if it is executable; it only passes information to the target `EditPart`.

The second part of the process is to define the target node for the connection. The tool uses the same request but retypes it as `REQ_CONNECTION_END`. The command that the source node returns is now stored on the request and passed during the second part of the interaction. The target is asked for the final command that performs the entire creation of the connection. Any command can be returned at this point, including the command provided upon the request, updated with the target node information. At this point, enablement is determined by asking the command if it can be executed. Creation ends by executing the command.

During the first and second steps, the `EditPart` being targeted as the source or target node is asked to show target feedback. The `EditPart` might visually highlight various attachment points or simply indicate that it is the target.

The source node `EditPart` is also asked to show source feedback during creation. The provided `GraphicalNodeEditPolicy` can display creation feedback. This policy creates a connection feedback figure and sets its anchors using the `NodeEditPart` interface. This mix-in interface for `GraphicalEditPart` provides anchor points both during creation feedback and when the connection's `EditPart` is created.

The "source" and "target" nodes should not be confused with "source" and "target" feedback. For feedback, *source* simply means show the feedback for the connection, and *target* means highlight the mouse target element.

Editing Connections

Table 9-7 details the elements involved in connection edit interactions.

Table 9-7 Connection Edit Interactions

Tools	Requests	Edit Policies and Roles	Actions
ConnectionEndpoint Tracker	ReconnectRequest	ConnectionEndpointEditPolicy	
	REQ_RECONNECT_ SOURCE	ENDPOINT_ROLE	
	REQ_RECONNECT_ TARGET	GraphicalNodeEditPolicy NODE_ROLE	

Dragging the endpoints of an existing connection changes its source or target. This includes changing "ports" on the same node EditPart. This interaction is called reconnecting.

A connection adds handles at its endpoints by installing a `Connection EndpointEditPolicy` with the `ENDPOINT_ROLE`. Each of these handles returns a tracker for reconnecting the corresponding end of the connection. This policy is also responsible for showing the connection's feedback during the interaction. This policy does not return commands and, therefore, is not abstract. The reconnect command comes from the new target node.

As the source or target endpoint is dragged, the tracker sends source feedback requests to the connection and target feedback requests to the current target, if there is one. The tracker uses a `ReconnectRequest` typed as either a source or target reconnect.

The target node's `GraphicalNodeEditPolicy` is responsible for showing target feedback and returning the actual command to perform the reconnect. As with creation, the target `EditPart` should implement the `NodeEditPart` interface, which allows the `ConnectionEndpointEditPolicy` to snap the feedback to the node's anchor(s).

Bending Connections

Table 9-8 details the elements involved in connection bend interactions.

Table 9-8 Connection Bend Interactions

Tools	Requests	Edit Policies and Roles	Actions
ConnectionBendpoint Tracker	BendpointRequest	BendpointEditPolicy	
	REQ_MOVE_ BENDPOINT REQ_CREATE_ BENDPOINT	CONNECTION_ BENDPOINTS_ROLE	

Certain connection routers accept routing constraints (typically a list of `BendPoints`). Install a `BendpointEditPolicy` using the `CONNECTION_BEND-POINTS_ROLE` for editing the connections routing constraints. This `EditPolicy` requires a router that takes a list of `BendPoints`. During selection, the policy adds normal handles to existing bendpoints on the connection. It adds smaller handles where the user can create new bendpoints.

Each handle provides a `ConnectionBendpointTracker`. This tool sends a `BendpointRequest` back to the connection `EditPart` to show feedback and obtain the command to perform the bend. For existing bendpoints, the request is typed as `REQ_MOVE_BENDPOINT`; otherwise, it is `REQ_CREATE_BENDPOINT`. The `EditPolicy` must determine when moving a bendpoint back to its natural placement should result in its removal.

9.3 Summary

In this chapter, we took a closer look at the GEF. As it's an underlying component of the GMF, it's important to understand how it works and how they work together, particularly when you start adding customizations to your domain-specific diagrams.

CHAPTER 10

Graphical Modeling Framework Runtime

This chapter describes in detail the Graphical Modeling Framework (GMF) runtime. Although Chapter 4, "Developing a DSL Graphical Notation," provides information on how to use both the tooling and runtime components in the development of the book's example projects, this chapter is meant to be a reference guide on the runtime itself (although it contains examples as well). Where applicable, this chapter references other Modeling projects and components.

10.1 Overview

The GMF runtime provides a set of frameworks to assist in the development of Eclipse graphical editors using Eclipse Modeling Framework (EMF) and Graphical Editing Framework (GEF). You can use the GMF runtime on its own or as a target of the GMF Tooling generative component. In either case, the runtime provides the following:

- ❍ A set of reusable diagramming components, such as action bars, connection handles, compartments, geometrical shapes, a diagramming toolbar, a set of diagramming actions, properties view, page setup and print preview, diagram export to image file, SVG support, border shapes, and system Clipboard support

- ❍ A standard notation model for storing diagram information separate from domain information

- ❍ A command infrastructure that bridges EMF and GEF

- ❍ Extensibility options for the notation model, palette, diagram elements, layout, decorators, and domain model

- ❍ A service provider infrastructure with priority and policy facilities

As implied by the second bullet, GMF provides a separation of diagram and domain model. Although both can be persisted in a single file, the runtime provides for automatic persistence of all notational information (position of elements, color, font, and so on), requiring the Toolsmith to provide only a domain model. From the Practitioner's perspective, it is likely irrelevant that two models are used under the hood; the Practitioner more likely will use the diagram as the primary editing interface and will not distinguish between the two. Note, however, that a diagram can display multiple domains, many diagrams can provide views of a single domain, or a diagram can even provide multiple visual elements for the same underlying domain element. The runtime handles all these cases, which were motivators for keeping visual and domain information persisted separately.

As we covered in Chapter 9, "Graphical Editing Framework," a Model-View-Controller (MVC) architecture is used in the framework. GMF's runtime builds upon this architecture, providing significant capabilities, but also introducing significant complexity. The goal of these enhancements is to provide a platform for extensibility so that editors can be scalable through plug-in points and service provider interfaces.

This chapter explores in detail the functionality that the GMF runtime provides, beginning with a closer look at what a GMF-based diagram offers.

10.1.1 General Diagram Features

This section looks at each of the provided diagram runtime features. Each diagram is provided these features by default, or by making certain property changes in the gmfgen model if using the tooling component of GMF. Although some of what's described here is available from GEF, much of it is provided by GMF.

Toolbar

Many common diagramming functions are available in the main toolbar. You can modify the properties of selected diagram elements that display text by using the toolbar font, font size, bold, and italic toolbar items. To their right, you can adjust the font color, fill color, and line color for the selected element. Note that all these functions are also available in the Properties view.

Table 10-1 covers each toolbar function and its options.

Table 10-1   Diagram Toolbar Elements

Tool	Description
Rectilinear Style Routing	Switches the routing style of the selected link(s) to rectilinear, which inserts bendpoints to route links at 90° turns. This and the other routing style options are typically used in conjunction with the Select All Links function.
Oblique Style Routing	Switches the routing style of the selected link(s) to oblique, which creates direct links between two objects.
Tree Style Routing	Applies a tree routing style to the selected link elements. This is typically used in organizational or hierarchical diagrams, such as to show inheritance in a class diagram. *
Apply Appearance Property	With multiple elements selected, applies the appearance properties of the first selected item to the rest.
Select All	Selects all diagram elements, including nodes and links.
Select All Shapes	Selects all diagram node elements.
Select All Links	Selects all diagram link elements. This is useful when making changes to link style, such as from oblique to rectilinear.
Arrange All	Arranges all diagram elements according to the active diagram layout policy. Note that for this to work on the diagram level, no diagram element should be selected.
Arrange Selected	Arranges selected nodes only. This is particularly useful when working with elements that contain other elements, and when the nested elements are to be arranged within the parent.
Align Left	Aligns the selected elements vertically along the same left edge location.
Align Center	Aligns the selected elements vertically along the same center line location.
Align Right	Aligns the selected elements vertically along the same right edge location.
Align Top	Aligns the selected elements horizontally along the same top edge location.

(continues)

Table 10-1 Diagram Toolbar Elements (continued)

Tool		Description
	Align Middle	Aligns the selected elements horizontally along the same center line location.
	Align Bottom	Aligns the selected elements horizontally along the same bottom edge location.
	Auto Size	Sizes the selected element to fit its contents, taking into account the minimum and preferred size dimensions. Typically, a shape that was manually resized larger has this action invoked to return it to its default size.
	Show Connector Labels	Reveals all hidden diagram connection labels.
	Hide Connector Labels	Hides all diagram connection labels, which is useful to remove diagram "noise."
	Name Compartment Only	Hides node compartments other than the name (top) "compartment." This is typically used in conjunction with the Select All Shapes feature.
	All Compartments	Restores the visibility of the compartments for the select node or nodes.
	Zoom	A combo box with zoom levels is available, but it can also accept any user value. Zoom to fit, selection, width, and height are available.

* Note that for Tree Style Routing to be available in generated diagrams, the Tree Branch property of the Gen Link must be set to `true`, as described in Section 11.4.3, "Gen Link." Also note that although this routing style can be selected for an individual link in the Properties view when selected, multiple links must be selected to enable this style using the toolbar.

Properties

Several property pages are associated with diagramming, each displayed with content relevant for the given context. When the diagram canvas itself is selected, a Rulers & Grid tab appears with the following options and default settings. The diagram to the right in Figure 10-1 is being displayed with connection labels hidden and with only the name compartment.

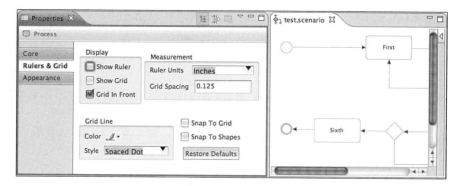

Figure 10-1   Rulers & Grid properties

The **Show Ruler** option displays a ruler along the left and top edges of the diagram and provides access to ruler guides, as shown in Figure 10-2. Guides are added by clicking anywhere in the ruler and are removed by pressing Delete when active.

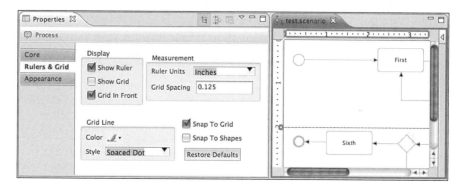

Figure 10-2   Diagram ruler and guide

The guide helps in the alignment of diagram elements, including a "sticky" feature shown in Figure 10-3. In this case, the Topic and Relationship nodes were positioned so that their top edge was along the guide. Using the guide handle, the elements can be moved vertically on the diagram. Note that you also can use guides vertically.

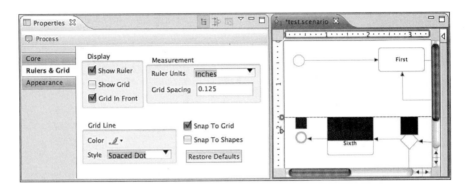

Figure 10-3   Alignment using guide

The Grid option is useful for alignment, but it also gives your diagram the look of having been drawn on graph paper, as shown in Figure 10-4. The Grid in Front option is turned off in this case. Having the grid over the top of diagram elements seems an odd choice, but this is the default. The Snap to Shapes option is useful in aligning elements, in addition to the alignment features of the toolbar and ruler guide.

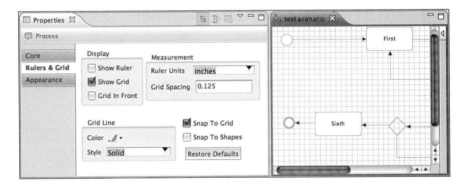

Figure 10-4   Diagram grid

Another useful alignment feature of GEF is activated using the Snap to Shapes feature. In Figure 10-5, we see a "laser line" appear as we move a shape. Lines appear for the node edges as well as the center line.

The other tabs available when the diagram canvas is selected are Core and Appearance, as shown in Figure 10-6. The Core tab displays the domain model information for the selected element. The name of the selected element appears at the top of the Properties view, adorned by its icon. The Appearance tab provides font and color options, similar to what's found on the toolbar.

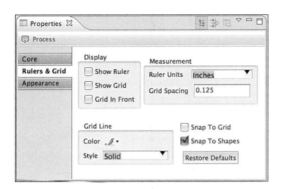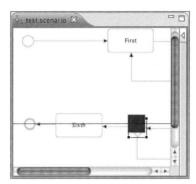

Figure 10-5 Diagram laser alignment

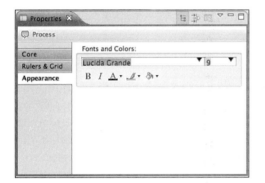

Figure 10-6 Appearance and Core properties

For diagram elements other than the canvas, only the Core and Appearance tabs appear, in addition to any custom tabs that you add. When one or more diagram links are selected, the Appearance tab displays the following additional properties.

The Smoothness properties add a "humanized" look to links, essentially giving them a hand-drawn appearance. The oblique routing style routes lines in a direct manner. Rectilinear inserts 90° bends when routing, and Tree routing combines links when they share a common target. Avoid Obstructions and Closest Distance are self-explanatory. Jump links provide the option to insert "jumps" where one line crosses another. Various styles and position options are available, as shown in Figure 10-7. Generally, line crossing is considered bad form, but it is sometimes unavoidable. Finally, the Lines and Arrows section enables you to change the line width, style, and end type of links. Currently, these capabilities are not available for generated diagrams.

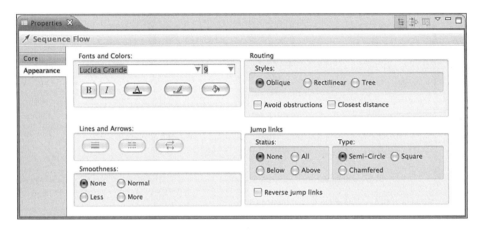

Figure 10-7   Link properties

Palette

Although the default location for the diagram palette is docked to the right side of the diagram editor, this is actually an Eclipse view that can be displayed by itself outside the editor pane, as seen in Figure 10-8. To restore the palette to its position within the diagram editor, simply close the view. Also note that the palette can be docked on either the left or right of the diagram, as well as collapsed to free up diagramming real estate. At the time of this writing, the GEF palette is undergoing some visual enhancements, so your environment might look somewhat different.

Figure 10-8   Palette view

Diagram Menu

The main Diagram menu contains many of the options found on the main toolbar and, to an extent, what's available for the given selection context. Items such as Font, Fill Color, Line Color, Line Style, Selection, Arrangement, Alignment, Zoom, and Filters are available. One important action available only from the Diagram menu is Make Same Size, which you might expect to appear on a context menu or even the toolbar. Table 10-2 lists the options provided.

Table 10-2   Diagram Menu Elements

Item		Description
	Both	Makes the selected elements equal in size (both width and height), based on the smaller element dimension
	Height	Adjusts the height dimension of the selected elements to match that of the smallest
	Width	Adjusts the width dimension of the selected elements to match that of the smallest

The Order menu item provides a list of its options, all of which affect the z-order of the selected element (see Table 10-3). Note that these actions are necessary only to reveal or hide overlapped elements, which is likely a rare situation.

Table 10-3   Order Menu Elements

Item	Description	
	Bring to Front	Moves the selected element to the top of the z-order
	Send to Back	Moves the selected element to the bottom of the z-order
	Bring Forward	Moves the selected element upward one level in the z-order
	Send Backward	Moves the selected element downward one level in the z-order

The View menu item provides the capability to toggle the Ruler and Grid and apply the Snap to Grid functionality (but not Snap to Shapes). Also available is Page Breaks and Recalculate Page Breaks. The Page Breaks action produces a thick blue border around the diagram contents, with a thin blue line to indicate the page boundary. Page numbers are also provided, as shown in Figure 10-9.

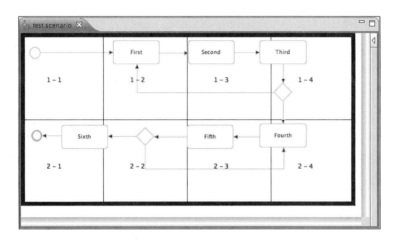

Figure 10-9   Page breaks

Note that the boundaries correspond to the settings defined in **File → Page Setup,** shown in Figure 10-10. A Print Preview option is also available in the File menu.

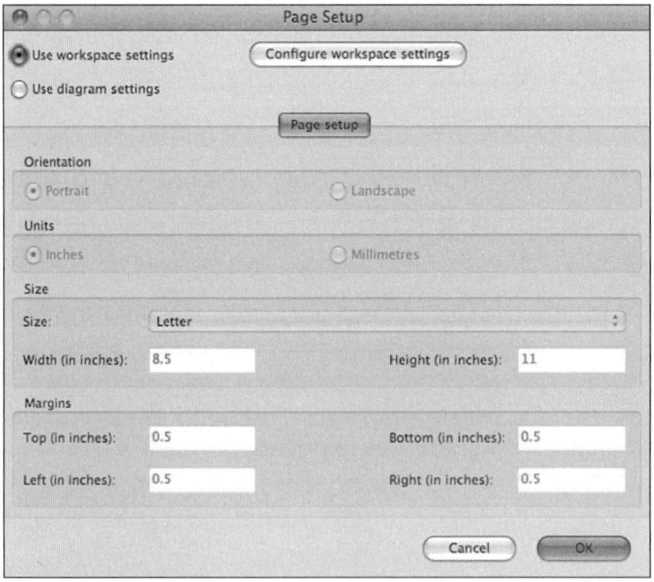

Figure 10-10   Page setup

Finally, the Filters item has a Sort/Filter Compartment Items option, although it seems always disabled.

Context Menu

Context menus provide a number of actions relevant to the current selection, with some of the more important ones covered next. Note that there are also new grouping capabilities in the runtime, although the generated diagrams do not yet leverage these.

The Add menu lets the user add a number of shapes, notes, or plain text to the diagram, each of which is persisted in the diagram file and is not available in the domain model. Following is a snippet from a diagram file, showing how a Text element and its style properties are persisted:

```
<children xmi:type="notation:Node" xmi:id="_Gy85wM5pEdymdqHGKqjE-g"
    type="Text">
    <children xmi:type="notation:Node" xmi:id="_Gy-H4M5pEdymdqHGKqjE-g"
    type="DiagramName">
     <element xsi:nil="true"/>
    </children>
    <children xmi:type="notation:Node" xmi:id="_Gy-H4c5pEdymdqHGKqjE-g"
     type="Description">
     <element xsi:nil="true"/>
    </children>
    <styles xmi:type="notation:ShapeStyle"
     xmi:id="_Gy85wc5pEdymdqHGKqjE-g"
     fontName="Lucida Grande"
     description="Some text associated with a class"/>
    <element xsi:nil="true"/>
    <layoutConstraint xmi:type="notation:Bounds"
     xmi:id="_Gy85ws5pEdymdqHGKqjE-g" x="423" y="261"
     width="97" height="32"/>
</children>
```

One of the more well-hidden features that the runtime provides is the capability to export a diagram as an image file. Although this is not available from the Eclipse main **File** menu as you might expect, it is available from **File → Save As Image File** on the diagram context menu, along with a **Print** action. The dialog is seen in Figure 10-11. Note that this is a context-sensitive feature; the selected element or elements appear in the image file. Selecting the canvas produces an image of the entire diagram.

The supported image file export formats are GIF, BMP, JPEG, JPG, PNG, and SVG. The Export to HTML option creates a simple HTML page and references the produced image.

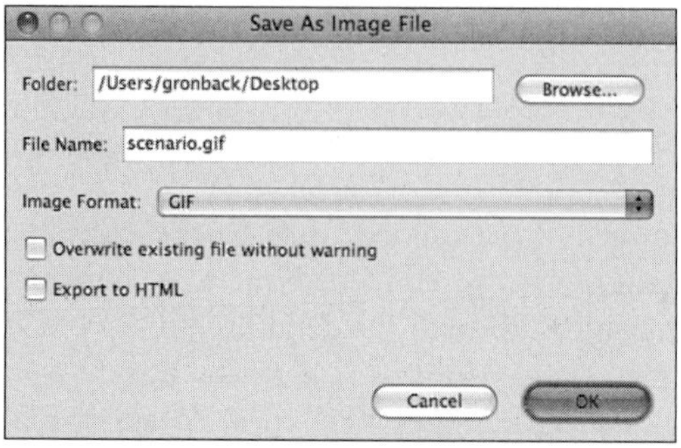

Figure 10-11   Save as Image File dialog

The diagram canvas has a number of other items duplicated in the Diagram main menu described earlier, but it also has a Show Properties View item that opens the Properties view, if it is not already open. Note that generated GMF diagrams also include a Load Resource option that is the same action available in generated EMF editors. This enables the user to load another model file into the resource set. Optionally, generated diagrams include a Create Shortcut menu item and allow the selection of related diagram elements to be added to the diagram. Section 11.4.2, "Contains Shortcuts To and Shortcuts Provided For," covers this capability.

Selected element context menus offer a number of specific menu items, including the familiar Cut, Copy, and Paste. A Duplicate action is also available. Finally, two delete menu items are available. Delete from Model is the functional menu item, while Delete from Diagram is one you would expect to see active in the case of diagram shortcuts, where only the notational element is to be removed from the diagram. Additionally, because the default generated diagrams are synchronized with the domain, the Delete from Diagram option doesn't make sense. A synchronization property in the GMF generator model determines the mode of operation.

Connection Handles

When the mouse is hovered over an element, whether it is selected or not, connection handles appear that you can use to create connections and even to prompt the user with possible options to create new diagram elements and a corresponding connection. Connection handles are shown in Figure 10-12.

Figure 10-12 Connection handles

Because the diagram is aware of the underlying domain elements, it can present the user with a legitimate list of options or allow for the selection of an existing element, as shown in Figure 10-13.

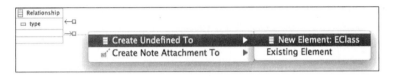

Figure 10-13 Connection handle prompts

Choosing the **Existing Element** option results in a dialog that lists the available types, as shown in Figure 10-14.

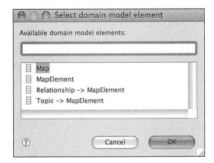

Figure 10-14 Select Domain Model Element dialog

Pop-Up Bars

A pop-up bar also appears when the mouse is hovered over any element, including the canvas itself, to present a list of available elements to create in the given context. A ToolTip is available for each, as shown in Figure 10-15 for the Ecore diagram.

Figure 10-15   Pop-up bars

TIP

These pop-up items are handy in some cases, but they often pop up at the wrong time—the worst case being just as you are about to click on an element, leaving you with a new element you didn't want. Generated diagrams include options to turn off connection handles and pop-up bars, and you might consider having them off by default. Another option is to modify the generated code to allow them to be activated explicitly, such as using Ctrl+spacebar.

Outline View

In textual editors, the Outline view provides just that: an outline of the file's contents, as seen in Figure 10-16. Diagram editors provide an outline of domain model elements, but they also provide an overview of the diagram for use in navigating large diagrams more easily.

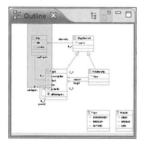

Figure 10-16   Outline view

Preferences

Although no limit exists for the number and type of preferences you can add, a number of default preferences are provided. Those discussed here are available to all generated editors.

Each diagram has its own root entry in the Preferences dialog, although a family of diagrams, such as the UML, should probably be placed under a common root. In the root of the diagram preferences are global options for enabling connection handles, pop-up bars, animated zoom and layout, and anti-aliasing, as seen in Figure 10-17.

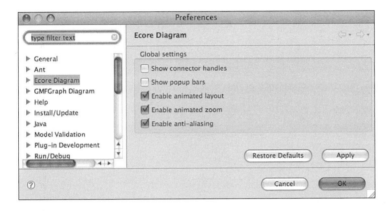

Figure 10-17   Diagram general preferences

In the Appearance category, options for colors and fonts are available, as seen in Figure 10-18. Note that changes made to default colors for a diagram apply to subsequently created elements only. Default connection style is set in the Connections category, with the options being Oblique and Rectilinear. This page is not shown because it's simply a drop-down list.

The Pathmaps page enables you to define a set of path variables for the diagram, as seen in Figure 10-19. Those registered using the `org.eclipse.gmf.runtime.emf.core.PathMap` extension-point are shown with a lock icon because you cannot modify them.

Printing itself is supported only by the GMF runtime for the Windows platform; printing preferences are available for all diagrams. The contents of this preference page are the same as the page setup options discussed in Section 10.1.1, "Diagram Menu."

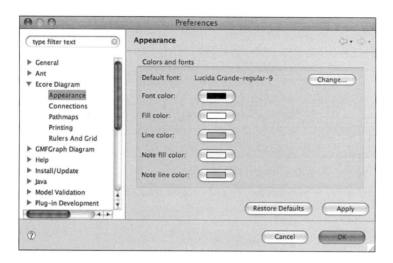

Figure 10-18   Diagram appearance preferences

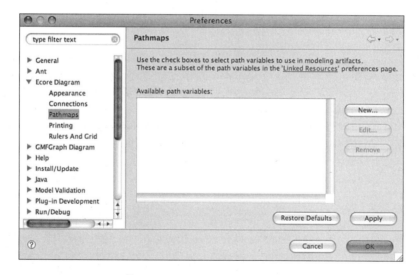

Figure 10-19   Diagram pathmap preferences

Finally, Rulers and Grid preferences are available and enable you to change the default options for ruler, grid, and snap-to functionality of new diagrams, as seen in Figure 10-20.

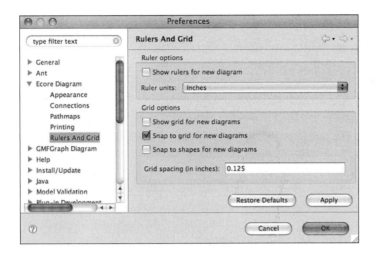

Figure 10-20   Diagram rulers and grid preferences

10.2 Notation Model

Used by the runtime to manage diagram element, position, and style attributes, the notation model also allows for persistence of diagrams to the file system. The notation model provides the link between GEF and EMF, and the GMF diagramming functionality is based on this model. Although it is general in its design, the notation model borrows some from GEF itself, similar to the tooling's graphical definition model.

Figure 10-21 is a diagram of the notation model. As you can see, the `View` class has an element reference to `EObject`. This is how the runtime provides a link to the domain model (or "semantic" model, as it's commonly referred to in the runtime documentation). `EditParts` will find their model element using this reference, although indirectly because the `View` object will be the GEF `EditPart`'s "model" element. Typically, code such as `((View) editPart.getModel()).getElement()` is used to access the underlying domain model from an `EditPart`.

`View` is the central class in the notation model, as you can tell from Figure 10-21. It contains the reference to the domain model element being represented and also does the following:

❍ Acts as the super type for `Diagram`, `Node`, and `Edge`

❍ Maintains a containment reference to children `Nodes` (transient and persistent)

○ Maintains a reference to the diagram itself

○ Has type, visibility, and mutable attributes

○ Maintains a list of all `Styles` applied to the element

○ Maintains a list of source and target `Edges`

The `Diagram` is the top-level container of views that has a name, `MeasurementUnit`, and containment references to all `Edges`. Note that, as with `View` children, Diagram `Edges` are either transient or persistent and are maintained in separate containment references.

A `Node` element is a `View` that can be composed in a container view and that can contain a `LayoutConstraint`. A layout manager uses a `LayoutConstraint` to set the `Bounds` of the `Node`'s visuals. The `Bounds` element holds size and position information.

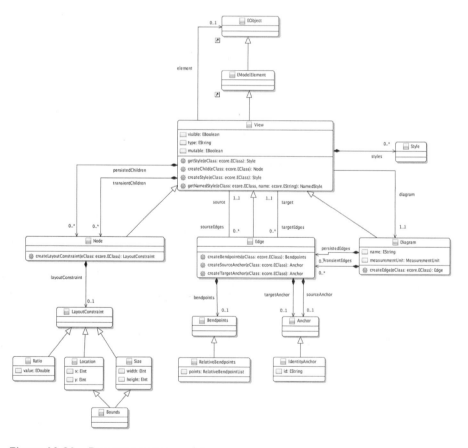

Figure 10-21   Diagram notation model

An `Edge` contains a list of `Bendpoint` and source/target `Anchors`. It also maintains a reference to its source and target `View` element. Note that `Bendpoint` and `LayoutConstraint` are designed with GEF's preference for relative coordinates in mind.

Diagram element appearance properties are handled by a number of Style model elements, as shown in Figure 10-22.

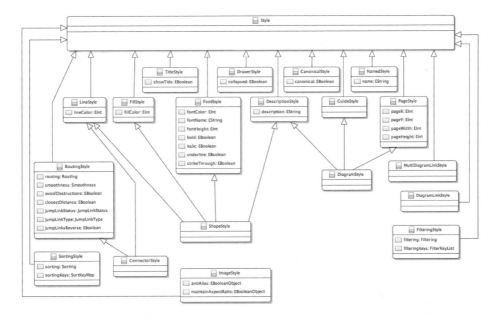

Figure 10-22　Notation styles

The `Style` interface provides an abstraction for appearance properties and has implementations in `FontStyle`, `LineStyle`, `RoutingStyle`, `CanonicalStyle`, `DrawerStyle`, `ImageStyle`, `FillStyle`, and so on. `Styles` are owned by the `View` and store properties used to display the shape and persist this information. One of the design considerations for the notation model was team collaboration. Separating styles into granular properties makes conflict merging easier to deal with when multiple modifications to the same resource occur. Additionally, `Styles` allow for flexibility as an extension-point for domain-specific properties and support the possibility of adding new `Styles` in future versions of the notation model.

COMMENT

The notation model is similar in its purpose to the Object Management Group's (OMG's) Diagram Interchange (DI) specification, which was developed to facilitate diagram exchange between Unified Modeling Language (UML) modeling tools; XML Metadata Interchange (XMI) for UML allows for the exchange of the model itself. With the introduction of the GMF runtime model into Eclipse, discussions have taken place regarding the update of the DI specification to align it with the GMF runtime model.

10.3 Extensibility Mechanisms

As you saw in Chapter 9, building a GEF editor means writing Java code that extends provided abstract classes and implementing required interfaces. GEF provides some integration with the Eclipse platform, but it offers no extension-points and limited hooks for extension. Furthermore, GEF does not require a clean separation of domain and notation information, although you can implement your graphical editor in this manner. In short, although GEF is a lightweight framework that is relatively easy to work with using conventional coding techniques, the GMF runtime provides a much richer set of extensibility frameworks and mechanisms that are specifically designed for building graphical editors for EMF models. As mentioned earlier, this comes at the price of some additional complexity (the usual trade-off).

As covered in Chapter 9, the main extensibility point of GEF comes with providing your own `EditPartFactory`, which the `Viewer` maintains to create `EditParts`, which create EditPolicies. With GMF, `EditParts` creation is modified to include a call to a service, where providers are registered and effectively replace the `EditPartFactory` concept in GEF. In fact, most aspects of diagram functionality are wrapped in services, including EditPolicies, views, palette, and layout. Section 10.4, "Services," covers the Service layer, along with detail on each of the provided services.

Although the extensibility of the GMF runtime is beneficial, it comes with the danger of malicious or malformed extensions that can be contributed to your diagram and can break its functionality. Also note that the current diagram code generated with the GMF tooling provides for normal runtime extensibility in a somewhat limited fashion. Not all extension-points are used because the team that wrote the tooling and generator did not see the value in contributing to each. However, the generation tooling is itself flexible, so if you want to alter the implementation of a generated diagram, you can do so by overriding or augmenting the models and Xpand templates. Furthermore, Bugzilla has an outstanding request to enhance the generator to provide for diagram extensions. Two approaches are considered for this extension:

○ Begin with the existing diagram definition models and provide extensions that, when regenerated, produce a new diagram that extends the original

○ Use a set of extension tooling models that target runtime extension-points opened in the diagram that the Toolsmith can extend

10.3.1 Extension-Points

The GMF runtime provides 27 extension-points for contribution in your diagram, while the tooling provides another 2 for its dashboard and validation. Of course, not all need to be used. The following sections provide information on each extension-point, most of which are found in the extension-points Reference section of the GMF help or can be viewed using PDE's Show extension-point Description feature. I provide this here for convenience, plus it contains additional examples, comments, and usage tips.

Note that every extension-point declaration includes an ATTLIST that is the same, including point, ID, and name attributes. These details are included in each schema description and are not reproduced here, to save space. Only the extension ELEMENT declaration is provided.

```
<!ELEMENT extension (elements)>
<!ATTLIST extension
point CDATA #REQUIRED
id CDATA #IMPLIED
name CDATA #IMPLIED>
```

point—The identifier of the extension-point—for example, org.eclipse. gmf.runtime.common.core.logListeners.

id—The identifier of the extension—for example, logListeners.

name—The name of the extension—for example, %ext.logListeners. (Note that %-prefixed Strings indicate localized Strings found in corresponding properties files.)

Additionally, several elements are used in multiple extension-point definitions. I list them here, to avoid duplication throughout this section.

```
<!ELEMENT staticMethod (value* , notValue*)>
<!ATTLIST staticMethod
name CDATA #REQUIRED
value CDATA #IMPLIED
notValue CDATA #IMPLIED>
```

This element specifies a static method to be called by reflection on the class. The static method has a name and a value. The value can be described by its String representation (`value` and `notValue`) or as an object (`value` or `notValue`). The rules of evaluation are as follows:

○ The return value String must be in the "`value`" String set.

○ The return value String must not be in the "`notValue`" String set.

○ The return value object must be in the "`value`" object set.

○ The return value object must not be in the "`notValue`" object set.

name—The name of the Static method. The format should be `PluginID\ClassName.method`, followed by an optional parameter set between parentheses. The parameter set can contain any number of primitive parameters or `%Context(pluginID/className)`, to use the context object as a parameter. Other parameter types are not supported. The method name can contain nested calling separated by a period (.). This is the general format for this method name:

```
<,param>*>?).<<,param>*>?)>*
```

value—A comma-separated list of String representations of the method return value. The String representation of the value is expected to be *one* of those in the list. The syntax to use is the following: `<,>*` If a comma (,) is expected to be in one of the Strings, it must be escaped by a forward slash (\). `null` is accepted as a String, and it means a null object.

notValue—A comma-separated list of String representations of the method return value that is not expected (the execution set). The String representation of the value is expected *not* to be *one* of those in the list. The syntax to use is the following: `<,>*` If a comma is expected to be in one of the Strings, it must be escaped by a forward slash (\). `null` is accepted as a String, and it means a null object.

```
<!ELEMENT method (value* , notValue*)>
<!ATTLIST method
name CDATA #REQUIRED
value CDATA #IMPLIED
notValue CDATA #IMPLIED>
```

This element specifies a `method` to be called by reflection on the object. The `method` has a `name` and a `value`. The value can be described by its String representation (`value` and `notValue`) or as an object (`value` or `notValue`). The rules of evaluation are the same as those for `staticMethod`.

```
<!ELEMENT value (method*)>
<!ATTLIST value
class CDATA #IMPLIED>
```

This element specifies a descriptor of an object that represents a method's returned value. The descriptor can include an optional set of methods to call on the `value` object.

    `class`—The fully qualified name of a class/interface that is assignable from or adaptable to the `value` object. The name could be followed (between parentheses) by the ID of a plug-in whose classloader can load that class. The final syntax is `className<(plugin id)>?`.

```
<!ELEMENT notValue (method*)>
<!ATTLIST notValue
class CDATA #IMPLIED>
```

This element specifies a descriptor of an object that represents a method's returned value that is not required. The descriptor can include an optional set of methods to call on the `notValue` object.

    `class`—The fully qualified name of a class/interface that is assignable from or adaptable to the `value` object. The name can be followed (between parentheses) by the ID of a plug-in whose classloader can load that class. The final syntax is `className<(plugin id)>?`.

10.4 Services

The GMF runtime provides a service layer and a collection of extension-points for use in contributing service providers. The service layer is designed to handle multiple providers, including dynamic contributions that reflect changes in runtime state. Providers can be loaded on demand and are assigned priorities to control their contribution to the runtime environment. Figure 10-23 illustrates the runtime services and their dependencies. Although the diagram shows all runtime extension-points and extensions to points within the runtime, those that are provided as services have a «service» stereotype in the label. Each service is described shortly, along with the rest of the extension-points. In the figure, empty pins indicate extension-points, while filled pins indicate extensions that are linked to their corresponding point.

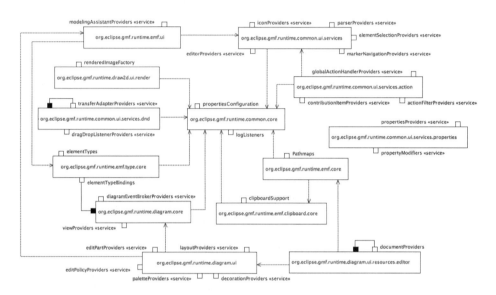

Figure 10-23   GMF runtime extension-points

Figure 10-24 is a diagram of the `org.eclipse.gmf.runtime.common. core.service` package, which contains the key elements of the service infrastructure and API.

The `IProvider` interface declares a `provides()` method for use in determining the applicability of a service to handle a given operation. As shown in the `IProvider` interface, a `Provider` can have change listeners attached. The `AbstractProvider` class implements the `IProvider` interface and has an abstract subclass `Service`, which is provided for clients to extend when creating new services. The `Service` class maintains a list of its providers, which are added with a `ProviderPriority` and `ProviderDescriptor`. The following priorities are defined in the `ProviderPriority` enumeration and specify the provider's relative importance: LOWEST, LOW, MEDIUM, HIGH, or HIGHEST.

In addition to the `ProviderPriority`, a provider is selected by taking into account an `ExecutionStrategy`. This enables you to specify an order during execution of a given `IOperation`, which complements the priority. Table 10-4 includes each strategy that the `ExecutionStrategy` enumeration defines and its meaning to the `Service`.

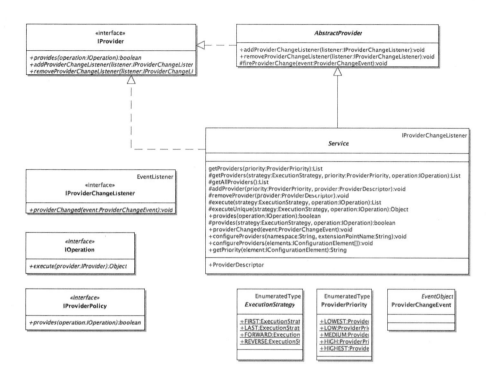

Figure 10-24   Runtime services core

Table 10-4   Service Execution Strategies

Strategy	Description
FIRST	Select the provider with the highest priority that is capable of servicing the request.
LAST	Select the provider with the lowest priority that is capable of servicing the request.
FORWARD	Invoke all providers in order of highest to lowest priority that are capable of servicing the request. The results of each provider are placed in a list of relative descending order of priority.
REVERSE	Invoke all providers in order of lowest to highest priority that are capable of servicing the request. The results of each provider are placed in a list of relative increasing order of priority.

The `Provider` implements the `IOperation` interface to fulfill the unit of work that the `Service` is designed to provide. The `Service` invokes the `IOperation`'s `execute()` method on its `Providers` using the `ExecutionStrategy`. The `Service` can provide the functionality if any of its registered `Providers` return `true` to the `provides()` operation when passed the `IOperation` instance.

Elements declared in the `Service` extension-point schema are populated by `Providers` and loaded using a configuration class. Not shown on the diagram is the `AbstractProviderConfiguration` class, which is intended to be subclassed to parse service provider descriptors. The `ProviderDescriptor` typically maintains an instance of the configuration that is initialized when the `Provider` is configured. The `Service` loads the `Provider` plug-ins when required, where its `startup()` method contains the required static initialization code.

You also can configure a `Service` with performance options, such as by using the `Service(boolean optimized)` constructor. Passing `true` causes the `Service` to cache providers when first retrieved for a given operation. Otherwise, the default behavior is to consider all `Providers` each time an operation is executed. Another `Service(boolean optimized, boolean optimistic)` constructor takes an additional optimistic Boolean parameter that, if `true`, causes the `Service` to trust its cache of `Providers`. Otherwise, it validates that the cache contents are still valid for the operation.

The `Service-Provider` infrastructure that GMF provides is used by many of its extension-points, as documented shortly. Note that you can use this infrastructure to create new services for your applications.

10.4.1 ViewService

Recall from the description of the notation model that `View` was the central element that contains the reference for the associated domain element. The `ViewService` is responsible for constructing `View` elements (`Diagram`, `Node`, `Edge`), typically by returning a `ViewFactory` class. This factory is responsible for creating notation view elements, setting `Style` elements, layout constraints, child views, and so on. In a similar recursive manner described for diagram creation in GEF, the `ViewService` is called with a *hint* to obtain the proper provider and factory for element creation.

As shown in Figure 10-25, the `ViewService` has a corresponding `AbstractViewProvider` that provides for a number of operations, including those used to create diagrams, nodes, and edges. Each diagram requires a view provider, which is typically a subclass of `AbstractViewProvider`. The method `get*ViewClass()` takes a hint that allows the custom logic to return the appropriate `ViewFactory` class.

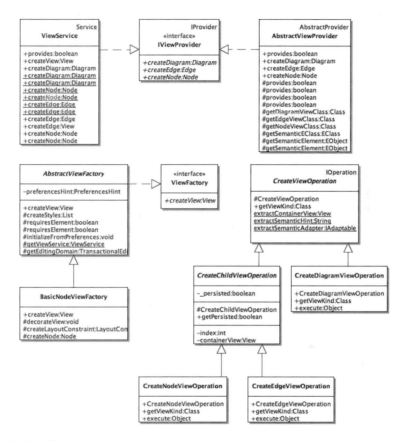

Figure 10-25 ViewService

ViewProviders Extension-Point

Identifier: `org.eclipse.gmf.runtime.diagram.core.viewProviders`
Description: This extension-point defines providers for the view service (`org.eclipse.gmf.runtime.diagram.core.services.ViewService`). The view service is responsible for creating view elements of the diagram notation model.

Configuration markup:

```
<!ELEMENT extension (viewProvider+)>

<!ELEMENT viewProvider (Priority , object* , context*)>
<!ATTLIST viewProvider
class CDATA #REQUIRED>
```

This element describes a `viewProvider`. A provider's description outlines zero or more objects to be referenced by the provider's contexts, and then lists zero or more contexts that the provider supports.

    `class`—The fully qualified name of the `viewProvider` class, which must implement `org.eclipse.gmf.runtime.diagram.core.providers.` `IViewProvider`. Typically, a subclass of `AbstractViewProvider` is specified.

```
<!ELEMENT Priority EMPTY>
<!ATTLIST Priority
name (Lowest|Low|Medium|High|Highest) >
```

This element defines the priority of the `viewProvider`.

    `name`—The priority of the provider. It can be one of the following values: `Lowest`, `Low`, `Medium`, `High`, or `Highest`. Dependencies must be considered when choosing the priority.

```
<!ELEMENT object (method* , staticMethod*)>
<!ATTLIST object
id CDATA #REQUIRED
class CDATA #IMPLIED>
```

This element describes an object that is examined by this provider. The object can have an optional set of methods to call upon.

    `id`—A unique (within the context of this provider XML definition) identifier for the object.

    `class`—The fully qualified name of a class/interface that is assignable from, or adaptable to, the object. The name can be followed (between parentheses) by the ID of a plug-in whose classloader can load that class. The final syntax is `className<(plugin id)>?`.

```
<!ELEMENT context EMPTY>
<!ATTLIST context
viewClass (org.eclipse.gmf.runtime.notation.Node |
org.eclipse.gmf.runtime.notation.Diagram |
org.eclipse.gmf.runtime.notation.Edge)
```

```
elements CDATA #IMPLIED
containerViews CDATA #IMPLIED
semanticHints CDATA #IMPLIED>
```

This element defines a context supported by the view provider that contains values for the different hint parameters needed to create views.

`viewClass`—A fully qualified name of a view class from a list of different kinds of views created by the view service that the provider can accept in this context. This field is an enumeration consisting of the qualified class names for `Node`, `Diagram`, and `Edge` notation elements.

`elements`—A comma-separated list of object IDs (from the provider XML definition) that represents elements that this provider can accept in this context.

`containerViews`—A comma-separated list of object IDs (from the provider XML definition) that represents container views that this provider can accept in this context.

`semanticHints`—A comma-separated list of Strings that represents semantic hints that this provider can accept in this context.

Examples:

Following is an example view provider extension-point contribution, as generated using the GMF tooling:

```
<extension-point="org.eclipse.gmf.runtime.diagram.core.viewProviders">
  <viewProvider
    class="org.eclipse.mindmap.diagram.providers.MindmapViewProvider">
    <Priority name="Lowest"/>
    <context viewClass="org.eclipse.gmf.runtime.notation.Diagram"
             semanticHints="mindmap"/>
    <context viewClass="org.eclipse.gmf.runtime.notation.Node"
             semanticHints=""/>
    <context viewClass="org.eclipse.gmf.runtime.notation.Edge"
             semanticHints=""/>
  </viewProvider>
</extension>
```

API information:

The class `AbstractViewProvider` (though technically not abstract) is provided as a base implementation that implements the required `org.eclipse.gmf.runtime.diagram.core.providers.IViewProvider` interface.

Notes:

The generated diagrams that the GMF tooling provides contribute to the view provider's extension-point.

By default, GMF diagrams provide geoshape elements and standard note, text, and description information. This functionality is provided by the internal

classes `org.eclipse.gmf.runtime.diagram.ui.geoshapes.internal.`
`providers.GeoshapeViewProvider` and `org.eclipse.gmf.runtime.`
`diagram.ui.providers.internal.DiagramViewProvider`, respectively.

10.4.2 EditPartService

An `EditPartService` is used to create `EditParts` that act as a controller for
the notation view and domain element. A corresponding `EditPartProvider`
supplies a `createGraphicEditPart()` method for this purpose, essentially
replacing GEF's `EditPartFactory.createEditPart(View)` method. The
main participants in the service are shown in Figure 10-26. The role of
an `EditPart` in GMF is no different than in GEF, except for the fact that
`createGraphicEditPart()` returns an instance of `IGraphicEditPart`. This
GMF runtime interface extends the GEF `GraphicalEditPart` interface to provide support for `EditParts` that use EMF `EObject` instances as their model.
Again, here *model* is the `View` object in the notation model, which maintains a
reference to the domain (semantic) model element. All `EditParts` used in the
GMF runtime should extend the abstract `org.eclipse.gmf.runtime.`
`diagram.ui.editparts.GraphicalEditPart` class. This class provides a
`getNotationView()` method to return the `View` model element, in addition to
a `resolveSemanticElement()` method to return the referenced domain model
element.

Providers are implemented by the Toolsmith, just as `EditPartFactory`
was supplied using GEF. Providers can provide `EditParts` for new or existing model element types, although it's more efficient to swap out EditPolicies on
an `EditPart` using the `EditPolicyService`.

EditPartProviders Extension-Point

Identifier: `org.eclipse.gmf.runtime.diagram.ui.`
`editpartProviders`

Description: The `EditPartService` is a factory for `EditParts`, given a
model and a context. An `EditPartProvider` extends the service by providing
for new `EditParts` or existing ones using a different combination of a model
and a context.

Configuration markup:

```
<!ELEMENT extension (editpartProvider+)>

<!ELEMENT editpartProvider (Priority , object* , context*)>
<!ATTLIST editpartProvider
class CDATA #REQUIRED>
```

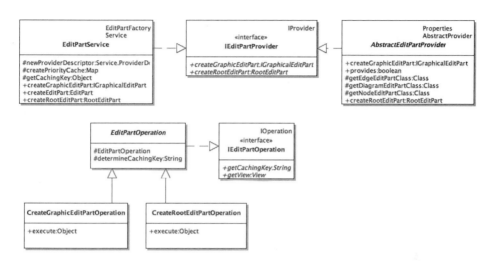

Figure 10-26 EditPartService

A provider's description outlines zero or more objects to be referenced by the provider's contexts and then lists zero or more contexts that the provider supports.

class—The fully qualified name of the `EditPartProvider` class that implements `org.eclipse.gmf.runtime.diagram.ui.internal.services.editpart.IEditPartProvider`.

```
<!ELEMENT Priority EMPTY>
<!ATTLIST Priority
name (Lowest|Low|Medium|High|Highest) >
```

name—The priority of the provider. It can be one of the following values: `Lowest`, `Low`, `Medium`, `High`, or `Highest`. Dependencies must be considered when choosing the priority.

```
<!ELEMENT object (method* , staticMethod*)>
<!ATTLIST object
id CDATA #REQUIRED
class CDATA #IMPLIED>
```

This element specifies a descriptor of an object that this provider examines. The object descriptor can include an optional set of methods to call on the object.

id—A unique (within the context of this provider definition) identifier for the object.

class—The fully qualified name of a class/interface that is assignable from, or adaptable to, the object. The name can be followed (between parentheses) by the ID of a plug-in whose classloader can load that class. The final syntax is className<(plugin id)>?.

```
<!ELEMENT context EMPTY>
<!ATTLIST context
views CDATA #IMPLIED
providesRootEditPart (true | false) "false">
```

This element defines a context supported by the EditPart provider.

views—A comma-separated list of view object IDs (from the provider XML definition) that this provider supports in this context.1

providesRootEditPart—true or false for whether this context represents the root EditPart.

Examples:

Following is an example EditPart provider extension-point contribution that the GMF tooling provides in generated diagrams:

```
<extension
  point="org.eclipse.gmf.runtime.diagram.ui.editpartProviders">
  <editpartProvider

class="org.eclipse.mindmap.diagram.providers.MindmapEditPartProvider">
    <Priority name="Lowest"/>
  </editpartProvider>
</extension>
```

API information:

The EditPart provider class that should implement the interface org.eclipse.gmf.runtime.diagram.ui.internal.services. editpart.IEditPartProvider. Note that this interface is in an internal package namespace, meaning that it is not yet public API. An alternative is to extend the public AbstractEditPartProvider, found in the package org. eclipse.gmf.runtime.diagram.ui.services.editpart.

Another internal class provided for support of rendered images is DiagramUIRenderEditPartProvider, which is found in the package org.eclipse.gmf.runtime.diagram.ui.render.internal.providers.

Notes:

As was the case with the View Service, two providers for the EditPartService are contributed by the geoshapes and the general diagram

provider (notes, text, and so on). These are `org.eclipse.gmf.runtime.`
`diagram.ui.geoshapes.internal.providers.GeoshapeEditPart`
`Provider` and `org.eclipse.gmf.runtime.diagram.ui.providers.`
`internal.DiagramEditPartProvider`, respectively.

10.4.3 EditPolicyService

As the previous section alluded to, you can install and remove EditPolicies on
`EditParts` using the `EditPolicyService`. In fact, clients can contribute new
`EditPolicy` implementations to existing diagrams without overriding the
`EditPart` class itself. Figure 10-27 shows the main elements of the service.

Note that GMF's `GraphicalEditPart` class overrides (final) the GEF
`AbstractEditPart` `createEditPolicies()` method. This override calls
`createDefaultEditPolicies()` and then invokes the `EditPolicyService`
to install EditPolicies for the `EditPart`. Those who want to install EditPolicies
programmatically must do so by overriding `createDefaultEditPolicies()`.

As with all services, the `EditPolicyService` offers all providers a chance
to install `EditPolicies` based on their stated priorities. To override an
`EditPolicy`, install a new one using the same role. To remove an `EditPolicy`,
contribute it using a `null` role.

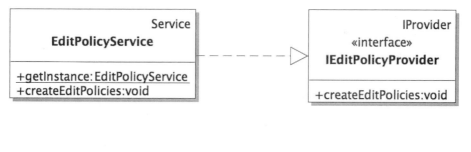

Figure 10-27 EditPolicyService

EditPolicyProvider Extension-Point

Identifier: `org.eclipse.gmf.runtime.diagram.ui.editpolicy`
`Providers`

Description: This extension-point defines `EditPolicyProviders` for the `EditPolicy` service. The `EditPolicyService` allows plug-ins to modify or enhance the behavior of an `EditPart` via an `EditPolicy` without modifying the `EditPolicy` code.

Configuration markup:

```
<!ELEMENT extension (editpolicyProvider+)>

<!ELEMENT editpolicyProvider (Priority , object* , context*)>
<!ATTLIST editpolicyProvider
class CDATA #REQUIRED>
```

`class`—The fully qualified name of the `EditPolicyProvider` class that implements `org.eclipse.gmf.runtime.diagram.ui.services.edit-policy. IEditPolicyProvider`.

```
<!ELEMENT Priority EMPTY>
<!ATTLIST Priority
name (Lowest|Low|Medium|High|Highest) >
```

`name`—The priority of the provider. It can be one of the following values: `Lowest`, `Low`, `Medium`, `High`, or `Highest`. Dependencies must be considered when choosing the priority.

```
<!ELEMENT object (method* , staticMethod*)>
<!ATTLIST object
id CDATA #REQUIRED
class CDATA #IMPLIED>
```

This element defines a descriptor of an object that this provider examines. The object can have an optional set of methods to call upon.

`id`—A unique (within the context of this provider XML definition) identifier for the object.

`class`—The fully qualified name of a class/interface that is assignable from, or adaptable to, the object. The name can be followed (between parentheses) by the ID of a plug-in whose classloader can load that class. The final syntax is `className<(plugin id)>?`.

```
<!ELEMENT context EMPTY>
<!ATTLIST context
editparts CDATA #IMPLIED>
```

This element defines a context that the `EditPolicyProvider` supports that contains the `EditParts` that this provider supports.

editparts—A comma-separated list of `EditPart` IDs (from the provider XML definition) that this provider supports.

Examples:

This is an example of a basic `EditPolicyProvider` extension-point contribution:

```
<extension
    point="org.eclipse.gmf.runtime.diagram.ui.editpolicyProviders">
    <editpolicyProvider class=
"org.eclipse.mindmap.diagram.providers.MindmapEditPolicyProvider">
        <Priority name="Lowest"/>
    </editpolicyProvider>
</extension>
```

API information:

The fully qualified class should implement the interface `org.eclipse.gmf.runtime.diagram.ui.services.editpolicy.IEditPolicyProvider`.

Notes:

Diagrams generated using the GMF tooling do not currently use this extension-point. EditPolicies are added to generated `EditParts` within the `createDefaultEditPolicies()` method.

10.4.4 Palette Service

You saw in Section 9.2, "GEF," that configuring a palette is straightforward. GMF adds a `PaletteService` to allow for palette definition using extension-point and service provider implementation, as shown in Figure 10-28. Contributions can be added or overridden by extender plug-ins, providing flexibility in palette definition and makeup. The runtime provides a `DefaultPaletteProvider` class, which is satisfactory for most diagrams. The only code that is required is to provide a palette factory, which links creation tools to model element types.

`PaletteProviders` can provide drawers, groups, separators, a palette tool, and template items using the extension-point, as defined next.

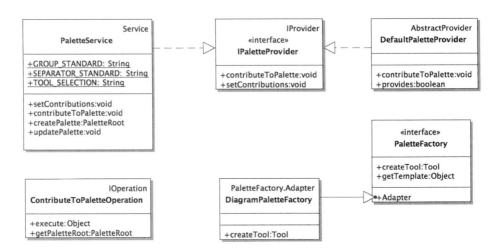

Figure 10-28   Palette service

PaletteProvider Extension-Point

Identifier: `org.eclipse.gmf.runtime.diagram.ui.paletteProviders`

Description: The `paletteProvider` extension-point allows for full declarative specification of a diagram palette.

Configuration markup:

```
<!ELEMENT extension (paletteProvider+)>

<!ELEMENT paletteProvider (Priority , editor? , content? ,
contribution*)>
<!ATTLIST paletteProvider
class CDATA
"org.eclipse.gmf.runtime.diagram.ui.providers.DefaultPaletteProvider">
```

A provider's description outlines the target context (the editor and the editor's content) and zero or more palette contributions in that context.

`class`—The fully qualified name of the `paletteProvider` class, which, by default, is the provided `org.eclipse.gmf.runtime.diagram.ui.` `providers.DefaultPaletteProvider`.

```
<!ELEMENT Priority EMPTY>
<!ATTLIST Priority
name (Lowest|Low|Medium|High|Highest) >
```

name—The priority of the provider. It can be one of the following values: Lowest, Low, Medium, High, or Highest. Dependencies must be considered when choosing the priority. A provider that adds contributions to paths (menus | groups) that other providers have contributed must have a higher priority than they do. Similarly, a provider that contributes palette entries that other providers have predefined must have a higher priority.

```
<!ELEMENT editor EMPTY>
<!ATTLIST editor
id CDATA #IMPLIED
class CDATA #IMPLIED>
```

This element specifies the target editor. The editor is not required when pre-defining palette entries.

id—The published ID of the targeted editor. Although this field is optional, at least one of the two fields (id and class) must be specified.

class—The fully qualified name of a class/interface that is assignable from or adaptable to the target editor. The name can be followed (between parentheses) by the ID of a plug-in whose classloader can load that class. The final syntax is className<(plugin id)>?. Although this field is optional, at least one of the two fields (id and class) must be specified.

```
<!ELEMENT content (method* , staticMethod*)>
<!ATTLIST content
class CDATA #IMPLIED>
```

class—The fully qualified name of a class/interface that is assignable from or adaptable to the target editor's content object. The name can be followed (between parentheses) by the ID of a plug-in whose classloader can load that class. The final syntax is className<(plugin id)>?.

```
<!ELEMENT contribution (entry* , predefinedEntry*)>
<!ATTLIST contribution
factoryClass CDATA #IMPLIED>
```

factoryClass—The fully qualified name of a class that represents the factory for the contributions. The class must implement the interface org.eclipse. gmf.runtime.gef.ui.internal.ui.palette.PaletteFactory.

```
<!ELEMENT entry (expand?)>
<!ATTLIST entry
kind (drawer|separator|template|tool|stack)
id CDATA #REQUIRED
path CDATA #IMPLIED
label CDATA #IMPLIED
description CDATA #IMPLIED
small_icon CDATA #IMPLIED
large_icon CDATA #IMPLIED
permission (None|HideOnly|Limited|Full)
defineOnly (true | false) >
```

This element specifies a palette entry that will be contributed to the palette.

kind—The kind of the entry (drawer I stack I separator I tool I template).

id—A user-defined ID for the entry (unique within a provider).

path—A fully qualified path of contribution. All path IDs should have been previously defined. *Previous* means either earlier in the XML file or in another one with a lower priority (order). If a path ends with a separator ID, the new entry is appended to the elements following the separator (just before the next separator, or at the end of the container, if it has no more separators below that one). If a path ends with a normal entry ID, the new entry is inserted after that entry. A path is required unless this palette entry is being defined only so that it can be contributed by another palette provider.

label—The palette entry label (not required for separators).

description—The palette entry description.

small_icon—The palette entry small icon.

large_icon—The palette entry large icon.

permission—The palette entry permission (None I HideOnly I limited I full).

defineOnly—If true, this palette entry is only being defined; it will not be contributed. In this case, the path is ignored and not required. When defining a palette drawer or palette stack, this flag needs to be set only on the palette drawer or stack, to indicate that all the entries on the drawer are being defined only. The palette entry can be contributed by another palette extension using a predefinedEntry.

```
<!ELEMENT expand (content?)>
<!ATTLIST expand
force (true | false) "false">
```

This element defines a condition to make palette drawers initially expanded.

force—true or false, used to force expansion.

```
<!ELEMENT predefinedEntry (expand?)>
<!ATTLIST predefinedEntry
id CDATA #REQUIRED
path CDATA #IMPLIED
remove (true | false) >
```

A descriptor for a palette contribution entry that another plug-in already has defined and that will now be contributed.

id—The ID given to the palette entry when it was defined. If the palette entry is in a palette container (the drawer or stack), the ID is considered the full path of this palette entry.

path—A fully qualified path describing where this palette entry should appear on the palette. All path IDs should have been previously defined. *Previous* means either earlier in the XML file or in another one with a lower priority (order). If a path ends with a separator ID, the new entry is appended to the elements following the separator (just before the next separator, or at the end of the container, if it has no more separators below that one). If a path ends with a normal entry ID, the new entry is inserted after that entry. The path is not required if this predefined entry is not being contributed. That is, a predefined entry can be used to expand an existing drawer or remove an existing entry from the palette.

remove—If true, an existing entry is removed.

Examples:

Following is a simple palette contribution with a single tool in a single drawer:

```
<extension-point="org.eclipse.gmf.runtime.diagram.ui.paletteProviders">
  <paletteProvider
  class="
org.eclipse.gmf.runtime.diagram.ui.providers.DefaultPaletteProvider">
    <Priority name="Highest"/>
    <editor
id="org.eclipse.mindmap.diagram.editor.MindmapDiagramEditorID"/>
    <contribution
    factoryClass="
org.eclipse.mindmap.diagram.providers.MindmapPaletteFactory">
        <entry label="Nodes"
               kind="drawer"
               description="Mindmap diagram nodes"
               path="/"
               small_icon="icons/obj16/MindmapDiagramFile.gif"
               id="nodeDrawer">
          <expand>
             <content/>
          </expand>
        </entry>
```

```
        <entry label="Topic"
               kind="tool"
               description="Create a new Topic"
               path="/nodeDrawer/"
               small_icon="icons/obj16/MindmapDiagramFile.gif"
               large_icon=""
               id="Topic"/>
      </contribution>
    </paletteProvider>
  </extension>
```

API information:

The interface `org.eclipse.gmf.runtime.diagram.ui.services.`
`IPaletteProvider` should be implemented by the class declared, if the
default `org.eclipse.gmf.runtime.diagram.ui.providers.Default`
`PaletteProvider` is not used.

Notes:

Diagrams generated using the GMF tooling do not currently use this
extension-point. Instead, a `*PaletteFactory` class is generated in the
`*.diagram.part` package.

10.4.5 Decoration Service

Validation errors, checkout state, or other decorations often need to be applied
to a diagram element. The runtime's DecorationService supports the addition of
decorator icons on top of figures in a declarative manner and without specific
knowledge of the underlying figure. It does this by using a layer placed above the
shapes, thereby allowing it to even span `EditPart` hierarchies. Figure 10-29
shows the main elements of the service.

To use this service, you must implement `IDecorationProvider`, where the
`createDecorators()` method supports the installation of a custom decoration
or image in a predefined location on the shape.

DecoratorProvider Extension-Point

Identifier: `org.eclipse.gmf.runtime.diagram.ui.`
`decoratorProviders`

Description: This extension-point defines decorator providers for the
Decorator Service (`org.eclipse.gmf.runtime.diagram.ui.services.`
`decorator`). The `DecorationService` enables clients to decorate diagram ele-
ments with an image or figure.

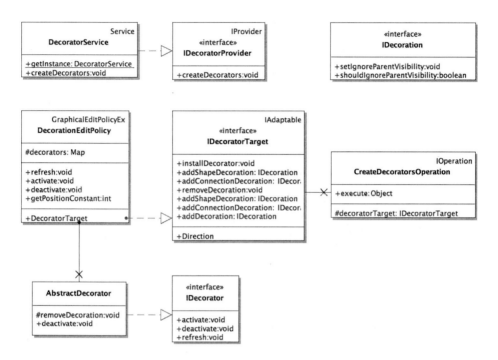

Figure 10-29 DecorationService

More specifically, the provider service enables implementors to do the following:

A provider of the `DecorationService` can add an adornment to any diagram element.

The decoration is typically an image but can be any sort of graphics object or figure. A provider of the decoration service is not restricted to any specific graphic type.

The provider can specify any of the following enumerated locations for a decoration on a shape, label, or list compartment item: center, north, northeast, northwest, south, southeast, southwest, east, or west. For a connector, the percentage of the distance from the source end of the connector provides a location for the decoration.

The decoration can be any size that fits within the shape or connector boundary.

The decoration is justified according to its position on the shape. For example, northwest is left-justified with an offset from the top-left side of the shape, and northeast is right-justified with an offset from the top-right side of the shape.

Each decoration can either be included in the printed output of the diagram or not.

If more than one provider adds a decoration to the same location, the decoration from the highest-priority provider appears on top of the other decoration(s).

Configuration markup:

```
<!ELEMENT extension (decoratorProvider)>

<!ELEMENT decoratorProvider (Priority , object* , context*)>
<!ATTLIST decoratorProvider
class CDATA #REQUIRED>
```

class—The fully qualified name of the decorator provider class that should implement the interface `org.eclipse.gmf.runtime.diagram.ui.` `services.decorator.IDecoratorProvider`.

```
<!ELEMENT Priority EMPTY>
<!ATTLIST Priority
name (Lowest|Low|Medium|High|Highest) >
```

name—The priority of the provider. It can be one of the following values: `Lowest`, `Low`, `Medium`, `High`, or `Highest`. Dependencies must be considered when choosing the priority. A provider at a higher priority takes a chance first at deciding provision.

If more than one provider adds a decoration to the same location, the decoration(s) from the highest-priority provider appears on top of decoration(s) supplied by lower-priority provider(s).

```
<!ELEMENT object (method* , staticMethod*)>
<!ATTLIST object
id CDATA #REQUIRED
class CDATA #IMPLIED>
```

This element specifies an object that this provider examines. The object can have an optional set of methods to call upon.

id—A unique (within the context of this provider XML definition) identifier for the object.

class—The fully qualified name of a class/interface that is assignable from or adaptable to the object. The name can be followed (between parentheses) by the ID of a plug-in whose classloader can load that class. The final syntax is `className<(plugin id)>?`.

```
<!ELEMENT context EMPTY>
<!ATTLIST context
decoratorTargets CDATA #IMPLIED>
```

The context contains a list of objects to be decorated using this provider. The list defined in decoratorTargets consists of items previously defined in the XML using the object element.

decoratorTargets—The decoratorTargets is a comma-separated list of objects that this provider supports. The xml defined object is specified using its id.

Examples:

An extension to the decorator service requires the implementation of the IDecorator and IDecoratorProvider interfaces. The following is an example decorator service provider extension:

```
<extension
     point="org.eclipse.gmf.runtime.diagram.ui.decoratorProviders">
   <decoratorProvider class=
"org.eclipse.gmf.runtime.diagram.ui.providers.MyDecoratorProvider">
      <Priority name="Lowest"/>
      <object class=
         "org.eclipse.gmf.runtime.notation.Node
         (org.eclipse.gmf.runtime.notation)"
      id="NODE">
         <method name="getType()" value="MyNodeType"/>
      </object>
      <context decoratorTargets="NODE"/>
   </decoratorProvider>
</extension>
```

API information:

For API information, see the classes and interfaces defined in the org.eclipse.gmf.runtime.diagram.ui.services.decorator package.

Clients that provide an extension to the decorator service need to create classes that implement the following interfaces:

```
org.eclipse.gmf.runtime.diagram.ui.services.decorator.IDecorator
org.eclipse.gmf.runtime.diagram.ui.services.decorator.IDecoratorProvider
```

Notes:

Diagrams generated using the GMF tooling use this extension-point when audits are defined for a diagram. Audit limit violations cause decoration of the diagram element. Additionally, enabling the diagram shortcut feature produces a generated extension to the decorator provider. Small arrow decorations appear in the bottom-left corner of shortcutted diagram elements.

A `DiagramDecoratorProvider` is available in the internal runtime package `org.eclipse.gmf.runtime.diagram.ui.providers.internal`. By default, this provider installs a `BookmarkDecorator` for the diagram layer.

10.4.6 IconService

The runtime's IconService allows for the retrieval of an icon based on a hint, such as the View class or ElementType. The service is simple in its implementation, but as with all Services, it allows for the substitution of icons for a diagram by contributing a provider of higher priority.

As shown in Figure 10-30, providers need to implement the `IIconProvider` interface, as is the case with the shown `DiagramIconProvider`. The runtime provides this provider, which handles icons for standard diagram notes and text. A `SharedImages` class provides the `DiagramIconProvider` with its `ImageDescriptors`.

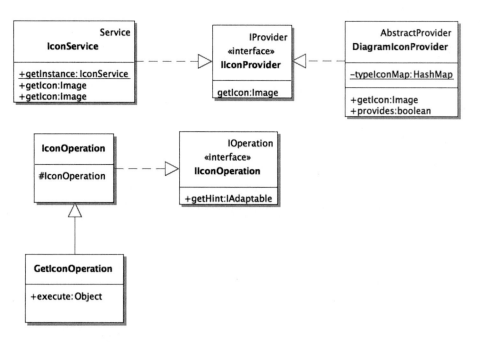

Figure 10-30   IconService

IconProvider Extension-Point

Identifier: `org.eclipse.gmf.runtime.common.ui.services.icon Providers`

Description: This extension-point defines icon providers for the icon service (`org.eclipse.gmf.runtime.common.ui.services.icon.IconService`). The icon service supplies an icon for a given element.

Configuration markup:

```
<!ELEMENT extension (IconProvider)>

<!ELEMENT IconProvider (Priority , Policy? , object* , context*)>
<!ATTLIST IconProvider
class CDATA #REQUIRED>
```

`class`—The provider class that must implement interface `org.eclipse.gmf.runtime.common.ui.services.icon.IIconProvider`.

```
<!ELEMENT Priority EMPTY>
<!ATTLIST Priority
name (Lowest|Low|Medium|High|Highest) >
```

`name`—The name of the provider priority—`Lowest`, `Low`, `Medium`, `High`, or `Highest`.

```
<!ELEMENT Policy EMPTY>
<!ATTLIST Policy
class CDATA #REQUIRED>
```

`class`—The provider policy class.

```
<!ELEMENT object (method*)>
<!ATTLIST object
id CDATA #REQUIRED
class CDATA #IMPLIED>
```

This element specifies an object that this provider examines. The object descriptor can include an optional set of methods to call on the object.

`id`—A unique (within the context of this provider definition) identifier for the object.

`class`—The fully qualified name of a class/interface that is assignable from, or adaptable to, the object. The name could be followed (between parentheses)

by the ID of a plug-in whose classloader can load that class. The final syntax is
className(plugin id).

```
<!ELEMENT context EMPTY>
<!ATTLIST context
elements CDATA #IMPLIED>
```

This element defines a context that the icon provider supports.

elements—A comma-separated list of element object IDs (from the provider XML definition) that this provider supports in this context.

Examples:

Following is an example of an icon provider extension, as contributed by generated code using the GMF tooling:

```
<extension
    point="org.eclipse.gmf.runtime.common.ui.services.iconProviders">
    <IconProvider class=
"org.eclipse.requirements.diagram.providers.RequirementsIconProvider">
        <Priority name="Low"/>
    </IconProvider>
</extension>
```

This is the Geoshapes contribution:

```
<extension
    id="iconProviders"
    name="%ext.iconProviders"
    point="org.eclipse.gmf.runtime.common.ui.services.iconProviders">
  <IconProvider class=
    "org.eclipse.gmf.runtime.diagram.ui.geoshapes.internal.providers.
    GeoShapeIconProvider">
    <Priority name="Medium"/>
    <object class="org.eclipse.gmf.runtime.notation.View
       (org.eclipse.gmf.runtime.notation)" id="GeoShape">
        <method name="getType()"
              value="oval,triangle,rectangle,shadowRectangle,
              rectangle3D,roundRectangle,hexagon,octagon,
              pentagon,diamond,cylinder,line"/>
        </object>
    <context elements="GeoShape"/>
  </IconProvider>
</extension>
```

API information:

The value of the class attribute must be the fully qualified name of a class that implements `org.eclipse.gmf.runtime.common.ui.services.icon.IIconProvider`.

10.4.7 MarkerNavigationService

The `MarkerNavigationService` and corresponding `IMarkerNavigation Provider` interface allow for a service-based implementation of the `gotoMarker()` method, as seen in Figure 10-31. Requests made in all editors are delegated to this Service and provided for based on priority and marker types supported. The runtime supports three `Abstract*MarkerNavigation Provider` classes and a concrete `DiagramMarkerNavigationProvider`.

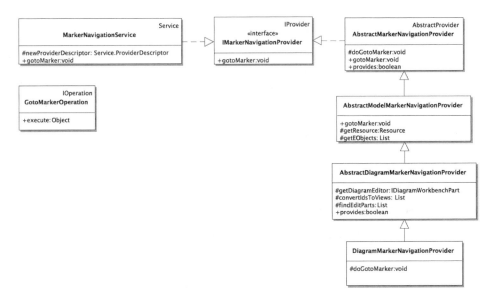

Figure 10-31 MarkerNavigationService

MarkerNavigationProvider Extension-Point

Identifier: `org.eclipse.gmf.runtime.common.ui.services.markerNavigationProviders`

Description: This extension-point facilitates the configuration of providers for the `MarkerNavigationService` (`org.eclipse.gmf.runtime.common.ui.services.marker.MarkerNavigationService`).

The `MarkerNavigationService` enables clients to perform the navigation feedback when the user double-clicks on or "goes to" a marker reference. The attribute values defined on the marker identify a location or locations in the resource that are of interest to the user. The feedback associated with navigation to that location depends on the resource and its associated editors. The feedback might simply be selecting the appropriate object(s) specified by the marker's location, or the feedback could involve a separate dialog to describe the reason for the marker (such as errors).

To use the `MarkerNavigationService`, a client should define its own marker types and create the marker instances on the appropriate resources. Markers created on the workspace root are not navigable.

Configuration markup:

```
<!ELEMENT extension (MarkerNavigationProvider)>

<!ELEMENT MarkerNavigationProvider (Priority , MarkerType+ , Policy?)>
<!ATTLIST MarkerNavigationProvider
class CDATA #REQUIRED>
```

`class`—The provider class that is a subclass of `org.eclipse.gmf.runtime.common.core.service.AbstractProvider` and implements `org.eclipse.gmf.runtime.common.ui.services.marker.IMarkerNavigationProvider`.

```
<!ELEMENT Priority EMPTY>
<!ATTLIST Priority
name (Lowest|Low|Medium|High|Highest) >
```

`name`—The name of the provider priority—`Lowest`, `Low`, `Medium`, `High`, or `Highest`.

```
<!ELEMENT MarkerType EMPTY>
<!ATTLIST MarkerType
name CDATA #REQUIRED>
```

name—The name of the marker type that the provider understands.

```
<!ELEMENT Policy EMPTY>
<!ATTLIST Policy
class CDATA #REQUIRED>
```

class—The provider policy class. Provider policies can optionally be specified to determine whether the providers support a given operation.

Examples:

Following is an example of a marker navigation provider extension, as contributed by the GMF tooling when audits or metrics are defined for a diagram:

```
<extension-point=
"org.eclipse.gmf.runtime.common.ui.services.markerNavigationProviders">
    <MarkerNavigationProvider
      class="org.eclipse.mindmap.diagram.providers.
      MindmapMarkerNavigationProvider">
        <MarkerType name="org.eclipse.mindmap.diagram.diagnostic"/>
        <Priority name="Lowest"/>
    </MarkerNavigationProvider>
</extension>
```

API information:

The value of the class attribute must represent a subclass of org. eclipse.gmf.runtime.common.core.service.AbstractProvider that implements org.eclipse.gmf.runtime.common.ui.services.marker. IMarkerNavigationProvider. For convenience, org.eclipse.gmf. runtime.common.ui.services.marker.IMarkerNavigationProvider. AbstractMarkerNavigationProvider is provided to be subclassed.

10.4.8 ParserService

When editing Strings on a diagram, the ParserService is responsible for returning an IParserProvider implementation that can handle Strings for the passed IAdaptable element. The provided parser itself must implement the IParser interface, shown in Figure 10-32. Section 4.6.7, "Custom Parsers," includes an example of a custom parser that was contributed to the color modeling diagram.

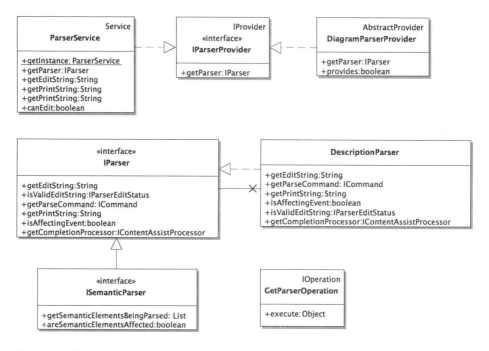

Figure 10-32   ParserService

ParserProvider Extension-Point

Identifier: `org.eclipse.gmf.runtime.common.ui.services.parserProviders`

Description: This extension-point defines parser providers for the parser service (`org.eclipse.gmf.runtime.common.ui.services.parser.ParserService`). The `ParserService` supplies and applies text associated with a given element, as shown in labels modified using an in-place editor.

Configuration markup:

```
<!ELEMENT extension (ParserProvider)>

<!ELEMENT ParserProvider (Priority , Policy?)>
<!ATTLIST ParserProvider
class CDATA #REQUIRED>
```

`class`—The provider class that implements `org.eclipse.gmf.runtime.common.core.services.parser.IParserProvider`.

```
<!ELEMENT Priority EMPTY>
<!ATTLIST Priority
name (Lowest|Low|Medium|High|Highest) >
```

name—The name of the provider priority—Lowest, Low, Medium, High, or Highest.

```
<!ELEMENT Policy EMPTY>
<!ATTLIST Policy
class CDATA #REQUIRED>
```

class—The provider policy class.

Examples:

Following is an example of a parser provider extension, as contributed by the GMF tooling generator. Note that a number of default parsers are also implemented using the generator, as specified in the mapping model:

```
<extension

point="org.eclipse.gmf.runtime.common.ui.services.parserProviders">
    <ParserProvider

class="org.eclipse.mindmap.diagram.providers.MindmapParserProvider">
    <Priority name="Lowest"/>
    </ParserProvider>
</extension>
```

API information:

The value of the class attribute must be the fully qualified name of a class that implements org.eclipse.gmf.runtime.common.core.services. parser.IParserProvider.

10.4.9 ModelingAssistantService

The GMF runtime provides a number of assistants to improve usability and extend the gestures used in modeling beyond what GEF provides. The ModelingAssistantService and corresponding ModelingAssistant Provider specify methods to be implemented to provide the content of pop-ups that appear on the diagram surface, as shown in Figure 10-33. An internal DiagramModelingAssistantProvider is provided to supply assistant functionality for diagram shapes in the form of pop-up bars and connection handles, as described in Section 10.1.1, "Connection Handles," and Section 10.1.1, "Pop-Up Bars."

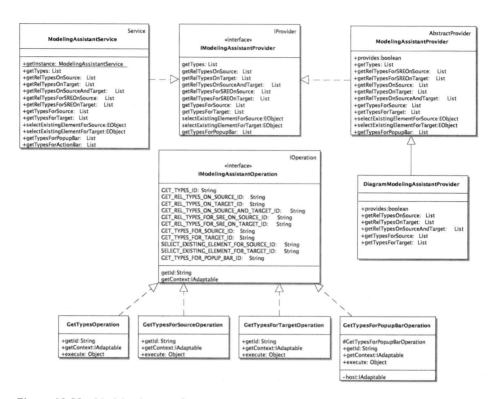

Figure 10-33   ModelingAssistantService

Modeling Assistant Provider Extension-Point

Identifier: `org.eclipse.gmf.runtime.emf.ui.`
`modelingAssistantProviders`

Description: This extension-point defines modeling assistant providers for
the `ModelingAssistantService`. The `ModelingAssistantService` allows
plug-ins to modify or contribute to the modeling assistant behavior (such as with
connector handles).

Configuration markup:

```
<!ELEMENT extension (modelingAssistantProvider+)>

<!ELEMENT modelingAssistantProvider (Priority , object* , context*)>
<!ATTLIST modelingAssistantProvider
class CDATA #REQUIRED>
```

class—The fully qualified name of the modeling assistant provider class that implements `org.eclipse.gmf.runtime.emf.ui.services.` `modelingassistant.IModelingAssistantProvider`.

```
<!ELEMENT Priority EMPTY>
<!ATTLIST Priority
name (Lowest|Low|Medium|High|Highest) >
```

name—The priority of the provider. It can be one of the following values: `Lowest`, `Low`, `Medium`, `High`, or `Highest`.

```
<!ELEMENT object (method*)>
<!ATTLIST object
id CDATA #REQUIRED
class CDATA #IMPLIED>
```

This element defines an object that this provider examines. The object descriptor can include an optional set of methods to call on the object.

id—A unique (within the context of this provider definition) identifier for the object.

class—The fully qualified name of a class/interface that is assignable from, or adaptable to, the object. The name could be followed (between parentheses) by the ID of a plug-in whose classloader can load that class. The final syntax is `className<(plugin id)>?`.

```
<!ELEMENT context EMPTY>
<!ATTLIST context
operationId CDATA #IMPLIED
elements CDATA #IMPLIED>
```

This element defines the context of a modeling assistant provider.

operationId—A String representation of the operation ID in this context (see `IModelingAssistantOperation`). If this field is omitted, the provider is considered for all operation types.

elements—A comma-separated list of object IDs (from the provider XML definition) that are valid element context(s) for the operation ID in this context description. If this field is omitted, the provider is considered for all element types.

Examples:

Following is an example of what the GMF tooling generates by default:

```
<extension-point=
  "org.eclipse.gmf.runtime.emf.ui.modelingAssistantProviders">
  <modelingAssistantProvider
    class="org.eclipse.mindmap.diagram.providers.
    MindmapModelingAssistantProvider">
    <Priority name="Lowest"/>
  </modelingAssistantProvider>
</extension>
```

The generated *ModelingAssistantProvider provides an example of how to implement a provider for your model types.

API information:

The declared class is one that implements `org.eclipse.gmf.runtime.emf.ui.services.modelingassistant.IModelingAssistantProvider`.

For convenience, the abstract class `org.eclipse.gmf.runtime.emf.ui.services.modelingassistant.ModelingAssistantProvider` is provided and supplies basic behavior.

10.4.10 LayoutService

The default toolbar and context menu provided for all GMF-generated diagrams (those that target the full runtime) have an arrange action. A basic layout algorithm is provided by default and can be overridden by using the LayoutService. Your domain-specific diagram likely will require a domain-specific layout to complement your notation and enhance its display of information.

The runtime supplies several layout providers for the LayoutService, as shown in Figure 10-34. Furthermore, the mindmap diagram example in Section 4.3.5, "Adding Custom Layout," gives an example of a layout provider contribution.

LayoutProvider Extension-Point

Identifier: `org.eclipse.gmf.runtime.diagram.ui.layoutProviders`

Description: This extension-point defines layout providers for the LayoutService. The LayoutService allows for the arrangement of diagram elements according to a specific layout style. Extensions to the service can provide additional layout behavior. For example, a new provider could implement a specialized inheritance layout.

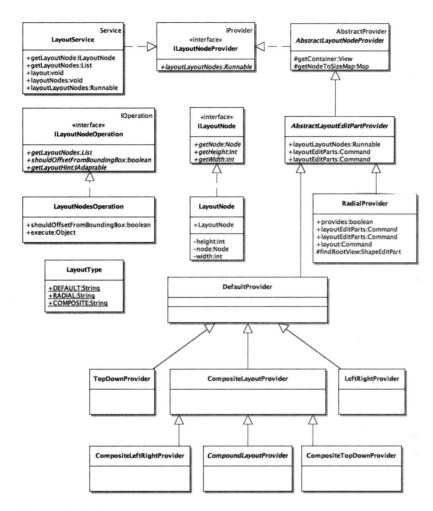

Figure 10-34   Layout service

Configuration markup:

```
<!ELEMENT extension (layoutProvider)>

<!ELEMENT layoutProvider (Priority)>
<!ATTLIST layoutProvider
class CDATA #REQUIRED>
```

class—The fully qualified name of the layout provider class. The specified provider class should implement the interface org.eclipse.gmf.runtime. diagram.ui.services.layout.ILayoutNodeProvider.

```
<!ELEMENT Priority EMPTY>
<!ATTLIST Priority
name (Lowest|Low|Medium|High|Highest) >
```

name—The priority of the provider. It can be one of the following values: Lowest, Low, Medium, High, or Highest. Dependencies must be considered when choosing the priority. The layout operation is executed on the first provider (in descending order of priority) that is found to provide the operation.

Examples:
The following is an example of a layout provider extension contribution:

```
<extension-point="org.eclipse.gmf.runtime.diagram.ui.layoutProviders">
    <layoutProvider class=
"org.eclipse.gmf.runtime.diagram.ui.providers.layout.RadialProvider">
        <Priority name="Lowest"/>
    </layoutProvider>
</extension>
```

API information:
For API information, see the interfaces defined in the package org.eclipse.gmf.runtime.diagram.ui.services.layout. Clients that provide an extension to the layout service need to create a provider class that implements the org.eclipse.gmf.runtime.diagram.ui.services. layout.ILayoutNodeProvider interface.

Notes:
Diagrams generated using the GMF tooling do not currently use this extension-point, which is understandable, given that currently no way exists to specify diagram layout in a diagram-definition model.

10.4.11 ContributionItemService

The ContributionItemService allows for the addition of items into an IWorkbenchPart contribution manager for action bars and pop-up menus, but with the added benefit of specified priority and execution strategy available in all runtime Services. The IContributionItemProvider interface specifies methods for these contributions, their update, and their disposal. The corresponding extension-point allows for these contributions to be made declaratively. An AbstractContributionItemProvider is provided, along with several concrete implementations, including the Diagram and Printing providers shown in Figure 10-35. These provide most of the generic contributions needed for most diagrams, including font properties, alignment actions, save, print, and so on.

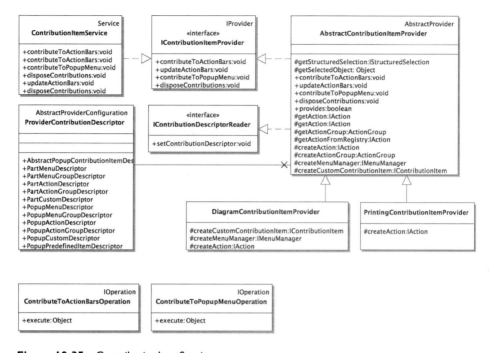

Figure 10-35 ContributionItemService

ContributionItemProvider Extension-Point

Identifier: `org.eclipse.gmf.runtime.common.ui.services.action.contributionItemProviders`

Description: This extension-point registers providers that contribute to different workbench parts' contribution managers. The contributions described in this extension-point can be for a workbench part's action bars (referred to as part contributions) or for a workbench part's pop-up menu (referred to as pop-up contributions). This extension-point provides an XML description of contributions to be read by the described providers. The extension-point provides an alternative to the following Eclipse extension-points:

`org.eclipse.ui.editorActions`

`org.eclipse.ui.viewActions`

`org.eclipse.ui.popupMenus` (viewerContribution)

However, this extension-point focuses on distinguishing the contribution criteria from the enablement and visibility of the described contributions. The description of each contribution has the following minimum information:

❍ Information to create the contribution (such as ID)

❍ Information to perform the contribution (such as path within manager)

❍ Information to consider the contribution (such as target ID, class)

Configuration markup:

```
<!ELEMENT extension (contributionItemProvider+)>

<!ELEMENT contributionItemProvider (Priority , (partContribution* ,
popupContribution*))>
<!ATTLIST contributionItemProvider
class CDATA #REQUIRED
checkPluginLoaded (true | false) "true">
```

This element is used to describe a contribution item provider that will contribute actions and toolbar items to a view's pop-up menus or action bars.

`class`—The name of a fully qualified class that extends the `org.eclipse.gmf.runtime.common.ui.services.action.contributionitem.AbstractContributionItemProvider` and `org.eclipse.gmf.runtime.common.core.service.IProvider` interfaces.

`checkPluginLoaded`—Indicates whether the service should consider contributions from this provider only if the declaring plug-in is already loaded (either `true` or `false`). The default value is `true`.

```
<!ELEMENT Priority EMPTY>
<!ATTLIST Priority
name (Lowest|Low|Medium|High|Highest) >
```

This element specifies the priority that this provider has relative to other `ContributionItemProviders` that are registered to provide the same kind of contribution to the same menu or toolbar. All providers have the opportunity to make their contributions. The provider with the lowest priority is chosen as the first contributor, while the provider with the highest priority is chosen as the last contributor. This means that a provider that wants to add contributions to menus or groups contributed by another provider must have the higher priority so that the menu or group has already been contributed by the time it is asked to make its own contributions.

`name`—The name of the provider priority—Lowest, Low, Medium, High, or Highest.

```
<!ELEMENT partContribution (partMenu* , partMenuGroup* , partAction* ,

partCustom* , partActionGroup*)>
<!ATTLIST partContribution
id CDATA #IMPLIED
class CDATA #IMPLIED>
```

This element adds a group of menus, groups, actions, and/or toolbar items to a workbench part. At least one of the attribute's ID or class must be specified for this element.

`id`—An optional unique identifier of a registered workbench part that is the target of this contribution.

`class`—An optional name of a fully qualified class or interface. Contributions are made to all workbench parts that subclass or implement this type.

```
<!ELEMENT popupContribution ((popupStructuredContributionCriteria |
popupTextContributionCriteria | popupMarkContributionCriteria)* ,

popupMenu* , popupMenuGroup* , popupAction* , popupCustom* ,

popupActionGroup* , popupPredefinedItem*)>
<!ATTLIST popupContribution
id CDATA #IMPLIED
class CDATA #IMPLIED>
```

This element adds a group of menus, groups, actions, and/or custom items to a context menu. At least one of the attribute's ID or class must be specified for this element.

Criteria for the visibility of this group of contributions can be specified by any number of the same kind of criteria elements, from among these:

> `popupStructuredContributionCriteria`
>
> `popupTextContributionCriteria`
>
> `popupMarkContributionCriteria`

`id`—An optional unique identifier of a registered context menu that is the target of this contribution. For a given part, there can be one or more context menus. This ID specifies the one the contributions are for.

`class`—An optional name of a fully qualified class or interface. Contributions are made to all context menus that subclass or implement this type.

```
<!ELEMENT partMenu EMPTY>
<!ATTLIST partMenu
id CDATA #REQUIRED
```

```
menubarPath CDATA #IMPLIED
toolbarPath CDATA #IMPLIED>
```

This element adds menu to a workbench part's action bars.

`id`—An optional identifier used to reference this menu contribution. It must be unique within the contribution item provider.

`menubarPath`—The contribution path of this menu within the part's menu bar. The path is a /-delimited String in the following format:

```
/<submenu_id/>*<group_id|contribution_id>
```

The path must start with a `/`, indicating the root of the contribution manager. Following that could be a `submenu_id` path that is also /-delimited. The final token in the path is either a `group_id` or a `contribution_id`. If the last token is a group, the contribution is appended to the end of the group. Otherwise, the contribution is inserted after the given `contribution_id`. If the field is omitted, the contribution does not take place with the menu bar.

`toolbarPath`—The contribution path of this menu within the part's toolbar. The path is a /-delimited String in the following format:

```
/<submenu_id/>*<group_id|contribution_id>
```

The path must start with a `/` indicating the root of the contribution manager. Following that could be a `submenu_id` path that is also /-delimited. The final token in the path is either a `group_id` or a `contribution_id`.

If the last token is a group, the contribution is appended to the end of the group. Otherwise, the contribution is inserted after the given `contribution_id`. If the field is omitted, the contribution does not take place with the toolbar.

```
<!ELEMENT partMenuGroup EMPTY>
<!ATTLIST partMenuGroup
id CDATA #REQUIRED
menubarPath CDATA #IMPLIED
toolbarPath CDATA #IMPLIED
separator (true | false) "true">
```

This element specifies a menu group to be contributed to a workbench part's action bars. Attributes are the same as described earlier.

```
<!ELEMENT partAction EMPTY>
<!ATTLIST partAction
id CDATA #REQUIRED
```

```
menubarPath CDATA #IMPLIED
toolbarPath CDATA #IMPLIED
global (true | false) "false">
```

This element specifies an action to be contributed to a workbench part's action bars. Attributes are the same as described earlier.

```
<!ELEMENT partCustom EMPTY>
<!ATTLIST partCustom
id CDATA #REQUIRED
menubarPath CDATA #IMPLIED
toolbarPath CDATA #IMPLIED>
```

This element specifies a custom contribution to a workbench part's action bars. Attributes are the same as described earlier.

```
<!ELEMENT popupMenu EMPTY>
<!ATTLIST popupMenu
id CDATA #REQUIRED
path CDATA "/additionsGroup">
```

This element specifies a menu to be contributed to a workbench part's pop-up menu.

id—The ID of the pop-up menu manager contribution. The ID is unique within a provider.

path—The contribution path of this menu within the pop-up. The path is a /-delimited String in the following format:

/<submenu_id/>*<group_id|contribution_id>

The path must start with a /, indicating the root of the contribution manager. Following that could be submenu_id path that is also /-delimited. The final token in the path is either a group_id or a contribution_id.

If the last token is a group, the contribution is appended to the end of the group. Otherwise, the contribution is inserted after the given contribution_id. If the field is omitted, the contribution does not take place with the pop-up menu.

```
<!ELEMENT popupMenuGroup EMPTY>
<!ATTLIST popupMenuGroup
id CDATA #REQUIRED
path CDATA "/"
separator (true | false) "true">
```

This element specifies a menu group to be contributed to a workbench part's pop-up menu.

`id`—The ID of the pop-up menu group contribution. The ID is unique within a provider.

`path`—The contribution path of this menu group within the pop-up menu. The path is a `/`-delimited String in the following format:

```
/<submenu_id/>*
```

The path must start with a `/`, indicating the root of the contribution manager. Following that could be a `submenu_id` path that is also `/`-delimited. There should be a `/` at the end of the path. The menu group is inserted at the end of the last submenu in the path. If the field is omitted, the contribution does not take place with the pop-up menu.

`separator`—A flag indicating whether the menu group is a separator (`true`—default) or a group marker (`false`).

```
<!ELEMENT popupAction EMPTY>
<!ATTLIST popupAction
id CDATA #REQUIRED
path CDATA "/additionsGroup">
```

This element specifies an action to be contributed to a workbench part's pop-up menu.

`id`—The ID of the pop-up action contribution. The ID is unique within a provider.

`path`—The contribution path of this action within the pop-up. The path is a `/`-delimited String in the following format:

```
/<submenu_id/>*<group_id|contribution_id>
```

The path must start with a `/`, indicating the root of the contribution manager. Following that could be a `submenu_id` path that is also `/`-delimited. The final token in the path is either a `group_id` or a `contribution_id`.

If the last token is a group, the contribution is appended to the end of the group. Otherwise, the contribution is inserted after the given `contribution_id`. If the field is omitted, the contribution does not take place with the pop-up menu.

```
<!ELEMENT popupCustom EMPTY>
<!ATTLIST popupCustom
id CDATA #REQUIRED
path CDATA "/additionsGroup">
```

This element specifies a custom contribution to a workbench part's pop-up menu.

id—The ID of the pop-up custom contribution. The ID is unique within a provider.

path—The contribution path of this custom contribution within the pop-up. The path is a /-delimited String in the following format:

```
/<submenu_id/>*<group_id|contribution_id>
```

The path must start with a /, indicating the root of the contribution manager. Following that could be submenu_id path that is also /-delimited. The final token in the path is either a group_id or a contribution_id.

If the last token is a group, the contribution is appended to the end of the group. Otherwise, the contribution is inserted after the given contribution_id. If the field is omitted, the contribution does not take place with the pop-up menu.

```
<!ELEMENT popupStructuredContributionCriteria (method* ,
staticMethod*)>
<!ATTLIST popupStructuredContributionCriteria
objectCount CDATA #IMPLIED
objectClass CDATA #IMPLIED
policyClass CDATA #IMPLIED>
```

This element defines a structured selection contribution criteria for a workbench part's pop-up menu. The criteria can have an optional set of methods to call on the "selected objects."

objectCount—The number of objects in the selection that this contribution applies to.

objectClass—The fully qualified name of a class/interface that is assignable or adaptable from the classes of objects in the selection. The name could be followed (between parentheses) by the ID of a plug-in whose classloader can load that class. This is the final syntax:

```
className <(plugin id)> ?
```

policyClass—The fully qualified name of a contribution policy class (that usually resides in a different plug-in/fragment that is assumed to be loaded), to determine whether this contribution should be considered. The class must implement the IPopupMenuContributionPolicy interface.

```
<!ELEMENT popupTextContributionCriteria EMPTY>
<!ATTLIST popupTextContributionCriteria
text CDATA #IMPLIED
policyClass CDATA #IMPLIED>
```

This element defines the text selection contribution criteria for a workbench part's pop-up menu.

text—The text in the selection. This is an optional field.

policyClass—The fully qualified name of a contribution policy class (that usually resides in a different plug-in/fragment that is assumed to be loaded), to determine whether this contribution should be considered. The class must implement the IPopupMenuContributionPolicy interface.

```
<!ELEMENT popupMarkContributionCriteria (method*)>
<!ATTLIST popupMarkContributionCriteria
documentClass CDATA #IMPLIED
policyClass CDATA #IMPLIED>
```

This element defines a mark selection contribution criteria for a workbench part's pop-up menu.

documentClass—The fully qualified name of a class/interface that is assignable or adaptable from the document of the mark selection. The name could be followed (between parentheses) by the ID of a plug-in whose classloader can load that class. This is the final syntax:

```
className <(plugin id)> ?
```

policyClass—The fully qualified name of a contribution policy class (that usually resides in a different plug-in/fragment that is assumed to be loaded), to determine whether this contributon should be considered. The class must implement the IPopupMenuContributionPolicy interface.

```
<!ELEMENT popupActionGroup EMPTY>
<!ATTLIST popupActionGroup
id CDATA #REQUIRED
path CDATA #IMPLIED>
```

This element defines an action group to be contributed to a workbench part's pop-up menu.

id—The ID of the pop-up action group contribution. The ID is unique within a provider.

path—The contribution path of this action group within the pop-up. The path is a /-delimited String in the following format:

```
/<submenu_id/>*<group_id|contribution_id>
```

The path must start with a /, indicating the root of the contribution manager. Following that could be a submenu_id path that is also /-delimited.

```
<!ELEMENT partActionGroup EMPTY>
<!ATTLIST partActionGroup
id CDATA #REQUIRED>
```

This element defines an action group contribution to a workbench part's action bars.

id—The ID of the part action group contribution. The ID is unique within a provider.

```
<!ELEMENT popupPredefinedItem EMPTY>
<!ATTLIST popupPredefinedItem
id CDATA #REQUIRED
path CDATA #IMPLIED
remove (true | false)>
```

This element defines a reference to a previously defined contribution to a workbench part's pop-up menu. The referenced contributed must be defined in a lower-priority provider.

id—The ID of the previously defined pop-up action contribution. The ID combined with the path is unique within the pop-up menu.

path—The contribution path of this previously defined item within the pop-up. The path is a /-delimited String in the following format:

```
/<submenu_id/>*
```

The path must start with a /, indicating the root of the contribution manager. Following that could be multiple submenu_id paths that are also /-delimited.

remove—If true, an existing contribution item is removed.

Examples:

The following is an example of a contribution item provider extension from the Logic Diagram where group and ungroup functionality is added. Note also that diagrams generated using GMF's tooling contribute to this extension-point for all delete actions.

```
<extension id="LogicExampleGroupContributionItemProvider"
    name="LogicExampleGroupContributionItemProvider"
    point="org.eclipse.gmf.runtime.common.ui.services.action.
```

```
                contributionItemProviders">
   <contributionItemProvider
     class="org.eclipse.gmf.runtime.diagram.ui.providers.
     DiagramContributionItemProvider">
      <Priority name="Low"/>
      <popupContribution
        class="org.eclipse.gmf.runtime.diagram.ui.providers.
          DiagramContextMenuProvider">
        <popupStructuredContributionCriteria
           objectClass="org.eclipse.gmf.runtime.diagram.ui.
           editparts.IPrimaryEditPart"
           objectCount="2+">
         <method
          name="getDiagramEditDomain().getEditorPart()
               .getEditorSite().getId()"
          value="LogicEditor"/>
        </popupStructuredContributionCriteria>
        <popupAction path="/formatMenu/miscellaneousGroup"
                     id="groupAction"/>
      </popupContribution>
      <popupContribution
         class="org.eclipse.gmf.runtime.diagram.ui.providers.
         DiagramContextMenuProvider">
        <popupStructuredContributionCriteria
           objectClass="org.eclipse.gmf.runtime.diagram.ui.
           editparts.GroupEditPart">
         <method
          name="getDiagramEditDomain().getEditorPart()
          .getEditorSite().getId()"
          value="LogicEditor"/>
        </popupStructuredContributionCriteria>
        <popupAction path="/formatMenu/miscellaneousGroup"
                     id="ungroupAction"/>
      </popupContribution>
    </contributionItemProvider>
  </extension>
```

API information:

The value of the contribution item provider class attribute must be a fully qualified name of a Java class that implements org.eclipse.gmf.runtime.common.ui.services.action.contributionitem.IContributionItemProvider.

For convenience, this can be a subclass of org.eclipse.gmf.runtime.common.ui.services.action.contributiontem.AbstractContributionItemProvider.

The order of contribution is given as follows, implying that a contribution path must fully exist before being used as a path of contribution:

The priority of the provider (lowest first)

The order of the definition within the XML file

10.4.12 GlobalActionHandlerService

The GlobalActionHandlerService provides a way to handle commonly used actions by providing an IGlobalActionHandler for an associated IGlobal ActionHandlerContext. A number of providers are available in the runtime, each extending the AbstractGlobalActionHandlerProvider class. The DiagramGlobalActionHandlerProvider uses the DiagramGlobalAction Handler to provide most of the common diagram behavior, such as cut, copy, paste, delete, print, and save. Most diagrams contribute this provider, in addition to DiagramIDEGlobalActionHandlerProvider and DiagramUIRender GlobalActionHandlerProvider. The main elements of the service are seen in Figure 10-36.

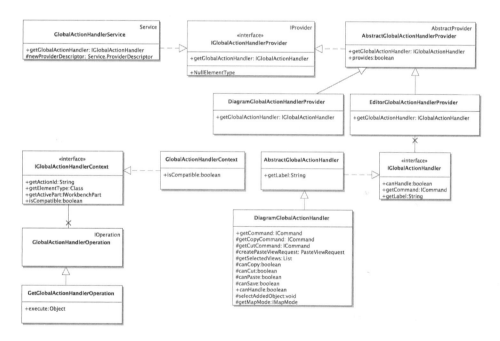

Figure 10-36 GlobalActionHandlerService

GlobalActionHandlerProvider Extension-Point

Identifier: org.eclipse.gmf.runtime.common.ui.services.action. globalActionHandlerProviders

Description: This extension-point configures providers for the `Global ActionHandlerService` (`org.eclipse.gmf.runtime.common.ui.serv-ices.action.global.GlobalActionHandlerService`).

This service provides an extensible way to handle commonly used (global) actions in different views and editors. These global actions might appear in a view part context menu or might be predefined retargetable actions. The service allows different handlers to be used, depending on the nature of the element(s) selected in the workbench part. Each `GlobalActionHandlerProvider` regis-ters itself for actions against a specific element type within a view part.

Configuration markup:

```
<!ELEMENT extension (GlobalActionHandlerProvider)+>

<!ELEMENT GlobalActionHandlerProvider (Priority , Policy? , ViewId+)>
<!ATTLIST GlobalActionHandlerProvider
id CDATA #REQUIRED
class CDATA #REQUIRED>
```

This element describes a `GlobalActionHandlerProvider` that will con-tribute handlers to a given view or views for one or more retargetable actions.

`id`—A unique identifier used to reference this provider.

`class`—The name of a fully qualified class that implements the `org.eclipse.gmf.runtime.common.ui.services.action.global.IGlobal ActionHandlerProvider` and `org.eclipse.gmf.runtime.common.core. service.IProvider` interfaces.

```
<!ELEMENT Priority EMPTY>
<!ATTLIST Priority
name (Lowest|Low|Medium|High|Highest) >
```

This element specifies the priority that this provider has relative to other `GlobalActionHandlerProviders` that are registered to handle the same global action for the kind of element in the same view. When such a conflict occurs, the provider with the highest priority is selected to provide the `Global ActionHandler`.

`name`—The name of the provider priority—`Lowest`, `Low`, `Medium`, `High`, or `Highest`.

```
<!ELEMENT ViewId (ElementType+)>
<!ATTLIST ViewId
id CDATA #REQUIRED>
```

This element specifies a group of global actions that this provider handles for the specified view and element types.

id—A unique identifier of a registered view.

```
<!ELEMENT ElementType (GlobalActionId+)>
<!ATTLIST ElementType
class CDATA #IMPLIED>
```

This element defines the set of global actions that this provider handles when objects of the specified type are selected.

class—A fully qualified name of the class or interface that at least one object in the selection must subclass or implement for this provider to be asked to handle the action(s).

```
<!ELEMENT GlobalActionId EMPTY>
<!ATTLIST GlobalActionId
actionId CDATA #REQUIRED>
```

This element describes a global action that this provider will handle.

actionId—The name of a global action that this provider handles. Global action names are specified in org.eclipse.gmf.runtime.common.ui. action.global.GlobalActionId.

```
<!ELEMENT Policy EMPTY>
<!ATTLIST Policy
class CDATA #REQUIRED>
```

This element optionally specifies a policy to use to further determine whether this provider should be considered to provide a handler for a global action, given that the view, element type, and action ID all match the specified criteria. To delay plug-in loading, the recommended strategy for policies is to define them in a separate package and add Bundle-ActivationPolicy: lazy in the MANIFEST.MF so that loading the policy class does not load the plug-in.

class—The fully qualified name of the class that implements org.eclipse.gmf.runtime.common.core.service.IProviderPolicy.

Examples:

The following is an example of the GlobalActionHandlerProvider extension contributions that are added by default to generated diagrams to handle common actions (such as save, cut, copy, paste, and bookmark):

```xml
<extension-point="org.eclipse.gmf.runtime.common.ui.services.action.
  globalActionHandlerProviders">
  <GlobalActionHandlerProvider
    class="org.eclipse.gmf.runtime.diagram.ui.providers.
      DiagramGlobalActionHandlerProvider"
    id="requirementsPresentation">
    <Priority name="Lowest"/>
    <ViewId id="org.eclipse.requirements.diagram.part.
      RequirementsDiagramEditorID">
      <ElementType
        class="org.eclipse.gmf.runtime.diagram.ui.editparts.
        IGraphicalEditPart">
        <GlobalActionId actionId="delete"/>
      </ElementType>
      <ElementType
        class="org.eclipse.gmf.runtime.diagram.ui.editparts.
         DiagramEditPart">
         <GlobalActionId actionId="save"/>
      </ElementType>
    </ViewId>
  </GlobalActionHandlerProvider>

  <GlobalActionHandlerProvider
    class="org.eclipse.gmf.runtime.diagram.ui.providers.
    ide.providers.DiagramIDEGlobalActionHandlerProvider"
    id="requirementsPresentationIDE">
    <Priority name="Lowest"/>
    <ViewId id="org.eclipse.requirements.diagram.part.
       RequirementsDiagramEditorID">
      <ElementType
        class="org.eclipse.gmf.runtime.diagram.ui.editparts.
        IGraphicalEditPart">
        <GlobalActionId actionId="bookmark"/>
      </ElementType>
    </ViewId>
  </GlobalActionHandlerProvider>

  <GlobalActionHandlerProvider
    class="org.eclipse.gmf.runtime.diagram.ui.render.
    providers.DiagramUIRenderGlobalActionHandlerProvider"
    id="requirementsRender">
    <Priority name="Lowest"/>
    <ViewId id="org.eclipse.requirements.diagram.part.
      RequirementsDiagramEditorID">
      <ElementType
        class="org.eclipse.gmf.runtime.diagram.ui.editparts.
        IGraphicalEditPart">
        <GlobalActionId actionId="cut"/>
        <GlobalActionId actionId="copy"/>
        <GlobalActionId actionId="paste"/>
      </ElementType>
    </ViewId>
  </GlobalActionHandlerProvider>
</extension>
```

API information:

The value of the `GlobalActionHandlerProvider` class attribute must be a fully qualified name of a Java class that implements both the `org.eclipse.gmf.runtime.common.ui.services.action.global.IGlobalActionHandlerProvider` and `org.eclipse.gmf.runtime.common.core.service.IProvider` interfaces. For convenience, this can be a subclass of `org.eclipse.gmf.runtime.common.ui.services.action.global.AbstractGlobalActionHandlerProvider`. As shown in the example, additional subclasses of `AbstractGloabalActionHandlerProvider` exist, such as `DiagramUIRenderGlobalActionHandlerProvider` (handles cut, copy, and paste) and `DiagramIDEGlobalActionHandlerProvider` (handles bookmarks).

10.4.13 ActionFilterService

The `ActionFilterService` provides a service-provider capability to the platform's `IActionFilter` functionality. Action filtering allows for a more fine-grained approach to controlling the contribution of actions to an item in the workbench. The runtime's `ActionFilterService` and corresponding `IActionFilterProvider` allow for priority and execution strategy enhancement of action filtering. The `DiagramActionFilterProvider` is an internal provider and extends `AbstractModelActionFilterProvider` as seen in Figure 10-37.

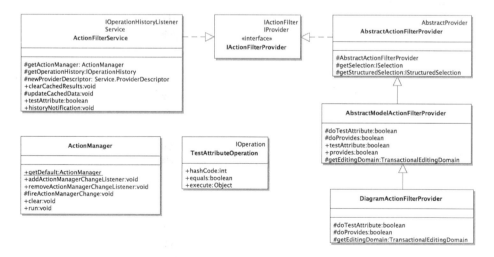

Figure 10-37 ActionFilterService

ActionFilterProvider Extension-Point

Identifier: `org.eclipse.gmf.runtime.common.ui.services.action.actionFilterProviders`

Description: This extension-point configures providers for the `Action FilterService` (`org.eclipse.gmf.runtime.common.ui.services.action.filter.ActionFilterService`).

This service allows ActionFilterProvider attributes to be added to existing types, as long as they adapt to `IActionFilterProvider` by returning the `ActionFilterService`. These ActionFilterProvider attributes can then be used inside the objectState element for enablement or visibility of static action contributions (see `org.eclipse.ui.popupMenus` extension-point). It also permits the entire workbench selection to be considered so that an action can be enabled if it is supported on one or more elements in the selection.

The ActionFilterService selects a provider using one of the following criteria:

○ **By provider descriptor**—This uses static XML to determine whether a provider provides the attribute test operation. A given provider can declare, in XML, that it supports zero or more name/value pairs (attribute elements); if the name/value of a given action expression matches any of these, it is assumed to provide the operation.

○ **By provider policy**—If no name/value pairs are specified in XML for a given provider, the service tries to load a policy for the provider (using the standard mechanism), if one is specified, and asks the policy whether it provides the operation.

○ **By the provider itself**—If no name/value pairs and no policy have been specified, the service loads the provider itself and asks whether it provides the operation. Typically, it is preferred to use one of the first two criteria for providers.

Note that the value attribute is optional. When available in the provider's XML, the value is used in conjunction with the name attribute to determine whether that provider should be considered. When not available, only the name is used to make the decision. For example, the value attribute for objectState elements of action expressions is sometimes set to either `enablement` or `visibility`. Some ActionFilterProviders use this information to determine whether the criteria are being tested to determine enablement or visibility for a contribution.

Configuration markup:

```
<!ELEMENT extension (ActionFilterProvider)>

<!ELEMENT ActionFilterProvider (Priority , Attribute* , Policy?)>
<!ATTLIST ActionFilterProvider
class CDATA #REQUIRED>
```

This element describes an ActionFilterProvider that contributes ActionFilter attributes to be used inside `objectState` elements for enablement or visibility of static action contributions.

class—The name of a fully qualified class that implements the `org.eclipse.gmf.runtime.common.ui.services.action.filter.IActionFilterProvider` and `org.eclipse.gmf.runtime.common.core.service.IProvider` interfaces.

```
<!ELEMENT Priority EMPTY>
<!ATTLIST Priority
name (Lowest|Low|Medium|High|Highest) >
```

This element specifies the priority that this provider has relative to other ActionFilterProviders that are registered to handle the same ActionFilter attribute. When such a conflict occurs, the provider with the highest priority is selected to provide the ActionFilter.

name—The name of the provider priority—`Lowest`, `Low`, `Medium`, `High`, or `Highest`.

```
<!ELEMENT Attribute EMPTY>
<!ATTLIST Attribute
name CDATA #REQUIRED
value CDATA #IMPLIED>
```

This element describes a new ActionFilter attribute.

name—The name of the ActionFilter attribute, which is used to identify the provider that should perform the test for `objectState` elements used in action enablement or visibility criteria.

value—The optional value of the ActionFilter attribute. When provided, it is also used to identify the provider that should perform the test for `objectState` elements use in action enablement or visibility criteria.

```
<!ELEMENT Policy EMPTY>
<!ATTLIST Policy
class CDATA #IMPLIED>
```

This element can specify a policy to determine whether this provider should be asked to test an ActionFilter attribute. The policy is used only if no attribute elements are defined for the provider. To delay plug-in loading, the recommended strategy for policies is to define them in a separate package and add `Bundle-ActivationPolicy: lazy` in the `MANIFEST.MF` so that loading the policy class does not load the plug-in.

`class`—The fully qualified name of the class that implements `org.eclipse.gmf.runtime.common.core.service.IProviderPolicy`.

Examples:
The following is an example of an ActionFilterProvider extension:

```
<extension-point="
org.eclipse.gmf.runtime.common.ui.services.action.
➥actionFilterProviders">
   <ActionFilterProvider class="
org.eclipse.test.project.ui.providers.action.
AllAreElementsActionFilterProvider">
      <Priority name="Highest"/>
      <Attribute name="AllAreElements" value="enablement"/>
      <Attribute name="AllAreElements" value="visibility"/>
   </ActionFilterProvider>
</extension>
```

API information:
For convenience, the provider can be a subclass of `org.eclipse.gmf.runtime.common.ui.services.action.filter.AbstractActionFilterProvider`. Additionally, `org.eclipse.gmf.runtime.emf.ui.services.action.AbstractModelActionFilterProvider` is available and wraps queries on this provider in the context of a read action using a `TransactionalEditingDomain`.

Notes:
Diagrams generated using the GMF tooling do not currently use this extension-point.

A `LogicActionFilterProvider` is used in the logic diagram example, although it seems to be a temporary workaround for a platform bug. Nevertheless, it illustrates how to filter the Add Circuit and Add Half Adder pop-up menu contributions from elements that are not `ContainerElement` types.

10.4.14 EditorService

The `EditorService` provides a means by which to open editors using the priority and execution strategy facilities of the Service layer. It's a simple API, as seen in Figure 10-38, that has no implementation example in the runtime or generated diagram code.

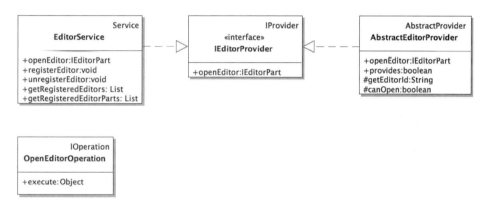

Figure 10-38   EditorService

EditorProvider Extension-Point

Identifier: `org.eclipse.gmf.runtime.common.ui.services.editorProviders`

Description: This extension-point facilitates the configuration of providers for the EditorService (`org.eclipse.gmf.runtime.common.ui.services.editor.EditorService`). Using this extension-point, providers are registered to manipulate editors, such as handling how to open an editor on a given input.

Configuration markup:

```
<!ELEMENT extension (EditorProvider)>

<!ELEMENT EditorProvider (Priority , Policy?)>
<!ATTLIST EditorProvider
class CDATA #REQUIRED>
```

class—Fully qualified String containing the provider class.

```
<!ELEMENT Priority EMPTY>
<!ATTLIST Priority
name (Lowest|Low|Medium|High|Highest) >
```

name—The provider priority as a String—Lowest, Low, Medium, High, or Highest.

```
<!ELEMENT Policy EMPTY>
<!ATTLIST Policy
class CDATA #REQUIRED>
```

class—Fully qualified String containing the provider class.

Examples:
Following is an example of an EditorProvider extension:

```
<extension
    point="org.eclipse.gmf.runtime.common.ui.services.editorProviders">
    <EditorProvider
        class="org.eclipse.test.project.providers.
➥MyDiagramEditorProvider">
        <Priority name="Lowest"/>
    </EditorProvider>
</extension>
```

API information:
The value of the class attribute must represent a subclass of org.eclipse.gmf.runtime.common.core.service.AbstractProvider that implements org.eclipse.gmf.runtime.common.ui.services.editor.IEditorProvider.

For convenience, org.eclipse.gmf.runtime.common.ui.services.editor.AbstractEditorProvider is provided.

Notes:
Diagrams generated using the GMF tooling do not currently use this extension-point.

10.4.15 ElementSelectionService

The ElementSelectionService and corresponding IElementSelectionProvider interface collect a set of elements matching some criteria. Although it is not shown in Figure 10-39, the `AbstractElementSelectionProvider` uses an `ElementSelectionServiceJob` class to run asynchronously in a separate job, sending matching objects to a listener. The runtime does not supply a concrete implementation of the provider, nor does the generated code contribute to its extension-point, described next.

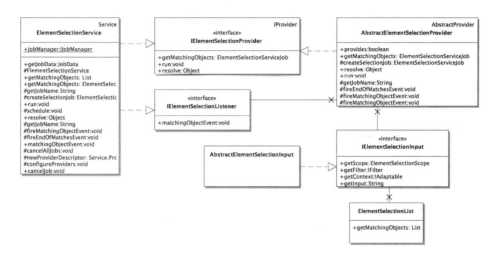

Figure 10-39 ElementSelectionService

ElementSelectionProvider Extension-Point

Identifier: `org.eclipse.gmf.runtime.common.ui.services.elementSelection`

Description: This extension-point facilitates the configuration of providers for the `ElementSelectionService` (`org.eclipse.gmf.runtime.common.ui.services.elementselection.ElementSelectionService`). Using this extension-point, providers are registered to provide a list of elements for the element selection composite and element selection dialog.

Configuration markup:

```
<!ELEMENT extension (ElementSelectionProvider)>

<!ELEMENT ElementSelectionProvider (Priority , Policy?)>
<!ATTLIST ElementSelectionProvider
class CDATA #REQUIRED>
```

`class`—Fully qualified String containing the provider class.

```
<!ELEMENT Priority EMPTY>
<!ATTLIST Priority
name (Lowest|Low|Medium|High|Highest) >
```

`name`—The provider priority as a String—`Lowest`, `Low`, `Medium`, `High`, or `Highest`.

```
<!ELEMENT Policy EMPTY>
<!ATTLIST Policy
class CDATA #REQUIRED>
```

`class`—The provider policy class. Provider policies can optionally be associated with providers to determine whether the providers provide a given operation.

Examples:

Following is an example of an element selection provider extension:

```
<extension
    point="org.eclipse.gmf.runtime.common.ui.services.
    elementSelectionProviders">
    <elementSelectionProvider
      class="org.eclipse.uml.ui.internal.providers.selection.
      UMLElementSelectionProvider">
      <Priority name="Highest"/>
    </elementSelectionProvider>
</extension>
```

API information:

The value of the class attribute must represent a subclass of `org.eclipse.gmf.runtime.common.core.service.AbstractProvider` that implements `org.eclipse.gmf.runtime.common.ui.services.elementselection.AbstractElementSelectionProvider`.

Notes:

Diagrams generated using the GMF tooling do not currently use this extension-point.

10.4.16 PropertiesService

The `PropertiesService` and corresponding `IPropertiesProvider` interface collect all property contributions from property source providers and assemble them into a property source object. Specifically, each provider contributes an ICompositePropertySource object for a given target. The runtime provides implementations of IPropertiesProvider in GenericEMF PropertiesProvider and DiagramPropertiesProvider, as shown in Figure 10-40.

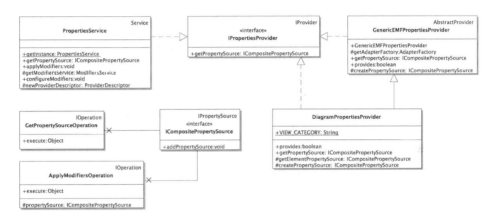

Figure 10-40   PropertiesService

PropertiesProvider Extension-Point

Identifier: org.eclipse.gmf.runtime.common.ui.services.properties.propertiesProviders

Description: This extension-point facilitates the configuration of providers for the PropertiesService (org.eclipse.gmf.runtime.common.ui.services.properties.PropertiesService). Using this extension-point, providers are registered to contribute properties to the Eclipse property sheet view part, given a workbench selection.

Configuration markup:

```
<!ELEMENT extension (PropertiesProvider)>

<!ELEMENT PropertiesProvider (Priority)>
<!ATTLIST PropertiesProvider
class CDATA #REQUIRED
verifyPluginLoaded (true | false) >
```

A PropertiesProvider element describes a client-defined PropertiesProvider object.

class—The class attribute must contain a fully qualified name of the PropertiesProvider class. The PropertiesProvider must implement the org.eclipse.gmf.runtime.common.ui.services.properties.IPrope rtyProvider interface.

verifyPluginLoaded—The verifyPluginLoaded attribute is used while testing the applicability of the given provider. If set to true, the service verifies that the provider's plug-in is loaded, before running the IProp ertyProvider.provides() test. If the declaring plug-in is not loaded, IPropertyProvider.provides() is not called and the provider then is considered not applicable. If the declaring plug-in is loaded, the service runs IPropertyProvider.provides() to determine whether the provider is applicable. When the verifyPluginLoaded attribute is set to false, verification is not performed and IPropertyProvider.provides() is called regardless of the plug-in being loaded.

```
<!ELEMENT Priority EMPTY>
<!ATTLIST Priority
name (Lowest|Low|Medium|High|Highest) >
```

The Priority element specifies the priority of the provider from Highest to Lowest. The providers are allowed to contribute to the property source in order of their priorities, from Highest to Lowest. This ensures the desired order of contribution and helps to exclude duplicate properties that were already contributed by others. For example, a provider with Lowest priority, when executed, can check whether there are any properties already contributed by any other providers. If none have been contributed, the provider might want to contribute; if some have been contributed, the provide might want to withdraw from contribution.

name—Enumeration with the following five values: Highest, High, Medium, Low, and Lowest.

Examples:
The following is an example of a provider extension:

```
<extension
 point="org.eclipse.gmf.runtime.common.ui.services.properties.
propertiesProviders">
    <PropertiesProvider
        verifyPluginLoaded="false"
        class="com.examples.MyPropertiesProvider">
        <Priority name="Medium"/>
    </PropertiesProvider>
</extension>
```

API information:

The value of the class attribute must represent a subclass of `org.eclipse.gmf.runtime.common.core.service.AbstractProvider` that implements `org.eclipse.gmf.runtime.common.ui.services.properties.IPropertiesProvider`.

Notes:

Diagrams generated using the GMF tooling do not currently use this extension-point.

10.4.17 PropertiesModifierService

The `PropertiesModifierService` provides the modification of properties contributed by the `PropertiesService`. The runtime provides a concrete implementation of the modifier service with `ReadOnlyDiagramProperties Modifier`, as seen in Figure 10-41. Install this provider on diagrams that do not allow for the editing of properties.

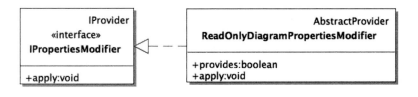

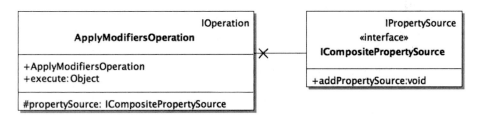

Figure 10-41 PropertiesModifierService

PropertiesModifier Extension-Point

Identifier: `org.eclipse.gmf.runtime.common.ui.services.properties.propertyModifiers`

Description: This extension-point facilitates the configuration of modifiers for the `PropertiesService` (`org.eclipse.gmf.runtime.common.ui.services.properties.PropertiesService`).

Using this extension-point, modifiers are registered to specific property providers, which contribute properties to the Eclipse property sheet view part. The role of a modifier is to write-protect and/or set flags for properties provided by the provider for which this modifier is contributed. The Provider element indicates the associated provider(s). One or more associated providers can exist. If the modifier is to be attached to all property providers, its Provider's element class should be set to *.

You can specify a policy to delay loading the modifier until it is applicable.

Configuration markup:

```
<!ELEMENT extension (PropertyModifier)>

<!ELEMENT PropertyModifier (Priority , Policy? , Provider+)>
<!ATTLIST PropertyModifier
class CDATA #REQUIRED>
```

class—Fully qualified String containing the provider class that implements `org.eclipse.gmf.runtime.common.ui.services.properties.IPropertiesModifier`.

```
<!ELEMENT Priority EMPTY>
<!ATTLIST Priority
name (Lowest|Low|Medium|High|Highest) >
```

name—This element specifies the priority that this provider has relative to other property modifier providers. All providers have the opportunity to make their contributions. The provider with the lowest priority is chosen as the first contributor, and the provider with the highest priority is chosen as the last contributor.

```
<!ELEMENT Policy EMPTY>
<!ATTLIST Policy
class CDATA #REQUIRED>
```

class—Fully qualified String containing the policy class.

```
<!ELEMENT Provider EMPTY>
<!ATTLIST Provider
class CDATA #REQUIRED>
```

`class`—Fully qualified String containing the provider class.

Examples:

The following is an example `PropertiesModifier` extension:

```
<extension
point="org.eclipse.gmf.runtime.common.ui.services.properties.
propertyModifiers">
<PropertyModifier class="org.eclipse.test.project.ui.
properties.providers.
ReadOnlyDiagramPropertiesModifier">
<Priority name="Highest"/>
<Provider class="*"/>
</PropertyModifier>
</extension>
```

API information:

The value of the class attribute must represent a class that implements `org.eclipse.gmf.runtime.common.ui.services.properties.IProp-ertiesModifier`.

Notes:

Diagrams generated using the GMF tooling do not currently use this extension-point.

10.4.18 DragDropListenerService

The `DragDropListenerService` works with the `IDragDropListener Provider` to provide `IDragSourceListener` and `IDropTargetListener` functionality for a specified context. The runtime supplies an `AbstractDrag DropListenerProvider`, leaving the methods `getDragSourceListener()` and `getDropTargetListener()` for implementation, as seen in Figure 10-42. By default, the `provides()` method is handled by the `ProviderDescriptor` inner class of `DragDropListenerService`, which extends `Service. ProviderDescriptor`. The configuration is loaded from the extension-point contribution for the provider, as discussed next.

DragDropListenerProvider Extension-Point

Identifier: `org.eclipse.gmf.runtime.common.ui.services.dnd. dragDropListenerProviders`

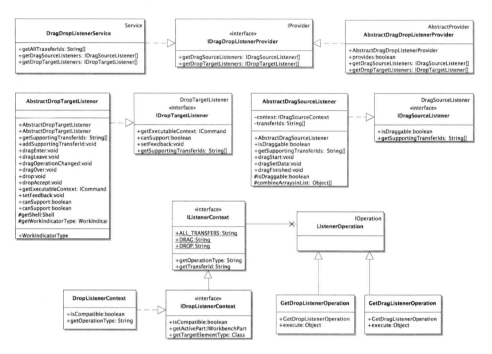

Figure 10-42   DragDropListenerService

Description: This extension-point registers drag source and drop target listeners for element types within view parts. This extension-point facilitates the configuration of providers for the `DragDropListenerService` (org. eclipse.gmf.runtime.common.ui.services.dnd.core.DragDrop ListenerService). The providers register listeners for drag-and-drop operations on specific element types within view parts.

Configuration markup:

```
<!ELEMENT extension (DragDropListenerProvider)>

<!ELEMENT DragDropListenerProvider (Priority , ViewId+)>
<!ATTLIST DragDropListenerProvider
id CDATA #REQUIRED
class CDATA #REQUIRED>
```

id—The identifier of the provider—for example, `my_dragDropListener Provider`.

class—The provider class. Providers implement service functionality (operations).

```
<!ELEMENT Priority EMPTY>
<!ATTLIST Priority
name (Lowest|Low|Medium|High|Highest) >
```

name—The name of the provider priority—Lowest, Low, Medium, High, or Highest.

```
<!ELEMENT ViewId (ElementType+)>
<!ATTLIST ViewId
id CDATA #REQUIRED>
```

id—The target view part ID—for example, org.eclipse.test. project.ui.views.MyView.

```
<!ELEMENT ElementType (OperationType+)>
<!ATTLIST ElementType
class CDATA #REQUIRED>
```

class—The element type within the view part—for example, org. eclipse.test.providers.MyElement.

```
<!ELEMENT OperationType (TransferId+)>
<!ATTLIST OperationType
operation (drag|drop) >
```

operation—The operation type being registered for within the view part— for example, drag or drop.

```
<!ELEMENT TransferId EMPTY>
<!ATTLIST TransferId
transferId CDATA #REQUIRED>
```

transferId—The ID for the transfer agent.

Examples:
The following is an example of the DragDropListenerProvider extension:

```
<extension
point="org.eclipse.gmf.runtime.common.ui.services.dnd.
dragDropListenerProviders">
<DragDropListenerProvider
   class="org.eclipse.test.project.ui.internal.providers.dnd.
```

```
        DragDropListenerProvider"
        id="myExplorerDragDropListenerProvider">
        <Priority name="Lowest"/>
        <ViewId id="org.eclipse.test.project.ui.views.MyExplorer">
            <ElementType
                class="org.eclipse.test.project.ui.internal.
                providers.myexplorer.MyElement">
                <OperationType operation="drag">
                    <TransferId transferId="selection"/>
                    <TransferId transferId="customData"/>
                    <TransferId transferId="file"/>
                    <TransferId transferId="text"/>
                    <TransferId transferId="richText"/>
                </OperationType>
                <OperationType operation="drop"/>
                    <TransferId transferId="selection"/>
                    <TransferId transferId="customData"/>
                </OperationType>
            </ElementType>
        </ViewId>
    </DragDropListenerProvider>
</extension>
```

API information:

The value of the class attribute must represent a subclass of `org. eclipse.gmf.runtime.common.core.service.AbstractProvider` that implements `org.eclipse.gmf.runtime.common.ui.services.dnd. core.IDragDropListenerProvider` (such as a subclass of `org.eclipse. gmf.runtime.common.ui.services.dnd.core. AbstractDragDrop ListenerProvider`).

Notes:

Diagrams generated using the GMF tooling do not currently use this extension-point.

10.4.19 TransferAdapterService

The `TransferAdapterService` and corresponding `ITransferAdapter |Provider` interface allow providers to supply transfer adapters for a specified transfer ID during drag-and-drop operations. An `AbstractTransfer AdapterProvider` is supplied, along with a concrete `TransferAdapter Provider` class, as seen in Figure 10-43. Providers work with `ITransfer DropTargetListener` and `ITransferDragSourceListener` implementations.

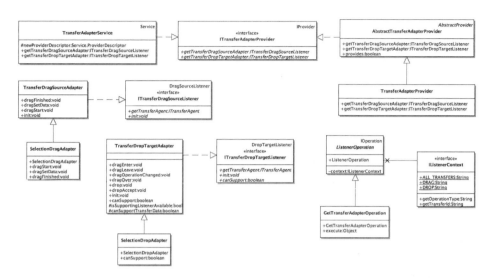

Figure 10-43 TransferAdapterService

TransferAdapterProvider ExtensionPoint

Identifier: `org.eclipse.gmf.runtime.common.ui.services.dnd.transferAdapterProviders`

Description: This extension-point registers transfer adapters for drag-and-drop operations. This extension-point facilitates the configuration of providers for the `TransferAdapterService` (`org.eclipse.gmf.runtime.common.ui.services.dnd.core.TransferAdapterService`). The providers register adapters for drag-and-drop operations on specific transfer IDs.

Configuration markup:

```
<!ELEMENT extension (TransferAdapterProvider)>

<!ELEMENT TransferAdapterProvider (Priority , AdapterType+)>
<!ATTLIST TransferAdapterProvider
id CDATA #REQUIRED
class CDATA #REQUIRED>
```

`id`—The identifier of the provider—for example, `my_transferAdapter Provider`.

`class`—The provider class. Providers implement service functionality (operations).

```
<!ELEMENT Priority EMPTY>
<!ATTLIST Priority
name (Lowest|Low|Medium|High|Highest) >
```

name—The name of the provider priority—Lowest, Low, Medium, High, or Highest.

```
<!ELEMENT AdapterType (TransferId+)>
<!ATTLIST AdapterType
operation (drag|drop) >
```

operation—The adapter type being registered—for example, drag or drop.

```
<!ELEMENT TransferId EMPTY>
<!ATTLIST TransferId
id CDATA #REQUIRED>
```

id—The unique transfer ID for the transfer agent—for example, customDataTransfer.

Examples:

The following is an example of the TransferAdapterProvider extension:

```
<extension
    point="org.eclipse.gmf.runtime.common.ui.services.dnd.
    dragDropListenerProviders">
    <DragDropListenerProvider
        class="org.eclipse.test.project.ui.internal.providers.dnd.
        MyExplorerDNDListenerProvider"
        id="myexplorerDragDropListenerProvider">
        <Priority name="Lowest"/>
        <ViewId id="org.eclipse.test.modeler.ui.views.MyExplorer">
        <ElementType
            class="org.eclipse.test.project.ui.internal.providers.
            explorer.MyElement">
            <OperationType operation="drag">
                <TransferId transferId="selection"/>
                <TransferId transferId="customData"/>
                <TransferId transferId="file"/>
                <TransferId transferId="text"/>
                <TransferId transferId="richText"/>
            </OperationType>
            <OperationType operation="drop"/>
                <TransferId transferId="selection"/>
                <TransferId transferId="customData"/>
            </OperationType>
```

```
        </ElementType>
      </ViewId>
    </DragDropListenerProvider>
</extension>
```

API information:
The value of the class attribute must represent a subclass of `org.eclipse.gmf.runtime.common.core.service.AbstractProvider` that implements `org.eclipse.gmf.runtime.common.ui.services.dnd.core.ITransferAdapterProvider` (such as a subclass of `org.eclipse.gmf.runtime.common.ui.services.dnd.core.AbstractTransferAdapterProvider`).

Notes:
Diagrams generated using the GMF tooling do not currently use this extension-point.

10.4.20 DiagramEvenBroker Service

As pointed out in its corresponding extension-point schema documentation, this is an advanced feature of the runtime; only those who understand its potential effects should use it. The `DiagramEventBrokerService` and corresponding provider allow for the contribution of an event broker for diagrams that replaces the default, provided by the class `DiagramEventBroker`. As shown in Figure 10-44, the functionality that the `DiagramEventBroker` provides is central to the operation of the event model of the diagram within its editing domain, hence the reason for the previous warning.

DiagramEventBrokerProvider Extension-Point

Identifier: `org.eclipse.gmf.runtime.diagram.core.diagramEventBrokerProviders`

Description: This extension-point is intended to be used only by GMF runtime experts because changing the diagram event broker could have severe implications on diagrams that share the same editing domain.

Configuration markup:
```
<!ELEMENT diagramEventBrokerProvider (Priority , editingDomain+)>
<!ATTLIST diagramEventBrokerProvider
class CDATA #REQUIRED>
```

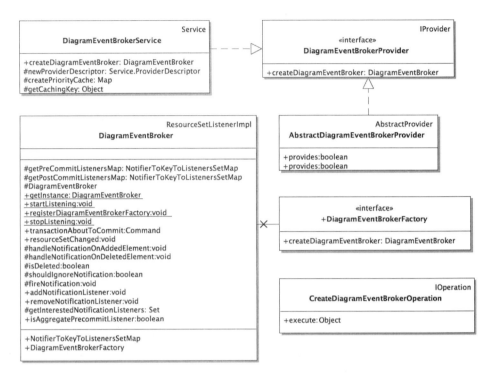

Figure 10-44   DiagramEventBrokerService

`class`—The fully qualified name of the `DiagramEventBrokerService` class.

```
<!ELEMENT editingDomain EMPTY>
<!ATTLIST editingDomain
ID CDATA #REQUIRED>
```

This element defines an editing domain to associate with the `DiagramEvent Broker`.

`ID`—The ID of the editing domain

```
<!ELEMENT Priority EMPTY>
<!ATTLIST Priority
name (Lowest|Low|Medium|High|Highest) >
```

This element defines the priority of the `DiagramEventBrokerService`.

`name`—The priority of the provider. It can be one of the following values: `Lowest`, `Low`, `Medium`, `High`, or `Highest`. Dependencies must be considered when choosing the priority.

Examples:

```
<extension
    point="org.eclipse.gmf.runtime.diagram.core.
    diagramEventBrokerProviders">
  <diagramEventBrokerProvider
      class="org.eclipse.pde.target.diagram.
      MyDiagramEventBrokerProvider">
    <Priority name="Highest"/>
    <editingDomain
        ID="org.eclipse.pde.target.diagram.EditingDomain">
    </editingDomain>
  </diagramEventBrokerProvider>
</extension>
```

Notes:

Diagrams generated using the GMF tooling do not currently use this extension-point. Furthermore, this service doesn't appear to be usable.

10.5 Additional Extension-Points

In addition to the extension-points described so far that incorporate the service-provider infrastructure, the GMF runtime provides a number of additional extension-points that I define here.

10.5.1 ElementTypes

Identifier: `org.eclipse.gmf.runtime.emf.type.core.` `elementTypes`

Description: The `org.eclipse.gmf.runtime.emf.type.core.ele-` `mentTypes` extension-point defines application specializations of metamodel types for the following purposes:

To extend (but not replace) the basic metamodel editing behavior for elements that match such specializations

To contribute icons and display names for such specializations

The `elementType` specializations can be used for menu or tool palette items for element creation.

You can extend editing behavior by associating an `editHelperAdvice` to a specialization or by contributing an adviceBinding that binds an `edit` `HelperAdvice` to an `elementType`. Edit `HelperAdvice` is applied before and/or after the behavior that the default metamodel editing behavior provides.

You can create custom `elementTypes` by declaring an `IElementType Factory` that is responsible for creating all `elementTypes` declaring the same "kind" as the factory. Custom parameters can be associated with `elementTypes` created this way.

Configuration markup:

```
<!ELEMENT extension (metamodel* , elementTypeFactory* ,
specializationType*)>

<!ELEMENT metamodel (metamodelType* , specializationType* ,

adviceBinding*)>
<!ATTLIST metamodel
nsURI CDATA #REQUIRED>
```

This element identifies the metamodel for which a set of `elementTypes` and advice bindings are defined. All eClass and eContainmentFeature values specified in the types must be found within this metamodel.

`nsURI`—The namespace URI of the metamodel.

```
<!ELEMENT elementTypeFactory EMPTY>
<!ATTLIST elementTypeFactory
factory CDATA #REQUIRED
kind CDATA #REQUIRED
params CDATA #IMPLIED>
```

This element contributes a `factory` that will create `elementTypes` declaring the same "`kind`" as the factory. Custom parameters can be associated with `elementTypes` created this way.

`factory`—The fully qualified name of a class that implements the `org. eclipse.gmf.runtime.emf.type.core.IElementTypeFactory`.

`kind`—String identifying the kind of element that this factory will create. `elementTypes` will declare the same "`kind`" String if they want to be created by this factory.

`params`—Comma-separated list of custom parameters that this `elementType` factory supports. Parameter values are read from the `element Type` element and passed to the factory when they are created.

```
<!ELEMENT metamodelType (param*)>
<!ATTLIST metamodelType
id CDATA #REQUIRED
icon CDATA #IMPLIED
name CDATA #IMPLIED
```

```
eclass CDATA #REQUIRED
edithelper CDATA #IMPLIED
kind CDATA #IMPLIED>
```

This element defines a new metamodel `elementType`.

`id`—The unique identifier for this metamodel `elementType`.

`icon`—The path of this metamodel `elementType` icon, relative to this plug-in location.

`name`—The I18N display name for this metamodel `elementType`.

`eclass`—The name of an `EClass` instance from the metamodel specified in the enclosing metamodel element.

`edithelper`—The fully qualified name of a class that implements `org.eclipse.gmf.runtime.emf.type.core.edit.IEditHelper`.

`kind`—The kind of element. Identifies the `IElementTypeFactory` that is used to instantiate the `elementType`. If it is not specified, a default factory creates the element.

```
<!ELEMENT specializationType (specializes+ , (matcher | enablement)? ,

param* , eContainer?)>
<!ATTLIST specializationType
id CDATA #REQUIRED
icon CDATA #IMPLIED
name CDATA #IMPLIED
edithelperadvice CDATA #IMPLIED
kind CDATA #IMPLIED>
```

This element defines a new specialization `elementType`.

`id`—The unique specialization edit type identifier.

`icon`—The path of this specialization `elementType` icon, relative to this plug-in location.

`name`—The I18N display name for this specialization `elementType`.

`edithelperadvice`—The fully qualified name of a class that implements `org.eclipse.gmf.runtime.emf.type.core.edit.IEditHelperAdvice`. This attribute specifies the class that provides editing advice for elements of this type. You can contribute editing advice before and/or after the default editing behavior.

`kind`—The kind of element. Identifies the `IElementTypeFactory` that is used to instantiate the `elementType`. If it is not specified, a default factory creates the element.

```
<!ELEMENT adviceBinding ((matcher | enablement)? , eContainer?)>
<!ATTLIST adviceBinding
typeId CDATA #REQUIRED
class CDATA #REQUIRED
inheritance (all|none) "none"
id CDATA #REQUIRED>
```

This element binds an `IEditHelperAdvice` with an `elementType`.

`typeId`—The `elementType` identifier.

`class`—The fully qualified name of a class that implements `org.eclipse.gmf.runtime.emf.type.core.edit.IEditHelperAdvice`. This attribute specifies the class that provides editing advice for elements of this type. You can contribute editing advice before and/or after the default editing behavior.

`inheritance`—Indicates the related `elementTypes` that should inherit this advice. Does not apply to specialization types, which always inherit (all).

`all`—Advice is inherited by all metamodel types whose `EClasses` are subtypes of the metamodel type to which it was applied, and to all specializations of those metamodel types.

`none`—Advice is not inherited by related metamodel types. It is applied only to the metatmodel type and its specializations.

`id`—The unique ID of this advice binding.

```
<!ELEMENT specializes EMPTY>
<!ATTLIST specializes
id CDATA #REQUIRED>
```

This element is used to identify another `elementType` (metamodel or specialization) that this type specializes.

`id`—Identifier of the metamodel type or specialization type that this type specializes in.

```
<!ELEMENT matcher EMPTY>
<!ATTLIST matcher
class CDATA #REQUIRED>
```

This element is used to specify the class that will determine whether an existing model element matches this type.

`class`—The fully qualified name of a class that implements `org.eclipse.gmf.runtime.emf.type.core.IElementMatcher`.

```
<!ELEMENT eContainer (eContainmentFeature* , (matcher | enablement)?)>
```

This element describes the qualities of the container model element for which this edit helper advice is relevant.

```
<!ELEMENT eContainmentFeature EMPTY>
<!ATTLIST eContainmentFeature
qname CDATA #REQUIRED>
```

This element specifies the containment feature for model elements for which this `EditHelper` advice is relevant.

`qname`—The name of the containment feature, qualified by its `EClass` name.

```
<!ELEMENT param EMPTY>
<!ATTLIST param
name CDATA #REQUIRED
value CDATA #REQUIRED>
```

This element defines a custom parameter name and value pair.

`name`—The parameter name.

`value`—The parameter value.

Examples:

```
<metamodel nsURI="http://www.eclipse.org/emf/2002/Ecore">
   <metamodelType
       id="org.eclipse.gmf.runtime.emf.type.core.eobject"
       icon="icons/eobject.gif"
       name="%EObject"
       eclass="EObject"
       edithelper="org.eclipse.gmf.runtime.emf.type.core.
       EObjectEditHelper">
   </metamodelType>

   <specializationType
       id="org.eclipse.gmf.runtime.emf.type.core.special"
       icon="icons/special.gif"
       name="%Special"
       edithelperadvice="org.eclipse.gmf.runtime.emf.type.core.
       SpecialEditHelperAdvice">
       <specializes
           id="org.eclipse.gmf.runtime.emf.type.core.eobject"/>
       <matcher
           class="org.eclipse.gmf.runtime.emf.type.core.
           specialMatcher"/>
   </specializationType>

   <specializationType
       id="org.eclipse.gmf.runtime.emf.type.core.special2"
       icon="icons/special2.gif"
       name="%Special2"
```

```
            edithelperadvice="org.eclipse.gmf.runtime.emf.type.
            core.Special2EditHelperAdvice">
            <specializes id="org.eclipse.gmf.runtime.emf.type.
                core.eobject"/>
                <eContainer>
                    <enablement>
                        <test property="special2"
                                value="special2Value"/>
                    </enablement>
                </eContainer>
                <enablement>
                    <test property="special2" value="special2Value"/>
                </enablement>
        </specializationType>

        <specializationType
            id="org.eclipse.gmf.runtime.emf.type.core.customType"
            icon="icons/customType.gif"
            name="%CustomType"
            kind="org.eclipse.gmf.runtime.emf.type.core.
            CustomElementKind"
            edithelperadvice="org.eclipse.gmf.runtime.emf.type.
            core.CustomEditHelperAdvice">
            <specializes
                id="org.eclipse.gmf.runtime.emf.type.core.eobject"/>
                <param
                    name="customParameter1"
                    value="value1">
                </param>
                <param
                    name="customParameter2"
                    value="value2">
                </param>
        </specializationType>

        <adviceBinding
            id="org.eclipse.gmf.runtime.emf.type.core.advisedType"
            typeId="org.eclipse.gmf.runtime.emf.type.core.eobject"
            class="org.eclipse.gmf.runtime.emf.type.core.
            advisedTypeEditHelperAdvice"
            applyToSubtypes="false">
            <eContainer>
                <enablement>
                    <test property="advised" value="advisedValue"/>
                </enablement>
            </eContainer>
        </adviceBinding>
    </metamodel>

    <elementTypeFactory
        factory="org.eclipse.gmf.runtime.emf.type.core.
        CustomElementTypeFactory"
        kind = "org.eclipse.gmf.runtime.emf.type.core.CustomElementKind"
        params = "customParameter1, customParameter2">
    </elementTypeFactory>
</extension>
```

API information:

See the `org.eclipse.gmf.runtime.emf.type.core` package in the `org.eclipse.gmf.runtime.emf.type.core` plug-in for the API description. Figure 10-45 shows the main elements of this service.

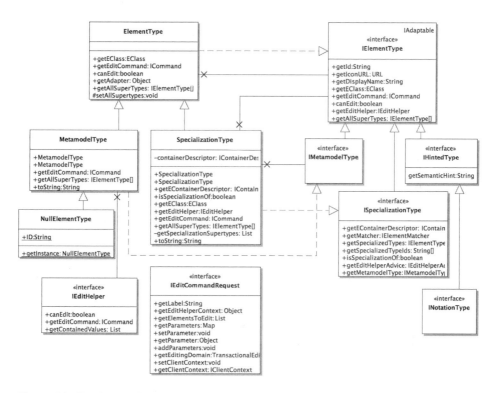

Figure 10-45   ElementTypes

10.5.2 ElementTypeBindings

Identifier: `org.eclipse.gmf.runtime.emf.type.core.element TypeBindings`

Description: This extension-point allows clients of the GMF extensible type registry to define "client contexts" that describe the objects that they are interested in editing, and to bind them to `ElementTypes` and advice that they want to have applied to these objects.

Configuration markup:

```
<!ELEMENT extension (clientContext* , binding*)>
<!ELEMENT clientContext (enablement | matcher)>
<!ATTLIST clientContext
id CDATA #REQUIRED>
```

This element defines a client context, representing a class of objects that a client wants to edit using a set of `ElementTypes` and advice.

A client context can declare an `<enablement>` expression that matches model elements that are included in the context. Where that is not sufficient, an alternative is to define a matcher class using a `<matcher>` element.

`id`—The unique ID of the client context.

```
<!ELEMENT matcher EMPTY>
<!ATTLIST matcher
class CDATA #REQUIRED>
```

This element specifies the class that determines whether an existing model element matches this client context.

`class`—The fully qualified name of a class that implements `org.eclipse.gmf.runtime.emf.type.core.IElementMatcher`.

```
<!ELEMENT binding (elementType* , advice*)>
<!ATTLIST binding
context CDATA #REQUIRED>
```

This element defines a binding between a client context and one or more `ElementTypes` or advice. The context itself can be declared by the same plug-in or by a different plug-in.

You can specify the constraints to be bound by any number of nested `<elementType>` and/or `<advice>` elements to reference multiple `Element Types` and/or advice.

`context`—References the ID of a context that is bound to one or more `ElementTypes` or advice.

```
<!ELEMENT elementType EMPTY>
<!ATTLIST elementType
ref CDATA #IMPLIED
pattern CDATA #IMPLIED>
```

This element defines an `ElementType` or a pattern of `ElementType` IDs in a client context `<binding>`.

ref—References the ID of an ElementType to bind the client context to. You cannot use this attribute in conjunction with the pattern attribute.

pattern—The pattern of ElementType IDs to be bound. Patterns are regular expressions that match unique identifiers. See the Java documentation for java.util.regex.Pattern for further details. You cannot use this attribute in conjunction with the ref attribute.

```
<!ELEMENT advice EMPTY>
<!ATTLIST advice
ref CDATA #IMPLIED
pattern CDATA #IMPLIED>
```

This element defines an advice or a pattern of advice IDs in a client context <binding>.

ref—References the ID of an advice to bind the client context to. You cannot use this attribute in conjunction with the pattern attribute.

pattern—The pattern of advice IDs to be bound. Patterns are regular expressions that match unique identifiers. See the Java documentation for java.util.regex.Pattern for further details. You cannot use this attribute in conjunction with the ref attribute.

Examples:

Consider this example of a context that includes only EObjects from the logic example's editing domain:

```
<extension-point="org.eclipse.gmf.runtime.emf.type.core.
      elementTypeBindings">
    <clientContext
        id="org.eclipse.gmf.examples.runtime.diagram.logic">
        <enablement>
            <test
              property="org.eclipse.gmf.runtime.emf.core.editingDomain"
              value="org.eclipse.gmf.examples.runtime.diagram.
              logicEditingDomain"/>
        </enablement>
    </clientContext>
</extension>
```

This is an example of binding a single advice to the logic context:

```
<extension-point="org.eclipse.gmf.runtime.emf.type.core.
      elementTypeBindings">
    <binding
        context="org.eclipse.gmf.examples.runtime.diagram.logic"/>
        <advice ref="org.eclipse.gmf.runtime.diagram.core.advice.
```

```
        notationDepdendents"/>
      </binding>
</extension>
```

Consider this example of binding multiple elementTypes and advice to the logic context:

```
<extension-
point="org.eclipse.gmf.runtime.emf.type.core.elementTypeBindings">
      <binding
context="org.eclipse.gmf.examples.runtime.diagram.logic"/>
            <elementType pattern="logic.*"/>
            <advice pattern="logic.*"/>
      </binding>
</extension>
```

10.5.3 LogListeners

Identifier: org.eclipse.gmf.runtime.common.core.logListeners

Description: This extension-point defines listeners for the Eclipse logging facility.

Configuration markup:

```
<!ELEMENT extension (LogListener)>

<!ELEMENT LogListener EMPTY>
<!ATTLIST LogListener
class CDATA #REQUIRED>
```

class—The listener class.

Examples:

The following is an example of a LogListener contribution:

```
<extension point="org.eclipse.gmf.runtime.common.core.logListeners">
   <LogListener
        class="org.eclipse.mindmap.listeners.MindmapLogListener"/>
</extension>
```

API information:

The value of the class attribute must be the fully qualified name of a class that implements org.eclipse.core.runtime.ILogListener.

Notes:

Diagrams generated using the GMF tooling do not currently use this extension-point.

This extension-point is not contributed to in the runtime itself, and the only implementations of the `ILogListener` interface are found in `PlatformLog Writer` and `StatusManagerLogListener`.

10.5.4 *PropertiesConfigurations*

Identifier: `org.eclipse.gmf.runtime.common.core.propertiesConfiguration`

Description: This extension-point defines plug-in-specific Strings in external properties files so that clients of the plug-in can refer to these Strings without loading the plug-in itself. (Loading of the plug-in is deferred.)

Configuration markup:

```
<!ELEMENT extension (PropertiesConfiguration+)>
<!ELEMENT PropertiesConfiguration EMPTY>
<!ATTLIST PropertiesConfiguration
path CDATA #REQUIRED>
```

`path`—The relative path to a properties file.

Examples:

The following is an example of a `PropertiesConfiguration` contribution:

```
<extension
    point="org.eclipse.gmf.runtime.common.core.propertiesConfiguration">
    <PropertiesConfiguration path="plugin.properties"/>
</extension>
```

Notes:

Diagrams generated using the GMF tooling do not currently use this extension-point.

10.5.5 *Document Providers*

Identifier: `org.eclipse.gmf.runtime.diagram.ui.resources.editor.documentProviders`

Description: This extension-point defines mappings between file types and `documentProviders`, or between types of editor inputs and document

providers that editors can use. DocumentProviders must implement the interface org.eclipse.gmf.runtime.diagram.ui.editor.IDocumentPro-
vider. Editor inputs must be an instance of org.eclipse.ui.IEditor
Input.

Configuration markup:

```
<!ELEMENT extension (provider*)>

<!ELEMENT provider EMPTY>
<!ATTLIST provider
extensions CDATA #IMPLIED
inputTypes CDATA #IMPLIED
class CDATA #REQUIRED
id CDATA #REQUIRED
documentType CDATA
"org.eclipse.gmf.runtime.diagram.ui.editor.IDocument">
```

extensions—A comma-separated list of file extensions.

inputTypes—A comma-separated list of qualified editor input class names
that must implement org.eclipse.ui.IEditorInput.

class—The qualified name of the document provider class that must implement the interface org.eclipse.ui.texteditor.IDocumentProvider.

id—The unique ID of this provider.

documentType—org.eclipse.gmf.runtime.diagram.ui.editor.
IDocument

Examples:

This example registers org.eclipse.ui.examples.javaeditor.
JavaDocumentProvider as the default provider for files with the extension
.jav:

```
<extension
    point="org.eclipse.gmf.runtime.diagram.ui.resources.
    editor.documentProviders">
    <provider
        extensions=".jav"
        class="org.eclipse.ui.examples.javaeditor.JavaDocumentProvider"
        id="org.eclipse.ui.examples.javaeditor.JavaDocumentProvider">
    </provider>
</extension>
```

This example registers org.eclipse.gmf.runtime.diagram.ui.
resources.editor.FileDocumentProvider as the default provider for all
editor inputs that are an instance of org.eclipse.ui.IStorageEditor
Input.

```
<extension
    point="org.eclipse.gmf.runtime.diagram.ui.resources.editor.
    documentProviders">
    <provider
        inputTypes="org.eclipse.ui.IStorageEditorInput"
        class="org.eclipse.gmf.runtime.diagram.ui.resources.editor.
        FileDocumentProvider"
        id="org.eclipse.gmf.runtime.diagram.ui.resources.editor.
        FileDocumentProvider">
    </provider>
</extension>
```

API information:

DocumentProviders registered for a file extension have precedence over those registered for input types. DocumentProviders must implement the interface org.eclipse.ui.texteditor.IDocumentProvider. Editor inputs must be instance of org.eclipse.ui.IEditorInput. Figure 10-46 is a diagram of the IDocumentProvider interface and its implementations provided by the runtime.

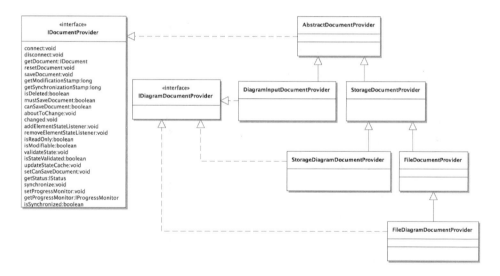

Figure 10-46   DocumentProvider

Notes:

Diagrams generated using the GMF tooling do not currently use this extension-point, but they do provide an implementation of IDiagramDocument Provider and extend AbstractDocumentProvider.

10.5.6 RenderedImageFactory

Identifier: `org.eclipse.gmf.runtime.draw2d.ui.render.`
`renderedImageFactory`

Description: This extension-point defines an image type to allow autodetection of an image buffer. The image type can instantiate a `RenderedImage`, which can subsequently be rendered using the `ScalableImageFigure` class. In the extension-point, the client points to a factory class that is created implementing the `RenderedImageType` interface. The `RenderedImageFactory` static class calls the extension-point to compile a list of image types to query. When the client calls the `RenderedImageFactory` to retrieve the proper `RenderedImage`, it asks each type whether it can handle the particular image buffer. If the type autodetects the image buffer, the type instantiates and returns a `RenderedImage` object.

Configuration markup:

```
<!ELEMENT extension (factory)>
<!ELEMENT factory EMPTY>
<!ATTLIST factory
class CDATA #REQUIRED>
```

`class`—Name of the image factory, such as the provided `org.eclipse.gmf.runtime.draw2d.ui.render.factory.RenderedImageFactory`.

Examples:

An extension to the `renderedImageFactory` would require implementation of the `RenderedImageType` interface. The following is an example contribution to the `renderedImageFactory` extension, as found in the runtime plug-in `org.eclipse.gmf.runtime.draw2d.ui.render.awt`:

```
<extension
    point="org.eclipse.gmf.runtime.draw2d.ui.render.
    renderedImageFactory">
     <factory
       class="org.eclipse.gmf.runtime.draw2d.ui.render.awt.
       internal.svg.SVGImageType">
     </factory>
  </extension>
```

API information:

For API information, see the classes and interfaces defined in the `org.eclipse.gmf.runtime.draw2d.ui.render` and `org.eclipse.gmf.runtime.draw2d.ui.render.factory` packages.

Clients that provide an extension to the `renderedImageFactory` extension-point must create classes that implement the following interfaces:

```
org.eclipse.gmf.runtime.draw2d.ui.render.RenderedImage
org.eclipse.gmf.runtime.draw2d.ui.render.factory.RenderedImageType
```

Notes:
Diagrams generated using the GMF tooling do not currently use this extension-point.

10.5.7 ClipboardSupport

Identifier: `org.eclipse.gmf.runtime.emf.clipboard.core.clip-boardSupport`

Description: Providers of EMF metamodels can contribute extensions to provide support for copying EMF objects to and pasting them from the system Clipboard. `ClipboardSupport` allows extensions to implement fairly complex metamodel-specific semantics for copy/paste operations, where some relationships between model elements need special treatment.

Configuration markup:

```
<!ELEMENT extension (factory+)>
<!ELEMENT factory EMPTY>
<!ATTLIST factory
nsURI CDATA #REQUIRED
class CDATA #REQUIRED
priority (lowest|low|medium|high|highest) "medium">
```

This element registers an implementation of the IClipboardSupportFactory interface that can create objects that provide metamodel-specific copy/paste semantics for EMF objects.

nsURI—Namespace URI identifying the `EPackage` for which the extension provides an `IClipboardSupportFactory` implementation. The `EPackage` represents an EMF metamodel.

class—The fully qualified name of a class implementing the `IClipboard SupportFactory` interface. This class is loaded and instantiated only when needed to copy an EMF object to the Clipboard or when pasting from the Clipboard.

priority—Indicates the priority, relative to other factories registered for the same metamodel. The default is medium. This attribute is deprecated; a new context-based approach will be devised soon.

Examples:

To register a `ClipboardSupport` factory for the EMF Library example model, follow this:

```
<extension
     point="org.eclipse.gmf.runtime.emf.clipboard.core.
     clipboardSupport">
     <factory
          nsURI="http:///org/eclipse/emf/examples/library.ecore"
          class="com.example.emf.library.clipboard.
          LibraryClipboardSupportFactory">
     </factory>
</extension>
```

API information:

Classes registered on this extension-point must implement the `org.eclipse.gmf.runtime.emf.clipboard.core.IClipboardSupportFactory` interface. A support factory is responsible for creating `IClipboardSupports` for the packages on which it is registered on this extension-point.

Notes:

Diagrams generated using the GMF tooling do not currently use this extension-point.

10.5.8 Pathmaps

Identifier: `org.eclipse.gmf.runtime.emf.core.Pathmaps`

Description: Extension-point for the definition of pathmap variables. Pathmap variables allow for the portability of URIs, in similar fashion to path Eclipse's core path variables. The actual location indicated by a URI depends on the runtime binding of the path variable. Thus, different environments can work with the same resource URIs even though the resources are stored in different physical locations.

Configuration markup:

```
<!ELEMENT extension (pathmap)>

<!ELEMENT pathmap EMPTY>
<!ATTLIST pathmap
name CDATA #REQUIRED
plugin CDATA #IMPLIED
path CDATA #REQUIRED>
```

This element specifies a `pathmap` variable to be registered with the runtime.
`name`—The variable name.

`plugin`—The plug-in that contains the path, if different from the plug-in
that defines the extension.

`path`—The path, relative to the plug-in location (as indicated by the plug-in
attribute, if specified, or the current plug-in, if not).

Examples:

This example illustrates the definition of a `pathmap` to locate libraries in the
UML2 project. Using this `pathmap`, you can use URIs such as the following to
reference UML2 library resources: `pathmap://UML2_LIBRARIES/Ecore.`
`library.uml2`.

```
<extension
        id="UML2Libraries"
        name="UML2 Libraries"
        point="org.eclipse.gmf.runtime.emf.core.Pathmaps">
    <pathmap
        name="UML2_LIBRARIES"
        plugin="org.eclipse.uml2.resources"
        path="libraries">
    </pathmap>
</extension>
```

API information:

This extension-point has no associated API.

Notes:

Diagrams generated using the GMF tooling do not currently use this
extension-point.

10.6 Element Creation

With the basics of the notation model and services under our belt, let's bring it
together and compare how GMF's runtime differs from what we learned about
GEF in Chapter 9. We look at element creation because it is the most fundamental use case and nicely illustrates how GMF differs from GEF. You might
want to compare Figure 10-47 and the following description of GMF element
creation with that of GEF element creation covered in Section 9.2.6,
"Interactions."

This initial sequence for element creation is similar to GEF, with the major
difference being GMF's use of a `CreationEditPolicy` that uses a compound

command to create both the domain (semantic) element and the view element that references it. Using the command infrastructure in GMF ensures that undo and redo are handled in a generic fashion and eliminates the need for orphan element creation.

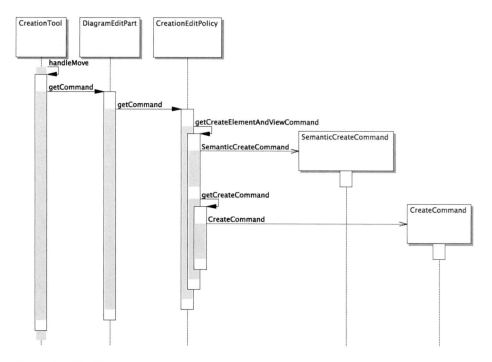

Figure 10-47   Element creation

Now let's consider the mouse click on the diagram surface, which is covered by Figures 10-48 and 10-49. First, we see that the compound command loaded into the creation tool is executed to create the domain and notation view elements. Note that the domain element is created first and then passed to the ViewService for notation element creation, leveraging the registered provider and corresponding ViewFactory.

When the domain element was created earlier, notification of the event went to its corresponding EditPart. This is done within the context of a write action so that undo/redo is possible. The EditPart then invokes refreshChildren(), which causes the creation of the corresponding EditPart and Figure for the child. Similar to the ViewService, an EditPartService finds the appropriate provider to obtain the corresponding EditPart.

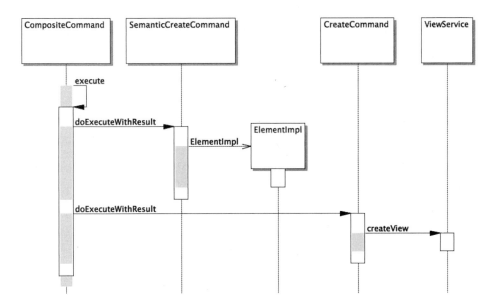

Figure 10-48 Create command

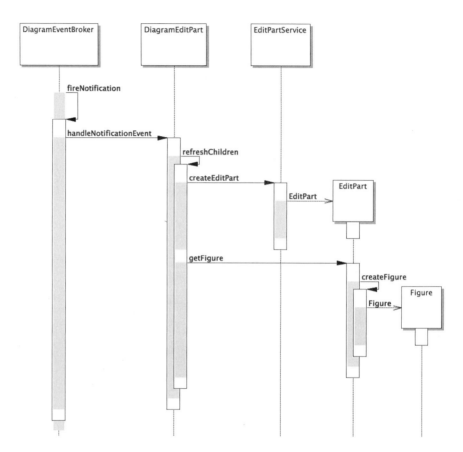

Figure 10-49   EditPart creation

10.7 Command Infrastructure

The GMF runtime's command infrastructure involves two aspects. The first
relates to commands that do not modify underlying EMF model elements (recall
that GMF uses EMF for both domain and notation, or diagram, models), such
as those used for opening a diagram, copying an image, and so on. The second
aspect is used to effect changes in the underlying EMF models and leverages the
EMF Transaction component.

10.7.1 Command Infrastructure

The heart of GMF's command infrastructure for non-model-modifying commands is the `AbstractCommand` class, found in the `org.eclipse.gmf.runtime.common.core.command` package. `AbstractCommand` extends the platform's `AbstractOperation` class, which provides general undoable/redoable command functionality.

Figure 10-50 is a diagram of the `org.eclipse.gmf.runtime.common.core.command` package.

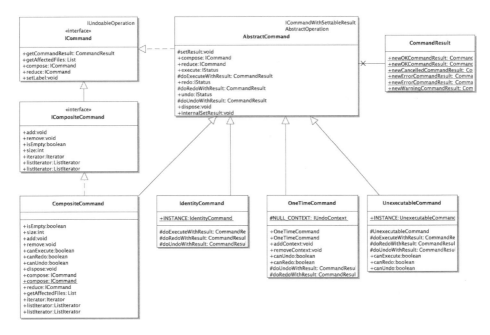

Figure 10-50 Core commands

10.7.2 Model Element Command Infrastructure

One of the main motivators for starting the GMF project was the need to provide a standardized way to work with GEF and EMF command infrastructures. Solutions to this problem had been covered in documentation, a GEF example, and many independently developed applications. GMF uses the EMF Transaction component for commands that impact the underlying model elements, which is built upon the platform's command infrastructure.

The heart of command support for undoable operations on model elements is `AbstractTransactionalCommand`, which has a number of provided subclasses, as shown in Figure 10-51, and is found in the package `org.eclipse.gmf.runtime.emf.commands.core.command`. Look to the `org.eclipse.gmf.runtime.diagram.core.commands` and `*.diagram.ui.commands` packages for many common commands for use in diagrams, such as these:

`AddCommand`

`CreateDiagramCommand`

`DeleteCommand`

`GroupCommand` and `UngroupCommand`

`RemoveBookmarkCommand`

`SetConnectionAnchorsCommand`

`SetConnectionEndsCommand`

`SetPropertyCommand`

`CreateCommand`

`DeferredCreateConnectionView`
`Command`

`DeferredLayoutCommand`

Commands have corresponding requests and are often invoked by a user Action. The `DiagramAction` abstract class is provided and has a number of subclasses to cover most diagram actions. Many of these are internal classes, but they can be examined to better understand how to use the command infrastructure of the diagram runtime. Figure 10-52 shows the `DiagramAction` class and a number of its available subclasses.

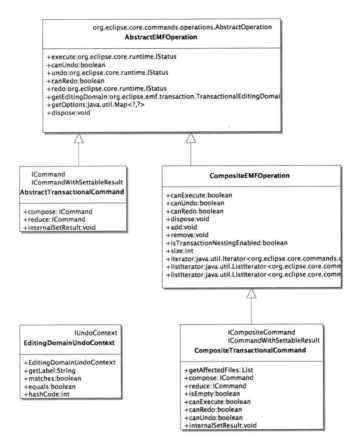

Figure 10-51 Transactional commands

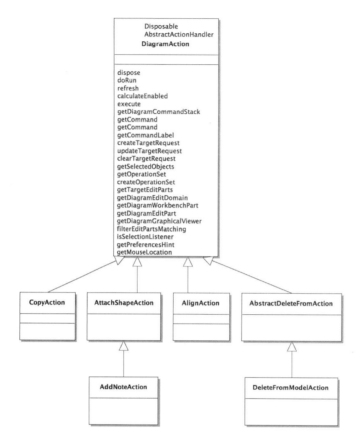

Figure 10-52   Diagram actions

10.8 Developing a Diagram

This section explores how to construct a diagram from scratch using the runtime functionality, without the generator. We build a mindmap diagram so that we can more easily compare with the code generated when using the tooling side of GMF, as outlined in Section 4.3, "Developing the Mindmap Diagram." The first step is to create the minimal working editor, to which we'll add properties support, diagram preferences, action bars, and so on.

10.8.1 Essential Diagram Elements

To begin, we create a new Plug-in Project in our workspace named `org.eclipse.mindmap.diagram.pure`, or a similar but necessarily different name from one that might have been created earlier. Note that you also need to have the mindmap model and edit projects in the workspace. When using the new Plug-in Project Wizard, select the option that indicates that the plug-in will make contributions to the user interface (UI), but don't use any of the provided templates. When finished, you'll have a basic plug-in with activator class that extends `AbstractUIPlugin`.

Diagram Editor

Using the plug-in manifest editor, add a new contribution to the `org.eclipse.ui.editors` extension-point. You can do this from the Extensions tab using the UI, or you can create it directly into the plugin.xml using its Text Editor tab. We need to supply only the basic information for ID, class, extension, matching strategy, and contributor class, as shown here:

```
<extension point="org.eclipse.ui.editors">
    <editor
        id="org.eclipse.mindmap.diagram.editor.MindmapDiagramEditorID"
        name="%editorName"
        icon="icons/obj16/MindmapDiagramFile.gif"
        extensions="mmd"
        default="true"
        class="org.eclipse.mindmap.diagram.editor.MindmapDiagramEditor"
        matchingStrategy="org.eclipse.gmf.runtime.diagram.ui.
        resources.editor.parts.DiagramDocumentEditorMatchingStrategy"
        contributorClass="org.eclipse.mindmap.diagram.editor.
        MindmapDiagramActionBarContributor">
    </editor>
</extension>
```

Use the provided quick fix support in the editor to add new classes where required, beginning with the editor class. In the wizard, indicate that the editor should extend `org.eclipse.gmf.runtime.diagram.ui.resources.editor.parts. DiagramDocumentEditor`. This superclass offers almost all the basic functionality we need, so the only content to add at this point is an ID field and getter. Note that the ID matches the ID field in our earlier plug-in manifest. If we plan to share the editing domain for this editor, we must enter the appropriate extension-point contribution and ID with getter in the editor code as well. We explore the sharing of editing domains in Section 4.4, "Developing a Requirements Diagram."

```
public class MindmapDiagramEditor extends DiagramDocumentEditor {

  public MindmapDiagramEditor() {
    super(true);
```

```
  }

  public static final String ID =
    "org.eclipse.mindmap.diagram.editor.MindmapDiagramEditorID";

  @Override
  public String getContributorId() {
    return MindmapDiagramEditorPlugin.ID;
  }
}
```

Notice in our manifest that we declare that `DiagramDocumentEditor`
`MatchingStrategy` provides our editor's matching strategy. This class is provided along with our editor's superclass by the GMF runtime and is sufficient for
our needs as is. However, we must implement our own contributor class. To do
this, we again use the quick fix and create a class to extend `DiagramActionBar`
`Contributor`, provided by the runtime in the `org.eclipse.gmf.`
`runtime.diagram.ui.parts` package. We need to override two methods, as
shown here. The superclass uses the contribution item service to initialize a
default set of action bars that are useful for most diagrams.

```
public class MindmapDiagramActionBarContributor

  extends DiagramActionBarContributor {

  @Override
  protected Class<MindmapDiagramEditor> getEditorClass() {
    return MindmapDiagramEditor.class;
  }

  @Override
  protected String getEditorId() {
    return MindmapDiagramEditor.ID;
  }
}
```

Domain Model

We must register each of the domain model elements used in our diagram within
an `org.eclipse.gmf.runtime.emf.type.core.elementTypes` contribution, declaring our mindmap model NS URI as the metamodel.

```
<extension point="org.eclipse.gmf.runtime.emf.type.core.elementTypes">
    <metamodel nsURI="http://www.eclipse.org/2008/mindmap">
        <metamodelType
         id="org.eclipse.mindmap.diagram.Map"
```

```
        icon="icons/obj16/MindmapDiagramFile.gif"
        name="Map"
        eclass="Map"
        kind="org.eclipse.gmf.runtime.emf.type.core.IHintedType">
        <param name="semanticHint" value="Map"/>
      </metamodelType>
      <metamodelType
        id="org.eclipse.mindmap.diagram.Topic"
        icon="icons/obj16/MindmapDiagramFile.gif"
        name="Topic"
        eclass="Topic"

        kind="org.eclipse.gmf.runtime.emf.type.core.IHintedType">
          <param name="semanticHint" value="Topic"/>
      </metamodelType>
    </metamodel>
</extension>
```

Note that both the `Map` and `Topic` classes from our domain model are registered as `metamodelType` elements with unique ID, name, eclass, and `IHintedType` kind attributes. The `semanticHint` parameter for each `metamodelType` supports the mapping of each type with its corresponding `View` and `EditPart`, as you will see in our `viewProviders` and `editpartProviders` extensions. Later, you'll see how these metamodel elements are mapped to palette tools and, therefore, diagram graphical elements. First, we need to complement our `elementTypes` contribution with an enumerator that returns an `IElementType` instance for each of our declared `metamodelType` IDs, as shown here in our `MindmapElementTypes` class. `IElementType` is an interface that the GMF runtime uses to define types that are displayed, created, edited, and destroyed. Each type has an associated icon, display name, `EClass`, and `EditHelper`, and they all return an edit command when provided an edit request.

```
public class MindmapElementTypes extends AbstractElementTypeEnumerator
{
    public static final IElementType MAP =
        getElementType("org.eclipse.mindmap.diagram.Map");
    public static final IElementType TOPIC =
        getElementType("org.eclipse.mindmap.diagram.Topic");
}
```

We need to add extension parser support for the diagram's notation model. The runtime provides one, so we simply declare a contribution using the `GMFResourceFactory` class for our editor extension `mmd` type.

```
<extension point="org.eclipse.emf.ecore.extension_parser">
      <parser
          type="mmd"
class="org.eclipse.gmf.runtime.emf.core.resources.GMFResourceFactory">
      </parser>
</extension>
```

Palette Definition

To create diagram elements, we need to define a palette. We can do this in a largely declarative manner using the `paletteProviders` extension-point. Following, we define a palette provider for our mindmap that uses the runtime's `DefaultPaletteProvider` class and is associated with our editor using its ID. Note that the Practitioner can customize the palette.

```
<extension point="org.eclipse.gmf.runtime.diagram.ui.paletteProviders">
   <paletteProvider
      class=
"org.eclipse.gmf.runtime.diagram.ui.providers.DefaultPaletteProvider">
      <Priority name="Highest"/>
      <editor
       id="org.eclipse.mindmap.diagram.editor.MindmapDiagramEditorID"/>
      <contribution
        factoryClass="org.eclipse.mindmap.diagram.providers.
          MindmapPaletteFactory">
      <entry id="nodeDrawer"
            label="Nodes"
            kind="drawer"
            description="Mindmap diagram nodes"
            path="/"
            small_icon="icons/obj16/MindmapDiagramFile.gif">
          <expand>
              <content/>
          </expand>
      </entry>
      <entry id="Topic"
            label="Topic"
            kind="tool"
            description="Create a new Topic"
            path="/nodeDrawer/"
            small_icon="icons/obj16/MindmapDiagramFile.gif"/>
      </contribution>
   </paletteProvider>
</extension>
```

We've declared a factory class `MindmapPaletteFactory` that we need to implement, along with a node drawer entry with a single `Topic` tool. Following is the implementation of our factory class, which extends the inner class

`PaletteFactory.Adapter` provided by the runtime. Note the aforementioned reference to the `IElementType` for our `Topic` domain element being passed as a constructor argument to the GMF runtime's `CreationTool` class.

```
public class MindmapPaletteFactory extends PaletteFactory.Adapter {

    @Override
    public Tool createTool(String toolId) {
        if (toolId.equals("Topic")) {
            return new CreationTool(MindmapElementTypes.TOPIC);
        }
        return null;
    }
}
```

View Definition

As you learned earlier, the creation tool of the palette first creates a domain element and then views using the view service. For this, we need to contribute to the `org.eclpse.gmf.runtime.diagram.core.viewProviders` extension-point. Below, we declare the contribution and our `MindmapViewProvider` class, which we will need to implement.

```
<extension point="org.eclipse.gmf.runtime.diagram.core.viewProviders">
    <viewProvider
        class="org.eclipse.mindmap.diagram.providers.MindmapViewProvider">
            <Priority name="Lowest"/>
    </viewProvider>
</extension>
```

Our `MindmapViewProvider` extends the provided `AbstractView Provider` and overrides the `getNodeViewClass()` and `getDiagramView Class()` methods. These methods use the `semanticHint` parameters to return the appropriate `ViewFactory` classes for the `Topic` node diagram, respectively.

```
public class MindmapViewProvider extends AbstractViewProvider {

    private final Map<String, Class<?>> diagramMap = new
        HashMap<String,
    Class<?>>();
    {
        diagramMap.put(MindmapDiagramEditor.ID,
DiagramViewFactory.class);
    }
```

```java
private final Map<String, Class<?>> nodeMap = new HashMap<String,
  Class<?>>();
  {
    nodeMap.put("Topic", TopicViewFactory.class);
  }

@Override
protected Class getDiagramViewClass(IAdaptable semanticAdapter,
  String diagramKind) {
  return diagramMap.get(diagramKind);
}

@Override
protected Class getNodeViewClass(IAdaptable semanticAdapter,
  View containerView, String semanticHint) {
  Class clazz = null;
  if (semanticHint != null && semanticHint.length() > 0) {
    clazz = nodeMap.get(semanticHint);
  }
  return clazz;
}
}
```

Note that as an alternative to using the `semanticHint` obtained from the `elementType` contribution in our plug-in manifest, we could use the `getSemanticEClass(semanticAdapter)` method to resolve the semantic element. Of course, we'd then have to modify our `Map` storage to use the `EClass` as the key, as shown here:

```java
private final Map<EClass, Class<?>> nodeMap = new HashMap<EClass,
Class<?>>();
{
  nodeMap.put(MindmapPackage.eINSTANCE.getTopic(),
    TopicViewFactory.class);
}

@Override
protected Class getNodeViewClass(IAdaptable semanticAdapter,
    View containerView, String semanticHint) {
  return nodeMap.get(getSemanticEClass(semanticAdapter));
}
```

The `TopicViewFactory` extends the provided `AbstractShapeView Factory` but provides no additional capabilities. The provided `DiagramView Factory` suffices for our mindmap's diagram view class.

At this point, we have registered `IElementTypes` that correspond to our domain model elements and are referenced by our creation tools in our palette. When creating a `Topic` on the diagram, the creation tool invokes a compound command that creates our domain element instance and passes it to the view service. The view service uses our registered `MindmapViewProvider` and obtains our `TopicViewFactory` based on the provided semanticHint.

For further clarification on how the runtime knows to create a new `Topic` object and store it in the proper feature in our `Map` class, let's take a closer look at the compound command that the creation tool uses and see how it works. First, we need to cover our `EditPart` definition.

EditPart Definition

We must define our `EditParts` for the diagram, which are provided by contributing to the `org.eclipse.gmf.runtime.diagram.ui.editpart Providers` extension-point. As with our view provider, we declare a provider class that we need to implement.

```
<extension
   point="org.eclipse.gmf.runtime.diagram.ui.editpartProviders">
   <editpartProvider class=
       "org.eclipse.mindmap.diagram.providers.MindmapEditPartProvider">
    <Priority name="Lowest"/>
 </editpartProvider>
</extension>
```

The implementation of our `MindmapEditPartProvider` is similar to that of our `ViewProvider`, with a `HashMap` that contains our shape `EditPart` classes keyed by their `semanticHint`, which is available from the passed `View` using the `getType()` method. For now, we have only a single entry for our `Topic` element. Our diagram `EditPart` is simply the default `DiagramEdit Part` class that the runtime provides.

```
public class MindmapEditPartProvider extends AbstractEditPartProvider {

private final Map<String, Class<?>> diagramMap = new HashMap<String,
   Class<?>>();
   {
     diagramMap.put(MindmapDiagramEditor.ID, DiagramEditPart.class);
   }

private final Map<String, Class<?>> shapeMap = new HashMap<String,
   Class<?>>();
   {
     shapeMap.put("Topic", TopicEditPart.class);
   }

   @Override
   protected Class getDiagramEditPartClass(View view) {
```

```
    return diagramMap.get(view.getType());
  }

  @Override
  protected Class getNodeEditPartClass(View view) {
    return shapeMap.get(view.getType());
  }
}
```

Here again, we could replace the use of the `semanticHint` as the key by the `EClass` of the element. The `EClass` can be resolved from the `View` using the provided `getReferencedElementEClass()` method, as shown here:

```
private final Map<EClass, Class<?>> shapeMap = new HashMap<EClass,

Class<?>>();
{
  shapeMap.put(MindmapPackage.eINSTANCE.getTopic(),
    TopicEditPart.class);
}

@Override
protected Class getNodeEditPartClass(View view) {
  Class clazz = null;
  final EClass eClass = getReferencedElementEClass(view);
  clazz = shapeMap.get(eClass);
  return clazz;
}
```

Taking a look at the provided `DiagramEditPart` class, you can see in its `createDefaultEditPolicies()` method that it installs a `CreationEdit Policy`. When our creation tool is selected in the palette, the `Topic IElementType` is set on the tool. When the mouse hovers over the diagram, the installed `CreationEditPolicy` on the `DiagramEditPart` receives a `CreateViewAndElementRequest` and returns a `CompositeCommand` containing a `SemanticCreateCommand`. Because we haven't specified the containment feature of our `Map` class in which to hold new `Topic` objects, the runtime uses the `PackageUtil.findFeature()` method to discover one. In our case, only one is appropriate: the `elements` containment reference. If there were multiple options, or if we wanted to explicitly declare the containment feature, we could provide our own `EditPolicy` that would set the containment feature on the request before creating the command. Or we could add an `EditHelper` for the `Map` class that would return the proper containment feature by overriding the `getDefaultContainmentFeature()` method.

The `getNodeEditPartClass()` method is passed a `View` object that, in turn, is passed to the `getReferencedElementEClass()` method of the superclass. The `View` object's element `EClass` is resolved and returned for use in retrieving the proper `EditPart` class from the shapeMap.

As you can see, we need to provide a `TopicEditPart` class. As usual, we extend a class provided by the runtime that offers most of the functionality we need. In this case, our `TopicEditPart` extends `ShapeNodeEditPart` and overrides `createNodeFigure()` to return a `DefaultSizeNodeFigure` with a child `RoundedRectangle` to provide the main figure.

```
public class TopicEditPart extends ShapeNodeEditPart {

  public TopicEditPart(View view) {
    super(view);
  }

  @Override
  protected NodeFigure createNodeFigure() {
    final NodeFigure figure = new
  DefaultSizeNodeFigure(getMapMode()
  .DPtoLP(40), getMapMode().DPtoLP(40));
    figure.setLayoutManager(new StackLayout());
    figure.add(new TopicFigure());
    return figure;
  }

  public class TopicFigure extends RoundedRectangle {
    public TopicFigure() {
      this.setCornerDimensions(new
        Dimension(getMapMode().DPtoLP(10), getMapMode().DPtoLP(10)));
    }
  }
}
```

Continuing from the last section, when a new `Topic` domain element and view are created, the diagram's `EditPart` receives the notification event and refreshes its children. As a `View` notification event, there is not yet an `EditPart` for the new domain element, so it invokes the `EditPartFactory` to create a new one and add it to its list of children. As you can see from the earlier `TopicEditPart` class, a new `RoundedRectangle` figure is created and displayed on the diagram.

New Diagram Wizard

To test our diagram, we need a wizard to create and initialize a new diagram editor instance. First, we contribute to the `org.eclipse.ui.newWizards` extension-point declaring a new `MindmapDiagramCreationWizard` that

extends the provided `org.eclipse.gmf.runtime.diagram.ui.`
`resources.editor.ide.wizards.EditorCreationWizard`.

```
<extension point="org.eclipse.ui.newWizards">
   <wizard
      category="org.eclipse.ui.Examples"
      class=
    "org.eclipse.mindmap.diagram.wizards.MindmapDiagramCreationWizard"
      icon="icons/obj16/MindmapDiagramFile.gif"
      id="org.eclipse.mindmap.diagram.wizards.MindmapCreationWizardID"
      name="%newWizardName">
      <description>%newWizardDesc</description>
   </wizard>
</extension>
```

You can see the implementation of the wizard in the provided sample code. Basically, the wizard provides a location and name selection page, with the option of separating the diagram and domain model into distinct files. By default, the two models are persisted into the same file, which our `MindmapDiagramEditor` initializes and opens.

If we launch the runtime workbench and test our diagram thus far, we can see that we can create a diagram using this wizard and add `Topic` elements to the diagram. We cannot set any properties yet, so we'll configure those next.

10.8.2 Configuring the Properties View

To configure a properties view for our diagram, we leverage the platform's tabbed properties extension-points. As shown shortly, `org.eclipse.ui.` `views.properties.tabbed propertyContributor`, `propertyTabs`, and `propertySections` extension-points are used to provide basic domain model properties for our diagram.

For the `propertyTab` contribution, we assign the `org.eclipse.` `mindmap.diagram` contributor ID that will be referenced in the remaining contributions. A `propertyTab` element in the domain category is declared, for which we'll configure a `propertyContributor` here:

```
<extension point="org.eclipse.ui.views.properties.tabbed.propertyTabs">
      <propertyTabs contributorId="org.eclipse.mindmap.diagram">
         <propertyTab
            category="domain"
            id="property.tab.domain"
            label="%tab.domain"/>
      </propertyTabs>
</extension>
```

The label provider is declared to be the `MindmapSheetLabelProvider` class, which we need to implement. The contributor ID and category match our `propertyTabs` definition. Following the extension-point contribution is the implementation of the label provider, which extends `DecoratingLabel Provider` and mainly consists of unwrapping methods to adapt our underlying EMF models.

```xml
<extension point=
    "org.eclipse.ui.views.properties.tabbed.propertyContributor">
    <propertyContributor
        contributorId="org.eclipse.mindmap.diagram"
        labelProvider=
          "org.eclipse.mindmap.diagram.sheet.MindmapSheetLabelProvider">
        <propertyCategory category="domain"/>
    </propertyContributor>
</extension>
```

```java
public class MindmapSheetLabelProvider extends DecoratingLabelProvider
{

  public MindmapSheetLabelProvider() {
    super(new AdapterFactoryLabelProvider(
      MindmapDiagramEditorPlugin.getInstance().
      getItemProvidersAdapterFactory()), null);
  }

  @Override
  public String getText(Object element) {
    final Object selected = unwrap(element);
    return super.getText(selected);
  }

  @Override
  public Image getImage(Object element) {
    return super.getImage(unwrap(element));
  }

  private Object unwrap(Object element) {
    if (element instanceof IStructuredSelection) {
      return unwrap(((IStructuredSelection)
          element).getFirstElement());
    }
    if (element instanceof EditPart) {
      return unwrapEditPart((EditPart) element);
    }
    if (element instanceof IAdaptable) {
      final View view = (View) ((IAdaptable)
          element).getAdapter(View.class);
      if (view != null) {
        return unwrapView(view);
      }
```

```
    }
    return element;
  }

  private Object unwrapEditPart(EditPart p) {
    if (p.getModel() instanceof View) {
      return unwrapView((View) p.getModel());
    }
    return p.getModel();
  }

  private Object unwrapView(View view) {
    return view.getElement() == null ? view : view.getElement();
  }
}
```

As you can see, we need to add an `AdapterFactory` for our plug-in, which can be configured in our `MindmapDiagramEditorPlugin` class, as shown here:

```
private ComposedAdapterFactory adapterFactory;
@Override
public void start(BundleContext context) throws Exception {
  super.start(context);
  instance = this;
  adapterFactory = createAdapterFactory();
}

protected ComposedAdapterFactory createAdapterFactory() {
final List<AdapterFactoryImpl> factories = new
    ArrayList<AdapterFactoryImpl>();
  factories.add(new MindmapItemProviderAdapterFactory());
  factories.add(new ResourceItemProviderAdapterFactory());
  factories.add(new ReflectiveItemProviderAdapterFactory());
  return new ComposedAdapterFactory(factories);
}

public AdapterFactory getItemProvidersAdapterFactory() {
  return adapterFactory;
}
```

The `propertySections` contribution appears here, along with the implementation of our `MindmapPropertySection` class. Input types are declared to be GEF `EditPart` types because they will be selected on our diagram. The implementation of `MindmapPropertySection` is standard for most diagrams and can be seen in generated code for the mindmap diagram.

```
<extension
point="org.eclipse.ui.views.properties.tabbed.propertySections">
    <propertySections contributorId="org.eclipse.mindmap.diagram">
        <propertySection
            id="property.section.domain"
            tab="property.tab.domain"
            class=
            "org.eclipse.mindmap.diagram.sheet.MindmapPropertySection">
            <input type="org.eclipse.gef.EditPart"/>
        </propertySection>
    </propertySections>
</extension>
```

We can easily configure additional provided property tabs and content contribution. Take a look at generated diagram code to see the contribution of visual property tabs and content for diagram appearance, rulers, grid, and so on.

10.8.3 Connections

We need to provide linking between `Topic` elements to establish subtopic relationships. We begin by extending our `paletteProviders` contribution to include a link drawer and tool, as seen here:

```
<entry id="linkDrawer"
        label="%palette.link.drawer.label"
        kind="drawer"
        description="%palette.link.drawer.desc"
        path="/"
        small_icon="icons/obj16/Link.gif">
    <expand>
        <content/>
    </expand>
</entry>
<entry id="Subtopic"
        label="%palette.link.label"
        kind="tool"
        description="%palette.link.desc"
        path="/linkDrawer/"
        small_icon="icons/obj16/Link.gif"/>
```

Next, we revisit our `MindmapPaletteFactory` to add the corresponding tool for this palette entry. This time, we use the `ConnectionCreationTool`, passing our soon-to-be-created `SUBTOPIC` element type.

```
public Tool createTool(String toolId) {
  if (toolId.equals("Topic")) {
    return new CreationTool(MindmapElementTypes.TOPIC);
```

```
    }
  if (toolId.equals("Subtopic")) {
    return new ConnectionCreationTool(MindmapElementTypes.SUBTOPIC);
  }
  return null;
}
```

In our `MindmapElementTypes` class, we add the new type, referencing an ID that we'll next add to our `elementTypes` extension.

```
public class MindmapElementTypes extends AbstractElementTypeEnumerator
{
  public static final IElementType MAP =
     getElementType("org.eclipse.mindmap.diagram.Map");
  public static final IElementType TOPIC =
     getElementType("org.eclipse.mindmap.diagram.Topic");
  public static final IElementType SUBTOPIC =
     getElementType("org.eclipse.mindmap.diagram.Subtopic");
}
```

```
<extension point="org.eclipse.gmf.runtime.emf.type.core.elementTypes">
    <metamodel nsURI="http://www.eclipse.org/2008/mindmap">
       <!-- ... -->
    <specializationType
          id="org.eclipse.mindmap.diagram.Subtopic"
          icon="icons/obj16/Link.gif"
          name="Subtopic"
          kind="org.eclipse.gmf.runtime.emf.type.core.IHintedType">
          <param name="semanticHint" value="Subtopic"/>
          <specializes
              id="org.eclipse.gmf.runtime.emf.type.core.null"/>
       </specializationType>
    </metamodel>
</extension>
```

The important point to note is that we've added a `specializationType` entry for our `Subtopic` element. The reason is that it represents a reference element in an existing element type, not an `EClass` itself. Our `Relationship` element in the mindmap model is a full `EClass` and is declared using the `elementType` element, as is the case with our `Map` and `Topic`. Note also that the specializes element declares an ID of `org.eclipse.gmf.runtime.emf.type.core.null`. This is the ID used in cases such as this, where the `specializationType` is represents a reference element. As before, we include the `semanticHint` parameter, which we'll see used in our `MindmapViewProvider`.

We know from Section 10.6, "Element Creation" that the semantic elements are created first when creating elements in our diagram. And, since our subtopic link represents a subtopics relationship element of our `Topic` class, we should consider adding a `SemanticEditPolicy` to our `TopicEditPart` in order to create the appropriate `CreateRelationshipCommand` for the subtopic link. If we were using GEF alone, we would use the `installEditPolicy()` method to do this; in GMF, we could use `createDefaultEditPolicies()`. However, we have an `editpolicyProvider` extension-point and Service in GMF that we can configure for this purpose, without requiring us to modify our `TopicEditPart`. Below is the contribution to the extension-point we will add to our `plugin.xml` file.

```
<extension
point="org.eclipse.gmf.runtime.diagram.ui.editpolicyProviders">
<editpolicyProvider
class=
"org.eclipse.mindmap.diagram.providers.MindmapEditPolicyProvider">
<Priority name="Lowest"/>
</editpolicyProvider>
</extension>
```

Our `MindmapEditPolicyProvider` class follows. We override the `createEditPolicies()` method to reinstall the new `TopicSemanticEdit Policy` on our `TopicEditPart`. We use the `provides()` method that declares this offering.

```
public class MindmapEditPolicyProvider extends AbstractProvider

implements IEditPolicyProvider {

  public void createEditPolicies(EditPart editPart) {
    if (editPart instanceof TopicEditPart) {

editPart.installEditPolicy(EditPolicyRoles.SEMANTIC_ROLE, new
        TopicSemanticEditPolicy());
    }
  }

  public boolean provides(IOperation operation) {
    if (operation instanceof CreateEditPoliciesOperation) {
      CreateEditPoliciesOperation op =
(CreateEditPoliciesOperation)operation;
      if (op.getEditPart() instanceof TopicEditPart) {
        return true;
      }
    }
    return false;
  }
}
```

For the implementation of the `TopicSemanticEditPolicy` class, we need only override the `getSemanticCommand()` method and check for an incoming `CreateRelationshipRequest`, returning a properly configured SubtopicCreateCommand wrapped in an `ICommandProxy`. We compare the element type of the request against our `Subtopic` element type, along with the values for source and target to return the proper command. Looking at our SubtopicCreateCommand, we find the logic that determines whether the returned command is executable.

```java
public class SubtopicCreateCommand extends EditElementCommand {

  private final EObject source;
  private final EObject target;

  public SubtopicCreateCommand(CreateRelationshipRequest request,
      EObject source, EObject target) {
    super(request.getLabel(), null, request);
    this.source = source;
    this.target = target;
  }

  public boolean canExecute() {
    if (source == null && target == null) {
      return false;
    }
    if (source != null && !(source instanceof Topic)) {
      return false;
    }
    if (target != null && !(target instanceof Topic)) {
      return false;
    }
    if (target == source) {
      return false;
    }
    return true;
  }

  protected CommandResult doExecuteWithResult(
  IProgressMonitor monitor,
  IAdaptable info) throws ExecutionException {
    if (!canExecute()) {
      throw new ExecutionException(
"Invalid arguments in create link command");
    }
    if (getSource() != null && getTarget() != null) {
      getSource().getSubtopics().add(getTarget());
    }
    return CommandResult.newOKCommandResult();
  }

  protected Topic getSource() {
```

```
    return (Topic) source;
  }

  protected Topic getTarget() {
    return (Topic) target;
  }
}
```

From `canExecute()`, we see that if the request source and target do not conform to the appropriate type (Topic, in this case), `false` is returned. A `false` is also returned if the target `Topic` is the same as the source `Topic` because it doesn't make sense for a `Topic` to be a subtopic of itself. Other validation could take place here, such as ensuring that the target is not already found in the source's subtopics reference.

The command extends the provided `EditElementCommand`, and we see how the target is added to the subtopics reference in `doExecuteWithResult()`. Now that we understand how the underlying semantic command is provided and validated against the model, it's time to look at the `View` and `EditPart` aspects of our `Subtopic` link.

Our `MindmapViewProvider` must be augmented to deal with edge views. We can add another `Map` for diagram edges and initialize it with the provided `ConnectionViewFactory` class, keyed to our `Subtopic` semantic hint, as shown here:

```
public class MindmapViewProvider extends AbstractViewProvider {

  private final Map<String, Class<?>> edgeMap = new HashMap<String,
  Class<?>>();
  {
    edgeMap.put("Subtopic", ConnectionViewFactory.class);
  }

  // . . .

  @Override
  protected Class getEdgeViewClass(IAdaptable semanticAdapter,
    View containerView, String semanticHint) {
    Class clazz = null;
    if (semanticHint != null && semanticHint.length() > 0) {
      clazz = edgeMap.get(semanticHint);
    }
    return clazz;
  }
}
```

In our `MindmapEditPartProvider`, we similarly add a `Map` and override `getEdgeEditPart()` to return our new `SubtopicEditPart` class.

```
public class MindmapEditPartProvider extends AbstractEditPartProvider {

  private final Map<String, Class<?>> edgeMap = new HashMap<String,
  Class<?>>();
  {
    edgeMap.put("Subtopic", SubtopicEditPart.class);
  }

  // . . .

  @Override
  protected Class getEdgeEditPartClass(View view) {
    return (Class) edgeMap.get(view.getType());
  }
}
```

Finally, we add our `SubtopicEditPart`, which simply returns a new `PolylineConnectionEx` as our link figure.

```
public class SubtopicEditPart extends ConnectionNodeEditPart {

  public SubtopicEditPart(View view) {
    super(view);
  }

  @Override
  protected Connection createConnectionFigure() {
    if (getModel() == null) {
      return null;
    }

    Connection connection = new PolylineConnectionEx();
    return connection;
  }
}
```

At this point, we can draw `Topic` rectangles and solid links between them to signify subtopic relationships, as shown in Figure 10-53. Without labels to indicate our `Topic` names on the diagram, it's still not terribly useful. Providing usable labels requires a bit of work that we'd rather generate, so let's move to the next section and compare this manual implementation of a simple mindmap with that generated by the tooling component. For another example of contributing a parser provider for labels, see Section 4.6.7, "Custom Parsers."

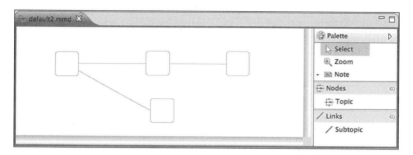

Figure 10-53 Basic mindmap diagram

10.8.4 Comparison to Generated Diagram

Now that we've manually created a diagram using the GMF runtime, let's compare the result with what the tooling component of GMF is generating. If we define a simple mindmap graphical, tooling, mapping, and generator model (see Section 4.3.4, "Mindmap Generator Model"), we can observe what is generated with what was created above by hand. Note that what's described below is only for a simple mapping of the `Topic` element to a node, subtopics relationship mapped to a link, and topic name label. No advanced options (such as printing support, shortcuts, audits, metrics, and so on) were selected, which would cause even more to be generated.

The generated diagram contributes extensions to a number of runtime extension-points, including `contributionItemProviders`, `globalAction HandlerProviders`, `iconProviders`, `parserProviders`, `viewProviders`, `editpartProviders`, `elementTypes`, `elementTypeBindings`, and `modelingAssistantProviders`. Notably missing are the `editpolicy Providers` and `paletteProviders` contributions. The tooling team did not think these were necessary, opting instead to add generated `EditPolicy` contributions directly in `EditParts` and generating a `PaletteFactory` implementation from the gmftool model directly. Figure 10-54 shows the runtime extension-points contributed to by the initial mindmap diagram defined in Chapter 4.

In addition to providing labels with parser providers for in-place editing, the generated diagram provides diagram preferences, generic navigator support, link reorientation commands, diagram initialization from an existing domain model instance, a diagram update command, and several other features. For larger diagrams with many domain elements and diagram representation, clearly, beginning with the tooling models and generating the base implementation is the preferred approach. For more information on producing diagrams using the tooling and extending the generative approach, see Chapter 4 and Chapter 11, "Graphical Modeling Framework Tooling."

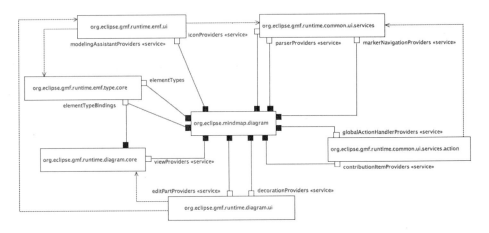

Figure 10-54   Mindmap generated extension-point contributions

10.9 Extending Diagrams

You learned in Section 4.3.5, "Adding Custom Layout," that it's possible to extend an existing diagram through the use of a customization plug-in. In this case, we were able to add a custom layout to our Mindmap diagram, along with an Insert Subtopic action using standard Eclipse UI contribution techniques. In Section 4.6.7, "Custom Parsers," we similarly were able contribute a custom parser for attributes in our Color Modeling diagram. In this section, we continue the extension story and demonstrate how to add custom figures to an existing diagram. Specifically, we add an SVG version of the BPMN Intermediate Event node for use in our Scenario diagram.

10.9.1 Scenario Diagram Custom View and Edit Providers

We begin by creating a new plug-in project named `org.eclipse.scenario.diagram.custom` in our workspace. Add a dependency to our `org.eclipse.scenario.diagram` plug-in, along with `org.eclipse.gmf.runtime.diagram.ui` and `org.eclipse.gmf.runtime.draw2d.ui.render`. To override the default `View` and `EditPart` providers in the generated diagram, we need to contribute our own providers and implementation classes in our customization plug-in. Beginning in the Extensions tab of our plug-in manifest editor, add a new `viewProviders` and `editpartProviders` extensions to match what's shown here. Notice that the `Priority` of both providers is set to `Medium`, thereby ensuring that they will override our generated providers, which are set to `Lowest`.

```
<plugin>
   <extension
        point="org.eclipse.gmf.runtime.diagram.core.viewProviders">
      <viewProvider
         class="org.eclipse.scenario.diagram.custom.providers.
         ScenarioViewProvider">
         <Priority name="Medium"/>
         <context viewClass="org.eclipse.gmf.runtime.notation.Node"
          semanticHints=""/>
      </viewProvider>
   </extension>
   <extension
      point="org.eclipse.gmf.runtime.diagram.ui.editpartProviders">
      <editpartProvider
         class="org.eclipse.scenario.diagram.custom.providers.
         ScenarioEditPartProvider">
         <Priority name="Medium"/>
      </editpartProvider>
   </extension>
</plugin>
```

We need to provide our two classes specified. The `ScenarioViewProvider` appears next and overrides the `getNodeViewClass()` method to return an `IntermediateEventImageViewFactory` class when the passed element's visual ID matches that of our `Event2EditPart`. This is the `EditPart` that represents the Intermediate Event nodes on our diagram, although we should probably return to our `scenario.gmfgen` model and give each `Event` a more descriptive name. This is the default naming scheme that the GMF generator applies when a single domain element represents multiple elements in the diagram.

TIP

The default `Export-Package` list in the `MANIFEST.MF` of a generated diagram plug-in includes only the `*.edit.parts`, `*.part`, and `*.providers` packages. If you expect that your diagram will be extended, such as in the manner described here, you must export additional packages before shipping your diagram.

```java
public class ScenarioViewProvider extends AbstractViewProvider {

  @Override
  protected Class getNodeViewClass(IAdaptable semanticAdapter, View
    containerView, String semanticHint) {
    if (containerView == null) {
      return null;
    }

    EObject semanticElement = getSemanticElement(semanticAdapter);
    int nodeVID =
        ScenarioVisualIDRegistry.getNodeVisualID(containerView,
        semanticElement);
    if (nodeVID == Event2EditPart.VISUAL_ID) {
      return IntermediateEventImageViewFactory.class;
    }
    return null;
  }
}
```

Technically, our `ViewFactory` is not required right now, but later we can override the `decorateView()` method to add custom style information. For now, simply create this class in a `*.custom.factories` package and extend the generated `Event2ViewFactory` class.

Our new `ScenarioEditPartProvider` class follows, with its override of method `getNodeEditPartClass()`. If the passed `View`'s domain model element is an instance of `Event` and its `type` is `INTERMEDIATE`, we return our `IntermediateEventImageEditPart` class.

```java
public class ScenarioEditPartProvider extends AbstractEditPartProvider {

  @Override
  protected Class getNodeEditPartClass(View view) {
    if (view.getElement() instanceof Event && ((Event)
      view.getElement()).getEventType().getValue() ==
      EventType.INTERMEDIATE_VALUE) {
      return IntermediateEventImageEditPart.class;
    }
    return super.getNodeEditPartClass(view);
  }
}
```

Our new `EditPart` class extends our `Event2EditPart` original and overrides the `createNodeShape()` method. As you can see here, an `ievent.svg` file is used to represent our intermediate event node, and it is located in an `/images` folder. Following is the EditPart code, followed by the `ievent.svg` file content. As you can see, we added a gradient effect to our SVG so that we can distinguish this figure from the original.

```
public class IntermediateEventImageEditPart extends Event2EditPart {

  public IntermediateEventImageEditPart(View view) {
    super(view);
  }

  protected IFigure createNodeShape() {
    URL url = FileLocator.find(Activator.getDefault().getBundle(),
        new Path("images" + IPath.SEPARATOR + "ievent.svg"), null);
      return new
        ScalableImageFigure(RenderedImageFactory.getInstance(url),
        true, true, true);
  }
}
```

```
<?xml version="1.0" standalone="no"?>
<!DOCTYPE svg PUBLIC "-//W3C//DTD SVG 1.1//EN"
"http://www.w3.org/Graphics/SVG/1.1/DTD/svg11.dtd">
<svg width="20" height="20" version="1.1"
xmlns="http://www.w3.org/2000/svg">
 <defs>
     <linearGradient id="blue_white" x1="0%" y1="0%"
     x2="100%" y2="0%">
            <stop offset="0%"
            style="stop-color:rgb(0,0,255);stop-opacity:1"/>
            <stop offset="100%" style="stop-color:rgb(255,255,255);
            stop-opacity:1"/>
     </linearGradient>
 </defs>
 <circle cx="10" cy="10" r="9" style="fill:white; stroke:black;
    stroke-width:1"/>
 <circle cx="10" cy="10" r="7" style="fill:url(#blue_white);
    stroke:black; stroke-width:1"/>
</svg>
```

If we launch our runtime instance, you'll see that our new intermediate event figure is displayed in place of our original figure. This very simple extension shows the usefulness of the service provider framework of the runtime for modifying an existing diagram. However, our Practitioner might prefer the original figure or would like to switch between the two. We'll add this capability through a menu action on our figure, allowing us to demonstrate the contributionItemProviders extension-point.

10.9.2 Custom Style

To add an action that facilitates the switching of figures for our intermediate event, we need someplace to store the current state. Clearly, the underlying domain model is an inappropriate place to store information regarding the visual display of its information, which leaves us with the runtime's notation model. As we saw from the discussion in Section 10.2, "Notation Model," the Style element can be extended to store the additional information we need. While we're at it, we'll add a field to store a URL to allow hyperlinking from our notation element to an external source.

TIP

Adding a new `Style` is one approach, but note that the `View` element of the runtime's notation model extends `ecore::EModelElement` and, therefore, is capable of holding `EAnnotation` elements. So instead of adding a new style, we could just create a new annotation on our `View` element and use that to hold additional information. In fact, the generated diagrams use this approach for shortcut decorators.

In a new `/model` folder within our custom diagram plug-in, we can create a `style.ecore` Ecore model. We' only need to create a single class named `CustomStyle` with `default:EBoolean` and `hyperlink:EString` attributes. Using **Load Resource** we'll browse the registered models and select our GMF runtime notation model, identified by its NS URI of `http://www.eclipse.org/gmf/runtime/1.0.1/notation`. Our `CustomStyle` class needs to extend the `Style` class in the notation model. Create an EMF generator model named `style.genmodel` and set the `Base Package` property of the style package to `org.eclipse.scenario.diagram.custom`. Generating the model code only to our custom diagram plug-in enables us to move forward with implementing our action for switching figures. In our `plugin.xml` file, we'll create a new extension to the `contributionItemProviders` extension-point.

```
<extension point="org.eclipse.gmf.runtime.common.ui.services.action.
  contributionItemProviders">
  <contributionItemProvider
     class="org.eclipse.scenario.diagram.custom.providers.
     ContributionItemProvider">
     <Priority name="Medium"/>
     <popupContribution
        class="org.eclipse.gmf.runtime.diagram.ui.providers.
```

```
        DiagramContextMenuProvider">
        <popupStructuredContributionCriteria
           objectClass="org.eclipse.scenario.diagram.custom.edit.parts.
           IntermediateEventImageEditPart" />
        <popupAction path="/additions"
                     id="displayDefaultFigureAction"/>
     </popupContribution>
   </contributionItemProvider>
</extension>
```

The `ContributionItemProvider` class declared in the extension is shown next. It extends the abstract provider supplied by the runtime and returns a new `DisplayDefaultFigureAction` class that we'll add to the `*.diagram.custom.actions` package. The action extends the provided `BooleanProperty Action` class, leaving us with just an ID field and initialization to add.

```
public class ContributionItemProvider extends
AbstractContributionItemProvider {

  protected IAction createAction(String actionId,
    IWorkbenchPartDescriptor partDescriptor) {
    if (actionId.equals(DisplayDefaultFigureAction.ID)) {
      return new
         DisplayDefaultFigureAction(partDescriptor.getPartPage());
    }
    return super.createAction(actionId, partDescriptor);
  }
}

public class DisplayDefaultFigureAction extends BooleanPropertyAction {

  static public final String ID = "displayDefaultFigureAction";

  public DisplayDefaultFigureAction(IWorkbenchPage workbenchPage) {
    super(workbenchPage, PackageUtil.getID(
       StylePackage.eINSTANCE.getCustomStyle_Default()),
          "Display default image");
       setId(ID);
       setText("Display default image");
     setToolTipText("Use the default image display
     for this element");
  }
}
```

We need to add the `org.eclipse.gmf.runtime.diagram.ui.actions` plug-in to our dependencies list. The ID declared in our extension matches the ID field in our action class, which uses the ID of our `default:EBoolean` attribute of our `CustomStyle` class. We're also declaring that the contribution item menu is applicable for our custom `EditPart` class added earlier, with 'Display default image' added to its context menu. Returning to our `ViewFactory` class, we'll add the following overrides to decorate the view with our new `CustomStyle`.

```
public class IntermediateEventImageViewFactory extends
Event2ViewFactory {

  @Override
  protected void decorateView(View containerView, View view, IAdaptable
  semanticAdapter, String semanticHint, int index, boolean persisted) {
    super.decorateView(containerView, view, semanticAdapter,
       semanticHint, index, persisted);
     CustomStyle style = (CustomStyle)
        view.getStyle(StylePackage.eINSTANCE.getCustomStyle());
     style.setDefault(false);
  }

  @Override
  protected List createStyles(View view) {
    List styles = super.createStyles(view);
    styles.add(StyleFactory.eINSTANCE.createCustomStyle());
    return styles;
  }
}
```

Our `EditPart` must be aware of the new `Style` element to create the appropriate figure. Additionally, as our action will set our `default:EBoolean` attribute in the `CustomStyle`, we'll need to respond to this event and update our model accordingly by overriding `handleNotificationEvent()`.

```
public class IntermediateEventImageEditPart extends Event2EditPart {

  public IntermediateEventImageEditPart(View view) {
    super(view);
  }

  protected IFigure createNodeShape() {
    CustomStyle style = (CustomStyle) getNotationView().getStyle(
        StylePackage.eINSTANCE.getCustomStyle());
    if (style == null || style.isDefault()) {
      return super.createNodeShape();
    }
    URL url = FileLocator.find(Activator.getDefault().getBundle(),
        new Path("images" + IPath.SEPARATOR + "ievent.svg"), null);
    return new ScalableImageFigure(
        RenderedImageFactory.getInstance(url), true, true, true);
  }

  protected void handleNotificationEvent(Notification notification) {
```

```
Object feature = notification.getFeature();
if (StylePackage.eINSTANCE.getCustomStyle_Default()
    .equals(feature)) {
  handleMajorSemanticChange();
} else {
  super.handleNotificationEvent(notification);
}
}
}
```

At this point, we can launch our runtime workspace and test our new action. At this point, we can launch our runtime workspace and test our new action. Figure 10-55 is an image of our SVG figure and the menu item that allows us to restore the original figure for display.

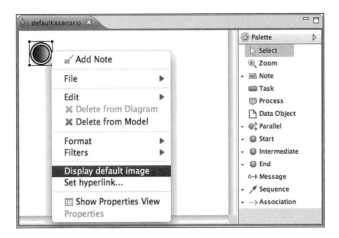

Figure 10-55   SVG image menu

10.9.3 Custom EditPolicy

We now add a custom `EditPolicy` to take advantage of the `hyperlink:EString` attribute on our `CustomStyle` notation element. We'll add the following contribution to the `editpolicyProviders` extension-point.

```
<extension
    point="org.eclipse.gmf.runtime.diagram.ui.editpolicyProviders">
  <editpolicyProvider
    class="org.eclipse.scenario.diagram.custom.providers.
    ScenarioEditPolicyProvider">
      <Priority name="High"/>
  </editpolicyProvider>
</extension>
```

The implementation of our provider appears next. For `EditParts` that are instances of our custom `IntermediateEventImageEditPart`, we install an `OpenHyperlinkEditPolicy` and assign it to the `OPEN_ROLE`. Therefore, double-click events on our node will trigger this new `EditPolicy`.

```
public class ScenarioEditPolicyProvider extends AbstractProvider

implements IEditPolicyProvider {

  public void createEditPolicies(EditPart editPart) {
    if (editPart instanceof IntermediateEventImageEditPart) {
      editPart.installEditPolicy(EditPolicyRoles.OPEN_ROLE,
        new OpenHyperlinkEditPolicy());
    }
  }

  public boolean provides(IOperation operation) {
    if (operation instanceof CreateEditPoliciesOperation) {
      CreateEditPoliciesOperation op =
          (CreateEditPoliciesOperation) operation;
      if (op.getEditPart() instanceof IntermediateEventImageEditPart)
      {
        return true;
      }
    }
    return false;
  }
}
```

The `OpenHyperlinkEditPolicy` follows, where the override of `getOpenCommand()` will return a `Command` that, when executed, opens the value of our hyperlink String in the underlying operating system's registered program—in this case, a browser for `http://` Strings.

```
public class OpenHyperlinkEditPolicy extends OpenEditPolicy {

  protected Command getOpenCommand(Request request) {
    return new Command("OpenHyperlinkCommand") {
      public void execute() {
        IGraphicalEditPart gep = (IGraphicalEditPart) getHost();
        CustomStyle style = (CustomStyle)
            gep.getNotationView().getStyle(
            StylePackage.eINSTANCE.getCustomStyle());
        if (style != null) {
          String location = style.getHyperlink();
          Program.launch(location);
        }
      }
    };
  }
}
```

The problem we face now is that there's no default way to access the custom style properties in our diagram. The standard properties view shows only domain model information, although the navigator gives us a read-only view of the CustomStyle and its property. We could extend our properties view to include our custom notation elements, or we could simply add another action that pops up a dialog to allow the Practitioner to enter a hyperlink. Because we already discussed custom property sheets in Section 4.4.6, "Properties Revisited," we take the second approach here.

To add a new context menu item on the node, we return to our contributionItemProviders extension contribution and add another entry. The setHyperlinkAction will be adjacent to our displayDefault FigureAction in the menu.

```
<popupContribution class="org.eclipse.gmf.runtime.diagram.ui.providers.
   DiagramContextMenuProvider">
   <popupStructuredContributionCriteria objectClass=
      "org.eclipse.scenario.diagram.custom.edit.parts.
      IntermediateEventImageEditPart"/>
   <popupAction path="/additions" id="setHyperlinkAction"/>
</popupContribution>
```

We need to augment the createAction() method in our Contribution ItemProvider for this new action ID, as shown here:

```
public class ContributionItemProvider extends
AbstractContributionItemProvider {

  protected IAction createAction(String actionId,
     IWorkbenchPartDescriptor partDescriptor) {
    if (actionId.equals(DisplayDefaultFigureAction.ID)) {
      return new
         DisplayDefaultFigureAction(partDescriptor.getPartPage());
    }
    if (actionId.equals(SetHyperlinkAction.ID)) {
      return new SetHyperlinkAction(partDescriptor.getPartPage());
    }   return super.createAction(actionId, partDescriptor);
  }
}
```

Finally, we need to implement the SetHyperlinkAction. We extend the runtime's PropertyChangeAction and initialize it with our hyperlink property ID, action ID, and text. Overriding the doRun() method lets us present the Practitioner with an InputDialog to provide the URL, which we use to update our target Request. We should probably add validation code, but this is fine for our contrived example.

```java
public class SetHyperlinkAction extends PropertyChangeAction {

  static public final String ID = "setHyperlinkAction";

  public SetHyperlinkAction(IWorkbenchPage workbenchPage) {
    super(workbenchPage, PackageUtil.getID(
      StylePackage.eINSTANCE.getCustomStyle_Hyperlink()),
      "Set hyperlink...");
    setId(ID);
    setText("Set hyperlink...");
    setToolTipText("Set a navigable hyperlink on this element");
  }

  @Override
  protected void doRun(IProgressMonitor progressMonitor) {
    String value = (String)
        getOperationSetPropertyValue(getPropertyId());
    ChangePropertyValueRequest request =
        (ChangePropertyValueRequest) getTargetRequest();
    final InputDialog inputDialog = new
        InputDialog(Display.getCurrent().getActiveShell(),
        "Hyperlink", "Enter the URL:", value, null);
    if (InputDialog.OK == inputDialog.open()) {
      request.setValue(inputDialog.getValue());
    } else {
      return;
    }
    super.doRun(progressMonitor);
  }

  @Override
  protected Object getNewPropertyValue() {
    String value = (String)
        getOperationSetPropertyValue(getPropertyId());
    if (value != null) {
      return value;
    }
    return null;
  }
}
```

BEST PRACTICE

By extending the `PropertyChangeAction` class, we've violated an Eclipse plug-in development best practice. The class is abstract and extended by public classes within the runtime, but it is itself located in an `*.internal.*` package namespace. The right thing to do would be extend from its public superclass `DiagramAction` and reimplement the functionality we need from `PropertyChangeAction`, or submit a bug to the GMF project and ask that the class be made an API.

Launching again to test our new action and dialog, we find that it works as desired, as shown in Figure 10-56. We are able to enter a new hyperlink value using the menu item, which marks the diagram as dirty, as we expect. A double-click of the node opens our Web browser to the specified address.

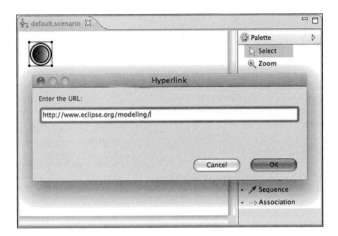

Figure 10-56 Hyperlink dialog

10.9.4 Custom Decorator

Continuing our tour of runtime extensibility, we now look at how to add a decorator to our event node to indicate to the Practitioner whether a hyperlink has been added. Currently, a double-click of an event does nothing if no hyperlink has been set, but there's no way to know that one has been set by looking at the diagram. We want a small decorator near the node that indicates that it has a hyperlink set. We can use the decorator service in our customization plug-in to accomplish the task. To begin, we contribute the following extension to our plugin.xml file:

```
<extension
   point="org.eclipse.gmf.runtime.diagram.ui.decoratorProviders">
   <decoratorProvider
      class="org.eclipse.scenario.diagram.custom.providers.
      LinkDecoratorProvider">
      <Priority name="Lowest"/>
   </decoratorProvider>
</extension>
```

Our `LinkDecoratorProvider` class appears next. It extends the `AbstractProvider` and implements the `IDecoratorProvider`. In both the `provides()` and `createDecorators()` methods, we use the `getDecorator` `TargetNode()` static method on our `LinkDecorator` class, which is listed below our provider code.

```java
public class LinkDecoratorProvider extends AbstractProvider implements
IDecoratorProvider {

  public static final String HYPERLINK_DECORATOR_ID = "hyperlink";

  public boolean provides(IOperation operation) {
    if (false == operation instanceof CreateDecoratorsOperation) {
      return false;
    }
    IDecoratorTarget decoratorTarget =
    ((CreateDecoratorsOperation) operation).getDecoratorTarget();
    return
    LinkDecorator.getDecoratorTargetNode(decoratorTarget) != null;
  }

  public void createDecorators(IDecoratorTarget decoratorTarget) {
    Node node =
    LinkDecorator.getDecoratorTargetNode(decoratorTarget);
    if (node != null) {
decoratorTarget.installDecorator(HYPERLINK_DECORATOR_ID, new
      LinkDecorator(decoratorTarget));
    }
  }
}

public class LinkDecorator extends AbstractDecorator {

  private static final Image LINK;

  static {
    URL url = FileLocator.find(Activator.getDefault().getBundle(),
        new Path("images" + IPath.SEPARATOR + "link.gif"), null);
    ImageDescriptor imgDesc = ImageDescriptor.createFromURL(url);
    LINK = imgDesc.createImage();
  }

  public LinkDecorator(IDecoratorTarget decoratorTarget) {
    super(decoratorTarget);
  }

  static public Node getDecoratorTargetNode(IDecoratorTarget
    decoratorTarget) {
    CustomStyle style = null;
    View node = (View) decoratorTarget.getAdapter(View.class);
    if (node != null && node.eContainer() instanceof Diagram) {
      style = (CustomStyle)
          node.getStyle(StylePackage.eINSTANCE.getCustomStyle());
      if (style != null) {
```

```
          return (Node) node;
        }
      }
      return null;
    }

  public void refresh() {
    removeDecoration();
    Node node = getDecoratorTargetNode(getDecoratorTarget());

    if (node != null) {
      CustomStyle style = (CustomStyle)
          node.getStyle(StylePackage.eINSTANCE.getCustomStyle());
      if (style != null) {
        boolean linked = style.getHyperlink() !=
          null && style.getHyperlink().length() > 0;
        if (linked) {

setDecoration(getDecoratorTarget().addShapeDecoration(
            LINK, IDecoratorTarget.Direction.NORTH_EAST, 1, false));
        }
      }
    }
  }

  private NotificationListener notificationListener = new
    NotificationListener() {

    public void notifyChanged(Notification notification) {
      refresh();
    }
  };

  public void activate() {
    IGraphicalEditPart gep = (IGraphicalEditPart)
        getDecoratorTarget().getAdapter(IGraphicalEditPart.class);
    assert gep != null;

    DiagramEventBroker.getInstance(
      gep.getEditingDomain()).addNotificationListener(
      gep.getNotationView(),
      StylePackage.eINSTANCE.getCustomStyle_Hyperlink(),
      notificationListener);
  }

  public void deactivate() {
    removeDecoration();

    IGraphicalEditPart gep = (IGraphicalEditPart)
        getDecoratorTarget().getAdapter(IGraphicalEditPart.class);
    assert gep != null;
     DiagramEventBroker.getInstance(
      gep.getEditingDomain()).removeNotificationListener(
      gep.getNotationView(), notificationListener);
  }
}
```

A static initializer loads our link image, which is just the Eclipse internal Web browser icon. The `getDecoratorTargetNode()` method returns the View node if it contains our `CustomStyle` added earlier. The `refresh()` method is responsible for installing the decorator on the node if the hyperlink property of our custom style is present. The decorator is added to the top-right corner of the node, as shown in Figure 10-57. Notice also from the code that a `NotificationListener` invokes the `refresh()` method, while the `activate()` and `deactivate()` methods add and remove the listener for our Custom Style hyperlink property, respectively.

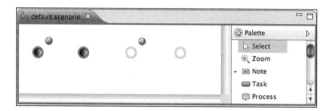

Figure 10-57   Figure decorator

10.10 Beyond GEF and Draw2d

In a number of places, the GMF runtime extends GEF. In this section, we look into the `org.eclipse.gmf.runtime.*gef*` and `*draw2d*` packages to see what additional layouts, figures, and so on are available from GMF. Some of these classes possibly will move into GEF in the future, and some of the elements currently found in `*.internal.*` namespaces might become public. Either way, they provide a good source of additional capabilities and inspiration for creating your own GEF elements.

Figure 10-58 is a diagram of the `org.eclipse.gmf.runtime.draw2d.ui.figures` package. You've seen some of these elements in our generated and custom code, such as the `OneLineBorder` and `WrappingLabel` classes.

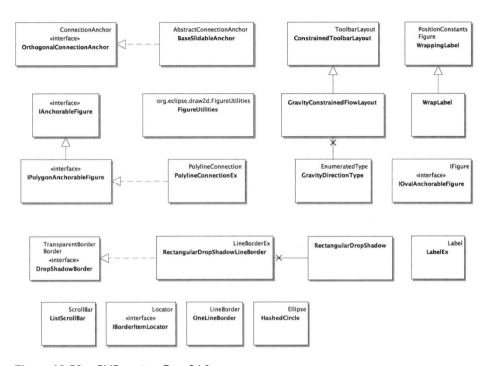

Figure 10-58   GMF runtime Draw2d figures

The `FigureUtilities` class is helpful when manipulating figures, converting between Color, RGB, and Integer values. Additional figures are available in the internal package, with those ending in `*Ex` providing Hi-Metric-enabled GEF alternatives. A number of other classes found in the `*.draw2d.ui` plug-in deal with Hi-Metric units, including the `IMapMode` interface. In the text package, extensions to the GEF text classes provide capabilities such as underlining, strikethrough, and truncation.

You saw some of the `org.eclipse.gmf.runtime.draw2d.render` and `*.render.awt` plug-ins in Section 10.9.1, "Scenario Diagram Custom View and Edit Providers," with the addition of an SVG figure. These plug-ins have image render factories, converters, and utilities.

The `org.eclipse.gmf.runtime.gef.ui` plug-in contains a number of public figures and palette customization classes. You can see the figures in Figure 10-59, and many additional figures are found in the corresponding `*.internal.*` package, including `CircleFigure`, `DiamondFigure`, and `OvalFigure`.

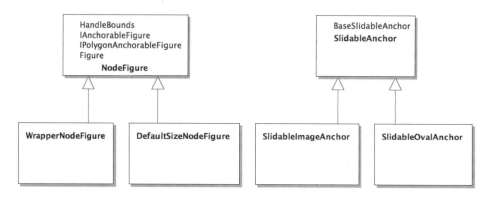

Figure 10-59   GMF runtime GEF figures

10.11 Summary

In this chapter, we took a look into the GMF runtime and its many provided services and APIs. We also included a discussion of how to start from scratch developing a diagram with the runtime and how to extend diagrams produced by the tooling or others. Next, we take a closer look at the generative GMF tooling component.

CHAPTER 11

Graphical Modeling Framework Tooling

This chapter covers each of the Graphical Modeling Framework (GMF) models in detail and is intended to be used as an Application Programming Interface (API) reference and usage guide. Each of the tooling models is described as exposed in the user interface instead of than by strict Ecore representation, to provide a more usable reference section.

11.1 Graphical Definition Model

The GMF graphical definition model (`gmfgraph.ecore`) is designed to be generic, although its constructs closely resemble that of the Graphical Editor Framework (GEF) project. Conceivably, GMF could target alternative graphical frameworks or technologies (such as Scalable Vector Graphics [SVG]), even though today it targets only GEF.

You can think of the graphical definition model as having three "layers": First, figures define visual representations of diagram elements. Second, figure descriptors and accessors reference figures in the first layer for use in the next. Third, diagram elements are defined for use in the mapping model and can contain element-specific layout information. These three layers provide flexibility in the graphical definition model because reuse is allowed throughout. Figures can be reused to construct other figures, figure descriptors can be used by multiple diagram elements, and the same diagram element can be used in multiple mappings.

Figure 11-1 illustrates the first two layers in the model. A `Figure Descriptor` maintains a containment reference to a figure, which can be either a `RealFigure` or a figure reference (`FigureRef`). A `FigureDescriptor` also can contain a number of `ChildAccess` elements, which, in turn, reference a figure. A `FigureRef` maintains a reference to a `RealFigure`, which can contain a number of children figures.

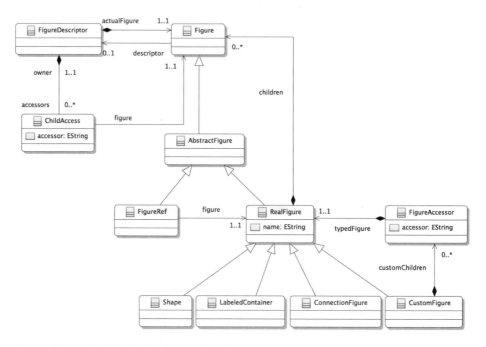

Figure 11-1   Graphical definition model—figures

Figure 11-2 illustrates the third layer and completes the previous figure. A `Canvas` contains a number of `FigureGallery` elements, which contain descriptors and figures. The `Canvas` also contains elements that represent diagram surface nodes, connections, compartments, and labels.

Looking at Figure 11-2 for reference, a `FigureGallery` contains `FigureDescriptor` and `RealFigure` elements. Both of these contain `Figure` elements, which can be either `FigureRef` or `RealFigure` elements. A `FigureRef` is a placeholder that references a `RealFigure` and provides a way to reuse figures in the gallery. `Figures` defined with a `FigureDescriptor` can be accessed using a `ChildAccess` element. The accessor is a method or field name.

Note that the `CustomFigure` element can contain a `FigureAccessor` that contains a `RealFigure`. This enables you to nest custom figures in the figure hierarchy because the provided method in the accessor returns an instance of the figure (as long as the custom figure declares such a method). Custom figures can be nested within other figures or can have other figures nested within them using provided accessor methods.

Consider the case of a label figure within another figure, such as a rectangle. A Figure Descriptor element is created in the Gallery and contains a Rectangle figure and a Child Access element with a reference to the nested Label figure. Generated figure code will contain a getter of the same name as the value of the Child Access element's accessor property. By default, this will be getFigure plus the name of the referenced child Figure.

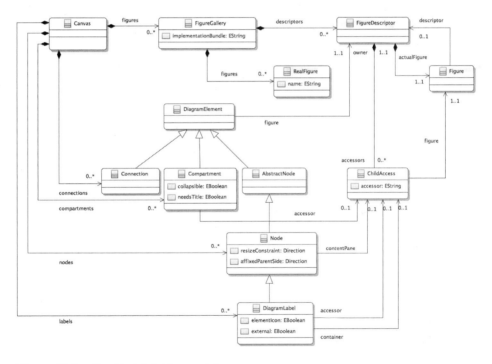

Figure 11-2   Graphical definition model—canvas

The graphical definition model has its own code-generation templates, which are invoked either during the creation/recreation of the GMF generator model or to generate a standalone figures plug-in. The model and its code-generation templates are found in the org.eclipse.gmf.graphdef and org.eclipse.gmf.graphdef.codegen plug-ins, respectively. Also found in the org.eclipse.gmf.graphdef plug-in are some standard models that contain figure definitions for basic, class diagram, and state machine diagram elements. Of course, the UML2 Tools project provides an extensive set of additional example GMF models.

In most cases, you can define custom elements for a graphical definition and specify any existing classes that you developed previously using GEF. Or you might want to code certain figures by hand and reference them in your graphical definition model. You can also use this capability when generating standalone figure plug-ins; the produced `mirrored.gmfgraph` model will contain references to custom elements generated from the original graphical definition model. Section 4.5.5, "Generating the Figures Plug-In," illustrates the technique of using a standalone figure plug-in.

11.1.1 The Canvas

At the root of every graphical definition model is the `Canvas`. This root element has a name property and containment references to one or more `Figure Galleries`, `Nodes`, `Connections`, `Compartments`, and `Labels`. Note the distinction between figures and diagram elements. In a GMF graphical definition, a `Figure` is defined within a `Figure Gallery`, which is then referenced by `Node`, `Connections`, `Compartment`, and `Label` diagram elements, via `Figure Descriptors` and `Accessors`. These diagram elements are siblings to `Figure Gallery` elements, although they can reference figure definitions from other graphical definition models. The idea is to promote reuse of figure definitions without adding the complexity of yet another GMF model.

11.1.2 The Figure Gallery

As mentioned, a `Canvas` can contain a number of `Figure Gallery` elements, which, in turn, contain figures, figure descriptors, and an optional implementation bundle property.

TIP

Be careful not to name your `Canvas` the same as any of the contained `Figure Gallery` elements because this will cause a name clash. This will be detected during validation of the graphical definition model, but it will result in exceptions when trying to load the `Canvas` mapping in the mapping definition model. Validation is performed upon transformation from the mapping model to generator model, or when invoked manually from the context menu.

The implementation bundle property is currently used only when generating standalone figure plug-ins. The idea is that the `Figure Gallery` entry in the mirrored diagram definition indicates the plug-in where custom figures are found and referenced. Upon generation, these bundle names are added to the `Require-Bundle` list of the generated plug-in so that custom figures whose fully qualified names are specified can be resolved.

A `Figure Descriptor` has a name and describes a figure by holding a reference to a Figure and its accessors, if any. Figure descriptors enable figure galleries to be reused with figures nested within other figures without an explicit reference to their parent.

TIP

Note that the code-generation templates use the `Figure Descriptor` name when generating the figure code. Typically, the descriptor and its figure are given the same name, although it's fine to omit the name on the figure.

A `Figure Descriptor` contains a single `Figure`, while a `Figure Gallery` can contain a number of `Figure` elements. A `Figure Descriptor` can use a `Figure Reference` as its figure, but these are not allowed as contained elements of a `Figure Gallery`. A `Figure Reference` element merely holds a reference to another figure to allow for reuse.

Figures come in a variety of flavors and are typically generated as `org.eclipse.draw2d.Figure` subclasses. Note that it is also possible to define a figure to be used in a GMF diagram using SVG.

As you can see from the context menu on a `Figure Descriptor`, you can specify many types of figures. Each of these is described shortly, along with its individual properties. Because they all extend from the Figure element, they share a number of common properties, covered first.

Each `Figure` can be assigned the properties in Table 11-1.

Table 11-1   Figure Properties

Property	Description
Name	The name of the figure.
Foreground Color	The color of the figure's outline. Color can be specified using RGB values or using a set of color constants.
Background Color	The color of the figure's background, or the area inside the outline.
Size	The initial dimension (width and height) of the figure.
Maximum Size	The maximum dimension (width and height) of the figure.
Minimum Size	The minimum dimension (width and height) of the figure.
Preferred Size	The preferred dimension (width and height) of the figure.
Font	The name, size, and style (normal, bold, italic) of a font used for figure text.
Insets	The bottom, top, left, and right inset values for the figure, used with a Margin Border.
Border	A decoration on a figure with corresponding **Insets** elements used to determine how its children are positioned. See the upcoming "Borders" section for more information on the types of borders available.
Location	The location of the figure's top-left corner.

Shape Figures

A number of shape figures share a common set of properties, listed in Table 11-2. These properties correspond to `org.eclipse.draw2d.Shape` class properties.

Table 11-2   Shape Figure Properties

Property	Description
Outline	A Boolean property that indicates whether to draw the figure's outline
Fill	A Boolean property that indicates whether to fill the figure with the specified background color
Line Width	The width of the outline
Line Kind	The style of line used for the figure's outline: solid, dash, dot, dash-dot, dash-dot-dot, or custom

Property	Description
XOR Fill	A Boolean property that indicates whether an XOR-based fill is used in the figure
XOR Outline	A Boolean property that indicates whether an XOR-based outline is used for the figure

Rectangle and Rounded Rectangle

`Rectangle` and `Rounded Rectangle` are two popular shape figures. These generate subclasses of `org.eclipse.draw2d.Rectangle` and `Rounded Rectangle`, respectively. The `Rounded Rectangle` has two additional properties for `corner width` and `corner height`.

Ellipse

An `Ellipse` is another popular shape that, when generated, extends `org.eclipse.draw2d.Ellipse`. To create a circle, create a `Size` child element with equal `width` and `height` values.

Polyline and Polygon

A `Polyline` is a shape (although not a regular shape) that contains a series of points (x,y values) to define subclasses of `org.eclipse.draw2d.Polyline`. A `Polygon` is a `Polyline` that is closed and can be filled. A `Polygon` generates a subclass of `org.eclipse.draw2d.Polygon`. A `ScalablePolygon` is a `Polygon` that autosizes to fill the available bounds.

Note that, in the case of a `Polygon`, the first and last points automatically are closed to form the `Polygon`, so there's no need to explicitly list the start point at the end.

Template Point

`Polygons` are specified using a series of points. `Children TemplatePoint` elements of a `Polygon` draw a shape in the order they are added. It is helpful to have a piece of graph paper handy when designing `Polygons`. As an example, the points to draw a diamond decoration for use on a `Polyline` connection would be (0,0) (−2,1) (−4,0) (−2,−1).

Polyline Connection

A `Polyline Connection` is a special type of `Polyline` that can contain source and target end `Decoration` figures. `Decorations` come with three options: `Polyline`, `Polygon`, and `Custom`. In addition to `Polyline Connection`, a

`Custom Connection` exists and can be set to any fully qualified figure class name. A number of custom attributes can be added to the custom class as well.

Borders

A number of border types are available, including `Line  Border`, `Margin Border`, `Compound Border`, and `Custom Border`.

Line Border

A `Line  Border` has additional properties for color and width, and a `Margin Border` has a child `Insets` property, as mentioned earlier. A `Compound Border` has child inner and outer `Border` elements. Finally, a `Custom Border` is simply a custom figure class that you can set to any fully qualified class name with custom attribute properties.

Margin Border

You can add a `Margin  Border` to figures where space is desired between the outside edge and the children figures. An `Insets` element is added to the border to specify bottom, left, top, and right margins.

Compound Border

When you want to add more than one border to a figure, you can use a `Compound Border`. An inner and outer border (`Line`, `Margin`, `Compound`, or `Custom`) can be added to produce a great number of border effects. For example, if a `Compound Border` consists of an outer margin border and an inner line border, an inset line can be drawn inside a figure.

Custom Border

If you have a custom coded border class, you can enter its fully qualified name in a `Custom Border` element.

Labels

A `Label` figure has an additional `Text` property, used to set the default text value. A `Label` produces a generated `org.eclipse.gmf.runtime.draw2d. ui.figures WrappingLabel` class. This class does not extend the `org.eclipse.draw2d.Label` class, but it provides wrapping of the label's text at a given width and alignment.

Layout

Each figure also has layout properties for its `Layout` and `Layout Data`. A number of `Layout` classes are available, with corresponding `Layout Data` where appropriate. As usual, a `Custom Layout` element is available for those who want to specify a custom class name.

Flow Layout

`Flow Layout` corresponds to GEF's `org.eclipse.draw2d.FlowLayout` class and is used to arrange children of a figure in rows or columns. A number of options are available for Flow Layout, as presented in Table 11-3.

Table 11-3 Flow Layout Properties

Property	Description	Default
Vertical (Orientation)	A Boolean property that determines whether the components should be laid out vertically (true) or horizontally (false).	False
Force Single Line	Causes the generation of a ToolbarLayout, which allows elements to be compressed (resized) so that they fit into a single row/column.	False
Match Minor Size	In a horizontal layout, figures will have the same height. In a vertical layout, figures will have the same width.	False
Major Alignment	The alignment used for a row/column. [BEGINNING | CENTER | END | FILL]	BEGINNING
Major Spacing	The spacing in pixels between elements running parallel to the layout orientation.	5
Minor Alignment	The alignment used for elements within a row/column. [BEGINNING | CENTER | END | FILL]	BEGINNING
Minor Spacing	The spacing in pixels between elements within a row or column.	5

For example, Figure 11-3 shows what the default `Flow Layout` settings produce using a simple `Rectangle` that can accept children `Rectangles`. When the `Vertical` property is set to `true`, the children are added vertically, not horizontally, as shown.

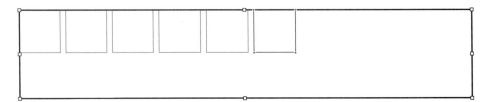

Figure 11-3   Flow layout

When changing the `Force Single Line` property to `true`, the generated `org.eclipse.draw2d.ToolbarLayout` causes the elements to shrink as more are added so that they fit on a single row. Note that they will not shrink below their `Minimum Size` property, if set.

Setting the `Major Alignment` property to `CENTER` instead of the default `BEGINNING` (top/left) for `Major Alignment` centers the inner elements either horizontally or vertically, depending on the `Vertical` setting. No difference exists between `CENTER` and `FILL`; both generate code that uses `FlowLayout.ALIGN_CENTER`.

Stack Layout

A `Stack Layout` causes elements to be added on top of one another, in the order they are added. This works well with one element to center it in another, as was the case with our `Topic` and `Task` labels in the mindmap and scenario diagrams, respectively.

XY Layout

`XY Layout` enables you to place an element wherever you want. A diagram canvas typically has an `XY Layout`, as does the rectangle in Figure 11-4 where three inner rectangles are positioned arbitrarily.

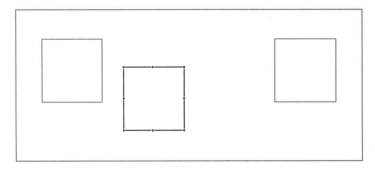

Figure 11-4   XY layout

Border Layout

`Border Layouts` allow for the placement of inner elements in the following locations: top, bottom, left, right, and center. In terms of GMF graphical definition properties, the values in Table 11-4 correspond to these options.

Table 11-4 Border Layout Properties

Border Layout Data	Alignment	Vertical
CENTER	CENTER	true	false
TOP	BEGINNING	true
BOTTOM	END	true
LEFT	BEGINNING	false
RIGHT	END	false

In Figure 11-5, a `Border Layout` is used on the outer rectangle, which also has a margin border to provide spacing between its outer edge and the inner elements. Additional rectangles are added to the top, bottom, left, and right locations. A rectangle is also added in the center position and has a compound border to achieve the (outer) margin border and (inner) line border. Each of these rectangles has child `Border Layout Data` elements with alignment and vertical property settings.

Figure 11-5 Border layout

Grid Layout

The `Grid Layout` is a powerful layout, although with additional complexity required to configure. Each figure added to a parent that uses `Grid Layout` provides its own `Grid Layout Data`. The `Grid Layout` itself has just two properties: `Equal Width` and `Num Columns`. The first indicates whether the columns in the grid are of equal width. The second determines the number of columns. When figures are added to a grid layout, they are laid out in columns, with new rows being added when this number is met.

`Grid Layout Data` elements have a number of properties, summarized in Table 11-5.

Table 11-5 Grid Layout Properties

Property	Values	Description
Grab Excess Horizontal Space	true | false	Determines whether the cell should be widened to fit the remaining space. Default is false.
Grab Excess Vertical Space	true | false	Determines whether the cell should be made tall enough to fit the remaining space. Default is false.
Horizontal Alignment	BEGINNING | CENTER | END | FILL	Determines how a figure is positioned horizontally within a cell. Default is CENTER. Note that in horizontal alignment, BEGINNING is LEFT and END is RIGHT. FILL resizes the figure.
Horizontal Indent	Integer	Specifies the number of pixels of indentation on the left side of the cell. Default is 0.
Horizontal Span	Integer	Specifies the number of column cells that the figure will occupy. Default is 1.
Vertical Alignment	BEGINNING | CENTER | END | FILL	Determines how a figure is positioned vertically within a cell. Default is CENTER. Note that in vertical alignment, BEGINNING is TOP and END is BOTTOM. FILL resizes the figure.
Vertical Span	Integer	Determines the number of row cells that the figure will occupy. Default is 1.

Figure 11-6 is an example of using `Grid Layout` to arrange figures within a rectangle.

In this example, four figures are arranged using grid data elements within a rectangle that uses grid layout settings equal `width = true`, number of `columns = 2`, as follows:

○ The hollow circle uses horizontal and vertical alignment of END, with horizontal span = 2. As you can see, it's situated at the bottom right of the top row.

○ The filled circle is added next and thus is put into the second row. It has default horizontal and vertical span values of 1, and it uses horizontal and vertical alignment values of END. As such, it is situated again at the bottom right of its cell.

○ The hollow square uses horizontal and vertical alignment values of BEGINNING, placing it at the upper left of its cell.

○ The filled square uses a horizontal and vertical span of 2, with vertical alignment CENTER. Its horizontal alignment is set to BEGINNING and has a horizontal indent of 20. This causes it to be situated the same distance from the left edge of its cell, but centered vertically. You can see this and other layout effects clearly when comparing the left and right images above where the parent rectangle is resized.

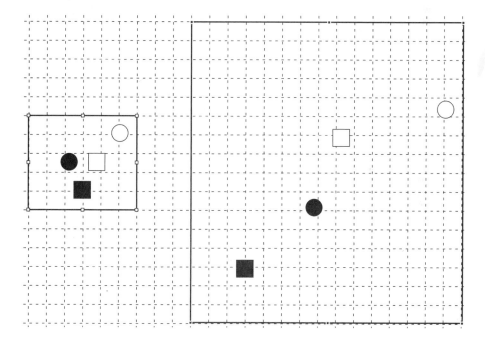

Figure 11-6   Grid layout

Combining Layouts in Complex Figures

You also likely will combine layouts when designing complex figures. The sample diagrams in this book and the UML2 Tools project provide many examples of how to use various layouts to achieve the desired arrangement of your figure elements. Specifically, the color modeling diagram archetype figures defined in Section 4.6.1, "Diagram Definition," illustrate how to use labels, nested rectangles, and compartments.

11.1.3 Diagram Elements

Before Figures can be used in a diagram, they must be referenced by a `Diagram Element`. These are siblings of `Figure Gallery` elements in the graphical definition model and, therefore, are children of the `Canvas` element. Note that diagram elements can reference the same `Figure`—or, put another way, each node on a diagram does not need to have distinct figures. Figures can be reused within the same graphical definition or from another graphical definition model.

In addition to a figure reference, a diagram element can contain `Visual Facets`. A `Visual Facet` is a way to add information to a diagram element for use in generation. Five types of visual facets exist: `General`, `Alignment`, `Gradient`, `Label Offset`, and `Default Size`. A General facet enables you to add arbitrary information, leaving it up to the template author to make use of the data.

Alignment facets are currently used only for diagram labels used with links, where constants from `org.eclipse.draw2d.ConnectionLocation` can be specified (`MIDDLE = Alignment.CENTER`, `TARGET = Alignment.END`, `SOURCE = Alignment.BEGINNING`).

`Gradient` is an unused facet, but it has a direction property and can be used in custom templates.

`Label Offset` specifies an initial offset that a label is created in relation to its figure, when a label is external to the node.

`Default Size` is useful in initializing a new element on a diagram to a certain set of dimensions. The code generated for this facet is in the `createNodePlate()` method of the node edit part, whereas the `Preferred Size` property of a figure sets its dimension of the figure itself. In other words, a figure can be nested within other figures, while a `Node` created as a diagram element that references a figure represents what is created on the diagram. Therefore, the default size facet on a node determines the initial size of a diagram element. Of course, if this facet on the node and the top-level figure has a preferred dimension that is larger, it is created at that size.

Nodes

In addition to the name, figure, and facets properties that all diagram elements share, nodes have the following properties: `Resize Constraint, Affixed`

Parent Side, and Content Pane. The Resize Constraint gives options of how the node is allowed to be resized, with the default being NSEW, which allows it to be resized using all eight points (each of the handles shown when selected). Affixed Parent Side is used primarily for port-type elements that are nodes attached to the side of another node. The default value for this property is NONE. The Content Pane property is currently not used.

TIP

With some modification, you can leverage the Content Pane in the generated code. The intention is to allow a Figure to specify child elements. In the generated EditPart, locate the setupContentPane() method and mark it @generated NOT to prevent overwriting on regeneration.

```
if (nodeShape instanceof <GeneratedFigure>) {
  nodeShape = ((<GeneratedFigure>)nodeShape)
    .<figureAccessorName>();
}
```

Introduce code such as this to assign the proper child Figure using the generated accessor.

Diagram Labels

Diagram Label extends Node in the graphical definition model and, therefore, has all of its properties. Additionally, it has the following properties: Element Icon, Accessor, External, and Container. Element Icon is a Boolean property that indicates whether the label uses an icon image to complement its text. The Accessor obtains the figure instance from the parent EditPart. An External label does not require such an Accessor because the figure is not contained within another—for example, link labels are always external. Therefore, the External property is set to false automatically if an accessor is selected for a Diagram Label.

Connections

Connections are simple diagram elements that have no additional properties. The figure reference, a name, and whatever facets you chose to add as children are sufficient to define a connection.

Compartments

A Compartment is defined as a diagram element, although it is always contained within another element, unlike connections, nodes, and (external) labels. Additional properties available for compartments are Accessor, Collapsible, and Needs Title.

Collapsible is a Boolean property that determines whether the compartment will have a handle that, when clicked, collapses and expands the compartment. The Needs Title property determines whether a string label is placed above the compartment. The title given to the compartment is the name of the Compartment element itself, but you can change this in the generator model.

An important aspect of using compartments is to set the proper layout on the container. It's best to specify a Flow Layout using CENTER alignment, Vertical orientation, and Force Single Line equal to true for compartments that have list items. Of course, it's possible not to define a layout at all, as it is possible to use just a labeled container as the compartment figure.

TIP

Keep in mind a couple things when dealing with collapsible compartments. First, the default size facet mentioned earlier helps keep a reasonable shrunken size of your node because one or two items added to a list in a compartment won't likely stretch the node beyond the default 40×40 size of a node plate. In this case, collapsing the compartment hides the list items, but the node itself does not shrink, as you might expect. Setting the default size facet to, say, 40×15 gives you the desired effect. Second, recall that, when manually resized, a node no longer collapses down, but it respects the sizing the user selected. To restore the node to autosizing, select it and use the Auto Size button on the diagram's main toolbar.

11.2 Tooling Definition Model

The Tooling model is one of GMF's simplest models, mainly because it is not yet complete. Primarily, the tooling model defines a diagram's palette—that is, the creation tools for creating nodes and links.

At the root of a tooling definition model is the Tool Registry. This element contains the Palette and any number of Menus and shared Action elements. At this time, GMF generates only code for Palette elements. The remaining elements are left to future versions of GMF.

A `Palette` element has a `Title` and a `Description`, although these strings appear only in the generated user interface for creation tools. A `Default` element determines the active entry to be displayed when a stack of palette tools is configured.

You can add a number of elements to the palette: `Icon Images`, `Palette Separator`, `Tool Group`, `Palette`, `Standard Tool`, `Creation Tool`, and `Generic Tool`. At the palette level, the icon image selections are not used. Also not currently used are the `Palette`, `Standard Tool`, and `Generic Tool` elements. This leaves `Tool Group` and `Separator` as valid elements to choose from.

A `Tool Group` is meant to hold `Creation Tool` entries that make sense to group together. Typically, a **Nodes** group and a **Links** group are created. The `Active` and `Stack` properties of a tool group are typically used together, but they require a parent tool group to work properly. This means that there must be a `Tool Group` element with its own child `Tool Group`. This second `Tool Group` must have its `Stack` property set to `true`. In this case, the tool selected as the palette's `Active` tool appears at the top of this stacked group by default. If the `Collapsible` property is set, the "drawer" feature of the generated GEF palette is enabled and the group collapses into a named drawer.

You can add a `Separator` anywhere between tool entries, resulting in a horizontal line in the generated palette. This can be helpful in large groupings of tools where a logical separation makes it easier to find tools but doesn't warrant separate groups or drawers.

A `Creation Tool` has image child elements. Specifically, there are large and small icon images that you can specify as either default or custom (bundle). If the default icons are used, the generator uses the same icons as specified for the element it creates. These typically are picked up from the Eclipse Modeling Framework (EMF) edit code icons. If the bundle icon elements are used, the bundle and path to the icon to be used must be entered. For example, if you want to use the wrench icon used for the GMF tooling model root as an image icon for your palette, you would enter `org.eclipse.gmf.tooldef.edit` for the `Bundle` property and `icons/full/obj16/GMFToolModelFile.gif` for the `Path` property.

11.3 Mapping Model

The mapping model is the heart of GMF models and itself represents a diagram. Until now, graphical definition and tooling models have been separate and available for reuse. A mapping model is transformed to one or more generator models that drive templates for code generation.

Although we do not cover this in detail, you might have noticed while using GMF that a fair amount of validation takes place when transforming to the generator model. If you look at the gmfmap.ecore model in the org.eclipse.gmf.map plug-in, you will notice a number of OCL constraints defined for elements in the model.

The root of the model is the Mapping element, which can take a number of elements as children: Top Node Reference, Link Mapping, Canvas Mapping, Audit Container, Metric Container, and Generic Style Selector. GMF does not yet leverage the Generic Style Selector.

Figure 11-7 shows the mapping model, to aid in the discussion that follows.

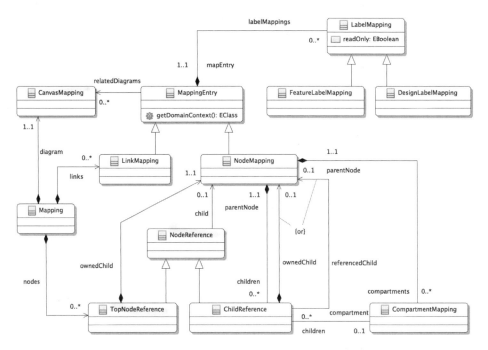

Figure 11-7   Mapping model

11.3.1 Canvas Mapping

The Canvas Mapping element is required and represents the diagram canvas. The mapping wizard populates this element with the selected Domain Model (EPackage), its root Element (EClass), the Diagram Canvas from a graphical definition model, and the Palette from the tooling definition model. GMF does not yet use the Menu and Toolbar Contributions elements.

11.3.2 Top Node Reference

A `Top Node Reference` represents elements that are created on the diagram surface. This element contains a `Child` reference to a single `Node Mapping`. Elements must be contained somewhere in the corresponding domain model when they are instantiated as diagram elements. The `Containment Feature` property specifies where to add these new objects and, by default, where to retrieve them.

A common pattern in modeling involves having a single containment reference for a generic type that is used to store model objects, while a derived attribute of a specific type is used to retrieve objects. As an example, consider the mindmap domain model used in this book, shown again in Figure 11-8 for convenience.

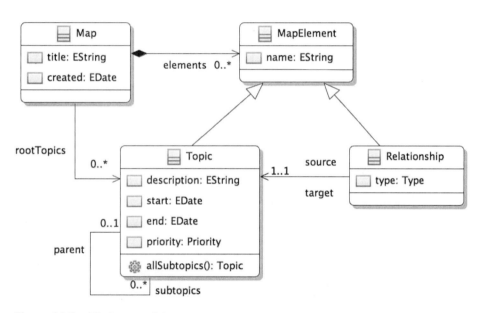

Figure 11-8   Mindmap model

Here, an `elements` containment reference is used to hold all `MapElement` objects in the `Map`. To obtain a list of root `Topic` objects, a derived `rootTopics` reference is provided and implemented using OCL (refer back to Section 3.3.5, "Adding OCL").

In some models, you might find it necessary to specify both the `Containment Feature` and a `Children Feature` for a `Top Node`

Reference element. By specifying both, the generated code knows both where to store newly created elements and where to retrieve existing elements.

11.3.3 Node Mapping

Each Top Node Reference and Child Reference contains a single Node Mapping. A Node Mapping element binds a Diagram Node, Tool, and domain model Element together. A number of properties and child elements are available to a Node mapping, so let's start with the basics.

The domain Element is the EClass from the domain model that this node mapping represents. Likewise, the Diagram Node is the node from the graphical definition used to display the graphical concrete syntax for this node. Finally, the Tool is the creation tool from the tooling definition that is used to create the node from the palette. As you might have predicted, GMF does not yet use the Appearance Style and Context Menu.

TIP

You can assign the same palette tool to multiple nodes. This results in a pop-up menu of the mapped nodes appearing when you use the tool, giving you the choice to select the proper element. It's not clear whether this is a better approach than using multiple palette tools, particularly considering that they can be stacked. When constraints are applied to each element that the tool can create so that no ambiguity exists for the target, no pop-up will appear when only one possibility exists, as was the case in the scenario diagram.

The Related Diagrams element maps to a Canvas Mapping so that this diagram node can be used to navigate to another diagram. This concept is known as *diagram partitioning*. It's rather straightforward to use this feature to create partitioned diagrams, or diagrams where a node maps to its own Canvas and thereby allows composite domain elements to be displayed on their own Canvas. For example, consider an Ecore or Unified Modeling Language (UML) diagram in which the package element is represented as a Canvas and can be created in a hierarchy. A package node is related to the diagram's Canvas; by default, double-clicking on a package opens a new diagram surface. The UML2 Tools project uses this feature, as does the Ecore diagram that GMF provides. Both use cases for using diagram partitioning are covered in Section 4.5.6, "Diagram Partitioning."

On the Canvas, a number of Top Node Reference elements can be added. The root object of your DSL maps to the Canvas, so top nodes on your diagram typically map to a Containment Feature of the root object. This setting tells the diagram where to store newly created objects to the domain model instance, but sometimes another feature is used to retrieve children for display. In this case, the Children Feature property is set, although for most models, it's not necessary. In Section 11.3.3, "References, Containment, and Phantom Nodes," we discuss how it is also possible to show elements that are not contained in the root object as top nodes on the Canvas, using a concept known as "phantom" nodes and connectors.

To a Top Node Reference, we can add a Node Mapping to define a domain element, its Node from the graphical definition, and its creation tool from our palette. You can add several elements to a Node Mapping. The most popular is a Feature Label Mapping. With this property, a Diagram Label from the graphical definition can be mapped to an attribute (or collection of attributes) from the domain element specified in the node mapping. An example in Figure 11-9 from our dnc.gmfmap model shows the mapping of our attribute label.

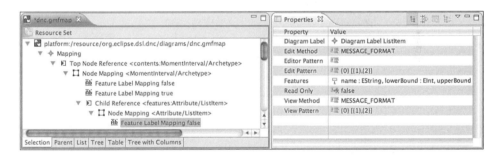

Figure 11-9   Feature label mapping

In this case, we are using three of our Attribute properties from the domain model: name, lowerBound, and upperBound. We've also specified that, using the MESSAGE_FORMAT method of parsing in-place edits of our label, it should display the name, a space, and then the lower- and upper-bound properties in square brackets, separated by a comma. Note that the default values you set in your domain model are important to how a new element is initially displayed on the diagram. Without specifying default values for the lower- and upper-bound properties, our label displays "[null,null]" and is not very user-friendly.

TIP

In the mapping model, order matters. This is obvious in feature initializers, but it might not be obvious in the case of node labels. For example, if a node has two labels, the top of which is read-only (for example, with a stereotype label), the default generated code does not allow the second label (for example, the node's name) to be activated with the in-place editor when the node is created on the diagram. So reverse the order of the label mappings to achieve the desired effect.

References, Containment, and Phantom Nodes

We've taken a look at how to map nodes to containment references using Top Level and Child Node elements in our mapping model. If your domain model has a straightforward mapping to a graphical display, particularly with respect to containment versus noncontainment references, you will have no problems. However, if you want to create a node on the diagram surface (a Top Level Node) but the domain element it represents is not a contained element of the element used for the Canvas, you can see a problem. How do we indicate where to store the created element represented by this node in the domain model instance?

We need to provide a link from this node to the element representing the domain element that has the containment reference for objects of this type. The problem is, we typically create nodes and then link them to other elements using a link tool. So for a short period of time, we have a so-called "phantom" element represented on our diagram surface that does not yet have a home. If you look at your domain model instance after creating this type of node, you'll see that the underlying domain element instance is held in the root of the model—that is, until it is connected with a link to the contained element. The solution in this case is to leave the Containment Feature property of the node mapping blank and indicate the containment feature as the Target Feature of the corresponding Link Mapping. Figure 11-10 is an example of our requirements model and its Link Mapping for Requirement children.

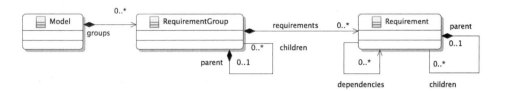

Figure 11-10   Requirements model

Table 11-6   Link Mapping

Element	Property	Value
Mapping		
Link Mapping	Target Feature	children : Requirement
	Diagram Link	Connection RequirementChild
	Tool	Creation Tool Child Requirement

On our diagram, we want to display `RequirementGroup` elements both as root elements on the diagram and as children elements, whereby a link indicates the containment of these elements in a `RequirementGroup` instance, not the Model instance representing the canvas. The problem is, because both are of the same type, the generated code from the GMF tooling cannot determine the proper node to use, particularly when initializing a diagram from an existing domain instance without a tip. To provide the tip, we can add a constraint to our root `RequirementGroup` node definition to check that its `eOpposite` parent is `null`; only root elements won't have a parent reference. In OCL, this would be `parent.oclIsUndefined()`.

In summary, a Toolsmith must be aware of how elements are created and their storage within domain model instances when creating diagram mapping definitions. Phantom nodes provide a solution when we do not want to represent a containment relationship in a domain model as a containment representation on a diagram. Inner nodes and compartments provide a straightforward way to represent contained elements on a diagram, but can we indicate noncontainment references in a domain model using these containment visual representations? It's possible, but it requires some code modification. To store a child diagram element in a separate model container, locate the generated `xxxCreateCommand.doDefaultElementCreation()` method and modify it so that the newly created element is stored in an appropriate place in the domain model, along with a corresponding reference. The diagram must be updated as well, to reflect the change.

Node Constraints

A `Constraint` child element can be added to a `Node Mapping`, usually to distinguish between types in case a containment reference holds several (sub)types. `Constraints` can be defined in Object Constraint Language (OCL), Java, regexp, and nregexp. The context of the constraint is the domain element selected in the node mapping.

Primarily, constraints provide hints to the generator so that code is written to obtain the proper visual ID for a node. A visual ID is an integer that the generator assigns to a node. At runtime, type checks are augmented by constraint evaluation to return the proper visual ID where there would otherwise be ambiguity. Note that this feature becomes important when initializing a diagram from an existing instance of a domain model. Normally, there is a user to eliminate ambiguity when diagramming by selecting the proper node tool from the palette. This also is useful when performing diagram updates with semantic refresh because these constraints are checked when comparing view and domain elements, as discussed in Section 4.3.5, "Subtopic Figure."

An example should make this point clear. Consider the Ecore metamodel and the following relationship between `EDataType` and `EEnum`. Both are `EClassifiers` and are held in the `eClassifiers` containment reference of `EPackage`, as shown in Figure 11-11. When creating node mappings for each of these, the `eClassifiers` reference is used as the `Containment Feature`. With mappings to distinct creation tools in the palette, and with each node mapping's `Element` property set to distinct `EClasses`, the diagram supports the creation of both `EDataType` and `EEnum` elements. However, when trying to determine the correct visual ID when pulling objects out of the `eClassifiers` reference, instances of `EEnum` are ambiguous because they also appear as `EDataType`. So which edit part visual ID to return?

Using a constraint on the node mapping for the `EDataType` that verifies (in OCL) that it is `not oclIsKindOf(ecore::EEnum)` removes the ambiguity in a straightforward manner. Alternative solutions exist, but this one falls into a general pattern of using OCL to more precisely define mappings in GMF, as you will see later.

Another use of constraints on a node is to distinguish between nodes that represent the same domain element but might have an attribute set when initialized. This is commonly the case with classes that have an enumerated type set to a value. These go hand in hand with feature sequence initializers, which are covered next.

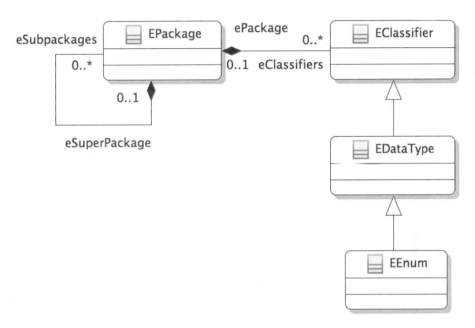

Figure 11-11   EClassifier model

11.3.4 Feature Initialization

Certain attributes of the underlying domain element might need to be initialized
to some value when a node is added to a diagram. To accomplish this, we can
use a `Feature Seq Initializer` child element on the `Node Mapping`. The
feature initialization is shown in Figure 11-12. It's also possible to initialize new
reference elements and their attributes, as shown in the initialization of the
`Requirement` element and its `Version` in Section 4.4.3, "Mapping Definition."
Another common application of initialization is in naming elements placed on a
diagram, such as archetypes on our color modeling diagram of Section 4.6,
"Developing the Color Modeling Diagram." If we added an OCL statement to
the initializer such as the following, each new archetype would be created with
the name ClassX, where X is the number of elements in the package: `"Class"`
`+ container.childElements->size()`.

   As mentioned earlier, feature initialization is commonly used in conjunction
with a node `Constraint` element. The constraint specifies the state of an object
to distinguish it from other instances, and it is required for the generator to produce a diagram that works when several nodes are mapped to the same diagram
element.

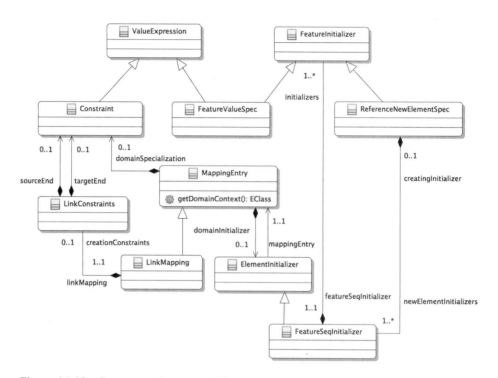

Figure 11-12   Feature initialization model

11.3.5   Implementing Side-Affixed Nodes (Pins and Ports)

As mentioned in the section on the graphical definition model, the `Affixed Parent Side` property of a `Node` diagram element triggers the generation of a side-affixed node. In fact, this is the only property that you need to set, aside from the normal child/parent node mappings. As an example, we create a fixed-size rectangle to attach to all sides of a parent rectangle below.

For the port itself, we've created a simple figure. The `Node` diagram element that uses this figure has the `Affixed Side Parent` property set to `NSEW`, which allows the port to float around all four sides of our parent rectangle. It also has a `Default Size Facet` with the dimension 10×10. (The normal default size of 40×40 is a bit large for a port/pin.) The parent is just a simple rectangle figure with `Default Size Facet` set to 80×80. The mapping to achieve this is straightforward as well—just a simple top-level node mapped to our simple rectangle and a child reference mapping the port node. A basic containment relationship exists in the domain model between the parent and child (port) elements. Figure 11-13 is an image of the port (side-affixed node) in action.

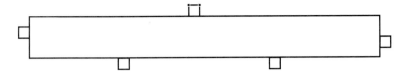

Figure 11-13 Side-affixed node

Looking at the generated code, you'll find that the edit part for the parent rectangle extends `AbstractBorderedShapeEditPart` and installs `BorderItemSelectionEditPolicy` on its child to restrict movement around the border. The port edit part extends `AbstractBorderItemEditPart` and installs a `NonResizableEditPolicy`, so it's not necessary to set Max/Min/ Preferred dimensions on the figure. Note that this approach applies to external labels as well.

11.3.6 Link Mapping

To map a `Connection` from the graphical definition to a domain model and palette creation tool, use the `Link Mapping` element. Four major use cases are supported for link mappings: design links, domain element references, links representing domain class elements, and phantom node links.

Note that it's possible to create links that do not map to domain elements, so-called design links. In this case, simply select a palette tool and diagram link, leaving all properties for the domain empty. Links created this way can be made between all top-level nodes on the diagram, although they represent no domain model information.

Links create connections between elements on the diagram and can represent several types of reference relationships found in a domain model. Regular references are the most typical use for links on a diagram and are the most straightforward to implement. Links can also represent full-fledged domain (`EClass`) elements, with source and target references. As mentioned already, containment references can be represented using links to top-level nodes on a diagram using the "phantom node" concept. We explore each of these in turn here.

In the case of a normal `EReference` between two elements, a link mapping simply requires specifying the target. Consider the following example, where `Topic` is linked to itself by a normal (noncontainment) `subtopics` reference, as seen in Figure 11-14. To create a link mapping to represent this relationship as a connection between two nodes on a diagram, the mapping properties are as indicated. The only property in the `Domain Meta Information` category that needs to be set is the `Target Feature`. The generator and runtime can infer the appropriate node types that are valid by specifying only this property.

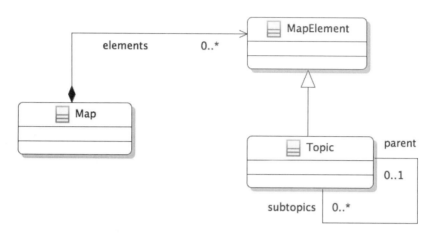

Figure 11-14   Simplified mindmap model

Table 11-7   Subtopic Link Mapping

Element	Property	Value
Mapping		
Link Mapping	Target Feature	subtopics : Topic
	Diagram Link	Connection TopicSubtopics
	Tool	Creation Tool TopicSubtopics

If a link is to be used to indicate a containment reference, we set the properties as discussed in the phantom node discussion of Section 11.3.3, "References, Containment, and Phantom Nodes."

When a domain element (`EClass`) is used to represent a relationship, more information is required in the mapping definition. In this case, the generator needs to create code that knows where to store the new instance of the class representing the link, as well as what features on this class to initialize with references to the source and target. Consider the `Connection` element in our scenario model, shown in Figure 11-15.

`Connection` has `source` and `target` references to the `Element` class, which have corresponding `eOpposite` relationships `outgoing` and `incoming`. Table 11-8 shows how this type of link is mapped. Because `Connection` is itself an `Element`, it is stored in the `elements` containment reference within `Process`, which, in this case, represents the `Canvas`. The mapping is for our `Association` class, which is the `Element` itself being mapped and representing the link. The Source Feature and Target Feature map directly to our source and target references.

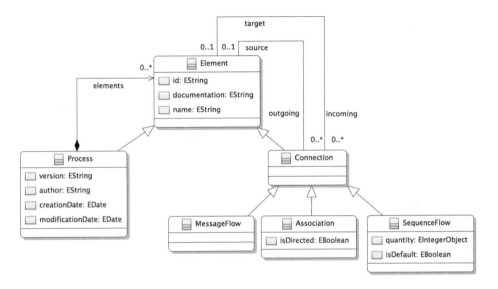

Figure 11-15 Connection model

Table 11-8 Connection Link Mapping

Element	Property	Value
Mapping		
Link Mapping	Containment Feature	elements : Element
	Element	Association -> Connection
	Source Feature	source : Element
	Target Feature	target : Element
	Diagram Link	Connection DirectedAssociation
	Tool	Creation Tool Directed Association
Constraint	Body	isDirected = true
Feature Seq Initializer	Element Class	Association -> Connection
Feature Value Spec	Body	true
	Feature	isDirected : EBoolean

Notice from the mapping that the link also has a `Constraint` and `Feature Seq Initializer` element. `Constraints` specify conditions for which the underlying relationship is valid, or remove ambiguity if multiple links are mapped for a single element. In this case, the `isDirected` property is set to `true`. The initializer mapping element that follows sets the property itself. The language defaults to OCL, and the expression is simply `true`.

A link can also have a label mapping. Naturally, the label will be of the "external" variety, able to be associated with an end of the link, as specified in the graphical definition model. Table 11-9 is our dependency link mapping from Section 4.3.5, "Updating the Mapping Definition," where two link mappings are required: one for the link name and the other for the stereotype.

Table 11-9 Relationship Link Mapping

Element	Property	Value
Link Mapping	Containment Feature	elements : MapElement
	Element	Relationship → MapElement
	Source Feature	source : Topic
	Target Feature	target : Topic
	Diagram Link	Connection Relationship
	Tool	Creation Tool Dependency
Feature Label Mapping	Diagram Label	Diagram Label RelationshipName
	Features	name : EString
Feature Label Mapping	Diagram Label	Diagram Label RelationshipType
	Features	type : Type
	View Pattern	«{0}»

11.3.7 Audits and Metrics

The root of the mapping model allows for the creation of an `Audit Container` and a `Metric Container`, as shown in Figure 11-16. An `Audit Container` contains audit rules or child containers. An audit rule has several properties, including name, ID, message, description, severity, and whether to use "live" mode. The alternative to live is batch, in which the Practitioner must explicitly run audits on models. An audit rule requires two child elements: a constraint, or the rule itself defined in OCL, Java, regexp, or nregexp, and a context. The context can be a domain element, domain attribute, diagram element, notation model element, or metric rule.

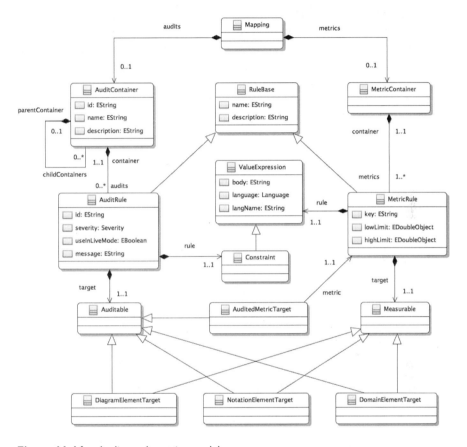

Figure 11-16 Audits and metrics model

You can find examples of applying audits and metrics in the mindmap diagram, in Section 4.3.5, "Audits and Metrics."

11.4 Generator Model

The GMF generator model is the largest model used in GMF and the one most likely to be extended to provide customizations, probably using a decorator model. Much of the model doesn't need to be covered in detail because most elements are simply Gen-prefixed elements from the input models. These elements are created and populated by GMF Mapping model to Generator model transformation. This transformation is currently implemented in Java code but might eventually be implemented in QVT Operational Mapping Language (OML).

GMF provides merge functionality to help in reconciling changes made to the generator model when retransforming from the mapping model. The Experimental Software Development Kit (SDK) provides a trace facility that helps maintain generated visual IDs consistent between regenerations. We recommend that you use these facilities if you plan to make changes or augment the generator model in any way.

The generator model has references to the EMF generator model for use in generating the diagram code. The figures used in the diagram are either serialized into fields in the generator model during the transformation from gmfmap to gmfgen, or they are referenced by class name from their corresponding generated figure plug-in.

Following are descriptions of the major elements of the generator model, with particular attention given to those that the Toolsmith most likely will change before generation.

11.4.1 Gen Editor Generator

This element is the root of the generator model and contains general properties and child elements for the generated diagram editor. Following is a description of each.

Copyright Text

Use this property to enter the copyright statements you want to appear at the top of your generated source code. Note that you do not need to enter the comment markers, such as `/*`, `*/`, `//`, `<!--`, or `-->`. These are added automatically, and the generated source code respects the line breaks you enter in the multiline dialog.

Note that copyright statements are added to Java and `plugin.xml` files only, not to `.properties` files or the OSGi bundle manifest (`MANIFEST.MF`). Also be aware that, thanks to current merge limitations, changes to this property do not affect existing files. Delete all files and regenerate if you want the copyright text updated.

Diagram File Extension

This is the file extension registered with the `org.eclipse.ui.editors` extension-point contribution in the generated diagram plug-in manifest. By default, it is the name of the domain model with `_diagram` appended. The extension you choose should be unique, if possible.

Domain File Extension

This is the file extension registered with the associated domain generator model. It is used for the pop-up menu UI contribution that invokes the generated diagram initialization feature, the New Diagram Wizard, and so on.

Domain Gen Model

This is a reference to the domain generator model. It is used primarily for the domain model element property tester, which requires knowing the accessor methods for the classes.

Dynamic Templates and Template Directory

When the `Dynamic Templates` property is set to `true`, the path specified in the `Template Directory` invokes the dynamic (custom) templates located there when diagram code is generated. Note that the path should begin from the workspace root, so templates located in a `/templates` directory of plug-in `org.eclipse.demo` would be entered as `/org.eclipse.demo/templates`. Also, it is possible to enter any valid Uniform Resource Identifier (URI) into this field—for example, `file:/c:/path`, `platform:/resource/org.eclipse.dsl.mindmap/templates`.

Model ID

By default, this is the value of the domain model name that identifies the generated diagram. As with the file extension property, this value should be unique to the environment. If multiple diagrams are defined for a single domain model, alter this property to make it unique; by default, it gets the same value as the first one.

This property creates the IDs and other names used to identify the diagram elements, such as the `globalActionHandlerProviders` extension-point contributions. It also identifies related diagrams when using the `Shortcuts Provided For` property (discussed later).

Package Name Prefix

As you can guess, this property forms the base package for generated diagram code.

Same File for Diagram and Model

By default, GMF creates a diagram in its own resource and references domain elements stored in a separate file. This is the preferred method, where domain and diagram (notation) information are separate, and thus allows for several diagrams (views) to be made for the same domain model instance.

Setting this Boolean property to `true` alters the generated diagram wizard code to persist the domain model within the same resource (file) as the diagram model. An XML Metadata Interchange (XMI) element serves as the root, with child elements for the domain and diagram (notation).

This property is also used in the template for generating the initialize diagram code. If the **Initialize xxx Diagram** is invoked on a domain model, using the `Domain File Extension`, the model content is copied into a file ending in the `Diagram File Extension` and persisted in the same file as the notation data.

11.4.2 Gen Diagram

This element contains properties and children related to the diagram itself. The rest of the properties relate to supporting elements, such as the generated plug-in, view, and navigator.

Many of the properties for the diagram are strictly names for generated classes and packages. This element includes names for edit parts, edit policies, edit commands, edit helpers, and so on. The remaining properties are listed next, along with the child elements of `Gen Diagram`.

Contains Shortcuts To and Shortcuts Provided For

Diagrams can have elements from other model instances placed as shortcuts on their `Canvas`, but only if the related diagrams are known at generation time. You should consider two properties here: `Contains Shortcuts To` and `Shortcuts Provided For`.

Adding the file extension of a domain model to the `Contains Shortcuts To` property makes elements of that model type appear as shortcuts on your diagram. Note that there must be a top-level node mapping for the selected element in a deployed GMF diagram definition before a shortcut can be placed on the diagram.

When this property is populated, a generated `Create Shortcut To` action on the diagram invokes a chooser dialog to allow the selection of model elements to be shortcut. Only those file types specified will be visible, and their content validated before selection will be permitted.

Most commonly, Toolsmiths will want a set of diagrams of the same type to allow shortcuts for each other's elements. Adding the `Model ID` of the related diagram in the `Shortcuts Provided For` property enables elements of that diagram to be added to the diagram.

Synchronized

This property determines the behavior of the diagram at runtime with respect to the state of its corresponding domain model. A synchronized diagram (default) updates automatically to reflect changes in the underlying domain model instance. For example, a package diagram node that contains classes will be updated automatically to reflect the addition of new classes to the package automatically. Note that default generated code from GMF does not synchronize a diagram when changes are made in another editing domain until the changes are saved—for example, if the model is also open in the EMF-generated editor and is modified but not yet saved. It's also possible to share the same editing domain among diagram editors that operate on the same underlying domain model, as is often the case with UML diagramming tools. You can find the process for accomplishing this on the GMF wiki. Section 4.4.6, "Integrating EMF and GMF Editors," covers sharing EMF and GMF editors when both use the same editing domain.

You can initially create a nonsynchronized diagram using the initialize diagram action for a given domain model, but it will not be updated to reflect changes in the model. More specifically, canonical updates occur, but the creation of new diagram elements that correspond to newly created elements in the underlying domain model does not occur. Labels and compartment items for existing diagram elements will reflect changes in their underlying domain properties.

You can also take a mixed approach, in which some diagrams are synchronized and others are not; this is another common use case for UML diagramming tools.

Units

This property refers to the unit of measure used to render the diagram in the display. The valid values are `Himetric` and `Pixel`. A `Himetric` unit is equal to 1/100 mm on any display. A `Pixel` can vary depending on the display resolution.

Validation Decorators and Validation Enabled

When validation is enabled for use with diagram audits and metrics, validation decorators can also be enabled to allow decoration of diagram elements. Setting `Validation Enabled` to `true` causes the generation of `_ValidationProvider` and `_MarkerNavigationProvider` classes for invoking the EMF validation framework and providing resource markers, respectively. Setting `Validation Decorators` to `true` causes the `_ValidationDecoratorProvider` class to be generated, which handles decorating diagram elements with validation errors.

Along with these properties, this section of the generator model has provider priority elements. By default, many of these are set to `Lowest` priority, which, unfortunately, might not allow them to be activated at runtime. For example, set the `Validation Decorator Provider Priority` to `Medium` if you aren't seeing decorators for audit violations. For metrics, set the `Metric Provider Priority` to something higher than `Lowest`. As mentioned in the runtime section, these providers are part of an extensibility framework that gives custom providers priority over the default or generated providers, according to the execution strategy that the service defines.

Creation Wizard Category ID and Icon Path

By default, GMF generates the Diagram Creation Wizard, sets it to the `org.eclipse.ui.Examples` category, and provides a standard icon. If you want to put your wizard in a custom category, specify it here, but be sure to use a valid category ID. Otherwise, you might find your wizard in the "Other" category.

Similarly, you can provide an alternative relative path to use a different icon. If you'd prefer to reuse the EMF wizard icon for the diagram wizard, enter `{reuseEMFIcon}` in the field. Note that this also impacts the file icon used in the navigator. Of course, you could just replace the generated icon with one you prefer and leave the filename and path set to the default.

Editing Domain ID

A unique identifier for the diagram is its editing domain, which uses its own resource set. Generated diagrams are given an instance of an editing domain for each open editor, so, by default, they cannot share instances of model elements that are open in another open diagram. You can alter the generated code so that several diagrams can share a single domain model instance.

Visual ID

The Visual ID is a number used to represent a diagram metaelement where various types are being edited within a single editor. Generally, you do not need to modify this value except when using a shared editing domain, as described earlier.

Without Domain

You can generate diagrams where no underlying domain model is mapped, in which case this property is `true`. This is useful when you want to experiment with notations or refine your figures.

11.4.3 Gen Link

To enable `Tree Style Routing` for links, you must set the `Tree Branch` property to `true`. This causes the generated `EditPart` for the link to implement `ITreeBranchEditPart` and allow for tree-style link routing, as described in Section 10.1.1, "Toolbar."

11.4.4 Custom Behavior

The `Gen Diagram` and child `Gen Node` and `Gen Link` elements can have a `Custom Behavior` child element, which enables the Toolsmith to add custom behavior to the parent element. Note that these elements are not created by default as part of the transformation from the mapping model, but they are features to be added by the Toolsmith.

From the description of GEF's Edit Policy concept in Section 9.2.3, "EditPolicies," we know that they are the mechanism for adding behavior to a diagram element. A `Custom Behavior` element simply allows for a `Key` and `Edit Policy Qualified Class Name` to be entered. The generator then adds the necessary code to install this `EditPolicy`. Of course, it's up to the Toolsmith to code the policy.

Another feature of `Custom Behavior` is to remove an `Edit Policy` that is already installed. To do this, simply enter the key of the policy and leave the class name blank. This signals the generator to enter the code to uninstall this policy. This is particularly useful for removing some of the default-installed policies available from the GMF runtime. For example, the diagram connection handles can be uninstalled using the key `org.eclipse.gmf.runtime.diagram.ui.editpolicies.EditPolicyRoles. CONNECTION_HANDLES_ ROLE`.

11.4.5 Open Diagram Behavior

The related diagram property of the mapping model allows elements to open other diagrams through a mapping to their `Canvas`. Specifying the `Related Diagrams` property in the mapping results in an `Open Diagram Behavior` element being added to the generator model and an `OpenDiagramEditPolicy` class being generated. This functionality is illustrated in Section 4.5.6, "Diagram Partitioning."

11.4.6 Gen Plugin

The `Gen Plugin` element contains properties for generating the diagram plug-in itself. Table 11-10 describes each of these properties. `Gen Plugin` has no child elements.

Table 11-10   Gen Plugin Properties

Property	Description
ID	The unique plug-in ID assigned to the generated diagram plug-in. It must be unique in the workspace because it will also be the name of the generated plug-in.
Name	The textual name of the generated plug-in. Technically, this string appears in the plugin.properties localization file, while %pluginName will appear in the MANIFEST.MF file.
Printing Enabled	Setting this value to true (default is false) generates the code required for Print and Print Preview functionality for the diagram.
Provider	The name of the generated plug-in provider. Again, the String is generated to the plugin.properties file, with %providerName in the MANIFEST.MF file.
Required Plugin Identifiers	A list of additional plug-in IDs that the generated diagram depends upon. For example, you can add custom figures found in a generated figure plug-in here.
Version	The version number of the generated plug-in, including version qualifier suffix by default. The suffix is replaced by the PDE build (from the workspace, or headless) to a value that reflects changes made since the last build.

11.4.7 Gen Editor View

The generated diagram editor has properties defined in this element.

Icon Path

Alter this property if you want to use a different icon for the editor, which is viewed in the navigator. As mentioned earlier for the diagram wizard icon, you can use the string {reuseEMFIcon} to force the use of the EMF editor icon. Again, the easiest way to use your own icon is to simply replace the generated one with a custom one using the default name and location.

ID

This is the unique ID used for the diagram editor, which is registered in the plug-in manifest as an eclipse.ui.editors contribution. This ID should be unique if you are working with several diagrams for the same domain model.

Generate as Eclipse Editor

By default, GMF generates a diagram that is an Eclipse editor. Alternatively, the lite runtime enables the Toolsmith to generate a diagram that functions in an Eclipse view.

11.4.8 Gen Navigator

The Gen Navigator element and children generate support for the common navigator (**Package Explorer** view). This allows diagram content—and, optionally, domain model content—to be displayed below the file in the navigator. Most of the properties of this element are ID and class names that need no explanation; the rest are described here.

Generate Domain Model Navigator

As mentioned, GMF also allows the content of a diagram's domain model to be exposed in the **Project Explorer**. The default value is true. When working with several generated diagrams for a single domain model, only one of the editors should have a value of true for this property. Otherwise, duplicate domain model structures will be observed in the navigator.

Gen Navigator Child Reference

This child element has properties that affect how diagram elements are displayed in the tree; see Table 11-11. By default, GMF generates logical groups for incoming and outgoing diagram links, including subelements for link source and target references.

Table 11-11   Gen Navigator Child Reference Properties

Property	Description
Group Icon	A relative path to the icon used to represent the logical group, typically displayed as a folder.
Group Name	The name given to a logical group. If this property is empty, child elements are displayed directly below the parent element. Note that each Gen Navigator Child Reference element has Parent and Child properties.
Hide If Empty	A Boolean property to filter empty logical groups from the navigator.
Reference Type	A number of options exist for how the notation model tree is traversed: children, out_target, in_source, and default.

11.4.9 Gen Diagram Updater

This element has properties to specify the names of the generated updater, commands, and descriptors. A `_DiagramUpdater` is generated and contains a number of static methods that can list all semantic children of a diagram element, in addition to diagram link information. The class is used by generated `_CanonicalEditPolicy` classes and the `_NewDiagramFileWizard` (for non-synchronized diagrams) for updating a diagram based on actual domain model content. The updater is also a handy utility class that can be used in custom code that needs to query model elements.

11.4.10 Property Sheet

GMF provides support for the enhanced tabbed properties view now available in the platform. The `Property Sheet` element and its children define the default properties sheet support, which is intended to be extended by the Toolsmith. One approach to extending property sheet support is to use a decorator model and custom templates, as shown in the gmfgraph editor itself.

The `Package Name` and `Label Provider Class Name` properties are straightforward. Note that if the property `Caption for the Sheet` is `false`, no label provider is generated. By default, the caption shows the name of the underlying domain element, if any.

The `Read Only` property is `false` by default but can be set to `true` if the Toolsmith wants all properties to be displayed but not editable by the Practitioner. Note that individual properties can be set to read-only by using the domain generator model's `Property Type` property set to `Readonly`.

If you'd rather have no property sheet for the diagram, simply remove the `Property Sheet` element from the generator model.

Standard Property Tab

GMF comes with standard tabs: Diagram, Advanced, and Appearance. These display diagram notation information, such as ruler, grid, line color, and type settings.

Custom Property Tab

GMF generates a Core property sheet to display the selected element's domain properties in the familiar grid view. A child `Typed Selection Filter` is responsible for controlling which elements the tab displays. Section 4.4.6, "Properties Revisited," describes custom property tabs.

11.4.11 Gen Application

When the RCP option is selected when transforming between the mapping and generator models, a `Gen Application` element is created. This element and its children provide the information required to generate an RCP-based application.

11.5 Summary

In this chapter, we took a deeper look into the GMF tooling component. While there is plenty left for the reader to discover within the models, templates, and code provided with GMF, this chapter should give you enough to get started developing your own diagrams. In the next chapter, we cover some of the most popular FAQs about GMF.

CHAPTER 12

Graphical Modeling Framework FAQs

Graphical Modeling Framework (GMF) is such an extensive framework and tooling infrastructure that many questions often appear on the newsgroup. Some have been collected into FAQ content on the GMF wiki pages, but here you find a collection of the most commonly asked questions about how to use GMF. Where possible, the answer references information within the book and its sample projects.

12.1 General FAQs

The FAQs in this section relate to general topics on GMF, the project.

How do I get started with GMF?

Aside from reading this book, you can find a number of wiki pages at http://wiki.eclipse.org/Graphical_Modeling_Framework that contain information on a wide range of GMF topics. Many tutorials on both the tooling side of GMF and its runtime have been posted, along with FAQs, new and noteworthy documents, and more.

What advantages does GMF offer over Graphical Editing Framework (GEF)?

GMF simplifies the integration of EMF as the underlying model for a GEF diagram. With that, it provides a separate notation model that is used to segregate the domain from diagram information. A number of services, extensionpoints, and APIs are provided with GMF to make developing diagrams easier than if you had started with GEF alone. Add to this the capability to define diagrams using a series of models and generate a large portion of the diagram code using the GMF tooling Software Development Kit (SDK). You can find discussions on the differences between GEF and GMF throughout Chapter 9, "Graphical Editing Framework"; Chapter 10, "Graphical Modeling Framework Runtime"; and Chapter 11, "Graphical Modeling Framework Tooling."

What are the prerequisites for GMF?

GMF depends on GEF, Eclipse Modeling Framework (EMF), the EMF Transaction and Validation components, Model Development Tools Object Constraint Language (MDT OCL) , and, when working with Scalable Vector Graphics (SVG) figure support, Apache Batik and Xerces. Furthermore, the Eclipse Packaging Project and Modeling Amalgam projects provide downloads that include GMF and all its dependencies.

How can I contribute to GMF?

Okay, so this isn't a *frequently* asked question—but since it's here…. The best way to contribute to GMF or any Eclipse project is to interact with project Committers in the newsgroup and, after reaching an agreement, apply a patch to a Bugzilla item. All contributions must go through Bugzilla, must be in the format of a CVS patch, and should have unit tests associated with the functionality or fix.

12.2 Diagramming FAQs

The FAQs in this section relate to figures—how to change them dynamically, alter their properties, and so on.

How do I change the figure of an existing element dynamically?

You can change the figure of an EditPart by configuring requests and executing commands to first remove the existing view element and add the new one; you must save the location information so that the new element is positioned properly. This is done within the UML2 Tools project. A different approach relies on the underlying diagram refresh method and layout invocation in Section 4.3.5, "Subtopic Figure." Yet another approach is to use the runtime's extensibility features, as illustrated in the scenario diagram customization of Section 10.9.1, "Scenario Diagram Custom View and Edit Providers."

How can I change a figure's appearance based on a preference change?

The basic process involves adding a `PreferencePropertyChange Listener` to the `EditPart` by overriding the `addNotationalListeners()` method and invoking the change on the corresponding figure when the corresponding `PropertyChangeEvent` is sent. Section 4.6.6, "Color Preferences," outlines an example of this.

How can I change a property of a figure when a domain property changes?

The most straightforward approach is to override the `handleNotifi-cationEvent()` method in the `EditPart` and determine whether the change was on the domain property of interest. If so, update the corresponding figure accordingly. Section 4.3.5, "Subtopic Figure," gives an example of a domain change being detected to invoke diagram layout.

How can I make my figure nonresizable?

Using code, you install a `NonResizeableEditPolicy` for the `EditPolicy.LAYOUT_ROLE`. To accomplish this in the definition model, set the Resize Constraint of the Node element to NONE and provide a Default Size Facet, as illustrated in Section 4.5.1, "Gateways."

What does *canonical* mean in the context of GMF?

In terms of the runtime, *canonical* refers to the capability of a container to maintain its children views in synchronization with their underlying domain elements. For example, consider a compartment within a Class element in a UML diagram. New elements added to the underlying domain model are synchronized with the compartment view automatically. In this case, the compartment is a canonical container and keeps track of changes to its children.

Why can't I see elements I place on the diagram?

This can happen when you use certain versions of Linux that might not have the Cairo graphics library installed or that have Windows 2000 without the GDI+ library. The selection border for elements typically is shown, so try using Select All (Ctrl+A) to verify this. If this is your issue, install the missing libraries. You can also disable anti-aliasing for the diagram to resolve the problem; this option is available in the preferences of your diagram.

12.3 Tooling FAQs

The FAQs in this section relate to using the GMF Tooling models for diagram generation.

How do I modify the output of the generation templates?

You can modify the templates for both figure generation and diagram code using the extensibility options provided by the underlying Xpand model-to-text framework. This book explores each of these techniques. See Section 4.2.3, "Customization Options," for a general overview and Sections 4.6.5, "Gradient Figures," and 4.6.6, "Color Preferences," for specific examples.

Do I have to use the tooling component to use GMF?

No. As described in Section 10.8, "Developing a Diagram," you can develop a diagram manually using the provided extension-points and APIs. Using the tooling to get started is generally recommended because you can generate a lot of the code you need to write from its models.

How can I include a diagram as one page in a multipage editor?

The process for doing this is currently long and involved, although it eventually might become easier if the generation of both EMF and GMF is modified to facilitate this common request. You can refer to an Eclipse Corner article on this topic (see Section 4.4.6, "Integrating EMF and GMF Editors").

How can I get nodes to stick to the border of a parent?

In the Node element of the graphical definition model, set the Affixed Parent Side property to something other than NONE. Based on the Node mapping for the parent, or the domain element that has a containment reference that holds instances of the child, the generated EditPart has a `BorderItemSelection EditPolicy` installed for its `EditPolicy.LAYOUT_ROLE`. Section 4.5.6, "Requirement to Scenario Partition," illustrates this.

Why does GMF have its own version of Xpand?

Historically, GMF adopted Xpand to replace Java Emitter Templates (JET) as the primary template engine, but Xpand had some IP cleanliness issues. The GMF team refactored Xpand to use the LALR Parser Generator (LPG) parser generator, in addition to some other enhancements. Currently, additional refactoring is underway to replace Xtend with Object Constraint Language (OCL)/QVT Operational (QVTO), so this variant of Xpand likely will migrate to the Model-to-Text Transformation (M2T) project as a distinct, though similar, alternative to the original Xpand. Furthermore, the Xpand team is working to implement its next version, based on Xtext.

12.4 Summary

In this chapter, we look into some typical FAQs about the GMF runtime and tooling. While not exhaustive, many other FAQs can be found on the project website.

CHAPTER 13

Query/View/Transformation Operational Mapping Language

The Meta-Object Facility (MOF) Query/View/Transformation (QVT) specification includes three languages: the Relations language, the Core language, and the Operational Mapping Language (OML). The first two are related, in that the Relations language is transformed into the Core language for "execution." The Relations language is a high-level, declarative language that is intended to be more user-friendly than low-level, imperative languages. It can support complex pattern matching between objects, creating a trace file implicitly that allows for bidirectional transformation.

The Core language is semantically equivalent to the Relations language but is defined at a lower level of abstraction. Therefore, transformations written in Core are more verbose than those written in Relations. Trace models must be defined explicitly, unlike in Relations, where they are derived from the transformation definition.

Both the Relations language and OML are currently under development within the Model-to-Model Transformation (M2M) project. At the time of this writing, only the OML is available, so it is the focus of this book. Note also that this book focuses on aspects of OML that have an implementation available, but it also discusses some aspects of the language that are planned to be supported in the future.

The OML is intended to provide an imperative alternative, which can be invoked from the Relations and Core languages in a "black-box" manner. OML makes extensive use of Object Constraint Language (OCL), which this book does not cover in detail. As with Eclipse Modeling Framework (EMF), OCL is covered by a book of its own, which is recommended reading before, or in parallel with, this book. This chapter covers the extensions to OCL added in the QVT spec.

OML is an imperative language that most programmers will find familiar. The language is used to define unidirectional transformations, although a second transformation can always be written to provide bidirectionality. It can provide implementations of mappings for the Core or Relations languages when declarative approaches prove difficult, which is known as a hybrid approach. Transformations defined exclusively using OML are known as operational mappings.

As you will see in the language description that follows and throughout the examples in this book, you can write equivalent QVT scripts in many ways. The decisions made by the transformation author to use particular techniques and constructs will be determined by experience, style preference, reusability, and maintainability factors. As the language and tooling support matures, features for navigation, refactoring, and optimization of QVT scripts are expected to improve the experience of working with QVT from its current state.

13.1 Transformation Declaration

A QVT transformation is defined in a file that includes a transformation signature and `main` mapping to serve as an entry point. One or more `modeltype` declarations can also be included to explicitly define the metamodels used in the transformation. Following is a transformation declaration with modeltype and main mapping elements:

```
modeltype UML uses
        simpleuml('http://www.eclipse.org/examples/1.0.0/simpleuml');
modeltype RDB uses rdb('http://www.eclipse.org/examples/1.0.0/rdb');

transformation uml2rdb(in uml:UML, out rdb:RDB) {

  -- The main entry point of the transformation
  main() {
    -- Standard model element access and mapping invocation
    uml.objects()[Class]->map class2table();
  }
}
```

As you can see, a transformation definition is much like a class declaration, with import statements, a signature, and a `main()` mapping entry point. The analogy between operational QVT and object-oriented languages is accurate: Transformations are instantiated and have properties and (mapping) operations. Note that the mappings of the transformation are enclosed within curly braces following the transformation signature. This is not required if the file has only one transformation, in which case the transformation declaration is terminated by a semicolon. At the time of this writing, QVT Operational (QVTO) currently supports only one transformation per file, so the previous syntax would result in a compiler error. Instead, declare transformations as follows:

```
transformation uml2rdb(in uml:UML, out rdb:RDB);
```

Each model parameter is associated with an MOF extent. The transformation itself can be considered a class that is instantiated, causing the initialization of the parameter extents. Output parameters are initialized to empty model extents. All are accessible using the this variable, which refers to the transformation instance itself. When instantiating objects, the model extent can be declared to remove ambiguity when multiple models of the same type are in use. This is done using the @ sign followed by the name, as shown here:

```
transformation mindmap2requirements(in inModel : mindmap,

  out oneModel : requirements, out outModel2 : requirements);

main() {
  object Model@oneModel {
  }
}
```

The modeltype declaration assigns an alias to a metamodel used in the context of the transformation. The uses part of the declaration specifies the model name and registered URI that the environment uses to resolve the MOF metamodel definition. In the case of Eclipse QVT OML, MOF is equivalent to EMF's Ecore metamodel. Therefore, URIs used here are those found in the NS URI field of packages registered in EMF. To see a list of the models registered in the environment, use the **Metamodel Explorer** view provided by the M2M OML component. It's also possible to specify modeltypes using Eclipse platform:/plugin and platform:/resource Uniform Resource Identifiers (URIs).

Note that it's not necessary to place the URI within parentheses following the model name. The following is equivalent to our Unified Modeling Language (UML) modeltype declaration earlier:

```
modeltype UML uses 'http://www.eclipse.org/examples/1.0.0/simpleuml';
```

You also can simply state the model name, which, in the case of M2M OML, corresponds to the EMF registered package. This allows some flexibility because several versions of a model could be registered in the environment, but it also can cause some conflicts because you cannot guarantee that the model name is unique. Technically, the NS URI is no guarantee of uniqueness, but it gives a much higher degree of confidence. Following is another modeltype declaration that uses just the model name:

```
modeltype UML uses simpleuml;
```

A modeltype declaration can also include a `strict` qualifier. By default, model types are effective and flexible, in that they allow the transformation to work with similar model types. For example, slight version changes of a metamodel might not impact a QVT definition, so the `effective` declaration allows these instances to be processed. If the transformation author requires a specific metamodel to be used, adding `strict` before the `uses` clause provides the required enforcement. For example, this is a fully qualified modeltype declaration using `strict` compliance:

```
modeltype UML 'strict' uses

simpleuml('http://www.eclipse.org/examples/1.0.0/simpleuml');
```

You also can restrict the model type using a `where` clause. For example, the following declaration imposes the restriction that a model must have at least one `Class`. This capability allows for a degree of validation of input models without executing the transformation.

```
modeltype UML uses

simpleuml('http://www.eclipse.org/examples/1.0.0/simpleuml') where

{self.ownedElements->closure(oclIsKindOf(UML::Class))->size() > 0};
```

Currently, the M2M QVTO implementation produces a warning that metamodel conditions are not supported.

NOTE

The use of `closure()` in the previous statement is nonstandard. Although QVT extends standard OCL libraries, this is not a QVT function. The `closure` iterator is provided by MDT's OCL component and works nicely in this case.

The previous signature states that the uml2rdb transformation will take as an input a uml model instance of type UML and return an rdb model instance of type RDB. From the modeltype statements, we know that these map to models found in our environment by name or URI. Parameters have a direction (in, out, or inout), an identifier, and a type. Parameters that are designated as in parameters are not changed, those designated as inout are updated (these are sometimes referred to as *in-place* transformations), and those designated as out are assigned the newly created result. Note that it's possible to have abstract transformations, where the main() mapping is disallowed.

13.1.1 In-Place Transformations

It is possible to invoke a transformation for the purpose of modifying an existing model. Potential uses for this capability are model cleansing, refactoring, or refinement. Section 6.2, "Model Refactoring," provides an example of an in-place transformation. Part of this example is provided again here:

```
transformation requirements2requirements(inout model : requirements);

property groupCounter : Integer = null;
property reqCounter : Integer = null;

mapping main(inout req : requirements::Model@model) {
   -- ...
}

mapping inout requirements::RequirementGroup::resetValues() {
   -- ...
}
```

The key to using QVT for in-place transformations is to use inout declarations in the transformation signature, main mapping, and mapping definitions that modify the model.

13.1.2 Extends and Access

A transformation can extend another transformation or library. For example, suppose that we have a BaseUml2Rdb transformation and UmlUtil library that we want to extend. Furthermore, we want to access a typeUtil library. To indicate this, we simply add the following extends and access keywords with transformation names to the end of our signature. In the case of extension, mapping definitions can override those in the extended transformation.

```
transformation uml2rdb(in uml:UML, out rdb:RDB)
extends BaseUml2Rdb
extends library UmlUtil
access library typeUtil;
```

At this time, M2M OML does not support access and extension of transformations and libraries. The M2M project does not yet have a Relations language implementation, so it also does not yet support the `refines` keyword.

13.1.3 Intermediate Elements

OML supports the definition of `intermediate` classes and properties, which can be helpful in some transformation definitions. Essentially, the definition of an `intermediate` class and associated property allows for metamodel extension in the context of the transformation. The example used in the specification follows; here, a `LeafAttribute` class is defined to help with mapping complex type attributes to relational database columns. An `intermediate` property allows for the storage of `LeafAttributes` in a `Sequence`, accessible as a feature of the `Class` element.

```
intermediate class LeafAttribute {
  name : String;
  kind : String;
  attr : Attribute;
};

intermediate property Class::leafAttributes : Sequence(LeafAttribute);
```

Elsewhere in the transformation, the `leafAttributes` property can be accessed in the same manner as any other feature of the metamodel. For example:

```
self.leafAttributes := self.attribute->map attr2LeafAttrs();
```

Unfortunately, intermediate classes are not yet implemented in Eclipse M2M OML. Intermediate properties are supported and can be a Tuple type, providing somewhat of a workaround for the lack of intermediate classes, as shown next. Another workaround is to define an intermediate class in a separate `*.ecore` model and use it within the context of the transformation.

```
intermediate property UML::Class::leafAttributes :

Sequence(Tuple(name:String, kind:String, attr:Attribute));
```

13.1.4 Configuration Properties

External properties might need to be passed into a transformation, which you can accomplish using a `configuration property` declaration. For example, say that you are transforming a model into a Java model and need to specify the package namespace, but it's not a property in the source model. Assuming that you know this value at invocation time, it can be passed to the transformation and set in a configuration property. A name and type are required, as shown in the following example.

```
configuration property namespace : String;
```

Using Eclipse OML, the launch configuration dialog has a **Configuration** tab that is aware of all configuration property entries in the specified transformation. Values entered are passed into the executing transformation instance to initialize the corresponding properties.

13.1.5 Renaming Elements

Sometimes a clash arises between the name of elements in a metamodel and, say, keywords in OML. In this case, the `rename` facility can provide an alternative naming in the context of the transformation. In the following example, the `library` attribute of the `java::Class` element is renamed to `lib` to avoid a clash with the `library` keyword:

```
rename java::Class.lib = 'library';
```

This feature of the QVTO implementation is not generally required because name clashes are handled automatically by prefixing the element with an underscore. So using the previous example, the `library` element would be accessed as `_library` within the transformation.

13.1.6 Predefined Variables

Within the context of a transformation definition, a number of predefined variables are available. You can access the transformation itself, or the instance thereof, using the `this` variable. You can therefore use `this` to access configuration properties, mappings, helpers, and so on. For example, to reference a property defined at the transformation level, you can access it as follows:

```
this.dependencies := mmap.dependencies();
```

As you will see shortly, within the context of a mapping or query, the contextual parameter is accessed using the `self` variable. The final predefined variable, also discussed in detail soon, is the `result` variable, which accesses the result parameter or tuple of a mapping or helper.

13.1.7 Null

Within the context of a transformation, the literal `null` complies to any type and is used to mean the absence of value. It can be used as the return of an operation, either explicitly or implicitly. From OCL, the type OclAny also represents an object of any type, while the type OclVoid represents an undefined value and conforms to all types. The OclAny operation oclIsUndefined returns `true` when its argument is undefined.

13.2 Libraries

Often you can reuse query, mapping, and type definitions in transformations. When this is the case, they are defined in `library` modules and imported as discussed earlier using `access` or `extends` statements in a transformation signature. Using `access` implies import semantics, whereas `extends` implies inheritance semantics.

The main differences between a library and a transformation are that no `main` entry point is defined for execution in a library and that models listed in its signature are those it operates on, not parameters. Following is a library definition `UmlRdbUtil` that operates on UML model instances, extends the `UmlUtil` library, and accesses the `RdbUtil` library:

```
library UmlRdbUtil(UML)
extends UmlUtil
access RdbUtil;
```

Note that QVT defines a standard library `StdLib` that is implicitly imported in every transformation definition. This is similar in concept to the `java.lang.*` package, which is imported automatically in every Java class.

13.3 Mapping Operations

OML `mapping` operations are the refinement of a relation and provide the fundamental behavior of transformations. Mappings take one or more source model elements and return one or more target model elements. Following is the general syntax of a mapping operation, where <direction> is one of in, out, or inout. A mapping is either contextual, as seen here, where X represents the type and prefixes the mapping name, or noncontextual, where the input parameter is explicitly declared, as in **mapping** XtoR(in x : X) : R.

```
mapping <direction> X::name
      (<direction> p1:P1, <direction> p2:P2)  : r1:R1, r2:R2
   when { ... }
   where { ... }
{
   init { ... }
   population { ... }
   end { ... }
}
```

A mapping has a name, which, by convention, follows either an X::<input_ element>2<output_element>() or X::to<output_element>() pattern, where x represents the input element type. The mapping name is prefixed by the fully qualified input element, separated by double colons. This is standard OCL namespace syntax. The input object is referenced using self within the mapping. Note that a mapping can be declared as abstract.

Parameters are comma separated and indicate direction in|out|inout followed by name and type information. Input parameters cannot be modified, while inout parameters can be updated. The out parameter receives a new value but cannot be newly created if a previous mapping invocation for the input instance has been processed. The following example specifies a single input parameter named targetType and conforms to the type UML::DataType. In this case, UML is defined by a modeltype declaration at the top of the transformation.

The result is declared following a single colon after the parameter list. In the following example, the return conforms to the type RDB::TableColumn, where RDB is also defined by a modeltype declaration. Note that it's possible to have multiple results for a mapping. The result keyword is used to reference the return object, or tuple, in the case of multiple result objects.

```
mapping UML::Property::primitiveAttribute2column(in targetType :

UML::DataType) : RDB::TableColumn
  when { self.isPrimitive() }
{
  isPrimaryKey := self.isPrimaryKey();
  name := self.name;
. . .
}
```

Before the mapping body are optional when and where sections, both of which evaluate contained Boolean expressions. The when clause acts as either a *precondition* or *guard,* while the where clause acts as a *post-condition.* In the previous example, the input Property object is validated as being primitive using a call to the isPrimitive() query. If the when clause evaluates to false, the mapping is not executed and a return object is not created (null is returned). If the mapping is invoked using strict semantics (xmap), the mapping is not executed and an exception is thrown. Currently, M2M OML does not support the where clause.

13.3.1 Mapping Body

Within the body of the mapping, marked by open and closing curly braces, are optional init, population, and end blocks. These are optional, in that init and end blocks are not required, and the population section is implied as the remaining area within the mapping body itself. The specification describes situations when it is required to use an explicit population section, but it's not generally used.

The init section is where computation can take place to initialize variables, explicit setting of output parameters, and so on before the effective instantiation of the mapping output. A possible use for init is to instantiate an object that is a subtype of that defined as the result in the mapping definition. The output values are set in the population section, and finalization of computation occurs in the end section before the mapping returns.

You can consider yet another section to exist implicitly between the init and population section where return objects that are not initialized are instantiated. What's important to realize here is that if you want to assign an existing object to a return parameter, you must do this in the init section. The end block is a finalization section for placing additional code that must be invoked before the mapping operation returns.

Execution Semantics

To better understand a mapping operation's execution semantics, consider the following sequence:

1. When resolved, a mapping is executed with all parameters passed as a tuple. This includes the context parameter (first) and the result parameter (last).

2. All out parameters are initialized to null, while all input parameters are passed by reference.

3. The type compliance of all parameters and evaluation of the when clause takes place. If failure occurs, `null` is returned.

4. If the guard succeeds, the trace is consulted to see whether the mapping has previously been satisfied for the given input. If so, the out parameters are populated using the previous result and are returned. Otherwise, the mapping body is entered.

5. The expressions found in the `init` section (if present) are executed in sequence.

6. Following `init`, the "implicit instantiation" section is entered, where all output objects are initialized, if still `null`. Collection types are initialized with empty collections, and trace data is recorded for the mapping.

7. Each expression in the population section is executed in sequence, typically operating on the `out` or `inout` objects.

8. The `end` section expressions are then executed in sequence.

The execution semantics change when a mapping inherits, merges, or is a disjunction of another mapping, as described in Section 13.3.3, "Inheritance, Merger, and Disjunction."

return

During execution of a mapping operation or helper, you can control the flow using explicit `return` statements. If a value is provided, it is assigned to the `result` object of the mapping.

13.3.2 Entry Operation

A special form of mapping, known as the entry operation, is marked with the `main` keyword. There can be only one `main` per transformation—or, in the case of abstract transformations, no `main` operation at all. If used without `mapping`, this entry point takes no parameters and has no `init`, `population`, or `end` block. A `main` can be used with the `mapping` keyword and combines the aspects of the transformation entry point and those of a regular mapping operation. Following is a `main` that does not declare that it's a mapping operation. The output is assigned the result of the `toRequirementsModel()` mapping. As you can see, QVTO allows parameters in `main` operations, although it's technically not allowed in the specification.

```
main(in mmap : mindmap::Map@inModel, out req :

requirements::Model@outModel) {
  req := mmap.map toRequirementsModel();
}
```

An example of using `main` without parameters follows. Strictly speaking, this is what all `main()` operations should look like. In most cases, the `in` model parameter is accessed directly and is used to invoke the mapping operation. The `rootObjects()` operation is available on all Model objects. The use of brackets in the statement is an example of the `collectselect` statement shorthand.

```
transformation mindmap2requirements(in inModel : mindmap,

out outModel : requirements);

main() {
  inModel.rootObjects()[Map]->map toRequirementsModel();
}
```

13.3.3 Inheritance, Merger, and Disjunction

Mappings can extend other mappings through inheritance, can have their result merged with the result of another mapping, or can be executed based on the success of their guard conditions. Each of these is discussed next, along with how they impact the execution semantics at runtime.

inherits

Mapping operations can inherit from other mapping operations. During execution, the inherited mapping is invoked *after* the initialization section of the inheriting mapping. This includes the implicit instantiation section. The effect of this is that output parameters are non-`null` when the inherited mapping is invoked.

Following is an example of `inherits` used in the context of our `dnc2jee`. `qvto` transformation found in Section 6.9, "Transforming a Business Model to Java."

```
mapping dnc::Archetype::toClass() : java::JavaClass {
  name := self.name;
  fields += self.getAttributes().map toField(result);
  methods += self.getOperations().map toMethod();
}
```

```
mapping dnc::Archetype::toSerializableClass() : java::JavaClass
  inherits dnc::Archetype::toClass {
  implementsInterfaces += 'java.io.Serializable'.map toClass();
}

mapping dnc::Archetype::toStateful() : java::JavaClass
  inherits dnc::Archetype::toSerializableClass {

  eAnnotations += toAnnotation('description', self.description, null);
  eAnnotations += toAnnotation('annotation', '@Stateful', null);
  classImport += 'javax.ejb.Stateful'.map toClass();
}
```

In this example, `toStateful()` inherits from `toSerializableClass()`, which, in turn, inherits from `toClass()`.

merges

Sometimes a mapping operation produces multiple outputs or results in an object that is the logical combination of other defined mappings. By allowing for the merging of mapping operations, the language of the transformation more closely approximates a natural language. In terms of execution semantics, the merged mappings are invoked following the end of the merging mapping. All mappings, including `out`, are passed to the merged mapping.

We can modify our previous `inherits` example to include `merges` for the serializable aspect of the stateful class. In this case, a stateful bean is a class that also is serializable.

```
mapping dnc::Archetype::toClass() : java::JavaClass {
  name := self.name;
  fields += self.getAttributes().map toField(result);
  methods += self.getOperations().map toMethod();
}

mapping dnc::Archetype::toSerializableClass() : java::JavaClass {
  implementsInterfaces += 'java.io.Serializable'.map toClass();
}

mapping dnc::Archetype::toStateful() : java::JavaClass
  inherits dnc::Archetype::toClass
  merges dnc::Archetype::toSerializableClass {

  eAnnotations += toAnnotation('description', self.description, null);
  eAnnotations += toAnnotation('annotation', '@Stateful', null);
  classImport += 'javax.ejb.Stateful'.map toClass();
}
```

Disjunction

Another option when structuring mappings is to specify several mappings from which the first that satisfies its guard conditions (type and when clause) is executed. This is done by specifying a list of mappings after the `disjuncts` keyword in the mapping declaration.

During execution, each guard is executed in a series until one is satisfied. The first successful disjuncted mapping is executed. If none of those listed satisfies the conditions, `null` is returned. Following is an example adopted from the specification, for illustration:

```
mapping uml::Feature::convertFeature () : java::Element
    disjuncts convertAttribute, convertOperation, convertConstructor {}

mapping uml::Attribute::convertAttribute : java::Field {
    name := self.name;
}

mapping uml::Operation::convertConstructor : java::Constructor
    when {self.name = self.namespace.name} {
    name := self.name;
}

mapping uml::Operation::convertOperation : java::Constructor
    when {self.name <> self.namespace.name} {
    name := self.name;
}
```

13.4 Helper Operations

Although I've mentioned `mapping` and `query` operations, I've not made a formal distinction between these two constructs. According to the QVT specification, a query is a special kind of `helper` operation. But unlike a `query`, a `helper` *may* have side effects on the parameters passed into it.

Queries are intended to simplify expression writing in mapping operations because complex queries are not required to be implemented within an expression. The main restriction on queries is that they cannot create or update object instances, other than for predefined and intermediate types. A query is an operation that has no side effects.

A mapping operation does not return a new instance of the specified model object for a given input instance upon subsequent invocations, based on its trace model. Instead, it returns a reference to the previously mapped instance. With a helper operation, the result is always a new instance.

This query operation returns all objects of type Topic from the elements reference of a Map instance:

```
query mindmap::Map::getTopics() : Sequence(mindmap::Topic) {
  return self.elements->select(oclIsTypeOf(mindmap::Topic))
  ->collect(oclAsType(mindmap::Topic));
}
```

In queries, it's possible to define and assign local variables. For example, the following query returns a dot-delimited fully qualified name for a class based on its package namespace:

```
query oocore::Class::fullyQualifiedName() : String {
  var fqn : String := self.name;
  var pkg : oocore::Package := self._package;
  while (not pkg.oclIsUndefined()) {
    fqn := pkg.name + '.' + fqn;
    pkg := pkg._package;
  };
  return fqn;
}
```

13.5 Implementing Operations

Within mapping and query operations, objects are created, initialized, passed as parameters, returned as parameters, and more. Although much of the syntax you will use within mapping and query bodies is OCL, QVT provides additional features. This section covers essential OCL and QVT operations, mapping and query invocation, object creation, and population.

13.5.1 Operations and Iterators

All the common OCL operations and iterators form the basis of QVT, with imperative versions provided to support side effects and strict semantics.

select

The select() operation comes from OCL and allows for the filtering of collections to work with a subset. The conditional argument provides for the specification of the filter and can have an optional iterator variable. Following is an example of select in which all objects of type mindmap::Topic are returned from the elements collection:

```
elements->select(oclIsTypeOf(mindmap::Topic))
```

The select operation has a shorthand notation that uses square brackets, as shown here. This expression is equivalent to the previous one.

```
elements[oclIsTypeOf(mindmap::Topic)]
```

collect

The `collect()` operation comes from OCL and allows for the creation of one collection from another, typically of different element types. The resulting collection is flattened; `collectNested()` and QVT's `xcollect()` can be used when nested collections are required. `collect()` is commonly used to gather the elements of a class into a new collection, as illustrated here:

```
topics->collect(t | t.name);
```

Here, `topics` represents a collection of Topic elements, which have a name attribute of type String. Therefore, the result of this `collect()` operation is a collection of Strings representing the name attribute values of each Topic element in topics. This can be written without the iterator variable as simply this:

```
topics->collect(name);
```

Collect() also has a shorthand notation, where a dot (.) can be used in lieu of the `->collect()` syntax. This makes the previous statement even more simply stated as follows:

```
topics.name;
```

It's common to find `select()` and `collect()` used together to obtain a collection of commonly typed elements from a reference that can contain multiple subtypes. For example, consider the `elements` reference in the Map class that is of type MapElement. Two subtypes exist: Topic and Reference. To obtain just the Topic elements, use the following expression:

```
var topics : Sequence(Topic) :=
self.elements->select(oclIsTypeOf(Topic)->collect(oclAsType(Topic));

-- using shorthand, the following is equivalent:
var topics : Sequence(Topic) :=
self.elements[oclIsTypeOf(Topic)].oclAsType(Topic);
```

13.5.2 Imperative Operations

QVTO provides a number of imperative operations, including forEach, forOne, while, and switch. Additionally, imperative versions of OCL are available. This section describes each and provides examples of their use.

forEach

The forEach imperative loop expression executes the loop for all the elements in the collection for which the conditional expression holds. QVTO currently does not support this expression.

forOne

The forOne imperative loop expression executes the loop for only the first element in the collection that satisfies the conditional expression. QVTO currently does not support this expression.

while

The while control expression iterates on an expression until its condition is false. You can terminate a while using a break, or you can direct execution to the beginning of the next iteration at any point using the continue expression. Following is an example of a while loop used to create a table name from a class name:

```
/**
 * Replaces camel case with underscore, e.g. firstName -> FIRST_NAME
 */
query String::toColumnName() : String {
  var name : String := '';
  var digit : String := '';
  var pos : Integer := 1;
  while (pos <= self.size()) {
    digit := self.substring(pos, pos);
    if digit.toLowerCase() <> digit then {
```

```
      name := name + '_' + digit;
    } else {
      name := name + digit;
    } endif;
    pos := pos + 1;
  };
  return name.toUpperCase();
}
```

switch

The switch imperative expression evaluates condition-based alternatives. It is popular when dealing with enumeration types, as shown in the following example. Note that the more familiar case syntax is also available, in addition to what's shown here.

```
query mindmap::Topic::getPriority() : String {
  var pri : String := null;
  switch {
      (self.priority = Priority::HIGH) ? pri := 'High';
      (self.priority = Priority::MEDIUM) ? pri := 'Medium';
      (self.priority = Priority::LOW) ? pri := 'Low';
      else ? assert fatal (false)
      with log('Priority unsupported', self);
  };
  return pri;
}
```

In the example, the priority is evaluated against the enumeration literal, with a String returned for each match. If no matches are found, the else statement invokes a fatal assertion to terminate execution and log the appropriate message.

13.5.3 Imperative Iterate Expressions

A set of six imperative iterate expressions are available: xcollect, collectOne, collectselect, collectselectOne, xselect, and selectOne. Each of these iterates over the source collection to populate the target using iterator variables, a body, and a condition expression. These are similar to their OCL counterparts but can be interrupted using break, continue, raise, and return expressions. Perhaps the most important difference is that null values are not included in the result set.

The xcollect imperative iterate expression is similar to its collect counterpart, but with the important distinction that it does not flatten the result. This makes it more comparable to the OCL collectNested() operation. This means that xcollect can return nested collections such as {1, {2, 3}}, which collect would otherwise return as {1, 2, 3}.

As for the collection types xcollect operates on and returns, Sets and Bags result in a Bag, while OrderedSets and Sequences result in a Sequence. In both cases, duplicates are possible.

You can think of the collectselect imperative iterate expression as a single loop combination of collect and select, where *null* values are removed from the result. The remaining iterators are self-explanatory.

The type of objects contained within the results of these iterators depends on the use of its conditional, if specified. When a Type is specified as the conditional, it is evaluated using the Boolean oclIsKind(Type) and returns a sequence casted to the specified Type.

Shorthand notation is available for these imperative expressions, as described in the following examples. Notice that the shorthand is also available to operations, as shown in the last two examples.

```
-- An example of collectselect
self.elements->collectselect(i; a=i.name | a.startsWith('A'));

-- An equivalent collectselect using shorthand notation
self.elements->name[a | a.startsWith('A')];

-- An equivalent collectselect shorthand without a target variable
self.elements->name[startsWith('A')];

-- An example of xcollect
self.elements->xcollect(a | a.name);

-- An equivalent xcollect using shorthand notation
self.elements->name;

-- An example of xselect
self.elements->xselect(Topic);

-- An equivalent xselect using shorthand notation
self.elements[Topic];

-- An example of collectselect shorthand with an operation
main() {
  inModel.rootObjects()[Map].map toRequirementsModel();
}

-- An example of collectselectOne shorthand using '!'
main() {
  inModel.rootObjects()![Map].map toRequirementsModel();
}
```

13.5.4 Object Creation and Population

As mentioned earlier, a mapping invocation implicitly creates an instance of the declared return type or types. The features of instantiated elements are set using the assignment operator (:=), as shown earlier with the `name := self.name` statement. Although this works for mappings of simple attributes of the same type, more complex mappings necessarily require more complex expressions. Note that a second assignment operator (+=) is available for adding to collections.

To create an object within the context of an operation, use the `object` keyword. Following is a basic `object` expression that creates an instance of `PrimitiveDataType` and assigns it to the type reference in the `TableColumn` object created by the mapping:

```
type := object RDB::datatypes::PrimitiveDataType {
  name := 'int';
};
```

In fact, the entire body of a mapping can be contained within an `object` block, as shown in the complete mapping definition. This is not necessary, however, because the return type of the mapping is enough to determine what the body is instantiating.

```
mapping UML::Property::primitiveAttribute2column(in targetType:

UML::DataType) : RDB::TableColumn
  when { self.isPrimitive() }
{
  object RDB::TableColumn {
    isPrimaryKey := self.isPrimaryKey();
    name := self.name;
    type := object RDB::datatypes::PrimitiveDataType {
      name := umlPrimitive2rdbPrimitive(self.type.name);
    };
  }
}
```

A common use of `object` is to initialize variables in the init section. For example, the following snippet has a variable `primitiveType` assigned to an object that was created and initialized using the `umlPrimitive2rdbPrimitive()` query, which is later used to set the `TableColumn`'s type reference.

```
mapping UML::Property::primitiveAttribute2column(in targetType:

UML::DataType) : RDB::TableColumn
  when { self.isPrimitive() }
{
  init {
    var primitiveType : RDB::datatypes::PrimitiveDataType :=
        object RDB::datatypes::PrimitiveDataType {
        name := umlPrimitive2rdbPrimitive(self.type.name);
      };
  }
  isPrimaryKey := self.isPrimaryKey();
  name := self.name;
  type := primitiveType;
}
```

As stated earlier, objects that are created are first checked for existence. If they are `null`, a new object of the stated type is instantiated and initialized in the order of the statements in the body. If the object already exists, its contents are updated according to the statements in the body. This implies that update semantics are used in object statements where an object has already been instantiated. Consider this example:

```
mapping UML::Property::primitiveAttribute2column(in targetType:

UML::DataType) : RDB::TableColumn
  when { self.isPrimitive() }
{
  init {
    result := object RDB::TableColumn {
      isPrimaryKey := self.isPrimaryKey();
      type := object RDB::datatypes::PrimitiveDataType {
        name := umlPrimitive2rdbPrimitive(self.type.name);
      };
    };
  }
  name := self.name;
}
```

This example shows the use of the `result` keyword, in addition to the inlining of mapping operations. By default, the returned model instance of a mapping is assigned to the `result`, which we're explicitly setting here in the `init` section. We're then updating the result in the mapping body to set the name property. Technically, the implicit instantiation section that exists between the `init` section and the `population` section (or the mapping body, in this case) recognizes the existence of the instantiated result and incorporates update semantics.

If you examine the output of this mapping, you'll find that `isPrimaryKey` and `type` are both set correctly during the `init`, while the name of the returned instance is simply updated in the mapping body without instantiating a new `TableColumn`. Similarly, access to the result is available in the `end{}` block, as shown next. Here again, update semantics are in effect in both the body and end blocks because there is an implicit instantiation of the return object.

```
mapping UML::Property::primitiveAttribute2column(in targetType:

UML::DataType) : RDB::TableColumn
  when { self.isPrimitive() }
{
  name := self.name;

  end {
    result.isPrimaryKey := self.isPrimaryKey();
    result.type := object RDB::datatypes::PrimitiveDataType {
      name := umlPrimitive2rdbPrimitive(self.type.name);
    };
  }
}
```

Another reason to explicitly create an object is for assignment to return parameters where more than one is defined for a mapping. Consider this example:

```
mapping X::toYZ() : y:Y, z:Z {
  object y:Y {
  };
  object z:Z {
  };
}
```

13.5.5 Mapping Invocation

When invoking a mapping, use either the `map` or `xmap` keyword, where `xmap` represents invocation with strict semantics. The `map` keyword is used after a dot (.) or alternatively after an arrow (->) when using the collect shorthand. When invocated, as long as the mapping can be resolved using the actual context and the guard conditions are satisfied (if present), the trace is consulted to look for target instances produced from the given source object. If present, the relation holds and the previous result is returned. Otherwise, the mapping body is executed.

In this first example, the input is being mapped using nonstrict semantics to a requirements Model using the more popular form of invocation.

```
main(in mmap : mindmap::Map@inModel, out req :

requirements::Model@outModel) {
  req := mmap.map toRequirementsModel();
}

mapping mindmap::Map::toRequirementsModel() : requirements::Model {
  . . .
}
```

If we simply change map to xmap, we change the invocation semantics to strict. In this case, if the called mapping has a when clause that is not satisfied, an exception is thrown. Using map, the mapping simply returns null.

```
main(in mmap : mindmap::Map@inModel, out req :

requirements::Model@outModel) {
  req := mmap.xmap toRequirementsModel();
}
```

Both map and xmap can be called using an arrow instead of the dot notation. This implies that the mapping operation is the body of an xcollect imperative collect construct.

13.5.6 Resolution Operators

OML provides resolve, resolveone, resolveIn, and resolveoneIn resolution operators that reference trace data to resolve created objects, or objects used as the source of an object creation, in the case of their inverse variants. These can be useful to update or reference objects created from executed mappings. We cover each of these in turn, along with their late versions, which are designed to improve transformation efficiency.

resolve

The most fundamental resolution operator is resolve. It returns an object created from a mapping operation. The resolve operator can take no arguments, a type argument, or a Boolean type condition. Consider an example of each:

```
source->resolve();  -- select any object
source->resolve(Type);     -- select only Type instances
-- select Type instances where the name attribute equals 'aName'

source->resolve(t:Type | t.name = 'aName');
```

The type returned from a resolve operation matches that provided, or a collection (Sequence) of the type. If no type is specified, `OclAny` is the result type. Technically, the specification calls for a return type of `Object`, but the current QVTO implementation returns its subclass `OclAny`.

TIP

The conditional version of `resolve` can result in a performance advantage over filtering the results because it avoids intermediate collection creation.

Let's consider our mindmap-to-requirements transformation to describe the `resolve` functions. As you might recall, a mindmap has a collection of Relationship elements that are mapped to Requirement dependency references when the type of Relationship is of `Type::DEPENDENCY`. To create this mapping, we first need to obtain the Requirement object that was created from the source Topic in the Relationship. For this, we can use the following `sourceReq` variable assignment:

```
mapping mindmap::Relationship::toDependency()
  when { self.type = mindmap::Type::DEPENDENCY }
{
  init {
    var sourceReq : requirements::Requirement :=
      self.source.resolve(requirements::Requirement)->any(true);
  }
...
}
```

This mapping is invoked from the `end` block of our main mapping, so all Topic to Requirement mappings are completed. In this case, the `resolve` operation returns all Requirement objects that were created from the Topic object referenced in our `source` reference. We know that there is a one-to-one mapping in this case, so we can filter the resulting `Sequence` using `any(true)`.

Having obtained the Requirement mapped from the `source` Topic in our Relationship, we now need to find the Requirement object created from the Topic referenced by the `target` reference and add it to our collection of `sourceReq` dependencies. We can accomplish this using another `resolve` operation. Although `resolve` returns all possible mappings, we know that only one will be possible.

```
sourceReq.dependencies +=

  self.target.resolve(requirements::Requirement);
```

resolveone

When we're interested in only the first suitable result when using resolve, we can use the `resolveone` alternative. If no suitable results are found, a `null` is returned.

Returning to our example, although `resolve` worked in the last case, we can improve it a bit by specifying that we want only the first result. So combining the two fragments and replacing `resolve` with `resolveone`, we have the following equivalent version:

```
mapping mindmap::Relationship::toDependency()
  when { self.type = mindmap::Type::DEPENDENCY }
{
  init {
    var sourceReq : requirements::Requirement :=
      self.source.resolveone(requirements::Requirement);
    sourceReq.dependencies +=
      self.target.resolveone(requirements::Requirement);
  }
}
```

resolveIn and resolveoneIn

If we want to further restrict the possible results to objects created by a specific mapping, we can use the `resolveIn` and `resolveoneIn` variants. These take an additional argument to represent the qualified identifier of the mapping. If multiple mappings have the same name with different signatures, an ambiguity error is reported.

In the case of our mindmap-to-requirements mapping, we have only one mapping that produces Requirement objects from Topic objects, but if there are more in the future, we can restrict those resolved by specifying the current mapping as follows:

```
var sourceReq : requirements::Requirement :=
  self.source.resolveoneIn(mindmap::Topic::toRequirement,
  requirements::Requirement);

sourceReq.dependencies +=
  self.target.resolveoneIn(mindmap::Topic::toRequirement,
  requirements::Requirement);
```

inv

Sometimes we're interested in the inverse resolution, or finding the source object that was used in a mapping to create or update an object. By prefixing the resolve operators with inv, we can achieve the inverse—for example, invresolve, invresolveone, invresolveIn, and so on.

late

When performing transformations, resolving objects that were not yet created during the execution of a mapping might require more than one pass over a model. To solve this problem, you can modify resolution operators with a late operator to defer evaluation until the end of the transformation. This technique is always used with assignment operators, where a null assignment is created until resolution is completed. Use transformation properties instead of local variables so that they are valid when the transformation ends.

Keep in mind that the left side of a late resolution statement is not re-executed along with the right-side deferred statement. This means that you cannot expect to use the result of the deferred assignment in a later expression. For example, the following assignment of the variable p is not the result of the resolve operation; the result is null because that was assigned during the normal execution.

```
mapping mindmap::Topic::toRequirement() : requirements::Requirement {
  parent := self.parent.late resolve(requirements::Requirement)
    ->asSet();
  end {
    var p := result.parent->asOrderedSet();
  }
}
```

Furthermore, late resolutions are invoked sequentially at the end of the transformation in the order they were encountered during normal execution. Don't rely on the result of a late resolution that might not have been executed.

As we mentioned earlier, invoking our example mapping from the end block ensures that we can resolve Requirement objects created from our Topic objects. We can alter this approach using the late resolution operator, which defers resolution until the end of the transformation and provides the same outcome. Following is an example of this approach:

```
property dependencies : Set(Relationship) = null;

mapping main(in mmap : mindmap::Map, out req : requirements::Model) {
  init {
    this.dependencies := mmap.dependencies();
      . . .
  }
}
```

```
mapping mindmap::Topic::toRequirement() : requirements::Requirement {
  title := self.name;
  children += self.subtopics.map toRequirement();
  dependencies += this.dependencies
    ->select(source = self).target.late
  resolveIn(mindmap::Topic::toRequirement,
    requirements::Requirement);
}
```

Here we've reworked our example a bit to illustrate late resolveIn. A dependencies property is declared in the transformation and initialized in our main mapping using a query that selects all Relationships of Type::DEPENDENCY (not shown). When mapping our Topic elements to Requirement elements, we add to the Requirement's dependencies list those Requirements that were resolved using the toRequirement() mapping, where the Topic is specified as the target of the Relationship and where the current Topic is the source. During execution, all Topics might not yet have been processed, so late enables us to avoid a second pass. Section 6.6, "Transforming a Mindmap to Requirements," fully explains this example.

Note that although it's legal to combine the inv variant with a late operator, it doesn't make much sense to do so. This is because the source object would always be available using a non-late resolve operation.

13.5.7 Executing Transformations

Some things that occur during execution of a QVT script are more clear when we have a debugger, trace model, or log facility. This section discusses the execution facilities that are available in the QVTO runtime. Unfortunately, no debugger is yet available from M2M QVTO.

Trace Model

Execution of a transformation results in one or more target models and a corresponding trace model. The trace model contains a recording of each mapping, including input model element and target model element instance data. The trace model is consulted during execution and for reconciliation during subsequent transformation, to allow for model update semantics.

When an object is created within a transformation, an entry in a trace file is made. When using M2M OML, you'll find a .qvtotrace model file created when you execute a transformation, as specified in the launch configuration. Feel free to examine this model to better understand its contents and how it works.

Log

To output information on transformation execution to the environment, a `log` expression is provided and has the following syntax. This expression is helpful when debugging QVT scripts or for understanding how they work.

```
log(message, [object], [level]) [when condition];
```

Only the first argument is required, but the output also can include a reference to the relevant object and a level. The conditional is also optional and can reference the relevant object. For example:

```
init {
    log('Input map:', mmap, 3) when mmap.elements->size() > 0;
}
```

Using M2M QVT OML, this outputs to the console the `toString()` result of the mmap object, prefixed by `Level 3 -` and the String `Input map:`, as shown here:

```
Level 3 - Input map:, data:

org.eclipse.emf.ecore.impl.DynamicEObjectImpl@6fa74a (eClass:

org.eclipse.emf.ecore.impl.EClassImpl@d467a6 (name: Map)

(instanceClassName: null) (abstract: false, interface: false))
```

The level value has no strict meaning in QVT for `log` messages, and M2M QVT OML allows any integer value, leaving it up to the user to specify and interpret levels.

Log output in M2M QVT OML is displayed in the Eclipse Console view. Optionally, the launch configuration can redirect the output to a file, as discussed in Section 6.5.4, "Launch Configuration."

Assert

If a condition needs to be checked during transformation execution, you can use the `assert` expression and combine it with the `log` expression to output information. You can assign severity to an assertion with the levels `warning`, `error`, or `fatal`, with `error` being the default. If a `fatal` severity is declared, the transformation execution terminates if the assertion fails. This is the general syntax of the `assert` expression:

```
assert [severity] condition [with log]
```

For example, the following assertion checks whether a Topic element's name attribute begins with an underscore and logs a message if it does:

```
init {
  assert warning (not name.startsWith('_')) with
    log('Topic name begins with underscore', name);
}
```

Note that the surrounding parentheses are required per the grammar provided in the spec, although this is not shown in Section 8.2.2, "AssertExp."

The default output is the severity level prefixed by `ASSERT` and followed by `failed at <line_number>`, with optional `log` output shown here:

```
ASSERT [warning] failed at (UknownSource:27) :

Topic name begins with underscore, data: _A sub-subtopic
```

Transformation Composition

You can invoke one transformation from another transformation using the `transform()` operation. At this time, transformation composition is not available in QVTO.

13.6 Library Operations

An implicitly imported library for all QVT transformations is the Stdlib library. This section covers the types and operations defined in this library. Some operations that are not currently available are not covered here or are indicated as such. For a complete list of standard library features, refer to the QVT specification.

13.6.1 Object Operations

A couple operations are defined for use on Objects.

repr

```
Object::repr() : String
```

Returns a String representation of an object, similar to the Java `toString()` method. This is handy in `log()` statements.

asOrderedTuple

`Object::asOrderedTuple() : OrderedTuple(T)`

Converts objects not already ordered into an ordered Tuple. This operation is not yet implemented.

13.6.2 Element Operations

In addition to MOF (Ecore) reflective operations, several operations are available on all Elements.

_localId

`Element::_localId() : String`

Returns a local internal identifier. This operation is not currently implemented.

_globalId

`Element::_globalId() : String`

Returns a global internal identifier. This operation is not currently implemented.

metaClassName

`Element::metaClassName() : String`

Returns the name of the metaclass. For example, where `self` is of type `mindmap::Map`, the output of the following `log()` operation is `Map`.

`log(self.metaClassName());`

subobjects

`Element::subobjects() : Set(Element)`

Returns all immediate children objects of the Element.

allSubobjects

```
Element::allSubobjects() : Set(Element)
```

Recursively returns all children objects of the Element.

subobjectsOfType

```
Element::subobjectsOfType(OclType) : Set(Element)
```

Returns all immediate children objects of the Element that are of the specified type.

allSubobjectsOfType

```
Element::allSubobjectsOfType(OclType) : Set(Element)
```

Recursively returns all children objects of the Element that are of the specified type.

subobjectsOfKind

```
Element::subobjectsOfKind(OclType) : Set(Element)
```

Returns all immediate children objects of the Element that are of the specified kind (type plus subtypes).

allSubobjectsOfKind

```
Element::allSubobjectsOfKind(OclType) : Set(Element)
```

Recursively returns all children objects of the Element that are of the specified kind (type plus subtypes).

clone

```
Element::clone() : Element
```

Creates a new instance copy of the model element. The clone is placed in the first model extent. The copy is of only the first-level object, not subobjects. For cloning subobjects as well, see `deepclone`.

deepclone

`Element::deepclone() : Element`

Creates a new instance copy of the model element, including subobjects.

markedAs

`Element::markedAs(value:String) : Boolean`

An operation that is defined for each model type. It can determine whether an element is marked, as is the case when accessing an `MOF::Tag`. This operation is not currently implemented.

markValue

`Element::markValue() : Object`

An operation used to return the value associated with a marked element. This operation is not currently implemented.

stereotypedBy

`Element::stereotypedBy(String) : Boolean`

An operation used to determine whether an element is stereotyped. This operation is not currently implemented.

stereotypedStrictlyBy

`Element::stereotypedStrictlyBy(String) : Boolean`

An operation similar to `stereotypedBy()`, except that the base stereotype is not considered. This operation is not currently implemented.

13.6.3 Model Operations

Model objects that are declared in a transformation signature are available to be accessed throughout the transformation definition. A number of operations are available on these objects and are covered here.

M2M QVT OML provides access to the Ecore features available on the **Model** objects as well. It's possible to access a model's `eAnnotations` property or eContainer() method, for example. For a list of what's available in Ecore, refer to EMF documentation [38].

objects

```
Model::objects() : Set(Element)
```

Returns a list of objects in the model extent, or a flattened set of all objects contained in the passed model instance.

objectsOfType

```
Model::objectsOfType(OclType) : Set(Element)
```

Returns a list of objects from the set of flattened model objects that are of the specified type. Following is an example in which objects of type mindmap::Map are selected from the input model:

```
inModel.objectsOfType(mindmap::Map).map toRequirementsModel();
```

rootObjects

```
Model::rootObjects() : Set(Element)
```

Returns a list of objects found at the root of the model—that is, those not contained within any other model object. In the case of typical Ecore models, this is a single model object. In the case of XMI files, there can be multiple root objects. In the case of XSD-based model instances, the root object is the DocumentRoot object.

removeElement

```
Model::removeElement (Element) : Void
```

Removes an object from the model, including all links to other objects. This can be useful when cleaning up a model created when intermediate or unwanted objects exist.

asTransformation

```
Model::asTransformation(Model) : Transformation
```

Casts a model that complies to the QVT metamodel to a transformation instance, for invocation of dynamically defined transformations. This operation is not yet implemented.

copy

Model::copy() : **Model**

Creates a new instance of a model from an existing model, including all objects in the model extent. This operation is not yet implemented.

createEmptyModel

static **Model**::createEmptyModel() : **Model**

Creates and initializes a model of the specified type. This operation is intended for use when creating intermediate models within a transformation. This operation is not yet implemented.

13.6.4 List Operations

QVT provides a number of list operations, in addition to the collection operations that OCL provides.

add

List(T)::add(T) : **Void**

Adds an element to the end of a mutable list of this type of element. A synonym operation is append(). This operation is not yet implemented.

prepend

List(T)::prepend(T) : **Void**

Adds an element to the beginning of a mutable list of this type of element. This operation is not yet implemented.

insertAt

List(T)::insertAt(T, int:**Integer**) : **Void**

Inserts an element into a mutable list of this type of element at the specified index location. This operation is not yet implemented.

joinfields

```
List(T)::joinfields(sep:String, begin:String, end:String) : String
```

Creates a String of list items separated by sep that is prefixed by begin and suffixed by end Strings. This operation is not yet implemented.

asList

```
Set(T)::asList()  : List(T)
OrderedSet(T)::asList(T)  : List(T)
Sequence(T)::asList(T)  : List(T)
Bag(T)::asList(T)  : List(T)
```

Converts a collection from the specified type into an equivalent mutable List. This operation is not yet implemented.

13.6.5 Numeric Type Operations

Only one operation defined in the specification for use on numeric types. Beyond the range() operation, M2M QVT OML provides additional operations that are covered here.

range

```
Integer::range (start:Integer, end:Integer) : List(Element)
```

Returns the list of Integers in the range between the passed start and end Integers. This operation is not currently implemented.

toString

```
Integer::toString()  : String
```

Returns a String of the Integer value.

13.6.6 String Operations

QVT builds upon OCL, so the normal OCL String operations are available within your scripts and are described in the OCL specification. Additionally, the following Strings are available in the standard library.

format

```
String::format (value:Object) : String
```

Similar to the Java `format()` method and the C `printf()` function, this operation prints a message substituting parameters `%s` (String), `%d` (Integer), and `%f` (Float) with a value. If multiple parameters are declared, a Tuple is passed as the value, with its elements used for substitution. Additionally, a Dictionary can be used for the value, in which case the format of the parameter is `%(key)s`, where `key` is looked up in the Dictionary.

This operation is not currently implemented.

size

```
String::size () : Integer
```

Returns the number of characters in the String. A synonym operation `length()` is called out in the specification but is not implemented in M2M QVT OML. Following is an example of `size()` and its output from within a log expression where `toString()` is used to convert the Integer:

```
log('This string has 29 characters'.size().toString());
result: 29
```

substringBefore

```
String::substringBefore (match : String) : String
```

Returns the substring that appears in the character sequence before the sequence to match passed as a parameter. If no match is found, the entire String is returned.

```
log('test'.substringBefore('s'));
result: te
```

substringAfter

```
String::substringAfter (match : String) : String
```

Returns the substring that appears in the character sequence after the sequence to match passed as a parameter. If no match is found, an empty String is returned.

```
log('test'.substringAfter('s'));
result: t
```

toLower

```
String::toLower () : String
```

Returns a String with all characters from the original converted to their lowercase equivalents. For example, the following String outputs what follows to the console:

```
log('RemovE tHe UpPerCaSe ChAracterS'.toLower());
result: remove the uppercase characters
```

Note that M2M QVT OML provides a synonym operation `toLowerCase()` as well.

toUpper

```
String::toUpper () : String
```

Returns a String with all characters from the original converted to their uppercase equivalents. For example, the following String outputs what follows to the console:

```
log('RemovE tHe LoWerCaSe ChAracterS'.toLower());
result: REMOVE THE LOWERCASE CHARACTERS
```

Note that M2M QVT OML provides a synonym operation `toUpperCase()` as well.

firstToUpper

```
String::firstToUpper () : String
```

Converts the first character in a String to its uppercase equivalent, as shown here:

```
log('test'.firstToUpper());
result: Test
```

lastToUpper

String::lastToUpper () : **String**

Converts the last character in the String to its lowercase equivalent, as shown here:

```
log('test'.lastToUpper());
result: test
```

indexOf

String::indexOf (match : **String**) : **Integer**

Returns the index of the first character found in the match String on the target String. If the match is not found, -1 is returned. Following is an example with corresponding log output.

```
var s : String := 'Find me in the string';
log(s.indexOf('me').toString());
result: 5
```

Note that M2M QVT OML provides another variant of this operation not listed in the specification:

```
String::indexOf(match : String, startIndex : Integer) : Integer
```

Following is an example of this version of indexOf(), which provides the index of the first character in the match String after the startIndex argument position. In this case, the second me String begins at index 17:

```
var s : String := 'Find me and then me in the string';
log(s.indexOf('me', 6).toString());

result: 17
```

endsWith

```
String::endsWith (match : String) : Boolean
```

Returns `true` if the String terminates with the match String provided as an argument. Following is an example of an assertion that looks for sentences ending without a period and logs a warning if found:

```
var sentence : String := 'I end without a period';
assert warning (sentence.endsWith('.'))

  with log('Sentence ends without a period', sentence);
```

startsWith

```
String::startsWith (match : String) : Boolean
```

Returns `true` if the String begins with the match String provided as an argument. Following is an example of an assertion that looks for sentences beginning with whitespace and logs a warning if found:

```
var sentence : String := ' I start with a space.';
assert warning (not sentence.startsWith(' '))

  with log('Sentence starts with a space', sentence);
```

trim

```
String::trim () : String
```

Returns a String with leading and trailing whitespace removed. Note that the `sentence` variable in the previous `startsWith()` example could be corrected using `trim()`:

```
sentence.trim();
```

normalizeSpace

```
String::normalizeSpace() : String
```

This operation goes one step further than the `trim()` operation by removing excess whitespace within a String and also removing leading and trailing whitespace. Whitespace sequences are replaced by a single space in the returned String.

```
log('A  sentence with   extra spaces '.normalizeSpace());
result: A sentence with extra spaces
```

replace

```
String::replace (m1:String, m2:String): String
```

Returns a String with all occurrences of String `m1` replaced with String `m2`. Following is an example of package . (dot) notation replaced with directory path delimiters (/). (Note the escape character before the dot:

```
var pkg : String := 'org.eclipse.mindmap';
log('Converted package to path', pkg.replace('\.', '/'));
```

The specification indicates that `replace()` will work on all occurrences, but we see here that only the first is replaced:

```
Converted package to path, data: org/eclipse.mindmap
```

Eclipse M2M QVT OML provides a `replaceAll()` operation that does what we expect:

```
var pkg : String := 'org.eclipse.mindmap';
log('Converted package to path', pkg.replaceAll('\.', '/'));
```

Now we get what we wanted in the console output:

```
Converted package to path, data: org/eclipse/mindmap
```

If we had not used the escape character in the first example, the output would have been this:

```
Converted package to path, data: /rg.eclipse.mindmap
```

match

String::match (matchpattern:**String**) : **Boolean**

Returns `true` if the regex *matchpattern* is found in the String. If the pattern is not found, it returns `false`. The following example outputs `true`.

```
log('xxxy'.match('x*y').repr());
```

equalsIgnoreCase

String::equalsIgnoreCase (match:**String**) : **Boolean**

Returns `true` if the String is the same as the match String, without taking case into account. Returns `false` otherwise. The following example outputs true.

```
log('a simple test'.equalsIgnoreCase('A Simple Test').repr());
```

find

String::find (match:String) : Integer

Returns the index of the start of the substring that equals the match String, or -1 otherwise. The following example returns 10.

```
log('find the x character'.find('x').repr());
```

rfind

String::rfind (match:**String**) : **Integer**

Returns the index of the start of the substring beginning from the right that equals the match String, or -1 otherwise. The following example returns 10.

```
log('find the x character'.rfind('x').repr());
```

isQuoted

```
String::isQuoted (s:String) : Boolean
```

Returns `true` if the String begins and ends with the argument String, and returns `false` otherwise. The following example returns `true`.

```
log('"is quoted?"'.isQuoted('"').repr());
```

quotify

```
String::quotify (s:String) : String
```

Returns a String that begins and ends with the argument String. The following example outputs the String `"quote me"`.

```
log('quote me'.quotify('"'));
```

unquotify

```
String::unquotify (s:String) : String
```

Returns a String that has the argument String removed from the beginning and end of the String, if it's found. Otherwise, it returns the content of the source String. The following example returns the String `do not quote me`.

```
log('"do not quote me"'.unquotify('"'));
```

matchBoolean

```
String::matchBoolean (s:String) : Boolean
```

This non-case-sensitive operation returns `true` if the String is `true`, `false`, `0`, or `1`. The following example outputs `true true`.

```
log('true'.matchBoolean(true).repr() + ' ' +

  '0'.matchBoolean(false).repr());
```

matchInteger

```
String::matchInteger (i:Integer) : Boolean
```

Returns `true` if the String represents an Integer. The following example outputs `true`.

```
log('0'.matchInteger(0).repr());
```

matchFloat

`String::matchFloat (f:Float) : Boolean`

Returns `true` if the String represents a Float. The following example outputs `true`.

```
log('0.117'.matchFloat(0.117).repr());
```

matchIdentifier

`String::matchIdentifier(s:String) : Boolean`

Returns `true` if the String represents an alphanumeric word. The following example returns `false`.

```
log('a8s(c'.matchIdentifier('').repr());
```

asBoolean

`String::asBoolean() : Boolean`

Returns a Boolean value if the String can be interpreted as a Boolean and `null` otherwise. The following returns `false`.

```
log('0'.asBoolean().repr());
```

asInteger

`String::asInteger() : Integer`

Returns an Integer value if the String can be interpreted as an Integer, and null otherwise. The following example returns 99.

```
log('99'.asInteger().toString());
```

asFloat

String::asFloat() : **Float**

Returns a Float value if the String can be interpreted as a Float, and null otherwise. The following example returns 99.9.

```
log('99.9'.asFloat().toString());
```

startStrCounter

String::startStrCounter (s:**String**) : **Void**

Creates and initializes a counter with the String. When used with the following counterparts, this operation can provide a convenient means to create indexes. The following example outputs 0, 1, 0, 1 for the sequence of counter operations.

```
var index : String := 'index';
String.startStrCounter(index);
log(String.getStrCounter(index).toString());
log(String.incrStrCounter(index).toString());
index.restartAllStrCounter();
log(String.getStrCounter(index).toString());
log(String.incrStrCounter(index).toString());
log(index.addSuffixNumber());
```

getStrCounter

String::getStrCounter (s:**String**) : **Integer**

Returns the current value of the counter associated with the String. See the example in startStrCounter() for its usage.

incrStrCounter

```
String::incrStrCounter (s:String) : Integer
```

Increments the value of the counter associated with the String. See the example in startStrCounter() for its usage.

restartAllStrCounter

```
String::restartAllStrCounter () : Void
```

Resets all String counters. See the example in startStrCounter() for its usage.

addSuffixNumber

```
String::addSuffixNumber () : String
```

Appends the current value of the counter associated with the String to the String. This operation can generate unique internal names. See the example in startStrCounter() for its usage.

13.7 Syntax Notes

The OML language has many of the same syntax features as programming languages such as Java, plus a number of shorthand notations. This section covers these, along with variations from the specification as implemented by M2M QVT OML.

13.7.1 Comments

The QVT specification defines three comment styles. Only two are supported:

```
-- A single line comment to end of the current line
// A single line comment style that is not supported
/*
 * A multiple line comment style that is
 * similar to Java.
 */
```

13.7.2 Strings

Literal Strings are delimited by either single or double quotation marks, according to the specification. M2M QVT OML supports only single quote marks:

```
var s1 : String := 'a string';
```

Literal Strings that fit in multiple lines can be notated as a list of literal Strings. In the specification, they do not require the concatenation operator +, although M2M QVT OML requires this. For example:

```
var s : String := 'This string is split ' +
    'across two lines';
```

Escape sequences are provided and are the same as those found in the Java language. Table 13-1 lists the supported escape sequences.

Table 13-1   QVT Escape Sequences

Escape Sequence	Unicode Value	Name
\ b	\u0008	Backspace BS
\ t	\u0009	Horizontal Tab HT
\ n	\u000a	LineFeed LF
\ f	\u000c	Form Feed FF
\ r	\u000d	Carriage Return CR
\ "	\u0022	Double Quote "
\ '	\u0027	Single Quote ' (Note: not currently supported)
\ \	\u005c	Backslash \

13.7.3 Shorthand

Repeatedly typing lengthy operation names in a QVT script, such as oclIsKind Of(), is tiresome. In addition, superfluous text hinders readability. To address this issue, QVT provides a number of shorthand notations.

○ The `oclIsKindOf()` operation is used frequently, and you can substitute the unary # operator for it. Typing `#Topic` is equivalent to typing `oclIsKindOf(Topic)`. This shorthand notation is not currently supported.

○ The `oclIsTypeOf()` operation is also commonly used, and you can substitute the unary ## operator for it. Typing `##Topic` is equivalent to typing `oclIsTypeOf(Topic)`. This shorthand notation is not currently supported.

○ You can substitute the unary * operator for the `stereotypedBy()` operation. Typing `*aStereotype` is equivalent to typing `stereotypedBy("aStereotype")`. The multiplication operator brings up no ambiguity because of the type involved (String vs. Float/Integer). This shorthand notation is not currently supported.

○ You can substitute the unary % operator for the `format()` operation. Typing `'the name is %s\n' % name` is the equivalent to typing `'the name is %s\n'.format(name)`. Again, ambiguity is eliminated because of the type involved. This shorthand notation is not currently supported.

○ Instead of using the single equals sign (=) equality operator, you can use the more familiar double equals sign (==) for comparison operations. * This shorthand notation is not currently supported.

○ You can replace the not-equal operator <> with the familiar != operator. * This shorthand notation is not currently supported.

○ You can use the binary operator + for String concatenation, thereby replacing `'append'.concat('me')` with `'append' + 'me'`. Again, ambiguity is eliminated by the type involved (String vs. Integer/Float).

○ When adding to lists, you can replace the `add()` operation with the binary operator +=—for example, `allSubtopics += topic.subtopics()`.

  * Note that using == and != shorthand notation requires a directive comment at the top of the source file. This makes the traditional OCL operators = and <> illegal within the file. Following is an example directive comment (although it seems that use-contemporary-syntax would be a more fitting name):

```
-- directive: use-traditional-comparison-syntax
```

13.7.4 OCL Synonyms

For each of the `ocl`-prefixed operations and types available from OCL, QVT provides a synonym operation that drops the `ocl`. For example, you can use `isKindOf()` in QVT in addition to the traditional `oclIsKindOf()`. Note that this support is not yet part of the M2M QVT OML implementation.

Table 13-2 lists synonyms for predefined OCL operations.

Table 13-2   OCL Operators

Type	Operator	Operation
String	+	concat
Integer	+	plus
	- (binary)	minus
	- (unary)	unaryminus
	*	multiply
	/	divide
Real	+	plus
	- (binary)	minus
	- (unary)	unaryminus
	*	multiply
	/	divide

13.8 Simple UML to RDBMS Example

The QVT specification uses a simplified UML and relational database meta-model to illustrate the capabilities of QVT. Both a Relations language and OML solution are provided in the spec, with the latter found in Appendix A. The example provided in M2M QVTO is significantly different from the one in the specification, although an updated one is under development as the implementation matures. For example, to implement the specification's example, M2M QVTO first needs to support intermediate classes.

The OML implementation from the M2M project includes this transformation as a sample project, which is available at **New → Examples → QVT Transformation (Operational) → SimpleUML to RDB Transformation Project**. The wizard also creates a launch configuration.

The models used in the transformation are installed as part of the QVTO examples feature. To see the structure of the models, you can use the Metamodel Explorer (**Window** → **Show View** → **Other** → **Operational QVT** → **Metamodel Explorer**), or you can obtain the Ecore models themselves from the Eclipse CVS repository and render a diagram. Alternatively, placing the cursor on the `modeltype` declaration at the top of the `Simpleuml_to_Rdb.qvto` file and pressing **F3** opens the Metamodel Explorer and selects the model in the tree.

The M2M QVTO example Simple UML model is slightly more complicated than the one in the specification, but it remains simpler than the actual UML metamodel.

The `rdb.ecore` model provided in the sample is much more complex than the model used in the specification. The example model includes additional datatypes, views, and constraints subpackages.

The sample project also includes an instance of the Simple UML model to allow for invocation of the script. To run, expand the **Run** button on the main toolbar and select the **SimpleUML to RDB** launch configuration. A `Simpleuml_to_Rdb.rdb` model appears in the root of the sample project. You can open this and the source `pim.simpleuml` model to compare input and output results in the context of the discussion to follow.

The mapping between these two models is straightforward. Although the OML has no graphical notation, the notation used to describe the Relational implementation can be helpful in understanding the mapping. In fact, you could use GMF to implement a similar notation and diagram for QVTO. This exercise is left to you, with the suggestion that you consider contributing the solution to the M2M project.

Let's begin with the transformation declaration. Both the Simple UML and RDBMS models are declared using `modeltype` statements at the top of the file, along with the `transformation` declaration itself. Note that there is no `strict` qualifier in the modeltype statements, leaving you free to modify the model and reuse this script—that is, as long as you don't change it so that it breaks the script. Also, no `where` clauses restrict our input model from being passed to the transformation.

```
modeltype UML uses
    'http://www.eclipse.org/qvt/1.0.0/Operational/examples/simpleuml';
modeltype RDB uses
    'http://www.eclipse.org/qvt/1.0.0/Operational/examples/rdb';
transformation Simpleuml_To_Rdb(in uml : UML, out RDB);
```

Notice that the sample uses a shorter notation for the `uses` clause, compared to the version in the specification, opting to not surround the URI with the model

name. Also, the sample uses the URI declared by the models in their EMF registration, which align better with the EMF convention. It would be possible to
import each model into the project and add **Metamodel Mappings** in the project
properties and assign the original URI, as shown next. The only other difference
is the model names, which, in this case, reflect the names assigned in the Ecore
models.

```
modeltype UML uses simpleuml("omg.qvt-samples.SimpleUML");
modeltype RDBMS uses rdb("omg.qvt-samples.SimpleRDBMS");
transformation Uml2Rdb(in srcModel:UML,out RDBMS);
```

Looking at the `transformation` declaration, because only one transformation is defined in the file, no braces are required to surround its contents. Note
also that a name is assigned to the input UML model but not to the RDBMS output model.

The entry point of a QVTO transformation is its `main` mapping. As you can
see here, the `UML::Model` class is passed in as the root object, and the `out`
parameter instantiates and returns an `RDB::Model` object. Both the input and
output parameters are given a name to be accessed by within the body of the
mapping.

```
main(in model: UML::Model, out rdbModel: RDB::Model) {
  rdbModel:= model.map model2RDBModel();
}
```

In the body, the `rdbModel` output is assigned the results of the
`model2RDBModel()` mapping, which is invoked by appending `.map` to the
model element, indicating that it will be passed as the input to the mapping.

The `model2RDBModel()` mapping is straightforward and could have been
folded into the main mapping. The `name` of the UML model is mapped to the
name of the RDB model, and the `UML::Model` element is passed to the `pack-
age2schemas` query.

```
mapping UML::Model::model2RDBModel() : RDB::Model {
  name := self.name;
  schemas := self.package2schemas();
}
```

The `package2schemas()` query returns an `OrderedSet` of Schema
objects, which are created from the package and its subpackages. In the body of
the query, the `UML::Package` is mapped to an `RDB::Schema` object by the
`package2schema()` mapping. The result is unioned with a mapping of

subpackages, recursively obtained with calls to `package2schemas()` for each subpackage.

```
query UML::Package::package2schemas() : OrderedSet(RDB::Schema) {
  self.map package2schema()->asSequence()->
    union(self.getSubpackages()->collect(package2schemas()))
    ->asOrderedSet()
}
```

Looking at the `package2schema()` mapping, you can see our first when clause in the script. We want to map UML Package elements to RDB Schema elements only if they contain persistent classes. The `hasPersistentClasses()` query can determine this; you can see it here along with the `isPersistent()` query it uses. As you can see, a class is persistent if it contains a stereotype equal to the String `'persistent'`.

```
query UML::Package::hasPersistentClasses() : Boolean {
  ownedElements->exists(
    let c : UML::Class = oclAsType(UML::Class) in
      c.oclIsUndefined() implies c.isPersistent())
}

query UML::ModelElement::isPersistent() : Boolean {
  stereotype->includes('persistent')
}
```

The mapping from package to schema involves selecting and collecting all the `UML::Class` instances from the package and invoking the `persistentClass2table()` mapping.

```
mapping UML::Package::package2schema() : RDB::Schema
  when { self.hasPersistentClasses() }
{
  name := self.name;
  elements := self.ownedElements->select(oclIsKindOf(UML::Class))->
  collect(oclAsType(UML::Class).map persistentClass2table())
    ->asOrderedSet()
}
```

The `persistentClass2table()` mapping appears next. A when clause eliminates classes that are not persistent using the same query that was used earlier to determine whether a package contained at least one persistent class. The name of the table is mapped from the name of the class. The columns of the table are created by the `class2columns()` query and sorted by name. Primary keys are created using the `class2primaryKey()` mapping, while foreign keys are created using the `class2foreignKeys()` query.

```
mapping UML::Class::persistentClass2table() : RDB::Table
  when { self.isPersistent() }
{
  name := self.name;
  columns := self.class2columns(self)->sortedBy(name);
  primaryKey := self.map class2primaryKey();
  foreignKeys := self.class2foreignKeys();
}
```

The class2columns() query combines the results of the dataType2columns() and generalizations2columns() for the class passed as a parameter, returning the union as an ordered set.

```
query UML::Class::class2columns(targetClass: UML::Class) :

  OrderedSet(RDB::TableColumn) {
  self.dataType2columns(targetClass)->
    union(self.generalizations2columns(targetClass))
      ->asOrderedSet()
}
```

The dataType2columns() query combines the results of queries that create columns from primitive, enumeration, relationship, and association attributes, rejecting those that are undefined.

```
query UML::DataType::dataType2columns(in targetType : UML::DataType) :

  OrderedSet(RDB::TableColumn) {
  self.primitiveAttributes2columns(targetType)->
    union(self.enumerationAttributes2columns(targetType))->
    union(self.relationshipAttributes2columns(targetType))->
    union(self.assosiationAttributes2columns(targetType))
    ->reject(c|c.oclIsUndefined())->asOrderedSet()
}
```

The generalizations2columns() query uses the class2columns() query on the general class, rejects those undefined, and returns an ordered set.

```
query UML::Class::generalizations2columns(targetClass : UML::Class) :

  OrderedSet(RDB::TableColumn) {
  self.generalizations->collect(g |
    g.general.class2columns(targetClass))
    ->reject(c|c.oclIsUndefined())->asOrderedSet()
}
```

The `primitiveAttributes2columns()` query simply invokes the `primitiveAttribute2column` query for each attribute, returning the results as an ordered set.

```
query UML::DataType::primitiveAttributes2columns(in targetType:

  UML::DataType) : OrderedSet(RDB::TableColumn) {
  self.attributes->collect(a |
    a.primitiveAttribute2column(targetType))->asOrderedSet()
}
```

Primitive types are filtered using the `isPrimitive()` query in the when clause, which checks to see that the `targetType` parameter is of type `UML::PrimitiveType`. The column's `isPrimaryKey` property is set using the `isPrimaryKey()` query, which checks to see that a stereotype is present equal to the String `"primaryKey"`. The name of the primitive type passed in is used as the column name, and the type is set to a `PrimitiveDataType` object whose name is initialized by the `umlPrimitive2rdbPrimitive()` query. This query uses a simple String comparison of basic types.

```
mapping UML::Property::primitiveAttribute2column(in targetType:

  UML::DataType) : RDB::TableColumn
  when { self.isPrimitive() }
{
  isPrimaryKey := self.isPrimaryKey();
  name := self.name;
  type := object RDB::datatypes::PrimitiveDataType { name :=
    umlPrimitive2rdbPrimitive(self.type.name); };
}

query UML::Property::isPrimitive() : Boolean {
  type.oclIsKindOf(UML::PrimitiveType)
}

query UML::Property::isPrimaryKey() : Boolean {
  stereotype->includes('primaryKey')
}

query umlPrimitive2rdbPrimitive(in name : String) : String {
  if name = 'String' then 'varchar' else
    if name = 'Boolean' then 'int' else
      if name = 'Integer' then 'int' else
        name
      endif
    endif
  endif
}
```

When mapping enumeration attributes to columns, the `enumeration Attributes2columns()` query invokes the `enumerationAttribute2column()` mapping for each attribute. A when clause checks that the passed property is an enumeration using the `isEnumeration()` query, which checks that its type attribute is of type `UML::Enumeration`.

Again, the `isPrimaryKey` property is set using the `isPrimaryKey()` query, and the `name` attributes are directly mapped. The column's type is set to a new `PrimitiveDataType` object initialized with a name of `'int'`.

```
query UML::DataType::enumerationAttributes2columns(in targetType:

  UML::DataType) : OrderedSet(RDB::TableColumn) {
  self.attributes->collect(map
    enumerationAttribute2column(targetType))->asOrderedSet()
}

mapping UML::Property::enumerationAttribute2column(in targetType:
  UML::DataType) : RDB::TableColumn
  when { self.isEnumeration() }
{
  isPrimaryKey := self.isPrimaryKey();
  name := self.name;
  type := object RDB::datatypes::PrimitiveDataType { name := 'int'; };
}

query UML::Property::isEnumeration() : Boolean {
  type.oclIsKindOf(UML::Enumeration)
}
```

Relationships are mapped to columns using the `relationshipAttributes 2columns()` query. Unlike the primitive and enumeration types, which map to simple columns, relationships involve the creation of foreign keys. The input `targetType` parameter is passed to the `relationshipAttribute 2foreignKey()` mapping, where a when clause checks that it is a relationship type using the `isRelationship()` query. In this case, valid relationships are data types that are persistent.

Looking closer at our `relationshipAttributes2columns()` query, after the collection of `ForeignKey` elements, those that are undefined are rejected. From this collection, the `TableColumn` objects from each `includedColumns` attribute of the foreign keys are collected and returned in an ordered set.

```
query UML::DataType::relationshipAttributes2columns(in targetType:

  UML::DataType) : OrderedSet(RDB::TableColumn) {
  self.attributes->collect(map
    relationshipAttribute2foreignKey(targetType))->reject(a |
```

```
      a.oclIsUndefined())->
      collect(includedColumns)->asOrderedSet();
}
```

To create a `ForeignKey` object from a `DataType` that is a Relationship, first the key's `name` is set to the relationship name prefixed with `FK`. The `included Columns` attribute is set using the `dataType2primaryKeyColumns` query, which passes a Boolean value equal to the result of the `isIdentifying()` query. This query looks for a stereotype String equal to `identifying`.

Finally, the `referredUC` property is set using a `late resolveoneIn class2primaryKey()` mapping. Using `late` means the mapping will be invoked at the end of the transformation, which allows for the resolution of objects that might not yet be created. Using `resolveoneIn` returns a primary key object that has previously been created by the type attribute of the passed in property. This is accomplished by examining the trace model that is created during the transformation and avoids creating duplicate object instances.

```
mapping UML::Property::relationshipAttribute2foreignKey(in targetType:

  UML::DataType) : RDB::constraints::ForeignKey
  when { self.isRelationship() }
{
  name := 'FK' + self.name;
  includedColumns :=
    self.type.asDataType().dataType2primaryKeyColumns(self.name,
    self.isIdentifying());
      referredUC := self.type.late
      resolveoneIn(UML::Class::class2primaryKey,
      RDB::constraints::PrimaryKey);
}

query UML::Property::isRelationship() : Boolean {
  type.oclIsKindOf(UML::DataType) and type.isPersistent()
}
```

To create primary key columns from data types, two parameters are passed in addition to the data type: a `prefix` String for the column name and a Boolean to set the `isPrimaryKey` property. The body is a little complicated. First the `dataType2columns()` query is called, and those that are primary keys are selected. Then a collection based on `TableColumn` objects created using passed parameters is returned as an ordered set.

```
query UML::DataType::dataType2primaryKeyColumns(in prefix : String,

  in leaveIsPrimaryKey : Boolean) : OrderedSet(RDB::TableColumn) {
```

```
  self.dataType2columns(self)->select(isPrimaryKey)->
    collect(c | object RDB::TableColumn {
      name := prefix + '_' + c.name;
      domain := c.domain;
      type := object RDB::datatypes::PrimitiveDataType {
        name := c.type.name;
        };
      isPrimaryKey := leaveIsPrimaryKey
    })->asOrderedSet()
}

query UML::Property::isIdentifying() : Boolean {
  stereotype->includes('identifying')
}

mapping UML::Class::class2primaryKey() : RDB::constraints::PrimaryKey {
  name := 'PK' + self.name;
  includedColumns :=
    self.resolveoneIn(UML::Class::persistentClass2table,
    RDB::Table).getPrimaryKeyColumns()
}
```

The final mapping for our data types to columns is the association
Attributes2columns() query. First, attributes that are persistent association
types are selected. Columns that are mapped to columns are collected and
returned as an ordered set.

```
query UML::DataType::assosiationAttributes2columns(targetType :

  UML::DataType) : OrderedSet(RDB::TableColumn) {
  self.attributes->select(isAssosiation())->
    collect(type.asDataType().dataType2columns(targetType))
    ->asOrderedSet()
}

query UML::Property::isAssosiation() : Boolean {
  type.oclIsKindOf(UML::DataType) and not type.isPersistent()
}
```

13.9 Summary

In this chapter, we explored the QVT Operational Mapping Language in detail, as
supported by the current release of the M2M QVTO component. Improved support of the Operational language is expected, along with the introduction of support for the Relations language in subsequent releases. In the next chapter, we take
a deeper look at the Xpand template language for model-to-text transformation.

CHAPTER 14

Xpand Template Language

From model instances, it's common to generate code, text files, reports, and so on. Query/View/Transformation Operational Mapping Language (QVT OML) provides our language for Model-to-Model Transformation (M2M), and we turn to Xpand to provide for Model-to-Text Transformation (M2T). Alternative choices exist within the M2T project, namely Java Emitter Templates (JET) and the new Model to Text Language (MTL) component.

JET is the default M2T technology that EMF itself uses, but other projects within Eclipse have found success and discovered advantages to using Xpand. JET borrows heavily from Java Server Pages (JSP), but Xpand has a significantly different syntax to offer those who might not be fond of JSP. This is not to say that JET is not worth consideration as the default template technology in your DSL Toolkit; this book just does not cover it. Hopefully a future book will include details on using JET.

Xpand itself has minimal syntax and relies on the Xtend language and underlying expression language and type system to complete its syntax and semantics. Xpand also provides aspect-oriented capabilities, which lends to its extensibility features. Invoking Xpand templates is primarily done through the EMFT Modeling Workflow (MWE) component. This chapter covers all these topics, in addition to example code throughout to illustrate Xpand's capabilities.

One important note about the future of Xpand is important at this point. Two versions of Xpand exist within the Modeling project. I cover the traditional Xpand here, and a refactored version will soon be available in the context of the Graphical Modeling Framework (GMF) project. This version uses OCL and QVT OML as the expression language and will be invoked primarily from Java or Ant files. The latter represents an attractive workflow alternative to MWE, particularly because QVT OML also provides Ant integration. For now, however, let's continue our coverage of the Xpand language.

14.1 Xpand Language

Xpand templates are written in text files that end with an .xpt extension. An Eclipse editor is provided for authoring templates, complete with syntax highlighting, code completion, and code templates. As guillemets (French quotation marks, « and ») are used as delimiters in the language, it's important to first configure your environment to the right encoding. For PC installations of Eclipse, use UTF-8 encoding; ISO-8859-1 works on Mac OS X. Furthermore, learn to use Ctrl+< and Ctrl+> on the PC to type guillemots (Alt+| and Alt+Shift+| work on the Mac). Alternatively, you can use an empty «» template by pressing Ctrl+spacebar.

Regarding the use of guillemets, when outputting text into a file, you can remove trailing whitespace by adding a hyphen before the closing guillemot: «...-».

With the preliminaries out of the way, let's take a look at the Xpand language itself. Each of the following sections covers the main elements of the language: «IMPORT», «DEFINE», «EXPAND», «FILE», «FOREACH», «EXTENSION», «IF», «PROTECT», «LET», «ERROR», and «REM».

14.1.1 IMPORT

At the top of an Xpand template, metamodel imports are listed using the «IMPORT» statement. The concept of importing is similar to import statements in Java and modeltype statements in OML. As with modeltype statements, imports in Xpand let you declare metamodels by either their package or their registered Eclipse Modeling Framework (EMF) Namespace URI (NS URI) Uniform Resource Identifier (URI). In the case of their package, discovery of models along the containing project's source path resolves the model declared.

This is a simple import statement for the Ecore metamodel:

```
«IMPORT ecore»
```

Alternatively, the import below uses the NS URI method, available in the GMF Xpand implementation.

```
«IMPORT "http://www.eclipse.org/emf/2002/Ecore"»
```

After a metamodel is imported, you can reference its elements throughout the template without fully qualifying their names. Xpand currently does not have the flexibility to assign an alias for use within the template, as you saw with QVT OML.

14.1.2 DEFINE

Although an .xpt file is called a template file, in Xpand, the content of a
«DEFINE» block is considered the template. This book uses the word *template*
to reference both. A «DEFINE» block represents a fragment that is expanded in
the context of executing the template. A «DEFINE» block has a name and
optional list of parameters, along with a FOR clause that specifies the applicable
element of the metamodel. An «ENDDEFINE» tag terminates the «DEFINE»
block. This is the general syntax for a «DEFINE» statement:

```
«DEFINE templateName (parameterList) FOR MetaClass»
. . .
«ENDDEFINE»
```

This is a simplistic template that describes «DEFINE» and other Xpand elements. It takes a mindmap instance and produces a Comma-Separated Values
(CSV) file.

```
«IMPORT mindmap»

«DEFINE Main FOR Map»
«FILE title + ".csv"-»
«FOREACH elements.typeSelect(Topic) AS topic-»
«topic.name»,«topic.start»,«topic.end»
«ENDFOREACH»
«ENDFILE»
«ENDDEFINE»
```

The «DEFINE» statement includes the name Main and indicates that the
mindmap model's Map class is the metamodel element used in the definition.
This example passes no parameters. Within the body of the «DEFINE» block,
output text is placed, along with other Xpand statements. I explain the contents
of the example in detail shortly, but it's not hard to see that an output file is created and will contain a series of Topic attributes separated by commas. Consider
this sample output:

```
A Topic,Tue Nov 20 10:16:00 EST 2007,Fri Nov 23 12:46:20 EST 2007
A Subtopic,Wed Jun 20 00:00:00 EDT 2007,Sat Aug 09 00:00:00 EDT 2008
Another Topic,Sun Sep 09 00:00:00 EDT 2007,Wed Dec 12 00:00:00 EST 2007
Another Subtopic,Sat Dec 01 00:00:00 EST 2007,
Tue Jan 01 00:00:00 EST 2008
A SubSubtopic,Mon Oct 22 00:00:00 EDT 2007,Sat Dec 08 00:00:00 EST 2007
```

When invoking a template, Xpand uses fully qualified namespaces, including directory structures, the .xpt filename, and the «DEFINE» name. If this example template were in a file named mindmap2csv.xpt within the folder /templates/deploy, this «DEFINE» would be addressed as deploy::mindmap2csv::Main from another template or the workflow used to execute the template. This assumes that the /templates folder is set to a source path in the project properties, or, in the case of GMF, that it is the folder specified as the dynamic templates location.

14.1.3 EXPAND

The «EXPAND» statement directs execution to another «DEFINE» template block or expands it, similar to invoking a subroutine. This is the general syntax for an «EXPAND» statement:

«**EXPAND** definitionName [(parameterList)] [**FOR** expression |

FOREACH expression [**SEPARATOR** expression]]»

The definitionName must be a fully qualified namespace, including the filename and path, unless it's a «DEFINE» within the same file. In that case, a simple name is sufficient. When referencing a «DEFINE» block outside the file, it might be more convenient to add the appropriate IMPORT statement to the template file. For example, let's say we wanted to modify our simple mindmap2csv.xpt template to output a CSV file for Relationship elements, in addition to the one for Topic elements. Our original «DEFINE» would then include two «EXPAND» statements, as shown here. In this case, the Topic version of the template is located in a directory /topic relative to a project source path in a file named topic.xpt with a main «DEFINE». The relationship template is structured similarly.

```
«IMPORT mindmap»

«DEFINE Main FOR Map»
«EXPAND topic::topic::Main FOR this»
«EXPAND relationship::relationship::Main FOR this»
«ENDDEFINE»
```

Alternatively, if the topic and relationship folders were located below our /template root folder, we could add IMPORT statements to our template and shorten our «EXPAND» statements slightly.

```
«IMPORT mindmap»
«IMPORT topic»
«IMPORT relationship»

«DEFINE Main FOR Map»
«EXPAND topic::csv FOR this»
«EXPAND relationship::csvFile FOR this»
«ENDDEFINE»
```

Note that each «EXPAND» statement explicitly includes FOR this, meaning that the context of the enclosing «DEFINE» is passed along. Technically, we could have eliminated FOR this altogether. An alternative is to pass another element, such as a list of Topic or Relationship elements. In the following example, the Relationship elements are filtered out and passed to a «DEFINE» that takes a list.

```
«DEFINE Main FOR Map»
«EXPAND topic::csv»
«FILE title + "-relations.csv"-»
«EXPAND relationship::csv FOR elements.typeSelect(Relationship)-»
«ENDFILE»
«ENDDEFINE»

«DEFINE csv FOR List[mindmap::Relationship]»
«FOREACH this AS relation-»
«relation.name»,«relation.type.toString()»,«relation.source.name»,
«relation.target.name»
«ENDFOREACH»
«ENDDEFINE»
```

Another option would be to have a «DEFINE» that accepts a single Relationship element, enabling us to use a FOREACH clause in the «EXPAND» to iterate over the collection:

```
«EXPAND relationship::csv FOREACH elements.typeSelect(Relationship)»

«DEFINE csv FOR Relationship»
«relation.name»,«relation.type.toString()»,«relation.source.name»,
«relation.target.name»
«ENDDEFINE»
```

As you can see, we can accomplish the same result in many ways using Xpand, as is the case for most languages. Before we describe how to accomplish this using polymorphism, let's look at the final feature of our «EXPAND» statement: the SEPARATOR.

Suppose we wanted to simply output a comma-separated list of `Topic` names instead of the details of each `Topic` element. We could use the `SEPARATOR` feature of «EXPAND» to accomplish this, as shown in the following example. A nice feature of `SEPARATOR` is that it places a comma (or specified separator) between each element, with no trailing separator at the end of the list. Note the judicious use of the hyphenated closing guillemet (-»), to avoid whitespace in the output.

```
«DEFINE Main FOR Map»
«FILE "topics.csv"-»
«EXPAND topicList FOREACH elements.typeSelect(Topic) SEPARATOR ","»
«ENDFILE»
«ENDDEFINE»

«DEFINE topicList FOR Topic-»
«this.name-»
«ENDDEFINE»
```

This is a sample output of the Topic list:

```
A Topic,A Subtopic,Another Topic,Another Subtopic,A SubSubtopic
```

Polymorphism

Xpand templates include polymorphism support for metaclasses declared in «DEFINE» blocks. If a metaclass has two subclasses and each has its own «DEFINE» block, template execution invokes the proper «DEFINE» to match the instance.

Let's refactor our `mindmap2csv` template to take advantage of this capability. We can do this in two steps, just to illustrate more completely. First, we modify the template as shown here:

```
«IMPORT mindmap»

«DEFINE Main FOR Map»
«EXPAND csvFile(title) FOR elements.typeSelect(Topic)»
«EXPAND csvFile(title) FOR elements.typeSelect(Relationship)»
«ENDDEFINE»

«DEFINE csvFile(String title) FOR List[mindmap::MapElement]»
«ENDDEFINE»

«DEFINE csvFile(String title) FOR List[mindmap::Topic]»
«FILE title + "-topics.csv"-»
«FOREACH this AS topic-»
«topic.name»,«topic.start»,«topic.end»
```

```
«ENDFOREACH»
«ENDFILE»
«ENDDEFINE»

«DEFINE csvFile(String title) FOR List[mindmap::Relationship]»
«FILE title + "-relations.csv"-»
«FOREACH this AS relation-»
«relation.name», «relation.type.toString()», «relation.source.name»,
«relation.target.name»
«ENDFOREACH»
«ENDFILE»
«ENDDEFINE»
```

As you can see, this is not quite polymorphism at its best, but it is a working example that illustrates the proper dispatching of «DEFINE» statements based on type—in this case, a list of a particular type. This example also illustrates the use of parameters: The title from the Map is passed to both MapElement subclass «DEFINE» blocks for use in creating their output files.

Also note that an empty «DEFINE» for a list of MapElement types is provided. This seems to be an Xpand limitation; without a «DEFINE» for the superclass, Xpand could not properly invoke the subclass «DEFINE» blocks.

Even better is the next example, where true polymorphism is used in place of the explicit typeSelect() filtering. Notice that the FILE statements specify outlets now. This is because it's possible to set an append attribute to an outlet; otherwise, each invocation of csvFile would create a new file. Outlets are specified in the workflow file that invokes this template and are covered in detail later.

```
«IMPORT mindmap»

«DEFINE Main FOR Map»
«EXPAND csvFile(title) FOREACH elements-»
«ENDDEFINE»

«DEFINE csvFile(String title) FOR MapElement»
«ENDDEFINE»

«DEFINE csvFile(String title) FOR Topic»
«FILE title + "-topics.csv" TOPIC_OUTLET-»
«name», «start», «end»
«ENDFILE»
«ENDDEFINE»

«DEFINE csvFile(String title) FOR Relationship»
«FILE title + "-relations.csv" RELATIONS_OUTLET-»
«name», «type.toString()», «source.name», «target.name»
«ENDFILE»
«ENDDEFINE»
```

As you can see, this is a much nicer use of polymorphism, although our obligatory «DEFINE» for the MapElement still exists. If you're curious, consider this portion of the workflow file that sets up the outlets and invokes this template:

```
<outlet path="${out}"/>
<outlet name="RELATIONS_OUTLET" path="out" append="true"/>
<outlet name="TOPIC_OUTLET" path="out" append="true"/>
<expand value="mindmap2csv::Main FOR model"/>
```

14.1.4 FILE

The previous sections have already covered most of how «FILE» works, so if you've skipped to this section, you might want to go back and read up the EXPAND topic. This is the syntax for «FILE»:

```
«FILE expression [OUTLET_NAME]»
 . . .
«ENDFILE»
```

As you've seen, you can possibly combine strings and model element values using + to form the «FILE» name, or expression. A previous example used the title of the Map element combined with the string -topics.csv.

OUTLET_NAME is optional and corresponds to a named <outlet/> element defined in a workflow file. One way to think about this is to consider the use of outlets as named streams. In fact, future versions of Xpand might provide more formal support for the named stream concept. The GMF version of Xpand relies on the stream concept because the output files used for persistence are determined externally in Java code. This feature should become available in M2T Xpand in the future, where file output likely will be specified within the workflow instead of within the Xpand template itself.

14.1.5 FOREACH

When working with collection types, it is often necessary to iterate through their contents. You've already seen FOREACH used within an EXPAND statement for this purpose. However, frequently iteration is required within «DEFINE» blocks, which is where «FOREACH» comes into play.

```
«FOREACH expression AS varName [ITERATOR iterName]

[SEPARATOR expression]»
. . .
«ENDFOREACH»
```

The expression can be any collection element within the current context or a statement that results in a collection. Within the block, each element in the collection is accessed using the varName you provide. The body of the FOREACH block can contain other Xpand statements, including nested FOREACH elements. A special Xpand-provided iterator is accessible by name within the block if the ITERATOR is specified. A common use for the ITERATOR is to access its counter for outputting a numerical sequence within the body of the statement. As you saw earlier, you can declare a SEPARATOR and insert it between elements in the collection. Section 14.1.13, "Type System," covers the full list of features that an iterator offers.

To illustrate the use of an ITERATOR, consider this «DEFINE» block:

```
«DEFINE NumberedCsvFile FOR Map»
«FILE "numbered-" + title + "-topics.csv"-»
«FOREACH elements.typeSelect(Topic) AS topic ITERATOR i-»
«i.counter0», «topic.name», «topic.start», «topic.end»
«ENDFOREACH»
«ENDFILE»
«ENDDEFINE»
```

In this case, we're prefixing each line in our output CSV file with an index obtained by our iterator's counter0 property. The output looks like the following.

```
0,A Topic,Tue Nov 20 10:16:00 EST 2007,Fri Nov 23 12:46:20 EST 2007
1,A Subtopic,Wed Jun 20 00:00:00 EDT 2007,Sat Aug 09 00:00:00 EDT 2008
2,Another Topic,Sun Sep 09 00:00:00 EDT 2007,
Wed Dec 12 00:00:00 EST 2007
3,Another Subtopic,Sat Dec 01 00:00:00 EST 2007,
Tue Jan 01 00:00:00 EST 2008
4,A SubSubtopic,Mon Oct 22 00:00:00 EDT 2007,

Sat Dec 08 00:00:00 EST 2007
```

14.1.6 EXTENSION

Xpand supports the extension of the underlying metamodel through the «EXTENSION» statement. Declaring an «EXTENSION» import in a template means that additional features of the metamodel can be added using the Xtend language. This is analogous to QVT's use of libraries.

For example, consider the `rootTopics` derived feature added to the mindmap model in Section 3.3.5, "Adding OCL." We explicitly extended the metamodel and provided an implementation using OCL. The same type of extension can be provided using Xtend and made available to our Xpand templates. Consider the following implementation of `rootTopics` in a file named `util.ext`.

```
import mindmap;

List[Topic] rootTopics(Map mindmap) :
  let topics = mindmap.elements.typeSelect(mindmap::Topic) :
  topics.without(topics.subtopics)
;
```

When used within a template, this extension can be declared at the top of the file and used within the body as if it were part of the metamodel itself. The only difference between the use of `rootTopics()` in our extension and the `rootTopics` element in the model is the parentheses used in the former. This example shows the use of both:

```
«IMPORT mindmap»

«EXTENSION util»

«DEFINE Main FOR Map»
«EXPAND csvFile(title) FOREACH this.rootTopics()»
«EXPAND csvFile(title) FOREACH this.rootTopics»
«ENDDEFINE»
```

14.1.7 IF

As you might expect, Xpand supports conditional expansion using the «IF» if statement. «ELSE» and «ELSEIF» statements complement the «IF» block. This is the general syntax of the «IF» statement:

```
«IF expression»
  . . .
[ «ELSEIF expression» ]
  . . .
[ «ELSE»
  . . . ]
«ENDIF»
```

This is an example of «IF» and «ELSE» from the `PropertySection.xpt` template used in GMF's diagram generation:

```
«IF createLabel() && isExpandable()-»
  «EXPAND createControls(name()+"Control") FOREACH contents-»
  «name()».setClient(«name()»Control);
  «name()».addExpansionListener(getExpansionListener(«parentVar»));
«ELSE-»
  «EXPAND createControls(name()) FOREACH contents-»
«ENDIF»
```

14.1.8 PROTECT

To mark sections of generated code that are designated for user modification, Xpand provides a «PROTECT» statement. During regeneration, these regions are protected from being overwritten. This is the general syntax for «PROTECT» statements:

```
«PROTECT CSTART expression CEND expression ID expression (DISABLE)?»
  . . .
«ENDPROTECT»
```

The CSTART and CEND expressions should be valid comment markers for the target language—for example, /* and */ for Java comments. The ID expression should be unique for the execution of the generator. By default, a protected region is enabled, but you can disable it by adding the DISABLED keyword.

To use protected regions, you must configure a resolver in your workflow file.

EMF uses the recommended approach for dealing with user-modified code, and JMerge follows this upon regeneration. To use this approach, insert @generated JavaDoc comments above class, field, and method declarations. Removing this tag and modifying it (such as by adding NOT to the end, as in @generated NOT) signifies that the block should not be overwritten.

14.1.9 LET

Sometimes it's convenient to create a local variable for use in your template. The «LET» statement enables you to bind an expression to a variable name using the following syntax:

```
«LET expression AS varName»
. . .
«ENDLET»
```

Statements using the variable are nested within the block. For example, if we wanted to use a «LET» statement for our Topic CSV filename, we could refactor our template as shown next. When accessing «LET» or metamodel elements within a body, simply place the name within guillemets, as in «fileName».

```
«LET title + "-topics.csv" AS fileName»
«FILE fileName TOPIC_OUTLET-»
«name»,«start»,«end»
«ENDFILE»
«ENDLET»
```

14.1.10 ERROR

You can terminate the execution of a template by inserting an «ERROR» statement. The expression will be used as the message of an XpandException, which is thrown if the «ERROR» is processed. Note that it's typically best to validate input model elements before executing templates, so using the «ERROR» statement is rarely required. This is the general syntax:

```
«ERROR expression»
```

This simple example reports when the passed Map class has no title set:

```
«DEFINE Main FOR Map»
«IF title == null || title == ''-»
«ERROR 'No title'»
«ELSE»
...
«ENDIF»
«ENDDEFINE»
```

14.1.11 REM

Comments can be added to templates to provide documentation using the «REM» statement. «REM» tags cannot be nested. They follow this general syntax:

```
«REM»Text comment here...«ENDREM»
```

14.1.12 AROUND

One of the more powerful features used in Xpand templates is the aspect-oriented capabilities provided by the «AROUND» statement. Using «AROUND», you can augment templates noninvasively. This is convenient when you want to augment the capabilities of templates that you cannot or do not want to modify, or, in the case of multiple products generated in a product line, when you seek to avoid conditionals throughout your MDD artifacts. This is the general syntax of «AROUND»:

```
«AROUND fullyQualifiedDefinitionName(parameterList)? FOR Type»
. . .
«ENDAROUND»
```

The aspect-oriented part is in the point cut `fullyQualifiedDefinition Name`, which can contain wildcards (*). For example, `mindmap::topic2csv:: csvFile` can provide a fully qualified name, while `mindmap::topic*` can match templates that begin with `mindmap::topic`.

Similarly, parameter types can be specified in our point cut. Types specified are matched to their definition parameter type or super type. The wildcard (*) can be used in parameter lists as well. For example, you can use `mindmap::topic2csv::csv(String name)` or `mindmap::topic2csv:: csv(String name,*)` if there might be additional parameters.

Consider some examples of «AROUND» definitions.

To match all templates:

```
«AROUND *(*) FOR Object»
```

To match all templates ending in *topic* and with any number of parameters:

```
«AROUND *topic(*) FOR Object»
```

To match all templates in the `mindmap` namespace that have no parameters for `MapElement` types (including subclasses):

```
«AROUND mindmap::* FOR MapElement»
```

To match all templates with a single `String` parameter:

```
«AROUND *(String s) FOR Object»
```

To match all templates with at least one `String` parameter:

```
«AROUND *(String s,*) FOR Object»
```

You can call the underlying definition using `proceed()` on the implicit variable `targetDef`. The original parameters are passed to the underlying definition, but you can modify this with the advice beforehand. You can achieve total control over the parameters passed using `proceed(Object target, List params)`, although no type checking occurs when you do so.

Let's take a look at a simple example of using «AROUND». Consider this portion of a previous version of the `mindmap2csv` file template:

```
«DEFINE Main FOR Map»
«FILE title + "-topics.csv"-»
«EXPAND listElements FOR elements.typeSelect(Topic)»
«ENDFILE»
«ENDDEFINE»

«DEFINE listElements FOR List[mindmap::Topic]-»
«FOREACH this AS topic-»
«EXPAND csv FOR topic-»
«ENDFOREACH»
«ENDDEFINE»

«DEFINE csv FOR Topic-»
«name»,«start»,«end»
«ENDDEFINE»
```

Here, the `Topic` elements are expanded into CSV line entries where their name, start date, and end date values are written. Let's assume that it's legal to enter a comment at the top of a CSV file to describe each entry, preceded by a # sign. If we weren't given access to the template, or if we did not want to modify it, we could use «AROUND» to noninvasively add a comment line before each `Topic` line in our output. This is a new `.xpt` file with an «AROUND» statement that lets us do just that:

```
«IMPORT mindmap»

«AROUND templates::mindmap2csv::listElements FOR List[mindmap::Topic]-»
# Topic Name, Start Date, End Date
«targetDef.proceed()»
«ENDAROUND»
```

Using the qualified name of the «DEFINE» that we want to augment instructs the generator that this block will be executed in its stead, stating that it should output a simple comment line and then proceed with the original statement using `targetDef.proceed()`. It's possible to place the `proceed()` in the beginning, thereby providing *before advice*. To execute the template so that the generator knows about our advices, we can modify our workflow file. Section 14.1.16, "Aspects," covers this, so for now we just show the new output.

```
# Topic Name, Start Date, End Date
A Topic,Tue Nov 20 10:16:00 EST 2007,Fri Nov 23 12:46:20 EST 2007
A Subtopic,Wed Jun 20 00:00:00 EDT 2007,Sat Aug 09 00:00:00 EDT 2008
Another Topic,Sun Sep 09 00:00:00 EDT 2007,Wed Dec 12 00:00:00 EST 2007
Another Subtopic,Sat Dec 01 00:00:00 EST 2007,
Tue Jan 01 00:00:00 EST 2008
A SubSubtopic,Mon Oct 22 00:00:00 EDT 2007,Sat Dec 08 00:00:00 EST 2007
```

In general, the aspect-oriented capabilities of Xpand (and Xtend and Workflow) are key to providing flexibility in your MDD artifacts. Knowing these capabilities when writing templates helps to keep a fine-grained approach to «DEFINE» blocks and even inserts extensibility points. These are all recommended practices in general and are exemplified by these capabilities.

14.1.13 Type System

Before moving on to the expression language and Xtend language description, it's important to understand the underlying type system. You've seen the List type used in the preceding Xpand examples, so let's cover this and the rest in detail.

Type System API Documentation

This section provides basic information on the properties and operations available for each of the underlying type system elements, as seen in Table 14-1 and Table 14-2.

Table 14-1   Object Properties

Type	Name	Description
Type	metaType	Returns this object's meta type. This can be useful when dealing with enumeration types, as in this example:

```
Boolean isEntity(Class c) :
      c.metaType == dnc::MomentInterval ||
      c.metaType == dnc::MIDetail ||
      c.metaType == dnc::Party ||
      c.metaType == dnc::Place ||
      c.metaType == dnc::Thing ||
      c.metaType == dnc::Description
  ;
```

Table 14-2 Object Operations

Return Type	Name	Description
Boolean	< (Object)	Less than.
Boolean	!= (Object)	Not equal to.
Boolean	>= (Object)	Greater than or equal to.
Boolean	<= (Object)	Less than or equal to.
Boolean	> (Object)	Greater than.
Integer	compareTo (Object)	Compares this object with the specified object for order. Returns a negative integer, a zero, or a positive integer when this object is less than, equal to, or greater than the specified object, respectively.
Boolean	== (Object)	Equality.
String	toString ()	Returns the String representation of this object. (Calls Java's toString() method.)

The super type of String is Object.

Table 14-3 String Properties

Type	Name	Description
Integer	length	The length of this String

Table 14-4 String Operations

Return Type	Name	Description
String	toUpperCase ()	Converts all the characters in this String to uppercase using the rules of the default locale (from Java).
String	toLowerCase ()	Converts all the characters in this String to lowercase using the rules of the default locale (from Java).
List	split (String)	Splits this String around matches of the given regular expression (from Java 1.4).
String	trim ()	Returns a copy of the String, with leading and trailing whitespace omitted (from Java 1.4).
String	+ (Object)	Concatenates two strings.

Return Type	Name	Description
String	replaceAll (String, String)	Replaces each substring of this String that matches the given regular expression with the given replacement.
String	subString (Integer, Integer)	Returns a portion of the String beginning at the index defined by the first parameter, through the index defined by the second parameter. If no second parameter is provided, the remainder of the String is returned.
Boolean	endsWith (String)	Tests whether this String ends with the specified suffix.
Integer	asInteger ()	Returns an Integer object holding the value of the specified String (from Java 1.5).
Boolean	contains (String)	Tests whether this String contains the specified substring.
String	toFirstUpper ()	Converts the first character in this String to uppercase using the rules of the default locale (from Java).
String	toFirstLower ()	Converts the first character in this String to lowercase using the rules of the default locale (from Java).
String	replaceFirst (String, String)	Replaces the first substring of this String that matches the given regular expression with the given replacement.
Boolean	startsWith (String)	Tests whether this String starts with the specified prefix.
List	toCharList ()	Splits this String into a List[String] containing Strings of length 1.
Boolean	matches (String)	Tells whether this String matches the given regular expression (from Java 1.4).

The supertype of Integer is Real.

Table 14-5 Integer Operations

Return Type	Name	Description
Boolean	<= (Object)	Less than or equal to.
Integer	+ (Integer)	Add.
Integer	* (Integer)	Multiply.
Boolean	> (Object)	Greater than.

(continues)

Table 14-5   Integer Operations (continued)

Return Type	Name	Description
List	upTo (Integer, Integer)	Returns a list of integers starting with the value of the target expression, up to the value of the first parameter, incremented by the second parameter—for example, 1.upTo(10, 2) evaluates to {1,3,5,7,9}.
Boolean	!= (Object)	Not equal to.
Integer	/ (Integer)	Divide.
Integer	- ()	Negate.
List	upTo (Integer)	Returns a list of integers starting with the value of the target expression, up to the value of the specified integer, incremented by 1—for example, 1.upTo(5) evaluates to {1,2,3,4,5}.
Boolean	< (Object)	Less than.
Integer	- (Integer)	Subtract.
Boolean	== (Object)	Equals.
Boolean	>= (Object)	Greater than or equal to.

The superclass of Boolean is Object.

Table 14-6   Boolean Operations

Return Type	Name	Description
Boolean	! ()	Not equal

The supertype of Real is Object.

Table 14-7   Real Operations

Return Type	Name	Description
Boolean	== (Object)	Equal to
Boolean	!= (Object)	Not equal to
Boolean	<= (Object)	Less than or equal to
Real	/ (Real)	Divide
Boolean	< (Object)	Less than

Return Type	Name	Description
Real	* (Real)	Multiply
Boolean	> (Object)	Greater than
Real	- ()	Negate
Real	- (Real)	Subtract
Boolean	>= (Object)	Greater than or equal to
Real	+ (Real)	Add

The supertype of Collection is Object. Note that Set is a subclass of Collection but offers no properties or operations beyond that of Collection.

Table 14-8 Collection Properties

Type	Name	Description
Integer	size	Returns the size of this Collection
Boolean	isEmpty	Returns true if this Collection is empty

Table 14-9 Collection Operations

Return Type	Name	Description
Collection	remove (Object)	Removes the specified element from this Collection, if contained, and returns this Collection.
Set	toSet ()	Converts this collection to a Set.
List	toList ()	Converts this collection to a List.
Boolean	containsAll (Collection)	Returns `true` if this collection contains each element contained in the specified collection; otherwise, returns `false`. Returns this Collection.
Collection	removeAll (Object)	Removes all elements contained in the specified collection from this Collection, if contained, and returns this Collection.
Collection	addAll (Collection)	Adds all elements to the Collection and returns this Collection.
String	toString (String)	Concatenates each contained element (using toString()), separated by the specified String.

(continues)

Table 14-9   Collection Operations (continued)

Return Type	Name	Description
Boolean	contains (Object)	Returns `true` if this collection contains the specified object; otherwise, returns `false`. Returns this Collection.
Set	intersect (Collection)	Returns a new Set, containing only the elements contained in this and the specified Collection.
Set	without (Collection)	Returns a new Set, containing all elements from this Collection without the elements from the specified Collection.
List	flatten ()	Returns a flattened List.
Set	union (Collection)	Returns a new Set, containing all elements from this and the specified Collection.
Collection	add (Object)	Adds an element to the Collection and returns this Collection.

Table 14-10   List Operations

Return Type	Name	Description
Object	last ()	Returns the last Object in the List
Object	first ()	Returns the first Object in the List
Integer	indexOf (Object)	Returns the index of the specified Object in the List
Object	get (Integer)	Returns the Object at the specified index
List	withoutLast ()	Returns the list without its last Object
List	withoutFirst ()	Returns the list without its first Object

The supertype of Type is Object.

Table 14-11   Type Properties

Type	Name	Description
String	name	The name of the Object
Set	superTypes	The Set of Object supertypes
Set	allProperties	The Set of all Object Properties

Type	Name	Description
Set	allFeatures	The Set of all Object Features
Set	allOperations	The Set of all Object Operations
Set	allStaticProperties	The Set of all Object StaticProperties
String	documentation	The Object documentation

Table 14-12 Type Operations

Return Type	Name	Description
Property	getProperty (String)	Returns a Property that matches the provided name
Operation	getOperation (String, List)	Returns an Operation that matches the provided name and List of parameters
StaticProperty	getStaticProperty (String)	Returns the StaticProperty that matches the provided name
Feature	getFeature (String, List)	Returns the Feature of the provided name and Type
Boolean	isAssignableFrom (Type)	Returns true if the Type is assignable from the specified Type
Boolean	isInstance (Object)	Returns true if the specified Object is an instance
Object	newInstance ()	Returns a new instance of the Object

The supertype of Feature is Object.

Table 14-13 Feature Properties

Type	Name	Description
Type	owner	The owner of the Feature
Type	returnType	The return Type of the Feature
String	documentation	The documentation of the Feature
String	name	The name of the Feature

The supertype of Property is Feature.

Table 14-14 Property Operations

Return Type	Name	Description
Void	set (Object, Object)	Sets the first Object to the second Object
Object	get (Object)	Returns the Object specified

The supertype of `Operation` is `Feature`.

Table 14-15 Operation Operations

Return Type	Name	Description
Object	evaluate (Object, List)	Evaluates the Operation and provided parameters
List	getParameterTypes ()	Returns a List of parameter Types for the Operation

The supertype of `StaticProperty` is `Feature`.

Table 14-16 StaticProperty Operations

Return Type	Name	Description
Object	get ()	Returns the static value

The supertype of `AdviceContext` is `Object`.

Table 14-17 AdviceContext Properties

Type	Name	Description
List	paramNames	The List of parameter names
String	name	The name of the AdviceContext
List	paramTypes	The List of parameter Types
List	paramValues	The List of parameter values

Table 14-18   AdviceContext Operations

Return Type	Name	Description
Object	proceed ()	Evaluates the extension
Object	proceed (List)	Evaluates the extension with List of Objects

The supertype of `Definition` is `Object`.

Table 14-19   Definition Properties

Type	Name	Description
List	paramNames	List of the parameter names
List	paramTypes	List of the parameter types
Type	targetType	Type of the target definition
String	name	Name of the target definition

Table 14-20   Definition Operations

Return Type	Name	Description
String	toString ()	Returns a String of Definition Type, name, and parameters
Void	proceed (Object, List)	Evaluates the extension and parameters
Void	proceed ()	

The supertype of `Iterator` is `Object`.

Table 14-21   Iterator Properties

Type	Name	Description
Boolean	firstIteration	A Boolean property that signals that this is the first iteration
Boolean	lastIteration	A Boolean property that signals that this is the last iteration
Integer	counter1	An incrementing Integer value starting at 1
Integer	elements	An Integer value indicating the number of elements in the collection
Integer	counter0	An incrementing Integer value starting at 0

14.1.14 Expression Language

To provide support for metamodel element access, aggregation, and iteration, Xpand uses an underlying expression language. This language is also available within Xtend, and this section covers it. You've already seen uses of this expression language, such as in the `typeSelect()` function used in our earlier example template.

The syntax of the expression language is a mixture of OCL and Java. On one hand, this is good because it's familiar to many. On the other hand, it's not OCL. The underlying implementation does not leverage the MDT OCL project, as does QVT OML, which is also based on OCL. To provide side effects, QVTO itself could be used in place of Xtend/OCL in Xpand, which is exactly the approach that the forthcoming Xpand variant from GMF takes.

General Syntax

Let's begin with some of the basics of accessing properties, invoking operations, and so on. Following are examples that should form a self-explanatory basis of the expression language.

To access a property of a model element, use a simple dot notation:

```
modelElement.name
```

To access an operation defined in the model, use a dot notation with parentheses:

```
modelElement.anOperation()
```

To perform basic arithmetic, use the usual suspects:

```
(1 + 1 * 2) / 4
```

Boolean logic is specified using Java-like constructs and semantics:

```
! ((text.startsWith('t') && text.length > 0 ) | | ! false)
```

Literals and Special Operators for Built-In Types

Several literals exist for built-in types, each of which is described next.

Object
Naturally, no literals exist for Object, but there are two operators:

```
obj1 == obj2   // equals
obj1 != obj2   // not equals
```

Void
The only possible instance of Void is the `null` reference. Therefore, just one literal exists: `null`.

Type Literals
The literal for types is simply the name of the type—for example:

```
String            // the type string
my::special::Type // evaluates to the type 'my::special::Type'
```

The literal for static properties (also known as enumeration literals) is similar to type literals:

```
my::Color::RED
```

Two different literal syntaxes are used for Strings (with the same semantics):

```
'a String literal'
"a String literal"
```

For Strings, the expression language supports the plus operator that is overloaded with concatenation:

```
'The element ' + element.name + ' is ' + element.state
```

The Boolean literals are `true` and `false`.
These are the Boolean operators:

```
true && false      // AND
true || false      // OR
! true             // NOT
```

The syntax for Integer and Real literals is as expected:

```
5             // Integer
4456          // Integer
8.9           // Real
0.95          // Real
```

Additionally, common arithmetic operators are used:

```
1 + 2         // addition
4 - 3         // subtraction
2 * 3         // multiplication
3 / 7         // divide
- 32          // unary minus operator
```

Finally, the well-known compare operators are defined:

```
4 > 5             // greater than
4 < 5             // smaller than
4 >= 5            // greater than or equal
4 <= 5            // smaller than or equal
```

Collections

A literal exists for lists:

```
{1,2,3,4}              // a List with four integers
```

No other special concrete syntax is used for collections. If you need a Set, you must call the `toSet()` operation on the List literal:

```
{1,2,4,4}.toSet()      // a Set with 3 Integers
```

As with OCL, the expression language defines several special operations on collections. These operations are not members of the type system, so they cannot be used in a reflective manner.

select

Sometimes an expression yields a large collection, but one is interested in only a special subset of the collection. The expression language has special constructs to specify a selection out of a specific collection. These are the `select()` and reject() operations. The select() operation is analogous to the OCL select() operation and specifies a subset of a collection as follows:

```
collection.select( v | boolean-expression-with-v )
```

Select returns a sublist of the specified collection. The list contains all elements for which the evaluation of boolean-expression-with-v results in true. For example:

```
{1,2,3,4}.select(i | i >= 3)      // returns {3,4}
```

typeSelect

A special version of a select expression is the typeSelect() expression. The metaclass name is provided as the argument.

```
collection.typeSelect( classname )
```

typeSelect() returns a sublist of the specified collection that contains only objects that are an instance of the specified class. For example:

```
elements.typeSelect(mindmap::Topic)
```

reject

The reject operation is similar to the select operation, but with reject we get the subset of all the elements of the collection for which the expression evaluates to false. The reject syntax is identical to the select syntax:

```
collection.reject( v | boolean-expression-with-v )
```

For example:

```
{1,2,3,4}.reject(i | i >= 3)      // returns {1,2}
```

collect

As shown in the previous section, the select() and reject() operations always result in a subcollection of the original collection. Sometimes we want to specify a collection that is derived from another collection but that contains objects not in the original collection (it is not a subcollection). The collect operation does this using the same syntax as the select and reject expressions:

```
collection.collect( v | expression-with-v )
```

collect() iterates over the target collection and evaluates the given expression on each element. In contrast to select, the evaluation result is collected in a list. When the iteration is finished, the list with all results is returned. For example, if the name property of the objects in the collection elements is a String, a list of Strings is returned:

```
elements.collect(e | e.name)        // returns a list of Strings
```

Navigation through many objects is common, so a shorthand notation for collect() makes the expressions more readable. This is just as in OCL, so instead of using:

```
self.employee.collect(e | e.birthdate)
```

You can simply write this:

```
self.employee.birthdate
```

In general, when a property is applied to a collection of Objects, it automatically is interpreted as a collect() over the members of the collection with the specified property.

forAll

Often a Boolean expression must be evaluated for all elements in a collection. The forAll() operation enables you to specify a Boolean expression that must be true for all objects in a collection for the operation to return true:

```
collection.forAll( v | boolean-expression-with-v )
```

The result of forAll() is true if boolean-expression-with-v is true for all the elements contained in the collection. If boolean-expression-with-v is false for one or more of the elements in the collection, the expression evaluates to false.

For example:

```
{3,4,500}.forAll(i | i < 10) // evaluates to false
```

exists

Often you need to know whether there is at least one element in a collection for which a Boolean is `true`. The `exists()` operation enables you to specify a Boolean expression that must be `true` for at least one object in a collection:

```
collection.exists( v | boolean-expression-with-v )
```

The result of the `exists()` operation is `true` if `boolean-expression-with-v` is `true` for at least one element of collection. If the `boolean-expression-with-v` is `false` for all elements in collection, then the complete expression evaluates to `false`.

For example:

```
{3,4,500}.exists(i | i < 10)        // evaluates to true
```

sortBy

If you want to sort a list of elements, you can use the function `sortBy()`. The list processed using `sortBy` is sorted by the results of the given expression.

For example:

```
elements.sortBy(e | e.name)
```

In the example, the list of elements is sorted by the name of the `element`. Note that no Comparable type exists in the expression language. If the values returned from the expression are instances of `java.util.Comparable`, the `compareTo()` method is used; otherwise, `toString()` is invoked and the result is compared.

Consider some more examples. (The following expressions return `true`.)

```
{'C','B','A'}.sortBy(e | e) == {'A','B','C'}
{'AAA','BB','C'}.sortBy(e | e.length) == {'C','BB','AAA'}
{5,3,1,2}.sortBy(e | e) == {1,2,3,5}
```

Ternary Expression

Conditional expressions come in two different flavors. The first one is the ternary expression, with this syntax:

```
condition ? thenExpression : elseExpression
```

For example:

```
name != null ? name : 'unknown'
```

switch

The second conditional expression is the `switch` expression, with this syntax:

```
switch (expression) {
   (case expression : thenExpression)*
   default : catchAllExpression
}
```

The default part is mandatory because `switch` is an expression; therefore, it needs to evaluate to something in any case. This is an example from GMF, found in GenModelUtils.ext:

```
String getClassifierAccessorName(genmodel::GenClassifier gc) :
      switch (gc.getEcoreClassifier().name) {
            case "Class" : "Class_"
            case "Name" : "Name_"
            default : gc.getEcoreClassifier().name
      }
;
```

Boolean expressions have an abbreviation:

```
switch {
   case booleanExpression : thenExpression
   default : catchAllExpression
}
```

Chain Expression

Expressions and functional languages should be as free of side effects as possible. But sometimes side effects are necessary. In some cases, expressions don't have a return type (that is, the return type is Void). If you need to call such operations, you can use the `chain` expression, with this syntax:

```
anExpression -> anotherExpression -> lastExpression
```

Each expression is evaluated in sequence, but only the result of the last expression is returned. For example:

```
person.setName('test') -> person
```

This chain expression sets the name of the person first, before it returns the person object itself.

Create Expression

The `create` expression instantiates new objects of a given type:

```
new Topic
```

Let Expression

The `let` expression lets you define local variables. The syntax is as follows:

```
let v = expression : expression-with-v
```

This is especially useful together with a `chain` and a `create` expression. For example:

```
Topic newTopic() :
    let t = new Topic : t.setName('A topic') -> t
;
```

Casting

The expression language is statically type checked, although sometimes it's necessary to perform a cast. The syntax for casts is very Java-like:

```
((String)unTypedList.get(0)).toUpperCase()
```

14.1.15 Xtend Language

The Xtend language is commonly used with Xpand templates to provide reusable operations and simple expressions by extending the underlying metamodels. Xtend is based on the expression language covered in the previous section and is also used for model transformation definition. We limit our use of Xtend in the scope of this book to its use in Xpand templates because we rely on the QVT OML for model transformation.

Xtend files have an .ext file extension and corresponding editor in Eclipse. They are typically arranged in libraries and imported by Xpand templates using the «EXTENSION» statement.

Xtend Syntax

The syntax for Xtend is simplistic because most of an extension file's content is made up of the underlying expression language syntax.

Import

The import keyword is used at the top of a file and indicates the name space of different types used within the extension file. As usual, double colon (::) characters delimit elements in the namespace, and a semicolon ends the statement. For example, the following import statement imports our mindmap model namespace.

```
import mindmap;
```

No support exists for wildcard or static imports in Xtend, so the following examples are incorrect:

```
import org::eclipse::*;      // incorrect
import mindmap::Map;         // also incorrect
```

Extension Import

It is possible to import another extension file using the «EXTENSION» keyword at the top of the file. Again, fully qualified namespace declaration is required. Following is an example.

```
extension org::eclipse::mindmap::Util;  // full path with no *.ext
```

If you want to export an extension used in a file with your own extensions, add the `reexport` keyword to the end of the extension statement.

extension `org::eclipse::mindmap::Util` **reexport**`;`

Comments

Comments in Xtend come in two flavors: single line and multiline. Single-line comments are like those in Java: two forward slashes (//) demark the start of a comment that goes until the end of the line.

```
// An example single line comment
```

A multiline comment is also like comments in Java, with /* marking the start and */ marking the end of comments that can span multiple lines.

```
/*
 * A multi-line comment.
 */
```

Extensions

The basic syntax for an extension expression indicates an optional return type, extension name, parameter list, and expression body following a single colon and terminated with a semicolon. Following is the general syntax.

ReturnType `expressionName(`**ParamType1** `param1, …)  :  expression-body;`

Consider this simple example that returns a standard setter method name for a passed element:

String `setterName(`**NamedElement** `element)  :  'set' +`

`element.name.toFirstUpper();`

Extension Invocation

You can invoke an extension in two ways. The first is by passing the element instance as a parameter, as shown here:

```
setterName(myFeature);
```

The implicit first parameter represents the element instance, so we can use the "member syntax" to seemingly invoke an extension on the instance. This gives us more of the feeling that we're truly extending the underlying metamodel. This is an equivalent example to the first:

```
myFeature.setterName();
```

Remember that even though we're seemingly extending the metamodel, these extensions are not available using reflection and cannot be used for specialization of metamodel operations. During evaluation, an operation matched in the metamodel takes precedence in execution.

Type Inference

It's not strictly required that a return type be declared because the type can be inferred from the expression and depends on its context of use. For example, consider this expression:

```
asList(Object o) : {o};
```

When invoking this extension and passing an Integer, as shown next, it has the static type `List[Integer]`. So the use of `upTo()` is statically type safe.

```
asList(55).get(0).upTo(60);
```

Recursion

One exception to the rule regarding type declaration is with recursive expressions. Because the type cannot be inferred, it must be stated explicitly, as shown in this example:

```
String fullyQualifiedName(JavaPackage p) :
  p.eSuperPackage == null ? p.name :
  fullyQualifiedName(p.eSuperPackage) + '.'
  + p.name
;
```

Consider another example from GMF's `xpt::editor::palette::Utils` extensions:

```
private List[gmfgen::ToolGroup] collectSubGroups(gmfgen::ToolGroup
  group) :
  let rv = group.entries.typeSelect(gmfgen::ToolGroup) :
  rv.addAll(rv.collect(g| g.collectSubGroups()).flatten())
;
```

Cached Extensions

If you expect to have an extension called multiple times for a given set of parameters, you might want to have the result cached for performance reasons. This is accomplished by adding the `cached` keyword to the expression, as in this example from GMF's `xpt::navigator::Utils` extensions:

```
cached List[gmfgen::GenCommonBase]

  getNavigatorContainerNodes(gmfgen::GenNavigator navigator) :
  getNavigatorNodes(navigator).select( n |
  getChildReferencesFrom(navigator, n).size() > 0)
;
```

Private Extensions

If you do not want to expose an extension outside its file, you can add the `private` keyword, as shown in this example from GMF's `xpt::navigator::Utils` extensions:

```
private List[gmfgen::GenCommonBase]

  getNavigatorNodes(gmfgen::GenNavigator navigator) :
  let diagram = navigator.editorGen.diagram :
  { diagram }
    .addAll(diagram.topLevelNodes)
    .addAll(diagram.childNodes)
    .addAll(diagram.links)
    .addAll(diagram.compartments)
    .typeSelect(gmfgen::GenCommonBase)
;
```

Java Extensions

Sometimes you need to call a Java method. The JAVA keyword provides the means by which to declare that a Java public static method is called. This is the general syntax for defining a Java public static method:

```
Type aJavaExtension(ParamType param, …) :
  JAVA package.Type.staticMethod(package.Type, …)
;
```

Following is an example from GMF's `xpt::EMFUtils` extensions:

```
String toStringLiteral(String strValue) :
  JAVA org.eclipse.gmf.internal.codegen.util.EmfUtils.toStringLiteral(
  java.lang.String)
;
```

Xtend Examples

The first example provides the same functionality we expressed in our mindmap model using OCL. Although the derived feature for `rootTopics` was created and annotated with OCL to provide the value, this snippet of Xtend completes the story by showing what otherwise we would need to do to accomplish the same thing if we had not "pulled up" the capability into our metamodel. This is an extension that returns the list of root Topic elements from a Map:

```
import mindmap;

cached List[mindmap::Topic] rootTopics(Map mindmap) :

  let topics = mindmap.elements.typeSelect(mindmap::Topic) :

  topics.without(topics.subtopics)

;
```

To compare, this is the OCL we added to the metamodel after creating a derived, transient, volatile `rootTopics` reference in our Map class:

```
let topics : Set(mindmap::Topic) = self.elements
  ->select(oclIsKindOf(mindmap::Topic))
  ->collect(oclAsType(mindmap::Topic))->asSet() in
  topics->symmetricDifference(topics.subtopics->asSet())
```

Finally, this is the QVT we used in our transformation from mindmap root Topic to RequirementGroup objects:

```
var topics : Set(mindmap::Topic) := mmap.elements
  ->select(oclIsTypeOf(mindmap::Topic))
  ->collect(oclAsType(mindmap::Topic))->asSet();

var rootTopics : Set(mindmap::Topic) := topics
  ->symmetricDifference(topics.subtopics->asSet());
```

As you can see, the three are similar. Because QVT OML is based on OCL, it's understandably the same syntax as the OCL annotation. And because Xtend borrows from OCL, it is similar except where `without` is used instead of `symmetricDifference()`, and where `typeSelect()` is used instead of `select()->collect()`.

In the context of our `mindmap2csv` Xpand template, you can see the use of our `rootTopics()` extension here. In this case, only the root `Topic` elements of our `Map` will be written out in CSV format.

```
«DEFINE csvFile FOR Map»
«EXPAND csvFile(title) FOREACH this.rootTopics()-»
«ENDDEFINE»
```

Chapter 7, "Developing Model-to-Text Transformations," has additional examples of Xtend and Xpand usage.

14.1.16 Workflow Engine

Although it is possible to invoke Xpand templates using Java and even Ant, the "native" method is to use the Model Workflow Engine (MWE) component of EMF Technology (EMFT). The workflow engine uses configuration files, which are Ant-like XML files executed using the Eclipse launcher. Note that this section concentrates on using the workflow engine in the context of Xpand templates only. Although additional capabilities exist, such as constraint checking and Xtend-based model transformation, they fall outside the scope of this book.

Properties

Workflow configuration files support Ant-like properties. The following example would set a `model` property that could be used as `${model}` elsewhere in the workflow. The use of full URIs, such as `platform:/resource/`... shown here, is recommended practice.

```
<property name="model"

  value="platform:/resource/org.eclipse.dsl.mindmap/model/Map.xmi"/>
```

Note that properties passed into a workflow invocation via Java or Ant override those defined in the workflow itself. This is a convenient means by which to develop and later deploy a workflow when the environment of execution changes.

EMF Setup

When using EMF models, configuring a bean element with the `Standalone Setup` class is required in the workflow. A number of elements are available to be used within the `StandaloneSetup` component, as described next.

platformUri

This element points to the platform, and, in most cases, the value used is simply `../`, as shown in the following example. In a project in which the .ecore file is within a source path of the project and uses a local dynamic instance model as input, this is all that setup requires.

```
<bean class="org.eclipse.emf.mwe.utils.StandaloneSetup">
  <platformUri value="../" />
</bean>
```

uriMap

The `uriMap` element enables you to specify a map from the package's registered NS URI to another URI, such as a `platform:/resource/...` URI. For example, working with a mindmap instance model, not a local dynamic instance model that references an *.ecore model, you can map its NS URI to a workspace *.ecore model for resolution, as follows:

```
<bean class="org.eclipse.emf.mwe.utils.StandaloneSetup">
  <platformUri value="../" />
  <uriMap

  from="http://www.eclipse.org/2008/mindmap"
  to="platform:/resource/org.eclipse.dsl.mindmap/model/mindmap.ecore"/>
</bean>
```

RegisterGeneratedEPackage

Models in the environment that have contributed to the EMF generated_ package extension-point can be referenced using the `RegisterGenerated EPackage` element. The package element's class attribute of the contribution is used as the value, as shown here:

```
<bean class="org.eclipse.emf.mwe.utils.StandaloneSetup">
      <platformUri value="../" />
     <RegisterGeneratedEPackage
    value="org.eclipse.jem.java.JavaRefPackage"/>
</bean>
```

In this example, the Java EMF Model (JEM) is referenced by its gener-
ated_package, as shown here in its plugin.xml file:

```
<extension point="org.eclipse.emf.ecore.generated_package">
    <package
        uri="java.xmi"
        class="org.eclipse.jem.java.JavaRefPackage" />
</extension>
```

RegisterEcoreFile

To explicitly register a metamodel using its .ecore file, use the
RegisterEcoreFile element. In this example, the mindmap.ecore file is referenced from another project in the workspace:

```
<bean class="org.eclipse.emf.mwe.utils.StandaloneSetup">
    <platformUri value="../" />
    <RegisterEcoreFile value=
    "platform:/resource/org.eclipse.dsl.mindmap/model/mindmap.ecore"/>
</bean>
```

Note that it is possible to use any valid URI scheme in the value attribute.
For example, if you want to reference a file within a *.jar file, declare the path
as follows:

```
<RegisterEcoreFile value="jar:/file:/my.jar!/model/my.ecore"/>
```

ExtensionMap

If the EMF extension_parser extension-point is to be used to load a model,
you can use the ExtensionMap element, as shown here. Also shown is the contribution from the corresponding model plugin.xml file.

```
<bean class="org.eclipse.emf.mwe.utils.StandaloneSetup">
    <platformUri value="../" />
    <ExtensionMap from="gmfgen"
    to="org.eclipse.gmf.internal.codegen.util.GMFGenResource$Factory"/>
</bean>

<extension point="org.eclipse.emf.ecore.extension_parser">
    <parser type="gmfgen" class=
    "org.eclipse.gmf.internal.codegen.util.GMFGenResource$Factory"/>
</extension>
```

Reader

A Reader must be configured and populated with the input model instance for use in the Generator component. The default `org.eclipse.emf.mwe.utils.Reader` has a number of nested elements, which are covered next. At a minimum, a Reader is configured with a `uri` and `modelSlot` element to indicate where to load the model from and which slot to populate, respectively. Following is an example:

```
<component class="org.eclipse.emf.mwe.utils.Reader">
    <uri value="${model}" />
    <modelSlot value="model" />
</component>
```

uri

The `uri` element contains the path to the model to be loaded. As mentioned in the previous properties section, this is a path that is typically expressed using a `uri` value. It's common to set a property to this value so that it can be substituted with a runtime parameter during deployment.

modelSlot

The `modelSlot` element defines the default `model` slot that is used in the expand element of our Generator element. Typically, the `uri` element is used to populate this slot with a model instance, as in the previous example.

firstElementOnly

Set this element's value attribute to `false` if the input model has multiple root elements that require processing. The default for EMF models is to have a single root element, so the default value for this element is `true`, meaning that it does not normally need to be defined. However, sometimes multiple roots are present and should be passed to the template, as is the case in GMF when diagram and domain models are persisted in the same file.

Xpand Component

A predefined workflow component provided with Xpand is the `org.eclipse.xpand2.Generator` class. The use of this component is complemented by workflow properties, metamodel references, and model readers. Following is a basic configuration that was used to invoke our earlier template examples that produced CSV files from our mindmap model.

```xml
<?xml version="1.0"?>
<workflow>
    <!-- Specify model and output locations -->
    <property name="model" value=
    "platform:/resource/org.eclipse.dsl.mindmap/model/Mindmap.xmi"/>
    <property name="out" value="out" />

    <!-- Configure EMF and specify platform location -->
    <bean class="org.eclipse.emf.mwe.utils.StandaloneSetup">
        <platformUri value="../" />
    </bean>

    <!-- Configure model reader to populate model slot -->
    <component class="org.eclipse.emf.mwe.utils.Reader">
        <uri value="${model}" />
        <modelSlot value="model" />
    </component>

    <!-- Configure Xpand generator for EMF metamodel invocation -->
    <component class="org.eclipse.xpand2.Generator" id="generate">
        <metaModel id="mm" class=
        "org.eclipse.xtend.typesystem.emf.EmfRegistryMetaModel"/>
        <expand value="mindmap2csv::Main FOR model" />
        <outlet path="${out}"/>
    </component>
</workflow>
```

The comments throughout make this workflow example fairly straight-forward. The `bean` element for `org.eclipse.mwe.emf.StandaloneSetup` supports the registration of Ecore models using URIs, generated packages, and those models in our project source path, such as our mindmap.ecore model.

An `org.eclipse.mwe.emf.Reader` is then configured to fill our `model` slot with our dynamic instance. In the Generator component that follows, this slot is referenced by name in the «EXPAND» element. Note that an «EXPAND» element in a workflow takes in its `value` attribute an «EXPAND» expression, minus the «EXPAND» keyword (as it is provided by the element name). Note also the assignment of the ID attribute. When we discuss the use of aspects with Xpand in Section 14.1.16, "Aspects," you'll see that this is a required attribute.

BEST PRACTICE

To allow for the execution of a workflow that adds extensibility to your Xpand templates using «AROUND» elements, be sure to specify an ID attribute of the workflow `org.eclipse.xpand2.Generator` component.

Before invoking the template with the «EXPAND» element, a metaModel is declared and uses the org.eclipse.m2t.type.emf.EmfRegistryMeta Model class. The outlet directs our template result to the out directory, relative to the project location. Each of the elements and their properties are described next.

metaModel

The metaModel element takes an ID and class attribute, with the default class being org.eclipse.xtend.typesystem.emf.EmfRegistryMetaModel for working with EMF models.

expand

The expand element determines the template that is invoked and the model element that is passed. These are specified in the value attribute, which contains an Xtend expression that is the same as an «EXPAND» expression in an Xpand template, without the «EXPAND» statement itself. In the previous example, the Main definition is invoked in the mindmap2csv.xpt template file, passing the model slot, which is populated with our Mindmap.xmi dynamic instance.

Outlet

The outlet element of the Xpand generator component provides five attributes: name, append, overwrite, path, and fileEncoding.

Additionally, we set up outlet elements to direct the output of the template. We covered earlier the concept of named outlets, as shown with the RELA-TIONS_OUTLET and TOPIC_OUTLET declarations. Note that we are specifying that the output should be appended with append="true" because the default is false. An overwrite flag is also available and is set to true by default. In our example, the default outlet points to the path /out, which is created in the root of the containing project (if it doesn't already exist). «FILE» statements that do not specify an outlet write to the default location.

Postprocessor

Although it's possible to write your templates so that they produce nicely formatted output, code formatters are available for most languages and can be invoked using the postprocessor element within the outlet element. It's likely more important for your templates to be readable, so leveraging a formatter for your generated output gives you the benefit of both readable templates and generated code.

Xpand workflow provides two beautifiers, specified using `org.eclipse.xpand2.output.JavaBeautifier` and `org.eclipse.xpand2.output.XmlBeautifier`. You enter these into your Generator elements, as shown in the following example:

```
<outlet path="src-gen">
   <postprocessor class="org.eclipse.m2t.xpand.output.JavaBeautifier"
      configFile="config/org.eclipse.jdt.core.prefs"
</outlet>
```

The Java post-processor uses the JDT's code formatter and picks up preferences as long as they are found in the classpath. To create a preferences file for use in your post processor, enable project-specific settings in **Preferences** → **Java** → **Code Style** → **Formatter** and save the file into the path specified in your `configFile` attribute.

The XML post-processor provides default support for `.xml`, `.xsl`, `.wsdd`, and `.wsdl` file extensions. Use the `fileExtensions` attribute to add alternate extensions.

If you are generating something other than Java or XML, you can create your own post-processor by implementing the `org.eclipse.m2t.xpand.output.PostProcessor` interface. When deploying the provided or custom processors, be sure to include the required dependencies to your plug-in.

Aspects

To use the aspect-oriented features of Xpand or Xtend when invoking the generator, you need to configure them in your workflow. As you might recall from Section 14.1.12, "AROUND," which covered using «AROUND» in templates, the workflow used to leverage aspects must be made aware of them. Following is the workflow file used to invoke the `mindmap2csv.xpt` template, including the advices defined in `aspects::mindmap2csv.xpt`:

```
<?xml version="1.0"?>
<workflow>
      <cartridge file="mapsample.mwe" inheritAll="true"/>

      <component class="org.eclipse.xpand2.GeneratorAdvice"
      id="reflectionAdvice" adviceTarget="generate">
            <advices value="aspects::mindmap2csv"/>
      </component>

</workflow>
```

This workflow file simply invokes the original, as defined in the `cartridge` element. The `GeneratorAdvice` component is configured to use `reflectionAdvice` and targets our component with ID equal to `generator`, which is the ID attribute of the Generator component defined in the original workflow. The advices contributed are defined in the child `advices` element, which points to our `aspects::mindmap2csv` template.

Java Invocation

A `WorkflowRunner` class is provided to allow for invocation at the command line or from within an Eclipse application. The syntax for the command line follows, where `-p` lets you override properties.

```
java org.eclipse.emf.mwe.WorkflowRunner

  -pbasedir=/base path/workflow.mwe
```

To invoke from within Eclipse, a `Map` of properties and a `Map` of slot contents are required, along with a `String` path to the workflow file. Following is the `run()` method signature:

```
public boolean run(final String workFlowFile,
 final ProgressMonitor theMonitor,
 final Map<String, String> theParams,
 final Map<String, ?> externalSlotContents)
```

For example:

```
Map<String, String> properties = new HashMap<String, String>();
properties.put("model", modelURI);
properties.put("out", outputDirectory);
new WorkflowRunner().run(workflowFile.getPath(),
new NullProgressMonitor(), properties, null);
```

Note that the contents of the properties map override those defined in the workflow, and you can pass a model already in memory as a slot content. Also note that the `ProgressMonitor` and `NullProgressMonitor` shown here are workflow classes, not Eclipse platform classes.

Section 8.1.2, "Actions," includes a complete example of Java invocation in a deployed plug-in.

Using Ant with Workflow

It is possible to invoke a workflow and pass it parameters using Ant. Following is a simple example to illustrate the basic configuration:

```
<target name='generate'>
    <taskdef name="workflow"
             classname="org.eclipse.emf.mwe.core.ant.WorkflowAntTask"/>
    <workflow file='path/workflow.mwe'>
      <param name='baseDir' value='/base/'/>
    </workflow>
</target>to i
```

14.2 Summary

In this chapter, we looked closer at the Xpand template language, including its underlying expression and Xtend languages. We also learned how to invoke a template for generating text using the Model Workflow Engine.

PART IV

Appendixes

This part of the book contains additional reference and background information. Specifically, this part provides a Graphical Modeling Framework (GMF) runtime set of keyboard shortcuts and a discussion on how the Eclipse Modeling Project and the Object Management Group's Model-Driven Architecture (MDA) initiative come together.

APPENDIX A

Graphical Modeling Framework Key Bindings

The Graphical Modeling Framework (GMF) runtime provides many convenient keyboard bindings and diagram-manipulation options using both the keyboard and mouse. This table comes from the GMF's Help documentation and is copied here for convenience.

Table A-1 Cycling between the Diagram Editor and Palette

Current State	Keyboard Key(s)	Description	New State
Diagram name in focus	Tab	Navigates to the palette	Palette in focus
Palette in focus	Tab	Navigates to the palette Minimize button.	Palette Minimize button in focus
Palette Minimize button in focus	Tab	Navigates to the palette items.	Palette item in focus
Palette item in focus	Tab	Navigates to the Diagram Editor and places focus on any selected item.	Diagram Editor in focus
Diagram Editor in focus	Shift+Tab	Navigates to the palette items. The last palette item used is selected; otherwise, it defaults to the Select option.	Palette item in focus
Palette item in focus	Shift+Tab	Navigates to the palette Minimize button.	Palette Minimize button in focus

(continues)

Table A-1   Cycling between the Diagram Editor and Palette (continued)

Current State	Keyboard Key(s)	Description	New State
Palette Minimize button in focus	Shift+Tab	Navigates to the palette.	Palette in focus
Palette in focus	Shift+Tab	Navigates to the Diagram Editor.	Diagram name in focus

Table A-2   Palette Item Navigation

Current State	Keyboard Key(s)	Description	New State
Drawer in focus	Spacebar	Collapses or expands the selected drawer in the palette	Drawer in focus
Palette item in focus	Spacebar	Selects the current palette item in focus	Palette item in focus
Palette item in focus	Up/down arrow	Moves the focus between the palette items	Palette item in focus
Shape palette item in focus	Enter	Creates a new shape on the diagram	New shape selected in diagram
Connection palette item in focus	Enter	Creates a new connection between the two selected items in the diagram	New connection selected in diagram
Palette item in focus	Tab	Tab—Navigates to the diagram	Diagram Editor in focus with Select Palette tool
Palette item in focus	Escape	Esc—Deselects the palette item	Enabled
Stack palette item in focus	Alt+down arrow	Makes the stack pop-up list appear	Stack pop-up list in focus
Stack pop-up list in focus	Up/down arrow	Navigates between the available palette tools on the stack	Stack pop-up list in focus
Stack pop-up list in focus	Enter	Selects an item from the pop-up list	Selected palette item

Table A-3 Diagram Navigation

Current State	Keyboard Key(s)	Description	New State
Selected diagram	Alt+down arrow	Selects shape in diagram	Selected shape
Selected diagram	Arrow keys	Cycles through the shapes that exist in the selected diagram	Selected shape
Selected diagram	Shift+arrow keys	Multiselects shapes on the diagram	Selected shapes
Selected diagram	Shift+F10	Invokes the context menu for the shape	Diagram context menu

Table A-4 Shape Navigation

Current State	Keyboard Key(s)	Description	New State
Selected shape	Shift+F10	Invokes the context menu for the shape.	Shape context menu
Selected shape	. (period)	Cycles through the following handles: position handle, 8 side and corner size handles, position handle (clockwise rotation).	Selected shape handle
Selected shape	Shift+. (period)	Cycles through the following handles: position handle, eight side and corner size handles, position handle (counterclockwise rotation).	Selected shape handle
Selected shape	/ (forward slash)	Selects any available connection. Navigates clockwise among the existing connections.	Selected connection
Selected shape	\ (backslash)	Selects any available connection. Navigates counterclockwise among the existing connections.	Selected connection

(continues)

Table A-4   Shape Navigation (continued)

Current State	Keyboard Key(s)	Description	New State
Selected shape	Alt+down arrow	Selects the shape compartment.	Shape compartment selected
Selected shape	Ctrl+spacebar	Deselects the selected shape by showing the shape in an outline.	Shape outline
Selected shape handle	Arrow keys	Changes shape size or position. A shaded shape is displayed showing the new size or position.	Shaded shape
Selected shape handle	Ctrl+arrow keys	Changes shape size or position respecting the aspect ratio. A shaded shape is displayed showing the new size or position.	Shaded shape
Selected shape handle	Shift+arrow keys	Changes shape size or position respecting the shape's center. A shaded shape is displayed showing the new size or position.	Shaded shape
Selected shape handle	Ctrl+shift+ arrow keys	Changes shape size or position respecting the aspect ratio and shape's center. A shaded shape is displayed showing the new size or position.	Shaded shape
Selected shape handle	Escape	Deselects the selected shape handle.	Selected shape
Selected shape	Enter	Accepts the current shaded shape.	Selected shape
Selected shape	Escape	Reverts to the original shape size or position.	Selected shape
Selected shape	Alt+down arrow	Selects a compartment within the shape.	Compartment selected
Compartment selected	Up/down arrow	Navigates between the available compartments.	Compartment selected

Current State	Keyboard Key(s)	Description	New State
Compartment selected	Alt+down arrow	Selects the shape compartment items. The first compartment item is selected.	Compartment item selected
Compartment selected	Alt+up arrow	Deselects the compartment and selects the shape.	Selected shape
Compartment item selected	Alt+up arrow	Deselects the compartment item and selects the compartment.	Compartment selected
Compartment item selected	Up/down arrow	Navigates between the available compartment items.	Compartment item selected

Table A-5 Connection Navigation

Current State	Keyboard Key(s)	Description	New State
Selected connection	Shift+F10	Invokes the context menu for the connection.	Connection context menu
Selected connection	Alt+down arrow	Cycles through all the connection labels. A connection label is selected when the four corner size handles are shown. Connection labels are navigable in the same way that shapes are.	Selected connection label
Selected connection label	Alt+up arrow	Deselects the connection label and selects the connection.	Selected connection
Selected connection	Arrow keys	Deselects the connection and selects the shape.	Selected shape
Selected connection	Ctrl+spacebar	Deselects the selected connection by showing the connection in an outline.	Connection outline

(continues)

Table A-5   Connection Navigation (continued)

Current State	Keyboard Key(s)	Description	New State
Selected connection	. (period) or Shift+. (period)	Cycles through the endpoints, bendpoints, and midpoints of a connection.	Selected endpoint, bendpoint, or midpoint
Selected endpoint	Arrow keys	Allows the connection endpoint to be moved to a new shape.	Selected connection
Move cursor over bendpoint	Arrow keys	Moves the connection bendpoint.	Selected bendpoint
Move cursor over bendpoint	Enter	Accepts the current location.	Selected connection
Move cursor over bendpoint	Escape	Reverts to the original location.	Selected connection
Add bendpoint cursor	Arrow keys	Moves the new bendpoint.	Selected bendpoint
Add bendpoint cursor	Enter	Accepts the new bendpoint.	Selected connection
Add bendpoint cursor	Escape	Removes the bendpoint.	Selected connection

To navigate to the Properties View: Press Ctrl+F7 and choose the Properties View, or Select Show Properties View from the context menu of a diagram, shape, or connection.

Table A-6   Properties View Navigation

Current State	Keyboard Key(s)	Description	New State
Selected properties field	Shift+Tab	Cycles through the fields in the property section and eventually highlights the currently active properties tab. Shift+Tab cycles through the UI of the Properties view.	Properties tab highlighted
Properties tab highlighted	Tab	Cycles through the fields in the property sections of the active tab. Tab cycles through the UI of the Properties view in the opposite direction of Shift+Tab.	Selected properties field
Properties tab highlighted	Up/down arrow	Move focus among tabs in Properties view.	Properties tab highlighted

APPENDIX B

Model-Driven Architecture (MDA) at Eclipse

The OMG has defined a set of standards for use in what it calls Model-Driven Architecture (MDA). Although the approach of MDA is more or less the same as most other approaches to a general model-driven software development, MDA requires technologies that implement the stated OMG standards. The Modeling project provides support for many of these standards, so using the Modeling project for MDA is definitely an option. However, where standards compliance is not a requirement, or where you need a capability for which no implementation yet exists, the Modeling project provides a range of alternatives.

As stated in its charter,

> the importance of supporting industry standards is critical to the success of the Modeling project, and to Eclipse in general. The role of the Modeling project in the support of industry standards is to enable their creation and maintenance within the Eclipse community. Furthermore, as standards bodies such as the Object Management Group (OMG) have a strong modeling focus, the Modeling project needs to facilitate communication and outreach through its PMC and project contributors to foster a good working relationship with external organizations.

When the OMG introduced MDA to the world in 2001, Eclipse was an incipient community. In the past seven years, MDA and Eclipse have experienced success while concurrently undergoing changes in focus, positioning, and applicability to the world of software development. Eclipse is no longer "just a Java IDE," and MDA is now based on a more complete set of specifications, making it much more well defined than seven years ago.

Although the Eclipse Modeling Project makes little mention of MDA proper, it is nonetheless supported to a large degree, as discussed shortly. In fact, Eclipse has significantly contributed to the success and realization of MDA, providing an open source platform and de facto reference implementations for many of the MDA specifications. Unfortunately, this has been done with minimal collaboration with the OMG. Improved collaboration likely will increase the success of both organizations as they strive to increase the adoption of model-driven development.

Implemented Standards

The Eclipse Modeling Project is a top-level Eclipse project that is logically structured into projects that provide abstract syntax definition, concrete syntax development, Model-to-Model Transformation (M2M), and Model-to-Text Transformation (M2T). Additionally, the Model Development Tools (MDT) project focuses on providing implementations of industry-standard metamodels and exemplary tools for developing models based on those metamodels. This range of functionality provides its community with a full range of model-driven software development (MDSD) capabilities, many of which conform to published MDA specifications.

Although the top-level Modeling project is the primary location for MDA-related activity at Eclipse, other projects within Eclipse have modeling-related technology and specification implementations. For example, the Software Process Engineering Model (SPEM) [4] is implemented as part of the Eclipse Process Framework (EPF) [5] project, while BPMN diagramming [18] is provided by the SOA Tools project [19].

It's also worth pointing out that the Eclipse Modeling Project provides alternative technologies for several of the OMG's MDA specifications. These are discussed shortly because they are popular technologies with strong user communities. In most cases, their implementations precede the corresponding OMG specification.

Altogether, these projects fulfill most of the MDA vision, while certainly fulfilling general MDSD and domain-specific language (DSL) tooling requirements. The following is a list of the relevant MDA specifications and their implementation status within Eclipse. This is not an exhaustive list of MDA specifications, but these are the most relevant within the current scope of the Eclipse Modeling Project.

Meta-Object Facility (MOF)

We cannot overstate the importance of having a common underlying metamodel, provided by the Meta-Object Facility (MOF) [11] specification. MOF—or, more specifically, EMOF (Essential MOF)—is closely aligned with the Ecore meta-model of the Eclipse Modeling Framework (EMF) [12] and forms the basis of most Modeling project technologies.

The topic of aligning the Ecore metamodel with the EMOF specification has been ongoing for years and will likely continue because the implications of alignment are not trivial. EMF is such a popular technology used within many Eclipse projects and commercial products that changing its structure and API is not a viable solution. As has been discussed, updating the EMOF specification to align with Ecore might be a better solution.

Although EMF forms the bedrock of nearly every Modeling project, room for improvement still exists. Discussions are ongoing in the areas of large-scale models, metamodel enhancements, alternative persistence mechanisms, and so on. When considering the evolution of EMF and all Eclipse open source projects, it's important to keep in mind that it is contribution based. EMF itself consists of a small team that must maintain and preserve its current client base.

Unified Modeling Language (UML)

Unified Modeling Language (UML) [6] is implemented within the UML2 component of the Model Development Tools (MDT) project [8] and currently conforms to the 2.1 version of the specification. This implementation of the UML2 metamodel is based on EMF and has been part of Eclipse for quite some time.

Diagramming capabilities for the UML2 metamodel implementation are now provided by the MDT project's UML2 Tools component. These diagrams are generated using the Eclipse Graphical Modeling Framework (GMF) project, itself an example of model-driven software development using Eclipse technologies.

Both the metamodel and diagramming components provide support for the definition of UML Profiles. Profiles play an important role in MDA and in the definition of UML-based DSLs. Although no UML Profiles are available at Eclipse today, they could be implemented and provided to the community in the future. Ideally, a catalog of profiles and other MDA artifacts would be contributed to and maintained by the community for general consumption.

Object Constraint Language (OCL)

Object Constraint Language (OCL) [9] is an important element of Model-Driven Architecture (MDA) and is used in several Modeling projects. OCL is provided as a component of the Model Development Tools (MDT) project, with a complementary OCL Tools component coming in the near future. The OCL implementation conforms to the 2.0 version of the specification and has bindings to both Ecore and the UML2 metamodel implementations.

Diagram Interchange (DI)

UML Diagram Interchange (DI) [16] is not currently provided at Eclipse, but it has prompted many questions from the community regarding its implementation, particularly with the introduction of UML diagramming from the MDT project.

The team that designed and implemented the notation model for the GMF runtime found this specification to be insufficient. It has been suggested that the DI specification be revised to align with the GMF notation model because the original version of the specification was not broadly adopted and because GMF is so popular.

A related topic is the Diagram Definition RFP [24], which itself was inspired by the mapping that GMF provides between Ecore models, their notation elements, and their tooling. This RFP will help bridge the current gap in modeling specifications from the OMG.

XML Metadata Interchange (XMI)

XML Metadata Interchange (XMI) [13] is supported by EMF and is used by the UML2 project and others. EMF also can read serialized EMOF models, in addition to several other format import options, including XML Schema Definition (XSD).

MOF Query/View/Transformation (QVT)

Query/View Transformation (QVT) [14] is part of the M2M project [15] and currently provides an implementation of the QVT Operational Mapping Language (OML). The QVT Relations and Core languages are also being implemented within M2M.

The M2M project provides another model-to-model transformation technology with its Atlas Transformation Language (ATL) component. ATL was a contender among responses to the QVT RFP and has fostered a large and successful community of its own.

MOF Models to Text Transformation Language

MOF2Text is being implemented within the MOFScript [26] component of the Generative Modeling Technologies (GMT) project. This is a recent specification and implementation in an area that has no shortage of alternative technologies.

Java Emitter Templates (JET) [27] originated as EMF's code-generation framework and borrows heavily from Java Server Pages (JSP). JET is undergoing an update to enhance its capabilities, and it resides within the M2T project.

Xpand [28] is an increasingly popular template-based M2T component that provides an alternative syntax and expression language to JET. Xpand provides additional extension capabilities and continues to be enhanced via community contributions.

JET and Xpand are well used within the community. Although MOF2Text is relatively new and unproven, the benefits it might offer likely will prompt the reimplementation of existing templates. Nonetheless, a MOF2Text contribution exists within the Modeling project for those looking for a specification-compliant M2T solution.

Human-Usable Textual Notation (HUTN)

Human-Usable Textual Notation (HUTN) [17] is not currently implemented, but it relates to the proposed Textual Modeling Framework (TMF) project [30] within Modeling. A great deal of interest in tooling for the support of textual concrete syntaxes for modeling languages has arisen, particularly as the interest in DSLs and "language workbenches" [28] has grown.

The TMF proposal states that it will allow for the definition of concrete textual syntaxes for abstract syntaxes defined using EMF. A full-featured textual editor will be generated, likely targeting the capabilities of the proposed IDE Meta-Tooling Platform (IMP) [31] project. Therefore, TMF will provide complementary concrete syntax to the graphical concrete syntax that the Graphical Modeling Framework (GMF) project provides.

Business Process Modeling Notation (BPMN)

The SOA Tools Project at Eclipse provides Business Process Modeling Notation (BPMN) diagramming, mainly for the purpose of generating BPEL [34]. The diagramming is based on GMF, and the underlying model is based on EMF, thereby making this project compatible with other Modeling technologies.

Because BPMN provides no well-defined metamodel, the introduction of the Business Process Definition Metamodel (BPDM) [32] will hopefully lead to a new contribution of this capability at Eclipse. As standards-based model implementations, the implementation of the BPDM metamodel and BPMN diagramming for working with these models would fall within the scope of the MDT project.

Software Process Engineering Metamodel (SPEM)

As mentioned, the Eclipse Process Framework supports Software Process Engineering Metamodel (SPEM) [4]. Although SPEM is mentioned in the list of MDA specifications, no real requirement specifies its use in the application of MDA. Within Eclipse, currently no connection exists between EPF and the Modeling project, aside from the fact that the SPEM metamodel is implemented using EMF.

Working Relationship

To date, very little formal communication has taken place between the OMG and the leadership of the Eclipse Modeling Project regarding a working relationship. Lately, the most promising discussions have been with respect to a series of symposia, to be held at EclipseCon [35] and during OMG technical meetings. The focus of these events will be to discuss individual specification implementations and ways the two organizations can strive for more constructive cooperation.

The current situation raises a number of questions about the nature of the relationship, which hopefully these meetings can address. The relationship could remain informal, with no explicit commitment or expectation that implementations found in the Modeling project must represent so-called "reference implementations" of OMG standards, as described in OMG Specification and Products [3].

In the past, specifications such as UML have suffered from interoperability issues among vendors who had different interpretations or implementation goals. The introduction of XMI, well-defined compliance levels, DI specification, and so on were meant to improve the situation but have largely failed to deliver and now compound the problem. Developing a reference implementation in parallel with the specification can identify ambiguities and defects earlier and can serve the larger community by delivering a platform upon which to implement commercial products.

That said, the UML2 implementation at Eclipse is the de facto reference implementation for the UML2 specification, and its development exemplifies the model we would like to achieve with the OMG for all implemented standards within Eclipse. Only through communication and feedback between implementers and specification authors can our respective communities be best served.

Membership

Currently, the Eclipse Foundation is a member of the OMG, and the OMG is a member of the Eclipse Foundation. This is a start, but it raises the question of what level of interaction and commitment this brings, particularly because corporate members of each are often involved in and provide contributions to both of these organizations.

What are the best techniques for aligning standards organization activities with reference implementation project team activities? Should members be required to participate in both contribution areas, where applicable? What does it really mean for the Eclipse Foundation to be a member of the OMG, and vice versa? What role would the Foundation representative have within the context of the OMG, and how would this person coordinate with fellow members from the Eclipse community? What if members have competing goals? Are there new working models that would be more productive—and perhaps have never before explored in this context?

Specification Delivery

Specifications with defined metadata should be delivered in a serialized format, preferably XMI. The standard RFP template requires this for new specifications, but it has not been mandated or required for all specifications currently published by the OMG.

Graphical notations (concrete syntax) are typically provided by drawings and natural language descriptions. Although these are typically sufficient for describing the elements, they are not as precise as they could be and must be manually implemented for use in modeling tools.

The delivery of specifications in formats that are machine consumable, particularly if used as inputs to generative tooling frameworks, should be an obvious benefit to those involved in specification, implementation, and consumption of these technologies. This includes metamodel constraints, which should be serialized and interpreted by the underlying tooling. Currently, no standard way exists for EMF to define constraints (such as OCL) or interpret constraints on models even if they were provided.

The UML specification contains domain (abstract) syntax and semantics, OCL constraints, and graphical (concrete) syntax, accompanied by natural language description and mapping to the domain. It would seem reasonable for specifications to be delivered in a manner that describes the abstract model separately from the concrete syntax and that uses a mapping definition. This approach provides proper separation of concerns and supports the generation of graphical editors for various domain models.

As mentioned previously, the RFP for Diagram Definition should address the issue, which leaves the graphical notation definition issue. Should graphical notations be defined in term of a graphical definition metamodel, SVG, or another standard?

With respect to mapping definitions—for example, the myriad mappings from UML2 Profiles to Information Management Metamodel (IMM) (among others)—should QVT be provided as part of these specifications?

Specification Compliance

A generally provided set of conformance criteria must be met when implementing a specification. With improved collaboration between implementation and specification organizations, some level of minimum compliance level can be expected, to provide a proper reference implementation. In some cases today, implementations at Eclipse are well aligned, or nearly aligned, with OMG specifications. For example, the Eclipse UML2 project provides a compliant implementation of the UML 2.1 metamodel using the nearly EMOF-compliant Eclipse EMF project.

Should implementations be required to provide the highest level of compliance to defined specification acceptance criteria? Or is a "best effort" approach adequate? What actions can or should be taken to provide specification alignment or conformance?

Implementations Influencing Specifications

As indicated previously, in some cases, existing implementations are close to a specification yet are not fully compliant. With a large existing client base on a high-quality, open source implementation, why not align a specification with the implementation? For example, consider the previously mentioned case of EMF's Ecore model being not quite aligned with the EMOF specification.

A precedent exists for this type of influence between an open source implementation and OMG specification in the UML. The DI and Diagram Definition RFP are two more areas where this type of cooperation can be mutually beneficial.

Most often, specifications are themselves driven from implementations, although typically from a commercial vendor. Wouldn't an open source approach to implementations influencing specifications be a more equitable solution? This leads us directly to the next topic.

Open and Transparent Nature

In the case of Eclipse, contributions are done in the open, with an emphasis on meritocracy as the basis for achieving more responsibility within the community.

Transparency is essential to the open source process at Eclipse, yet this is somewhat different from the specification development process at the OMG [21]. Perhaps this is an area in which the two organizations can influence one another.

If the development of a reference implementation were done in the open, it follows that the developing version of the specification itself must be available. Otherwise, there would need to be a serial process of first developing the specification, publishing it, and then implementing it, which eliminates the benefits of validating the specification while developing an implementation in parallel.

Can the process of developing standards be done in a more open and transparent manner, with an emphasis on addressing the needs of a developing reference implementation? Alternatively, could Eclipse support a model whose source is not open until it reaches a required level of alignment with ongoing specification work?

Future Outlook

In summary, the promise of MDA can be realized to a large extent today using the capabilities provided by the Eclipse Modeling Project. As MDA encompasses a collection of specifications that align well with the implementation goals of the Eclipse Modeling Project, the future of delivering a solid open source infrastructure for MDA tooling seems bright.

Practically speaking, many challenges remain before realizing the statement in the Modeling project's charter related to its relationship with standards bodies such as the OMG. A relationship that is too informal will not likely yield the desired results, whereas a relationship that is strictly defined and enforced will likely limit the progress of implementation. The right balance will clearly benefit both of these organizations, their members, and, ultimately, the customers of standards-based commercial products.

References

[1] Object Management Group (OMG), www.omg.org.

[2] Eclipse Modeling Project, www.eclipse.org/modeling.

[3] OMG Specification and Products, www.omg.org/gettingstarted/specsandprods.htm#SpecProd.

[4] Software Process Engineering Metamodel (SPEM) specification, www.omg.org/technology/documents/modeling_spec_catalog.htm#SPEM.

[5] Eclipse Process Framework (EPF), www.eclipse.org/epf/.

[6] Unified Modeling Language (UML) specification, www.omg.org/technology/documents/modeling_spec_catalog.htm#UML.

[7] Eclipse UML2 Project, www.eclipse.org/uml2.

[8] Eclipse Model Development Tools (MDT) Project, www.eclipse.org/mdt.

[9] Object Constraint Language (OCL) specification, www.omg.org/technology/documents/modeling_spec_catalog.htm#OCL.

[10] EMF Technology OCL Project, www.eclipse.org/emft/projects/ocl#ocl.

[11] Meta-Object Facility (MOF) specification, www.omg.org/technology/documents/modeling_spec_catalog.htm#MOF.

[12] Eclipse Modeling Framework (EMF) Project, www.eclipse.org/emf.

[13] XML Metadata Interchange (XMI) specification, www.omg.org/technology/documents/modeling_spec_catalog.htm#XMI.

[14] MOF Query/View/Transformation (QVT) specification, www.omg.org/technology/documents/modeling_spec_catalog.htm#MOF_QVT.

[15] Eclipse Model-to-Model Transformation (M2M) Project, www.eclipse.org/proposals/m2m.

[16] UML Diagram Interchange (DI) specification, www.omg.org/technology/documents/modeling_spec_catalog.htm#UML_DI.

[17] UML Human-Usable Textual Notation (HUTN) specification, www.omg.org/technology/documents/modeling_spec_catalog.htm#HUTN.

[18] Business Process Modeling Notation (BPMN) specification, www.omg.org/technology/documents/bms_spec_catalog.htm#BPMN.

[19] Eclipse SOA Tools Project (STP), www.eclipse.org/stp.

[20] Eclipse Graphical Modeling Framework (GMF) Project, www.eclipse.org/gmf.

[21] OMG Technology Adoption Process, www.omg.org/gettingstarted/processintro.htm.

[22] Model to Text Transformation (M2T) Project, www.eclipse.org/modeling/m2t/.

[23] Architecture-Driven Modernization (ADM), http://adm.omg.org/.

[24] Diagram Definition RFP, www.omg.org/techprocess/meetings/schedule/Diagram_Definition_RFP.html#RFP_Issued.

[25] Business Process Definition Metamodel, http://doc.omg.org/dtc/2007-07-01.

[26] MOFScript component, www.eclipse.org/gmt/mofscript/.

[27] Java Emitter Templates (JET), www.eclipse.org/modeling/m2t/?project=jet.

[28] Xpand template engine, www.eclipse.org/modeling/m2t/?project=xpand.

[29] Language Workbenches, http://martinfowler.com/articles/languageWorkbench.html.

[30] Textual Modeling Framework (TMF) Proposal, www.eclipse.org/ proposals/tmf.

[31] IDE Meta-tooling Platform (IMP) Proposal, http://www.eclipse.rog/ proposals/imp.

[32] Business Modeling Definition Metamodel (BPDM), http://doc.omg.org/ dtc/2007-07-01.

[33] Catalog of OMG Domain Specifications, www.omg.org/technology/ documents/domain_spec_catalog.htm.

[34] Business Process Execution Language, http://docs.oasis-open.org/ wsbpel/2.0/wsbpel-v2.0.html.

[35] EclipseCon 2008, www.eclipsecon.org/2008.

[36] Mindmap, http://en.wikipedia.org/wiki/Mind_map.

[37] GMT Zoos, www.eclipse.org/gmt/am3/zoos/.

[38] Frank Budinsky, David Steinberg, Ed Merks, Raymond Ellersick, and Timothy J. Grose, *Eclipse Modeling Framework* (Boston, MA: Addison-Wesley, 2004).

[39] Krysztof Czarnecki and Ulrich Eisenecker, *Generative Programming: Methods, Tools, and Applications* (Boston, MA: Addison-Wesley, 2000).

[40] Jack Greenfield, Keith Short, Steve Cook, and Stuart Kent, *Software Factories: Assembling Applications with Patterns, Models, Frameworks, and Tools* (Indianapolis, IN: Wiley, 2004).

[41] Thomas Stahl, Markus Voelter, and Krzysztof Czarnecki, *Model-Driven Software Development: Technology, Engineering, Management* (London, UK: Wiley, 2006).

[42] Emfatic, www.alphaworks.ibm.com/tech/emfatic

[43] IBM Redbook: Eclipse Development Using the Graphical Editing Framework and the Eclipse Modeling Framework, www.redbooks. ibm.com/abstracts/sg246302.html.

[44] Christian W. Damus, "Implementing Model Integrity in EMF with MDT OCL," www.eclipse.org/articles/article.php?file=Article-EMF-Codegen-with-OCL/index.html.

[45] David S. Frankel, *Model Driven Architecture: Applying MDA to Enterprise Computing* (Indianapolis, IN: Wiley, 2003).

[46] Peter Coad, Eric Lefebvre, and Jeff De Luca, *Java Modeling in Color with UML: Enterprise Components and Process* (Upper Saddle River, NJ: Prentice Hall, 1999).

[47] Volker Wegert and Alexander Shatalin, "Integrating EMF and GMF Generated Editors," www.eclipse.org/articles/article. php?file=Article-Integrating-EMF-GMF-Editors/index.html.

[48] Martin Taal, "Using Teneo Hibernate in a Graphical Framework Editor," www.elver.org/hibernate/gmftutorial/tutorial1.html.

[49] Tony Clark, Paul Sammut, and James Willans, *Applied Metamodelling: A Foundation for Language Driven Development, Second Edition* (Sheffield, UK: Ceteva, 2008), www.ceteva.com/docs/ Applied%20Metamodelling%20 (Second%20Edition).pdf.

[50] Graphical Editing Framework (GEF) project, www.eclipse.org/gef Programmer's Guide to Draw2d/GEF: http://help.eclipse.org/ help33/topic/org.eclipse.gef.doc.isv/guide.html.

[51] Remko Popma, "JET Tutorial Part 1 (Introduction to JET)," www.eclipse.org/articles/Article-JET/jet_tutorial1.html.

Index

X-Y-Z

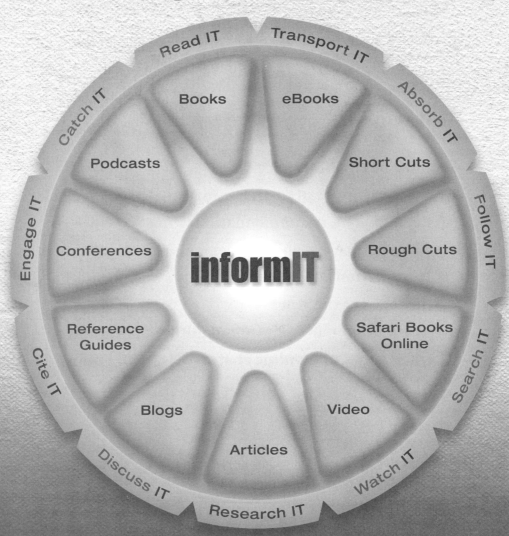

LearnIT at InformIT

Go Beyond the Book

11 WAYS TO LEARN IT at **www.informIT.com/learn**

The online portal of the information technology
publishing imprints of Pearson Education

 Addison Wesley   **Cisco Press**   EXAM/**CRAM**   **IBM Press**   que   PRENTICE HALL   SAMS

FREE Online Edition

Your purchase of **Eclipse Modeling Project** includes access to a free online edition for 45 days through the Safari Books Online subscription service. Nearly every Addison-Wesley Professional book is available online through Safari Books Online, along with more than 5,000 other technical books and videos from publishers such as Cisco Press, Exam Cram, IBM Press, O'Reilly, Prentice Hall, Que, and Sams.

SAFARI BOOKS ONLINE allows you to search for a specific answer, cut and paste code, download chapters, and stay current with emerging technologies.

Activate your FREE Online Edition at
www.informit.com/safarifree

> **STEP 1:** Enter the coupon code: HMEBAAA.

> **STEP 2:** New Safari users, complete the brief registration form.
> Safari subscribers, just log in.

If you have difficulty registering on Safari or accessing the online edition, please e-mail customer-service@safaribooksonline.com